STUDENTS!
Information for HM Video Cases That Accompany This Book

Are you interested in what *really* happens in the classroom? Do you want to know how teachers handle challenging situations? Watch the Houghton Mifflin Video Cases and see how new and experienced teachers apply concepts and strategies in real K–12 classrooms. These 4- to 6-minute video clips cover a variety of different topics that today's teachers face, and allow you to experience real teaching in action.

To access the Houghton Mifflin Video Cases and other premium, online resources, look for your passkey which is packaged with your new text.

ENHANCE YOUR LEARNING EXPERIENCE.

Houghton Mifflin Video Cases are integrated into your new copy of Cooper/Kiger's *Literacy: Helping Students Construct Meaning*, Seventh Edition, throughout the text and assignments. The cases include video clips and a host of related materials to provide a comprehensive learning experience. See the listing of Video Cases at the end of each chapter.

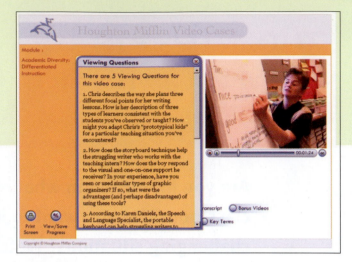

Reflect on the teacher's approach and assess how you might handle the situation by considering the **Viewing Questions**.

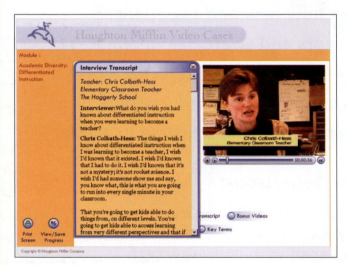

Read detailed **interviews with the teachers** as they explain their approach, how they engage students, and how they resolve issues.

View **handouts and materials used in the class**, and gain ideas for your own portfolio.

SEVENTH EDITION

LITERACY

Helping Students Construct Meaning

J. David Cooper
Ball State University, Retired

Nancy D. Kiger
University of Central Florida, Retired

with an introduction by
Kathryn H. Au

DATE DUE			
GAYLORD			PRINTED IN U.S.A.

Houghton Mifflin Company   *Boston   New York*

To the memory of my mother Isabelle who continues to give me the strength to succeed, and to Michael, Lucas, Melissa, David, Molly, Cooper, and Tallulah, the most important people in my life.

—J. David Cooper

To my daughters Laura and Katherine and the memory of my mother and my son Michael.
—Nancy D. Kiger

Executive Publisher: Patricia A. Coryell
Editor in Chief: Carrie Brandon
Sponsoring Editor: Shani B. Fisher
Marketing Manager: Amy Whitaker
Discipline Product Manager: Giuseppina Daniel
Senior Development Editor: Lisa A. Mafrici
Senior Project Editor: Margaret Park Bridges
Senior Media Producer: Philip Lanza
Senior Content Manager: Janet Edmonds
Art and Design Manager: Jill Haber
Cover Design Manager: Anne S. Katzeff
Senior Photo Editor: Jennifer Meyer Dare
Senior Composition Buyer: Chuck Dutton
Senior New Title Project Manager: Pat O'Neill
Editorial Assistant: Amanda Nietzel
Marketing Assistant: Samantha Abrams

Cover Image: All of the artwork was done in the spring of 2007 by children at the Baldwin School, Cambridge, Massachusetts, under the direction of their art teacher, Abby Pepin. © Jemima Joseph, 5 yrs. old, kindergarten—front left flower (multicolored). © Dorothy Anna Bacci, 13 yrs. old, 7th grade—front middle flower (orange). © Ayana Starr Aubourg, 13 yrs. old, 7th grade—front right flower (red & orange) & handwriting on back cover. © Samira Begum Pinke, 7 yrs. old, 1st grade—red & pink flower on back cover. © Henderson Gregory Sykes, 7 yrs. old, 1st grade—red flower on blue background & handwriting, both on back cover. © Taylor Lynn Vandick, 13 yrs. old, 7th grade—flower on spine. © Hannah Mueck, 10 yrs. old, 4th grade—handwriting on front cover. © Sebastien Roberts, 10 yrs. old, 4th grade—handwriting on front cover.

Page 64: Reprinted with permission from BRIDGES TO LITERACY by Diane DeFord, Carol Lyons, and Gay Su Pinnell. Copyright © 1991 by Diane DeFord, Carol Lyons, and Gay Su Pinnell. Published by Heinemann, Portsmouth, NH. All rights reserved. **Page 65:** Table "Criteria for Leveling Books for Grades 3–8" from SOAR TO SUCCESS!: The Reading Intervention Program Teacher's Manual, Level 7, in Houghton Mifflin Reading: Invitations to Literacy, by J. David Cooper. Copyright © Houghton Mifflin Company. All rights reserved. Reprinted by permission of the publisher. **Pages 122–128:** Excerpt from GLADIATOR, by Richard Watkins. Copyright © 1997 by Richard Watkins. Reprinted by permission of Houghton Mifflin Company. All rights reserved. **Pages 224–236:** NO, NO TITUS! By Claire Masurel. Illustrated by Shari Halpern. Copyright © 1997 North South Books. **Pages 283–290:** EVERGLADES FOREVER: RESTORING AMERICA'S GREAT WETLAND. Text copyright © 2004 by Trish Marx. Photographs Copyright © 2004 by Cindy Karp. Permission arranged with Lee & Low Books, Inc., New York, NY 10016. **Page 469:** Figure adapted from L. Morrow, "Using Story Retelling to Develop Comprehension" by D. Muth et al. in CHILDREN'S COMPREHENSION OF TEXT, © 1989. Reprinted by permission of International Reading Association.

Printed in the U.S.A.

Library of Congress Control Number: 2007931284

ISBN-10: 0-618-90708-4
ISBN-13: 978-0-618-90708-3

123456789-VH-12 11 10 09 08

Brief Contents

Contents

Effective Literacy Teachers   1

A Comprehensive Balanced Literacy Program   23

3 Prior Knowledge: Activating and Developing Concepts and Vocabulary

4   How to Teach Strategies for Constructing Meaning   137

Beginning Literacy

Intermediate Grades and Middle School: Decoding, Vocabulary, and Meaning

9 Helping Struggling Readers   375

Developing a Management System for a Comprehensive Balanced Literacy Classroom   401

Assessment and Evaluation in the Comprehensive Balanced Literacy Classroom   455

Preface

Our goal in writing this text has never wavered and is very simple: **to help teachers help every student learn to read and write**. Now titled *Literacy: Helping Students Construct Meaning,* this edition continues to provide preservice and in-service teachers the information, techniques, and strategies to help all students become literate.

Focus of This Revision

The mission of Houghton Mifflin's Education list is to provide quality content, technology, and services to ensure that new teachers are prepared for the realities of the classroom—thus bridging the gap from preservice to practice to foster teachers' lifelong career success. In this revision, as always, we strive to meet the needs of preservice and in-service teachers. Here are some of the changes that we think make this edition even more helpful than before:

- **Chapter 1 has been completely rewritten.** Now titled "Effective Literacy Teachers," this chapter has been rewritten to make even more clear what is necessary to teach literacy.

- **Standards for Students.** To illustrate that standards are more alike than different from one state to another, we have used sample standards from different states in our Standards-Based Literacy Lessons.

- **Standards-Based Literacy Lessons.** We have added Multilevel Notes within each lesson to illustrate how a lesson can be used with students of varying abilities and backgrounds. Each literacy lesson is based on a piece of literature that is included in the text. Each lesson is tied to sample standards from a different state and we show where in the lesson each standard might be assessed.

- **New Literacy Lesson.** A new nonfiction book, *Everglades Forever* (Marx, 2004), has been used for the sample literacy lesson in Chapter 6. This book provides an introduction to the wetlands in a time of increased awareness of our ecology.

- **Houghton Mifflin Video Cases.** At appropriate places within every chapter, a special feature alerts the reader to a Houghton Mifflin Video Case (to be viewed at the Student Website) related to the subject matter. These award-winning Video Cases show teachers in real classrooms interacting with students and discussing the methods they are using. The Video Cases feature includes reflective questions to guide your viewing.

- **New Key Points.** The main ideas of each chapter are listed in bulleted, easy-to-use format at the end of each chapter.

- **New How Do I Teach? Feature.** Each strategy and technique presented in a chapter is listed at the end of the chapter with the page on which it is explained for easy reference.

- **More Visual Presentation of Material.** Throughout the text we have reorganized information into bulleted lists and boxes to facilitate ease of use and make important ideas stand out.

- **Levels of Intervention.** We have added information to Chapter 9 to help teachers understand, identify, and manage whatever level of intervention a student might require. This is important in today's schools because educators are currently discussing Response to Intervention and Tiers of Intervention.

- **Continued emphasis on decoding, vocabulary, and meaning.** Throughout the text, emphasis is placed on the importance of decoding, vocabulary, and meaning. We have addressed the concept of Tiers of Vocabulary Instruction to help teachers determine which words to teach and how to teach them.

- **New Literature Feature, "*Good Books and Where to Find Them.*"** Throughout the text, where appropriate, references to new pieces of literature are given. Near the end of the text, a new feature appears that lists all literature referred to within the text, and we also include lists of major award-winning books and other resources to help teachers keep up with new literature.

- **Updated references and research.** To maintain the strong research base, references and research have been updated where appropriate.

- **For Additional Reading.** New suggestions have been added to each chapter.

- **Websites.** We have updated and added to the websites at the end of each chapter.

- **Online Support.** To improve the integration of the text with all the online support resources, throughout the book, a marginal icon alerts the reader to places where the text is supported by online material.

Chapter-by-Chapter Organization

The eleven chapters and the Handbook Resource provide complete coverage of the topics needed to help all teachers develop a Comprehensive Balanced Literacy Program that will lead all students to make adequate yearly progress.

"To the Student Reading This Text" is a brief introduction that provides guidance to the reader, focusing on what to do before reading, during reading, and after reading each chapter. It also introduces students to the numerous online resources which accompany this text.

Chapter 1, "Effective Literacy Teachers," provides **new guidelines** for teachers who strive to be effective literacy teachers: (1) paying attention to how children learn, (2) understanding listening, speaking, reading, and writing, (3) creating a Comprehensive Balanced Literacy Program, (4) learning to use standards and benchmarks to plan and differentiate instruction based on students' needs, (5) learning to teach using a variety of instructional strategies and routines, (6) recognizing that diversity among students is a strength in the classroom, (7) involving the families or caregivers of students, and learning about the community in which the students live, and (8) keeping up with research about literacy learning and teaching.

Chapter 2, "A Comprehensive Balanced Literacy Program," presents a model of a literacy program for grades K–8. We **revised and expanded** our explanation of how all students should experience the same text during some instruction while reading in text appropriate to their reading ability during other times. Basic skills that teachers need are developed, including the Standards-Based Literacy Lesson, the Minilesson, and the listening lesson. Guidelines for selecting texts for the literacy program are provided. A complete discussion about the components of basal reading systems is provided. A sample listening lesson is included. The "Educators Speak" feature focuses on using different modes of reading to accommodate diversity in the classroom.

Chapter 3, "Prior Knowledge: Activating and Developing Concepts and Vocabulary," stresses the importance of connecting prior knowledge and vocabulary development and presents strategies that lead students to become independent in developing their own prior knowledge and vocabulary, including the **new** student strategy "making connections." The Standards-Based Literacy Lesson focusing on prior knowledge is based on *Gladiator*. Three **new features** accompany this lesson: a sample set of standards from one state (Kansas), suggested places within the lesson to assess standards (Assessment Notes), and Multilevel Notes throughout the lesson that show how one lesson can work with varying ability levels and needs. The "Educators Speak" feature focuses on using projects that cut across the curriculum.

Chapter 4, "How to Teach Strategies for Constructing Meaning," provides information that is important at all literacy levels. It shows teachers how to model strategies for students systematically and explicitly. **Two new strategies** are included: making connections and evaluating. Eight strategies supported by the research are presented: visualizing, making connections, monitoring, inferencing, identifying important information, generating and answering questions, synthesizing and summarizing, and evaluating. Sample lessons are provided. Two "Educators Speak" features show how an elementary school teacher and a middle school teacher use strategies to meet the needs of students.

Chapter 5, "Beginning Literacy: Decoding, Vocabulary, and Meaning," presents instructional routines for beginning literacy instruction. A Standards-Based Literacy Lesson using the book, *No, No, Titus!* is provided. Again, three **new features** accompany this lesson: a sample set of standards from one state (Oregon), Assessment Notes, and Multilevel Notes. Two "Educators Speak" features show how teachers are using various routines to meet the diverse needs of learners.

Chapter 6, "Intermediate Grades and Middle School: Decoding, Vocabulary, and Meaning," has a **new** title that more accurately reflects the content. It focuses on reading instruction in the upper elementary grades and the middle school. A **new** section address tiers of vocabulary instruction. The **new** Standards-Based Literacy Lesson uses *Everglades Forever*. Sample standards from Texas show that this lesson can meet any state standards. Assessment suggestions and Multilevel Notes are added to the lesson. The "Educators Speak" feature provides an example of how a classroom teacher meets the needs of diverse learners.

Chapter 7, "Responding and the Construction of Meaning," presents ideas for making responding an integral part of comprehension development. A variety of techniques are presented. Two "Educators Speak" features show how classroom teachers incorporate responding into their literacy programs.

Chapter 8, "Writing and the Construction of Meaning," illustrates the role of writing in the comprehensive literacy program. Ideas are presented for connecting reading and writing, teaching spelling, and teaching grammar. The "Educators Speak" feature focuses on using technology to improve writing instruction.

Chapter 9, "Helping Struggling Readers," provides teachers a framework and guidelines for helping struggling readers in the classroom. A **new section** describes tiers, or levels, of intervention along with suggested ways intervention can be managed. The "Educators Speak" feature shows how one teacher provides intervention help for struggling beginning readers.

Chapter 10, "Developing a Management System for a Comprehensive Literacy Classroom," identifies the steps required for developing a management system for a comprehensive literacy classroom. A **new explanation and graphic** clarify how to use guided reading with leveled books. Organizing for this instruction is illustrated with a **new** sample guided reading plan for three groups. The chapter presents guidelines for creating a literate environment, organizing the classroom, and keeping needed records. Procedures for developing student routines are included. One of the "Educators Speak" features shows how one teacher approaches organization and management in her classroom.

Chapter 11, "Assessment and Evaluation in the Comprehensive Literacy Classroom," focuses on how to provide assessment and evaluation in a classroom guided by standards. The section on fluency checks has been **expanded**. The "Educators Speak" feature shows how a curriculum specialist helps teachers use assessment in diverse classrooms.

"Good Books and Where to Find Them" presents resources that will help you stay current with children's and young adult literature and awards.

The **Handbook Resource, "Word Skills: Phonics and Structural Analysis for Teachers,"** is designed to help teachers develop the content of phonics and structural analysis. It includes information on the scope and sequence of decoding instruction and practice exercises. The Handbook Resource can serve as a useful reference.

Materials to Support Preservice and In-Service Instruction

The complete package accompanying *Literacy: Helping Students Construct Meaning*, Seventh Edition, provides resources to assist the college instructor and the staff development leader in providing effective training for teachers.

Instructor's Resource Manual

The Instructor's Resource Manual (IRM) has been completely revised. It contains many suggestions for using this text in preservice courses as well as in-service training. The manual provides suggestions for using the PowerPoint slides that accompany the text as well as other ancillary items available online. It also includes ways to use text features if one choose not to use online features, for example, chapter outlines and Key Points, questions and activities to encourage discussion and active learning, and other pedagogical aids to reinforce key concepts in the text. The IRM is available online on the instructor's website, or in print upon request.

HM Testing CD

New to this edition, we provide a full test bank for instructors in computerized form for ease of use. It includes assessment items for each chapter consisting of multiple-choice, short-answer, and essay questions.

HM TeacherPrepSPACE Student and Instructor Websites

This edition is accompanied by a rich website resource for both students and instructors. Highlights of the website include student study materials such as ACE self-test quizzes and interactive glossary flashcards, additional Standards-Based Literacy Lessons, the HM Video Cases (described fully in the next section), web links, and an enhanced version of the "Educators Speak" features from the text. The site can be accessed at http://college.hmco.com/pic/cooperliteracy7e. Students can access HM TeacherPrepSPACE content at any time via the Internet. Some content may be passkey protected.

Houghton Mifflin Video Cases

Available online (and also in a DVD of all sixty Video Cases to adopters on request) and organized by topic, each "case" is a 3- to 5-minute module consisting of video and audio files presenting actual classroom scenarios that depict the complex problems and opportunities teachers face every day. The video and audio clips are accompanied by "artifacts" to provide background information and allow preservice teachers to experience true classroom dilemmas in their multiple dimensions.

HM TeacherPrepSPACE with Eduspace

For instructors who use a course management system, Eduspace, Houghton Mifflin's Course Management System, offers instructors a flexible, interactive online platform to help them communicate with students, organize material, evaluate student work, and track results in a powerful gradebook. In addition to the grade book and other course management tools, Eduspace includes special interactive components such as graphic organizers, videos, a discussion board, reflective journal questions, test items, and additional materials to aid students in studying and reflecting on what they have learned.

Acknowledgments

This seventh edition of *Literacy: Helping Students Construct Meaning* is a reflection of the ideas from many preservice and in-service teachers across the country. We are very appreciative of the suggestions and ideas we received from them. Many individuals have provided support that helped to make this book a reality.

Michael D. Robinson for his wonderful support both personally and professionally. Thanks to our families and friends for their support and encouragement.

Kathy Au, whose wonderful introductions have been a part of this book since the second edition.

Carolyn Shute, Literature Content Research Manager in the Houghton Mifflin School Division, for her excellent assistance in identifying and selecting new literature for the Standards-Based Literacy Lesson.

Our Advisory Board of reviewers, including Tara S. Azwell (Emporia State University), Patricia Becker (University of Texas at El Paso), Cindy M. Bird (State University of New York at Fredonia), Diane Bottomley (Ball State University), Grace Mwninimudzi Chiuye (Niagara University), Bette P. Goldstone (Arcadia University), Diane L. Lowe (Framingham State College), Linda H. Lord (State University of New York at Oswego), Kathleen M. McNamara (Stonehill College), Lina L. Owens (Arkansas State University), Pamela W. Petty (Western Kentucky University), Ruth E. Quiroa (National–Louis University), Joanne L. Ratliff (University of Georgia), Lem Londos Railsback (Texas A&M International University), Penée W. Stewart (Weber State University), Irene Welch-Mooney (University of New Mexico), Ann A. Wolf (Gonzaga University).

Melissa Kelleher, Development Editor, for her outstanding suggestions and guidance on the seventh edition and her unbelievably hard work. She has been greatly appreciated!

Lake Lloyd at Electronic Publishing Services, Inc., for her careful work in seeing the final production of the text to publication.

Margaret Park Bridges, Senior Project Editor, shepherded the manuscript through the stages of production.

Lisa Mafrici, Senior Development Editor, who has been involved with this text since the early editions and in a variety of roles, for her enthusiastic support of this project.

To the memory of John T. Ridley, friend and former Vice President and Publisher in the Houghton Mifflin School Division, who was the first person in 1985 to believe in this book and support its publication.

To Loretta Wolozin, who sponsored the first edition of this text for Houghton Mifflin. As the Sponsoring Editor she believed it would have a long life and bright future. Twenty-four years and seven editions later, her beliefs have been verified.

To every teacher who has used this book in one or more editions and each student who has been touched by those teachers.

To each of these individuals and groups we extend a very special THANK YOU!

The seventh edition of this text continues to reflect what we know to be true about helping teachers help students while including new viewpoints and thinking. We are thankful that we have been able to provide college instructors and in-service trainers a resource that has consistently improved in its effectiveness over twenty-four years.

J. David Cooper
Nancy D. Kiger

Introduction

A joke in the real estate business goes like this:

Question: What are the three most important factors to consider when buying property?
Answer: Location, location, location.

A parallel question and answer in education might be the following:

Question: What are the three most important factors to consider when teaching literacy?
Answer: Achievement, achievement, achievement.

Student achievement is the name of the game these days. This is the reality in many schools, and no joke at all.

Two years ago, I resigned my position at the University of Hawaii to spend more time working in public schools. My goal was to help schools in Hawaii raise literacy achievement through an approach called the Standards-Based Change (SBC) Process. This approach brings teachers in a school together as a professional learning community, with the goal of coherent curriculum across the grades. I follow the achievement results of schools in the SBC Process closely, because I want to be sure I'm doing all I can to help them succeed.

The ramifications of the emphasis on achievement and accountability are never more evident than at this time of year. It's early August, and the Hawaii public schools, which are all on a year-round schedule, are already back in session. Results of last spring's state testing reached the schools two weeks ago.

Last Friday I conducted a workshop at a school that had met all of the state targets for reading and math achievement. The principal made a banner that read, "We made Adequate Yearly Progress!" to hang on the fence in front of the school. "I want our community to know what you and the students accomplished," she told the teachers. Everyone applauded. About 54 percent of the students at this school are from low-income families. The teachers have worked hard over the past three years, following the SBC Process to pull together as a faculty around writing instruction.

The mood has been far less jubilant at another SBC Process school with a similar percentage of students from low-income families. This school fell out of "good standing" due to the rate of testing participation by special education students. Parents of special education students had the option of having their children not take the state tests, and a number had chosen to exercise this option. This was probably the right decision for the children, shielding them from a potentially frustrating and discouraging experience. But it caused the participation rate of special education students at this school to fall below the target of 95 percent.

In the newspapers, it appeared that this school had failed to make adequate progress in raising student achievement. Yet over the past year this school increased the percentage of students meeting or exceeding proficiency on the state reading test, from 57 percent to 67 percent this past spring. Even better, given that the school had focused on math improvement, the percentage of students meeting or exceeding proficiency on the state math test jumped from 33 percent to 55 percent. Sigh! If only the full story had been made known to the general public.

But wishing won't change anything. We need to roll up our sleeves and get on with the job of bringing all students to high levels of literacy, regardless of what seems fair or unfair about existing systems of accountability. That means focusing on delivering powerful, effective instruction to all students, especially those who struggle with learning to read.

When I looked at the seventh edition of *Literacy: Helping Students Construct Meaning,* I had one thought in mind: Will this book support teachers faced with the daunting challenge of raising the literacy achievement of the wide range of students likely to be found in their classrooms? I am pleased to report that the answer is a resounding yes. J. David Cooper and Nancy Kiger have updated an already successful text to serve as a valuable resource to teachers motivated to teach literacy effectively. What I have always liked about this text is its focus on powerful instruction: how to teach strategies for constructing meaning, how to activate prior knowledge and build vocabulary, how to teach decoding by analogy. These topics and more receive thorough treatment with specific lesson examples and new video cases.

Educators at many schools are discovering that packaged programs alone are not the answer. A well-designed program might help to jumpstart change, but as the saying goes, programs don't teach—teachers teach. In the past, an overreliance on programs led many schools to focus all of their professional development on implementing programs the "right way." Schools discovered over time that rigid implementation of programs was not the way to meet the needs of all learners. Students whose needs as learners happened to coincide with a program's design did well, while other students—whose needs as learners went unmet—lagged behind. If we really want to meet the literacy learning needs of all students, we must support teachers in adapting and differentiating instruction appropriately.

Last week I met with the leadership team at a suburban elementary school. As the discussion unfolded, I found out that the three resource teachers were planning to spend the majority of their time over the coming school year tutoring individual children in reading. I spoke rather bluntly to the group about the dangers of this plan. When such a large number of children require tutoring to reach grade-level benchmarks in reading, it's a sure sign that classroom instruction must be strengthened. This should be the first priority rather than tutoring, which addresses the effect rather than the cause of the problem. Tutoring is always a supplement to strong classroom instruction, never a replacement for it. But in this case, the unspoken message being sent to the classroom teachers was "Don't worry about your struggling readers, because we'll be tutoring them." This message could easily have the unintended effect of reducing teachers' attention to struggling readers. I recommended that the resource teachers spend their valuable time working to improve classroom instruction. They should go into the classrooms of teachers who need support, to demonstrate powerful instructional strategies and effective groupings, and to provide scaffolding until these teachers can carry out the new approaches on their own.

Teachers must be consummate professionals, informed about current literacy research and theory and knowledgeable in the flexible application of research-based instructional strategies. This is where *Literacy: Helping Students Construct Meaning* can serve as a valuable resource. While this text would work well in an undergraduate methods course, it would also be an excellent choice for study groups of in-service teachers intent on exploring issues of literacy instruction and assessment. A new first chapter provides teachers with a thorough grounding in a developmental view of children's growth as speakers, readers, and writers. This chapter goes a long way toward helping teachers understand the why as well as the what of the instructional strategies and organization approaches presented later in the text.

Notable in this new edition is the emphasis on standards. David and Nancy provide teachers with much needed guidance for working with standards as targets for students' learning. Standards have won grudging acceptance from teachers over the years. I like to remind teachers that the original vision of the standards movement was to initiate a public conversation about the goals of public education. The early advocates of standards wanted the goals of education—standards describing what students should know and be able to do—to move out of the pages of textbooks and the minds of teachers. Standards were to be accessible to parents and the general public and (radical thought!) to students themselves.

With its new focus on standards and continued emphasis on powerful instruction, the seventh edition of this well-received text keeps up with changing times and rigorous demands for literacy achievement. This text can give teachers the conceptual grounding and practical guidance they need to meet the literacy learning needs of all their students. The answer to the demand for higher test scores is not tutoring, test preparation, narrowly focused drill and skill, or still another packaged program. No, there is only one sensible response to calls for achievement, achievement, achievement—professional development focused on helping teachers to provide powerful, evidence-based instruction. David and Nancy have provided us with a valuable text to help in this endeavor.

Kathryn H. Au
Honolulu, Hawaii

To the Student

Reading This Text

Literacy: Helping Students Construct Meaning, Seventh Edition, was written for pre-service and in-service teachers. How you use this text will depend on your purpose for using it. Be sure to take advantage of the many online resources noted by icons throughout the book. The following ideas will help you gain the most knowledge and skills possible from each chapter:

Before Reading

- Preview the chapter by reading over the graphic organizer presented at the beginning of each chapter.
- Review the list of "Terms You Need to Know" found at the conclusion of each graphic organizer.

During Reading

- As you read, think back to the chapter preview and terminology.
- Highlight key points or make notes as you read.
- List questions that you have.

After Reading

- Review the "Key Points" and "How Do I Teach" feature listed at the end of each chapter.
- Review the "Terms You Need to Know."
- Seek answers to questions you still have by using some of the sources in the "For Additional Reading" and "Websites" sections.

On the Website

The *Literacy* Student Website offers many helpful resources. Go to http://college.hmco.com/pic/cooperliteracy7e and select the *Student Website*

to find self-quizzes, glossary flashcards, lesson plan templates, and more.
For example:

- To review the "Key Points," see the ACE practice tests.
- To review the "Terms You Need to Know," see the interactive glossary flashcards.
- Watch the HM Video Cases presented in each chapter.
- Find links to the websites listed in the text.
- Review the Educators Speak features and the reflective questions.
- Find an online version of the "Good Books and Where to Find Them" section, with links to complete lists of the major award-winning books cited in the text version.

Effective Literacy Teachers

1

*W*e are visiting Mr. Mejia's fifth grade where students are working in three small groups, each group with a different informational text on the topic of tropical rain forests. In one group partners are taking turns reading sections of the book aloud. We notice that some students are recording words in their journals as they read and discuss the book. After a few minutes, the entire group comes together to discuss the book using prompts Mr. Mejia has provided on a chart.

Students in the second group are reading independently. Some are writing summaries of what they have read. Mr. Mejia calls this group to a table in the back of the room where they discuss what they have learned about the tropical rain forest. Students take turns sharing what they have written in their journals. Mr. Mejia asks the group to compare the book they just read with the one on the same topic that they read last week. Cooper and Molly disagree about some points, so Mr. Mejia suggests that each student prepare a Venn diagram like the one shown in Figure 1.1, showing how the two books are alike and how they are different. Mr. Mejia leaves the group to complete the assignment and moves on to the next group.

The third group has been working at centers, locating words in their book about rain forests that have some of the prefixes and suffixes they had learned yesterday. Mr. Mejia asks the students to bring the books to the table. Tallulah, Michael, Melissa, and Dave seem excited to discuss the book. Carmen, Nancy, and Iñaqui sit quietly and listen to the discussion. Mr. Mejia asks students to find places in the text to support the points they are making. Carmen does not agree

FIGURE 1.1	**Sample Venn Diagram**

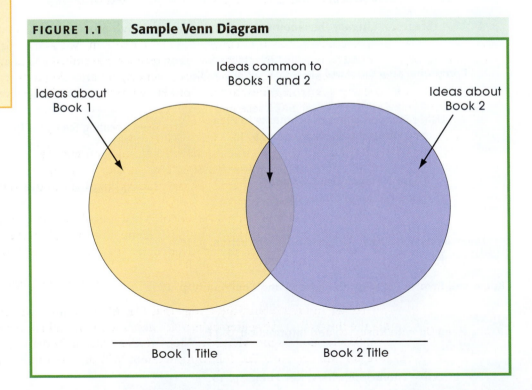

with Dave and she is able to find a place in the text that supports her point of view, which she reads aloud. Dave agrees that she was "probably right."

Mr. Mejia then has all of his students form groups with at least one person who is reading each book in each group. Everyone is eager to share, and they all want to read each other's books. This activity lasts about five minutes, and then Mr. Mejia calls the entire class together for a shared writing lesson on writing reports.

The HM TeacherPrepSPACE Student Website offers many helpful resources, such as self-quizzes, glossary flashcards, lesson plan templates, and more. college.hmco.com/pic/cooperliteracy7e

During our brief visit to Mr. Mejia's classroom we saw a lot of activity related to literacy learning taking place. We saw:

- three groups of students, each group reading informational books appropriate to their reading levels.
- students were all responding in various ways—some were writing in journals, some were having discussions, and some were writing summaries.
- discussions were both student-led and teacher-directed.
- both whole-class and small-group activities occurred.
- reading and writing were connected—the texts were informational and the related writing lesson was report writing.
- teacher modeling took place through shared writing.

Based on our observations and discussions with Mr. Mejia, we could tell that his was a comprehensive balanced literacy classroom. We asked Mr. Mejia how he learned to be such an effective literacy teacher. He smiled and said he wasn't really sure. Then he told us what he focused on or paid attention to when he first started teaching—and continues to focus on, knowing that there is always room for growth in his effectiveness. These include:

1. Paying attention to how children learn.
2. Understanding listening, speaking, reading, and writing.
3. Creating a Comprehensive Balanced Literacy Program.
4. Learning to use standards and benchmarks to plan and differentiate instruction based on students' needs.
5. Learning to teach using a variety of instructional strategies and routines.
6. Recognizing that diversity among students is a strength in the classroom.
7. Involving the families or caregivers of his students, and learning about the community in which the students lived.
8. Keeping up with research about literacy learning and teaching.

As we thought about the things that Mr. Mejia told us, we realized that these are the things that every literacy teacher needs to focus on in order to become effective. We decided to use what Mr. Mejia shared with us as the organizational structure for this chapter. The following sections will discuss each of the eight points listed above.

How Children Learn

Knowing how children and young adults learn helps you know how to plan instruction. Teachers, reading specialists, and researchers have learned a great deal about how individuals learn to read and write, or become literate. Although there are several theories about learning (Hergenhahn & Olson, 2004), all include the understanding that individuals learn in different ways:

- Some students learn by having someone model or show them how to do something. For example, the teacher thinks aloud; he verbalizes the process he uses as he reads to help him infer the main idea. This would be considered **direct** or **explicit instruction.** This is the type of instruction the teacher would use to teach students a strategy, skill, or process.
- Some students learn implicitly by participating in different activities or experiences. For example, your students might read a book that is appropriate to their reading ability and carry out a discussion afterward. This would be **student-centered instruction.**
- Most students learn in both ways—some things they learn through explicit instruction, and others learn through more student-centered instruction.

No teacher should rely on only one type of instruction. Effective literacy teachers are aware of how students learn and are able to use both types of instruction.

Understanding Listening, Speaking, Reading, and Writing

There are many definitions of **literacy** (Harris & Hodges, 1995). Over the years, most definitions have focused on just reading and writing (Venezky, 1995). Now, discussions of literacy have broadened to include listening and speaking and other types of literacy, such as mathematics literacy and technology literacy. This broadened concept of literacy makes it a term that includes all of the communication and calculation skills needed in today's society.

How Literacy Develops

Children and young adults develop literacy by participating in a variety of real literacy experiences and a considerable amount of direct or explicit instruction. They begin by developing **oral language** (listening and speaking) and then later learn to read and write. All of the elements of literacy—speaking, listening, reading, writing, and thinking—continuously develop together (Wilkinson & Silliman, 2000). Understanding how these components develop helps us create an effective literacy program for our students.

An Expanded Definition of Literacy: Meaningful Ways to Use Technology

Watch the video clip, study the artifacts in the case, and reflect on the following questions:

1. Based on reading Chapter 1 and watching this Video Case, how would you define *literacy* in your own words?

2. Describe what the students in this Video Case are doing that will help their literacy develop. Explain your thinking.

3. This text focuses on the communication aspects of literacy, which include listening and speaking (oral language), reading, and writing. An integral part of each of these elements is the process of thinking. Another aspect of communication literacy that is often discussed is viewing: using the various strategies and skills involved in listening, speaking, reading, writing, and thinking when watching television, viewing a movie or video, and so forth. The goal of communication literacy is twofold: to construct meaning from what is heard and read and to convey meaning through speaking and writing (National Reading Panel, 2000a, b). To reach this goal, we must answer the question, How do individuals develop literacy?

Theories of Oral Language Acquisition

The process of acquiring language is lifelong; each of us continues to acquire new aspects of language through our interactions and experiences. Therefore, language acquisition is first and foremost a social process (Cook-Gumprez, 1986; Wells, 1990). Taylor and Dorsey-Gaines (1988) report that inner-city families "use literacy for a wide variety of purposes (social, technical, and *aesthetic* purposes), for a wide variety of audiences, and in a wide variety of situations" (p. 202). Thus, *all children come to school with a language base,* though this base may or may not match the base on which the school is trying to build. Since a strong connection between oral language and reading has been clearly established for all learners (Cazden, 1972; Garcia, 2000; Loban, 1963; Menyuk, 1984; Ruddell, 1963; Snow et al., 1998; Wilkinson & Silliman, 2000), it is important that schools build literacy experiences around whatever language a child has developed.

There are several theories of language acquisition. *Nativists* believe that children acquire language innately, without practice or reinforcement (Chomsky, 1965; Lenneberg, 1967; McNeil, 1970). Those who hold the *cognitive development* point of view stress that children acquire language through their various activities (Piaget & Inhelder, 1969). Vygotsky (1978) proposed a concept known as the *zone of proximal development,* a range in which a child can perform a task only with the help of a more experienced individual. Halliday (1975) views language acquisition as an active process in which children try out their language and make approximations of real language. Therefore, according to Halliday, we should accept errors during literacy development, because it is through these approximations that children gradually develop their perfected forms of language.

All of these theories contribute to our understanding of how children acquire language. Basically, we know that children acquire language:

- when they have a need that is meaningful and real.
- through interactions with peers and adults.
- by making approximations of real language.
- at varying rates and in various stages, even though they all go through similar phases of development.
- by having language modeled for them both directly and indirectly.

This understanding provides a solid basis on which to develop a literacy program that fosters students' abilities to construct meaning.

Reading and Writing Acquisition

Reading and writing are complex processes that grow from oral language and are built on listening and speaking. For example, the child who develops a good listening and speaking vocabulary has formed many concepts and ideas. This is known as **prior knowledge,** and it is critical for effective reading and writing (Anderson & Pearson, 1984; Pressley, 2000).

Chapter 3 deals with prior knowledge.

Reading involves two basic processes—**decoding** and **comprehension.** Decoding is the ability of the individual to figure out the pronunciation of printed words and ultimately determine the word's meaning (Harris & Hodges, 1995). The only way a child knows that a word has been pronounced correctly is by checking it against his or her oral language. For example, suppose Meredith reads the sentence, "We had eggs and *bācon* for breakfast." If she does not immediately recognize the word *bacon,* she tries to sound it out. First, she says *băcun,* but that does not sound like a real word. Next, she says *båcun,* which sounds like a word she knows. The child mentally compares the word to his or her oral language to determine if it has been pronounced correctly and makes sense—that is, it is something that goes with eggs. A child with limited oral language or limited English may not be able to determine the accuracy of the word's pronunciation. In other words, the word must be in the child's head before pronunciation can be verified. However, even without the word *bacon* in the child's head, thinking can verify that—based on the context of the sentence—the word probably names a food that people eat for breakfast.

Oral language is also critical to comprehension, which is the ability to construct meaning by interacting with a text. Think back to the sentence read above: "We had eggs and bacon for breakfast." As the child decodes the word *bacon,* he or she uses the meanings developed in oral language to associate meaning with the written word. A child who does not have these meanings in his or her oral language cannot associate meaning with the word or text. For example, read the following sentence to yourself:

The Gayzorniplatz was noving his tonk.

FIGURE 1.2	A Gayzorniplatz

Since you have good reading skills, you obviously recognize the words *The, was,* and *his.* You may recognize the inflected ending -*ing* in the word *noving* and decide it must be a verb. Because of the noun markers *The* and *his,* you also know that *Gayzorniplatz* and *tonk* are probably nouns, and that *Gayzorniplatz* is probably a proper noun, since it is capitalized. You are also able to come up with some semblance of pronunciation for the words. However, since these words are not in your oral language, you cannot be absolutely sure of their pronunciation or construct their meaning. If, on the other hand, I show you a picture of a Gayzorniplatz (see Figure 1.2) and give you the meanings of *noving* and *tonk,* you begin to be able to construct meaning.

Decoding and comprehension are the two big jobs in the process of learning to read. Refer to Figure 1.3. Notice that as an individual moves from beginning reading to mature reading, the emphasis in learning shifts from more focus on decoding to more focus on comprehension. Both comprehension and decoding are *always* a part of the process. However, as students become adept at decoding, they are free to pay more attention to constructing meaning. This process is not as smooth and linear as the diagram shows; it is a "jerky continuum" (Cooper & Kiger, 2008).

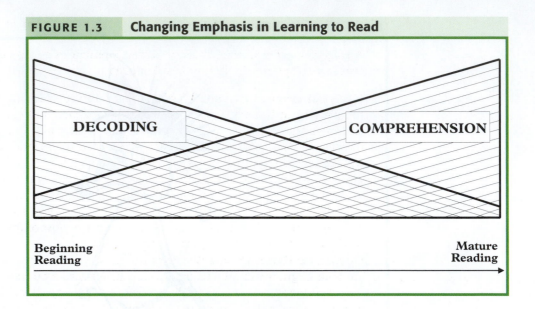

FIGURE 1.3   **Changing Emphasis in Learning to Read**

DECODING   COMPREHENSION

Beginning Reading   Mature Reading

Writing is the process of conveying meaning or ideas by using graphic symbols. For very beginning writers, this may be drawing or scribbling, as shown in Figure 1.4. This type of writing occurs long before the child can form letters. Once the child begins to form letters, he or she uses invented or temporary spelling (see Figure 1.5).

Writing involves the reverse of decoding, the process that is used in reading; writing involves encoding or spelling—writing symbols to represent words. Using the concepts and ideas you have developed through your own prior knowledge and oral language, you convey your ideas for others to read. You use the knowledge of language you have gained to express your ideas.

Throughout the processes of speaking, listening, reading, and writing, children learn to think. As they learn language, they become more adept at expressing themselves, solving problems, and making judgments. The process of thinking (often referred to as critical thinking or higher-order thinking skills) develops along with all of the other aspects of literacy. Exactly what happens as children develop literacy?

Stages of Literacy Development

There is general agreement among researchers and literacy specialists that children and young adults go through various stages as they develop literacy (Adams, 1990; Chall, 1983; Cooper & Kiger, 2008; Ehri, 1991, 1997; Juel, 1991; Rupley, Wilson, & Nichols, 1998). Although detailed study of these stages is beyond the scope of this text, it is important that we be aware of these stages and know the role that they play in literacy instruction. For detailed discussions about the **stages of**

literacy development, see Cooper and Kiger (2008), listed in "For Additional Reading."

A stage is a point in time during the development of an overall process. There are five stages or phases in literacy development:

1. **Early Emergent Literacy.** This is the stage during which children develop the foundations of literacy. It usually occurs before the child enters kindergarten, and includes such aspects of literacy as developing oral language, writing by drawing or scribbling, and being curious about print. Second-language learners have usually done these things in their first language.

2. **Emergent Literacy.** During this stage, the child becomes more interested in literacy. He or she uses more standard oral language patterns, and forms and names letters. Concepts about print, such as recognizing a letter or word, also develop during this stage. Most children complete most of this stage by the end of kindergarten or at the beginning of grade 1.

3. **Beginning Reading and Writing.** In this stage, oral language expands, and students begin to actually read and write in conventional ways. They figure out the pronunciation of words and also develop **fluency** (the ability to recognize words automatically, accurately, and rapidly) in reading (Samuels & Farstrup, 2006). They understand the meanings of more and more words. This stage continues through first grade for most students and into second or third grade for some.

Almost fluent readers work collaboratively.
© Cleo Photography/ Photo Edit

FIGURE 1.4   A Beginning Writer's Scribbles

4. **Almost Fluent Reading and Writing.** During this stage, the child is growing more sophisticated with all aspects of literacy. He or she reads silently more than in the previous stage, does more writing, and has a larger oral language vocabulary. For most students, this stage may begin toward the end of second grade, and may continue into the beginning of fourth or fifth grade.

5. **Fluent Reading and Writing.** By this stage, the student is using reading, writing, and oral language for a variety of purposes. He or she has attained most of the skills of reading and writing. This stage may begin for some students in fourth grade; it continues through the upper elementary grades and into middle

FIGURE 1.5   Sample of a Kindergartner's Writing

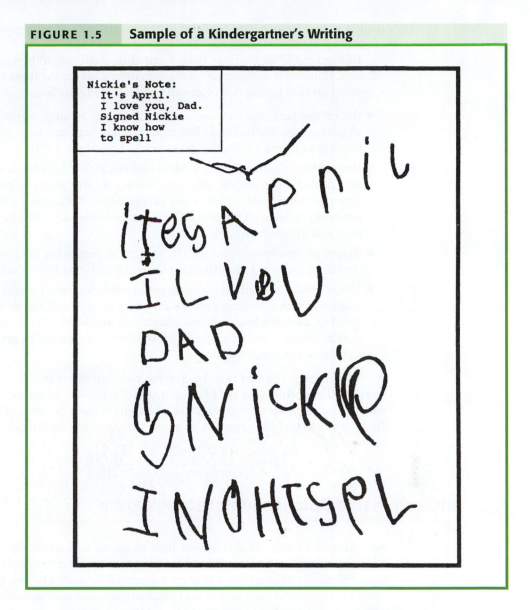

school and high school. In fact, fluent reading and writing development continues throughout one's life.

There is much overlap between the stages. No student ever completely finishes one stage and then moves into another. Some students reach a plateau and remain at a particular stage for a period of time.

For many years, literacy development was viewed as having a period of "readiness," a time when children developed a discrete set of "prerequisite" skills. At some magical moment, they were supposedly ready to learn to read. Research evidence eventually indicated that this is not true (Durkin, 1966). In the past, educators also tended to rigidly associate levels of achievement with specific grades; they did not allow for variation in individual development.

In the light of all that has been learned through research over the past several decades, thinking about literacy development in stages is the most reasonable way to approach literacy instruction. Consider the following findings:

- All of the language arts—speaking, listening, reading, writing, viewing, and thinking—are interrelated. Essentially, what happens to a student's development in one area affects the other areas (Shanahan, 1990).

- Researchers (Yaden, Rowe, & MacGillivray, 2000) have been able to document and describe the earliest stages of literacy as an emergent literacy stage. Students do not develop or learn one part or piece of literacy at a time. Rather, they gradually develop all the parts. They grow into literacy with the appropriate support and instruction.

- Stages of development are clearly evident in beginning readers as they develop decoding and word identification skills (Ehri, 1991, 1997; Juel, 1991).

- When students' reading comprehension abilities have been studied in the elementary grades, evidence shows that they go through stages or phases as they develop their reading abilities (Rupley et al., 1998). As their comprehension builds, students use a consistent set of strategies repeatedly, gradually becoming more sophisticated in their use.

Within each stage of literacy development, students exhibit certain behaviors, strategies, and skills that are identified through the use of **standards** and **benchmarks** that form the core content for a Comprehensive Balanced Literacy Program. First, let's define this program and see why it is important for effective literacy instruction.

Comprehensive Balanced Literacy Program

An effective literacy teacher knows how to create and maintain a Comprehensive Balanced Literacy Program, which is a plan for literacy instruction that includes the essential blocks of instruction that are supported by research. This plan incorporates both explicit direct instruction and student-centered instruction and includes the extra support needed by some students. Research on literacy clearly supports the idea of providing a Comprehensive Balanced Literacy Program that is designed to help all children succeed (Snow, Burns, & Griffin, 1998). Having a framework or concept for a Comprehensive Balanced Literacy Program ensures that everything needed to help students develop literacy effectively is included in the classroom.

Sometimes you will hear educators refer to this type of program as a comprehensive program, and others you will hear it called a Balanced Literacy Program. In most instances, the individuals are referring to the same type of program. We use the more inclusive term: Comprehensive Balanced Literacy Program. Chapter 2 is devoted to developing a concept for such a program.

Using Standards and Benchmarks to Plan and Differentiate Instruction

When you look at individual state standards, you find that the terms *standards* and *benchmarks* are not always used the same. Usually, standards are statements that express what is valued or expected in a given field or area at certain times. Benchmarks are descriptions of behaviors that indicate whether students have achieved a given standard or reached a certain stage of development. However, in some states, a standard is just the name of the area, such as reading. Then, benchmarks say what is expected, with *indicators* to describe what students should be doing.

For example, if a benchmark (or indicator) says, "The student reads 20 books independently during the semester," you as the teacher can use this to evaluate student performance in relation to independent reading. Educators sometimes use the terms *standards* and *benchmarks* interchangeably. Regardless of terminology, your state standards will play an important part in how you carry out your literacy program.

At the present time, the U.S. government has not recommended or required any national standards for literacy. However, this situation could change during the next decade (Education Commission of the States, 2001).

Standards and benchmarks become the foundation for differentiating literacy instruction for each student. There are two basic steps that you follow:

1. First, familiarize yourself with your state standards for the grade level you are teaching as well as those for the previous grade. This information will let you know the content students should have learned in the previous grade and what you are expected to cover for all students in their current grade.
2. Next, look at each student's performance in relation to the content from the previous grade to make sure the student has really learned what the standards indicate should have been learned. This process is known as a **diagnosis,** which means that you do some type of testing or assessment to identify each student's strengths and needs. This information helps you plan instruction that fits the needs of each student. This process is known as **differentiated instruction** or **differentiating instruction.**

The use of standards and benchmarks for literacy instruction (and other subject areas) is a significant issue for schools. In many instances, standards and benchmarks are designated for each stage of literacy development (Cooper & Kiger, 2008). These serve as the guidelines for both assessment and instruction.

Locating Standards for Your State

As we have noted, each state usually has its own set of standards. If you do not have a copy of the standards for your state, use the Internet to locate them. Use a search engine; type in "(the name of your state) Department of Education" and click Search or Go. Then look for a link to information on the standards for that state. In this book, we use sample standards from different states to help you understand that though the language varies, the intent of standards from one state to another is virtually the same.

Video Case

Teacher Accountability: A Student Teacher's Perspective

Watch the video clip, study the artifacts in the case, and reflect on the following questions:

1. Do you agree with the current emphasis on national and state standards in schools? In your own words, what are the pros and cons of standards-based education?

2. In this Video Case, one master teacher states that standardized test results "provide an opportunity to reflect on one's own teaching practice." Explain this statement in your own words and discuss whether or not you agree.

Learn to Teach Using a Variety of Instructional Strategies

Teaching is the process of imparting knowledge, a skill, or a strategy to someone. It involves the teacher knowing how to model the skill, strategy, or process for students and being able to tell when a student has learned what is being taught. Teaching is more than assigning students one task after another. It involves modeling a skill, strategy, or process, then having students practice and apply what is being taught.

Children at the beginning reading stage profit from teacher read aloud.
© Leah Warkentin/ Design Pics/Corbis

Educators Speak

Sixth-Grade Literacy Block Enhanced with Computers

"Meeting the individual needs of thirty-four sixth-grade students can be a daunting task. One thing that helps me is using a 45-minute block of time each day when every student reads at his or her level. During this time I am able to work in a small group with my most critical students. Technology is extremely beneficial during this time. My students do extensive research projects that are often related to our social studies curriculum, such as an ancient civilization that we are studying. They use the computers to conduct research, practice word processing skills, and turn their research into slide show presentations to share with the rest of the class.

Computers give students access to information that otherwise would not be available. They are developing critical thinking skills as they locate the necessary information, pull out relevant facts, and sift through extraneous information. The reading strategies of summarizing, clarifying, and questioning that have been ingrained in these students are now used at a much higher level.

Word processing skills may not seem to tie into literacy, but if students are quick and accurate with keyboarding skills, it will help them throughout their education. The less they have to concentrate on where the keys are, the more attention they can pay to the content of what they are writing. Allowing students access to computers during research time gives students the application and practice they need.

After students have completed their research and typed a paper, they share what they learned with the class through a presentation in the form of a slide show on the computer. For this, they need to again gauge the importance of the information they have found and whittle it down to the main details. They also must think about the sequencing of events.

As students complete these projects independently, while I am working with a small group, they apply several reading as well as improve on a variety of technology skills that are a necessity in today's world."

—Jill Baker, Sixth-Grade Teacher
Grand Oaks Elementary School
Citrus Heights, California

Throughout this text the focus is on *how to teach*. Knowing how to teach means the effective literacy teacher can use a variety of teaching strategies and routines to meet the needs of all students.

Technology as a Part of Instruction

Technology is a significant part of nearly everyone's life (Valmont, 2003). Computers, CD-ROMs, audio and video resources, and DVDs offer real possibilities for improving literacy instruction and thereby improving literacy learning. Research in literacy learning and technology suggests possibilities for enhancing literacy instruction, but it offers few clear guidelines as to the *best* use of technology (National Reading Panel, 2000a). Educators must continue to study how technology can

Academic Diversity: Differentiated Instruction

Watch the video clip, study the artifacts in the case, and reflect on the following questions:

1. Describe some specific ways in which this classroom teacher adapts the lesson for the diverse learners in her classroom. What tools and strategies does she use?

2. If you could ask this classroom teacher any questions about how to "do" differentiated instruction, what would you ask? As a future classroom teacher, what are your biggest questions and concerns about this important instructional approach?

enhance literacy learning. The ISTE website (listed at the end of the chapter) helps you keep up with changing technology in education.

Throughout this text, we incorporate ways to use technology to enhance the quality of literacy learning, to differentiate literacy instruction, and to keep up in the field of literacy. The Educators Speak feature for this chapter (on page 15) illustrates how a sixth-grade literacy block is enhanced with computers. Each chapter concludes with a section entitled "Websites."

Diversity as a Strength for Classroom Instruction

Classrooms throughout the United States are diverse in that they include students who are English Language Learners (ELLs) or second-language learners, as well as students with a variety of special needs, such as learning disabilities, giftedness, reading problems, and the wide cultural and familial differences that exist in any community. We consider **diversity** a strength in the classroom. The diverse classroom reflects the real world, allowing students to learn in a setting that more realistically represents the world outside the classroom.

Diversity in the classroom means that teachers must adjust instruction to the needs of students. Think back to Mr. Mejia's classroom, which we read about at the beginning of this chapter. Although most of his ELL students had made the transition to English, as he taught, he made sure that all students, including the ELL students, had the needed background and concepts to understand the texts they were going to read. This is just one example of how Mr. Mejia was providing differentiated instruction. Regardless of the types of diversities, we must adjust our instruction to meet the needs of our students.

We must keep in mind the truism that "good teaching is good teaching." "Considerable evidence supports the conclusion that the differences in achievement between students of mainstream and non-mainstream backgrounds are not the result of differences in their ability to learn, but rather of differences in the quality of instruction they have received in school" (Association for Supervision and Curriculum Development, 1995, p. x). There are no specific procedures that are designed just for learning-disabled students or ELL students. We must tailor our instruction to meet the needs of *all* students, because instruction has a great impact on how *all* students learn. Throughout this text, we will continually focus on how to meet the needs of diverse students by differentiating instruction.

Know and Involve Families, Caregivers, and Community

Knowing about your students helps you understand them and plan instruction more effectively (National PTA, 1998). This includes getting to know about each student's family or caregivers and the community in which they live and finding ways to involve them in the school and classroom. When families and schools work together, evidence shows that:

- students achieve more, regardless of their socioeconomic level.
- students get better grades and have higher test scores.
- students have more positive attitudes about school and learning.

There are many ways to get to know students' families and caregivers. Some include:

- have conferences with family members and/or caregivers.
- hold a school open house—invite family members and caregivers to visit the classroom and see what is happening.
- make home visits when appropriate.
- invite family members and caregivers to visit the classroom and share interesting things about their interests, such as hobbies, special talents, and so forth.
- establish a website for your classroom.
- invite families to stay in touch with you via e-mail.

Keep Up with Research and Information

An effective literacy teacher stays current with the latest information and research about literacy and literacy instruction. There are many ways to do this (Cooper, Chard, & Kiger, 2006):

1. **Join professional organizations.** Belonging to a professional organization gives you an opportunity to interact with other teachers who have interests similar to yours and gives you access to some of the most recent research and

newest teaching procedures. Two good organizations that support literacy teaching and learning are:

International Reading Association (IRA)
800 Barksdale Road
P.O. Box 8139
Newark, DE 19714-8139
1-800-336-READ; 1-302-731-1600
www.reading.org

National Council of Teachers of English (NCTE)
1111 W. Kenyon Road
Urbana, IL 61801-1096
1-877-369-6283
www.ncte.org

2. **Read journals and periodicals.** Reading journals, periodicals, and magazines for teachers keeps you informed with a variety of new ideas and some of the latest research on literacy instruction. The two professional organizations mentioned above provide some good professional journals for teachers:

    IRA—*Lectura y vida,* a Spanish-language journal for teaching second-language learners at all levels.

    The Reading Teacher provides research and professional articles for preschool and elementary teachers.

    Journal of Adolescent & Adult Literacy contains information and research on literacy instruction for middle school, high school, and adult learners.

    Reading Research Quarterly, a pure research journal, focuses on literacy at all levels.

    NCTE—*Language Arts*, a journal for preschool and elementary literacy teachers, includes research and practical applications.

    School Talk, a newsletter about current issues in reading and writing instruction.

    Voices from the Middle, a newsletter with ideas for literacy instruction for middle school teachers.

3. **Read professional books.** Reading professional books is another good way to keep you up to date. Listen for recommendations from colleagues, visit Internet bookstores such as www.amazon.com, listen for the recommendations of educational speakers you hear, and so forth.

4. **Attend workshops and classes.** Attending workshops and taking courses is another good way to keep current. Watch the bulletin board in your school lounge or office for announcements of offerings from local universities, professional organizations, and publishers.

5. **Search the Internet.** Type the topic of interest into any search engine. Consider the source as you read information online; some are more reliable than others.

6. **Collaborate with colleagues.** Collaborating and working with your colleagues is another good way to keep up with current information and activities.

Working with colleagues is an important part of effective teaching.
© Michael Newman/ Photo Edit

Take time to talk with other teachers about what they are reading and what workshops they are attending. Share with others the things you are doing. Participate in faculty meetings, grade-level meetings, and team meetings. Talk with colleagues about how students are performing and share different ideas that are working.

Following these guidelines to keep yourself current will help to make you a more effective literacy teacher.

Effective Literacy Teachers: Key Points

To review the Key Points, see the ACE practice tests at the HM TeacherPrepSPACE Student Website.

- The effective literacy teacher needs to understand how children learn.
- The effective literacy teacher needs to understand listening, speaking, reading, and writing.
- The effective literacy teacher needs to have a concept of a Comprehensive Balanced Literacy Program.
- The effective literacy teacher needs to think about using standards and benchmarks to plan and differentiate instruction.

- The effective literacy teacher needs to focus on the importance of learning to teach using a variety of strategies.
- The effective literacy teacher needs to recognize diversity as a strength for the classroom.
- The effective literacy teacher needs to develop an understanding of the importance of getting to know students' families or caregivers and their community.
- The effective literacy teacher needs to know how to keep up with the research.

Video Cases in This Chapter

- **An Expanded Definition of Literacy: Meaningful Ways to Use Technology**
- **Teacher Accountability: A Student Teacher's Perspective**
- **Academic Diversity: Differentiated Instruction**

For Additional Reading

Armbruster, B. B., & Osborn, J. (2003). *Put reading first: The research building blocks for teaching children to read (K–3)* (2nd ed.). Ann Arbor: Center for the Improvement of Early Reading Achievement, University of Michigan.

Blair, T. R., Rupley, W. H., & Nichols, W. D. (2007). The effective teacher of reading: Considering the "what" and "how" of instruction. *The Reading Teacher, 60*(5), 432–438.

Cooper, J. D., & Kiger, N. D. (2008). *Literacy assessment: Helping teachers plan instruction* (3rd ed.). Boston: Houghton Mifflin.

McTavish, M. (2007). Constructing the big picture: A working class family supports their daughter's pathways to literacy. *The Reading Teacher, 60*(5), 476–485.

National Reading Panel. (2000). *Teaching children to read: An evidence-based assessment of the scientific research literature on reading and its implications for reading instruction.* Washington, DC: National Institute of Child Health and Human Development.

Ortiz, R. W., & Ordoñez-Jasis, R. (2005). Leyendo juntos (reading together): New directions for Latino parents' early literacy involvement. *The Reading Teacher, 59*(2), 110–112.

Padak, N., & Rasinski, T. (2006). Home-school partnerships in literacy education: From rhetoric to reality. *The Reading Teacher, 60*(3), 292–296.

Peregoy, S. F., & Boyle, O. F. (2005). *Reading, writing, and learning in ESL: A resource book for K–12 teachers* (4th ed.). Boston: Pearson/Allyn & Bacon.

Wepner, S., Valmont, W., & Thurlow, R. (2000). *Linking literacy and technology: A guide for K–8 classrooms.* Newark, DE: International Reading Association.

Websites

Helping all children become literate has always required that teachers keep up with new materials, new practices, and new research. The following websites will help you learn about changes in a variety of areas of educational interest, especially technology.

The Educator's Reference Desk
At this site you can find more than two thousand lesson plans, more than three thousand links to online education information, and more than two hundred archived responses to questions.
http://www.eduref.org

Discovery School: Kathy Schrock's Guide for Educators to Literature and Language Arts
Kathy Schrock's Guide for Educators is a categorized list of sites useful for enhancing curriculum and professional growth. It is updated often to include the best sites for teaching and learning.
http://school.discovery.com/schrockguide/arts/artlit.html

Educational Resources Information Center
The Educational Resources Information Center (ERIC) is a national information network of education information from all sources maintained by the U.S. Department of Education. Search the ERIC database to find education-related journal articles, research reports, curriculum and teaching guides, conference papers, books, and more.
http://www.eric.ed.gov

Houghton Mifflin's Education Place for Reading and Language Arts
Graphic organizers, resources, lesson plans, and links for K–8.
http://www.eduplace.com/rdg/index.html

International Reading Association
The International Reading Association (IRA) provides resources for teachers, reading specialists, tutors, and others concerned about literacy. Topics range from performance-based assessment to classroom discussion strategies, integrated instruction, motivation for reading, and teaching English as a Second Language. Visit the IRA's website to learn about books, journals, videos, and multimedia products about reading comprehension and literacy. You may be particularly interested in the IRA's five professional journals mentioned in this chapter.
http://www.reading.org

International Society for Technology in Education
The International Society for Technology in Education (ISTE) helps K–12 teachers and administrators share effective methods for enhancing student learning through the use of new classroom technologies. The website offers information about publications as well as about conferences and workshops.
http://www.iste.org

National Council of Teachers of English

The National Council of Teachers of English (NCTE) is devoted to improving the teaching of English and the language arts at all levels. NCTE publishes a member newspaper, three monthly journals (mentioned earlier in the chapter), and ten quarterlies. It also publishes position papers, teaching ideas, and other documents on professional concerns, such as professional standards. Explore the website to learn more.

http://www.ncte.org (Also see http://www.ncte.org/about/over/standards/ 110846.htm for a list of the twelve standards for English language arts developed by the National Council of Teachers of English (NCTE) and the International Reading Association.)

U.S. Department of Education's Just for Teachers Site

The U.S. Department of Education's mission is to ensure equal access to education and to promote educational excellence throughout the nation. At its Just for Teachers Site, check out the Toolkit for Teachers and the Reading Resources compendium.

http://www.ed.gov/teachers/landing.jhtml

A Comprehensive Balanced Literacy Program

2

EDUCATORS SPEAK

Using a Classroom Speaker System and the Read-Aloud Mode to Meet the Needs of Diverse Listeners, p. 42
—*Joy Nelson, Allentown, Wisconsin*
Using Listening Across the Curriculum, p. 54
—*Diane Alsager, Cedar Rapids, Iowa*

Terms
YOU NEED TO KNOW

- adequate yearly progress
- authentic literature
- automaticity
- basal series or system
- comprehensive balanced literacy instruction
- core instruction
- corrective feedback
- created text
- decodable text
- focus lesson or minilesson
- guided listening lesson
- high-frequency words
- literacy lesson
- metacognition
- modes of reading
- modes of writing
- predictable text
- scaffolding

L et's visit two second-grade teachers, Ms. Marks and Mr. Anzo. As you look at their class-rooms, think about how they are alike and how they are different.

Ms. Marks has twenty-three second graders: twelve boys and eleven girls. Three of her students speak mainly Spanish, and the child from Bosnia speaks a little English. Four students are having difficulty learning to read; they attend a special reading program for 30 minutes a day, three days a week, for extra instruction.

Ms. Marks uses a published reading and language arts program. She divides her class into three groups for language arts and reading instruction and uses the second-grade book for all groups. She follows the manual and uses all of the practice pages provided with the program. One group contains three English Language Learner (ELL) students and four native English speakers who all need English-language development work. Ms. Marks usually reads the stories aloud to the students, because they are unable to read them on their own. Her second group has twelve students who are making good progress in language arts and reading; one is an ELL student. Her third group consists of her four best readers.

Ms. Marks explained that the school is currently focusing on standards for language arts. She says that she doesn't have time for any additional instruction, and can't see how she will ever have time to meet the standards.

Mr. Anzo teaches across the hall from Ms. Marks and uses the same published reading and language arts program. He is also supposed to be focusing on the new language arts standards and has compared the standards for second grade to what the teacher's manual provides to support the standards. Mr. Anzo has twenty-four students: thirteen boys and eleven girls. He has five ELLs: three speak primarily Spanish and can read in Spanish; the two children from Bosnia speak only their native language.

Mr. Anzo has literacy instruction planned in blocks. He starts each morning with a 15-minute block for independent reading. During this time, he has conferences with a few students. His ELLs sometimes read books in their native language or listen to English books on tape. Three days each week, Mr. Anzo's entire class works in the grade-level book from the published program. He varies instruction by having students work with the same text differently. For example, today Mr. Anzo is directing one group, while other students are reading aloud with partners. Later in the morning, another group meets with Mr. Anzo for a phonics lesson, while other students do phonics practice activities at centers and on the computer. On the other two days of the week, all students are placed in books appropriate to their reading level.

Just as we are getting ready to leave, Mr. Anzo says that it is time to start the writing block. He explains that this takes place every day. He adds that his ELLs also go to English Language Development class each afternoon, and his struggling readers attend the special reading program for 30 minutes, three days per week.

The HM TeacherPrepSPACE Student Website offers many helpful resources, such as self-quizzes, glossary flashcards, lesson plan templates, and more.

Although our visits to these two classrooms were brief, we can begin to see the differences in the approaches of these two teachers. Ask yourself several questions:

- Which teacher tried to focus on the standards?
- Which teacher provided a balance of reading and writing instruction?

- Which teacher provided direct instruction in skills?
- Which teacher appeared to do more to differentiate instruction to meet students' needs?
- Which teacher was trying to provide a more Comprehensive Balanced Literacy Program?

If you answered *Mr. Anzo* to all of these questions, you are correct. Overall, Mr. Anzo was providing **comprehensive balanced literacy instruction** for his class. Certainly Ms. Marks was attempting to meet the needs of her students in the ways that she knew best. However, there are areas where she needs to change her instruction. For example, the group with the students who need English language development also needs books that these students can read. Just reading aloud to them will not teach them to read. Mr. Anzo came much closer to having a Comprehensive Balanced Literacy Program because he:

- looked at how to differentiate instruction using the published program to meet the new language arts standards.
- organized daily independent reading time.
- provided instruction using the grade-level text as well as texts appropriate to the students' abilities.
- provided direct instruction in the skills his students needed.
- had a block for daily writing instruction and he incorporated technology.

In this chapter, we focus on developing a framework for comprehensive balanced literacy instruction. We concentrate on key concepts that are needed to provide differentiated instruction within a comprehensive balanced literacy classroom.

Comprehensive Balanced Literacy Instruction

Over the years, considerable research has been conducted in the field of reading and literacy. Given the current state of our knowledge, some type of a balanced, comprehensive approach to literacy instruction is recommended to ensure that all children and young adults achieve success in literacy (Armbruster & Osborn, 2003; Chen & Mora-Flores, 2006; Gambrell, Morrow, & Pressley, 2007; Lyon & Chhabra, 2004; Snow, Burns, & Griffin, 1998). First, let us answer the question: *What is comprehensive balanced literacy instruction?*

Comprehensive Balanced Literacy Instruction Defined

Many educators and researchers discuss comprehensive balanced literacy instruction (sometimes referred to as comprehensive literacy, sometimes as balanced literacy) (Au, Carroll, & Scheu, 1997; Freppon & Dahl, 1998; Gambrell, Morrow, & Pressley, 2007; Pressley, 1998; Snow, Burns, & Griffin, 1998; Strickland, 1994). When the various models and points of view are examined, it is clear that comprehensive balanced literacy instruction always combines teacher-directed instruction and student-centered activities. Some individuals feel that research supports more teacher-directed instruction (Chall, 2000), and some think that research supports more student-centered activities (Weaver, 1994). However, in the big picture, a comprehensive balanced approach appears to be the most effective for all students (Pressley, 1998; Snow, Burns, & Griffin, 1998). We use the term *Comprehensive Balanced Literacy Program* (or *instruction*) throughout this text.

Teacher-directed instruction involves systematically and explicitly modeling or showing students how to use a skill, strategy, or process. For example, in writing, we model the process of writing a good sentence. Then students write their own sentences.

In student-centered instruction, students perform a given task, from which they are expected to learn certain things. For example, in reading, we have students read a short story that includes two or three words they do not know, expecting that they will learn the meanings of each word by using the context in which the word occurs; this might be a sentence, a paragraph, or the entire story. If we had used teacher-directed instruction, we would have taught the word meanings prior to reading.

Some students may learn one task better with more direct instruction, whereas others might learn better with more student-centered instruction. An effective literacy teacher differentiates instruction for students in accordance with their strengths, their needs, and the tasks they are performing. All students need both teacher-directed instruction and student-centered instruction, depending on what they are learning. Thus, comprehensive balanced literacy instruction is a combination of teacher-directed instruction and student-centered activities.

A Model for Comprehensive Balanced Literacy Instruction

In order to develop an effective Comprehensive Balanced Literacy Program, you need a model or framework. The basic framework presented in Figure 2.1 is the same for kindergarten through grade 8. Modifications are made across the grades as needed.

The Comprehensive Balanced Literacy Program has six blocks that make up **core instruction,** instruction that is needed by all students.

- Daily Independent Reading
- Daily Independent Writing
- Reading: Learning Skills and Strategies
- Reading: Application of Skills and Strategies
- Writing: Learning to Write
- Writing: Developmentally Appropriate Writing

The seventh block, intervention, provides additional instruction for struggling readers who are not making **adequate yearly progress.**

Let's see what takes place in each block:

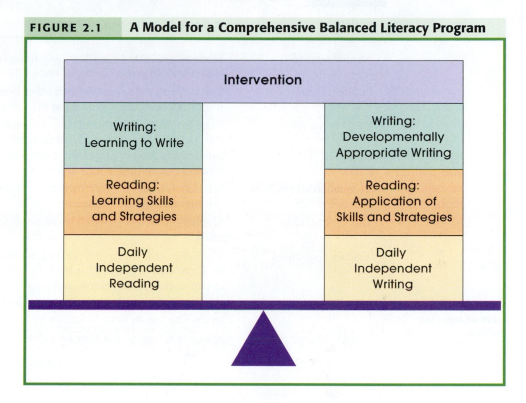

FIGURE 2.1   **A Model for a Comprehensive Balanced Literacy Program**

Intervention

Writing:
Learning to Write

Writing:
Developmentally
Appropriate Writing

Reading:
Learning Skills
and Strategies

Reading:
Application of
Skills and Strategies

Daily
Independent
Reading

Daily
Independent
Writing

Daily Independent Reading

See Chapter 10 for a discussion of creating a learning environment in the classroom.

Two activities—*self-selected reading* and *reading for fluency practice*—take place during this block. For self-selected reading, students read books of their own choosing. Beginning in preschool, children usually look at the pictures and often pretend to read the text by running their fingers along the lines of print. As children develop their skills through instruction in reading, they begin to read a greater variety of texts. This time in the program establishes the habit of independent reading.

To support self-selected reading, you need many different books, children's and young adult periodicals, and some newspapers. These can be displayed in the library area.

Starting in preschool, children usually select books by looking at the covers and illustrations. As they learn to read, you help them learn to select books they can read. Teach and model a procedure that many teachers use called "Thumbs Up." Tell children to read a page in the book. Each time they come to a word they don't know, they fold a finger down on one hand. If the child's thumb is still up at the end of the page, the text is probably appropriate for the child.

See Chapter 5 for routines for fluency practice.

A second part of daily independent reading is time for fluency building. For this, you will need books that are at the students' independent and instructional reading levels. Books used in previous instruction can be used for practice through

TABLE 2.1	Daily Fluency-Building Activities
Activity	**Description**
All students read	Students read aloud a book at their independent reading level. Everyone reads (softly) at once.
Partner reading	Two students read aloud to each other from the same text. Both students must be reading at the same reading level.
One-minute reads	Same as "All Students Read" except teacher times for 1 minute. Teacher directs students to start and stop at designated times. Students mark their stopping places and then count the number of words they read.
Tape-recorded readings	Students read on to a tape recorder and then listen to their reading and check for accuracy.
Teacher coaching	Teacher listens and provides corrective feedback as student reads.
Teacher read-aloud	Teacher models fluent oral reading. Have a copy of the text on a transparency or in a big book to show students where to pause, change expression, and stop.
Repeated reading	Teacher and students read aloud the same text several times. This can be done in groups by level or individually.
Readers theater	Students act out stories they have read by taking parts and reading a script.

See Chapter 5 for more on repeated reading.

repeated reading (Rasinski, 2003). Table 2.1 presents a number of activities that can be used for fluency practice at all grade levels.

Self-selected reading at the beginning of kindergarten should last about 5 minutes each day. As the year progresses, this time can be extended to 10 minutes. In first and second grades, independent reading is usually 10 to 15 minutes per day. In grades 3 through 8, independent reading increases to 15 to 20 minutes per day. Approximately 5 minutes per day should be allotted for fluency practice. It may also occur at other times in the two reading blocks.

Daily Independent Writing

During this time, children write what they want to write. In preschool, kindergarten, and the beginning of first grade, this "writing" may actually be drawing a picture with a few scribbles under it. Independent writing, like independent reading, provides students with the needed practice time to become proficient and establishes the habit of writing daily. As students progress through the grades, they will write a greater variety of products on varying topics.

The amount of time for independent writing will range from 5 minutes per day at the beginning of kindergarten to 10 minutes or more by the end of the year. In first and second grades, the amount of time for independent writing is usually 10 to 15 minutes per day. For grades 3 through 8, the amount of time should be 15 to 20 minutes per day.

Reading: Learning Skills and Strategies

Focus of This Block In this block, students receive instruction centered on the anthology of the basal series being used or a core book selected for the grade level, which helps develop grade-level skills and strategies and exposes students to grade-level background, vocabulary, and concepts. Explicit, direct instruction and student-centered instruction are used to teach the skills and strategies involved in decoding, comprehension, and study skills as needed. For example, in this block, beginning readers are systematically and explicitly taught to decode words through phonics and other skills and strategies. As they develop their ability to figure out words, they immediately begin to read **decodable texts** that allow them to practice and apply the skills they are learning. These texts may be in little book form and/or in the anthology of the basal program.

These various kinds of texts, including authentic literature, are discussed later in this chapter.

As children become more skilled at reading words, they should move beyond decodable texts to **authentic literature** that has been selected to help them continue to practice and apply the skills they have learned. As children gain power in decoding and as they develop independence, they will read more and more authentic literature. Independence in decoding for most children usually occurs by the end of second grade; for others, this might take longer.

During this block, children are also taught a number of **high-frequency** words, ones that occur often in English. They practice reading these words in the decodable texts being used for practice and application of phonics and other decoding skills and strategies.

See Chapters 4 and 5 for instructional routines to use during this block.

Constructing meaning, or comprehension, and research and study skills and strategies are also taught during this block. Various teaching routines are used throughout this block.

Managing This Block When Students Read at Different Levels When using a grade-level anthology or single core text for the Learning Skills and Strategies block, you may face the challenge of having some students for whom the text is too difficult to read independently or some for whom the text is so easy that learning will not take place. To accommodate all students, you must differentiate the way the text is read so that students read in accordance with their abilities. This requires small groups and having students read in a mode, or way, that helps them succeed. Modes are discussed in more detail in the "Modes of Reading as Forms of Instruction" section on page 33. Remember—when using a single grade-level text or core text, you must vary the way students read the text so that every student can be successful.

Summary In the Reading: Learning Skills and Strategies block students at all grade levels are taught the skills and strategies of reading using the grade-level anthology or core book, either with the whole class or small groups. If the book is too difficult for some students, you adjust your instruction to meet individual needs. All chapters that follow will help you learn to do this.

Reading: Application of Skills and Strategies

This is the block of the core instruction where students apply the skills and strategies they have been learning in texts appropriate to their reading levels. This means

Video Case

Elementary Reading Instruction: A Balanced Literacy Program

Watch the video clip, study the artifacts in the case, and reflect on the following questions:

1. Does the classroom depicted in this Video Case include all the components of a Comprehensive Balanced Literacy Program (see Figure 2.1 on page 27)? Which components can you identify, and which ones might be missing?

2. In your opinion, what is most effective about this teacher's approach to literacy instruction?

that students are able to read the texts independently or with minimal guidance and support. The texts used may include created, or specially written, texts, as well as authentic literature. This block requires the teacher to manage several reading groups in the classroom.

Writing: Learning to Write

See Chapter 8 for writing, spelling, and grammar instructional routines.

In this block, children are taught how to write, either in groups or as a whole class. In preschool, kindergarten, and first grade, you begin by modeling how to form letters, words, and sentences. As students develop their ability to write, you model different types of writing; spelling and grammar are taught as appropriate.

Writing: Developmentally Appropriate Writing

In this block, students write their own pieces. They do the same type of writing taught in the previous block, *but they select their own topics*. In the beginning, they may draw pictures and write a few letters or single words as captions for their pictures; gradually they begin to write stories, reports, and other pieces. In this block, students practice and apply grammar and spelling.

Intervention

For a detailed discussion of intervention, see Chapter 9.

This block is provided *in addition to the six blocks of core instruction for students experiencing difficulty learning to read and special education students*. Intervention is designed to stop or prevent failure for those students. The intervention block is supported by the six blocks of the classroom program, showing that students who need intervention also need strong, quality classroom instruction.

The amount of time required for the six blocks varies from grade level to grade level. In kindergarten, you need a minimum of 3 hours per day. In grades 1–8, most schools are trying to provide a 90-minute block for reading and a 30–45 minute block for writing; for students needing intervention, an additional 30–40 minute block is provided. Most first and second grades have another 30–60 minutes, as 90 minutes in grades 1 and 2 is not sufficient for reading instruction.

In summary, the model we have presented for comprehensive balanced literacy instruction provides a framework for planning instruction in line with *all students' needs* as they progress through the stages of literacy development. Although this program model stops at grade 8, literacy instruction should continue through grade 12 (Biancarosa & Snow, 2004).

Standards and Instruction in a Comprehensive Balanced Literacy Program

As we have already discussed, a Comprehensive Balanced Literacy Program includes a combination of teacher-directed instruction and student-centered instruction. Instruction within the program may be delivered in many forms. The teacher is key to planning this instruction, which is based on the standards to be covered and the individual students' needs.

The Role of Standards

The standards for your state or district guide the content that should be taught in your classroom's Comprehensive Balanced Literacy Program. State standards will help you determine what you teach in your program. Individual student needs will determine exactly where each student is in relationship to the standards for your grade. This is called *assessment-based* or *diagnostic literacy instruction* (Cooper & Kiger, 2008).

The Role of the Teacher

For a detailed discussion of modeling and sample lessons using think-alouds, see Chapter 4.

The teacher creates the circumstances and conditions within the classroom that support learning. **Focus lessons,** or **minilessons,** are concise lessons that teach a specific skill, strategy, or process. These lessons may use *modeling;* that is, they may show or demonstrate for students how to use the processes of reading or writing or how to use particular strategies that might help in decoding words or constructing meaning. For example, when teachers read a story to the class, they are modeling fluent reading; when they write a group story with the class, they are modeling writing. Many times, modeling involves the use of "think-alouds," sessions in which teachers share the thought processes they have gone through in constructing the meaning of a text (Clark, 1984; Meichenbaum, 1985).

In other instances, the teacher may set up an activity in which students work together on a task. This is known as *cooperative learning*. The teacher observes the activity while students are working, and provides directive support or coaching through questions and suggestions.

Instruction also gives students the opportunity to respond to their reading and writing. *Responding* is the essence of literacy: it is the construction of personal meanings (Rosenblatt, 1938/1976, 1978). Students may react to, talk about, or do something appropriate with a piece of literature they have read or listened to, or a story

TABLE 2.2	**Examples of Responding**

- *Before reading:* Students might look at a book and predict what will happen based on their knowledge of the topic or the author. This is the beginning of responding.
- *During reading:* As students are reading, they might have a reaction to a particular character and write a note about it in their journal or change a prediction in the light of new information.
- *After reading:* Because students loved the book they read, they may select another book by the same author, or may choose to retell the story to someone else.

For more discussion of responding, see Chapter 7.

they have written. For example, after writing a mystery, a student might want to read it aloud to some classmates or have it read and reacted to by others. Students who have read a book such as *Bridge to Terabithia* (Paterson, 1977) might respond to it by discussing it in a group. Responding must be authentic in that it must be the type of activity one naturally does with reading and writing. It may take place before, during, or after students read or write. See Table 2.2 for examples of responding.

The teacher plans and supports the activities and experiences that encourage responding. Teachers should prompt students to respond in ways of their own choosing or direct them by offering suggestions for the type of response they might make.

Reading in a variety of ways is an important part of instruction. The support the teacher provides while students are involved in reading or writing is called **scaffolding** (Collins, Brown, & Newman, 1987). This might be questioning that helps students understand what they have read or modeling to show students how to think through a particular piece of text or to learn a strategy. As students become increasingly competent, the teacher begins to remove the scaffolding, providing less and less support. This is what Pearson (1985) calls the "gradual release of responsibility." In other words, the teacher gradually gives more responsibility to the students. This process occurs in any learning situation. For example, young children who learned to read before formal instruction learned in this way: first someone read to them, and then gradually that person read less and less, and the children read more and more.

Instruction may be planned or unplanned (Durkin, 1990), and both types are necessary. However, once you have learned how to provide quality planned instruction, you are more likely to be comfortable seizing the teachable moment, or responding spontaneously to a situation that arises unexpectedly during a lesson or activity. For example, suppose your children have read *Today Was a Terrible Day* (Giff, 1980). In the discussion that follows, you realize that several children do not understand why Ronald Morgan is feeling so unhappy in school. Therefore, you begin by directing them to the first unhappy incident: when Ronald Morgan drops his pencil. By questioning and discussing, you help the children see how dropping the pencil and Miss Tyler's response make Ronald unhappy. You continue through the story in this way, looking at all events that take place. You are providing the support, or scaffold, when it is needed, to help the children construct meaning.

Another important part of the instruction is using different types of reading and writing to scaffold the support that students need. In the following section, we look at different modes of reading and writing. Knowing how to use different modes of

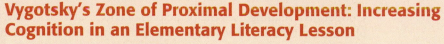

Video Case

Vygotsky's Zone of Proximal Development: Increasing Cognition in an Elementary Literacy Lesson

Watch the video clip, study the artifacts in the case, and reflect on the following questions:

1. Explain how the teacher in this Video Case illustrates the concept of "scaffolding" that is discussed in the chapter.

2. In your opinion, which of this teacher's scaffolding strategies are most effective? Which specific practices allow her to get the most out of her students?

reading and writing along with explicit, direct instruction provides you with a powerful combination of teaching tools that will ensure that *all* students succeed in reading and writing.

Modes of Reading as Forms of Instruction

Students may read a piece of text differently, depending on their stage of literacy development, as well as the complexity of the literature. No one mode is exclusively for reading at one stage or another. Rather, decisions as to which mode to use in a given instructional situation should be made by the teacher and/or students on the basis of the text, the students' reading abilities, and the particular lesson or situation. The teacher must be aware of each of the possible ways to approach reading and when, why, and how to use them. We will discuss five **modes of reading:**

- independent reading
- cooperative reading
- guided reading
- shared reading
- read-aloud

Independent Reading

During independent reading, students read all or part of a selection by themselves. As a mode of instruction, independent reading should not be confused with the independent, self-selected (voluntary) reading portion of the literacy program discussed earlier in this chapter. Since independent reading involves the least support possible, it is used when students have sufficient ability to read a piece of text without any support from the teacher or peers. It can also be used for rereading after students have received sufficient support through other modes of reading. Unfortunately, struggling readers may get few, if any, opportunities to read whole pieces of quality literature independently (Allington, 1977, 1983; Allington & Walmsley, 1995). *All students at all levels need to have instructional experiences in independent reading.*

Cooperative Reading

Cooperative reading uses the principles of cooperative learning (Slavin, 1990). Pairs of students take turns reading portions of a text aloud to each other, or they read silently to a designated spot and then stop to discuss what they have read. The students predict what they think will happen next and continue reading the next portion of the text, either aloud or silently, and stop again for discussion. This pattern continues until they have finished the book or selection. If reading aloud, students may take turns reading a sentence, paragraph, or page. Be sure that they are allowed to pass if they do not feel prepared to read the text.

    Cooperative reading is sometimes called *buddy reading, partner reading,* or *paired reading* (Tierney, Readence, & Dishner, 1990). It should be used when students need *some support* and are not quite able to handle an entire selection independently. The guidelines in Table 2.3, based in part on the successful reciprocal teaching

---

TABLE 2.3	**Guidelines for Cooperative Reading**

1. *Preview and predict.* Have the students look through the text and examine the illustrations or pictures; ask them to read the beginning portion of the text and predict what they think will happen or what they will learn.

2. *Read orally or silently.*

Oral Version	**Silent Version**
Skim silently. Each student skims the text silently before beginning oral reading.	*Read.* Each student reads the same portion of text silently, keeping in mind the predictions made.
Read orally. One student reads aloud the first part of the text while the other(s) follow along.	*Discuss, respond, and check predictions.* The students stop and retell or summarize what they have read. They tell how they feel about what they have read or what they have learned, and they talk about whether their overall predictions were verified or need to be changed.
Discuss, respond, and check predictions. The students stop and retell and/or discuss how they feel about what was read. They talk about whether they have verified or need to change their overall predictions.	
Predict and read. The students predict what they think will happen or what they will learn in the next section. The second student then reads aloud the next section. This pattern continues until the selection is completed.	*Predict and read.* The students predict what they think will happen next or what they will learn. They continue reading the next section silently. This pattern is followed until the entire piece has been completed.

3. *Summarize and respond.* After completing the entire selection, the students summarize what they have read. They respond by discussing how they feel about what they have read and deciding what they might do with it (tell someone about it, write their own summaries, use art to share what they read, and so forth).

model (Palincsar & Brown, 1986), should help you use cooperative reading in your class. You may want to model this process for your students.

Guided Reading

Detailed use of observational guided reading is discussed in Chapter 5.

Guided reading or *leveled reading* is an important part of helping readers develop fluency (National Reading Panel, 2000a). The two basic types of guided reading are: *observational* and *interactive*. Observational guided reading (our term) is the type discussed by Fountas and Pinnell (1996). Students read a text that has a minimal number of new concepts and skills. The teacher introduces the text, and students make some predictions. As they read, the teacher observes and coaches them in their use of strategies. The text is usually a short book or text that is read in its entirety.

With *interactive guided reading*, the teacher carefully guides, directs, or coaches students through the silent reading of a meaningful chunk of text by asking them a question, giving prompts, or helping them formulate a question that they then try to answer as they read the designated section of text. Sometimes the teacher helps students make predictions. At the end of each chunk, the students stop and discuss with the teacher the answer to the question or their predictions, as well as other points. The teacher encourages students to reflect on the strategies they have used and to discuss how those strategies have helped them construct meaning. At each stopping point, the teacher encourages students to respond to what they have read.

Interactive guided reading, as the name implies, involves both students and teacher participating in the process. It is used when students need a great deal of support in constructing meaning because of the complexity of the text or their limited abilities. This approach allows the teacher to adjust the scaffolding according to students' needs. For example, suppose your students are reading *Matilda* (Dahl, 1988) and you are guiding them through the first chapter, "The Reader of Books." As students are reading the first part of the chapter, you realize they do not have the appropriate or sufficient background needed to construct meaning. Perhaps they cannot relate to a child who begins school already reading as well as Matilda. Therefore, you provide the background they need. This type of unplanned instruction uses the "teachable moment." *The lesson scenario using interactive guided reading might go as follows. The annotations in parentheses should help you see what is happening.*

(*Relate prior knowledge to first chapter.*)

> *Teacher:* We have previewed the book *Matilda* and know that it is about a little girl who is gifted. We are now ready to read the first chapter. Who can find it in the book and read the title?
>
> *Sammy:* "The Reader of Books."

(*Get students to think about what might happen.*)

> *Teacher:* What do you think that title tells you about Matilda?
>
> *Megan:* She might read books.
>
> *Beth Ann:* I think the teacher reads books.
>
> *Teacher:* Let's turn through the chapter and look at the illustrations that Quentin Blake, the illustrator, drew. What does Matilda seem to be doing?

> *Tara:* She's reading lots of books.
>
> *Sammy:* It looks like she is in the library.
>
> *Juro:* Maybe she just looks at the pictures. She's so young to read.

(Guides students to predict. Helps students set purpose for reading.)

> *Teacher:* What would you predict is going to happen in this chapter?
>
> *Sammy:* Matilda is going to read a lot of books.
>
> *Juro:* Matilda is a little girl, but she reads a bunch of books.
>
> *Teacher:* [Records predictions on chalkboard.] Let's read pages 7, 8, and 9 silently to see if either of these predictions is correct. (Students read.)

(Follow up by having students check predictions. This is all a part of the scaffolding.)

> *Teacher:* Were either of our predictions confirmed?
>
> *Larry:* No. The author just told us that some parents think their kids are geniuses.

(Support students in clarifying.)

> *Teacher:* Did he mean the kids really are geniuses?
>
> *Juro:* No. Parents just think they are.
>
> *Teacher:* How can you tell that Roald Dahl is making fun of these types of parents?
>
> *Analise:* Because of the funny things he would write about the kids.
>
> *Teacher:* Like what?
>
> *Beth Ann:* He said he would write that Maximillian is a total washout and that he hopes there is a family business for him.
>
> *Sammy:* That's funny.
>
> *Teacher:* Why?
>
> *Sammy:* Because it just is. Maximillian must be lazy or dumb.
>
> *Megan:* No, he isn't. Roald Dahl is just being funny.

(Coach students to notice how authors motivate readers.)

> *Teacher:* Do you think he is trying to get us interested in his book?
>
> *Most students:* Yes.

(Encourage personal response.)

> *Teacher:* How did these pages make you feel?
>
> *Larry:* They were kind of funny.
>
> *Beth Ann:* Sad. I hope a teacher wouldn't really write those things.

(Support students in thinking about their predictions.)

> *Teacher:* Do you think we should change our predictions?
>
> *Juro:* No, we haven't read enough yet.

(Support students in having a purpose for reading.)

> *Teacher:* Let's read pages 10 and 11 silently and think about our predictions.

(Follow up on purpose for reading.)

> *Larry:* She's smart.
>
> *Juro:* She's a little kid.
>
> *Analise:* Her mother and dad don't like her.
>
> *Juro:* That's sad.
>
> *Teacher:* It is sad. Why do you think they feel that way?
>
> *Sammy:* I don't think they understand her.
>
> *Teacher:* Are there books for her to read?
>
> *Beth Ann:* No. Just one on cooking.

(The lesson would continue in this manner.)

Interactive guided reading is a very flexible tool; you can provide more support for students at the beginning of the reading, and gradually release the responsibility to them as the reading progresses. In this process, you control the amount of support through:

1. the types of questions you ask or the prompts you give before reading and during discussion,

2. the amount of text you have students read, and

3. the type of discussion held between reading sessions.

When students need more support, you can direct the discussion; then, as you give students more responsibility, they may carry out and direct the discussion with a partner.

Simply asking children about what they have read is not going to teach them how to construct meaning (Durkin, 1978, 1981). However, we know that the questions and prompts during interactive guided reading can help if they are of the appropriate types (National Reading Panel, 2000b). Effective questions or prompts meet the following criteria:

■ Questions or prompts given before reading should lead students to the important ideas in the text. In narrative text, they should focus on the setting of the story (time and place), the major characters, the story problem, the action, the resolution, and the overall moral or theme. In expository text, they should focus on the main ideas. For example:

> Narrative text: *Who are the two important characters introduced in the story, and what do they do?*
>
> Expository text: *Think about the important things we know about plants.*

■ Questions and prompts used during discussion *between* the sections of reading should pull together ideas brought out in reading and should help build relationships among ideas. For example:

> Narrative text: *Who were the two characters? What did you learn about them and how they usually work together?*
>
> Expository text: *What was the first important thing you found out about plants? How is this likely to help people?*

■ Questions and prompts should follow the order of the text.

By using these guidelines, you will help students develop what Beck calls an overall mental picture of the text being read (Beck, 1984).

Students who still need structured support during reading can use a *monitoring guide* independently. Sometimes called a *study guide* by content-area teachers, this is a sheet that poses questions and gives activities that carefully guide students through the reading of the text. Although often used in content classes, it can be used in reading any text. Figure 2.2 shows a portion of a monitoring guide that students could use while reading the first chapter of *Matilda*.

FIGURE 2.2	**Monitoring Guide for *Matilda***

by Roald Dahl, illustrated by Quentin Blake
Chapter 1, "The Reader of Books," pages 7–21

Previewing and Predicting
- Try to get an idea about this chapter
  —Look at the illustrations
  —Read page 7
- Write your prediction about what you think will happen in this chapter:

  _____

  _____

Reading Pages 7–11
- Now read pages 7–11 to see if your prediction was verified. Maybe you will want to change your prediction. As you read, make notes about any thoughts you have about the chapter.

- Notes: _____

  _____

  _____

After Reading Pages 7-11
- What did you learn about your prediction?

  _____

  _____

- Complete this chart showing what you learned about Matilda. Add other ovals if you need them.

Shared Reading

Holdaway (1979) developed a procedure known as the *shared book experience* for introducing beginners to reading by using favorite stories, rhymes, and poems. In this procedure, the teacher reads aloud a story and invites children to join in the reading or rereading when they feel comfortable. Stories are read several times, and children receive many opportunities to respond through writing, art, drama, discussion, and in other ways. In Holdaway's early description of this procedure, some of the children's favorite books were enlarged for group study; this is the basis for the "big book" concept that many teachers use. The shared book experience has come to be known as *shared reading*.

For a detailed discussion of how to use shared reading, see Chapter 5.

Shared reading provides very strong support for learners. It allows for the modeling of real reading and mimics the ways "natural readers" have learned to read by being read to, reading along with an adult or older child, and ultimately reading on their own. Although shared reading can be used for beginning reading, it can also be used with students at other levels.

Read-Aloud

Sometimes the best way to help children understand a particular piece of text is to read it aloud to them and discuss it with them. This type of reading helps to activate knowledge that the students already have and to develop their background vocabulary and concepts. It also is a way for the teacher to model oral reading. The Educators Speak feature about read-alouds on page 42 in this chapter illustrates how a fifth-grade teacher uses a classroom speaker system and the read-aloud mode to meet the needs of diverse learners.

Reading aloud for instructional purposes provides very strong teacher support for students. It is used when a particular piece of text has difficult concepts or words, would be hard for students to decode, or is difficult to follow. After the teacher has read a piece aloud, students may then read it with the teacher's guidance, cooperatively, or independently.

Combinations of Reading Modes

Table 2.4 summarizes the five modes of reading. Figure 2.3 shows how these modes of reading provide different amounts of scaffolding. Frequently, it is appropriate to combine several modes of reading. For example, if students are reading a short story or a chapter in a book, you might begin by reading aloud the first portion of the piece and discussing it with them. Next, you might put students into pairs and have them do the oral version of cooperative reading. Finally, you might have students read part of the text independently. This combined instructional reading strategy can be called *read aloud, read along, read alone*. By combining these forms of reading, you provide a scaffold for learning that gradually releases responsibility to the students. At the same time, you activate prior knowledge, develop background, and model real reading.

Remember that you can create different combinations as you work to meet the differing needs of your students. Sometimes, let students select their own mode of reading. Sometimes, vary the mode of reading to add fun and variety to your instruction.

TABLE 2.4	Modes of Reading	
Mode	**Description**	**When to Use**
Independent reading	Students read text alone without support, usually silently.	When students are likely to have no difficulty with the text or are highly motivated about the text or text topic.
Cooperative reading	Students read with a partner or partners, either orally or silently.	When students' abilities show need for some support. May also be done just for fun.
Guided reading	Teacher talks, coaches, and walks students through sections of text with questions and student predictions.	When text or students' abilities show need for much support. May be used for variety.
Shared reading	Teacher reads aloud as students view the text. Students chime in when they are ready to do so.	When students need a great deal of support for reading. Often used with beginning readers.
Read-aloud	Teacher reads text aloud. Students usually do not have a copy of the text.	Used when text is too difficult, when background needs to be developed, or for fun or variety.

Modes of Writing as Forms of Instruction

Chapter 8 discusses the writing process along with spelling and grammar.

Throughout the literacy program, students will be writing in response to text and for other purposes. When they write, they will frequently do *process writing;* that is, they will follow the same steps that effective writers use (Graves, 1983; Hillocks, 1987a, 1987b): selecting the topic, drafting, revising, proofreading, and publishing.

Five basic **modes of writing** may be used as part of instruction and learning:

- independent writing
- collaborative/cooperative writing
- guided writing
- shared writing
- write-aloud

Independent Writing

Independent writing is what students do when they write alone. It assumes that they are able to develop their product with little or no support. Independent writing builds power and fluency.

FIGURE 2.3 | **Varying Modes of Reading Provide Differing Amounts of Instructional Support**

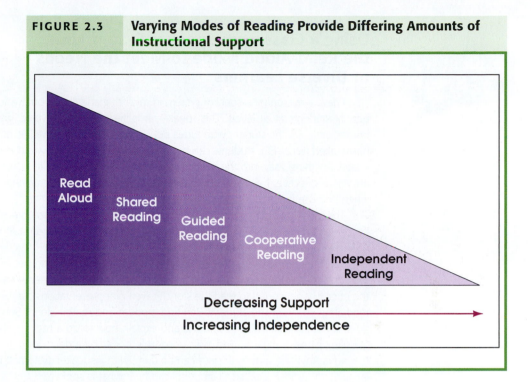

Collaborative/Cooperative Writing

When students write collaboratively/cooperatively, they work with one or more partners on a single product, often taking turns doing the actual writing. This mode of writing (comparable to the cooperative reading mode) gives students support by letting them work together and share ideas. It is often a good way to support writers who are unmotivated.

Guided Writing

This type of writing is comparable to guided reading. Students work on their own products, and the teacher is available to guide them through prompting and questioning. Routman (1991) suggests that this is the heart of the writing program.

Shared Writing

Just as there is shared reading, so there can be shared writing (McKenzie, 1985), sometimes called *interactive writing*. In this type of writing, teacher and students work together to write a group story (using the chalkboard, chart paper, an overhead projector, or a computer) following the steps of process writing. In the beginning, the teacher might do the actual writing, but as the class progresses, different students take turns writing parts of the story. You may also address problems that you

Educators Speak

Using a Classroom Speaker System and the Read-Aloud Mode to Meet the Needs of Diverse Learners

"I have a microphone speaker system in my fifth-grade classroom, which has proven to benefit students at all levels. The speaker amplifies my softest voice, grabbing attention immediately. For the student who tunes out or cannot attend as well as others, the system has worked nicely. ESL students can benefit by hearing proper slow diction of the new language. Anything I say into the microphone is definitely heard by all. My daily read-alouds are more effective. I do not, however, use it exclusively, thus ensuring its effectiveness when I do use it.

The students also love to use the microphone and eagerly volunteer to read aloud. I have seen improvement in oral reading, decoding, and pronunciation skills with the system. A teacher could even use a karaoke machine.

Various activities help students with diverse needs to become better readers. I show old filmstrips with text at the bottom of each frame, and the students take turns handing the microphone around to read the story. PowerPoint presentations can be developed and read aloud in class. The students can find a poem and read it aloud. Sometimes children go to the board with the microphone and explain how to do a math problem. Vocabulary guessing games can be played, with one student reading a definition and others guessing the word. Anything spoken in class can be done with a speaker system. It improves all oral language activities, because all students can hear what is spoken."

—Joy Nelson, Fifth-Grade Teacher
Allenton Elementary School
Allenton, Wisconsin

know students are having, modeling a particular aspect of grammar or spelling for the group without pointing out individual problems. At the same time, you model the full process of writing and can share the thinking processes involved in the construction of meaning.

Figure 2.4 shows a sample of shared descriptive writing that a teacher and students have revised. You can use shared writing when you think students need a great deal of support to help them expand their writing abilities. It is a powerful vehicle for developing minilessons to help students overcome problems in writing at all grade levels.

Write-Aloud

This mode of writing allows the teacher to model the thinking process that occurs during writing. As the teacher writes at a chart or overhead, he or she thinks aloud to share with students his or her thought process. Students listen and read what is being written. This modeling process may be used at any grade level to teach writing.

FIGURE 2.4	Sample of a Shared Writing Experience

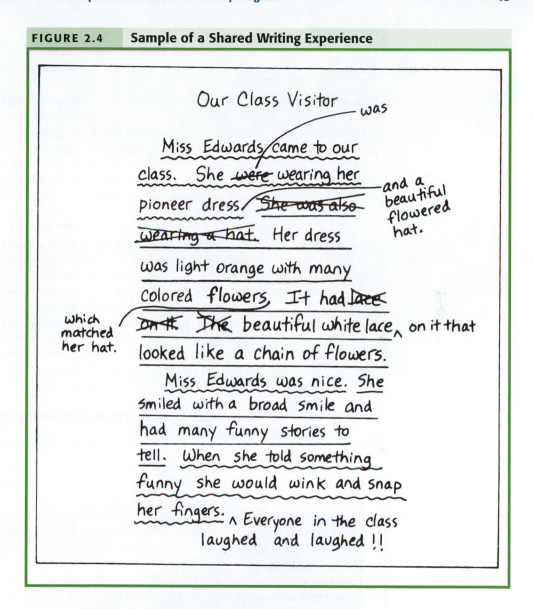

Combinations of Writing Modes

Table 2.5 summarizes the five modes of writing. You may use these modes with any students at any grade level, and you may also combine them. For example, you might begin with shared writing and move to collaborative/cooperative writing, and then independent writing, depending on the amount of support you believe students need. *All students at all levels* need to have the experience of independent writing. You will need to vary the modes of writing you use in the light of students' needs and growth stage. Figure 2.5 shows that by changing the mode of writing you use with students, you change the amount of support you give them. You should encourage students to select the mode of writing that most appropriately meets their stage of development.

TABLE 2.5	Modes of Writing	
Mode	**Description**	**When to Use**
Independent writing	Students write alone.	Students need little or no support.
Collaborative/ cooperative writing	Students write with one or more partners on a single product.	Students need limited support in their writing.
Guided writing	Students write their own product; teacher prompts and guides.	Students have had models of writing but need support in learning how to write their own product.
Shared writing	The group or class writes together, working with the teacher.	Students need a large amount of support in their writing, or teacher sees the need to focus on a particular writing convention.
Write-aloud	Teacher writes at a chart or overhead, sharing the thinking process being used.	Students need to have the process of writing modeled for a particular type of writing.

FIGURE 2.5 **Varying Modes of Writing Provide Differing Amounts of Instructional Support**

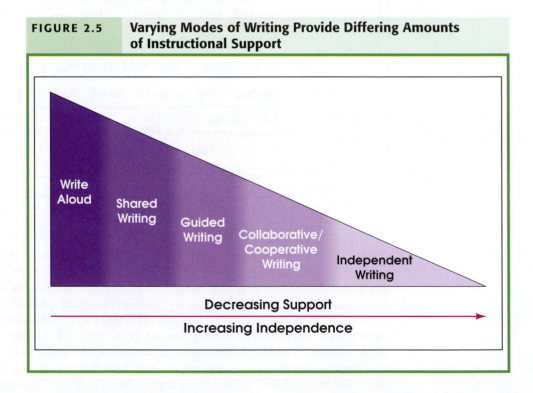

Formats for Developing Standards-Based Literacy Lessons

To plan effective literacy instruction based on standards, you need lesson plans to organize what you do. In this section, we discuss two frameworks that help you achieve this goal: a literacy lesson and a minilesson or focus lesson.

A Literacy Lesson

Various formats have been suggested for reading lesson plans. These include the DRTA, or Directed Reading Thinking Activity (Stauffer, 1969); the DRA, or Directed Reading Activity (Burns, Roe, & Ross, 1988; Harris & Sipay, 1985); and the DRL, or Directed Reading Lesson (Cooper, 1986; Cooper, Warncke, Ramstad, & Shipman, 1979), among others. Although these plans differ somewhat, they are similar in that they focus primarily on reading. The following **literacy lesson** format focuses on both reading and writing and helps the teacher and students relate both activities as integrated literacy learning processes. It has three simple parts: Introducing the Text, Reading and Responding to the Text, and Extending the Text.

First, you must know the standards you want to develop in your lesson. List these standards, remembering that a given standard will be addressed many times. Next, read the text that is to be used for the lesson. If it is a story, identify the parts, such as setting, characters, and problem. If the text is informational (expository), identify the main ideas and supporting details.

Introducing the Text

Chapter 3 is about prior knowledge, vocabulary, and concept development.

When you introduce each piece of text, two things must happen:

1. Students' prior knowledge must be activated and assessed, and pertinent additional background and concepts must be developed. This should include the recognition of key concept vocabulary.
2. Students must develop their purpose(s) for reading.

These two things are accomplished in different ways and with differing levels of teacher support, depending on the text and the students' needs. Sometimes, you teach words that are key to understanding the text, or use the illustrations in the text. For example, if students in a second-grade class are going to read *The Art Lesson* (de Paola, 1989), you might have them preview the story by looking at the pictures and discussing what they think the book will be about. Their purpose for reading then becomes seeing whether their predictions are verified. Throughout, you provide support according to their needs. Often you may incorporate writing into this part of the lesson; for example, you may have students do a "quick write" (an activity in which students are given a topic and a short time to write on it) to activate prior knowledge or to write predictions they will check during and after reading.

Reading and Responding to the Text

Reading and responding to the text take place concurrently; that is, students respond while they are reading as well as after they have read.

Different text requires different modes, depending on the text and students' abilities. Beginning readers and writers and those having difficulty need more scaffolding than others. Moreover, some pieces of text are more complex than others and require more teacher support even for students who are progressing well.

See Chapter 4 for information about strategies for constructing meaning.

The primary focus of this part of the lesson is reading and getting to know the text. As students read, remind them to monitor their reading by asking themselves whether what they are reading makes sense. This process is **metacognition,** knowledge of one's own thinking process. If the text does not make sense, the students should know and use appropriate strategies to help overcome the problem and construct meaning. Metacognitive development is a vital part of constructing meaning and comprehension (Paris, Wasik, & Turner, 1991).

You should not always select the mode of reading that students use. This decision should be made in part by your students. When students choose their own modes of reading, they select those that are most appropriate for their own needs and take greater ownership of their learning.

When responding to the text, students need to do something: *think about it, talk about it, write about it, or do something creative with it involving art, music, or drama.* Responses may be personal and creative. An important part of responding is summarizing or retelling what was read. Some students and some pieces of text require more teacher support than others. By observing how students respond, you can determine whether they need additional support or lessons to develop needed skills and strategies further.

See Chapter 7 for more information on responding.

Let's suppose your class is now ready to read *The Art Lesson*. This book seems easy enough for all students in your class to read independently. However, you offer them the option of reading it independently or cooperatively. You remind students to check whether their predictions were verified or changed as they read and encourage them to make running notes about their feelings or reactions in their journals. After reading, the students could form small groups to retell the story and share their favorite parts. From the responses, you may discover that some students do not understand why Tomie was upset about the art lessons. You then go back to the book and model how Tomie's expectations for art lessons had been built up and how he became disappointed in school. You might do this by developing a graphic organizer like the one shown in Figure 2.6. Throughout the reading-and-responding component, students should be encouraged to reflect on both the meanings they have constructed and how various strategies they have used helped them construct meaning.

Extending the Text

See Chapter 3 for more about making connections.

Extending the text involves further instruction as well as making connections with and integrating other language arts and other curricular areas. Students are

FIGURE 2.6 **Chart Modeling Tomie's Disappointment in *The Art Lesson* (de Paola, 1989)**

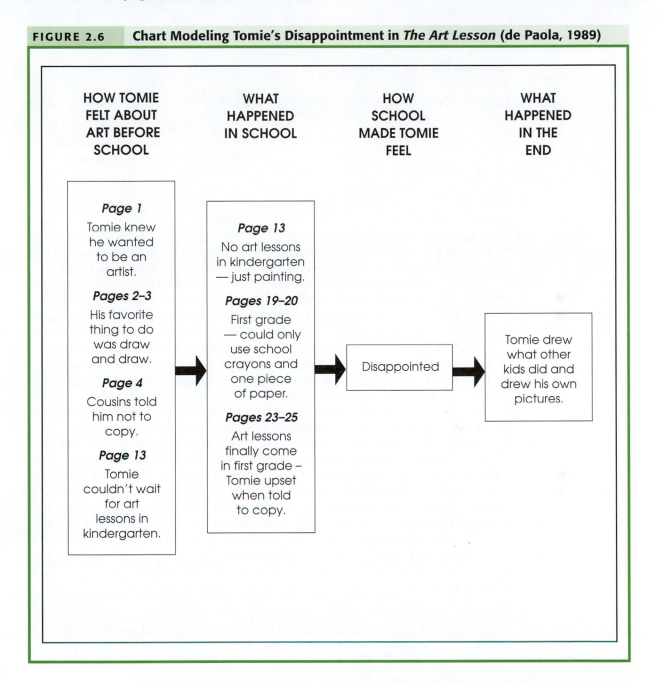

encouraged to use what they have learned in various ways or in different curricular areas such as science, social studies, art, music, and writing. Minilessons or focus lessons may be taught at this point, as well as at other places in the lesson.

Writing may also be tied directly to reading by using the text as a model for a certain type of writing. For example, a natural writing extension for *The Art Lesson*

TABLE 2.6	Summary of the Standards-Based Literacy Lesson Format	
Lesson Part	**Purposes**	**Remarks**
Introducing	Activate and assess prior knowledge and develop background.	The amount of teacher support provided will depend on both the text and the students' needs. Sometimes the support will include development of key concepts and vocabulary.
	Help students set purposes for reading.	Activities used will incorporate reading, writing, speaking, listening, and thinking.
Reading and responding	Read and have access to the entire selection. Do something creative and personal during and/or after reading the selection.	The mode for reading the selection is determined by students' needs and the text. This portion of the lesson focuses on the personal construction of meaning.
	Summarize what has been read.	By observing students' responses, you will be able to determine the need for additional support or mini-lessons.
	Reflect on the text and how various strategies helped in constructing meaning.	This part of the lesson helps students develop their metacognitive abilities, which leads to more effective comprehension.
Extending	Use the understandings and ideas gained from the literature. Use the literature as a model for writing.	Extension of the text will use the knowledge gained in many creative ways or in other curricular areas. Writing may be taught using the text as a model for the type of writing being developed.

is writing a story. Of course, you would vary the mode of writing according to students' needs.

This simple, easy-to-use literacy lesson is flexible and can be used throughout all grades. Make adjustments and variations in accordance with the students' stages of development, the text being read, and the needs of individual students. Table 2.6 summarizes the parts of the literacy lesson.

A Minilesson or Focus Lesson

Throughout all literacy lessons, you need to provide different levels of support to help students continue their process of learning to read and write. Sometimes you provide this support when *introducing* the text, sometimes while students are *reading* and *responding*, and sometimes as they are *extending* the text. *You provide this support in many forms and ways. Minilessons* or *focus lessons*, introduced earlier, are one way to provide the systematic direct instruction that makes instruction effective by breaking it down into smaller units, or chunks.

Minilessons may be used to model the construction of meaning, a skill, or a strategy and may take place before, during, or after reading or writing. They can be based on the text that students have just read or on the students' own writing. You determine the need for a focus lesson by observing how students read and respond to the literature or how they write and respond to their writing. Figure 2.7 shows how all of these elements fit together.

Minilessons may be informal or formal. For example, suppose your students are reading *Mufaro's Beautiful Daughters: An African Tale* (Steptoe, 1987), which tells a version of the Cinderella story. As students are responding and discussing the fairy tale, you realize they have not understood that the snake, the hungry little boy, and

FIGURE 2.7 **Model of Reading and Writing with Minilessons**

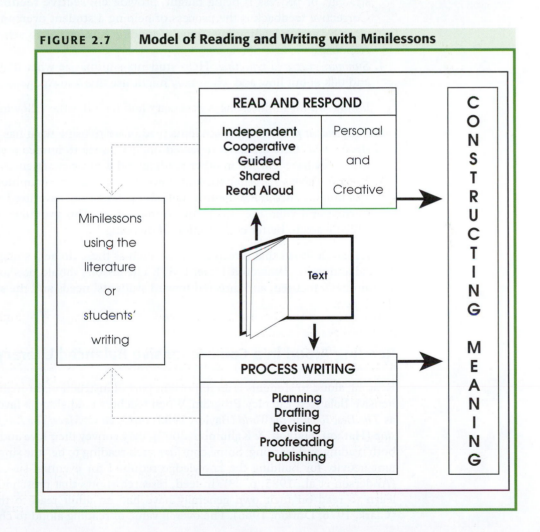

the old woman are all the same person—the king, Nyoka. You immediately have students go back to the story and locate the places where each character appeared and show them that each is the king, who has changed himself into these characters. This is an example of a minilesson taking place when a "teachable moment" arises.

See Chapter 4 for a discussion of think-alouds and three sample minilessons.

Most minilessons are more formal and more carefully and thoroughly planned. First, you identify the standard(s) for the lesson. Then, a typical planned minilesson incorporates the following steps:

1. *Introduction:* Tell students what they will learn and relate it to the text or their writing.
2. *Teacher modeling:* Model the element being taught using the text or writing to show examples. Incorporate think-alouds as needed.
3. *Student modeling and guided practice:* Guide students in modeling and using what is being taught by finding other examples in the text or in their writing. If a skill, strategy, or process is being taught, provide **corrective feedback** as needed. Corrective feedback is the process of helping a student overcome a mistake or error by asking leading questions or guiding him or her to achieve the correct response.
4. *Summarizing and reflecting:* Help students summarize what they have learned, and talk about how and when they might use this knowledge.

Follow-up for minilessons is necessary and includes the following three parts:

1. *Independent practice:* Have students read or write using what has been taught.
2. *Application:* Give students repeated opportunities to immediately use or apply what they have learned in other reading and writing experiences.
3. *Reflecting about use:* After students have had several opportunities to apply what was taught, encourage them to talk about how they have used what they have learned and what they might do to improve it. This promotes metacognition, which leads to better construction of meaning.

Research shows that directed lessons such as these do help some students learn to read and write (Pearson & Dole, 1987). The lessons should be short (usually 5 to 15 minutes), focused, and directed toward students' needs and the standards being developed.

Reading Aloud in a Comprehensive Balanced Literacy Program

Reading aloud to students is an important part of instruction throughout a Comprehensive Balanced Literacy Program. When teachers read aloud a favorite book such as *The Best Town in the World* (Baylor, 1982) or *Owen & Mzee: The Language of Friendship* (Hatkoff, Hatkoff, & Kahumbu, 2007), they convey their love and excitement for both reading and learning. Some consider such reading to be "the single most important activity for building the knowledge required for eventual success in reading" (Anderson et al., 1985, p. 23). Indeed, research shows that preschool children who learn to read on their own generally have had an adult read to them repeatedly (Clark, 1976; Durkin, 1966). The overall value of reading aloud to children at home has been clearly documented (Cain, 1996; Strickland & Taylor, 1989). As teachers, we should encourage all parents to read to their children as much as possible.

Research also verifies the value of reading aloud to children as part of the classroom program (McCormick, 1977). It helps to motivate students and also provides a basis for expanding oral language and prior knowledge (Feitelson, Kita, & Goldstein, 1986), especially for children who have not been read to at home. Reading aloud also influences children's writings (Dressel, 1990). Children who hear a great variety of stories reflect story features in their writing. While there is no substitute for reading to children at home, classroom read-aloud periods can provide some of the same benefits (Strickland & Taylor, 1989; Taylor & Strickland, 1986). There are three important purposes for reading aloud in a Comprehensive Balanced Literacy Program:

1. *Provide motivation and enjoyment.* When we read aloud a good book such as *Snowflake Bentley* (Martin, 1998) or *Not Norman: A Goldfish Story* (Bennett, 2005), we encourage students to read this book as well as others and allow them to enjoy the book.

2. *Build background and develop vocabulary.* Reading aloud exposes students to new ideas and lets them hear and learn new vocabulary. This is important for all students but is especially important when teaching ELLs and other students who do not have a well-developed oral language. Also, reading aloud books such as *The Little Painter of Sabana Grande* (Markun, 1993), *Hurricane Hunters* (Demarest, 2006), or *Bridges* (Simon, 2005) exposes students to many forms of expression, as well as a variety of vocabulary.

3. *Teach specific strategies and skills for comprehension.* Learning to construct meaning, or to comprehend, begins at the oral language level. Strategies for effective comprehension should first be taught through listening and then taught through reading.

See Chapter 4 for a full discussion of this process.

There are two kinds of read-alouds: *general* and *instructional.* General read-aloud primarily provides motivation and enjoyment. Instructional read-aloud builds background, introduces vocabulary and concepts, models fluency, or teaches a particular comprehension strategy or skill. Read-aloud may take place during any of the blocks of a Comprehensive Balanced Literary Program. Each occasion is likely to have more than one purpose. The following guidelines will help you plan read-aloud sessions in your program:

■ *Provide instructional read-alouds.* For instructional purposes, a **guided listening lesson** format should be used that includes the same basic parts as the literacy lesson presented earlier, except that the mode of operation is listening. The parts of this lesson are:

1. Introduce the text.
2. Listen and respond to the text.
3. Extend the text.

The parts of this lesson are described in Table 2.7. In most schools, one or more reading/language arts standards focus on listening (National Council of Teachers of English & International Reading Association, 1996). The Educators Speak feature "Using Listening Across the Curriculum" later in this chapter shows how

TABLE 2.7	Guided Listening Lesson Format	
Component	**Description**	**Comments**
1. Introduce the text.	■ Show the book or other text. ■ Read aloud the title and give the author's name. ■ Ask students to predict what the text is about or what they will learn. Record these for later use.	■ Builds background, vocabulary, and concepts and develops a purpose for listening.
2. Listen and respond to the text.	■ Remind students to keep their predictions in mind as they listen. ■ Read aloud part or all of the text, depending on the length of text and time available. ■ After listening, return to students' predictions. ■ Discuss and revise as needed. ■ Model any strategies or skills you want students to learn.	■ Keeps students focused on their purpose for listening. ■ Helps students learn that predictions change as they get more information. ■ Provides a place to teach strategies for constructing meaning at the listening level.
3. Extend the text.	■ Do one or more of the following: complete a graphic organizer, focus on words, or discuss the strategy or skill taught.	■ Provides a time to pull the parts of the lesson together.

one teacher integrated teaching listening into a content area. A sample guided listening lesson is presented in the next section of this chapter.

■ *Read aloud every day.* Set a consistent time so that children will look forward to the reading session. Many teachers prefer first thing in the morning because it gets the day off to a positive start. Any unexpected extra time is a good time for additional read-alouds.

■ *Have a comfortable, inviting place in the classroom for reading aloud.* Use the library area if it is large enough; sit in a favorite or special chair such as a rocker as you read to the children.

A list of Shel Silverstein and Jack Prelutsky's better-known works and a list of poetry anthologies appear at the end of this chapter.

■ *Select books that both you and the children will enjoy.* Some books may relate to specific themes or topics of study, but they do not have to. If you find you have selected a book the class is not enjoying, stop reading it and take some time to discuss why you have stopped. You should vary the types of books you read, and be sure to include some poetry, since children of all ages enjoy poetry that rhymes and has humor. Two favorite poets of most children are Shel Silverstein and Jack Prelutsky.

■ *Read with expression and feeling.* Make the book come alive for children. Trelease (2006) suggests adding a real-life dimension to your read-aloud session; for example, if you are reading a classic such as *Blueberries for Sal* (McCloskey, 1948) or a more recent favorite such as *Popcorn!* (Landau, 2003), have a bowl of fresh blueberries or some popcorn for children to taste.

■ *Allow time for discussion during and after each read-aloud period.* If students have questions during the reading, take time to discuss them, and use the discussion to talk about favorite parts, feelings, or reactions. Also, be sure to share your own thoughts about a book or story.

■ *Don't allow the discussion to become a time to "test" children on the book.* When you simply ask students a series of questions that require "right" answers, this is not a discussion. Instead, encourage students to share their thoughts, being careful to curb digressions.

■ *Allow students to write or draw as they listen.* Some may find it easier to pay attention if they are allowed to write or draw while listening. Of course, they should not be completing work assignments at this time.

The **Read-Aloud Handbook** *by Trelease listed in "For Additional Reading" will be helpful in planning general read-aloud periods.*

Sample Guided Listening Lesson

The following sample guided listening lesson illustrates how to use the listening lesson format summarized in Table 2.7 (page 52). The lesson also illustrates how to incorporate standards into your lessons. When we discuss classroom organization and management in Chapter 10, you will see how to work listening lessons into the daily schedule of your Comprehensive Balanced Literacy Program.

Before Reading the Lesson

1. Review the parts of a guided listening lesson.
2. Locate and read the book used as a basis for this lesson: *Raising Yoder's Barn* by Jane Yolen, paintings by Bernie Fuchs (Boston: Little, Brown, 1998). The Yoders are an Amish family who encounter a devastating fire that engulfs the windmill and barn on their farm. Their neighbors and friends come to help fight the fire. Once the ashes are raked away, Samuel Stulzfoot is summoned with plans for a new barn. Teams of men haul in beams and boards, and wagons of women and children arrive with hampers of food. The community, family, and friends work to raise Yoder's barn in one day.

Reading the Lesson

1. Note the standard focus for the lesson (see below). This focus is on the standards list for several states.
2. Make notes about questions you want to discuss.

After Reading the Lesson

1. Meet with a colleague to discuss the lesson.
2. Identify ways you might change the lesson.

Using Listening Across the Curriculum

"Listening is a skill that I assumed my students had conquered, so I was puzzled when they didn't follow directions after I had told them exactly what to do. They would ask me questions that I had just answered. I realized after directly teaching listening skills that, like other literacy skills, the ability to listen can be improved. Because of time limitations, I integrated the teaching of listening skills into one content area, science.

First I chose a nonfiction text, *A River Ran Wild: An Environmental History* by Lynne Cherry (1992), to accompany the environmental unit. I discovered that just like other literacy behaviors, there are things listeners do before, during, and after listening.

Before listening to the read-aloud, students were given guidance and instruction on listening skills and strategies. I prepared a graphic organizer listening guide to assist students in focusing on key pieces of information as they listened to the book. Together, we generated a list of questions we had: What is the author's purpose? Do I know something about this topic? What is my purpose for listening? Should I take notes on subject matter? We filled in the listening guide together and displayed it on the overhead.

Next, we discussed what we would do during listening. This list of questions included: Am I learning what I need to know about pollution? Am I putting information about pollution into categories? Am I thinking about the story?

I then read *A River Ran Wild* aloud, twice. Once was for the experience of hearing the story, and the second reading was to focus on the important information about pollution. I stopped at key points during the second reading. I did this to show students how to respond to the questions on the listening guide. We filled in the graphic organizer together on the overhead.

Finally, we considered what good listeners do. The questions generated were: Do I have questions for the author? Was any part unclear? What was the most interesting thing I learned? Is the listening guide complete? Students selected one of the above questions to respond to in writing. The completed listening guide was posted in the classroom.

We completed two more listening guides over the course of the week. One listening guide was used when directions were read for a recycling experiment. A video on litter was the source for our next listening guide. Students were then ready to fill out listening guides in groups. Eventually, students were able to create their own listening guides. The guides were extended to a variety of listening events (guest speakers, intercom announcements, assemblies). This taught students how to listen and shifted the responsibility for listening to them.

—Diane Alsager, Reading Facilitator
Cedar Rapids Community School District
Cedar Rapids, Iowa

Lesson Format

Approximate grade level: second or third grade

Standard focus: Students listen to material and retell it in their own words.

Support for English Language Learners: Since this is a listening lesson, all ELLs can participate. Lesson notes indicate activities that might be needed to support these learners.

Introduce the Text

- Show students the cover of the book and read aloud the title, author, and artist. Point out that *Yoder* is the family's last name.
- Ask students to describe what they see on the cover. (Ask ELLs to describe what they can; if students are just becoming fluent in English, have them work with an English-speaking partner.)

- Ask students what they think the word *raising* means. Discuss the multiple meanings: *lifting, building, bringing up (as children)*.
- Modeling prediction: Tell students that you are going to show them how to think about what is likely to be in the story by using the prediction strategy. For example:

  Teacher models: "I see a man and woman in a wagon in front of the barn. I predict that this is Mr. and Mrs. Yoder going to visit their neighbors."

- Ask several students to make predictions. Record predictions for later use.
- Tell students that after listening to the story, you will help them learn to retell it in their own words.
- Present the story map. Review the parts.
- Tell students as they listen to think about these parts of the story. Remind students to keep their predictions in mind as they listen.

Listen and Respond to the Text

- Read aloud the text in its entirety or in parts, as time permits.
- As you read, show each illustration.
- After listening, review all predictions. Discuss whether they were verified.
- Summarize the story using the story map. As students provide information, record their thoughts on the story map.

Extend the Text

- Using the completed story map as a prompt, demonstrate how you would retell the story in your own words.
- Have students work with partners to retell the story. Depending on the level of your ELLs, have them retell in their native language or in English.

Texts for a Comprehensive Balanced Literacy Program

An effective Comprehensive Balanced Literacy Program uses many types of texts. The goal is for students to read real, or authentic, literature. However, as students develop through the various stages of literacy, different texts may be needed to serve different purposes. As students develop their reading ability, they need texts that are sequenced from simple to complex until they can decode independently (Clay, 1991). Many schools use a published set of materials referred to as a **basal series or system** for their literacy program.

Basal Series or Systems and a Comprehensive Balanced Literacy Program

A basal series or system is a set of published materials that schools adopt and purchase for use as the core instructional materials for their literacy program. These series, which are usually for grades K–6 or K–8, come with various texts and support materials, which usually include the following:

- **Anthologies.** These are collections that usually include specially written texts and excerpts from original literature. They typically include both narrative and expository material, as well as poetry. Anthologies usually begin with the first grade. At the kindergarten level, some big books and sets of little books are provided.

- **Practice books.** Often called workbooks, practice books provide support for instruction, guided practice, and independent practice. Many include work on spelling, grammar, and writing.

- **Teacher's manual.** The manual contains directions and lesson plans for the teacher. It is often correlated to the standards of each individual state.

- **Paperback books.** These are usually authentic works of literature, both narrative and expository.

- **Decodable texts.** For beginning readers, there are usually little books that have been written to provide practice and application of the specific phonics and decoding skills being taught. These are usually available through second grade.

- **Other support materials.** Examples of these are transparencies, CD-ROMs and other technology, books on tape, posters, and charts.

No basal series provides all the materials you will need to meet the needs of all students. Therefore, the remainder of this section addresses three issues:

1. What are the different types of texts needed?
2. How do you select appropriate texts and literature?
3. How can texts be leveled and placed on a continuum of difficulty for appropriate instruction?

Let's examine each of these issues.

Types of Texts

There are four major categories of text in an effective literacy program:

- wordless books
- predictable texts

TABLE 2.8	Types of Texts for a Comprehensive Balanced Literacy Program	
Type	**Description**	**Major Use**
Wordless books	Text composed of only illustrations or photographs. No print is given.	Used to help children develop a concept of themselves as readers, develop oral language, and develop self-expression.
Predictable texts	Texts that use a repeated pattern of some type. May be authentic literature or created text.	Used to introduce children to literature through shared reading and to provide practice through repeated readings.
Created texts	Published texts that may be decodable or written to control high-frequency words, concepts, skills, strategies, and overall difficulty.	Used for practice and application of decoding skills for beginning readers. Also used for practice and application of skills for students who may be experiencing difficulty in certain aspects of learning to read.
Authentic literature	Stories and informational texts in which no attempts have been made to control the words, patterns, or decoding elements used in the text. The unedited and unabridged text is in the original form as written by the author.	Used for practice and application of reading once students have developed beginning decoding skills. Also used for shared reading and read-aloud at any point in the literacy program.

- created texts
- authentic literature

Table 2.8 summarizes the major uses of each type of text.

Wordless Books

Wordless books are children's *picture books* that tell their story or present their information through illustrations or photographs without printed words. Wordless books have varying degrees of detail and complexity, so they can be used for various purposes at various levels.

Wordless books have been recommended for developing oral language and self-expression for all students (Strickland, 1977). They are especially useful for working with ELLs (Peregoy & Boyle, 2005). Examples of well-known wordless books are *Bobo's Dream* (Alexander, 1970), *Do You Want to Be My Friend?* (Carle, 1971), *The Mysteries of Harris Burdick* (Van Allsburg, 1984), *Tuesday* (Wiesner, 1991), and *Sector 7* (Wiesner, 1999).

Wordless books are useful for introducing concepts such as the parts of a book and the idea that a book presents a story or information. Because there is no threat from print on the page, these books are fun. Use them at the early stages of literacy development to develop vocabulary, oral language, and self-expression. Tiedt (2000) recommends using wordless books even in middle school. For ELLs, wordless books help build connections between first languages and English. For all learners, they can motivate students to write.

Predictable Texts

Predictable texts have a repeated pattern of some type. Bridge, Winograd, and Haley (1983) identified seven patterns of predictability in texts:

1. Phrase or sentence repeated. Examples: *Mary Wore Her Red Dress and Henry Wore His Green Sneakers* (Peek, 1985) and *"Slowly, Slowly, Slowly," said the Sloth* (Carle, 2002).
2. Repetitive-cumulative pattern in which a phrase or sentence is built. Examples: *Nobody Listens to Andrew* (Guilfoile, 1957) and *This is the House That Jack Built* (Taback, 2002).
3. Rhyming patterns. Example: *Mrs. McNosh Hangs Up the Wash* (Weeks, 1998).
4. Familiar cultural sequences, such as cardinal and ordinal numbers. Examples: *Feast for Ten* (Falwell, 1993) and *Ten Little Ladybugs* (Gerth, 2000).
5. Familiar cultural sequences, such as the alphabet. Examples: *Dr. Seuss's ABC* (Seuss, 1963), *Old Black Fly* (Aylesworth, 1992), and *Girls A to Z* (Bunting, 2002).
6. Familiar cultural sequences, such as days, months, and colors. Examples: *Chicken Soup with Rice* (Sendak, 1962) and *One Lighthouse, One Moon* (Lobel, 2000).
7. Predictable plots. Examples: *Mr. Gumpy's Outing* (Burningham, 1970) and *We're Going on a Picnic* (Hutchins, 2002).

Predictable texts help children very quickly come to think of themselves as readers (Holdaway, 1979). For example, hearing or reading aloud a book such as *Brown Bear, Brown Bear* (Martin, 1967) in a shared fashion several times soon allows children to be able to recite the text. Often children memorize the text and can repeat it without looking at it. In this way, they think of themselves as readers and have fun reading.

However, too great a reliance on predictable text can cause beginning readers to over-rely on the illustrations rather than focus on the print. Brown (2000) has developed a strong case for limited use of predictable texts to get children who need oral language development started in the process of reading. After students experience success with some predictable text, Brown recommends moving them into what she calls transitional and decodable texts (defined below) to help students develop sequential decoding.

Created Texts

Created texts are written for students at all stages of literacy development so that they can apply various skills and strategies in a text that is usually easy for them to read. Within this category of texts, there are two basic types, decodable texts and other easy-to-read texts.

Decodable texts contain a high percentage of words that use the sound-letter relationships that children are currently being taught, as well as a limited number of high-frequency words (Chard & Osborne, 1999). These texts *may* also include a limited number of "special words" or "story words." For example, if students know the letter-sound relationships for *m* /m/, *s* /s/, *t* /t/, *p* /p/, *e* /e/, and *a* /a/ and the high-frequency and special words *the, elephant, said, no,* and *thank you,* they can read the following story:

Pat and the elephant

> *Pat met the elephant.*
> *The elephant met Pat.*
> *Pat sat.*
> *The elephant sat.*
> *The elephant sat on the mats.*
> *The elephant sat and sat.*
> *Pat sat and sat.*
> *Pat said, "Elephant, pat the pets."*
> *The pets said, "No, thank you, Elephant."*

(Chard & Osborne, 1999, p. 113)

The benefit of this type of text is that it allows students to practice sequential decoding, which is reading through a word from left to right, and develop fluency and **automaticity,** the ability to read words quickly and accurately. These are critical parts of beginning reading instruction (National Reading Panel, 2000a). Students are able to experience immediate success since the text is based on the instruction they have received.

The first major use of text similar to this type occurred in the 1960s (Bloomfield & Barnhart, 1961). It was referred to as *linguistically controlled text.* In 1967, Chall proposed that some of the control in beginning reading materials needed to result from a consideration of the phonic elements previously taught. In the example presented above, *beginning* readers are given an opportunity to apply their decoding skills in a real reading situation.

A major issue related to decodable text is the percentage of decodability (number of words that students can decode based on phonic elements taught thus far) that should be required. Limited research suggests that some decodable texts should be used for beginning reading instruction (Juel & Roper/Schneider, 1985), but there is little research to guide the decision about the percentage of decodability a text should have. The best rule of thumb is to use decodable text only until students become independent in sequential decoding. Recently, some researchers have recommended that, especially for potentially low beginning readers, decoding should be systematically taught quickly up through about February of the school year (Juel & Minden-Cupp, 2000). Although decodable texts are most important in the beginning reading program, they may be needed in later grades for students who have not yet achieved independence in decoding. In all instances, *decodable texts must be used along with other types of texts to help students continue to broaden their oral language base, develop vocabulary, and develop the use of comprehension strategies and skills.*

Easy-to-read texts, the other type of created text, are written for students beyond the beginning level of reading. For students who are progressing normally, easy-to-read texts provide a chance for practice and application of strategies and skills using text that is easy to decode. Students can then return to grade-level material and apply the strategies and skills in more challenging texts. Easy-to-read texts are also appropriate to help students build fluency. However, easy-to-read texts should not comprise a student's entire reading experience. Rather, they, like decodable texts, serve as a stepping stone to authentic literature.

Authentic Literature

Authentic literature (often referred to as trade books) consists of narrative and expository texts in the original form as written by the author. Narratives tell a story and have a structure known as a story grammar that is represented by a story map (see Figure 2.8). Expository texts present information and are organized around various structures. They are usually more challenging for readers because they incorporate several structures rather than having a single structure like a narrative text. They come in the form of books, anthology selections, magazine articles, newspaper articles, and others.

Authentic literature is motivating for students; it captivates their attention and engages them in learning (Huck, 1989; Sanders, 1987). It provides students with natural language texts that continually help them develop and expand their own language structures (Sawyer, 1987). Real (authentic) literature is generally easy for most students to understand (Simons & Ammon, 1989).

Sometimes beginning readers find authentic literature too difficult because they lack the skills to sequentially decode the words and have not yet been taught many of the high-frequency words. For this reason, authentic literature must be used concurrently with other types of texts.

In beginning reading, authentic literature should be used in read-alouds to develop and expand students' oral language, vocabulary, background, and prior knowledge. The listening experiences at these levels should serve as the basis for directly and systematically teaching critical comprehension strategies (National Reading Panel, 2000a).

FIGURE 2.8   **A Story Map**

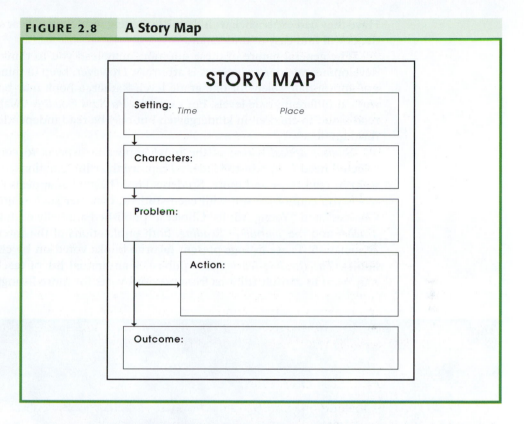

Having students read authentic literature, rather than text contrived for the sole purpose of building skills, is the goal of the literacy program. As soon as students develop some degree of independence in decoding, they should have repeated instructional and independent opportunities to read authentic literature. This literature should continue as the core of the literacy program. It should be carefully selected so that it is appropriate for the students' reading abilities.

Selecting Authentic Literature

Selecting the appropriate texts and authentic literature for the literacy program is both a critical and a challenging process. What constitutes "good literature" is a much-debated topic (Goodman & Goodman, 1991). Even so, it is possible to select quality literature for your students. Since thousands of new books are published annually, literature selection is an ongoing process that should involve you, other readers, the librarian or media specialist, students, parents, and other interested persons. There are four basic criteria to consider in selecting literature: developmental appropriateness, student appeal, literary quality, and cultural and social authenticity.

The developmental appropriateness of a book is determined by looking at the concepts and general complexity of the text. Will your students know the concepts?

Have they had experience with them? Is the text written in a clear style that your students will find easy to understand?

The general nature of these questions may lead you to think that determining developmental appropriateness is arbitrary. However, keep in mind that literature is not appropriate solely for one grade level. Rather, a book may be used in different ways at different grade levels. For example, *Ira Says Goodbye* (Waber, 1988) may be read aloud to children in kindergarten but may be read independently by second or third graders.

Student appeal is one of the most important aspects to consider. The books selected need to appeal to students, capture their imaginations, and entice them to want to read more and more. Students know best what appeals to them. However, when you cannot consult with each student, consider such sources as "Children's Choices" and "Young Adults' Choices," published annually each fall in *The Reading Teacher* and the *Journal of Reading,* both publications of the International Reading Association. These listings present favorite books voted on by children and young adults. *The Reading Teacher* also publishes an annual list of teachers' choices. You may want to consult editions from previous years for those listings.

The librarian helps students select new books.
© Will Hart/PhotoEdit

Literary quality is judged by looking at elements of plot, characterization, setting, theme, style, and point of view. Determining the literary quality of books is a large task for a busy teacher. A major reason that many schools use a basal series is that groups of professionals have already selected the quality literature. Even so, you need to know how to select additional books for your class. The following sources can help you evaluate new books as they become available:

- The *Horn Book Magazine* reviews books from many perspectives. Write to The Horn Book Magazine, 56 Roland Street, Suite 200, Boston, MA 02129.
- *Book Links* presents reviews of books that have been grouped by thematic areas. Published bimonthly by the American Library Association, 50 East Huron Street, Chicago, IL 60611.

In addition, the following professional journals review literature in each edition:

- *The Reading Teacher* (elementary), published by the International Reading Association
- *Journal of Adolescent & Adult Literacy* (middle school, junior high school, high school), published by the International Reading Association
- *Language Arts* (elementary), published by the National Council of Teachers of English

You can keep up with reviews of new books or books about children's literature by contacting the National Council of Teachers of English (NCTE) website at http://www.ncte.org and the International Reading Association (IRA) website at http://www.ira.org.

Cultural and social authenticity must also be considered when selecting literature. Reading and responding to books about a variety of cultural and social situations helps students develop an appreciation and understanding of how others live and work together. "Through multicultural literature, children of the majority culture learn to respect values and contributions of minority groups in the United States and the values and contributions of people in other parts of the world. . . . The wide range of multicultural themes also helps children develop an understanding of social change" (Norton, 1999, p. 581). Books such as *The Patchwork Quilt* (Flournoy, 1985), *Hawk, I'm Your Brother* (Baylor, 1976), *Felita* (Mohr, 1979), and *The Rainbow People* (Yep, 1989) are examples of the types of literature that should be a part of every literacy program.

Leveling Books for Instruction

Texts and literature for the literary program need to be placed in a sequence of difficulty, especially at the beginning levels of reading instruction. This is essential until students become independent in decoding, which occurs by the end of grade 2 for most students. Even beyond the beginning reading levels, however, there are times when books need to be placed in order of difficulty for instructional purposes. For many years, difficulty was determined by using a readability formula; however, many

TABLE 2.9	Criteria for Leveling Books for Beginning Reading
Levels 1–4	Consistent placement of print Repetition of 1–2 sentence patterns (1–2 word changes) Oral language structures Familiar objects and actions Illustrations provide high support
Levels 5–8	Repetition of 2–3 sentence patterns (phrases may change) Opening, closing sentences vary Or, varied simple sentence patterns Predominantly oral language structures Many familiar objects and actions Illustrations provide moderate to high support
Levels 9–12	Repetition of 3 or more sentence patterns Or, varied sentence patterns (repeated phrases or refrains) Blend of oral and written language structures Illustrations provide moderate support
Levels 13–15	Varied sentence patterns (may have repeated phrases or refrains) Or, repeated patterns in cumulative form Written language structures Oral structures appear in dialogue Conventional story, literary language Specialized vocabulary for some topics Illustrations provide low-moderate support
Levels 16–20	Elaborated episodes and events Extended descriptions Links to familiar stories Literary language Unusual, challenging vocabulary Illustrations provide low support

Source: Reprinted by permission from *Bridges to Literacy: Learning from Reading Recovery* by Diane DeFord, Carol Lyons, and Gay Su Pinnell. Published by Heinemann, a division of Reed Elsevier, Inc., Portsmouth, NH. All rights reserved. Copyright © 1991 by Barbara Peterson. Originally appeared in *Characteristics of Texts That Support Beginning Readers* by Barbara Peterson and published by The Ohio State University.

problems are associated with the various readability procedures (Weaver & Kintsch, 1991). It is best to use criteria other than a score derived from a formula to place texts in a sequence or gradient of difficulty. Table 2.9 presents criteria for leveling texts for beginning reading, and Table 2.10 presents criteria for leveling books in grades 3–8. There are several variations of these criteria (Fountas & Pinnell, 1996, 2001).

A committee of teachers usually carries out the leveling procedure. Each teacher reads the text under consideration and compares it to the criteria to determine the level of placement; a consensus is then reached. This procedure involves judgment; it takes into consideration more factors than a score derived from a mathematical formula. Many publishing companies now use similar criteria for their books.

TABLE 2.10	Criteria for Leveling Books for Grades 3–8
Category I	Small amount of print per page. (The majority of pages have 1–3 sentences.)
	Pictures/illustrations are clear and uncluttered and directly support the text.
	Text for both fiction and nonfiction is narrative, with a clear, easy-to-follow story line.
Category II	Still a small amount of print per page, but text can increase to 1–2 paragraphs on the majority of pages.
	Short lines of dialogue may increase the amount of text per page.
	Pictures/illustrations still give direct text support; 2–3 spot vignettes on a page are appropriate.
	Expository nonfiction on highly focused topics with simply stated main ideas and few supporting details. (Often a picture or photograph illustrates each main idea.)
	Short captions (a word, a phrase, or one sentence) may accompany pictures. Simple diagrams with clear labels are appropriate.
	Narrative story lines remain simple.
Category III	Increasing print with several paragraphs per page. Books themselves become longer.
	Pictures/illustrations are less supportive of text. Captions may increase in length.
	Clear story line, but now multiple characters are appropriate (narrative texts).
	Topics may broaden; main ideas increase in complexity with more supporting details (expository texts).
	Text may contain a secondary element, such as sidebars or speech balloons.
	More inferencing is required by the nature of the text.
Category IV	Text increases to fill the page.
	Story lines become more complex: there may be subplots, mysteries, or multiple problems (narrative texts) that require critical thinking.
	Topics expand to include subtopics, which may be organized by chapter; main ideas increase in complexity and contain more details, requiring readers to organize and analyze information.
	Picture support is less direct; pages may be designed more for visual effect than to help readers with the text. Chapter books may contain spot art or none at all.

(continued)

TABLE 2.10	Criteria for Leveling Books for Grades 3–8 *(continued)*
Category V	Number of chapters increases.
	Size of print decreases as amount of text per page increases.
	Picture support is minimal or nonexistent. Book length may increase to 80–100 pages.
	Greater inferencing skills are required to follow complex story lines containing multiple characters. Problems, which are multiple, are more sophisticated (narrative texts).
	Increasing amount of new information is presented with more complex text organization. Readers may be required to sift through information and make decisions about how relevant each detail is to the topic at hand.
Category VI	Book may increase in length past 100 pages.
	Size of print may decrease, reflecting the style of on-level literature.
	Pictures as support tools are nonexistent. Photos or illustrations may appear as resources in expository texts.
	Complex story lines require retention of details and application of inferences based on cumulative reading of text. Text may require readers to make judgments about characters and events.
	Expository text organization is increasingly complex and specific. Text may explore issues that arise within certain historical, social, or scientific topics. Readers will need to evaluate information to distinguish fact from opinion.

Source: From *Soar to Success!: The Reading Intervention Program* Teacher's Manual, Level 7 in *Houghton Mifflin Reading: Invitations to Literacy* by J. David Cooper and John J. Pikulski, et al. Copyright © 2001 by Houghton Mifflin Company. All rights reserved. Reprinted by permission of the publisher.

A Comprehensive Balanced Literacy Program: Key Points

To review the Key Points, see the ACE practice tests at the HM TeacherPrepSPACE Student Website.

- A Comprehensive Balanced Literacy Program combines teacher-directed instruction and student-centered activities.

- The model for the Comprehensive Balanced Literacy Program includes six core components: Daily Independent Reading, Daily Independent Writing, Reading: Learning Skills and Strategies, Reading: Applying Skills and Strategies, Teacher Modeled Writing, and Developmentally Appropriate Writing. An additional Intervention block is provided for struggling readers who need additional instruction.

- The classroom teacher creates the circumstances and conditions that support instruction.

- Scaffolding instruction is essential as students move toward independence.

- The five modes of reading are: independent reading, cooperative reading, guided reading, shared reading, and read-aloud.

- The five modes of writing are: independent writing, collaborative/cooperative writing, guided writing, shared writing, and write-aloud.

- By using various modes of reading and writing, you scaffold instruction to meet the individual needs of students.

- Three important frameworks for developing standards-based lessons are: the literacy lesson, minilessons or focus lessons, and guided listening lessons.

- Different types of texts are used in a Comprehensive Balanced Literacy Program: wordless books, predictable texts, created texts, and authentic literature. The first three types are particularly appropriate as students acquire strategies and skills.

- The goal of all literacy instruction is for students to read authentic literature.

- Guidelines for selecting quality authentic literature include: focusing on developmental appropriateness, student appeal, literary quality, and cultural and social authenticity.

- Books should be leveled for appropriate instructional use. Two sets of criteria were presented for leveling texts.

Video Cases in This Chapter

- **Using a Classroom Speaker System and the Read-Aloud Mode to Meet the Needs of Diverse Listeners**
- **Using Listening Across the Curriculum**

For Additional Reading

Au, K. H., Carroll, J. H., & Scheu, J. A. (2001). *Balanced literacy instruction: A teacher's resource book* (2nd ed.). Norword, MA: Christopher-Gordon Publishers.

Brassell, D. (2006/2007). Inspiring young scientists with great books. *The Reading Teacher, 60*(4), 336–342.

Broemmel, A. D., & Rearden, K. T. (2006). Should teachers use the Teachers' Choices books in science classes? *The Reading Teacher, 60*(3), 254–265.

Donovan, H., & Ellis, M. (2005). Paired reading—More than an evening of entertainment. *The Reading Teacher, 59*(2), 174–182.

Drucker, M. J. (2003). What reading teachers should know about ESL learners. *The Reading Teacher, 57*(1), 22–29.

Dzaldov, B. S., & Peterson, S. (2005). Book leveling and readers. *The Reading Teacher, 59*(3), 222–229.

Falk, B. (2000). *The heart of the matter: Using standards and assessment to learn.* Portsmouth, NH: Heinemann.

Hyde, A., Zemelman, S., & Daniels, H. (2005). *Best practice: Today's standards for teaching and learning in America's schools* (3rd ed.). Portsmouth, NH: Heinemann.

Ivey, G. (2003). "The teacher makes it more explainable" and other reasons to read aloud in the intermediate grades. *The Reading Teacher, 56*(8), 812–814.

Jenkins, J. R., et al. (2003). Decodable text—Where to find it. *The Reading Teacher, 57*(2), 185–189.

Kurkjian, C., Livingston, N., & Cobb, V. (2006). Inquiring minds want to learn: The info on nonfiction and informational series books. *The Reading Teacher, 60*(1), 89–96.

Leu, Jr., D. J., Castek, J., Henry, L. A., Ciro, J., & McMullan, M. (2004). The lessons that children teach us: Integrating children's literature and the new literacies of the Internet. *The Reading Teacher, 57*(5), 497–503.

Moss, B. (2005). Making a case and a place for effective content area literacy instruction in the elementary grades. *The Reading Teacher, 59*(1), 46–55.

Peterson, B. (2001). *Literacy pathways: Selecting books to support new readers.* Portsmouth, NH: Heinemann.

Risko, V. J., & Bromley, K. (Eds.). (2001). *Collaboration for diverse learners.* Newark, DE: International Reading Association.

Sekeres, D. C., & Gregg, M. (2007). Poetry in third grade: Getting started. *The Reading Teacher, 60*(5), 466–475.

Trelease, J. (2006). *The read-aloud handbook* (6th ed.). New York: Penguin Books.

Vardell, S. M., Hadaway, N. L., & Young, T. A. (2006). Matching books and readers: Selecting literature for English learners. *The Reading Teacher, 59*(8), 734–741.

Williams, N. L., & Bauer, P. T. (2006). Pathways to affective accountability: Selecting, locating, and using children's books in elementary school classrooms. *The Reading Teacher, 60*(1), 14–22.

Wutz, J. A., & Wedwick, L. (2005). BOOKMATCH: Scaffolding book selection for independent reading. *The Reading Teacher, 59*(1), 16–32.

Poetry by Shel Silverstein and Jack Prelutsky

Where the Sidewalk Ends (Silverstein, 1974)
A Light in the Attic (Silverstein, 1981)
Falling Up (Silverstein, 1996)
The Baby Uggs Are Hatching (Prelutsky, 1982)
The New Kid on the Block (Prelutsky, 1984)
Ride a Purple Pelican (Prelutsky, 1986)
Tyrannosaurus Was a Beast (Prelutsky, 1988)
Poems of a Nonny Mouse (Prelutsky, 1989)
Beneath a Blue Umbrella (Prelutsky, 1990)
Something Big Has Been Here (Prelutsky, 1990)
A Pizza the Size of the Sun (Prelutsky, 1996)
It's Raining Pigs and Noodles (Prelutsky, 2000)
Awful Ogre's Awful Day (Prelutsky, 2001)
Dog Days: Rhymes Around the Year (Prelutsky, 2001)
The Frog Wore Red Suspenders (Prelutsky, 2002)

Anthologies of Poetry

A Child's Garden of Verses (Stevenson, 1885/1981)
Cool Melons—Turn to Frogs (Gollub, 1998)
For Laughing Out Loud: Poems to Tickle Your Funnybone (Prelutsky, 1991)
I, Too, Sing America: Three Centuries of African-American Poetry (Clinton, 1998)
Insectlopedia (Florian, 1998)
Joyful Noises: Poems for Two Voices (Fleischman, 1988)
Neighborhood Odes (Soto, 1992)
A New Treasury of Children's Poetry: Old Favorites and New Discoveries (Cole, 1984)
The Norton Anthology of Children's Literature: The Traditions in English (Zipes, Paul, Vallone, Hunt, & Avery, 2005)
The Poetry of Black America: Anthology of the 20th Century (Adoff, 1973)
The 20th Century Children's Poetry Treasury

Websites

Online Children's Literature Journals

ALAN: The Assembly of Literature for Adolescents
ALAN, an NCTE special-interest group, is made up of teachers, authors, librarians, publishers, teacher-educators and their students, and others who are particularly interested in the area of young adult (YA) literature. ALAN also publishes *The ALAN Review,* which has articles on teaching YA literature, author interviews, reports on publishing trends, research on YA literature, and reviews of new books.
http://www.alan-ya.org/

Book Links

This online magazine is designed for teachers, librarians, library media specialists, booksellers, parents, and other adults interested in connecting children with high-quality books. *Book Links* provides comprehensive information for using books in the classroom, including thematic bibliographies with related discussion questions and activities, author and illustrator interviews and essays, and articles by educators on practical ways to turn children onto reading. Reviews are from quality journals such as *Horn Book, Library School Journal, Book Links,* and *Kirkus.* Each issue focuses on a core curriculum area (science, social studies, language arts, history, geography, or multicultural literature). At this site you will find highlights of the current issue, a searchable index, information about subscribing, and submissions guidelines.
http://www.ala.org/BookLinks/

The Bulletin of the Center for Children's Books

One of the nation's leading children's book review journals for school and public librarians, this *Bulletin* is devoted entirely to the review of current books for children. It provides summaries and critical evaluations; information on content, reading level, strengths and weaknesses, and quality of format; and suggestions for curricular use.
http://alexia.lis.uiuc.edu/puboff/bccb/

Carol Hurst's Children's Literature Site

This site provides information on featured and reviewed children's literature, curriculum and thematic topics, and professional resources, including a free online newsletter. The newsletter contains reviews of great books for kids, ideas for use in the classroom, and collections of books and activities about particular subjects, curriculum areas, themes, and professional topics.
http://www.carolhurst.com

The Children's Corner of the *Boston Book Review*

The Children's Corner of the *Boston Book Review* seeks out and promotes the highest achievements in contemporary writing. Bringing readers into the ongoing project of literary life, *BBR* features independent comment from preeminent writers, scholars, and intellectuals on today's most important children's books. Together with fiction, poetry, interviews, and essays, provocative reviews assess works in a wide variety of topics. *BBR* provides high-quality book reviews.
http://www.bookwire.com/bookwire/bbr/children/children.html

The Horn Book Guide Online

Instant access to more than thirty-five thousand reviews can be found at *The Horn Book Guide Online*. All reviews are searchable by author, illustrator, title, subject, bibliographic information, as well as by rating. This site is available by subscription.
http://www.hornbookguide.com/

The Lion and the Unicorn

A theme- and genre-centered journal of international scope committed to serious, ongoing discussions of children's literature.
http://muse.jhu.edu/journals/lion_and_the_unicorn/index.html

The Looking Glass
An electronic journal about children's literature that combines an interest in the traditional with an eye for the modern. Includes scholarly articles of interest to both specialists and nonspecialists.
http://www.the-looking-glass.net/

School Library Journal Online
Provides librarians who work with young people in school and public libraries with indispensable information needed to manage libraries—from creating high-quality collections to understanding how technology can assist (or hinder) learning.
http://www.schoollibraryjournal.com/

Websites on Children's Literature

KIDStack
This page, part of the Andy Holt Virtual Library, provides links to *Collections of Children's Literature*. Collections are divided into "English," "French," and "Spanish" sections. Clicking any link provides you with a list of books and further links. Plan to spend some time exploring where this site takes you.
http://www.utm.edu/vlibrary/docust5.shtml

Barahona Center for the Study of Books in Spanish for Children and Adolescents
The Barahona Center at California State University, San Marcos, provides information about recommended books in Spanish for children and adolescents. More than six thousand books are in the center's database, selected because of their quality of art and writing, presentation of material, and appeal to the intended audience.
http://www.csusm.edu/csbs/english/

The Center for Children's Books
The Center for Children's Books (CCB) houses a noncirculating collection of more than fourteen thousand recent and historically significant trade books for youth, birth through high school, plus review copies of nearly all trade books published in the United States in the current year. At the site you can find annotated bibliographies and links to The Children's Literature Database.
http://bccb.lis.uiuc.edu/

Children's Book Council
The Children's Book Council (CBC) is a nonprofit trade organization of U.S. publishers and packagers of children's and young adult trade books "dedicated to encouraging literacy and the use and enjoyment of children's books." Every other month, Showcase features a thematic bibliography of books published by members, featuring more than forty poetry books for children, with a link to cover art and a detailed summary for each book. The *Showcase Archives* contains about thirty bibliographies on topics such as multicultural books, nature and science, folk- and fairy tales, historical fiction, and biographies, holidays, mysteries, and the African American experience.
http://www.cbcbooks.org

Children's Literature: Beyond Basals
This site provides hundreds of in-depth guides for using children's literature in K–12 classrooms, curriculum ideas, picture books for older and reluctant readers, and links to other Web sources on children's literature.
http://www.umanitoba.ca/faculties/education/edlab/child-lit.html
NOTE: Enter "Children's Literature: Beyond Basals" for many other sites with this concept as their focus.

Children's Literature Web Guide
This site gathers together and categorizes the growing number of Internet resources related to books for children and young adults; authors and stories on the Web; readers theater; resources for teachers, parents, storytellers, writers, and illustrators; book awards; recommended book lists; journals; reviews; indexes; research on children's books; and much more. Much of the information comes from fans, schools, libraries, and commercial enterprises.
http://www.acs.ucalgary.ca/~dkbrown/index.html

Database of Award-Winning Children's Literature
Search this database to create a tailored reading list of quality children's literature or to find out if a book has won one of the indexed awards. Designed primarily for use by librarians or teachers intervening for a child-reader, but anyone can use it to find the best in children's literature, including parents, book store personnel, and children and young adults themselves. *DAWCL* has more than six thousand records from *fifty awards* across five English-speaking countries (United States, Canada, Australia, New Zealand, and the United Kingdom).
http://www.dawcl.com/

Jim Trelease on Reading
This site offers a complete guide to Jim Trelease's work and is aimed at parents, teachers, librarians, and college students—anyone interested in children's reading and education. Stresses the importance of reading aloud to children of all ages.
http://www.trelease-on-reading.com/

Kathy Schrock's Guide for Educators: Literature and Language Arts
This comprehensive site lists numerous websites on children's literature, including poetry, fables and multicultural stories, lesson plans, and writing and grammar.
http://school.discovery.com/schrockguide/arts/artlit.html

Kay E. Vandergrift's Special Interest Page
This site on children's literature is an outstanding resource for educators of all levels. It provides information on gender and culture in picture books, young adult literature, research, literature and technology, the history of children's literature, censorship, intellectual freedom and the Internet, and copyright laws and the World Wide Web.
http://www.scils.rutgers.edu/~kvander/

Once Upon a Time
This site contains many resources on children's literature. Includes information on professional associations, children's literature around the world, children's literature awards, poetry, authors and illustrators, and professional resources.
http://www.bsu.edu/classes/vancamp/ouat.html

Random House's Teachers' Resource Center
This site has teacher's guides on books for reluctant readers, thematic instruction, authors and illustrators, books by grade level, and Newbery Award winners.
http://www.randomhouse.com/teachers/

Read-Aloud Books Too Good to Miss
The Read-Aloud Books Too Good to Miss program is a project of the Association for Indiana Media Educators. Each year, a committee of media specialists, classroom teachers, reading teachers, principals, bookstore operators, and university faculty members is formed to develop five read-aloud lists—one each for primary school, intermediate school, middle school, high school, and ageless.
http://www.ilfonline.org/AIME/ReadAloud/ReadAloud.htm

For Further Online Reading

Electronic Collaboration: Children's Literature in the Classroom
This article is based on a project that explored whether electronic discussion can increase students' breadth and depth of thinking about issues in complex children's literature. Another goal was for teachers to extend their experience into the classroom by engaging their own students in similar projects.
http://www.readingonline.org/electronic/elec_index.asp?HREF=/electronic/RT/9-99RT.html

"A Horizon of Possibilities": A Critical Framework for Transforming Multiethnic Literature Instruction
http://www.readingonline.org/articles/art_index.asp?HREF=willis/index.html

Inclusion Literature
This article from the *ALAN Review* includes children's and adolescent literature written by parents and teachers related to inclusion issues such as self-esteem and individuality.
http://scholar.lib.vt.edu/ejournals/ALAN/spring98/andrews.html

Reading Aloud—Are Students Ever Too Old?
This article on the *Education World* site discusses why children are never too old to be read to. Includes a list of resources on reading aloud.
http://www.education-world.com/a_curr/curr081.shtml

Using the Internet and Children's Literature to Support Interdisciplinary Instruction
This article describes several types of resources on the Internet for children's literature that may be used to support interdisciplinary instruction: central sites, project sites, author websites, lesson plans, and electronic mailing lists to support others as they seek to integrate the Internet and children's literature with classroom instruction.
http://www.readingonline.org/electronic/elec_index.asp?HREF=/electronic/RT/9-00_column.html

Mailing Lists

Mailing lists, or listservs, can provide support for people interested in children's literature.

CHILDLIT (listserv@email.rutgers.edu)
This is a list for people interested in the criticism and theory of children's literature. Subscribers include librarians, K–12 teachers, teacher educators, publishers, authors, illustrators, and parents who are supportive.

KIDLIT-L (listserve@bingvmb.cc.binghamton.edu)
This is a list for people interested in children's literature. Many librarians, teachers, and teacher educators subscribe. It is also a very supportive list.

Prior Knowledge: Activating and Developing Concepts and Vocabulary

3

EDUCATORS SPEAK

Using a Project That Cuts Across the Curriculum, p. 114
—*Lynne Pistochini, Folsom, California*

Terms
YOU NEED TO KNOW

- anticipation guide
- background knowledge (or prior knowledge)
- concept development
- expository text
- graphic organizer
- K-W-L
- making connections
- narrative text
- picture walk
- prediction
- preview and predict
- prior knowledge
- project
- quick writing
- role playing
- schema theory (pl. schemata)
- semantic mapping
- story map
- strategy
- structured preview
- text structure
- text walk
- vocabulary

The HM TeacherPrepSPACE Student Website offers many helpful resources, such as self-quizzes, glossary flashcards, lesson plan templates, and more.

Let's visit a fourth-grade classroom where the teacher and students are beginning a unit about Abraham Lincoln. Mr. Willett needs to find out what his students already know about Lincoln, and about the historical period in which Lincoln lived, concepts related to trouble between the North and South, and vocabulary used to discuss those concepts, such as the word emancipation.

Mr. Willett uses several strategies to engage students from the beginning. First, he gave his students five minutes to write what they knew about Lincoln. He then had students work in small groups to pool what they, as a group, knew about the topic. Groups were also to brainstorm about what they would like to learn during the unit of study. One student in each group served as a recorder, writing the information to be shared with the class later.

After the small-group discussions, Mr. Willett brought the groups together and displayed a chart. (The K-W-L chart will be discussed later in this chapter.) Each group reported what it had discussed and recorded, and Mr. Willett summarized the information on the chart, giving a picture of the collective background knowledge and interests of his students.

The chart showed that the students already knew a great deal about Lincoln, though some of that knowledge was erroneous and there were some gaps in their background knowledge. During the unit, Mr. Willett would lead students to correct mistaken ideas as well as increase their background knowledge and make connections to today's world. The chart also showed that the students were very interested in learning more about Lincoln.

In this example, Mr. Willett was activating his class's prior knowledge before starting the unit on Abraham Lincoln in order to determine what additional background he needed to develop before introducing the first book, the Newbery Award winner *Lincoln: A Photobiography* (Freedman, 1987). Mr. Willett used four techniques for activating prior knowledge: a quick-writing exercise, brainstorming, the K-W-L strategy (Ogle, 1986), and small- and large-group discussion. Through these techniques, Mr. Willett determined the level of prior knowledge students had of vocabulary likely to be met in reading about this historical period and something about their understanding of the concepts such as the issues confronting Lincoln.

We have already talked about the importance of prior knowledge to successful literacy learning for students of all ages. In this chapter, we focus on techniques and strategies that help students activate and develop their prior knowledge of concepts and vocabulary in thematic units and literacy lessons. Two major points are stressed:

- *Purpose:* Students must have a purpose for reading and writing; in part, activating and developing prior knowledge, vocabulary, and concepts create this purpose.
- *Independence:* Students must become independent in activating and developing their own prior knowledge and developing vocabulary if they are to construct meaning effectively.

All of the strategies presented in this chapter lead to these two goals.

Understanding Prior Knowledge, Concept Development, and Vocabulary in Literacy Learning

Essentially, *prior knowledge* is the sum of a person's previous learning and experience (Harris & Hodges, 1995) including **concept development** and **vocabulary.** For many years, teachers have tried to make sure that their students have the appropriate background for reading a given selection, because such background was believed to enhance learning (Smith, 1965). When assessment revealed that student background, or prior, knowledge was insufficient, teachers developed it in class using various strategies. The information Mr. Willett gained from his students through quick writing, brainstorming, discussion, and the use of K-W-L constituted their collective prior knowledge about Abraham Lincoln.

Research has established that the process of constructing meaning through reading, writing, speaking, and listening is based on the **background knowledge,** or **prior knowledge** that individuals bring to the situation (Alexander & Jetton, 2000; Snow, Burns, & Griffin, 1998). The term *prior knowledge* always includes both understanding of concepts contained in the text to be read and the vocabulary, or language, used to talk about those concepts. After reviewing extensive research, Tierney and Cunningham (1984) concluded that "intervention research has supported the existence of a causal relationship between background knowledge and comprehension" (p. 612). No research has refuted this. The terms *prior knowledge, background, background knowledge or information*, and *world knowledge* are interchangeable; in this text, we use the term *prior knowledge* throughout.

Prior knowledge affects construction of meaning for everyone—emergent reader as well as competent reader. Educators recognize that for readers to construct meaning, they must be able to make connections with what they already know, with their own feelings, and with the world at large. A three-year-old child without relevant personal experience will not understand a story he or she hears. The most sophisticated reader will not understand written text when the concepts and language are unfamiliar. We are able to learn from texts only when we can, in effect, hook them onto something that is already in our background of experience. Prior knowledge, therefore, also includes concepts and vocabulary that are developed in the classroom.

Schema Theory

Our understanding of the importance of prior knowledge in literacy learning has developed through research based on **schema theory** (plural, *schemata*), which assumes that individuals develop a cognitive structure of knowledge in their minds (Bartlett, 1932; Rumelhart, 1980). As individuals experience the world, they add new information to their schemata, which are divided into various interrelated categories. One way to picture this concept more concretely is to think of the mind as a large system of file folders. As one gains new knowledge and information, the mind creates a new file folder, or schema, or adds the information to an existing schema (Anderson & Pearson, 1984; Rumelhart, 1980). Then, as individuals develop and expand their schemata, they construct meaning by drawing from various schemata and building connections among them; that is, they make inferences. This process goes on continuously while a person engages in literacy tasks. Example 3.1 illustrates how the experience of reading increases one's schemata.

Example 3.1

> You are going to read a magazine article about the pleasures of sailboat racing. As you begin to read, you think about what you know about sailboat racing; in the process you activate your schemata, which probably formed over many years of experience. If your schemata include positive, pleasant ideas, you will read the article differently than if they included negative, unpleasant ideas. If you have no schema or very limited schemata for sailboat racing, you will begin to form a schema as you read the article, and you will relate the information you gain to any other schemata you have about boats. For example, you may have a schema that relates racing to danger; if you read about how training reduces the dangers, you may form a new, broadened schema. Throughout the process of reading, you take the information from the text and either add it to an existing schema or form a new schema.

Schema theory contends that individuals understand what they read only as it relates to what they already know. Anderson, Reynolds, Schallert, and Goetz (1977) demonstrated this very clearly through their research. They asked students in an educational psychology class and students in a weightlifting class to read the following passage and tell what they thought it was about. Read this passage for yourself and see what you think:

> *Rocky slowly got up from the mat and planned his escape. He hesitated a moment and thought. Things were not going well. What bothered him the most was being held, especially since the charge against him had been weak. He considered his present situation. The lock that held him was strong but he thought he could break it. He knew, however, that his timing had to be perfect. Rocky was aware that it was because of his early roughness that he had been penalized so severely—much too severely from his point of view. The situation was becoming frustrating; the pressure had been grinding on him far too long. He was being ridden unmercifully. Rocky was getting angry now. He felt he was ready to make his move. He knew that his success or failure depended on what he did in the next few seconds.* (p. 372)

What was the focus of this paragraph? What topic came to your mind as you read? Most psychology students interpreted the passage as a prison escape, whereas the weightlifting students related it to a wrestling match, supporting the idea that individuals construct meaning in light of their prior knowledge and interests.

Misconceptions in Prior Knowledge

There is evidence that students sometimes bring incomplete or erroneous ideas to learning tasks. Such misconceptions can interfere with meaning construction (Driver & Erickson, 1983; Lipson, 1982, 1983), and numerous researchers have addressed this (Alvermann, Smith, & Readence, 1985; Dole & Smith, 1989; Hynd & Alvermann,

1986; Pace, Marshall, Horowitz, Lipson, & Lucido, 1989). In all instances, they found that an individual's interpretation of the text was clearly influenced by erroneous or incomplete prior knowledge. Strategies for overcoming misconceptions are discussed later in this chapter.

Prior Knowledge of English Language Learners

In classrooms throughout the country, many children are learning English as a second (or third) language; such children may be referred to as multilingual, ESL (English as a Second Language) students, LEP (Limited English Proficiency) students, Students Acquiring English, or English Language Learners (ELLs).

Some students whose first language is not English may have learned to read in their first language. Research has shown that second-language learners are able to learn to read in their first language and in English at the same time (Barrera, 1983). They develop literacy and the ability to construct meaning through essentially the same process as first-language learners, but with differences in language structure, vocabulary, and cultural prior knowledge (Weber, 1991). Because second-language learners have an extensive base of prior knowledge that may not have been developed around English and the cultural traditions of the place where they now attend school, their prior knowledge needs special attention. What children know in one language, they can access in a new language; they just need the English words for known concepts (Cummins, 1981).

Rigg and Allen (1989) have proposed five principles regarding the literacy development of second-language learners:

1. *People who are learning another language are, first of all, people.*
2. *Learning a language means learning to do the things you want to do with people who speak that language.*
3. *A person's second language, like the first, develops globally, not linearly.*
4. *Language develops best in a variety of rich contexts.*
5. *Literacy is part of language, so writing and reading develop alongside speaking and listening.* (p. viii)

These principles do not differ significantly from what we already have said about helping all students learn to construct meaning. Second-language learners bring their own language and prior knowledge to the classroom, which teachers must build on and expand. As Rigg and Allen (1989) conclude, "We should offer our second-language students a rich bath of language, not a string of language beads, one bead at a time" (p. xi). Research continues to demonstrate that there are many strategies that are effective in helping English Language Learners be effective in learning in the classroom (Hill & Flynn, 2006).

One way for English Language Learners to access prior knowledge is through the technique called "preview, view, review" (Freeman & Freeman, 2000). A teacher, aide, or bilingual student previews the lesson in the student's first language, which activates background knowledge. If possible, students can discuss the topic with others who speak the same language. The lesson itself is the "view" portion and is taught in English. Then the "review" covers the key concepts in the student's first

For further reading on this topic, see Au (1993) and Hill & Flynn (2006), listed in "For Additional Reading."

Video Case

Bilingual Education: An Elementary, Two-Way Immersion Program

Watch the video clip, study the artifacts in the case, and reflect on the following questions:

1. Does the classroom shown in the Video Case use the "preview, view, review" model described in this chapter? If so, describe the various steps of the model that you see demonstrated by these students and teachers.

2. Today's schools use a variety of models for teaching English Language Learners. Share your thoughts about the two-way model that is depicted in this Video Case. What are the potential pros and cons of using this approach?

language; this can be done in pairs or small groups of students who speak the same language. After the review, students report to the teacher in English.

What does this mean for you as a teacher? Given the vast quantity of research related to schema theory and prior knowledge, you need to remember these points as you develop and conduct your literacy program:

- Prior knowledge is crucial to the successful construction of meaning for *all* learners.

- Some students will have incomplete or erroneous prior knowledge related to a topic. Therefore, it is important to assess a student's prior knowledge before any learning experience.

- When students have erroneous or incomplete prior knowledge, it is possible to alter it and help them construct meaning more successfully.

In the remainder of this chapter, we focus on how to help students achieve independence in activating their own prior knowledge and how to build necessary prior knowledge when it does not already exist. We help students make connections before, during, and after reading and support them as they achieve independence.

Components of Prior Knowledge

An individual's prior knowledge includes concept development as well as the vocabulary, or language, to talk about concepts. We can also think about prior knowledge in these two ways: (1) as overall prior knowledge and (2) as prior knowledge for a particular topic or theme; this can be text-specific and/or topic-specific.

Overall prior knowledge is the entire base of knowledge that students possess as a result of their accumulated experiences both in and out of school, such as being read to, taking trips, watching television, or attending events. The *independent reading and writing* component of the literacy program is critical for expanding this knowledge base (Center for the Study of Reading, n.d.) because the more students read and write, the more extensive prior knowledge they build, which in turn improves their ability to construct meaning.

The prior knowledge that is important for a particular topic or theme is further divided into two kinds. The first is called *text-specific knowledge;* it refers to knowledge about the structure of the text. Students need to know that informational text isn't organized like stories and that not all informational texts are organized alike. The second kind is called *topic-specific knowledge;* it refers to information related to the topic about which students are going to read. For example, suppose your students are going to read *The Boys' War* (Murphy, 1990), a book about the experiences of the young boys who fought in the Civil War. Your students need both kinds of background: text-specific knowledge about how this book is organized and topic-specific knowledge about the Civil War.

Knowledge About the Text

Recall the two basic types of prose text: narrative and expository. Since students need knowledge about both types of text, it is important that you have a basic understanding of them.

Narrative Texts **Narrative texts** tell a story and are usually organized into a sequential pattern that includes a beginning, a middle, and an end. Within this pattern, a narrative may be composed of several episodes, each consisting of characters, a setting, a problem, action, and a resolution of the problem (the outcome). These elements are the story's grammar, or basic plan. A graphic representation of these elements is called a **story map,** which can take many different forms. The exact map for a story depends on the story's structure.

The *theme* of a story is the basic idea around which the whole story is written. Often the theme is unstated, requiring the reader to infer it. The *plot* is the way in which the story is organized; it is made up of episodes. The *setting* is the place and time at which the story occurs. The *characters* are the people or animals that carry out the action in the story. The *problem* is the situation or situations that initiate, or lead to, other events in the story. Finally, the *action* is what happens as a result of the problem; it is composed of events that lead to the solution of the problem, which is called the *resolution*, or outcome.

Expository Texts **Expository texts** present information organized around main ideas. These are the types of materials commonly found in informational books, textbooks, online, on CD-ROMs, and in newspapers and magazines. Students may have more difficulty reading expository texts than narrative texts because they have had less experience with them and because these texts may not follow a clear-cut pattern; instead, the organization depends on the type of information and purpose of the text. There are five commonly used organizational patterns of expository writing (Meyer, 1975; Meyer & Freedle, 1984):

- description
- collection (sometimes called listing or sequence)
- causation, or cause-effect
- response, problem-solution, question-answer, or remark-reply
- comparison

Let's take a look at each of these patterns:

■ *Description* presents information about a particular topic or gives characteristics of the topic. Unlike the other types of expository text structure, descriptive passages may not provide readers with clue words to aid in comprehension; therefore, readers must use the strategies they have learned for noting details and selecting important information from the passage. The structure of descriptive passages helps readers anticipate the type of content that is likely to follow.

■ *Collection* presents a number of ideas or descriptions in a related group. This structure is often called a *listing* or *sequence,* and the author frequently uses clue words such as *first, second, next,* and *finally* to introduce the points. Readers must infer the relationship between the listed points and the overall topic, noting details and identifying the sequence of ideas.

■ *Causation,* or *cause-effect,* presents ideas so that a causal relationship is either stated or implied. This structure is frequently used in content-area textbooks and in newspaper and magazine articles. The author often uses clue words: *therefore, consequently, because, as a result of, since,* or *the reasons for.* The reader must identify the elements being related and either recognize or infer the cause-effect relationships.

■ *Response* presents a problem, question, or remark followed by a solution, answer, or reply. This structure is often used in mathematics, science, and social studies. Sometimes (as in mathematics) the reader is expected to provide the solution. The author may use clue words such as *the problem is, the question is, one reason for the problem is, a solution is,* or *one answer is.*

■ *Comparison* requires the reader to note the likenesses and differences between two or more objects or ideas. This structure is frequently found in social studies and science texts. The author uses clue words and phrases such as *like, unlike, resemble, different from, same as, alike,* or *similar to* to make comparisons. The reader must recognize the objects or ideas being compared and the points of similarity or difference among them. Often these points are not directly stated.

Table 3.1 presents an example of each of the five types of expository **text structure.** Remember that one paragraph is not sufficient to determine the overall structure of a particular text, and within a given expository text several structures may be present.

Students need to know enough about text structure to understand the basic differences between narrative and expository texts and to realize how this will help them construct meaning. This knowledge is gained through reading and writing and through mini-lessons, if needed. Your knowledge of text structure will assist you in helping students activate the appropriate prior knowledge; it will also help you identify which words (vocabulary) are key to understanding a selection and the types of questions to ask when using interactive guided reading.

See Chapter 5 for more about key vocabulary.

See Chapter 2 for more about interactive guided reading.

Knowledge About the Topic

The second kind of specific prior knowledge has to do with the topic of the materials to be read, which includes the key concepts and key terminology. This knowledge must be activated along with knowledge of text structure.

TABLE 3.1	Examples of Expository Text Structures
Expository Structure	**Example**
Description	The tiger is the master of the Indian jungle. It stalks its prey in deadly silence. For half an hour or more, it carefully watches and then slowly, placing one foot softly in front of the other, closes in.
Collection, listing, or sequence	As master of the Indian jungle, the male tiger plays many roles. First, he is the hunter of prey who stalks in deadly silence. He is the beauty of the jungle, an expert at doing nothing so that he can rest to be ready for his hunt. Finally, the lord of the jungle is the active seeker of mates, who begins his mating with a nuzzle, but ends with a roar.
Causation or cause-effect	We observed the tiger from our vehicle as it stalked the herd of deer. As a result of the slight noise from our running camera, the tiger turned and knew we were there. This didn't stop it from returning to its intended prey. Slowly and carefully it moved forward, not making a sound. The deer were initially unaware of its presence, but because of the shifting winds they caught the tiger's scent. This was enough to scare them away.
Response, problem-solution, question-answer, or remark-reply	One problem to be resolved in tiger watching is transportation. How is it possible for observers to get close enough to a tiger without scaring it away or being attacked? Nature has helped solve this problem by making the tiger and the elephant friends. It is possible for an elephant carrying several people to get very near a tiger without even being noticed. If it weren't for this natural friendship, tiger watching would be virtually impossible.
Comparison	The power of the great tiger is like that of no other animal in the jungle. With one steady lunge, it can destroy its prey, seemingly without any effort at all. Unlike other predators, the tiger basks in the sun after an attack to prepare for its next kill. The actions of the tiger resemble those of no other animal in the Indian jungle.

If your students were going to read *Ronald Morgan Goes to Bat* (Giff, 1988), you might think you needed to activate prior knowledge of baseball, but this book isn't about baseball. It's a narrative about a boy whose problem is that although he really wants to play baseball, he can't catch or hit. The prior knowledge that is most likely to improve students' ability to construct meaning from this text is an understanding of what it is like to really want to do something even though one is not very good at it. This is what Beck (1984) refers to as *schema-directed prior knowledge development*.

While the prior knowledge needs for narrative text are determined by the story line, the needs for expository text are determined by the topic, main ideas, and structure of the text, and strictly topical prior knowledge activation and development without consideration of the actual structure of the text do not improve students' ability to construct meaning (Beck, Omanson, & McKeown, 1982).

Suppose your students are about to read an article entitled "Birds in Winter," which describes the survival of birds during a blizzard. To construct meaning from this article, students must understand both the words and the concepts of *survival* and *blizzard*. Study Examples 3.2 and 3.3 to see the incorrect and correct ways to activate prior knowledge.

Example 3.2

Incorrect Method of Activating Prior Knowledge

Today, we are going to read the article "Birds in Winter." Have you ever seen birds during the winter? What kinds of birds do you usually see in winter? How do birds get food in winter?

While the discussion in Example 3.2 is topical, it is too general. It does not access prior knowledge or develop background knowledge related to the main point or key concepts of the article. The discussion in Example 3.3, in contrast, clearly requires students to use whatever past experiences or schemata they have developed about birds and winter to make predictions. The teacher develops what students already know by relating that information to the concepts of *survival* and *blizzard*. Key-concept vocabulary is developed within the context of the background development. Finally, the teacher guides the students in summarizing the key points to make sure they have a schema for reading that relates directly to the article's main point.

Example 3.3

Correct Method of Activating Prior Knowledge (Schema Directed)

Today, we are going to read the article "Birds in Winter." Before we read it, I want you to think about some important ideas that will help you understand what you read. From the title, what would you say this article is going to be about? (Record student responses, and discuss them.) This article is about how birds survive during a blizzard. (Relate the students' predictions to surviving in a blizzard.) What is a blizzard? (Students respond. Write a sentence on the chalkboard that contains the word *blizzard*, and discuss its meaning.) What does it mean to survive in a blizzard? What kinds of problems might birds have surviving during a blizzard? (Discuss these questions; list students' responses on the board, and discuss them. Add your own points to the discussion.)

Example:

1. A blizzard is a bad snowstorm with high winds.
2. Birds could have many problems surviving in a blizzard. These could include:
   getting food.
   not freezing to death.
   having water to drink.
   having a place to sleep that is protected from the wind.

Standards, Prior Knowledge, Vocabulary, and Concept Development

Students are more likely to meet reading standards when teachers help them activate and develop the vocabulary and concepts that make up prior knowledge. Though all students have been acquiring concepts and vocabulary since birth, not all are able to bring that knowledge to their reading. The interaction and guidance suggested in this book will help you help students draw on their prior knowledge, as well as develop new concepts and vocabulary that expand prior knowledge.

The Role of the Teacher

Whether planning literacy lessons within thematic units or for individual pieces of text, it is important to think about two things in relation to prior knowledge:

1. What prior knowledge probably needs to be activated and/or developed for the overall theme, for each book to be read during the theme, and for writing to be done? Or, what is needed for this particular piece of literature?

2. How independent are your students in using strategies to activate their own prior knowledge?

To make the first decision, you must consider three elements: (1) the theme goals, (2) the theme topic, and (3) the literature.

Begin by considering what you want your students to accomplish in relation to the theme in terms of their attitudes and habits and their ability to construct meaning.

Next, think about the theme topic. What are the big ideas or concepts that students need to understand? For example, for a science fiction theme, do students know what science fiction is? Have they had prior experiences with it?

Then think about the books or selections to be read. Are they narrative or expository? What are the story lines for the narratives? What are the main ideas of the expository texts? Knowing this helps you determine the prior knowledge that is most likely to help students construct meaning.

To judge students' independence, assess your students in relation to the theme goals, the theme topic, the literature to be read, and their ability to use various strategies by observing them and using the strategies and techniques suggested in the next section of this chapter. *Good instruction incorporates assessment, and every instructional activity can also be used for assessment.* Therefore, the assessment of prior knowledge becomes a natural part of instruction.

Holmes and Roser (1987) identified and compared five techniques for assessing prior knowledge during instruction:

■ *Free recall:* "Tell me what you know about _____."

■ *Word association:* "When you hear the words *thief, stolen,* and *detective,* what do you think of?"

■ *Recognition:* Display the following key terms (phrases or sentences may be used), and ask students to tell which ones they think may be related to the book they are about to read, *The Polar Express* (Van Allsburg, 1985): *train, North Pole, wagon, conductor, sand, snow.*

■ *Structured question:* In preparation for reading the book *Martin Luther King, Jr.: Free at Last* (Adler, 1986), ask students a set of prepared questions that will help you assess their prior knowledge: "Who was Martin Luther King, Jr.?" "What was Martin Luther King's concern in life?" "How did Martin Luther King try to reach his goal in life?"

■ *Unstructured discussion:* "We are going to read about outer space. What do you know about it?" Holmes and Roser (1987) found this procedure to be *least* effective and useful for assessing prior knowledge.

Assessment and evaluation are discussed in detail in Chapter 11.

Note that each of these techniques is designed to activate, or access, as well as *assess* prior knowledge.

When working with many students in a group, it may not be possible to know everything about each student's prior knowledge of a particular theme, but you can get a sense of what the group knows and the group's level of independence by using the teaching strategies suggested in the next section and by helping students develop independence in activating their own prior knowledge. The sample lesson presented at the conclusion of this chapter illustrates the process of selecting prior knowledge for a theme and for one book. You might want to look at that lesson now to get an overview of how the lesson functions.

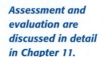

Strategies for Helping Students Achieve Independence in Activating and Developing Prior Knowledge

There are many ways to help learners become more strategic and independent readers (Paris et al., 1991), and prior knowledge activation and development may occur at three points:

1. When introducing a unit theme, at which time the focus is on the broad concepts and ideas needed to understand the theme
2. When each piece of literature is introduced within the lessons
3. Throughout the unit when you observe that certain students need more prior knowledge to better understand what they are reading or writing

A **strategy** is a plan selected deliberately to accomplish a particular goal (Paris, Lipson, & Wixson, 1983; Paris et al., 1991). When students reach the point where they can use a strategy automatically, they have achieved independence in its use. A *student strategy* is one that students can use on their own to construct meaning. A *teaching strategy* is a plan or an activity that the teacher can use to accomplish a desired outcome.

This section presents three student and twelve teaching strategies used to activate and develop the concepts and vocabulary, or terminology, that constitute prior knowledge in various places throughout a thematic unit or for a specific piece of text. For each, we provide a description, procedures, advice on when to use, assessment value, and sometimes comments related to how the use might vary at different grade levels or ability levels.

Three Student Strategies Leading to Independence

Three basic strategies students can use to activate their prior knowledge and set their own purposes for reading are **preview and predict, K-W-L,** and **making connections.** Table 3.2 presents an overview of these strategies and indicates when they should be used.

Preview and Predict

Description This strategy combines the processes of previewing and **prediction,** both of which have been shown to be effective in helping students construct meaning (Fielding, Anderson, & Pearson, 1990; Graves & Cooke, 1980; Graves, Cooke, & LaBerge, 1983; Hansen, 1981). Students look over, or preview, the material to be read and then predict what they think will happen (narrative text) or what they will learn (expository text). This is the first step in inferencing, which is ongoing in the process of constructing meaning. As they read or after completing the reading, students decide whether their predictions have been confirmed, verified, or changed.

Procedures Students begin by reading the title. Then they look at the pictures or illustrations to get a sense of what will be covered. They decide whether this is a story or informational text. Using their prior knowledge and the information gained from their preview, students predict what will happen or what they will learn. For

TABLE 3.2	Student Strategies for Activating and Developing Prior Knowledge		
Strategy	**Type of Text**	**Comments**	
Preview and predict	Narrative or expository	For all students; variations may	
■ Story map prediction	Narrative	be used to increase motivation	
■ Preview and self-question	Expository	and interest in using the strategy.	
K-W-L	Expository	For all students; good for introducing a thematic unit.	
Making connections	Narrative or expository	For all students before reading and during reading.	

beginning readers and primary children, the preview should be very simple, focusing on the title and illustrations. Older students can read the first few paragraphs of the text and/or captions under the illustrations.

See Chapter 4 for a discussion of monitoring strategies.

Chapter 4 discusses modeling in detail.

After previewing, students read to verify predictions. They monitor their reading (thinking about their predictions and changing them as they read). One way to help students learn and remember to use this and other strategies is to display a strategy poster such as is shown in Figure 3.1, adjusting the wording for different grade levels. Remember that strategies must be modeled if they are to be learned effectively (Pressley et al., 1990).

When to Use The preview and predict strategy is effective with both narrative and expository text and is most effective when students have some knowledge of the topic. With second-language learners or students having difficulty constructing meaning, this strategy works best under the teacher's direction and/or in combination with another strategy. When students are just beginning to learn any strategy, teacher guidance is needed.

Assessment Value By observing responses during the preview and predict process, you can assess the students' prior knowledge of type of text, concepts, and vocabulary and determine the need for additional prior knowledge development activities.

> **Discussion** The real power of preview and predict will become evident when students use it on their own. If students do not see its importance or refuse to use it, you should discuss and model its importance and be sure students have repeated successful opportunities to use the strategy.
>
> A variation of preview and predict is story map prediction, used for narrative texts. Training in the use of story maps has proven to be effective in helping students improve their comprehension (Pressley et al., 1990). Beginning readers should predict about one or two elements of the story. For example, the title and pictures may be sufficient to predict setting and characters. Of course, students can't predict all the action in a story; if they could, there would be little point to reading the story.
>
> Another variation, preview and self-question, is used with expository texts. Students preview the text and then pose questions they think they can answer from their reading.

K-W-L Strategy

Description K-W-L is another strategy for activating students' prior knowledge and helping them determine their purpose for reading expository texts. This strategy, developed by Ogle (1986), requires students to focus on three questions, two before they read, what I *know* (K), what I *want* to learn (W), and one after they read, what I *learned* and still need to learn (L). The two before-reading questions help students activate their prior knowledge and set their purposes for reading by raising questions they want to answer. The driving force behind this strategy is the students and their ideas and questions.

FIGURE 3.1   **Strategy Poster for Preview and Predict**

FIGURE 3.2   K-W-L Strategy Sheet

K-W-L STRATEGY

1. K—What we *know*	W—What we *want* to find out	L—What we *learned* and still need to learn

2. Categories of information we expect to use
   A.   E.
   B.   F.
   C.   G.
   D.

Procedures Each student has a worksheet such as the one in Figure 3.2. For the first two steps, the teacher leads students in a discussion of the topic for the selection they are going to read. During the last step, students write their answers to the questions posed before reading.

1. *Step K—what I know* begins with students brainstorming what they know about the topic. In keeping with the need to have schema-directed prior knowledge activation and development, the teacher selects a topic specific to the main ideas and key concepts of the material students will read. For example, students who are going to read *Spiders and Their Webs* (Murawski, 2004) could use K-W-L to activate their ideas about spiders. Ogle (1986) states the following:

   When the class will read about sea turtles, use the words sea turtles as the stimulus, not "What do you know about animals in the sea?" or "Have you ever been to the ocean?" A general discussion of enjoyable experiences on the beach may never elicit the pertinent schemata. . . . If there appears to be little knowledge of sea turtles in your students' experiences, then ask the next more general question, "What do you know about turtles?" (p. 565)

   Students record what they know (or think they know) on their worksheets and add to it as they share ideas. At the same time, the teacher records these ideas on a large version of the worksheet on the chalkboard, chart, or overhead projector. To broaden and deepen students' thinking during the discussion, Ogle suggests that the teacher ask students such questions as, "Where did you learn that?" or "How might you prove it?" When disagreement occurs, students must look for answers in the reading. If they seem to have little knowledge about the topic, you should ask more specific questions to draw out what information they do have.

The second part of the brainstorming involves identifying *categories of information* students might find in the material they will read. Students look over the list of what they know to see if any items fit into categories of information that might be found in their reading: for example, "foods turtles eat" or "use of sea turtles by humans."

2. *Step W—what I want to learn* is a natural outgrowth of step K. As students continue to share ideas, areas of uncertainty or lack of knowledge will arise, and you can help them turn these into questions they may answer by reading the text. Record these on the group chart. Just before the students begin to read, ask them to write questions on their worksheets that *they* want answered. This step helps students set individual purposes for reading. If the text is long or complex, you may preview it with students before they read or have students read the text in parts.

3. *Step L—what I learned* requires students to write the answers to their questions after reading. This helps them determine which questions they still need to answer or whether they have additional questions and can lead students to further reading.

When to Use K-W-L is used with expository texts, with students of any age. Primary children and students experiencing difficulty constructing meaning may need a version that focuses just on the K-W-L without the additional "categories of information." More capable readers may use the strategy independently.

Because it is so interactive, K-W-L gives students opportunities to learn from one another. It is especially strong for second-language learners and students experiencing difficulty constructing meaning; it immerses them in a natural discussion and offers a strong scaffold provided by teacher support and student interaction. Sometimes, it helps to combine K-W-L with other teaching strategies, such as previewing and the use of concrete materials, to further develop prior knowledge.

This strategy is a good way to initiate a thematic unit, because it sets students up to continue to read several selections on a given topic. It is also useful when reading chapters in textbooks in areas such as science, social studies, or health.

Assessment Value Teachers can assess students' prior knowledge during all three steps. During the K and W steps, you can tell whether students have prior knowledge relative to the topic and how accurate it is. During the L step, you can tell whether students have gained new knowledge and how well they have integrated that knowledge with what they already know.

See Chapter 4 for a discussion of modeling.

 **Discussion** Initially, the teacher should model the use of the strategy. Repeated opportunities to use the strategy under teacher direction are important.

Although K-W-L was designed as a teaching strategy, students can learn to use it as an independent study strategy in working alone or cooperatively. A poster such as the one shown in Figure 3.3 may be helpful.

FIGURE 3.3   K-W-L Strategy Poster

Making Connections

Description This strategy encompasses and goes beyond the thinking students use in the preview and predict and K-W-L strategies. A strategic reader is making connections all the time, before, during, and after reading—to his or her own experiences, to other texts, and to the world knowledge he or she has. Students need to learn that no individual piece of text should be read in isolation, but rather should always be understood in the context of where it fits into the reader's own experiences, what other texts it relates to in some way (genre, author, illustrator, form, topic, organization, conflict, and so forth), and how it relates to what is going on in the world.

Procedures Students begin by activating their prior knowledge for a text they are going to read by using preview and predict or K-W-L. Then they access further personal experiences by thinking about what connections they might make. They can do this by asking themselves questions such as the following:

- What connections can I make from this topic/text to my own experiences?
- What other texts have I read that have connections to this text or topic?
- What connections can I make between this text or topic and the world?

The answers to these questions may be shared orally or may be written for use after reading.

As students begin to read, whether with teacher guidance or independently, they continue to make the same connections. They will find that some ideas they had before reading need to be dropped or adjusted. New connections will emerge as they read. A poster such as the one shown in Figure 3.4 can remind students of how they can make connections while reading.

FIGURE 3.4   Making Connections Poster
Strategy Poster for Making Connections

Make Connections Before, During, and After Reading

For additional ideas about how to use making connections, see Oczkus in "For Additional Reading."

You should explicitly model how you make connections as you read. Then, until it becomes automatic, stop and ask students directly to "Make a connection." Ask them to tell whether the connection they are sharing is to self (their own experience), to other texts, or to the world.

When to Use The making connections strategy is effective with both narrative and expository material, as well as with poetry, propaganda (such as ads and commercials), and graphic materials (such as tables and charts).

Assessment Value Observed responses before, during, and after reading will alert you to gaps in prior knowledge (like preview and predict and K-W-L). Observation and direct questions will also alert you to whether students are indeed making connections as they read.

> **Discussion** In Chapter 4, you will see that we include making connections as a strategy for constructing meaning. Even adults who think of themselves as competent readers may not fully employ the strategy of making connections. Frequent teacher modeling followed by student modeling and reminders will be needed for most students to help it become automatic.

Twelve Teaching Strategies Leading to Student Independence

This section presents twelve teaching strategies for supporting students in *becoming independent* in activating their prior knowledge and setting their purpose(s) for reading. Each strategy will help students bring to mind the concepts and vocabulary they already know about the topic, as well as develop new concepts and vocabulary. The twelve strategies are discussion, brainstorming, quick writing, picture walk/text walk, semantic mapping, prequestioning and purpose setting, anticipation guides, structured previews, reading aloud to students, role playing, projects, and concrete materials and real experiences.

Table 3.3 shows when to use each strategy. Each strategy will benefit ELL students, and each can be used successfully for all students, from beginning readers to fluent readers. Remember that your goal is to move students toward independence as quickly as possible.

1. Discussion

Description While discussion is widely used for activating students' prior knowledge before reading or writing, much of what is done in the name of discussion is nothing more than teacher assessment of students' comprehension (Durkin, 1978, 1981) or conducting of a recitation period (Dillon, 1984). Such unstructured discussions have been found to be ineffective in activating appropriate prior knowledge (Holmes & Roser, 1987).

An effective discussion is an interactive procedure whereby the teacher and students talk about a given topic; it is not simply the teacher telling students a body of

TABLE 3.3	Teaching Strategies for Activating and Developing Prior Knowledge

Strategy	Type of Text	Comments
1. Discussion	Narrative or expository	For all students.
2. Brainstorming	Narrative or expository	Use when students have some knowledge of topic; for all students.
3. Quick writing	Narrative or expository	For all students; often needs to be combined with other strategies.
4. Picture walk/text walk	Narrative or expository	For students requiring a very structured framework for what they are going to read.
5. Semantic mapping	Most effective with expository; can be used with narrative	For all students; gives a visual picture of concepts.
6. Prequestioning and purpose setting	Narrative and expository	For beginning learners or those having difficulty constructing meaning; usually combined with other strategies.
7. Anticipation guides	Best with expository; may be used with narrative	Useful for overcoming misconceptions in prior knowledge; for all students.
8. Structured previews	Narrative or expository	Especially for second-language learners or students experiencing difficulty constructing meaning.
9. Reading aloud to students	Narrative or expository	Good to use when students have limited or erroneous knowledge; for all students, especially second-language learners.
10. Role playing	Narrative; sometimes expository, especially in social studies	For students needing more concrete prior knowledge development.
11. Projects	Narrative or expository	For all students; develops long-term prior knowledge throughout a theme.
12. Concrete materials and real experiences	Narrative or expository	For students with limited prior knowledge and second-language learners.

information. According to Alvermann, Dillon, and O'Brien (1987), discussions must meet three criteria:

■ Discussants should put forth multiple points of view and stand ready to change their minds about the matter under discussion;

■ students should interact with one another as well as with the teacher;

■ and the interaction should exceed the typical two- or three-word phrase units common to recitation lessons. (p. 7)

Procedures Conducting an effective discussion requires careful planning, as well as on-the-spot decisions during the discussion. The following guidelines should be helpful:

1. *Review the text to be read.* Determine the story line or main ideas to decide what key background concepts and vocabulary are needed to comprehend the text. For example, if your class is going to read the expository text *Monarch Butterfly* (Gibbons, 1989), focus your discussion on what students know about monarch butterflies (or, if nothing is known about monarchs, then butterflies in general) and their life cycle. If your students are reading the story (narrative) *Imogene's Antlers* (Small, 1985), the discussion should focus on how they might react if a strange or unusual circumstance occurred in their lives.

2. *Ask questions that require students to respond with more than yes or no.* Questions should require students to elaborate on and explain their answers. Unless very experienced, teachers should plan questions in advance. The suggested guidelines that accompany basal anthologies, content texts, or some trade books can be helpful.

3. *Encourage students to raise their own questions about the topic or about other students' answers.* Model such behavior and tell students that they can ask similar questions of you or other students.

4. *Call on individual students to answer questions; don't always wait for volunteers to answer.* Encourage participation by all students, even those who are sometimes reluctant to respond.

5. *When calling on individual students to answer questions, ask the question before calling on the student.* This practice encourages everyone to listen.

6. *After asking a question, give students sufficient time to answer.* You'll know which students need extra time.

7. *Participate in the discussion and model good questioning and question-responding behavior.* Encourage students to ask questions in a discussion in the same manner you do.

8. *Keep the discussion focused on the topic.* A short, lively discussion is better and more motivating than a lengthy one.

9. *Conclude the discussion by having students summarize the points that were made.* For the discussion to be of value to them, students must be able to internalize and verbalize the points that were developed.

Discussions may be planned for the whole class or small groups. Sometimes you may begin with small-group discussions and then use the whole-class format to pull

TABLE 3.4	Sample Discussion Guidelines Developed by One Fifth-Grade Class

Our Discussion Guidelines

1. Stick to the topic.
2. Pay attention to the person talking.
3. Ask questions about ideas given.
4. Give everyone a chance to participate.
5. Think about what is being said.
6. Try not to interrupt others.

together the ideas discussed in each group. This is a natural way to lead to a summary and to involve all students in a more interactive lesson. In either instance, the preceding nine guidelines apply. It is helpful to develop with students a set of guidelines or suggestions to follow during discussions. Table 3.4 presents a sample set of guidelines developed by a group of fifth graders and their teacher.

When to Use Discussion is a teaching strategy you can use with any group at any time to activate and develop prior knowledge. When students have limited or incorrect knowledge or difficulty constructing meaning, combine discussion with other strategies to make prior knowledge activation and development more concrete. For example, a group that has limited prior knowledge about frogs will profit from a discussion combined with photographs, a film, or a filmstrip on frogs. To help students move toward independence, encourage them to take the lead in small-group discussions.

Assessment Value A structured discussion is an excellent way to assess students' prior knowledge; responses and interactions will reveal their knowledge and their misconceptions.

Discussion Your job is to try to match your teaching strategies and procedures to fit not only the students' language base but also their cultural values. Mason and Au (1990) found that Hawaiian children responded best when the teacher asked a question and all children were allowed to respond if they had something to say. Several children spoke at once, and the teacher then repeated the highest-quality response for the group. Mason and Au point out that this pattern reflects the Hawaiian emphasis on the group rather than the individual.

See Chapter 7 for additional uses.

2. Brainstorming

Description Brainstorming requires students to tell all they know about a particular topic or idea, which begins to activate their prior knowledge.

Video Case

Elementary School Language Arts: Inquiry Learning

1. Describe how the students in this Video Case engage in discussion and brainstorming to activate their prior knowledge.

2. Do you think Ms. Williams strikes an effective balance between encouraging students to independently access their knowledge and providing instructional support (when needed)? Evaluate this aspect of her teaching practice.

Procedures Students can work individually or in pairs, first generating all of the ideas they have for a particular topic and then sharing their ideas with the group. The teacher lists the ideas on the chalkboard, and then they are discussed. By hearing others' ideas, students may activate additional information in their memories or learn new information. The following steps offer one way to carry out a brainstorming activity:

1. Provide cards on which students can write.
2. Tell students they are to list any words, ideas, or phrases they know about the given topic. Provide a time limit.
3. Have students read their lists aloud to the group as you record all of their ideas on the chalkboard or overhead projector.
4. Discuss the information recorded, pointing out ideas that directly relate to the selection students are going to read. If incorrect information is on the list, you may leave it until after reading; through discussion and responding, students may correct themselves. However, if the error is significant and is likely to interfere with meaning construction, discuss it at this point.
5. Direct the discussion of the ideas generated by the students to the story line or main ideas of the selection. Conclude the discussion by helping the students set a purpose for reading or giving them a purpose for reading.

When to Use Use brainstorming when students have some knowledge of the topic. It is useful as an opening activity for a thematic unit, or for reading a story or informational text. For example, if your sixth graders are going to read *Cousins* (Hamilton, 1990), brainstorming will help them think about what might happen when conflicts between cousins arise.

The following script shows how a teacher used brainstorming to introduce an article about whales:

(Teacher focuses the brainstorming.)

Teacher: Today we are going to read an article about whales and why they are in trouble. On your card write all the things you can think of about whales. Don't worry about spelling. [The ideas of two students are shown on the accompanying cards. After a few minutes, the teacher asked the students to stop writing.]

Ted

Whales are mammals.
Whales live in the ocean.
These are killer whales.
Whales can talk.

Elsie

fish
big
eat people

Teacher: I want each of you to read what you have written on your card, and I will write your ideas on the board. [The teacher accepted all responses from each student, unless it was a duplicate.]

(Students are looking for incorrect information.)

Teacher: Let's look at our list of ideas to see if there is anything that is incorrect.

Whales are mammals

Whales live in the ocean

There are killer whales

Whales can talk

Fish

Big

Eat people

Can be made into oil

Can be eaten

Are hunted by fishermen

Student: Whales aren't fish.

Teacher: Yes, they look like fish, but are much bigger. We will learn why they are not fish in our reading. [The teacher removed *fish* from the list.]

Teacher: You know that dinosaurs once lived on earth, but for many reasons they disappeared. The same thing is happening to whales. Look at our list to see if you can identify any reasons that whales might be in danger of disappearing. [The students responded. The teacher discussed their answers and identified items the students missed.]

Teacher: We are going to read the article entitled "Disappearing Whales." Based on the information we have just discussed about whales and why they might be in danger of disappearing, what do you think would be a good thing for us to think about or look for as we read?

Student: Maybe we could look to see if our reasons about why whales disappear are right, and maybe we can find some others.

(Setting a purpose for reading.)

Teacher: That's a good idea. [The teacher wrote the student's response on the board and had students read the article silently, telling them they would later discuss the article based on that purpose.]

Assessment Value Through student brainstorming, the teacher is able to identify and *begin* to correct errors in students' prior knowledge, as shown in the above dialogue about whales.

> **Discussion** It is important to keep the brainstorming focused without controlling it. If students have limited knowledge about the subject, a small-group activity might be more effective because it would help them to learn from one another.
>
> Brainstorming is often more effective if used in conjunction with another strategy, such as preview and predict or purpose setting. This helps you more effectively meet individual student's needs. Also, varying your teaching strategies keeps student interest high.

3. Quick Writing

Description Writing has been shown to be an effective way to activate prior knowledge before students read (Marino, Gould, & Haas, 1985; Moore, Readence, & Rickleman, 1989). **Quick writing** is structured by the teacher and is done in a brief amount of time.

Procedures The procedures are general because they depend on the selection being read and what is to be written. The following guidelines should be helpful:

1. *Select what students are to write about.* This should relate directly to the story line or main ideas in the text. For example, if students are going to read *The Stupids Have a Ball* (Allard & Marshall, 1978), you might ask them to pretend they are a person who does everything the opposite of normal and tell funny things that might happen to them. (The characters in this story do just that.) Quick writing can focus on a character, on the story problem, or on the major topic developed in an expository text.
2. *Have students write.* Allow students 3 to 5 minutes to complete the writing. Remind them that these papers will not be evaluated or graded.
3. *Invite students to share what they have written.* Direct students in a discussion of the ideas shared.
4. *Help students formulate a purpose for reading.* For example, they can now read *The Stupids Have a Ball* to see how the Stupids are like the characters they have written about.

When to Use Writing can be used as soon as students begin to be able to write and express their ideas. Use a different strategy if you know students have limited prior knowledge relative to the topic. Second-language learners should, in most instances, have an activity that introduces key words and phrases prior to writing; discussion combined with more concrete materials such as pictures would accomplish this goal.

Assessment Value Although writing is a valuable way to assess students' prior knowledge, some students may be hampered by limited writing skills or a dislike for writing rather than by limited prior knowledge. It is wise to look at two or more samples from different sources before drawing conclusions.

For more discussion of writing, see Chapter 8.

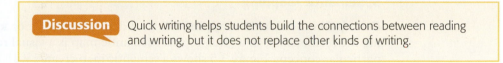

Discussion   Quick writing helps students build the connections between reading and writing, but it does not replace other kinds of writing.

4. Picture Walk/Text Walk

Description   A **picture walk** or **text walk** is a technique whereby the teacher guides students through a piece of literature to be read, using the pictures, illustrations, or other graphics to develop the big idea of what the text is about. This technique sets the reader up to succeed with the text by developing key concepts, vocabulary, and a general picture of the text before it is read. This technique has been used in New Zealand (Goldenberg, 1991) in regular classrooms and in special support programs such as Reading Recovery in New Zealand (Clay, 1985) and the United States (DeFord, Lyons, & Pinnell, 1991; Hiebert & Taylor, 1994). Clay (1985) says that carrying out this type of procedure before reading ensures that "the child has in his head the ideas and the language he needs to produce when prompted in sequence by printed cues" (p. 68). The term *picture walk* is used when referring to a picture book, and *text walk* is used when referring to an informational text.

Procedures   You may adapt the following procedures to any level, including middle school or high school content classes:

1. Before working with students, read the text to get a picture of important ideas developed, the story line, key terms, and so forth.
2. If appropriate, show students the cover, and have them predict what the text is likely to be about or what is likely to happen.
3. Turning through the pages and using the pictures, illustrations, or graphics as prompts, tell key things that will happen in the text, or have students predict what is likely to happen. As you tell the major elements of the text, use some of the key vocabulary students will encounter in the text.
4. In most instances, tell the entire text that is to be read. In some cases, however, tell only enough to develop a framework to avoid giving away a surprise or exciting ending.

When to Use   Picture walk or text walk is especially helpful when working with students who need a great deal of extra support to construct meaning. For example, students who are going to read *Look What Whiskers Can Do* (Souza, 2007) would profit from a picture walk using the many beautiful photographs in the book to build background. You can also use the procedure any time students are going to read a text when you think they need very structured scaffolding to help them understand the material. For example, students reading a social studies chapter in grade 6 may need the structured support of a text walk to help them build background concepts and vocabulary for the chapter.

For more information on using observation, see Chapter 11.

Assessment Value Observe and listen as students respond during the picture walk or text walk to get a sense of their prior knowledge, their ability to make predictions, their familiarity with key vocabulary, and their general ability to express themselves orally.

5. Semantic Mapping

Description **Semantic mapping** helps students develop prior knowledge by seeing the relationships in a given topic. A semantic map is a visual representation of a particular concept. Figure 3.5 shows a semantic map created with third graders who were preparing to read an article about the uses of pine trees. Ovals represent the concepts, and lines with arrows and words written above them represent the relationships. The relationships depicted on a map can be *class* (pine trees), *example* (white pine), or *property* (needles).

Procedures There are many ways to use semantic maps, and there is no one right way to develop one. The first set of guidelines that follows is structured and directed by the teacher; the second set is also teacher directed, but it incorporates brainstorming followed by grouping and labeling of concepts. The second set uses many of the ideas suggested by Taba (1967), as described by McNeil (1970).

Guidelines 1

1. Write the major concept being discussed on the chalkboard or overhead, and draw an oval around it. (In Figure 3.5, the concept is *pine trees*.)

FIGURE 3.5   Semantic Map for Pine Trees Using Guidelines 1

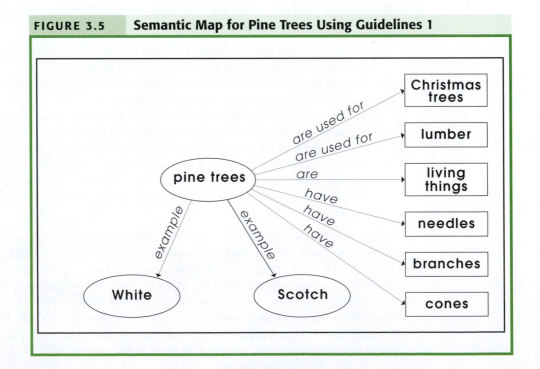

2. Ask students to think of words to describe the topic. Write those words in boxes, and link them with arrows to the main concept oval. Above the arrows, write words and phrases such as *have* or *are used for* to indicate the relationship between the main concept and the boxed words.

3. Ask students to give some examples of the topic, and write these in ovals with arrows indicating examples.

Guidelines 2

1. Present the concept to be discussed by placing it in an oval on the chalkboard or overhead.

2. Ask students to brainstorm words or ideas related to the concept. If necessary, probe for additional information.

3. Guide students in grouping the words or ideas to create the semantic map for the concept. Use different shapes to depict the different categories of information: rectangles for uses or descriptions, circles for examples, and squares for other types of information. Figure 3.6 shows how this process worked in one class.

The words written on the arrows to show relationships will vary according to the topic being discussed.

FIGURE 3.6   Semantic Map for Pine Trees Using Guidelines 2

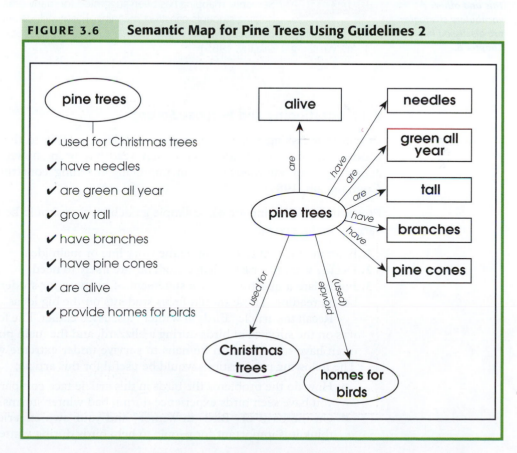

When to Use Semantic mapping is most effective when used with expository texts. If used with narratives, you must be certain that the concept used is central to the story line.

You can use semantic mapping with students from kindergarten through adulthood to help them visualize the relationships among ideas. Second-language learners and students with limited prior knowledge may respond best when the second set of guidelines is used, because they start out on a more global basis and move to specifics.

Semantic mapping is particularly effective when students will read several sources related to the same topic. The teacher and students can start the map before students begin the reading and add to it as they gain new information while reading. After they have completed their reading, they can return to the map to make additions or changes.

Assessment Value As students contribute to semantic mapping, you can assess their understandings of concepts and relationships, as well as key vocabulary.

This and other vocabulary strategies are discussed in Chapter 6.

> **Discussion** Semantic mapping has been suggested for many other uses in helping students construct meaning. These include summarizing the text, expanding their vocabulary, and writing (Noyce & Christie, 1989; Stahl & Vancil, 1986; Weisberg & Balajthy, 1985).

6. Prequestioning and Purpose Setting

Description Asking a question or giving students a topic to think about that will continue to focus their attention as they read has been shown to be effective in activating prior knowledge and in improving meaning construction (Tierney & Cunningham, 1984).

Procedures Following are some simple guidelines that should be used flexibly with various reading tasks:

1. Examine the text to determine the story line or main ideas.
2. Decide what prior knowledge students are likely to need.
3. Formulate a question(s) or a statement of purpose for students to think about before reading. These should focus students on the big ideas.

   Recall the article "Birds in Winter" discussed earlier. The focus of that article was on the survival of birds during a blizzard, and the main point was that birds often have to depend on humans to survive under extreme winter conditions. The following prequestions would be useful for this article:

   - How do the problems the birds in this article face compare to the problems you have seen birds experience during bad winter storms?
   - On the basis of "Birds in Winter" and your own experience, why do you think it is important for people to help birds during winter storms?

The following is an appropriate purpose-setting statement:

- You have discussed some of the problems that birds can have surviving in winter. Read this article to find out if there are other reasons that birds have difficulty surviving in blizzards.

Notice that the only real difference between this purpose statement and the prequestions is the form in which the purpose is stated.

The following prequestions would *not* be appropriate because they focus on specific points rather than the overall text and do not require readers to draw from their prior knowledge: "What two birds have the greatest difficulty surviving during blizzard conditions?" and "What three reasons does the author give to justify why people should help birds during blizzards?"

4. Have students read the text to answer the question or to accomplish the purpose given.
5. After reading, return to the question or purpose statement to see if students have achieved their goals and to discuss what they found. This helps students construct meaning.

When to Use This strategy should be used when students are not yet able to formulate their own purposes or prequestions or when the text is extremely difficult. Usually, you should combine prequestions and purpose statements with other strategies, such as discussion or brainstorming, to activate prior knowledge.

Assessment Value Prequestions and purpose statements are not as helpful as other strategies in assessing students' prior knowledge. Rather, their assessment value comes after reading, when students respond and show how well they have constructed meaning.

> **Discussion** Prequestions and purpose statements provide the scaffold for learning that some students need, and you will find you frequently use them when you employ the teacher-guided reading mode discussed in Chapter 2. Your goal, of course, is for students to learn to set their own purposes.

7. Anticipation Guides

Description An **anticipation guide** is a series of statements about a particular text that students are going to read. Students indicate whether they agree or disagree with the statements before reading and return to them after reading to do the same. This strategy is designed to activate prior knowledge and to give students a purpose for reading.

Procedures Readence, Bean, and Baldwin (1981, 1985, 1989) suggest eight steps in constructing and using anticipation guides:

1. *Identify major concepts.* Review the text to identify the major concepts or main ideas.

2. *Determine students' prior knowledge of these concepts.* Drawing on your experiences with your students, think about what they know about these concepts or ideas.
3. *Create statements.* Using the information from steps 1 and 2, write four to eight statements for students to react to that relate to the concepts to be learned and the students' prior knowledge. The number of statements depends on the amount of text to be read, the number of concepts in the text, and the age of the students. The statements should reflect information about which students have some, but not complete, knowledge. Statements should require students to think. Examples of good statements for a chapter on food and nutrition are:

> *An apple a day keeps the doctor away.*
> *If you wish to live a long life, be a vegetarian.*
> *Three square meals a day will satisfy all your body's nutritional needs.*
> *Calories make you fat. (Tierney, Readence, & Dishner, 1990, p. 48)*

4. *Decide on the statement order and presentation mode.* Sequence the statements to follow the text, inserting spaces for responses. Create a set of directions. Finally, decide whether the guide is to be presented individually or in a group mode, such as on the chalkboard or overhead.
5. *Present the guide.* Tell students they are to react to each statement by indicating whether they agree or disagree with it. Tell them they will share their responses with the group.
6. *Discuss each statement briefly.* Encourage students to share their opinions and tell why they feel as they do. You can tally the responses to each item.
7. *Direct students to read the text.* Have students read the text, keeping their opinions in mind. As they read, they should think about how the text relates to the statements on the guide.
8. *Conduct a follow-up discussion.* Ask students to respond to each statement in light of what they have read. Then have them discuss the statements, focusing on what they have learned and how their opinions and ideas have changed. Figure 3.7 presents a sample anticipation guide for a social studies chapter on transportation.

FIGURE 3.7   Anticipation Guide for Social Studies

Chapter 6, Transportation

Directions: Read each statement. Mark *A* for agree or *D* for disagree. Do the same after reading the chapter.

Before Reading		After Reading
_____	1. Travel has not changed much in the last 25 years.	_____
_____	2. The car is still considered the safest way to travel.	_____
_____	3. The safest way to travel is by air.	_____
_____	4. Large cities need to have more parking garages for increased populations.	_____
_____	5. Cars should be banned from the central business district of large cities.	_____

When to Use Anticipation guides may be used for any students at any level. They are most useful for expository texts. This strategy is particularly effective when students have misconceptions in prior knowledge, because when students interact with the text and compare prior opinions with what they learned from reading, they are likely to correct their misconceptions.

Assessment Value By looking at and listening to students' responses, you can tell the state of their prior knowledge and easily recognize their misconceptions. Then, by looking at the after-reading responses, you can tell whether those misconceptions have changed.

8. Structured Previews

Description Some students may need a more structured preview than was described earlier. A **structured preview** is carefully guided by the teacher and often involves some type of graphic display of information to help students see the ideas that are upcoming in the text and how they are organized. The concept is based on research showing that students' prior knowledge needs to be directed toward the story line (Beck, 1984; Beck, Omanson, & McKeown, 1982).

Procedures The procedure for conducting a structured preview for narrative texts differs from one for expository texts, though there are similarities.

Narrative Structured Preview

Most narrative structured previews are similar because most narrative texts have the same basic structure.

1. Look through the book to get a sense of the story line. Identify the setting, characters, problem, action, and outcome.
2. Formulate questions or statements that direct students to read the title and the opening paragraph or two (depending on the level), and look at the first few illustrations. Have students share what they learn.
3. Display a story map (see Figure 3.8) and discuss with students the elements in the story. For beginning learners and those having difficulty constructing meaning, focus on only one or two elements at first.
4. Ask students to predict what they can about the story elements from their preview, keeping students focused on the story line.
5. Have students silently read the story in its entirety or in sections. Then, return to the story map to help them decide whether their predictions were verified or changed. Together, complete the story map.

Adjust the steps involved in the structured preview to fit the story content, illustrations, and level. The primary focus should always be to get students to think about the particular story problem and relate what they already know to it. If your third-grade students are going to read *Wilfrid Gordon McDonald Partridge* (Fox, 1985), a book about how a young boy helps an elderly woman in an old people's home get her memory back, you begin the structured preview by having the children look at the cover and tell who they think this book is going to be about. Next, while looking through the first three or four pages, ask the children to talk about old people's homes and the

FIGURE 3.8   **Story Map for Structured Preview**

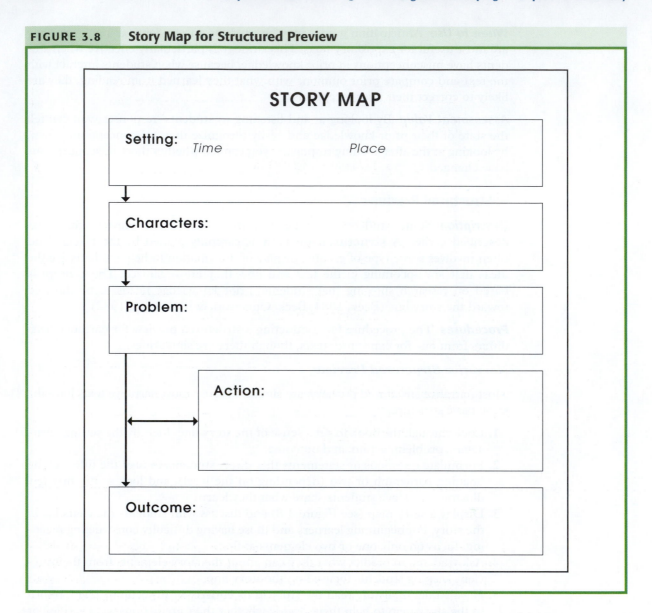

types of things that might be problems, focusing on the idea that some people become forgetful as they age. Complete the preview by presenting the story map and asking the children to predict the characters and the possible problem in the story.

Expository Structured Preview

Expository structured previews will vary because of varying text structures. Therefore, you will need to adapt the following guidelines to fit the structure of the text:

1. Review the text to determine the main ideas. Try to identify a **graphic organizer** that will help students see how the information fits together. For example, if the

FIGURE 3.9   **Graphic Organizer Showing Three Main Ideas in an Expository Text**

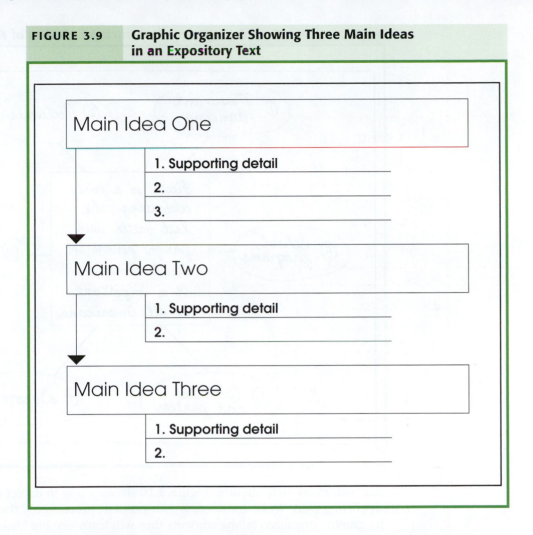

Main Idea One

    1. Supporting detail

    2.

    3.

Main Idea Two

    1. Supporting detail

    2.

Main Idea Three

    1. Supporting detail

    2.

text has three main ideas, the graphic organizer might be like the one shown in Figure 3.9, although many texts do not lend themselves to such a neat outline.

2. Formulate questions and statements to help students preview the text by reading the title, looking at the illustrations and captions, and reading subheads.

3. Guide students through a preview of the text, having them begin to predict the type of information they will learn.

4. Show the graphic organizer and tell students that the ideas are organized in that pattern.

5. Have students read to look for the main ideas in the organizer. As students become stronger readers, they can also identify information that supports the main ideas.

In preparing a structured preview for an expository text, pay close attention to how the main ideas are presented in the text. For example, if your second graders are going to read *Fiesta!* (Behrens, 1978), you know that this work has only one main

FIGURE 3.10   Graphic Organizer for Structural Preview of *Fiesta!*

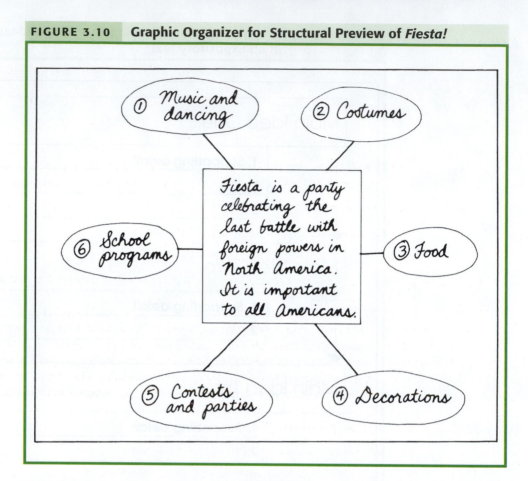

idea with many facts about it. Figure 3.10 shows a way to depict this idea with its supporting facts. When conducting your preview, present only the basic outline of the graphic organizer, telling students they will learn one big idea about fiesta and six kinds of information about what happens during fiesta. This type of structured preview activates prior knowledge about the topic and also gives students a framework to use in thinking about how the information is organized.

When to Use   Structured previews are useful on a number of occasions:

- When the text is particularly difficult
- When students are second-language learners
- When students are having difficulty constructing meaning
- When you know students have limited prior knowledge about either the topic or the type of text

Assessment Value   Students' responses during the preview session may help you determine the status of their prior knowledge and what they are gaining from the preview, but because the preview is so teacher directed, what you learn may be limited.

> **Discussion** Structured previews can be unnecessarily complicated. Keep your structured previews as simple as possible, making certain that any graphic organizers used actually *do* help students see how the text is organized. The structured preview may be combined with many of the other strategies.

9. Reading Aloud to Students

Description The importance of reading aloud to students was well established in Chapter 2. In this strategy, the reading is specific to a thematic topic or selection.

Procedures

Reading Aloud Background Material

Use the following guidelines to carry out this strategy:

1. Select a book, article, or other background material that relates to the topic or selection.
2. Tell students what it is about and why you will read it to them.
3. Give students a purpose for listening. For example, have them listen to identify some important idea or concept to retell an important part of the story. You can also ask them to make predictions about what they expect to learn as they listen.
4. After the read-aloud, discuss the material by checking the purpose for which students were to listen, or discuss whether predictions were confirmed.

Reading Aloud a Portion of a Selection

Guidelines for using this strategy are as follows:

1. Decide on the story or article students will read.
2. Identify how much of the initial part of the selection you are going to read aloud.
3. Introduce the selection, and give students a purpose for listening.
4. Read aloud the selected section.
5. Discuss the portion read aloud, checking the purpose given for listening.
6. Have students predict what they think will happen or what they will learn in the remainder of the text.
7. Have students read silently to check their predictions.
8. Discuss the entire selection, focusing on students' predictions.
9. Have students respond to the selection in their own way.

You may vary this second read-aloud strategy by reading aloud parts of the text and alternating these sessions with students reading cooperatively or independently. How much reading aloud you do will depend on the students' needs and the text. This is a variation of the read-aloud, read along, read alone strategy discussed in Chapter 2.

When to Use Use the read-aloud strategy when you know students have limited or erroneous prior knowledge. Use it with second-language learners to help them develop oral language.

Assessment Value As you read aloud, you can generally tell how well students comprehend through listening and how well they remember and organize ideas and understand key vocabulary, without having to figure out words in print. It is not as helpful as a way to assess students' specific prior knowledge.

> **Discussion** Reading aloud is also useful in building prior knowledge for writing.

10. Role Playing

Description In **role playing,** students take parts and act out a situation, which requires students to think about a problem or circumstance and bring their prior knowledge to bear on it.

Procedures Role playing can be fun, but it requires careful planning to make it a valuable experience for prior knowledge activation:

1. Select the book you want students to read. Determine the story line.
2. Select a situation that would be easy and fun for children to role-play. Make sure it relates to the story line but does not give away the story.
3. Describe the situation to the children. Divide them into small groups to decide on parts and determine how they will act out their situations.
4. Have each group perform. Then discuss the situations, focusing the discussion on the story to be read, not on an evaluation of their performances.
5. Have students read the story to compare it with their experience.

Suppose your sixth graders are going to read *Wayside School Is Falling Down* (Sachar, 1989), a hilarious book about the adventures of children in Louis Sachar's imaginary school. You could ask children to role-play the strangest and funniest thing they could imagine happening in school. As each group performs, you then discuss the incident, leading the children to focus on the book by directing them to see how their experiences compare with those of the Erics and other children in Wayside School.

When to Use Role playing is a good strategy for students who need concrete experiences. Often second-language learners who are reluctant to speak out individually in an open discussion will relate to and interact with their peers in a role-playing situation. Although role playing is often used with narrative texts, it may also be useful with expository texts, especially social studies.

For more discussion about observations, see Chapter 11.

Assessment Value Observing students in a role-playing situation can give you a sense of their prior knowledge as well as the ways they think and solve problems.

> **Discussion** If some students are too shy to participate, consider using puppets.

Video Case

Diversity: Teaching in a Multiethnic Classroom

Watch the video clip, study the artifacts in the case, and reflect on the following questions:

1. The chapter states that "projects help students learn new strategies and skills and gain new information. What new strategies and skills do you think the students within this Video Case have gained as a result of doing the Kamishibai project?

2. Based on watching the Video Case and reading the Lesson Plans (in the Classroom Artifacts for this Video Case), please describe the goals of this lesson and project. What kinds of prior knowledge does the Kamishibai project attempt to activate?

11. Projects

Description A **project** is a task undertaken to achieve a particular goal; it is usually long term, and because of its goal, you can tell when it is completed. Though often a culminating activity, projects can be an ongoing part of a thematic unit. Thus, a project may summarize what has been learned, activate prior knowledge, and develop new knowledge.

Procedures The following guidelines are useful with projects:

1. *Identify the project.* This can be done by you or your students.
2. *Select resources.* Assign the use of certain resources, or let students select them.
3. *Make a plan.* Decide what will be done and when.
4. *Decide how projects will be shared.* Will there be a display? An oral report? Something else?

When to Use While ongoing projects are not the most efficient way to activate prior knowledge for reading a particular text, as students use resources for such a project, they are developing prior knowledge for future reading of upcoming texts within the unit of study. Projects are also effective in helping ELLs develop prior knowledge.

Assessment Value As you observe students while they work, you can assess work habits, independence, and ability to use resources, as well as their developing background knowledge about the topic. Projects also lend themselves to student self-evaluation.

> **Discussion** Projects help students learn new strategies and skills and gain new information. They may require students to read and do research. They help students make connections, integrate new knowledge with prior knowledge, learn to work cooperatively and independently, and develop critical thinking. Students may do projects independently or in groups, depending on their purposes. They should be encouraged to select and plan their own projects. Be cautious when using this strategy. Sometimes students get so caught up in completing a project that it replaces most, if not all, of the reading and writing they should be doing. See the Educators Speak feature about projects in one school district.

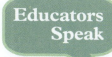

Using a Project That Cuts Across the Curriculum

"Cross-curricular projects are used by many teachers in our schools to meet the needs of our diverse population. Students are provided "structured choice" and are to select a number of items from a menu of activities that require reading, writing, and knowledge of content. The menu must include something for everyone in order to allow all students to participate. The depth and complexity of the items, as well as the reading and writing skill level required to complete the task, is an important feature of the project design. Some teachers assign a point value to each of the activities and require that each student select items that total a particular number. These are in addition to group tasks. The point value allows the teacher to include a variety of assignments that range in level of difficulty, complexity, and time required to complete, with the expectation that all students will take responsibility for demonstrating their knowledge of the content through reading and writing.

Teachers determine in advance the components that are to be completed by each individual and as a group. The students are then assigned to predetermined heterogeneous working groups. Each group is responsible for completing all of the menu items and is encouraged to take into account each member's strengths when dividing the responsibilities. Each group uses a preplanning sheet to establish a timeline for completion of each group activity, with check points along the way. They also list possible sources of information, materials, and other issues essential to completing the project. The teacher conferences with each group and guides and supports their decision making as the project components are distributed among the members.

Here are examples of activities teachers found to be meaningful and interesting to their students for a social studies unit on a particular time period:

- Develop a timeline that includes pictures or phrases that depict the major events of the period.
- Draw a cartoon and write a caption that illustrates a key point or main idea from the period.
- List ten quotes, paraphrase them, and describe their significance to the causes, effects, or events related to the period.
- Select ten of the most significant events from this period, and support their importance with factual information and personal commentary about why you selected these particular events.
- Select a song with lyrics that support some of the ideas brought forward during this time period. Explain the connections.
- Write two letters to the editor. One letter must be pro (select a key player in this time period) and the other must be con.

The purpose of the cross-curricular project is for students to apply their reading and writing skills across the curriculum as they demonstrate their knowledge of content through activities that range in level of difficulty and amount of reading and writing required. As

(continued)

teachers continue to brainstorm and share ideas, the menu of project activities continues to grow, and we work to ensure the activities do not become so elaborate that they overshadow the intent and we lose sight of their purpose.

—Lynne Pistochini, Curriculum Resource Specialist
San Juan Unified School District
Folsom, California

12. Concrete Materials and Real Experiences

Description Often the best way to activate and develop students' prior knowledge is to use concrete materials, and experiences such as the Internet, CD-ROMs, pictures, DVDs, videos, films, filmstrips, videos, field trips, or classroom planned experiences. For example, a classroom science experiment involving treating three plants

Fifth graders model Xian soldiers during an ancient civilization unit.
© David Young-Wolf/PhotoEdit

differently—one gets water and no light, one gets light and no water, and one gets water and light—can develop prior knowledge before a theme on plants or on air and water.

Procedures The only guideline is to ensure that the materials or experiences actually help to activate and develop prior knowledge that is relevant to the theme, the text to be read, or the writing experience.

When to Use Concrete materials and real experiences are most important when students lack prior knowledge on a particular topic. Second-language learners and students with limited background often need this type of support because it makes the input comprehensible (Krashen, 1982). This strategy is also useful for introducing a new topic to all students.

Assessment Value Since this strategy is used to develop prior knowledge, it has limited assessment value. However, students' responses will give you an indication of what they know and what they are learning.

> **Discussion** Always introduce real experiences by telling children their purpose, in order to make the connection to instruction clear. After the experience, you and the students should talk about what was learned and how it relates to the topic or theme. For example, in preparation for a thematic unit on wild animals, students should make predictions about certain animals before the real experience of going to the zoo on a field trip. Then, they can discuss which predictions were confirmed and summarize what they learned about the animals and how this knowledge will help them as they work in this unit.

Deciding Which Strategies to Use

Each of the fifteen strategies—three student strategies and twelve teaching strategies with variations just discussed—has as its primary focus activation and/or development of prior knowledge of concepts and vocabulary, leading students to set their purpose for reading. Some lessons will call for combining several strategies, and others will require only one strategy. Some will require heavy teacher support, others almost none. The following guidelines should help you decide which strategies to use and when to use them.

Motivation and Interest

Student motivation and interest for a topic or book directly influence the amount of prior knowledge activation and development needed. Usually students who select their own topics or books are either very highly motivated or have good prior knowledge about the topic; they will need little or no support. If students are highly motivated to read or write about a certain topic but have little prior knowledge about it, they will need support in developing this knowledge.

The Text

You must know the type of text (narrative or expository) and its difficulty when deciding which strategies to use. With narrative text, focus on the story line; for expository text, focus on the main ideas.

Complex concepts, ideas, or structures demand more prior knowledge activation, and some strategies will be more useful than others. Refer to Tables 3.2 and 3.3 for a summary of when to use the strategies presented in this chapter.

Student Needs and Level of Independence

As you become familiar with your students, you will know which ones need the most prior knowledge support. Students who have achieved independence may need no support, but this need will change from situation to situation. Students with limited English proficiency may benefit from pictures, objects, and gestures.

Lesson Variety

Using the same strategies over and over again becomes boring for everyone. Vary your strategies to keep interest and motivation for learning high.

Overcoming Inadequate Prior Knowledge

Students who experience difficulties in constructing meaning often have limited or erroneous prior knowledge (Lipson, 1984). They need more prior knowledge development that is *directed specifically to the reading or writing task* they are to perform. You can use all of the strategies presented in this chapter, but you may need to present them more thoroughly by covering more related concepts important to understanding the text to be read.

Limited Prior Knowledge

Our goal is to help all students expand and build on the prior knowledge they bring to school. Within the literacy program are many opportunities to expand students' world knowledge as well as knowledge and experience with literacy. Always value each individual and what he or she brings to school, even when some students' background experiences don't match what the school requires. The following suggestions should be helpful in planning classroom experiences that will help expand students' prior knowledge:

Sharing and Talking Create opportunities for students to share and talk about their own experiences and backgrounds; this shows that you value them. Opportunities can be provided in opening morning exercises, special sharing times, or throughout the day. Sharing should include time to talk about books students have read or writing they have done.

Read-Aloud Time Reading aloud to your students is one of the best ways to broaden their prior knowledge and language experiences. It is especially valuable if students have not been read to at home.

See Chapter 2 for suggestions.

Independent Reading and Writing Time Students who have limited prior knowledge need *more time to read and write independently*.

Use of Technology Some students with inadequate prior knowledge will be motivated to seek information on the Web and to share that information in meaningful ways with peers.

Plan Lessons and Experiences to Develop Prior Knowledge Use the strategies suggested in this chapter and those you learn from other sources to systematically develop prior knowledge when you start a new theme, when students read a selection, or when they begin a writing experience. Use the literacy lesson format presented in Chapter 2 with the strategies that lend themselves to more concretely developing prior knowledge for students. Students who have limited prior knowledge often need continued support throughout their reading lessons to develop and connect this newly developed knowledge to what they read.

Erroneous Prior Knowledge

Correcting misconceptions or erroneous prior knowledge is difficult, but research indicates it is possible to make these corrections and improve students' ability to construct meaning (Alvermann & Hynd, 1987; Alvermann et al., 1985; Dole & Smith, 1989; Hynd & Alvermann, 1986; Maria, 1988). The following guidelines may be helpful.

Activate and Assess Prior Knowledge Find out what students know and/or think about the topic by using the strategies in this chapter. As students respond, note misconceptions or errors.

Decide on the Best Time for Correcting the Error or Misconception This is not an easy decision. Research suggests that changing students' misconceptions is a long-term process that takes place through reading and writing over a period of time. Minor errors or misconceptions may be corrected before reading, but more serious ones will need to be viewed in the long-term process of instruction. Brainstorming and discussion may be natural strategies for correcting minor misconceptions before reading (Flood & Lapp, 1988). However, Maria (1990) cautions that too heavy a focus on correcting errors or misconceptions before reading may deter students from wanting to read.

Select the Strategies to Use Whereas all the strategies in this chapter might be useful in correcting minor misconceptions, those that involve longer-term thinking processes are more likely to be effective in overcoming more deeply rooted misconceptions. One such strategy is the anticipation guide presented earlier.

Research on the role of misconceptions in prior knowledge and the construction of meaning is continuing. Although the guidelines presented here are certainly supported by the limited amount of research that exists, you should be on the lookout for new information in this area.

Standards-Based Literacy Lessons

A Standards-Based Lesson Using *Gladiator*

This lesson focuses on introducing a theme and one of the books to be read during the theme. Global prior knowledge is activated and developed when introducing the theme and text-specific and topic-specific prior knowledge are activated and developed for the first chapter of the book.

This portion of the sample unit is based on a thematic unit plan on "Ancient Civilizations" designed for sixth grade in which one of the books to be read is *Gladiator* (Watkins, 1997).

Standards Used in the Plan

- Sample standards are the Sixth Grade Reading Standards from the Kansas Department of Education.
- The website at which you can find these standards is **http://www.ksde.org/Default .aspx?tabid=142.**
- In our lesson, some Kansas indicators are addressed during the introductory activities, some during the reading and responding activities, and some during the extending activities. We tell you how each indicator we included in our sample.
- Remember to look at your own state standards to see how they compare to these standards at this grade level.

Sixth Grade

Standard 1: Reading: The student reads and comprehends text across the curriculum.

Benchmark 2: The student reads fluently.

Indicators: The student . . .
  2. reads expressively with appropriate *pace*, *phrasing*, *intonation*, and *rhythm of speech*.

Benchmark 3: The student expands vocabulary.

Indicators: The student . . .
  1. determines the meaning of words or phrases using context clues (e.g., *definitions*, *restatements*, *examples*, *descriptions*, *comparison-contrast*, clue words) from sentences or paragraphs.
  3. understands and uses the references available in the classroom, school, and public libraries (e.g., dictionaries, thesauri, atlases, encyclopedias, Internet) that are appropriate to the task.

Benchmark 4: The student comprehends a variety of texts (narrative, expository, technical, *and* persuasive).

Indicators: The student . . .
  3. uses prior knowledge, content, and text type features to make, revise, and confirm predictions.
  4. generates and responds logically to literal, inferential, and *critical thinking* questions before, during, and after reading the text.
  10. identifies the *topic*, *main idea(s)*, supporting details, and *theme(s)* in text across the content areas and from a variety of sources in appropriate-level texts.

Standards-Based
Literacy
Lessons

continued

Before Reading the Plan

1. Think about what you have learned about prior knowledge activation and development.
2. Read the excerpt from *Gladiator*, which includes the cover, the Table of Contents, the Introduction, and the first chapter, "Ancient Rome."
3. Read the teacher preparation section to learn how we decided which prior knowledge to activate for the theme and for the literacy lesson. Then read the plan that follows the excerpt from *Gladiator*.

While Reading the Plan

1. Notice how prior knowledge was activated and developed for this theme and lesson.
2. Think about why each strategy was used. Note any questions.
3. Read the Multilevel Notes to see how the teacher accommodates different levels of students' reading when everyone in the class is using the same text.
4. Think of other ways you could have activated and developed prior knowledge for this theme and lesson.

 ## Teacher Preparation

The unit "Ancient Civilizations," with the literacy lesson using *Gladiator* (Watkins, 1997), was planned for a sixth-grade class. The school is in a small southern town and draws students from both the town and the surrounding rural area. Few students have computers with Internet access in their homes and there are limited technological resources in the school, with no computers in classrooms. The following section outlines the steps used to plan the lesson and gives a rationale for each step.

Unit Activities Prior to Reading the Book *Gladiator*

1. Several resources were gathered with the help of the school librarian. Some will be available only in the library (e.g., CD-ROMs), but many books will remain in the classroom for the duration of the unit. Because the topic will have wide appeal, all students will read *Gladiator;* therefore, we have multiple copies of the book. As students select other aspects of ancient civilizations to study, individuals and groups will read other materials and share what they learn.
2. We decided what text-specific and topic-specific background students would need in order to read the first chapter of the book with understanding.
   a. Text-specific background: Students will recall that historical information is often organized chronologically. (The class has been learning organizational patterns of informational text.) The content of the first chapter, "Ancient Rome," gives an overview of Roman history, from the traditional explanation of its founding in 753 B.C. by Romulus and Remus to its fall.
   b. Topic-specific background: Students may have some knowledge (whether correct or not) about Roman history in general and gladiators in particular. To activate prior knowledge about Roman history, we will use a map or globe and focused discussion. We will return to the map many times during reading. Prior knowledge about gladiators will be dealt with as we begin the book.

Specific Outcomes to Be Developed in This Lesson

You read earlier some Kansas state benchmarks and indicators met in this lesson.
1. Vocabulary: understands topic-specific words for the selection
2. Vocabulary: uses context to determine meaning of unfamiliar words

**Standards-Based
Literacy
Lessons**

continued

*See Chapter 2 for
discussion of modes
of reading.*

3. Comprehension: confirms predictions after reading a given text
4. Comprehension: determines topics, main ideas, important supporting details, and themes
5. Study skills: locates places on maps and globes and understands and uses references
6. Literary response: increases knowledge about an ancient civilization and relates to current civilizations; shares ideas with peers; demonstrates understanding through discussion and a project

About This Lesson

1. Prior knowledge of concepts and vocabulary will be activated and developed using semantic mapping, focused discussion, prequestioning, and concrete materials.
2. Because of the dense text and because of the students' scant, and probably inaccurate, prior knowledge, the lesson uses three modes of reading: read-aloud of the Introduction and the beginning of the chapter, then interactive guided reading, and finally cooperative or independent reading. Until we begin reading, we cannot determine at what point the final mode will occur.
3. We will not preteach additional vocabulary beyond that developed during the prior knowledge activity for the first chapter. Instead, students will draw on their ability to use context to determine the meaning of unfamiliar terms.
4. The lesson includes initial planning for independent or group activities that will result in a unit project.

Standards-Based
**Literacy
Lessons**
continued

GLADIATOR

Richard Watkins

Houghton Mifflin Company
Boston

CONTENTS

INTRODUCTION

On a sunny afternoon two thousand years ago, the fiercest and strongest men in the Roman Empire marched out onto the sand of the arena. Fifty thousand spectators roared as these men, the gladiators, came into view, their magnificent armor glistening in the sun. When they came to a halt in front of the emperor's box, slaves came forward to present each with a razor-sharp weapon: sword, dagger, or spear. As the slaves scurried away the crowd fell silent. The gladiators raised their weapons to the emperor and called out, "Hail, Emperor! We who are about to die salute thee!" Trumpets blared, the men paired off, and with a clash of swords began the deadly combats of the gladiators of ancient Rome.

I

ANCIENT ROME

The gladiator's world was a Roman world. The civilization that developed and exploited them was the most powerful empire of its time. At its height, it governed the lives of 60 million people, one-fifth of the world's population, all of whom obeyed its laws, paid taxes to its emperor, and were familiar with its language, religions, and customs.

According to tradition, Rome was founded on April 21, 753 B.C. The legend says that Romulus and Remus were the twin sons of the war god, Mars. As infants, they were abandoned in a basket by the River Tiber. There they were found by a she-wolf, who carried them back to her den and protected and nurtured them until they were old enough to survive on their own. It was as a young man that Romulus established the city that bears his name by carving its borders with a plow. Watching his brother hard at work and doing nothing to help, Remus teased Romulus mercilessly, making fun of his hard labor. When he could take it no

2

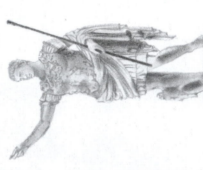

Augustus Caesar, Rome's first emperor

3

longer, Romulus flew into a rage and attacked his twin, killing him. Romulus was not only the founder of Rome, but also its first king.

From this legendary beginning Rome grew to become the most important city in the western world. In 509 B.C. Rome's last king was dethroned and the Roman Republic was founded, ruled by two consuls who were elected each year by the senate. Military conquest and colonization brought the rest of Italy under Roman rule by 268 B.C. First to be absorbed were the Latins, Samnites, and other Italian tribes, followed by the great Etruscan civilization in the north and the Greek colonies in the south. The Romans adopted many elements of both the Etruscan and Greek cultures. Gladiator fights and chariot racing were Etruscan in origin. Roman art, architecture, and literature borrowed heavily from the Greeks.

Carthage, Rome's principal competition for trade in the Mediterranean Sea, was finally defeated in 146 B.C., after one hundred years of war. Further conquests followed: Gaul (what is now France) was conquered by Julius Caesar in 49 B.C., Egypt in 30 B.C., and Britain in A.D. 43.

All this expansion was not without a price. The democratic principles established by the Republic sank under the weight of the growing empire. Victorious generals fought for power in a series of bloody civil wars. Julius Caesar, after proclaiming himself permanent dictator, was murdered by a conspiracy of senators in 44 B.C. In the struggle for power that followed, Caesar's adopted son, Octavian, defeated all his political and military rivals and became Augustus Caesar, first emperor of Rome, in 27 B.C.

THE ROMAN EMPIRE
IN THE 2ND CENTURY A.D.

Until its fall four hundred years later, Rome was ruled by eighty-six emperors, some wise and just, others insane and corrupt. At its height, the Roman Empire controlled all of southern Europe, Britain, Asia Minor, Syria, Egypt, and North Africa. Cities were established, trade was regulated, taxes were collected. Rome built 53,000 miles of roads, bridges, aqueducts, and sewers, some of which are still in use. Its laws, manners, and customs were adopted all over the empire.

But for all its glory, it's difficult to ignore the fact that the Roman Empire was won by military force and built by the labor of millions of slaves. To the average Roman citizen, life was hard, war was a constant threat, and slaves were just another piece of property. And in spite of their sophistication in government, business, and the arts, Romans had a crude taste for violence and cruelty. For almost a thousand years Roman society represented both the best and the worst of human civilization.

5

Standards-Based
Literacy
Lessons

continued

See Chapter 5 for discussion of word wall.

 Introducing Ancient Civilizations Unit

Activity	Procedures, Comments, and Multilevel Notes
Thematic opening activities; map/globe; brainstorm	Display a world map and/or a globe. Tell students they are going to begin their study of ancient civilizations with a study of one part of what is now known as Europe. Be sure students understand the meaning of the terms *ancient* in the historical sense and *civilization*. Brainstorm about the value of such study.
Focused discussion	Ask questions such as the following, keeping the discussion focused and brief: Where is Rome? What do we know about the role Rome played in history?
Word wall	Begin a word wall related to Rome by writing the name of the country and any topic-specific words or place names that arise during the discussion. Continue to add to the word wall as the unit progresses.
Introduce unit activities	Tell students to begin jotting down ideas for possible unit projects related to ancient civilizations and ancient Rome in particular. Explain what project resources will be made available during the unit of study: the library for reference books, CD-ROMs, and websites; additional books and maps within the classroom.
	Comment: *These activities activate global prior knowledge for future reading, motivate, and provide additional topic-specific vocabulary.*
	Multilevel Note: *Students of all reading levels can participate in some aspect of a project.*

 **Introducing *Gladiator***

Activity	Procedures, Comments, and Multilevel Notes
Picture; independent semantic mapping	1. Display the cover of the book.
	2. Have students work in pairs or small groups to make semantic maps of the term *gladiator*, with one student as the recorder.
	Multilevel Note: *Pairs or groups should be heterogeneous.*
	3. Tell students they will add to and/or revise these later.

Standards-Based Literacy Lessons

continued

Activity	Procedures, Comments, and Multilevel Notes (continued)
Word wall **Preview the book and the first chapter; note text structure**	Call students together in a large group, and ask for terms from independent activities to add to the word wall. 1. Have students preview the entire book by looking at the title and the table of contents and leafing through pages. 2. Discuss the cover art and the chapter titles, and record predictions about the content. 3. Have students locate the first chapter, and lead them to examine and discuss the pictures and the captions under them. 4. Recall with students what they know about how informational text might be organized. Ask them to predict how they think a chapter on this topic might be organized. Record these ideas and tell students you will return to them later. **Comment:** *These activities help students know that informational text is approached differently from story; it is a good idea to get a general idea about the entire text before beginning. Also, the chapter they will read has no organizational markers such as headings and subheadings. As they read, the organization will become clearer.*
Read aloud; predict	1. Read aloud the Introduction. Discuss how this introduction is unlike others in that it is designed to motivate one to want to read rather than provide an overview of the book. 2. Have students predict what they think they will learn from the first chapter based on the title. 3. Record the predictions, and tell students they will return to these predictions after completing the chapter. 4. Remind students they will return to their semantic webs to add (or change) information. **Comment:** *Reading aloud to students models fluent reading and motivates interest.* **Multilevel Note:** *Students of all levels can participate equally in all activities thus far.*

Assessment Note: Assess the following Kansas standard while introducing *Gladiator*: Standard 1, Benchmark 4, Indicator 3

**Standards-Based
Literacy
Lessons**

continued

✸ Reading and Responding to *Gladiator*

Activity	Procedures, Comments, and Multilevel Notes
Guided reading of the chapter	1. Read aloud the first paragraph or two. Lead students to compare the general information about the Roman civilization with their knowledge of current civilizations. Then have students read the next paragraph silently.
	2. Ask a volunteer to summarize the main idea of the paragraph.
	3. Ask students to suggest words to add to the word wall.
	4. Verify understanding of key terms, such as *legendary* and *colonization*.
	5. Have students predict what they will learn in the following paragraph(s).
	6. Continue guiding the reading until you think students will be able to carry on by reading with a partner or independently. You may want to discuss the content in great detail to be sure students understand the information and the terminology, and are able to place the information in time and place.
	Comment: *Guided reading models the value of summarizing, predicting, and dealing with concept vocabulary while reading informational text.*
	Multilevel Note: *Vary the depth of your guidance according to the needs of your group and of individual students.*
Cooperative or independent reading (when students are ready)	1. Have students continue reading the chapter.
	2. Remind students to summarize main ideas, details, and vocabulary as they read. If they are reading with a partner, they may discuss the reading.
	3. Have students list concept words as they read to add to the word wall later.
	Comment: *All students should be thinking about how they deal with unfamiliar words in context and be ready to talk about their strategies later.*
	Multilevel Note: *If some students are unable to read cooperatively or independently, they may continue guided reading with you.*

**Standards-Based
Literacy
Lessons**

continued

Activity	Procedures, Comments, and Multilevel Notes (continued)
Discussion	1. After all students have read the chapter, have students recall the main idea(s) and important details of this chapter.
	2. You may want to have students independently devise a graphic way of showing the important information in the chapter and then share this with the class.
	3. Display a current map of the same area as is shown in the map of the Roman Empire in the first chapter. Lead students to note what seems basically the same and what seems different. Lead a focused discussion about possible causes of such change.
	Comment: *During the chapter discussion, students may want to return to the text to support their ideas.*
	Multilevel Note: *All students can participate equally in discussion, regardless of mode used for reading.*
Return to predictions	Have students review the predictions they made before reading and confirm or revise them.
	Comment: *Returning to predictions helps students understand that ideas change as one reads.*

Assessment Note: Assess the following Kansas standards while reading and responding to *Gladiator:*

During guided reading:
- Standard 1, Benchmark 2, Indicator 2
- Standard 1, Benchmark 4, Indicator 3
- Standard 1, Benchmark 4, Indicator 4

During cooperative or independent reading:
- Standard 1, Benchmark 3, Indicator 1
- Standard 1, Benchmark 4, Indicator 4

During discussion:
- Standard 1, Benchmark 4, Indicator 10

As students return to predictions:
- Standard 1, Benchmark 3, Indicator 3

Extending "Ancient Rome" to the Remainder of the Book

1. Observation during the read-aloud, guided reading, and cooperative or independent reading of Chapter 1 will dictate how to have students read the remainder of the book. Some students may be able to read the rest of the book independently, with group discussions every chapter or two. Others may do better with continued guided reading and/or cooperative reading. It is not necessary that all students read the book in the same mode.

2. As students get ideas for projects, they will present them to me, and I will give whatever support individuals need to carry out their projects independently or with a partner. I will

Standards-Based
Literacy
Lessons

continued

help students choose projects they can completely successfully, depending on their strengths.

3. Throughout the unit, we will add to the word wall and to our group background knowledge about Rome and other ancient civilizations.

4. Throughout the reading of the book, I will hold individual conferences with students to assess their ability to deal with new vocabulary in context, summarize main ideas and supporting details, and predict. Based on these conferences, I will plan any needed direct skill instruction.

> **Assessment Note:** Assess the following Kansas standard during Extending Activities:
> - Standard 1, Benchmark 2, Indicator 2
>
> After Reading the Plan
> - Review the plan and discuss it with your peers. Focus on how prior knowledge was activated and developed before and throughout the lesson.
> - Plan a different lesson for the first chapter of *Gladiator* using two or three other strategies for activating prior knowledge.

Prior Knowledge: Activating and Developing Concepts and Vocabulary: Key Points

To review the Key Points, see the ACE practice tests at the HM TeacherPrepSPACE Student Website.

- Teachers must activate and develop the concepts and vocabulary that constitute prior knowledge.
- Second-language learners, students with limited prior knowledge, and students with misconceptions need special support.
- Student strategies and teaching strategies—help students call up their own prior knowledge and determine their purpose for reading.

How Do I Teach?

Preview and predict, p. 87
K-W-L, p. 88
Making connections, p. 92
Discussion, p. 94
Brainstorming, p. 97
Quick writing, p. 100

Picture walk/text walk, p. 101
Semantic mapping, p. 102
Prequestioning and purpose setting, p. 104
Anticipation guides, p. 105
Structured previews, p. 107

Reading aloud to students, p. 111
Role playing, p. 112
Projects, p. 113
Concrete materials and real experiences, p. 115
A Literacy Lesson, p. 119

Video Cases in This Chapter

■ Bilingual Education: An Elementary, Two-Way Immersion Program
■ Elementary School Language Arts: Inquiry Learning
■ Diversity: Teaching in a Multiethnic Classroom

For Additional Reading

Au, K. H. (1993). *Literacy instruction in multicultural settings*. Fort Worth, TX: Harcourt Brace.

Buehl, D. (2001). *Classroom strategies for interactive learning* (2nd ed.). Newark, DE: International Reading Association.

Dorr, R. A. (2006). Something old is new again: Revisiting language experience. *The Reading Teacher, 60*(2), 138–146.

Duke, N. K., & Purcell-Gates, V. (2003). Genres at home and at school: Bridging the known to the new. *The Reading Teacher, 57*(1), 30–37.

Dymock, S. (2005). Teaching expository text structure awareness. *The Reading Teacher, 59*(2), 177–182.

Gregg, M., & Sekeres, D. C. (2006). Supporting children's reading of expository text in the geography classroom. *The Reading Teacher, 60*(2), 102–110.

Henry, L. A. (23006). SEARCHing for an answer: The critical role of new literacies while reading on the Internet. *The Reading Teacher, 59*(7), 614–627.

Hill, J. D., & Flynn, K. M. (2006). *Classroom instruction that works with English language learners*. Alexandria, VA: Association for Supervision and Curriculum Development.

Lotherington, H., & Chow, S. (2006). Rewriting "Goldilocks" in the urban, multicultural elementary school. *The Reading Teacher, 60*(3), 242–252.

Nilsen, A. P., & Nilsen, D. L. J. (2003). A new spin on teaching vocabulary: A source-based approach. *The Reading Teacher, 56*(5), 436–439.

Websites

Use the following websites for additional ideas for developing prior knowledge:

Kidspiration
INSPIRATION or Kidspiration is a powerful visual learning tool that inspires students to develop ideas and organize their thinking. Teachers can download a free trial from the website.
http://www.inspiration.com

Kim's Korner
This website provides links to general information about anticipation guides and links to sample guides for specific novels or subjects.
http://www.kimskorner4teachertalk.com/readingliterature/readingstrategies/anticipation_guide.htm

Indiana University Clearinghouse on Reading, English, and Communication
This site offers a variety of teaching resources relating to the role of prior knowledge and schema in literacy development.
http://reading.indiana.edu/

Encarta
This online encyclopedia offers information, pictures, and additional Web resources on thousands of topics. This could be helpful in developing background and prior knowledge.
http://encarta.msn.com

The Library Lady
This online article discusses what teachers and parents can do to shorten the length of the assimilation process and help children process new information by encouraging the child to build a network of prior knowledge.
http://www.thelibrarylady.net/Childhood%20-%20From%20the%20Inside %20Out/building_a_network_of_prior_know.htm

ProTeacher
Lesson plans and information on Ancient Rome from proteacher.com.
http://www.proteacher.com/090084.shtml

History of Rome for Kids
http://www.historyforkids.org/learn/romans/

The Roman Empire for Children
http://www.roman-empire.net/children

How to Teach Strategies for Constructing Meaning

4

EDUCATORS SPEAK

Terms
YOU NEED TO KNOW

- application
- evaluating
- explicit modeling
- generating and answering questions
- guided practice
- implicit modeling
- inferencing
- making connections
- modeling
- monitoring/ clarifying
- reciprocal teaching
- reflection
- stop and think (see *monitoring*)
- student modeling
- summarizing
- synthesizing
- think aloud
- visualizing

The HM TeacherPrepSPACE Student Website offers many helpful resources, such as self-quizzes, glossary flashcards, lesson plan templates, and more.

*L*et's walk through Brownsville Elementary School to see what is happening in three different classrooms.

Mr. Robinson is reading the big book Pretend You're a Cat *(Marzollo, 1990) with his first graders. As he reads aloud each page, he reminds the children to make pictures in their heads. After reading the entire book aloud once, he briefly discusses with the children what they liked in the story. Then he talks about what they visualized while listening to the story.*

Down the hall, Ms. Garza's third-grade class is finishing story time. She has just read aloud Princess Furball *(Huck, 1989), after which all the students returned to their seats and immediately started independent reading time. Ms. Garza has several strategy posters displayed to remind students to apply the strategies they have learned.*

Upstairs, Mr. Lee shows his fifth graders a strategy poster for previewing and self-questioning. The class is looking at the book Lurkers of the Deep: Life Within the Ocean Depths *(Robison, 1978). Mr. Lee says, "As I look through this book, I can see from the section headings and photographs that I will find a lot of information about light in the ocean. One question I would like to answer as I read this book is: How does the light in the ocean affect life there? What question might you want to answer?" Terri volunteers that she would like to know how plants and animals grow in the dark.*

In each of these Brownsville Elementary School classrooms, a different activity was taking place, but one thing was common to all three: the students were learning to use strategies to construct meaning:

- Mr. Robinson guided students to use the strategy of visualizing to help enhance the construction of meaning.
- Ms. Garza used posters to remind students of the steps for various strategies.
- Mr. Lee modeled a particular strategy, preview and self-question, to help students do what expert readers do: determine their purpose for reading. By sharing his thinking as he used this strategy, Mr. Lee made his mental processes public to help the students think about this strategy.

These three scenes show how the use of strategies for constructing meaning is a part of every classroom's day-to-day activities. Mr. Robinson used the time when he read aloud to encourage his first graders to "make pictures in their heads," or visualize as they listened. Listening is a perfect time for visualizing, because children can close their eyes. Later, Mr. Robinson's students will visualize as they read for themselves. Ms. Garza has taught a number of minilessons on strategy use to her third graders. Whenever they are reading independently, she displays posters to remind her students to use strategies. Mr. Lee modeled a strategy he found useful in his own reading.

Strategies and Standards

Part of being a strategic reader is recognizing which strategy is appropriate and when to use it. A good reader often uses several strategies simultaneously.

As you develop your skills as a literacy teacher, you should pay close attention to the strategies identified as essential in your state. Virtually all state standards include a focus on helping students learn to use strategies. Let's examine the strategies for constructing meaning.

Strategies for Constructing Meaning

Research has clearly shown that reading comprehension is a process in which individuals construct meaning by interacting with the text (Pearson et al., 1990). This constructive interaction involves the individual's prior knowledge, the text, and the reading situation or context (Lipson & Wixson, 1986).

Expert readers have strategies or plans to help them solve problems and construct meaning before, during, and after reading (Paris et al., 1991). Although the number of strategies is small, they should be thoroughly developed (Pearson et al., 1990). You must address two major questions:

1. What strategies do my students need as they become expert constructors of meaning?
2. How are these strategies best taught in the literacy program?

We will examine these questions in this chapter.

Over the years, researchers and practitioners have attempted to identify the strategies that expert constructors of meaning use (Baker & Brown, 1984a, 1984b; Biancarosa & Snow, 2004; Dole et al., 1991; Harvey & Goudvis, 2000; Keene & Zimmermann, 1997; National Reading Panel, 2000; Oczkus, 2004; Paris et al., 1991; Pearson, Roehler, Dole, & Duffy, 1992; Pressley, 2000; Pressley, Johnson, Symons, McGoldrick, & Kurita, 1989). From these studies and others, eight important strategies emerge:

1. Visualizing
2. Making connections
3. Monitoring
4. Inferencing, including prediction
5. Identifying important information (story line in narrative texts and main ideas in expository texts)
6. Generating and answering questions
7. Summarizing—Synthesizing
8. Evaluating

Multiple Intelligences: Elementary School Instruction

Watch the video clip, study the artifacts in the case, and reflect on the following questions:

1. Explain how this Video Case illustrates the concept of "visualizing" that is described in this chapter.

2. Do you believe that classroom posters such as the "Word Paint" poster in the Video Case (see Classroom Artifacts) and the strategy posters presented in this chapter can influence the way children approach their work? Why or why not?

Video Case

Although the research discusses other strategies, these eight seem to have the greatest support for inclusion in the literacy program. They should be taught to students from kindergarten through grade 12, reteaching them as text becomes more challenging to students. In preschool, groundwork can be laid through read-alouds. Let's examine each of the eight strategies.

Visualizing

Strategic readers make pictures in their heads as they read. This process of **visualizing,** sometimes called *mental imaging,* enhances understanding. The mental picture we form as we read is a kind of inferential thinking that connects text with the questions we have mentally generated. Consider your own experience as you read a book such as a murder mystery. The author describes the discovery of a body, and you make a picture in your head of that scene. Perhaps you add some details that are not even in the text, drawing on your own prior knowledge about the setting, about dead bodies, and about the genre. This mental picture enhances your construction of meaning. You read on, adjusting your mental picture as you receive new information. Figures 4.1 and 4.2 show possible strategy posters that can remind students to make pictures in their heads as they read. A sample lesson on visualizing is presented on pages 168–171.

Making Connections

Strategic readers **make connections** between text and themselves, other texts, and the world. This strategy was presented in detail in Chapter 3, along with a poster (Figure 3.4) that can be used to remind students to use this strategy as they read. (See the Educators Speak feature "Can You Relate?" on page 162 in this chapter.)

FIGURE 4.1 Strategy Poster for Visualizing Narrative Text

VISUALIZING WHILE READING A STORY

Read the words.

One day everything changed. The ice began to melt from the trees. The birds came back. Little spikes of grass poked up through the snow.

Make pictures in your head.

Monitoring

Monitoring, sometimes called *clarifying,* is the process of knowing when what you are reading is not making sense, and then having plans for overcoming this problem. This is an important part of students' metacognitive development and is a developmental process that improves with age (Paris et al., 1991). Expert constructors of meaning are able to anticipate problems in reading and correct them as they occur. This "fix-up" process may involve these processes: rereading, reading ahead, raising

FIGURE 4.2   **Strategy Poster for Visualizing Expository Text**

VISUALIZING WHILE READING INFORMATIONAL TEXT

✔ **The words on the page can put pictures in your head. Pictures in your head help the words mean more.**

✔ **As you read, change the pictures in your head.**

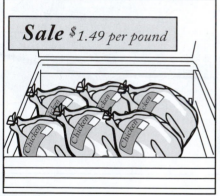

"Chickens are an important part of our economy."

"For one thing, eggs are a staple in the diet of many people."

Stop the point to think

FIGURE 4.3   **Strategy Poster for Stop and Think (Monitoring Narrative or Expository Text)**

new questions, changing predictions or making new ones, evaluating what is read, using strategies for identifying words, looking up words, or seeking help from an outside source. (See the Educators Speak feature, "Using Monitoring to Help the Diverse Learner," in this chapter.)

Figure 4.3 presents a strategy poster you can use in teaching students how to use the monitoring strategy known as **stop and think.** It is useful for both narrative and expository texts. A sample lesson for modeling this strategy appears on pages 171–174.

Educators Speak

Using Monitoring to Help the Diverse Learner

"I teach in a predominantly white middle-class suburban school district. Diversity exists primarily in learning styles and academic abilities. Seven students in my classroom are identified as gifted, and four are performing well below grade level in reading. The other thirteen students are reading on grade level.

We are currently enjoying Mark Twain's *The Prince and the Pauper* as an extension of the theme "Growing Up" from our reading series. Although this classic novel is identified as an early adolescent book, it is difficult for my students to comprehend. Monitoring has therefore become an extremely valuable tool in meeting my students' individual needs.

The monitoring strategy I am using actually involves a variety of reading strategies, including summarization, visualization, prior knowledge, rereading, questioning, inferencing, and predicting. As we read, we frequently pause so that a passage may be summarized. A volunteer explains a passage while his peers listen actively by visualizing this scene. Many of my students have prior knowledge of historical events of this time period and readily share their insight, which helps to clarify cultural differences presented in this novel. The complicated sentence structure, dialogue, and word choice in this historical fiction often requires that a passage be reread. After rereading, the class collectively asks questions, discusses, and interprets text meaning. Students often take an additional step and make inferences and predictions within the framework of this discussion. My role almost becomes secondary and that of a facilitator. I let the students take the lead as in a book discussion or literature circle.

Through monitoring and these other reading strategies, I am able to assess understanding and encourage students to look beyond the mechanics of simply reading the words. Monitoring works well with the diverse reading levels in my classroom and has also been effective in previous years when the diversity has been greater."

—*Monte Slaven, Sixth-Grade Teacher*
Maize East Elementary
Maize, Kansas

Inferencing

Inferencing, the process of judging, concluding, or reasoning from some given information, is the heart of meaning construction for learners of all ages (Anderson & Pearson, 1984). Even very young readers and readers performing a simple task such as reading a sentence use inferencing to supply information that is not given (Kail, Chi, Ingram, & Danner, 1977). When students make predictions before or during reading, they are *inferencing:* using available information and prior knowledge to construct meaning. A strategy poster such as the one in Figure 4.4 on page 145 can help students think about this process as they read both narrative and expository texts.

FIGURE 4.4   Strategy Poster for Inferencing

Identifying Important Information

Strategic readers identify the important information in what they read. In narrative texts or stories, they identify or infer the story line or story grammar (Mandler, 1984); in expository texts, they identify or infer the main ideas (Baumann, 1986). Although identification is similar in both types of texts, the task differs because the

FIGURE 4.5   Strategy Poster for Identifying Important Information in Narrative Text

IDENTIFYING IMPORTANT INFORMATION IN STORIES

As I read stories, I will look for:

Setting:
    Time   *Place*

Characters:

Problem:

Action:

Outcome:

text structures are different. Because text structures differ across languages, English Language Learners may not be familiar with the structures of texts in English. Teachers can help them by making explicit the typical structures of various genres of English writing (Kaplan, 1966).

Whatever terminology is used to describe this process, we know that construction of meaning can be improved when students learn a strategy for identifying important information in each type of text (Baumann, 1984; Short & Ryan, 1984; Winograd & Bridge, 1986). Figures 4.5 and 4.6 present strategy posters to help students learn this strategy for narrative and expository texts.

FIGURE 4.6 **Strategy Poster for Identifying Important Information in Expository Text**

IDENTIFYING IMPORTANT INFORMATION
IN EXPOSITORY TEXT
(Informational Text)

(1)  *The topic of this chapter is...*

Read to identify the topic by looking to see what most of the information is about.

(2)  *I don't see a summary sentence.*

Look for a sentence that summarizes the information of the paragraph or longer text.

(3)  *Some of this information doesn't seem important to the topic.*

Read to see what information is not important to the topic.

(4)  *I think the main idea of this is...*

Use the important information to think of your own main idea.

Generating and Answering Questions

Strategic readers improve their meaning construction by **generating and answering their own questions** (self-questioning) (Davey & McBride, 1986; Singer & Donlan, 1982). Students should be taught how to generate questions that require them to integrate information (make connections) and think as they read. For example, a good "think" question might be, "Why did the dinosaurs become extinct?" which helps the reader focus on more than just facts. Figure 4.7 presents a poster for

FIGURE 4.7 Strategy Poster for Question Generating and Answering (Expository Text)

QUESTION GENERATING AND ANSWERING STRATEGY
(Expository Text)

(1) **Preview the text.**
- Read titles and subheads.
- Look at pictures or illustrations.
- Read first paragraph.

(2) **Ask yourself a "think" question.**
- Write down your question.

(3) **Read to find important information to answer your question.**
- Write the answer.
- Think about whether your question was a good "think question."

(4) **Ask another think question.**
- If you answered your first one write down your question.

(5) **Read to answer your question. Continue to ask and answer questions as you read.**

(6) **Look back to see if you have other questions to answer.**

FIGURE 4.8   **Strategy Poster for Question Generating and Answering (Narrative Text)**

QUESTION GENERATING AND ANSWERING STRATEGY
(Narrative Text)

(1) **Preview the story.**
- Look at title, author, and other cover information.
- Look at illustrations.
- Read first paragraph.

(2) **Ask yourself a question about what will happen next in the story.**

(3) **Predict the answer to your question.**
- Read to find an answer to your question.
- Ask yourself if your question was a good one.

(4) **Make another prediction and ask another question.**

(5) **Continue to generate questions and read to find answers.**

(6) **Were all your questions answered? Why not?**
- Did you not understand something about the story?
- Was your question one that didn't really fit the story?
- Were there too many unfamiliar words?
- Were the events too different from what you know?
- Did the author choose to leave some things unsaid?

(7) **How will you change the questions you ask yourself the next time you read a story?**

See more information on reciprocal teaching later in this chapter.

using this strategy with expository text. Figure 4.8 is a poster for using this strategy with narrative text.

In addition to generating and answering questions of their own, readers often benefit from answering questions generated by others, such as the teacher or other students (National Reading Panel, 2000a, 2000b). This is an integral part of reciprocal teaching.

Summarizing and Synthesizing

For information on story grammar, see Chapter 2.

The two strategies of summarizing and synthesizing involve the same basic processes and can therefore be taught together even though you may teach each separately before students can move from one to the other smoothly. **Summarizing** is the process of pulling together the essential elements in a single longer passage of text. Research has shown that certain guidelines can help students develop this skill (Brown & Day, 1983). Although much of the research has focused on expository texts, the same guidelines can be applied to narrative texts using the story grammar concept. Figures 4.9 and 4.10 present strategy posters to use in teaching summarizing. A sample lesson using informational text is presented on pages 174–177.

Synthesizing is combining elements from multiple sources and integrating them into a new whole. When a reader synthesizes, he or she begins with the knowledge in his or her head, and then continually adds new information and recombines the old and the new. The new merges with the known and forms a new pattern—gives a new perspective—until in the end, the reader has constructed a meaning that is greater than what was in his or her head and/or in the text. The strategy of synthesizing can be applied to a single piece of text or across more than one text.

While reading a narrative, the reader may begin with visualizing and calling on prior knowledge about the setting or perhaps the problem. The reader's understanding of genre and story elements deepens with each narrative that is read through the process of synthesizing what is understood about the particular genre in the current narrative with what has been understood from prior narratives.

Fifth graders generate questions about social studies.

© Michael Zide

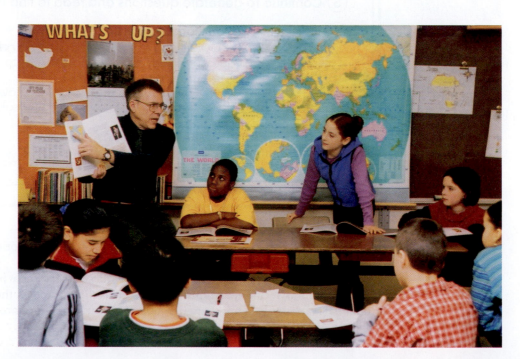

FIGURE 4.9   **Strategy Poster for Summarizing Narrative Text**

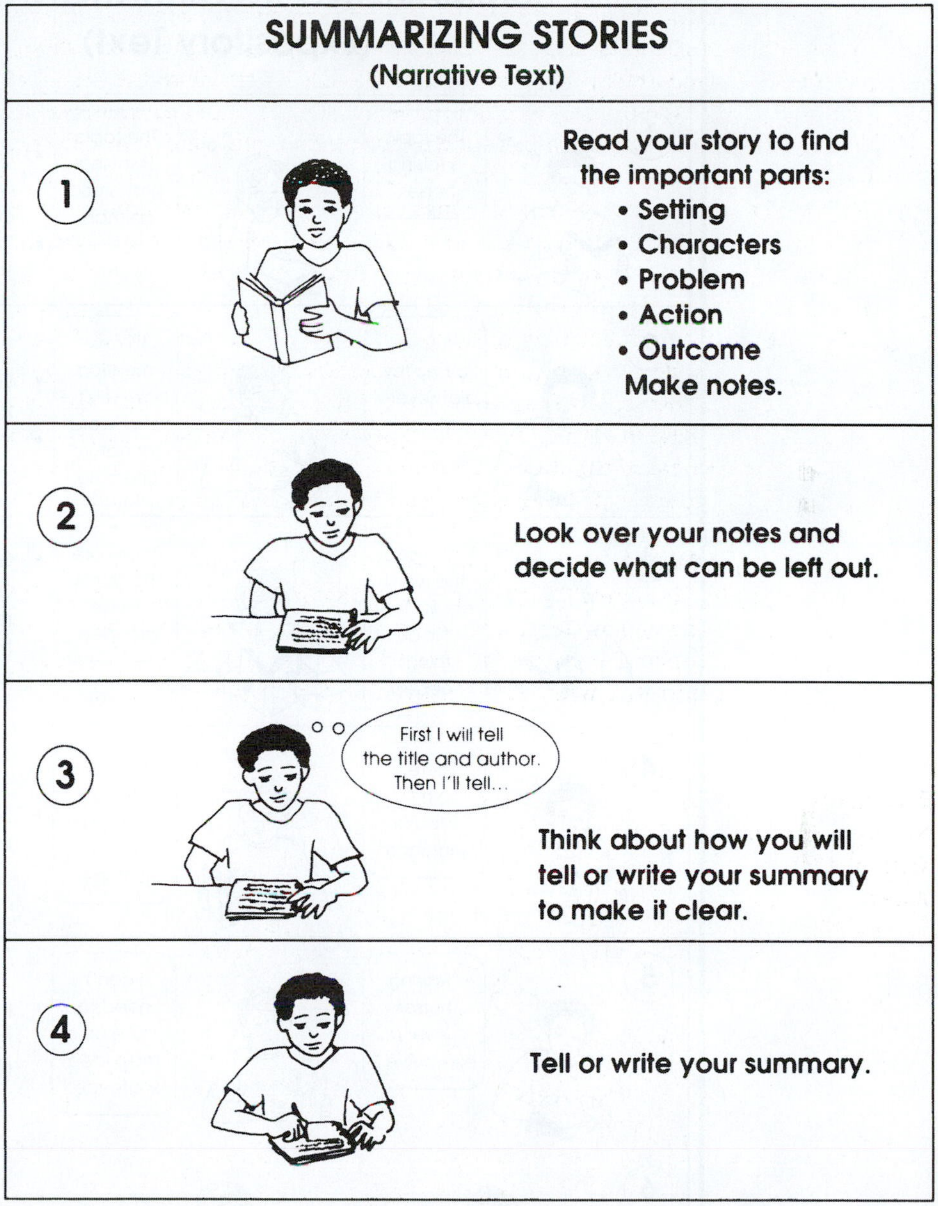

SUMMARIZING STORIES
(Narrative Text)

1. Read your story to find the important parts:
   - Setting
   - Characters
   - Problem
   - Action
   - Outcome

   Make notes.

2. Look over your notes and decide what can be left out.

3. *First I will tell the title and author. Then I'll tell…*

   Think about how you will tell or write your summary to make it clear.

4. Tell or write your summary.

With expository text, the process is similar, but the synthesis is more likely to be an accrual and integration of factual information, though inference will also contribute to the new perspective. Because synthesizing extends across texts as well as other sources of information, when reading a social studies text about the westward expansion, one might draw on and combine information already held based on

FIGURE 4.10 **Strategy Poster for Summarizing Expository Text**

SUMMARIZING INFORMATIONAL TEXT
(Expository Text)

1  The topic is raising horses. The topic is saving prehistoric animals.
- Look for the topic of the paragraph or text.
- Delete trivia.

2  It says a healthy diet several times. I'll only mention how helpful they were for nature one time.
- Look for information that is repeated.
- Include it once.

3  I'll use the word *equipment* for all things needed. There are no terms to be grouped.
- Group related terms or ideas under one term: *Example:* transportation for planes, buses, trains.

4  There is no main idea or sentence. The main idea sentence is the last one.
- Look for a main idea sentence.

5  "Raising horses is very expensive." I don't need to make up a main idea sentence.
- If there is no main idea sentence, make up one.

6
- Put your summary together.
- Check all rules.

FIGURE 4.11   Strategy Poster for Synthesizing Narrative Text

READING STORIES: ON THE PAGE AND IN MY HEAD

Before reading, ask yourself:
- What do I know about this kind of story?
- Have I read other stories by this author? Do I recognize the illustrator?
- Do I know already what the story is about?
- Did someone recommend the story to me? Why?

While you read, think:
- Do I understand the setting of this story?
- Do I understand the characters and the problem?
- Are the story events unfolding the way I thought they would?
- How are my ideas changing as I learn more about the story?

After you read, think:
- What were the important parts of the story? Could I retell them to someone?
- Would I recommend this to a friend? What would I say it is about?
- What have I learned about this kind of story? About how stories are told?

other texts about that period such as biographies, as well as films, CD-ROMs, informational programs on television, or even family journals.

Figures 4.11 and 4.12 show possible strategy posters to help students remember to synthesize as they read.

Evaluating

Strategic readers continuously decide whether the text they are reading is interesting or whether the arguments made in the text are credible (Pressley, 2000). This is the process of using the strategy of **evaluating** or making judgments. Evaluation involves many different processes depending upon what the reader is reading. It may include:

- Identifying what is important in a text such as the story elements in a narrative or main ideas in an expository text. As you can see there is overlap between evaluating and the strategy of identifying important information, which was discussed earlier.

FIGURE 4.12   **Strategy Poster for Synthesizing Expository Text**

FIGURE 4.13 **Strategy Poster for Evaluating**

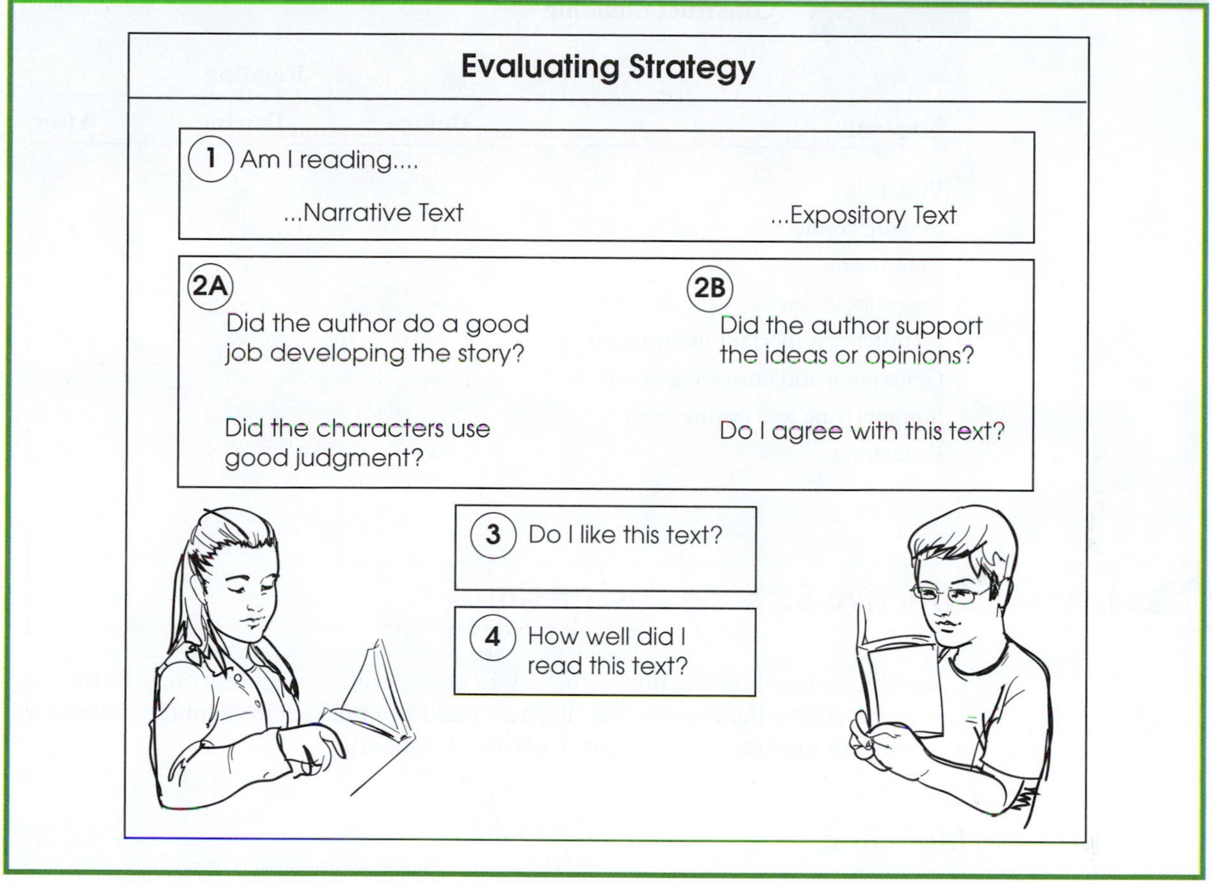

Evaluating Strategy

① Am I reading....

...Narrative Text　　　　　　　...Expository Text

2A Did the author do a good job developing the story?

Did the characters use good judgment?

2B Did the author support the ideas or opinions?

Do I agree with this text?

③ Do I like this text?

④ How well did I read this text?

- Making judgments about whether an author has used appropriate justification in an expository text to support an opinion or point of view.
- Deciding whether an author has done an effective job of developing a story line in a short story.
- Thinking about whether the characters in a story have used good judgment in making the decisions they have made.
- Doing self-evaluation of one's own reading as well as thinking about whether one liked a particular story or agreed with a certain point-of-view.

Overall, evaluating is the strategy that helps readers become more critical readers and make use of critical thinking. Figure 4.13 presents an example of a poster for use in teaching evaluating.

Some of these strategies can be used before reading, some during, some after, and some at more than one point. Table 4.1 shows where each of the eight strategies fit in an individual's reading.

TABLE 4.1	Points Where Strategies May Help Students Construct Meaning		

	Reading		
Strategy	**Before**	**During**	**After**
Visualizing	✓	✓	
Making connections	✓	✓	✓
Monitoring		✓	✓
Inferencing (includes predictions)	✓	✓	
Identifying important information	✓	✓	✓
Generating and answering questions	✓	✓	✓
Summarizing and synthesizing		✓	✓
Evaluating	✓	✓	✓

Planning Effective Strategy Instruction

Carefully planned instruction is the key to successful strategy learning. In this section we examine the factors that teachers need to consider in helping students use strategies to become effective constructors of meaning.

Modeling

Literacy learning is an interactive, constructive process. Children develop literacy by having real literacy experiences; as part of these experiences, they need carefully scaffolded instruction (Dole et al., 1991). Modeling is an important form of such support.

Modeling Defined

Modeling is the process of showing or demonstrating for someone how to use or do something she or he does not know how to do; most human behaviors are acquired in this way (Bandura, 1986). Modeling can also be described as the process by which an expert shows students (nonexperts) how to perform a task, so that they can build their own understanding of how to complete that task (Collins et al., 1987). With literacy learning, this expert may be an adult outside of school, an adult in school (usually the teacher), or a peer. When a child sees a parent writing a letter or reading a book, modeling is taking place. When Mr. Lee talked aloud using previewing and self-questioning, he was modeling. When a child sees a friend successfully complete a piece of writing and share it, modeling has occurred.

Culturally Responsive Teaching: A Multicultural Lesson for Elementary Students

Watch the video clip, study the artifacts in the case, and reflect on the following questions:

1. How does Dr. Hurley use the strategy of "explicit modeling" to effectively teach this lesson?

2. Identify the knowledge and skills that Dr. Hurley's students gain from being a part of this lesson. Use the Classroom Artifacts in this Video Case to help you answer this question.

Modeling can be implicit or explicit (Roehler & Duffy, 1991). **Implicit modeling** takes place when the processes or ideas being modeled occur as a part of an experience and are *not directly* identified or stated. Reading aloud to students and letting students see you write a letter are examples. Implicit modeling always occurs within the context of the complete process of reading and writing.

Explicit modeling involves directly showing and talking with students about what is being modeled using a **think-aloud** process (Roehler & Duffy, 1991). In this approach, teachers actually share with students the cognitive processes, or thinking, that they go through:

> *As I read through this paragraph, I can immediately tell that the topic of it is space travel because it mentions outer space, rockets, and planets. Even though mention is made of early pioneers, I can see that this is only a point of comparison. I notice that all of the points compared show me how early pioneer travel and space travel have been similar.*

Notice that the teacher is sharing his thinking to reveal the process one goes through in formulating or inferring a main idea.

An inherent danger in explicit modeling is that the activities are nothing more than the modeling of an isolated skill, which is not effective in helping students construct meaning (Pearson et al., 1990). *Explicit modeling must be done within the context of a specific text* (Duffy et al., 1987; Roehler & Duffy, 1991). All examples of modeling presented in this chapter and throughout the rest of the text adhere to this important guideline.

Although modeling helps students become more expert readers and writers and gives them better control over their metacognitive processes (Paris et al., 1991), the teacher must balance implicit and explicit modeling.

Where Modeling Takes Place

Modeling can occur at numerous points throughout the literacy program:

■ *During daily activities:* Although the daily activities will afford many opportunities for both implicit and explicit modeling, most will be *implicit.* Read-aloud times, shared writing experiences, periods for independent, self-initiated reading and writing, and cooperative reading are a few examples. Because the literacy-centered classroom operates on the premise that children learn to read and write by reading and writing, all of the activities associated with real reading and writing play a significant role in the modeling of these processes.

See Chapter 8 for information on writing.

■ *Process writing:* The process of writing, shared writing, and writing conferences present opportunities for both implicit and explicit modeling.

■ *Literacy lessons:* The literacy lesson consists of three parts: introducing, reading and responding, and extending. During the first two parts, there are opportunities for explicit modeling of prior knowledge, vocabulary, and particular strategies that students need to construct meaning. Implicit modeling by the teacher and peers will occur in all three parts of the lesson.

See Chapter 10 for information on reading and writing workshop.

■ *Minilessons:* Minilessons, developed on the basis of students' needs, include explicit modeling of strategies for both reading and writing. These lessons can be developed within the framework presented in Chapter 2. They may also take place during your reading workshop or writing workshop. Later in this chapter are three sample minilessons.

Guidelines

A great deal is known about effective strategy instruction (Duffy, 1993; Pressley & Harris, 1990). The following guidelines should be helpful in developing this instruction:

■ ***Determine the need for strategy instruction on the basis of student performance.*** Students will learn some strategies through their reading and writing experiences. When you observe that their construction of meaning would be enhanced by a minilesson involving modeling, provide it. *Students' needs should be the primary determining factor in using explicit modeling.*

■ ***Introduce all the major strategies early in the school year.*** This allows you to present the strategies you want students to learn and then have them focus on using the strategies while reading. At first, students may seem uncertain about a given strategy, but this uncertainty will fade. More time should be spent on using the strategy than on modeling and practicing the strategy in isolation.

■ ***Model and practice the strategy in the meaningful context of a reading experience.*** When strategies fail, it is often because they have been taught and practiced as isolated elements. A meaningful reading experience means students (1) work with a text where the strategy is useful, (2) use that text as the basis for having the strategy modeled by the teacher, and (3) use additional texts for practicing the strategy. No fill-in-the-blank, mark, circle, or underline types of exercises should be used, as such activities isolate the strategy.

■ ***Model each strategy at the point where it is most useful.*** Make the strategy modeling authentic by doing it when students are most likely to use it. For example, model the preview and predict strategy before reading a text, and then follow it up after reading.

■ *Make modeling and practicing interactive and collaborative activities.* Strategy learning and use is most effective when students are active participants and work alongside their peers. For example, students learning to summarize may first work together to help the teacher construct a summary and later work with a partner to write a collaborative summary of a story.

■ *Gradually transfer modeling from yourself to the students.* This is the scaffolding of instruction. Once you have modeled a strategy often enough for students to begin using it comfortably, have students model it for one another and then use it independently. If you see that more modeling is needed, provide it and then begin to release responsibility to the students again.

■ *Help students experience immediate success with each strategy.* Nothing encourages students more than success. Have students explain how the strategy helped them, and point out successes you have seen. If you notice that a particular strategy is not working for a student, discontinue using it and move on to another one.

■ *Encourage the use of a strategy across the curriculum.* Once students have started to use a strategy, model its use in curricular areas such as science and social studies. As students use strategies in these areas, have them reflect on and discuss how the strategies helped them understand more of what they read. This will help them see the value of the strategy and will motivate them to learn additional strategies.

■ *Guide students to become strategic readers.* Once students are familiar with each strategy, model and encourage the use of all strategies together. (This is discussed later in this chapter.)

These guidelines are applied in the sample minilessons beginning on page 168.

Using Different Types of Texts

See Chapter 3 for a discussion of text structures.

When planning effective strategy instruction, you must consider the types of texts students will be reading. Sometimes authors combine narrative and expository structures in the same text. For example, *The Popcorn Book* (de Paola, 1978) tells a story and at the same time presents information. This type of book is sometimes known as an informational story.

Content texts used in classes such as health, science, and history are usually expository texts. These books often combine several text structures; for example, a U.S. history chapter may have passages presenting information in sequence, combined with passages showing cause-effect; these passages may be combined with some narration that explains how things fit together. No matter where one reads text—whether the print is on paper or on a computer monitor—all of the strategies presented in this chapter are both applicable and necessary.

TABLE 4.2	Strategy Use in Different Types of Texts		
Strategy	**Narrative Texts**	**Expository Texts**	**Comment**
Visualizing	Yes	Yes	Adjust based on presence of pictures or other graphic information in text.
Making connections	Yes	Yes	Adjust based on type of text.
Monitoring	Yes	Yes	Adjust the monitoring strategies to the type of text.
Inferencing	Yes	Sometimes	Because expository texts present factual information, too much inferencing in a text reduces the text's quality.
Identifying important information	Yes; focus on story elements	Yes; focus on main ideas and supporting details	Must adjust strategy to structure of text.
Generating and answering questions	Yes; focus questions on story elements	Yes; focus questions on main ideas and key concepts	Must adjust strategy to structure of text.
Summarizing—synthesizing	Yes, focus summary on story elements; synthesis would involve stories from several sources	Yes, focus summary on main ideas and details; synthesis would involve information from several sources	Integrates new knowledge with prior knowledge. Must adjust strategy to structure of the text.
Evaluating	Yes	Yes	Adjust use of strategy to type of text.

Though all strategies work with any type of text, some modifications are needed to adjust to the different types. Table 4.2 shows the type of text and circumstances under which the eight strategies work best.

Integrating All Strategies: Focus on Strategic Reading

Strategic readers use several strategies simultaneously. Therefore, you must teach students how to select the strategy or strategies that will best help them construct meaning of a particular text.

First teach all of the strategies quickly, using suggestions and guidelines presented in this text. Then use the posters for the various strategies along with a poster such as that in Figure 4.14 to remind students about all of the strategies. Before students read any text, discuss with them which strategies they might use as they read that particular text. If you are guiding or coaching the reading, model and discuss the use of various strategies during reading. After reading, have students reflect on how the strategies helped them construct meaning. At any point before, during, or after reading, you may need to model the concept of strategic reading by modeling the use of one or more of the strategies.

FIGURE 4.14	Poster Promoting the Use of All Strategies Together

STRATEGIC READING

When I read, do I...

- Visualize
- Make Connections
- Monitor
- Infer/Predict
- Identify important information
- Self-question
- Summarize/Synthesize
- Evaluate

Teaching Strategies in Upper Elementary and Middle School

A goal for upper elementary and middle school is to help all students be strategic readers every time they read, no matter what kind of text. Each teacher, in each subject area, must focus on helping students learn how to read the texts that are particular to that content area. Since reading in each content area presents unique challenges for readers, the strategies should be taught anew with each subject area.

Can You Relate? Graphic Organizers, Strategies, and Literature in the Middle School

Helping middle-school students relate, or make a connection, to literature and therefore to life is one of the challenges that middle-school language arts teachers face every day. The use of graphic organizers and story maps has been most helpful.

Students enjoy predicting by trying to match wits with authors as they read. When I teach the poem "Barbara Frietchie" by John Greenleaf Whittier, we begin by brainstorming what it means to be a hero. Then students chart the names, beliefs, and actions taken of contemporary, historical, and fictional characters that they consider heroes. After reading the poem, they see if any of their predictions about heroes are true of Barbara.

Before reading the short story "The Landlady" by Roald Dahl, students have fun jotting down questions and predictions of what might happen based on the many clues offered in the story. The fun comes when Dahl outwits them, and their predictions turn out to be incorrect.

I use ready-made graphic organizers to help with visualizing and summarizing. Before students read the short story "The Treasure of Lemon Brown" by Walter Dean Myers, I have them create a Venn diagram that investigates the topics: "I value . . . Adults value . . . We all value . . ." After reading, the task is to compare this diagram to one they create based on the characters in the story.

Summarizing really helps the middle-school reader relate to the literature. We read "Broken Chain" by Gary Soto. I use a graphic organizer to help students organize a brief summary. Using the organizer, each student then relates orally what happened, who the main characters are, the sequence of events, and how the main problem is finally solved. For students who struggle getting started, try first thoughts to help get them started. "Alfonso wanted . . . but . . . so . . ."

One of the easiest and least time-consuming methods of using strategies is to have students keep a journal handy. (I store each class set in a plastic shoebox.) Readers relate by an ongoing dialogue with the text. They write questions, predictions, main points for summarization, and even visualizations of what is going through their minds. By learning to use these strategies, readers can relate to literature.

—David Burgess, Seventh- and Eighth-Grade Language Arts Teacher
New Castle Middle School
New Castle, Indiana

Nobody ever masters the ability to construct meaning; more challenging text can stump even the most strategic reader. Therefore, it isn't enough to teach strategy lessons only in the early grades, you must reteach them and reteach them as reading material becomes more complex. Some students, of course, may have greater need than others; they may need several minilessons. Other students may need only to be shown how the strategies they already know should be applied to a particular text.

FIGURE 4.15	Checklist to Help Students Focus on Using All Strategies in All Subject Areas

My Strategic Reading Guide

As I read, do I . . .

1. *Visualize*
   - Make pictures in my head?
   - Use mental images to answer my questions?

2. *Make Connections*
   - Make connections to my own experience?
   - Make connections to the world?
   - Make connections to the books Ive read?

3. *Monitor*
   - Ask: Does this make sense to me?
   - Does it help me meet my purposes?
   - Try fix-ups?
     - Reread
     - Read ahead
     - Look at illustrations
     - Ask for help
     - Think about words

4. *Infer/predict*
   - Look for important information?
   - Look at illustrations?
   - Think about what I know?
   - Think about what may happen or what I want to learn?

5. *Identify important information*
   - Look for story elements?
   - Look for main ideas and important details?

6. *Self-question*
   - Ask questions and look for answers?

7. *Summarize/Synthesize*
   - Summarize after I read?
   - Stories—think about story parts
   - Informational texts—think about main ideas and important details
   - Combine what I know with what I read?
   - Change my predictions as I read?
   - Integrate new knowledge with known?

8. *Evaluate*
   - What is important in this text?
   - Does the author use appropriate justification to support opinions or points of view?
   - Does the author develop the storyline effectively?
   - Do the characters use good judgment in making their decisions?
   - Do I agree with the ideas and opinions expressed in this text? Why?

As students develop in their literacy and face increasing textual demands, they must integrate the use of all strategies into the seamless process called "constructing meaning." Teachers must model and guide students in this integration. A checklist such as that shown in Figure 4.15 may help students remember to use the strategies they have been learning. Subject-area teachers may adapt such a checklist to suit their content areas.

Reciprocal Teaching

An excellent way to develop the use of strategies in upper elementary and middle school students is through the use of **reciprocal teaching** (Palincsar & Brown, 1986). Reciprocal teaching is an interactive process in which the teacher and students take turns modeling four strategies after reading a meaningful chunk of text—*predict, question, clarify,* and *summarize.* Though the labels differ somewhat, the strategies parallel those discussed in this chapter; in fact, the procedure works with any strategy. This reciprocal modeling process takes the place of the typical discussion that follows reading.

Reciprocal teaching begins with heavy teacher modeling, which helps students see how a competent reader deals with text by using different strategies, depending on the demands of the text (Oczkus, 2003). Teacher modeling also helps students see how a competent reader recognizes when text is challenging and knows which strategies to use in each situation. Gradually, as with all other modeling, the teacher's need to lead the process diminishes and students are able to model strategic reading themselves. The goal is for students to activate strategy use as they read independently. Reciprocal teaching helps them reach that goal.

Research has demonstrated that reciprocal teaching is effective in helping all students increase their comprehension ability. However, it is most effective in helping below-level readers accelerate their reading in a short amount of time (Rosenshine & Meister, 1994).

Strategy Lessons: The Minilesson

Explicit modeling may take place within the literacy lesson or through minilessons. For example, if, as part of a literacy lesson, you see the need to help students summarize stories, the most logical place to do this is at the conclusion of the literacy lesson, after a story has been read. As follow-up, students will practice using the strategy in reading the next selection.

This section presents three sample strategy lessons organized around the minilesson concept. These lessons may be taught before or after the literacy lesson or as part of it, depending on the particular strategy and where it needs to be placed.

The minilesson is a flexible plan based on the principles of effective instruction using explicit, or direct, teaching and effective strategy learning. The parts of the plan flow in an interactive dialogue throughout the entire lesson. As the name *minilesson* implies, the lesson is short and focused, usually lasting from 5 to 10 minutes and rarely longer than 15 minutes. Some lessons may need to be taught several times, depending on the students' stage of literacy development and how they respond, and some lessons may not work for certain students and should be discontinued as you move on to more effective experiences. The four parts of the minilesson are:

1. introduction
2. teacher modeling

3. student modeling and guided practice
4. summarizing and reflecting

Follow-ups occur over several days or more following the minilesson. The three parts of the follow-up to the minilesson are:

1. independent practice
2. application
3. reflection

Parts of a Minilesson

1. *Introduction:* During the introduction, you tell students what they are going to learn and relate it to reading or writing and their prior knowledge. You may point out relationships, or you may draw information from students through an interactive discussion. For example, when teaching a lesson on inferencing, you might say:

   Tell me some examples in the last book we read where the author gave clues about something but didn't tell you directly what was intended. [Students respond.] This happens many times in books. When you figured out information from the clues, you were using a strategy called inferencing. Today we are going to think more about inferencing.

   This focused introduction should take just a few minutes.

2. *Teacher modeling:* During teacher modeling, you show students how to use and think about the strategy by "thinking aloud" with them. You incorporate three elements:

   - Concept
   - Listening
   - Reading

   For example, with inferencing, develop the *concept* by starting with something concrete, such as a text illustration, and talk about what it shows and what you can infer from clues such as facial expressions or objects pictured. For *listening*, read aloud a piece of text and show students how to make inferences as they listen. Finally, for *reading*, have students read a piece of text. Make this part of the lesson interactive by drawing students into the modeling. *Think aloud*, showing students how you make inferences as you read. After you have modeled for students, gradually transfer the modeling to them and help them think aloud about how they are using the strategy as they read the text. This process flows naturally into the next part of the lesson.

3. *Student modeling and guided practice:* Students now use the strategy under your guidance, usually with the same text with which the strategy was originally modeled. They read sections silently, and you call on individuals to share their thinking aloud. For example, if you use a short story to model inferencing, have students continue through the story to find other places to use inferencing, and encourage them to share their thinking aloud as they work. If necessary, prompt

students with questions, examples, or additional modeling. Throughout, give students feedback about how they are doing in using the strategy. The teacher modeling, **student modeling,** and **guided practice** flow together so closely that it is often difficult to tell where one begins and the other ends. The purpose of this part of the lesson is to ensure that students are able to use the strategy before releasing them to practice it independently.

4. *Summarizing and reflecting:* Finally, prompt students to summarize what they have learned and have them reflect on how and where they might use the strategy. Use prompts such as the following:

   ■ How did we make inferences in this story?
   ■ What did we use besides story information?
   ■ Where do you think you will use this strategy?

Remember that *students* need to verbalize what they have learned and where and how they might use it.

Parts of the Follow-Up to the Minilesson

The follow-up to the minilesson consists of opportunities to practice, apply, and think about how the strategy has been useful to the student. This consists of independent practice, **application,** and **reflection:**

1. *Independent practice:* During independent practice students use the strategy in authentic reading or writing situations that are similar to those in which the strategy was developed and taught. For example, if you have modeled inferencing while reading a mystery, you can have students read other mysteries and ask them to write solutions to the mysteries in their journals to show how they have used the strategy. Many students will need repeated practice before they are comfortable applying it on their own. Remind students that they have been inferencing their whole lives; now they are transferring to reading something they already know how to do.

2. *Application:* Now students use the strategy in a different text from the one in which they have learned it. For example, for the inferencing strategy, they might self-select a mystery to read or write a mystery in which they provide clues. You may check application during conferences or group discussions. In further application, they would use inferencing in other genres. The application phase creates conditions that encourage transfer of the strategy to other areas and to different kinds of narrative.

3. *Reflection:* As students are practicing and applying the strategy, encourage them to reflect about how they have used it. Encourage them to talk about ways to improve and other situations where they might use the strategy. This activity helps students make the strategy their own and also helps them see how they have succeeded.

The basic minilesson with follow-up affords a flexible plan for helping students learn to use strategies to construct meaning. These procedures may need to be adapted and adjusted to fit the strategy being taught and the needs of the students. Table 4.3 summarizes the parts of the minilesson and follow-up.

TABLE 4.3	Summary of Minilesson and Follow-up Plan for Developing Meaning Construction Strategies	
	Purpose	**Possible Activities**
Minilesson		
Introduction	Let students know what they will learn. Relate it to prior knowledge and reading and writing.	Interactive discussion led by teacher
Teacher modeling	Show students how to use and think about the strategy. Incorporate concept, listening, and reading into your modeling.	Teacher-led "think-alouds" Student "think-alouds"
Student modeling and guided practice	Students gradually take charge of the strategy. Students try the strategy under teacher direction.	Student "think-alouds" Cooperative groups
Summarizing and reflecting	Pull together what has been learned. Think about when it might be useful	Teacher-prompted discussion Cooperative groups
Follow-up		
Independent practice	Try the strategy	Reading in text similar to type used in modeling Writing
Application	Use the strategy in a new situation	Self-selected books Writing Content-area work
Reflection	Think about how the strategy has been useful	Student-teacher discussion

Sample Strategy Lessons

Mini-lessons

Following are three strategy minilessons: visualizing narrative text, monitoring narrative text, and summarizing expository text. Each lesson should be viewed as a *generic model* to help you plan lessons of your own. Some parts of the lessons are scripted to show you the types of things you might say; these are *only examples* to help you plan. The Assessment and Discussion sections are merely suggestions.

Each lesson that follows would match the standards established by virtually any state. For example, here are samples related to strategies from Maryland. The same Indicators occur at all grade levels.

E. General Reading Comprehension

Indicator:
3. Use strategies to make meaning from text (during reading)
Indicator:
4. Use strategies to demonstrate understanding of the text (after reading)

For a complete listing of specific objectives under each Indicator, go to www.marylandpublicschools. org/MSDE/curriculum/reading/standard1/grade1.html. Change the grade level as needed.

Before Reading the Lessons

Review this chapter to clarify any questions you have on modeling or minilessons.

While Reading the Lessons

1. Think about how each element of the minilesson was developed.
2. Think about how you might vary the lesson.

Minilesson #1

Visualizing Narrative Text

Introduction

Purpose: To visualize while reading narrative text

Reading level: Primary (K–1)

Text: *No, No, Titus!* (Masurel, 1997; text shown beginning on page 224.)

In this sample lesson, assume that children will not have read the story or looked at the pictures, but that they have been involved in a unit about farms. This story will be used to model and teach visualizing. At the same time, students will activate prior knowledge and use prediction. Here, this book is being used for a strategy lesson. Later, the teacher will use this book for a literacy lesson. *No, No, Titus!* is a picture book, but for this strategy lesson, the children will see only the picture on the cover. The children's mental images may not match the art in the book, and that's just fine. In fact, when the children do see what the illustrator did, they can talk about how an artist illustrates a book using pictures in his or her head.

Mini-lessons

continued

Activity	Procedures, Comments and Multilevel Notes
Introduction	1. Ask children to discuss how they know what people and things in stories look like when there are no pictures. **Comment:** *Relates strategy to children's experience.* **Multilevel Note:** *This entire lesson can be taught to children at diverse literacy levels.* 2. Tell children they will learn to make pictures in their head to go with words in a story. **Comment:** *Lets children know what they will learn.* 3. Tell children they will listen to a story about a farm. **Comment:** *Relates lesson to a familiar unit of study.*
Teacher modeling *Develop the concept of visualizing*	1. Show the cover of the book *No, No, Titus!* Point to and talk about each of the items shown. Read the title. Tell the children you can already make pictures in your head that include more than what shows on the cover. **Comment:** *Tells children you know how to use the strategy.* 2. Model visualizing using the think-aloud below. *Teacher Think-Aloud* "When I look at the cover of *No, No, Titus!* I see a cow, a chicken, a cat, a dog in a doghouse, a girl, and a man. The cow and the chicken are big clues that this story probably takes place on a farm. In my mind, I have pictures of what farms look like. There is a barn, a farmhouse, more cows and chickens, and maybe a horse or goat or sheep. There might be fields of corn in the distance. I think it's a nice day. In my picture I see the sun shining and fluffy clouds in the sky."
Student modeling and guided practice	Have children make pictures in their heads and share them. **Comment:** *Gives children a chance to think aloud and practice visualizing.*
Teacher modeling	1. Tell students to listen as you read the words on the first page of the story and then listen as you think aloud about the pictures in your head that go with the words. **Comment:** *Models for children how to make pictures to go with words and also models how their prior knowledge contributes to visualizing.*

Mini-lessons

continued

Activity	Procedures, Comments and Multilevel Notes (continued)
	Teacher Think-Aloud "When I listen to the first page of the story, I learn that Titus (from the title, *No, No, Titus!*) is the dog, and I have a picture in my head from the cover. I now know that the man is a farmer and he is talking to the dog. I can see the dog wagging his tail. The farmer is patting the dog on the head. I think the girl may be there . . . and maybe other people in the family."
Reading to visualize student modeling and guided practice	2. Have students read the text on the next page as you read it aloud: The farm was big and everyone was busy.
	Multilevel Note: *Because you read the text aloud, all students can participate.*
	Teacher Think-Aloud "At first, I was picturing a snug little farm with just a few animals. Now I learn that the farm is big and busy, so I've changed and added to my picture. Now I think there is a huge barn and maybe other buildings besides the house, like a silo. And if it's busy, maybe there are trucks, and tractors, and people doing work."
	Comment: *Lets children see that visualizing changes as new information is revealed.*
	Continue by having students read as you read aloud, one page of text at a time. First, have children make and revise the pictures in their heads. Then ask volunteers to share their mental images by describing them.
	Comment: *Students try what has been learned.*
	Multilevel Note: *Some children may need prompting, and some may need continued teacher modeling with think-alouds. The teacher assesses the level of need as the lesson progresses. Very young children may need help understanding that though visualizing takes place in their heads, it must be based on a combination of their own knowledge and what the words say. Continue to emphasize how mental pictures change as one reads.*
Summarizing and reflecting	1. Ask children to explain what they can do when they hear or read stories to help them picture what is happening.
	Comment: *With continued minilessons, children will learn that even when there is art on the page of a story, they will still make pictures in their heads to enhance their understanding.*

Mini-lessons

continued

Activity	Procedures, Comments and Multilevel Notes (continued)
	2. Ask children to talk about when they might use this strategy.
	3. Show Strategy Poster (Figure 4.1) and discuss it.

Discussion Assess the lesson as students summarize and reflect and again as students listen to and read other texts. Most students will need repeated teacher modeling and guided practice; this can be done informally through the day. Separate minilessons should be planned to teach visualizing expository text.

Visualizing not only enhances comprehension; it enhances enjoyment. After this lesson, children should be reminded to visualize as they listen to and read stories and poems. As you continue to encourage children to visualize, help them understand that visualizing requires the use of other strategies, such as inferencing, identifying important information, monitoring, synthesizing, or summarizing. Strategies are not used in isolation, and should not be.

 **Minilesson #2**

Monitoring (Clarifying) Narrative Text

Introduction

Purpose: To monitor meaning construction while reading narrative text

Reading level: Third or fourth grade

Text: *Ananse's Feast* (Mollel, 1997)

Good strategic readers monitor their reading automatically. No longer needing to pay conscious attention, they continually ask: "Does this make sense? Do I understand what I'm reading?" And if the answer to such a question is, "No," then good readers use "fix-up" techniques to clarify meaning. These include rereading, reading ahead, looking up unfamiliar words, and seeking help. Minilessons on monitoring need to be taught, as it is unlikely that children will read strategically without direct instruction. Use of the strategy can be modeled by the teacher before reading and then continued during teacher-directed reading with teacher and students taking turns modeling. Children can be introduced to this strategy at the earliest literacy stage, when they are listening to stories read aloud to them, then taught and retaught the strategy as students advance through the literacy stages and through the grades. Even fluent readers may need occasional minilessons to remind them to make this strategy a part of every reading experience.

Mini-lessons

continued

Activity	Procedures, Comments and Multilevel Notes
Introduction	1. Tell students that good readers monitor their understanding as they read, which means they "stop and think" while reading to be sure what they are reading makes sense to them. Display the strategy poster in Figure 4.3. Explain each step on the poster.
	Comment: *Lets students know what they are going to learn.*
	2. Introduce the book *Ananse's Feast*. Have students examine the cover art (a spider at a table laden with dishes and food) and predict what will happen in the story.
Teacher modeling	1. Ask students if they have ever watched a video or DVD and missed something. What did they do? (They went back and watched it again.) Tell them that when they realized that they didn't understand something, they were monitoring their understanding.
Develop the concept of monitoring	2. Read aloud the first page of the story, stumbling on the word *drought*. Then stop and use the think-aloud shown below. Write the word *drought* on the chalkboard.
Modeling monitoring through listening	Comment: *Creates a "problem" situation. Though artificial, it is necessary in order to demonstrate monitoring.*
	Teacher Think-Aloud "I'm not sure of this word [mispronounce *drought*]. I don't know how to pronounce it and I don't know what it means. I haven't read far enough in the story to know if I even need to know what it means . . . and since I'm reading to myself, it's okay if I don't know exactly how to pronounce it. It seems to have something to do with the earth being hot, and no one having much to eat. I think I'll just read on without stopping to look up the word for now."
Student modeling and guided practice	1. Direct students to listen as you read aloud the next four pages. Tell them to decide if what they are listening to makes sense. Tell them you will call on volunteers to model their thinking during "stop and think."
	Comment: *Puts modeling at the listening level in the hands of students. Students may need prompting at first, but with repeated practice, they will become comfortable modeling.*

Mini-lessons

continued

Activity	Procedures, Comments and Multilevel Notes (continued)
	2. Prompt students who model thinking aloud: Were there any words you didn't know? What did you do about it? Was there anything you would reread? Why? Did you have to adjust your predictions as you read? Why?
Teacher modeling *Modeling monitoring through reading*	**1.** Have students read the next four pages silently and stop. Then model the monitoring strategy using the think-aloud shown.
	Comment: *Shows students how to use another fix-up technique.* **Multilevel Note:** *If necessary, have students read with a partner.*
	Teacher Think-Aloud "I understand most of what I'm reading just fine. I wasn't sure what all the foods were, but I decided it didn't matter if I didn't know what each one was—I knew they were foods the turtle wanted to eat. When Ananse told the turtle to wash his hands, I didn't quite "get it." I knew Ananse doesn't want to share his food, but I didn't see what sending the turtle off to wash his hands would accomplish. I read on and learned that Ananse is going to make the turtle go to the river. Then I figured out what was happening: the river was dry, so how could the turtle wash his hands? And when I read that the river was dry, I figured out what that word drought on the first page probably means. It probably means there hasn't been much rain; that's why the river is dry."
Student modeling/Guided practice	**2.** Continue having students read chunks of text, alternating between teacher modeling and student modeling, for the remainder of the story.
	Comment: *Releases more and more responsibility to students. Your decisions about how much teacher modeling is needed will be assessed as you teach.* **Multilevel Note:** *If some students need support, have them read with a partner or in a small group with you.*
Discussing the story	Encourage students to talk about the story and how it compares to other folktales.
	Comment: *Pulls the story together.*

Mini-lessons

continued

Activity	*Procedures, Comments and Multilevel Notes* (continued)
Summarizing and reflecting	Ask students to tell what they learned about the strategy of monitoring, or "stop and think." Encourage them to talk about when they plan to use this strategy.
	Comment: *Helps students verbalize the strategy and internalize it.*

Discussion Assess the lesson during guided practice and well as follow-up activities. Students will practice and apply this strategy with everything they read, whether narrative or expository text. Most students need direct instruction, as well as continued reteaching to activate use of the strategy. Younger children, or struggling readers, learn best if only one fix-up technique is introduced and practiced at a time. Early in the school year, after your first minilesson on this strategy, you should focus on it over several days to instill the habit of monitoring in your students.

When students have become adept at student modeling alternating with teacher modeling, they can read in a group or with a partner, with each student taking a turn modeling. During these activities, you can observe and assess how well students are verbalizing their monitoring; if any students are struggling, you can join in briefly for a session of teacher modeling.

✹ Minilesson #3

Summarizing Expository Text

Introduction

Purpose: To summarize informational (expository) text

Reading level: Upper elementary and higher

Text: "Ancient Rome," from *Gladiator* (Watkins 1997; partial text reproduced in Chapter 3.)

Summarizing informational or expository text requires the student to focus on main ideas and important details. The lesson here is based on rules developed by Brown and Day (1983) and successfully researched by others (Bean & Steenwyk, 1984). These steps are included in the strategy presented on the poster presented in Figure 4.10. It is best to teach this strategy after students have learned to identify important information in expository text. Early lessons should focus on summarizing paragraphs; later lessons can be extended to longer text. The lesson below would be taught after students had read the chapter "Ancient Rome" and already knew how to summarize paragraphs.

**Mini-
lessons**

continued

Activity	Procedures, Comments and Multilevel Notes
Introduction	Ask students to recall the strategy they have learned for summarizing paragraphs. Tell them they are going to learn how to apply this strategy to longer texts.
	Comment: *This relates what students will learn to what they already know.*
Teacher modeling	1. Display the strategy poster shown in Figure 4.10. Review each step with students.
Develop the concept of summarizing longer texts	2. Ask students to talk about times when they have had to write reports using information from several books. Point out that they needed to summarize from longer amounts of text.
	Comment: *Focuses students' attention on what they will learn.*
Modeling summarizing at the listening level	1. Ask students to recall "Ancient Rome" and briefly discuss it.
	Multilevel Note: *Everything through the listening level is appropriate for all readers.*
	2. Tell students you are going to show them how to apply the summarizing informational text strategy to more than one paragraph as they listen to text. Read aloud the first three paragraphs. Use the following think-aloud, along with a transparency of the first three paragraphs of the text. As you use the think-aloud, mark out the text and make notes in the margin.
	Comment: *Shows students how to think through the steps of the strategy.*
	Teacher Think-Aloud "As I listened to the first three paragraphs on pages 2 and 3, I could tell that ancient Rome was the main topic. Much of the other information presented was just interesting details. Even Romulus, the founder of Rome, liked fighting. As Romans conquered other countries or areas, they borrowed ideas from them—fighting and chariot racing were Etruscan; Roman art and architecture came from the Greeks. There isn't a main topic sentence in these three paragraphs. Therefore, I create one of my own: 'Ancient Rome was created by taking ideas from other countries through fights and conquests.'"
	Comment: *Pulls together ideas modeled.*

Mini-lessons

continued

Activity	Procedures, Comments and Multilevel Notes (continued)
Modeling summarizing at the reading level	**1.** Direct students to silently read the remainder of the chapter. Tell students that you will model the use of this strategy at the reading level.
	Multilevel Note: *If some students are unable to read the chapter independently, use a different mode.*
	2. Use a transparency of the pages and the following think-aloud to model the strategy.
	Teacher Think-Aloud "As I read these paragraphs, I see that the topic is how the Roman Empire came into existence. Each paragraph tells how Rome won a different war or took over someone or something else. The last paragraph on page 5 summarizes the entire chapter."
	Comment: *Models using the strategy in reading.*
	3. Have a student read aloud the last paragraph on page 5. Discuss additional items that need to be included.
	4. Assist students in writing a summary for these paragraphs.
Student modeling and guided practice	**1.** Use a transparency of Chapter 2, "The First Gladiators," and guide students in writing a summary.
	Comment: *Lets students try the strategy with teacher support if needed.*
	2. Have students work with a partner to develop the summary for Chapter 3, "Who Were the Gladiators?"
Summarizing and reflecting	Prompt students to summarize the parts of the strategy and talk about its uses: What steps do you follow when summarizing longer text? How is summarizing longer text different from summarizing paragraphs? How and when do you think you might use this strategy?
	Comment: *Helps students verbalize what they have learned and why it is important.*

Mini-lessons

continued

> **Discussion** After this lesson, students would read and summarize Chapter 4, "The Schools." Students could begin by working in cooperative pairs while you assess how well they are using the strategy. Most students will need repeated teacher modeling and guided practice. Since summarizing is difficult for students to learn, lessons are most effective if they are short and very focused. The poster shown in Figure 4.10 will help students stay aware of the steps to use in summarizing. Encourage students to help each other improve in their use of the strategy, and periodically invite students to reflect about their strategy use.
>
> At the same time, you will probably have taught synthesizing lessons. Students will then use both summarizing and synthesizing as they read.

After Reading the Plans

1. Select any strategy lesson plan presented in this chapter. Working with a partner, develop several more "think-alouds" that you would use to model the strategy.
2. Working with a partner, select any strategy you would like to teach, and prepare two lessons on it—one for expository text and one for narrative text. Teach the lessons to a small group, and discuss the results.
3. Select a grade level of your choice and observe for an hour or two, looking for evidence of students using the strategies mentioned in this chapter. Talk with the teacher to see how the children learned them. Were they taught? Did the students learn them through their literacy experiences?

A Final Word About Strategies

The strategy lessons in this chapter are models to help you develop your own lessons. Remember that just teaching the separate strategy lessons is not enough: in order for strategies to help students read more effectively, the students must be engaged in reading and using the strategies. You should introduce all the strategies early in the year and then provide repeated opportunities for students to use them in reading and writing throughout the year. Teaching strategies may be a helpful form of support for some students, but not necessary for others. *Many students may do very well by reading, writing, and interacting with their peers and you about their reading and writing.* Only an informed, observant teacher can decide whether students are profiting from strategy instruction. You must be that teacher!

How to Teach Strategies for Constructing Meaning: Key Points

To review the Key Points, see the ACE practice tests at the HM TeacherPrepSPACE Student Website.

- Strategies can help readers construct meaning.
- Eight essential strategies are visualizing, making connections, monitoring, inferencing, identifying important information, generating and answering questions, summarizing/synthesizing, and evaluating.
- Guidelines are helpful for planning and implementing strategy instruction in the classroom.
- Both implicit and explicit modeling, incorporating "think-alouds," are part of teaching students to use strategies.
- Minilessons are an appropriate way to teach strategies.
- A minilesson should include introduction, teacher modeling, student modeling and guided practice, and summarizing and reflecting.
- Follow-up to the minilesson includes independent practice, application, and reflection.
- Teachers should teach lessons when there is a need, but encourage independence whenever possible.

How Do I Teach?

Video Cases in This Chapter

- **Multiple Intelligences: Elementary School Instruction**
- **Culturally Responsive Teaching: A Multicultural Lesson for Elementary Students**

For Additional Reading

Applegate, M. D., Quinn, K. B., & Applegate, A. J. (2006). Profiles in comprehension. *The Reading Teacher, 60*(1), 48–57.

Barton, J., & Sawyer, D. M. (2003–2004). Our students are reading for this: Comprehension instruction in the elementary school. *The Reading Teacher, 57*(4), 334–347.

Cartwright, K. B. (2006). Fostering flexibility and comprehension in elementary students. *The Reading Teacher, 59*(7), 628–634.

Cortese, E. E. (2003–2004). The application of Question-Answer Relationship strategies to pictures. *The Reading Teacher, 57*(4), 374–380.

Fisk, C., & Hurst, B. (2003). Paraphrasing for comprehension. *The Reading Teacher, 57*(2), 182–185.

Fortenberry, C. L., & Fowler, T. W. (2006–2007). Mind magnets. *The Reading Teacher, 60*(4), 373–376.

Harvey, S., & Goudvis, A. (2000). *Strategies that work: Teaching comprehension to enhance understanding.* York, ME: Stenhouse Publishers.

Hashey, J. M., & Connors, D. J. (2003) Learn from our journey: Reciprocal teaching action research. *The Reading Teacher, 57*(3), 224–232.

Kragler, S., Walker, C. A., & Martin, L. E. (2005). Strategy instruction in primary content textbooks. *The Reading Teacher, 59*(3), 254–261.

Liang, L. A., & Dole, J. A. (2006). Help with teaching reading comprehension: Comprehension frameworks. *The Reading Teacher, 59*(8), 742–753.

McLaughlin, M., & Allen, M. B. (2002). *Guided comprehension: A teaching model for grades 3–8.* Newark, DE: International Reading Association.

McMackin, M. S., & Witherell, N. L. (2005). Different routes to the same destination: Drawing conclusions with tiered graphic organizers. *The Reading Teacher, 59*(3), 242–252.

Malloy, J. A., & Gambrell, L. D. (2006). Approaching the unavoidable: Literacy instruction and the Internet. *The Reading Teacher, 59*(5), 482–484.

Massey, D. D. (2003). A comprehension checklist: What if it doesn't make sense? *The Reading Teacher, 57*(1), 81–84.

Myers, P. A. (2005–2006). The princess Storyteller; Clara Clarifier; Quincy Questioner; and the Wizard: Reciprocal teaching adapted for kindergarten students. *The Reading Teacher, 59*(4), 314–324.

Neufeld, P. (2005–2006). Comprehension instruction in content area classes. *The Reading Teacher, 59*(4), 302–312.

Oczkus, L. D. (2003) *Reciprocal teaching at work: Strategies for improving reading comprehension.* Newark, DE: International Reading Association.

Oczkus, L. (2004). *Super six comprehension strategies: 35 lessons and more for reading success.* Norwood, MA: Christopher-Gordon Publishers, Inc.

Walmsley, S. A. (2006). Getting the big idea: A neglected goal for reading comprehension. *The Reading Teacher, 60*(3), 281–285.

Websites

The following websites have additional ideas for strategy instruction:

Reading Online
Stay abreast of research on strategy instruction at sites such as *Reading Online*, a journal of K–12 practice and research, published by the International Reading Association. Here you can find articles, discussions, ideas, and communities dedicated to serving teachers.
http://www.readingonline.org

International Reading Association
The International Reading Association (IRA) provides resources for teachers, reading specialists, tutors, and others concerned about literacy. Topics range from performance-based assessment to classroom discussion strategies, integrated instruction, motivation for reading, and teaching English as a Second Language. Visit the IRA's website to learn about books, journals, videos, and multimedia products about reading comprehension and literacy.
http://www.reading.org

National Council of Teachers of English
The National Council of Teachers of English (NCTE) is devoted to improving the teaching of English and the language arts at all levels. Explore the website to learn more.
http://www.ncte.org

Minilessons

Enter either minilesson or mini lesson in a search engine for hundreds, even thousands of possibilities. You are sure to find some that meet your needs. While the format may vary from what is presented in this book, you can use information and reshape it. Below are a couple of sites to get you started.

South Shore Regional School Board
This site was developed to assist educators by providing ideas for integrating technology in classrooms. It is maintained by the South Shore Regional School Board, Bridgewater, Nova Scotia, Canada. The Web address below takes you to the "Minilessons and More" page. Go to the home page for many more literacy topics.
http://ssrsbstaff.ednet.ns.ca/litandtech/interest.htm

Columbia Education Center
This site presents lesson plans from a summer workshop of teachers from fourteen states. Choose "Language Arts, Elementary" to see a list of dozens of minilessons.
http://www.youth.net/cec/cec.html

Beginning Literacy

Terms
YOU NEED TO KNOW

- alphabetic principle
- analogy
- concepts of print
- cueing systems
- grapheme
- phoneme
- phonemic awareness
- phonics
- rime
- routine
- structural analysis
- word wall

Beginning readers must learn to read words quickly, accurately, and automatically; this ability is critical to the process of constructing meaning, or comprehension (Adams, 1990). A look at how two first-grade teachers approach reading will help you understand this process.

Mr. Paredes and his students were rereading aloud the book *The Lady with the Alligator Purse* (Westcott, 1988). As Mr. Paredes read from the big book, the children chimed in: "Miss Lucy had a baby,/ His name was Tiny Tim." After rereading the whole book, the children talked about their favorite parts and found pages to show examples. Luanda said, "I like the pizza page" and showed the page where the characters are eating pizza in the bed. Mr. Paredes encouraged every child to respond.

After the discussion, Mr. Paredes returned to the first page and said, "Let's reread this page together: 'Miss Lucy had a baby,/ His name was Tiny Tim.'" All the children joined in. Mr. Paredes said, "What was the baby's name?" The children responded, "Tiny Tim." Mr. Paredes wrote the name on the board and asked, "What is the beginning letter of the baby's name?" Several children responded, "t." Mr. Paredes underlined the T and said, "This letter stands for /t/.* We are going to talk about the /t/ sound today."

"Does anyone in our class have a name that begins with the /t/ sound?" he asked. As the children called out names, Mr. Paredes listed them under Tiny Tim. He then asked different children to come up and underline the t and give the sound it stood for:

```
Tiny Tim
Terry
Tom
Tanisha
teacher
```

One child said, "Lisa." Instead of telling the child she was wrong, Mr. Paredes listed the name to the side of Tiny Tim and said, "Let's compare these two beginning sounds. Which one begins with /t/?" "Tiny Tim." "Which one begins with /l/?" "Lisa." "Are these the same sound?" asked Mr. Paredes. "No," the children chorused. Then he said, "Let's look at the lists on our word wall to see if we have one where Lisa's name will fit."

The children did not find a list for the letter L, because it had not been taught yet. Mr. Paredes tore off a long strip of paper, wrote Lisa at the top, and underlined the L. He said, "We will talk about this letter another day."

---

*When a letter is set off in slash marks, /t/, you are to give the sound for the letter. It is difficult to give the sound of a consonant without adding a schwa sound. Be aware of this difficulty and try to keep the sound as pure as possible. For example, the sound for t is not /tuh/; it is /t/ with quick, breathy sound.

Mr. Paredes returned to the list of t words, reread it with the children, and said, "Now we are going to play our game, Everyone Show. When I say a word that begins with the t sound /t/, everyone show the t-card. If it doesn't begin with /t/, show your No card." Mr. Paredes read teacher, top, dog, say, tiger, tap, run, toss. He had a class checklist for noting any child having difficulty for reteaching later. He then directed children back to the big book, The Lady with the Alligator Purse, and had the group reread it with him. Then he had the children read several pages to locate and read aloud words that began with /t/. Next, he gave each child a little book he had written and duplicated called Tip at the Top. This book contained many t-words and used only CVC (consonant-vowel-consonant) words that children could decode and sight words they already knew. He said, "Here is a book that will let you apply what we have learned about the letter t. It uses only skills and words you have learned. Read it to yourself to tell the others in the group what happened to the bird in the story."

Compare Mr. Paredes's class to Ms. Anderson's class.

"Boys and girls, we are going to meet a new phonics character today," said Ms. Anderson. She printed the letter B on the board. "His name begins with this letter. What is this letter?" The group called out "B." "Yes," said Ms. Anderson, who then showed a picture of a bear. "Here is a picture of our character. What is he?" "A bear," responded the children. "Our character's name is Boris Bear. You say it." The children all replied "Boris Bear." "Boris Bear is our character for the b sound. Listen to the /b/ sound at the beginning of his name /B/-/B/-Boris /B/-/B/-Bear. You say it." The children responded /B/-/B/-Boris /B/-/B/-Bear.

"Now, we are going to learn to read words that begin with /b/." Ms. Anderson printed the word book on the board. She modeled for the children how to read the word aloud. She placed her hand under the b and said: "This letter stands for /b/ and I remember /ook/; /b/-/ook/. I blend it faster /b/-/ook/—book. I can read the word. Now you will practice reading words together. I will point to the letter or letters and say SOUND. You say the sound; then I will say BLEND. You will blend the sounds to say the word. Let's try it again with book."

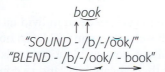

"SOUND - /b/-/o͞ok/"
"BLEND - /b/-/ook/ - book"

Ms. Anderson repeated the SOUND/BLEND process using bag, bug, boy, bump.

"Boys and girls, now take out your whiteboards. We are going to learn to spell words that begin with /b/. Number 1 to 5 down the side. I will say five words. Write b beside the number if the word I say begins with /b/ as in Boris Bear."

Ms. Anderson read "1. cap, 2. box, 3. baby, 4. sing, 5. bunny." She walked around looking to see who was having problems so she could give them help later.

"Now we are going to read a story using what you already know and what you have learned about the sound for b." Ms. Anderson passed out copies of a little book titled Bing, which is part of her published reading program. "Read this story silently to find out who the main character is and what he does. Remember, use the sound at the beginning of Boris Bear and what you already know to figure out the words." After silent reading, children discussed the story and read it aloud as a group.

The HM TeacherPrepSPACE Student Website offers many helpful resources, such as self-quizzes, glossary flashcards, lesson plan templates, and more.

Mr. Paredes and Ms. Anderson were each teaching students to read words. Think about how the two teachers were alike and different. Compare your ideas to the following:

- Mr. Paredes started with a big book, and returned to that big book after students had been taught the sound. Ms. Anderson started by teaching the individual sound.
- Both Mr. Paredes and Ms. Anderson explicitly modeled the sound being taught by isolating it for students.
- Ms. Anderson modeled for children how to read words sequentially.
- Ms. Anderson had the children learn to spell words using the sound being taught.
- Both teachers had children immediately practice reading a book in which vocabulary was controlled by containing only the sounds and words that had been previously taught.
- Both teachers were using procedures and practices that are supported by current research.

In Chapter 2, we presented a model for a Comprehensive Balanced Literacy Program. As you will recall, the model includes:

- blocks for daily independent reading and writing.
- learning reading skills and strategies.
- applying reading skills and strategies.
- learning to write.
- developmentally appropriate writing.
- an intervention block for students having difficulty learning to read.

Adjustments are made in individual blocks to suit student literacy development.

In this chapter, you will learn how to teach readers at the early stages of literacy development how to identify words using phonics and other **cueing systems,** to increase their vocabulary, and to construct meaning. Although the opening scenario showed first-grade classrooms, acquiring literacy is much the same whatever the age of the individual. If you are teaching an older beginning reader, you use material that matches the maturity of the student in terms of interest and experience, but the process is essentially the same.

What You Need to Know About Beginning Reading Instruction

Effective beginning reading instruction is critical for the success of readers of any age. Research has led to clear conclusions about beginning reading. These match what you learned in Chapter 1 about what makes an effective reading teacher.

Big Jobs in Learning to Read

Learning to read is not a simple process. While many factors and elements interact as a child learns to read (Juel, 1991), two big jobs work together: *decoding* and *comprehension*. Figure 5.1 shows how these jobs change in emphasis from beginning reading to mature reading.

Decoding is the process of translating written language into verbal speech (oral reading) or inner speech (thinking the words in one's head) (Eldredge, 1995). Decoding is necessary, but not sufficient, for reading. Reading occurs only when there is comprehension, the process whereby the reader constructs meaning by interacting with the text (Anderson & Pearson, 1984; Cooper, 1986).

See more about comprehension in Chapters 1, 3, and 4.

Decoding and comprehension interact as individuals learn to read. At first, most words children meet in print are already in their oral vocabulary; they understand them when listening and they use them when speaking. The task at the beginning stages of learning to read is how to recognize those words when they meet them in print. As readers gain skills and fluency, they learn to decode and comprehend words that may not yet be in their oral language; thus their vocabulary continues to grow. The element of vocabulary, then, is implicit in all decoding and comprehension instruction.

The two jobs of decoding and comprehension are not equal at the various stages; the amount of instructional emphasis shifts from one component to another, but *both are always included*. Figure 5.1 shows how the instructional emphasis needs to shift from the beginning to the mature stages. Let's focus on the "big job" of beginning reading—decoding.

FIGURE 5.1   Changing Emphasis in Learning to Read

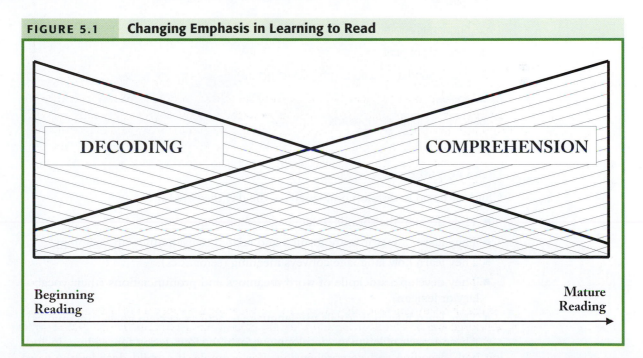

DECODING

COMPREHENSION

Beginning Reading

Mature Reading

186 ◆

Chapter 5 • Beginning Literacy

Elements Leading to Successful, Independent Decoding

The ultimate goal of reading words is fluency, which leads to comprehension. *Fluency is the process of automatically, accurately, and rapidly recognizing words* (LaBerge & Samuels, 1976; Perfetti, 1985; Rasinski & Hoffman, 2003; Stanovich, 1980, 1986). As students become fluent readers, they build a stockpile of *sight words,* or words that they recognize instantly and use decoding to hypothesize the pronunciation of the word (orally or silently) with words they do not recognize instantly.

In the beginning stages of learning to read, a learner must depend heavily on his or her decoding abilities to pronounce words. With repeated practice, the learner recognizes more words automatically, accurately, and rapidly (learns more sight words) and becomes a more fluent reader. Researchers have found that good comprehenders (constructors of meaning) are also fluent decoders (Carnine, Carnine, & Gersten, 1984; Chall, 1967; Lesgold & Curtis, 1981).

Teaching decoding systematically is a critical part of beginning literacy instruction. Students must develop six critical elements as they learn to independently decode words. In addition, readers must develop a stockpile of sight words, including a number of high-frequency words (words that occur most often in language). This combination of independent decoding and sight words helps individuals become efficient, independent readers.

Six Critical Elements

1. oral language

2. phonemic awareness

3. concepts of print

4. letter-sound associations (phonics/structure)

5. analogy

6. a way to think about words

Oral Language

Children begin to develop oral language the day they are born:

- They develop the sounds of language (phonology).
- They learn how words are formed and related to each other (morphology).
- They learn how language conveys meaning (semantics).
- They develop a stockpile of word meanings and pronunciations (their vocabulary or lexicon).
- They learn how individuals use language to achieve certain goals (pragmatics).

These aspects of language development form the foundation for reading, including both decoding and comprehension. For example, if a child decodes the word *horse,* his language base serves as the checking system to tell whether the word has been decoded properly as well as the basis for assigning meaning to the word *horse.*

Most children develop their use of language with ease (Snow, Burns, & Griffin, 1998). For these children, the school must provide activities that support continued language development. Children who come to school without a good language base, perhaps because of limited adult language models, or a neurological problem, need specific instruction and activities that develop oral language. For all learners, language development activities should include the following:

- Good language modeling provided by teachers' reading aloud to students and discussing what was read.

- Language lessons that model uses of language. For example, use a photograph as the basis for a discussion and model expansion of language by taking children's comments and adding more description.

> Child: *It's a dog.*

Teacher: *Yes, it is a big, brown dog. What else do you notice about this dog's face?*

> Child: *A white spot.*

Teacher: *Yes, the big, brown dog has a white patch or spot on its face.*

- Experiences such as field trips, class visitors, movies, videos, DVDs, and CD-ROM stories that expand students' background and knowledge followed by good discussions.

- Opportunities for children to use language in a variety of ways. This may occur in various centers in the kindergarten and first-grade classroom.

Continued language development forms and expands the foundation for children to develop their abilities to decode and comprehend. Weak or limited oral language may interfere with a child's ability to learn to read (Chard & Osborne, n.d.).

English Language Learners (ELLs) may have developed oral proficiency in their first language, but they may not yet have developed English oral language. They need extra support to develop English oral language as they are learning to read English.

Phonemic Awareness

An important element directly related to oral language development is **phonemic awareness,** the knowledge that spoken words are composed of a sequence of sounds, or **phonemes.** Phonemic awareness is a part of the broader category known as *phonological awareness,* which includes all the aspects of the sounds of language separate and apart from meaning. Research has supported the importance of phonemic awareness in relation to learning to read and learning to spell (Ball & Blachman, 1991; Juel, Griffith, & Gough, 1986; Liberman, Shankweiler, & Liberman, 1989).

English is an alphabetic language. The sounds of the language (phonemes) are represented by symbols—the alphabet (**graphemes**). For example, the word *cat* has three phonemes (/c/-/ă/-/t/) and three graphemes c-a-t. The word *goat* also has three phonemes /g/-/ō/-/t/ and three graphemes g-oa-t, but one of the phonemes, /ō/, is represented by a two-letter grapheme.

Most children do not naturally learn this **alphabetic principle**—that is, the idea that each sound of the language is represented by a graphic symbol (Eldredge, 1995). It must be explicitly taught (Adams, 1990). Phonemic awareness is a part of learning the alphabetic principle. If children have not yet acquired phonemic awareness, instruction in letter-sound associations will not be effective in helping them decode words. Researchers have identified several aspects of phonemic awareness (Adams, 1990; Eldredge, 1995). The following elements are common to most:

- *Rhyming words.* Being able to tell that two words rhyme (*hot-not; mat-fat*).
- *Counting words in sentences.* Being able to tell that the following is a four-word sentence: *This is my mother.*
- *Counting syllables in words.* Being able to tell that *horse* has one syllable, *listen* has two syllables, and so forth.
- *Counting phonemes in words.* Knowing that *hat* has three sounds /h/-/ă/-/t/.
- *Segmenting and blending syllables.* Hearing the word *happy* and giving the two syllables /hăp/-/ē/ is segmenting; hearing /rŭn/-/ing/ and giving the word *running* is blending.
- *Segmenting and blending onset and rime.* Hearing the word *brook* and identifying the onset /br/ and the rime /ōōk/ is segmenting; and hearing the onset /c/ and the rime /ard/ and being able to make the word *card* is blending.
- *Segmenting and blending phonemes.* Hearing the word *hot* and giving the three phonemes /h/-/ō/-/t/ is segmenting; hearing the phonemes /p/-/ă/-/t/ and saying the word *pat* is blending.
- *Substitution of sounds.* Taking the word *hot* and substituting the sound /c/ for /h/ and saying the word *cot*.

The two most important processes students must learn are segmentation of sounds and blending of sounds. Activities for teaching and developing phonemic awareness are discussed later in this chapter. (The Educators Speak feature on page 196 is about phonemic awareness and diverse learners.)

ELLs are still acquiring the English phonological system. Therefore, tests of phonemic awareness given in English, which is the students' second language, are not good indicators of their ability to use this process (Freeman & Freeman, 2000).

Concepts of Print

As children learn to identify words as an aid to constructing meaning, they must develop some **concepts of print.** Clay (1985) divides these concepts into four categories: *books, sentences, words,* and *letters* (see Table 5.1).

Beginning readers and writers must learn that books convey meaning through print. They also need to know the left-right, top-bottom orientation on a page, as well as concepts about a book, such as the cover, title, author, illustrator, beginning, and ending.

Students must develop some understanding of the sentences on the page. They need to recognize a sentence, know that it represents a spoken message, and be able to tell the beginning and ending by recognizing the capital letters and the end

TABLE 5.1	Concepts of Print

BOOKS

Knows:
- Cover
- Title, author, illustrator
- Beginning, ending
- Left-right orientation
- Top-bottom orientation
- Print tells story, not pictures

SENTENCES

Identifies:
- Sentence
- Beginning, ending of sentence
- Capital letter at beginning
- Punctuation: period, comma, question mark, quotation mark, exclamation point

WORDS

- Identifies words (knows that *day* is a word)

LETTERS

Knows:
- Letter order
- Capital and lowercase

Source: Based on Clay (1985).

See "Routines for Reading," page 207.

punctuation. They also need some understanding of other forms of punctuation, such as quotation marks.

Students must develop the concept of a word, and know that each word is composed of letters and that these letters appear in a certain order. Part of that learning includes knowing the difference between capital (uppercase) and lowercase letters. Many children come to school understanding these concepts about print, but some do not; so it may be necessary for you to teach these concepts to some children.

Letter-Sound Associations (Phonics and Structural Analysis)

A strong, consistent body of research has accumulated showing that beginning readers get their best start by being *explicitly* taught letter-sound associations (Adams, 1990; Anderson, Hiebert, Scott, & Wilkinson, 1985; Armbruster & Osborn, 2003; Chall, 1967, 1983; National Reading Panel, 2000; Snow, Burns, & Griffin, 1998). Instruction must include **phonics** and **structural analysis.** Phonics is the study of letter-sound (grapheme-phoneme) relationships. Structural analysis is the study of meaningful word parts. The instruction in and acquisition of phonemic awareness leads directly to teaching letter-sound associations.

For a detailed discussion of phonics and structural analysis, see the Handbook Resource, page 503.

Over the years, phonics has been a controversial issue (Allington, 1997; Flesch, 1955; Garan, 2001; National Reading Panel, 2000a, 2000b). Some educators and laypersons believe that phonics is the only and best way to teach children to read. Others disagree. The best way to be prepared to deal with phonics issues (or any other issues) is to:

- ■ **Be knowledgeable.** Make sure that you know what phonics is and understand the role it plays in learning to read and spell. "Word Skills: Phonics and Structural Analysis for Teachers," a special section presented in the Handbook Resource at the end of this text, is designed to help you learn the basic elements about phonics and structural analysis.

- ■ **Know the research.** Good research can guide decisions about phonics and other areas. Look for patterns in such research rather than depend on one isolated study to provide an answer.

You may want to read this section now (page 503).

Later in this chapter, we will look at how to teach phonics and structural analysis in ways that lead to effective reading and spelling.

Analogy

Analogy (when used in relation to decoding) is the process of noting similarities or patterns in words and using this to figure out an unfamiliar word. As beginning readers learn to read and spell words, they often use analogy to figure out the words (Gaskins et al., 1988). For example, if a child comes to the unknown word *ring*, she might recognize that the word looks like *sing*, a word she knows. Using letter-sound correspondences for the *r* and knowledge of the word *sing*, the child can make the analogy and decode the word *ring*. Analogy is *not* the process of looking for little words in big words—for example, *fat-her* in *father*. Such misinterpretation of analogy can lead beginning readers astray (Pinnell & Fountas, 1998).

Most readers don't use analogy immediately; they must learn some letter-sound correspondences (Ehri & Robbins, 1992) before they begin to use the process on their own. Then, analogy becomes an important strategy for independently decoding words.

A Way to Think About Words

Students must develop a strategy to apply what they have learned in order to decode words by themselves. Independent decoders use multiple cueing systems, or clues, to figure out unknown words:

- ■ phonics,
- ■ structural analysis,
- ■ context or meaning, and
- ■ their sense of language (syntax).

At the beginning stages, children are learning to "read through the word" or "sequentially decode" words. As they come to words they don't instantly recognize— for example, *horse*—they learn to use their letter-sound correspondence knowledge to read through the word starting at the beginning—/h/-/or/-/s/—and proceeding in order.

FIGURE 5.2   A Way to Think About Words

Analogy

Analogy (when used in relation to decoding) is the process of noting similarities or patterns in words and using this to figure out an unfamiliar word. As beginning readers learn to read and spell words, they often use analogy to figure out the words (Gaskins et al., 1988). For example, if a child comes to the unknown word *ring*, she might recognize that the word looks like *sing*, a word she knows. Using letter-sound correspondences for the *r* and knowledge of the word *sing*, the child can make the analogy and decode the word *ring*. Analogy is *not* the process of looking for little to the unknown word (known word: *base;* unknown word: *case*); or it may be recognizing a word pattern, or **rime,** such as *-op.* The student tries to decode the word and checks it by reading to the end of the sentence or paragraph. If this doesn't work, the student moves on to the next step.

2. The student tries to use the individual letter-sound associations and larger sound chunks (phonics and structural analysis). The student then sequentially decodes or sounds out the word and checks it by reading to the end of the sentence or paragraph. This places context in a checking or confirming position and focuses the student initially on the letter-sound correspondences that will lead to more accurate decoding (Adams, 1990; Stanovich, 1980).

3. Finally, if the student is unable to decode the word, he or she asks someone or refers to a dictionary as appropriate skills are learned.

The six elements we discussed in this section are critical to helping students become independent decoders. Keep in mind that while students are developing this independence in decoding, they are also learning high-frequency words and building a stockpile of sight words.

Standards and Beginning Literacy Instruction

State standards for each area of education, such as language arts, are available on the Internet. As you read the standards for your state, you will note that they are consistent with the instructional practices presented in this text. There may be several specific standards related to each aspect of word recognition, stating specific abilities students are expected to demonstrate at each grade level. The wording may vary slightly from one state to the next, but the intent is the same. There are certain abilities (standards) that all students must acquire in order to be literate. For each sample lesson in this text, we have presented standards from a different state to illustrate that our sample lessons meet standards from virtually any state. This text teaches you how to help students acquire those abilities.

Now let's focus on how to teach beginning reading by looking at routines for instruction.

Routines for Comprehensive Balanced Literacy Instruction

See Chapters 2 and 3 for teaching a literacy lesson, developing skills and vocabulary, and developing prior knowledge.

A **routine** is a set of procedures that can be used repeatedly. Within your classroom, you will use and develop many routines for instruction. You have already learned several in this text.

Fourteen routines are particularly effective for beginning literacy instruction. These, along with the others you have already learned, provide a resource from which to choose to meet the needs of your students. Table 5.2 lists the fourteen routines and indicates their functions. Some routines are for teaching, practicing, or

TABLE 5.2	Routines for Comprehensive Balanced Literacy Instruction

Routines	Functions				
	Teach	Practice	Apply	Develop Oral Language	Develop Concept of Print
Routines for Decoding					
■ Phonemic Awareness Routine					
■ Explicit Phonics Routine	X				
■ Analogy Routine	X				
■ Making Words Routine		X	X		
■ Word Wall Routine*		X			
■ Decodable High-Frequency Words Routine	X	X			
■ Irregular and Phonetically Unpredictable High-Frequency or other Words Routine	X	X			
Routines for Reading					
■ Decodable Text Reading Routine		X	X		
■ Fluency Reading Routine		X	X		
■ Read-Aloud Routine	X			X	X
■ Shared Reading Routine	X			X	X
■ Observational Guided Reading Routine		X	X		
■ Cooperative Reading Routine		X	X		
Routine for Comprehension					
■ Explicit Comprehension Strategy Routine	X				

*A word wall (a place on the wall to display words) may be used as a decoding routine and a high-frequency word routine. In this chapter it is described as a decoding routine with comments about how to use it as a high-frequency word routine.

applying some aspect of literacy, while others are for developing oral language or concepts of print. The three major groups of routines are:

- Routines for decoding
- Routines for reading
- Routine for comprehension

We will describe each routine by following a consistent format: purpose, when to use, description/procedures, and comments. As you study each routine, look for overlap. For example, when you are using a decoding routine, you are also developing vocabulary. The sample literacy lesson found on page 221 illustrates the use of some of the routines.

Elementary Reading Instruction: A Balanced Literacy Program

Watch the video clip, study the artifacts in the case, and reflect on the following questions:

1. How many of the routines listed in Table 5.2 can you find within the Video Case?

2. Watch the Video Case, then explain: Which of Ms. Jenoski's literacy routines do you find most effective? Why?

Routines for Decoding Unfamiliar Words and Learning High-Frequency Words

✱ Phonemic Awareness Routine

PURPOSE	Routines for phonemic awareness help children develop the awareness of sounds in words and the ability to blend sounds to make words. Since phonemic awareness involves several related components, there are different routines involving each component.
WHEN TO USE	Phonemic Awareness Routines are used in the Reading: Learning Skills and Strategies block of the Comprehensive Balanced Literacy Program in kindergarten through second grade or beyond if needed.
DESCRIPTION/ PROCEDURES	Three sample routines are presented for phonemic awareness. When you use a routine, it should be for short periods of time (5–10 minutes) repeatedly over several days or weeks until children have developed the component being taught.

For other activities for developing phonemic awareness, see "For Additional Reading."

Rhyming Routine

Teach:

1. Read aloud a book that contains many words that rhyme. (Examples are: *Sheep in a Jeep* [Shaw, 1986], *There's a Wocket in My Pocket* [Seuss, 1974], *Hop on Pop* [Seuss, 1963], *Truck Duck* [Rex, 2004], and *Skunk Dunk* [Rex, 2005].)
2. After reading the book, have children chant some of the lines with you: "Beep, Beep
   Sheep in a Jeep."
3. Identify several words from the text that rhyme (Example: *hop-pop*). Say the words slowly, noting that they rhyme. Give several other examples (*top-hop; pop-top*). Gradually have children tell when the words rhyme.

Practice:

- Play the game Stand Up/Sit Down. This game is like Simon Says.
- Say pairs of words that rhyme and pairs that don't rhyme. Children go from one position to the next only if the words rhyme (Sample words: *cat-hat*;

big-pig; *cat-pig*; *big-jig*; *hat-sat*; *sat-rat*; *sat-big*). Note how children respond to tell whether they are getting the concept.

■ Model and practice daily until children master the skill. Then drop the modeling, but continue to provide repeated practice.

Counting Sounds and Syllables Routine

Teach:

1. After reading aloud a favorite book to children, select a two- or three-sound word to model the number of sounds (Example: *top*).
2. Say the word slowly by stretching it out; tell children that this word has three sounds. Use several other examples (*red*, *cat*, *pig*). Model the number of sounds by slowly saying the word and clapping once for each sound. Ask children to clap with you.

Practice:

■ Play the Clapping Game. Use only words that have three phonemes. As you say words, have children clap for each sound heard. At first, stretch the words out; as children develop their ability to do this, say the words at a more normal speed.

■ Repeat this process over several days or weeks. Drop the modeling when it is no longer needed, and provide short daily practices until students develop the ability to hear sounds.

This same procedure may be used for counting syllables.

Segmenting and Blending Routines

Teach:

(Segmenting)

1. Select words of two syllables from a book that has been read aloud (examples: *baby*, *table*).
2. Say each word, slowly stretching it out /bā→//bē→/. Tell children that this word has two syllables (parts): *bāā* and *bēē*.
3. Repeat with several other words.

Practice:

■ Play the Match Game. Give each child a stack of colored tiles or colored squares of paper.

■ Use five to seven two-syllable words. Say each word slowly. Direct children to place a tile or colored square on their desks for each syllable they hear in the word. In the beginning, stretch the words by saying them slowly. As children become adept at using this skill, say the words normally.

Teach:

(Blending)

1. Select several two-syllable words from a book that has been read aloud.
2. Say the words in their parts /hăp//ē/. Model how you can blend these syllables together to make the word *happy*. Repeat the modeling using

Decoding Routines and Diverse Learners

"Teaching phonemic awareness is key for students who learn to read phonetically, but not all students learn to read this way. In my primary classroom, I use a number of different strategies to teach students about phonics.

Each week we have five new word wall words that we work with. One day a week, we work on rhyming words that we can think of for the word wall words. I start off another day with the students telling me the sounds they hear in the words. During this activity, we are able to divide the word into sounds that they hear, blends, digraphs, vowels working together, and ending sounds. Then different groups make the sound, and we blend them together to make the whole word. I believe that this really helps with "blending" words together. I try to use this phrase instead of "sounding" out words with both students and parents. When "training" my parents for our Wise Owl Book Club, I discuss with them how to blend sounds and to look for chunks inside words. Parents know which "chunk" we are working on by reading my weekly newsletter.

During guided reading, the students usually make words by manipulating the letters given to make new words that are important to the context of the book they have been reading, or a vowel or consonant blend that is noticeably a problem. They also use erasable marker boards.

During shared reading time, I refer to the 'chunk wall' and we discuss a chunk, for example, "ell," that we can use to make many words. This helps the students to use what they know when blending sounds to make an unknown word. They love coming up with rhyming words to go on the various shapes on our chunk wall. It is something that I can refer them to when they are writing on their own. It is a great tool that we leave up all year. This really helps my lower-level spellers when writing.

During the poetry time of the day, I use the *Fun Phonics* CDs that give various spellings for the sounds of the short and long vowels. These CDs are interactive, and the students are able to highlight which words make that vowel sound. Students often refer to their poetry folders when trying to figure out the spelling of a word. They can see the different patterns that make the various sounds. There are also CDs for the blends and digraphs; these give the children opportunities to hear and see the sound in a variety of words."

—Greg O'Connell, First-Grade Teacher
Grant Wood Elementary, Cedar Rapids Community School District
Cedar Rapids, Iowa

several more examples. Gradually ask children to take over the responsibility to blend the words.

Practice:

- Play the game Three Cheers!
- Identify five to seven words that you will say in parts. Say each word by giving the two syllables. Ask children to say the word three times as a cheer (example: Teacher: /bŏt•əl/ Children: *bottle, bottle, bottle*).

This same procedure can be used for blending onset and rime.

For more activities for teaching and practicing phonemic awareness, see "For Additional Reading."

Discussion The elements on page 188 present a possible sequence for teaching phonemic awareness; you may find others suggested elsewhere. It is important that you follow a sequence so that you can help children *systematically* develop phonemic awareness. All lessons for phonemic awareness should be *short, fun,* and *exciting.* They are more meaningful if they are connected to books that are being read aloud.

Explicit Phonics Routine

PURPOSE

This routine provides two patterns that can be used repeatedly for explicitly teaching phonic skills (letter-sound associations) as well as structural analysis. Two options are presented: *Option A,* Starting with Sounds, and *Option B,* Starting with Known Words. (Research supports explicitly and systematically teaching letter-sound associations, but it does not indicate whether it is better to start with sounds or with known words.) You may have some children who learn phonics and structural analysis better one way than the other. Therefore, you need to know both routines.

WHEN TO USE

The Explicit Phonics Routine (Option A and/or Option B) is used in the Reading: Learning Skills and Strategies block of the Comprehensive Balanced Literacy Program. Many teachers use Option B following the reading of text that contains some examples of the sound element to be taught (as Mr. Paredes did in the example at the beginning of this chapter). Others teach Option A, teaching the sounds before reading the text containing examples of the elements (as Ms. Anderson did at the beginning of this chapter).

DESCRIPTION/ PROCEDURES

This routine builds on the best research that we have to date on explicitly teaching phonics (Adams, 1990; Eldredge, 1995). Use the procedures that follow to explicitly teach phonics and/or structural analysis. Each of the five steps is incorporated within every phonics lesson, with adjustments to meet individual needs of students.

Five Steps in the Explicit Phonics Routine

1. *awareness*
2. *segmentation*
3. *association*
4. *reading*
5. *spelling*

The following examples provide guidelines to help you plan explicit letter-sound association instruction using both Option A and Option B:

Option A—Starting with Sounds
Illustration Using Short *a*

1. Awareness

a. Say, "Today you will learn to read and spell words with the short *a* sound—/ā/. Listen to each word I say; raise your hand when you hear /ă/ (/c/•/ă/•/t/ *cat*; /ă/•/p/•/əl/ *apple*; /t/•/ă/•/p/ *tap*)."

b. If students respond correctly, move on to the next step. If students do not respond correctly, provide more instruction in phonemic awareness.

2. Segmentation

a. Say, "You can hear /ă/ in the middle of *cap*. Sometimes /ă/ will be in the beginning of a word, as in *at*." Model using several other words (*apple, act, pat, pass*).

b. Say, "Listen to each of these words and tell me if you hear /ă/ and whether it is the middle or beginning of the word" (*at, cap, mat, dog, ask, cast*).

If students respond correctly, move on to the next step; if they do not, provide more teaching and practice in segmentation.

3. Association

A ă

Abby Astronaut

a. Tell children that they are now going to look at the letter that stands for /ă/. Write *a* on the board. Ask children to tell what letter this is.

b. Tell children they are going to meet a special character who will help them remember the sound for short *a*. Her name is Abby Astronaut. Ask children to repeat her name, say /ă/, and hold up the *a* letter card. Repeat two or three times.

4. Reading

a. Say, "Now let's read some words using /ă/." Print the word *mat* on the board. Remind children that they know the /m/ and /t/ sounds. Model sequential decoding saying the sounds together and showing the direction of reading by quickly moving your hand under the word:

/m//ă//t/

b. Print the following words on the board. Call on different children to come to the board and model sequential decoding, moving their hand under the word to show the direction of their reading. Remind children that they know all the sounds in the words (*at, lap, sat, Pam, man, rap, rat*).

c. Print a sentence or two on the board containing only words with sounds and high-frequency words children know. Guide individual children to read the sentences.

Tom is a man.
Tom sat on a mat.
Pam sat on a mat.
Pam has a cap.

Tom has a cap.
Cap! Cap!
Rap! Rap!

5. Spelling

a. Say, "Now we will learn to spell words with /ă/." Say the word *sap* slowly. Write the letters for each sound as you say the word slowly—*sap*. Remind children that they have already learned the *s* and *p* sounds. Model spelling two or three more words with short *a*.

b. Ask children to write (using paper or whiteboards) the letters for each word you say (*sat, man, tap, tan, map*).

c. Note children's performance.

Option B—Starting with Known Words
Illustration Using Initial Sound /b/

1. Awareness

a. Say, "Today you will learn to use the sound for the letter *b* to help you read and spell words."

b. "Listen to this word: /b/•/ō/•/t/." (Say it again slowly.) "How many sounds do you hear in this word?" (Students respond—three.) "What is the first sound you hear?" Repeat using words *big, boy, box.*

c. If students respond correctly, move on to the next step. If students do not respond correctly, provide more instruction in phonemic awareness (see page 194).

2. Segmentation

a. Say, "The first sound in *box* is /b/. What is the first sound in *barn*?" (Students respond—/b/.) Repeat using words *bet, bang, bake.*

b. If students respond correctly, move on to the next step; if they do not, provide more teaching and practice in segmentation.

3. Association

Bb

Boris Bear

a. Write the words *box, boy, bear* (use words from a book the students have listened to or read using shared reading) on the board. Underline the *b*. Say, "Each of these words begins with the same letter and the same sound. The letter is *b*; the sound is /b/." Say each word slowly, emphasizing the /b/ sound. Have children repeat with you.

b. Have a picture card with a bear. Show the card. Say, "This bear's name is Boris—Boris Bear. He will help us remember the sound for *b*—/b/."

c. Write groups of words on the board. Have students read the words with you and decide which ones begin with the same letter and sound as Boris Bear.
  - *band, car, bell*
  - *hat, beg, big*
  - *top, Bob, cap*

4. Reading

b

pig

a. On the board write a word that students know—*pig*.

b. Say, "This word is *pig*. If we change the beginning letter to *b*, what sound will be at the beginning of this word?" (/*b*/) "What is the new word?" (Students respond.) Repeat using other words.

c. Say, "Now let's use what we have learned about the *b* sound to read some more words." Use only letter-sound associations students have been taught. Print each word and model sequential decoding:

> *bat - /b/•/ă/•/t/*
> *ban - /b/•/ă/•/n/*
> *bug - /b/•/ŭ/•/g/*

Bab is a bug.
Bab is a big bug.

d. Write a sentence or sentences on the board using only letter-sound associations and high-frequency words students have been taught. Ask students to read, emphasizing the sound for *b*.

5. Spelling

a. Tell children that they are going to learn to spell words with /*b*/. Use words starting with *b* that have ending patterns that children know. Say, "I want to spell the word *bat*. I write *b* for /*b*/ and *at* for /*at*/. *b-a-t*." Model another word—*bit*.

b. Using small boards, whiteboards, or sheets of paper, ask students to write the following:

- The letter you hear at the beginning of *bake*
- The letter that stands for the /*b*/ sound

c. Dictate several words, mixing in words that begin with other sounds students know (*bank, best, cup, zoo, box*). Have students write the words. Look for accuracy in using the *b* and any other previously taught sounds.

Follow the instruction with practice by having students read and reread decodable texts. Gradually move students to authentic literature, encouraging them to apply what they have been learning and practicing in decodable texts.

See the Handbook Resource for ideas about sequencing phonics instruction.

Discussion   The use of routines for teaching phonics is not new (Cooper et al., 1979). Many teachers have found them effective for years. Placing a routine within the framework of a Comprehensive Balanced Literacy Program helps to make the program more effective. You should follow a sequence for teaching phonics. Use the one suggested in the published program your school uses, or identify one from some of the sources listed in the "For Additional Reading" section.

 **Analogy Routine**

PURPOSE
The purpose of this routine is to teach children to look at an unknown word such as *reach* and think about it in terms of a known word *(peach)* that will help them figure out the unknown word. The Analogy Routine should be used after children have learned quite a few sight words and have learned to use most letter-sound associations (Ehri & Robbins, 1992).

WHEN TO USE
This routine is used in the Reading: Learning Skills and Strategies block of the Comprehensive Balanced Literacy Program. It may be used at any stage of literacy development if the students are not effectively using analogy to decode words.

DESCRIPTION/ PROCEDURES
With this routine, children learn how to approach an unknown word by relating it to a word they know. This becomes a part of the strategy A Way to Think About Words (see page 191).

Teach:

1. Print a sentence on the board and underline a word that is unknown.

The <u>goat</u> drank milk.

2. "Let's say I'm reading along and I come to this sentence. I read *The*; the next word I don't know." (Point to *goat*.) "It looks like a word I know—*coat*. I see the *g* at the beginning of *g-o-a-t*. I know the *g* sound is /g/. Instead of /k/ I put /g/ at the beginning of *oat*. I say the word *goat*. I then read the sentence and it seems to make sense."
3. Print several more words in sentences on the board, and have children help you decode them and explain how they made the analogy (*lame/same; make/cake; willow/pillow*).

Practice:

■ Write sentences on the board containing one unknown word where children could make an analogy. Underline the unknown word. Samples are:

Unknown	Known
lark	mark
cable	able
spot	hot

Ask children to read the sentence and explain how they thought of a known word to help them with the underlined word.

■ When children are reading aloud and come to a word they cannot pronounce, prompt them to make analogies:

– Say, "Does some part of this word look like a word you already know?"

– "If so, say that word; then cover up the part you don't know. Say what you know. Then uncover the part you don't know. Give the sound for this part. Then blend the sound with the familiar part to pronounce the word."

■ Relate the use of analogy to A Way to Think About Words strategy presented on page 190. Help children internalize this process by prompting them to use it again and again.

 **Discussion** After children have learned to use the basic concept of analogy, teach other lessons focusing on word parts such as suffixes and prefixes. Always help students see how this skill fits into their overall strategy for independently decoding words.

✳ Making Words Routine

PURPOSE

Making Words (Cunningham & Cunningham, 1992) is a hands-on manipulative activity for practicing the use of letter-sound associations and word patterns to decode and spell words. Students at any level can use this routine. It can be a whole class or a small-group activity.

WHEN TO USE

This routine fits into the Reading: Learning Skills and Strategies block of the Comprehensive Balanced Literacy Program.

DESCRIPTION/ PROCEDURES

This routine may be done with the whole class using a pocket chart and large letter cards, or with small groups using individual trays (such as Scrabble™ letter holders) and letters. The following guidelines are for using this routine with a small group:

1. Select a target word such as *bathtub* from a book students have read. List the words you want students to make leading to the target word, progressing from two-letter words to the target word:

   – at
   – bat
   – bath
   – hub
   – tub
   – bathtub

   bathtub (target word)

   Print each word on a card to use for word sorting at the end of the lesson.

2. Give each student a set of letters for the target word and a tray. (The tray can be made by folding tagboard.) Make the vowels one color and the consonants another color.

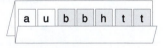

3. Before students begin, ask if anyone can guess the target word. Respond only by saying, "We'll check at the end." Ask students to make a word: *at.* Use in a sentence—"We are *at* school."

4. You make the word in your tray; show students. Say, "Does your word look like mine? If it doesn't, fix it." Have students show you their words.
5. Next, ask, "What one letter would you add to *at* to make *bat*?"
6. You make your word. Show students; have them check and show you.

7. Continue the lesson, building the words you want to have made: *bath*, *tub*, *bathtub*.
8. Throughout the lesson and at the end, help students see various patterns in the word building:

    at → *bat* (Add one letter; make a new word; could do more rhyming here, if needed)

    bat → *bath* (Add one letter; make a new word; if *th* has been taught, note the digraph *th*)

    hub → *tub* (Change one letter; make a new word)

    bath + *tub* → *bathtub* (Compound word)

9. Using the word cards for each word made, have children sort the words into various patterns as shown:

    At   hub   bath
    Bat   tub   bathtub

10. Add any or all of the words to the **word wall.**
11. Finally, locate the target word in the book from which it was taken to help children build the connection between what they are learning and reading.

> **Discussion**   Although "making words" is designated as a practice routine, it also teaches children about letter-sound associations and letter patterns. By regularly using this routine, children develop their abilities to decode words independently.

✴ Word Wall Routine

PURPOSE

Teachers put words on the wall in categories for various reasons. For decoding practice, the purpose is to help children see patterns in letter-sound associations. The Word Wall Routine helps students remember the sounds and words that they are learning and use them as they read and spell.

When using the routine for high-frequency words, the purpose is to help children learn the high-frequency word by alphabetizing it by the initial letter. For a science unit, the purpose might relate to science concepts and vocabulary.

WHEN TO USE

The Word Wall Routine is used in the Reading: Learning Skills and Strategies block of the Comprehensive Balanced Literacy Program. It is especially useful at the beginning literacy levels but may also be used at other levels for other purposes, such as to display an ongoing collection of words related to a particular topic.

DESCRIPTION/ PROCEDURES

The Word Wall Routine for decoding is used to display words that have the same sound patterns. A picture of a key word helps children remember the sound. The following guidelines will help you use the Word Wall Routine to reinforce the learning of letter-sound associations for both reading and writing:

1. As new letter-sound associations are taught, identify a key word that can be pictured to use as an exemplar of the sound:

Example:

Bb

Boris Bear

2. Display this on a bulletin board or on the wall.
3. As children learn to read words that contain the sound, add *some* of them to the wall. These words may be selected from any texts children are reading or from their writing. When a word is added to the wall, underline the common sound element.
4. At least once a week or oftener, play short games or do activities using the words on the wall:

Examples:

- READ AND THINK—Call on different children to *read* all the words under a particular sound and *think* of one or more to add.
- FIND AND READ—Say, "I'm thinking of words that start with /b/. Find the key word on the wall, read it, and read the list below."

Discussion When using the Word Wall Routine for letter-sound association instruction, group words by their common sound patterns even though the spellings are different. For example, words with the hard *c* or *k* sound, as in *cat,* should be grouped together or side-by-side to illustrate that the same sound is represented by different letters. Print the letters representing the common sound in a bright color. Figure 5.3 shows sections of a partial word wall.

Word walls are often used for high-frequency word practice (Cunningham, 2004). These words are also put up alphabetically but not by sound patterns. When using word walls for either letter-sound associations or high-frequency words, do follow-up activities such as "Read and Think" or "Find and Read."

FIGURE 5.3   **Partial Word Wall for Practicing Letter-Sound Associations**

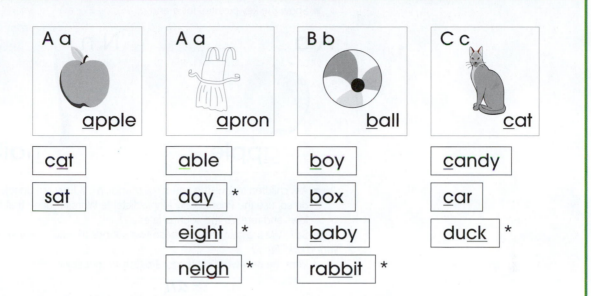

*These words are added as elements are taught. The most common elements are taught first. The variant spellings are not taught until the common spellings are learned.

Routines for High-Frequency Words

High-frequency words are those that occur many more times than other words in spoken or written language. These words must be given special attention in instruction because they occur in reading and writing so frequently (Hiebert, Pearson, Taylor, Richardson, & Paris, 1998). There are many lists of high-frequency words; one of the most common is the Dolch List of 220 Basic Sight Words (Dolch, 1936).

Decodable High-Frequency Words Routine

PURPOSE   This routine is used to teach high-frequency words that are completely decodable (examples: *at, it*) as soon as children have learned the decoding elements involved in the word.

WHEN TO USE   This routine can be used in both the Reading: Learning Skills and Strategies block and in the Reading: Application of Skills and Strategies block of the Comprehensive Balanced Literacy Program. It is used to introduce new high-frequency words before children read a text.

DESCRIPTION/ The following procedures should be used (Example—teaching *an*):
PROCEDURES
1. *Review the Sounds*
   - Show the key pictures for *a* and *n*.

   - Ask children to give the sounds /ă/ and /n/. If they are unable to do so, use the Phonetically Unpredictable Words routine that follows and reteach the sounds later.
   - Say, "We are going to use these two sounds to read a new word."
2. *Sound and Blend*
   - Print the new word on the board, but do not say it:

$$an$$

   - Point to each letter. Ask students to give the sound. Model or coach as needed.
   - Say, "Now let's blend the sounds to read the word [or "let's read the word"]."
   - Sweep your hand under the word as children blend. Model or coach as needed.
3. *Read the Word*
   - Print the word in a sentence:

$$I \ see \ \underline{an} \ apple.$$

(All words except *an* are known words or are decodable.)
   - Ask children to read the sentence.

See Chapter 6 for discussion of word banks.

Discussion Following the reading of the word in the sentence, give each child a 3" × 5" card. Tell the children to copy the word on one side and the sentence on the other side and then put the cards in alphabetical order in their word banks. Two or three times each week, have children play games with words in their banks, such as having them draw words from another person's bank and read it or play a game such as Fish.

Irregular and Phonetically Unpredictable High-Frequency Words Routine

PURPOSE

Use this high-frequency words routine with phonetically irregular and unpredictable words (ones that cannot be decoded, such as *the*) or with words for which children have not yet learned the necessary decoding skills.

WHEN TO USE

This routine can be used in the Reading: Learning Skills and Strategies and the Reading: Application of Skills and Strategies blocks of the Comprehensive Balanced Literacy Program.

DESCRIPTION/ PROCEDURES

Use the following procedures for this routine:

1. *Read the Word*
   - Write a sentence on the board with the word:

   ## The car is red.

   - Read the sentence aloud to the group. Ask children to read the sentence with you.
2. *Match the Word*
   - Distribute several 3″ × 5″ cards containing the word. Ask each child to find the word, match it by holding the card under it, and read the sentence aloud. Have the other children watching clap their hands softly if the child with the card is correct.
3. *Write the Word*
   - Hold up a word card containing the word or point to the word in the sentence. Say, "This word is *the, t-h-e*."
   - "Now you say and spell it."
   - Have children write the word on their papers or the board, saying and spelling the word as they write.

> **Discussion** Follow the instruction with many opportunities to read text containing the words taught. Provide repeated practice like that described in the Decodable High-Frequency Words Routine.

Routines for Reading

See Chapter 2 for a description of modes of reading.

Reading routines require students to read different types of texts in different ways. Many of the ideas related to the modes of reading concept also apply for these routines.

 ### Decodable Text Reading Routine

PURPOSE

Decodable texts provide beginning readers immediate opportunities to practice and apply in text what they are learning about decoding words and high-frequency words. Even though these texts are limited to a small number of words, they give children a chance to experience the pleasure of being able to read. Remember, children will find fun in books that may seem silly to an adult.

WHEN TO USE

This reading routine is used in the Reading: Learning Skills and Strategies block of the Comprehensive Balanced Literacy Program.

DESCRIPTION/ PROCEDURES

Decodable text reading is provided after each two or three skills are taught, in order to provide immediate practice and application. There is minimal focus on comprehension. You can use the literacy lesson to carry out this routine.

1. *Introduce the Text*
    - Show the cover of the text. Tell children that they are going to read this text to practice and apply the skills they have been learning.
    - Ask children to read the title.
    - Introduce any high-frequency words needed, using one of the routines presented earlier in this chapter.
2. *Read and Respond*
    - Direct children to read the text silently. Remind them to use the skill that has been taught. As they read, observe their behaviors and/or move from child to child asking each to read aloud softly to you. Note their ability to apply skills.
    - After reading, briefly discuss the story. Call on individuals to read aloud favorite parts, sentences that match illustrations, or places to prove or support their ideas.
    - Ask children to tell how they used the decoding skill being practiced or applied to figure out words.
3. *Extend the Text*
    - Provide opportunities for children to reread the text alone or use the Cooperative Reading Routine.
    - Reteach any decoding skills that seem to be causing difficulty.

> **Discussion**   The reading of decodable texts is a very short routine. In fact, at the very beginning stages of reading, you may use a new decodable text each day. Keep in mind that this reading is only one part of the literacy program. Your goal is to get children to the point of independent decoding and move them quickly to reading on their own using authentic literature.

 ## Fluency Reading Routine

PURPOSE

A major need for all children, but especially beginning readers, is to develop fluency (the ability to read texts quickly and accurately). The Fluency Reading Routine provides a procedure to help meet this goal. (See the Educators Speak feature on page 210 to see how to use technology to build fluency.)

WHEN TO USE

The Fluency Reading Routine is used in both the Reading: Learning Skills and Strategies block and the Reading: Application of Skills and Strategies block of the Comprehensive Balanced Literacy Program. Of course, fluency is also building during the Daily Independent Reading block when students read a book they choose. Here we discuss a planned routine for building fluency.

DESCRIPTION/ PROCEDURES

The texts used for the Fluency Reading Routine may be *any* of the texts used in your program after they have been read by the students. These texts should *always* be easy for children to read. Use the following guidelines to carry out this routine:

1. Select a book each child can read, or have children select their own from choices you provide. Often selections are made from baskets of books that children have read previously. Usually a small group will all be reading the same book.

2. Have children read their books silently.

Chapter 11 discusses evaluating oral reading in various ways.

3. As children read, move from child to child, asking him or her to read sections aloud to you. Note the child's fluency (i.e., speed of reading and accuracy). These observations will help you determine other skills that need to be taught. Students reading in a second language often read more slowly, and it is good to encourage them to increase their speed. An ELL mispronouncing some words does not reflect a lack of accuracy.

Note: Unless you are timing a child's oral reading fluency for evaluation purposes, simply note whether the child is reading quickly, smoothly, and accurately.

4. After reading, have children share and discuss their books with each other for a few minutes.

See Chapter 2, Table 2.1, for a complete description of several fluency building activities.

> **Discussion** The Fluency Reading Routine should be done regularly in your program. In the beginning, it should be a daily routine. You may also use the Cooperative Reading Routine for building fluency.

Read-Aloud Routine

PURPOSE

The Read-Aloud Routine is designed to help children develop vocabulary, oral language, and comprehension strategies. It is a critical part of helping children develop literacy. This routine uses wonderful, rich narrative and expository literature such as *Lucky Song* (Williams, 1997), *Goldilocks and the Three Bears* (Marshall, 1988), *The Real Slam Dunk* (Richardson, 2005), *Amazing Bats* (Simon, 2005), or *Great White Sharks Up Close* (Bredeson, 2006). The read-aloud routine can be used with students at all grade levels.

WHEN TO USE

The Read-Aloud Routine is used during the Reading: Application of Skills and Strategies block of the Comprehensive Balanced Literacy Program.

DESCRIPTION/ PROCEDURES

The format for the literacy lesson introduced in Chapter 2 can be adapted and used for the Read-Aloud Routine. You present and read aloud a wonderful book. However, here the primary focus is instructional. This routine does not replace the many times that you read aloud to children solely for pleasure. The following suggested procedures will help you use this routine.

1. *Introduce the Text*
   - Show the cover of the text and read the title; talk about other book parts. Briefly discuss content related to build background and concepts.

Educators Speak

Using Technology to Build Fluency

"My students are in their second year with me. They have bonded with each other and know each other and their personalities. I have some very creative individuals, as well as some very organized students. I have high achievers and students who struggle with learning. I have used lots of peer tutoring and projects to help build literacy learning. Here is one example of how I use technology to build fluency.

This project took us about three weeks to complete. We started to work on a class book that would cover number words and high-frequency words. My goal was to have the students take some ownership in the story, which would in turn make them want to reread their story over and over again for fluency.

Week 1: Students were asked to use the computers with the Kidspiration software program to develop their prewrite for a story about monsters. The students were asked to include some labeling with pictures in their webs. These were printed and kept for the next step. During this week, the students made lists of descriptive words for monsters. They gathered information from library books, their anthologies, and at home from the Internet. I assigned each student a partner to work to develop a page for the class book. By the end of this week, the pairs of students had been together to discuss their word lists, make some notes, and compare their graphic organizers.

Week 2: Students were assigned a number word. Their page would involve that number of monsters, and that number word would have to be used in their paragraph about their monster or monsters. They also knew to use some of the descriptive words we had compiled the week before. Students were assigned times to work on the computers while others developed their picture for their page. Each group printed what they produced during their computer time and saved to a disk for future use. I worked with each group to help revise and edit their work.

Week 3: Students took final copies of their work and illustrations and glued them to a page in our big book. I scanned each page and put it into a PowerPoint slide show and recorded myself reading the story. I burned the finished project to compact disks and placed one at each computer. The students were able to listen while reading and follow along with their story. They listened repeatedly to the story through the next week and still ask for it today. This project truly helped my students develop fluency.

—*Shari LaMunyon, First-Grade Teacher*
Vermillion Primary
Maize, Kansas

See Chapter 4 for a discussion of comprehension strategies.

- Ask children to *predict* what they think will happen or what they will learn or pose *questions* they think will be answered. During this time, you can begin to model comprehension, or construction of meaning, strategies. Record children's predictions or questions on the board or on a chart for later use.

2. *Read the Text*

- Remind the children to think about their predictions or questions as you read the text aloud.

Guidelines for reading aloud are in Chapter 2.

- Read aloud all or part of the text. Stop to discuss points or to clarify the meaning of words as needed.
- After reading, discuss children's predictions or questions. If you are reading a story, orally model summarizing by following the story map framework. If you are reading an informational book, summarize by listing the key points presented.
- From time to time, ask children to respond individually by drawing or by having brief discussions about favorite parts, characters, or what they learned.

3. *Extend the Text*
- Following the read-aloud, use the text to develop oral language, vocabulary, concepts, and additional background through discussion, role playing, puppets, or other oral activities.

Discussion The Read-Aloud Routine is used for instructional purposes. Every step teaches vital comprehension strategies. Keep in mind, however, that there should also be times when reading aloud is done just for pleasure.

Shared Reading Routine

See Chapter 9 on struggling readers.

PURPOSE

Shared reading, or the shared book experience, was developed by Holdaway (1979) as a means of introducing beginners to reading using favorite books, rhymes, and poems. Shared reading may also be adapted and used with older students. With this procedure, the teacher models reading for students by reading aloud a book or other text and ultimately inviting students to join in.

Shared reading builds on children's natural desire to read and reread favorite books. The repeated reading of texts over several days, weeks, or months deepens children's understanding of them (Yaden, 1988). Au (1991) suggests that such reading is not just random rereading. Rather, each time a child rereads a book with the teacher, the reading should be for a different purpose to extend, refine, and deepen the child's abilities to read and construct meaning.

Shared reading is especially good for ELLs because it helps make the written language comprehensible or understandable. Research has shown that shared reading improves English proficiency for ELL students (Elley, 1998).

WHEN TO USE

The Shared Reading Routine is used in the Reading: Application of Skills and Strategies block of the Comprehensive Balanced Literacy Program.

DESCRIPTION/ PROCEDURES

1. *Materials Needed*
- One copy of the book to be read in big-book form.
- Multiple copies of the book in little-book form for individual rereading after the big book has been read.

2. *Introduce the Book*
- Gather the children where they can all see the big book.
- Show and discuss the book cover; read the title, author, illustrator, and other appropriate book features.

- Motivate children by discussing the cover and some of the pages in the book, but don't give away the entire story. This activity also encourages children to activate and develop their prior knowledge.
- Invite children to predict what they think will happen in the book. If they have difficulty, model predicting by "thinking aloud" to show them how you would do it. Record predictions on the board or a chart for later reference. As the children gain experience, you can formally introduce the preview and predict strategy using the poster presented in Chapter 3 (page 89). The entire process for introducing the book should take no longer than 3 to 6 minutes.

3. *Read and Respond to the Book*
    - Read the book aloud to the children, holding it so they can see each page. Many teachers put the book on an easel. As you read, run your hand or a pointer under each line of print to help children develop a sense of left-to-right orientation, speech-to-print match, and other concepts of print. If some children wish to join in, encourage them to do so, though for a first reading, many children will just listen.
    - As you read, you may stop briefly to discuss the story or respond to reactions, but you should progress through the entire book rather quickly to give children a complete sense of the story.
    - At the conclusion of the reading, encourage children to respond, using questions such as the following prompts:

        Were your predictions right?
        What did you like in this story?
        What was your favorite part?
        What made you happy (or sad)?
        Who was your favorite character? Why?

    - Return to the book, rereading the story and inviting children to read along. Many will feel comfortable doing this right away, but others may not join in until another day. After the second reading, many children will say, "Let's read it again." This is especially true for books, songs, or rhymes that are lots of fun. Usually, when children want to reread, you *should* reread.
    - After you have read the book again, have children respond, using activities such as the following:
        - Talking with a friend about a favorite part
        - Retelling the story to a partner
        - Drawing a picture about the story and writing a word or a sentence about it
        - Drawing and writing about a favorite character
        - Writing a list of favorite characters

Help children become comfortable with making decisions about responding by giving them only a couple of choices initially. The amount of time devoted to reading and responding will be from 10 to 20 minutes, depending on the book and the children.

For more ideas for responding, see Chapter 7.

4. *Extend the Book*

You may want to wait until children have read a book several times before extending it or wait until they have read several books within a thematic unit and combine them for extension activities.

Each time you repeat a reading, you continue to model for the children. At the same time, you scaffold your instruction by transferring more and more responsibility to them. Although each repeated reading is fun, it carries important responsibilities for learning. The following suggestions should be helpful:

- Invite children to recall the title and what the book was about. Prompt and support them if needed.
- Tell children why they are rereading the book with statements such as the following:

"As we reread this book, let's think about who the important characters are." (comprehension)
"In our story today, notice how the author repeats lines over and over." (exploring language)
"Today, as we reread one of our favorite stories, look for places to use the phonic skills we have been learning." (decoding)

- After completing the rereading of the book, have children complete a response activity that again draws their attention to the purpose—for example:

Purpose: Comprehension
Prompt: Dramatize your favorite character.
Purpose: Explore language
Prompt: Write a group story using the story pattern. For example, after reading *Brown Bear, Brown Bear* (Martin, 1967), have children help write a story using the following pattern:

Brown Bear, Brown Bear, what do you see?

I see a redbird looking at me.

Red Bird, Red Bird, what do you see?

I see a _____ _____ looking at me.

_____ _____, _____ _____, what do you see?

I see a _____ _____ looking at me.

This response may also be done individually.

Purpose: Decoding
Prompt: List the words that have the sounds we have been learning. (Encourage children to use these words in stories they write.)

> **Discussion** Shared reading is powerful, versatile, and flexible. The activities allow children to apply what they are learning in the Reading: Learning Skills and Strategies block of the Comprehensive Balanced Literacy Program.

Observational Guided Reading Routine

PURPOSE

We refer to this routine as Observational Guided Reading to differentiate it from Interactive Guided Reading discussed in Chapter 2. Many just use the term *guided reading* and don't make the distinction given here. The Observational Guided Reading Routine is designed to help children use and develop the strategies of independent reading (Fountas & Pinnell, 1996). It provides children a time to apply what they are learning in the Reading: Learning Skills and Strategies block of the Comprehensive Balanced Literacy Program.

WHEN TO USE

The Observational Guided Reading Routine is used during the Reading: Application of Skills and Strategies block of the Comprehensive Balanced Literacy Program.

DESCRIPTION/ PROCEDURES

During Observational Guided Reading, children read texts that have a minimum of new words or skills to learn (Fountas & Pinnell, 1996). These texts are leveled and are at the students' developmentally appropriate reading level.

See the discussion on leveling texts in Chapter 2.

The children read in small groups (usually five to eight) with their teacher. The following guidelines, organized around the literacy lesson concept presented in Chapter 2, should be helpful to you in learning to use Observational Guided Reading.

1. *Introduce the Book*
   - Materials: Multiple copies of the book
   - Show the book cover. Read the title. Discuss other information on the cover. Ask students to *predict* what is going to happen in the text. Record the predictions. Do not give away the ending.
   - Conduct a picture walk using the book.

See Chapter 3 for an explanation of a text or picture walk.

2. *Read and Respond to the Book*
   - Direct students to read the book silently to see if their predictions are accurate. At the very beginning stages of reading, students may read aloud softly to themselves.
   - As the children read, observe their behaviors. Are some having difficulty with certain words or types of words? Are some tracking with their fingers while others are not?
   - Are children applying the decoding skills they have been taught? You can tell this when they read sections orally.
   - As you observe, look for one or two things you might help children with. For example, if several children seem to have trouble with the word *bent*, print it on the board and help them sequentially decode, or read through, the word by identifying each sound in order.
   - After reading, discuss students' predictions and what actually happened in the text.
   - Teach any decoding or comprehension skill or strategy needed.
3. *Extend the Book*
   - Have children reread the book alone or with a partner.
   - Children may also choose to act out or role-play the story with partners.

See Chapter 11 on running records.

 Discussion Observational Guided Reading should be a daily routine in the Comprehensive Balanced Literacy Program. It allows you to see children's progress and immediately help correct problems. When using this routine, you should take a running record on each child once every two weeks using books they have read.

Cooperative Reading Routine

For books on guided reading, see the "For Additional Reading" section.

PURPOSE As a routine for beginning reading instruction, cooperative reading involves partners' rereading texts that have been previously read. The primary purpose of this rereading is to build fluency and comprehension.

WHEN TO USE This routine may be used in either the Reading: Learning Skills and Strategies block or the Reading: Application of Skills and Strategies block of the Comprehensive Balanced Literacy Program.

DESCRIPTION/ PROCEDURES After the initial reading of any text, the Cooperative Reading Routine can be used to provide practice. It is best done with partners as opposed to triads (groups of three) because with the latter, there is always an odd person out. Use the following procedures with this routine:

1. Assign or have students select partners for cooperative reading.
2. Explain and model the process of cooperative reading with students:
   - Briefly discuss the book that has been previously read, drawing as much as possible from the children.
   - Have children take turns reading aloud sentences, paragraphs, or pages.
3. Observe the children to note their use of decoding skills and their fluency. Coaching or supporting some children may be needed during this time.
4. Direct students to briefly discuss what they have read with their partners.

Discussion The Cooperative Reading Routine is an effective way for children to practice reading of previously read text.

Routine for Comprehension

Explicit Comprehension Strategy Routine

PURPOSE The Explicit Comprehension Strategy Routine provides a pattern for explicitly teaching and modeling comprehension strategies. The strategies that should be taught include visualizing, making connections, monitoring, identifying important information, inferencing/predicting, monitoring/clarifying, generating and answering questions, summarizing/synthesizing, and evaluating.

See Chapter 4 for a detailed discussion of each strategy and teaching procedures.

WHEN TO USE This routine can be used in the Reading: Learning Skills and Strategies block or the Reading: Application of Skills and Strategies block of the Comprehensive Balanced Literacy Program.

DESCRIPTION/ PROCEDURES

This routine has three parts, with the teacher modeling the strategy at the *concept*, *listening*, and *reading* levels. The following sample is based on teaching the strategy of inferencing to beginning readers or struggling readers of any age.

1. Concept

a. Begin by developing the concept of inferencing. Use concrete materials and examples:

Say, "Look outside. Is the sun shining? Is it cloudy?" (Students respond.)

"What do these things indicate the weather is likely to be later in the day?" (Students respond.)

b. Discuss with students how they arrived at their answer (by looking outside, prior knowledge, logic). Tell students that this process is called *inferencing*.

2. Listening

a. Read aloud a short paragraph that requires students to infer.

Say, "Listen to this paragraph and tell what you think happened when Sara and Lisa went to the beach." Sara and her friend Lisa went to the beach. They took their beach ball, a blanket, and a picnic lunch. They wanted to play in the water and lie in the sun. As soon as they put out their blanket, the sun went behind a cloud. They heard a loud clapping sound.

b. Discuss students' responses. If they have difficulty with this process, model for them using a think-aloud and repeat the process using several additional examples.

c. Talk with students about how they arrived at their conclusion.

3. Reading

a. Select a piece of text students have read that requires inferencing.

b. Model the use of inferencing with a think-aloud.

Provide repeated practice and application through reading until students are comfortable using the strategy.

See Chapter 4 on procedures for teaching strategies.

Discussion For beginning readers, comprehension strategies can be modeled within the various reading routines. As texts become more challenging and readers become independent decoders, a more formal approach to modeling strategies should be used.

We have looked at a variety of beginning literacy routines. You will learn others as you teach. The routines presented in this section give you good resources to begin to plan a Comprehensive Balanced Literacy Program. Let's take a closer look to see how this can be done.

Planning Daily Instruction Using Routines

As you plan daily instruction for your class, you will use some routines every day and others only occasionally. The following four guidelines will help:

1. Keep in mind the model for the Comprehensive Balanced Literacy Program presented in Chapter 2. The six major blocks (Daily Independent Reading, Daily Independent Writing, Reading: Learning Skills and Strategies, Reading: Application of Skills and Strategies, Writing: Learning to Write, and Writing: Developmentally Appropriate Writing) should be included in each day's plan. There may be rare occasions when this is not true, but for the most part, this is your goal.

2. Lay out your daily schedule in blocks following the Comprehensive Balanced Literacy Program model. Often, blocks will overlap. (See Ms. Barbizon's schedule on page 218.)

3. Vary the routines you use. Although children like repetition and learn effectively when it is used, they also need some variety.

First and second graders work together in learning centers.
© Elizabeth Crews/The Image Works

For a discussion about how to organize and manage your classroom, see Chapter 10.

4. Select routines based on students' needs. Teaching is assessment; therefore, during all teaching-related activities, note student responses, and use this information to plan your instruction. For example, if during a Shared Reading Routine several children's responses show that they are not applying phonic elements that you have taught, you should return to the Explicit Phonics Routine and the Decodable Text Reading Routine for reteaching and more practice.

The following schedule from Ms. Barbizon, a first-grade teacher, shows how she uses a variety of routines each day. We added comments.

As You Read Ms. Barbizon's Plan

- Look for the variety of routines she uses.
- Note how she manages small groups by using independent reading and learning centers.
- Note how she schedules the six blocks of the Comprehensive Balanced Literacy Program.

Ms. Barbizon's Schedule
(19 first graders)
November 12

- Literacy block—8:45 to 11:45 daily
- Independent work—Five learning centers for writing, vocabulary, and spelling practice

TIME	ACTIVITY	ROUTINES	COMMENTS
8:45	READING: Application of Skills and Strategies – Reread the big book *The Lady with the Alligator Purse* (Wescott, 1988). – Discussion.	■ Shared Reading Routine	■ This previously read book provides application of previously taught letter-sound associations and high-frequency words. This also serves as a warm-up or opening activity.
9:00	Daily Independent Reading – Conference with Jeff, Lisa, Elaine, and Martha.		■ During this time students are practicing reading. Conferences help Ms. Barbizon check for decoding and other skill application to self-selected books.

TIME	ACTIVITY	ROUTINES	COMMENTS
9:10	READING: Learning Skills and Strategies – Teach digraphs *sh, ch, th*. – Practice and apply digraphs. ■ Read *Charlie's Shoes*.	■ Explicit Phonics Routine ■ Decodable Text Reading Routine ■ Observational Guided Reading Routine ■ Irregular and Phonetically Unpredictable Words Routine	■ Ms. Barbizon is continuing to teach the decoding skills students need. ■ Ms. Barbizon combines three routines. She meets with three small groups. While she meets with one group, the other children go to an assigned learning center.
10:10	Daily Independent Writing – Children add to journals.		■ Ms. Barbizon moves from child to child to see how they are spelling using the letter-sound associations taught so far this year.
10:20	WRITING: Learning to Write – Writing a group story. – Spelling words with *sh, ch, th*. *Spelling List* ■ chair ■ show ■ think ■ much ■ shop	■ Shared Writing Routine	■ Ms. Barbizon is connecting the explicit phonics instruction with spelling. The children help her write a group story. She works the spelling words into the story.
10:40	READING: Learning Skills and Strategies – Practice spelling words with digraphs *sh, ch, th*. – Add spelling words to word wall. – Review words on word wall.	■ Making Words Routine ■ Word Wall Routine	■ Ms. Barbizon returns to this block to provide more practice and connections for students.

See Chapter 8 for more information on the Shared Writing Routine.

TIME	ACTIVITY	ROUTINES	COMMENTS
11:00	WRITING: Developmentally Appropriate Writing – Children write own stories. – Encourage use of words from word wall.		■ This is a follow-up to the teacher-modeled writing. Ms. Barbizon moves from student to student to provide coaching. She is looking for application of skills previously taught and evidence of students' writing abilities.
11:15	READING: Application of Skills and Strategies – Read aloud *The 500 Hats of Bartholomew Cubbins* (Seuss, 1938) to teach noting important details using a simplified story map.	■ Read-Aloud Routine	■ Ms. Barbizon is teaching listening comprehension.
	– Partner practice reading (select any book already read).	■ Cooperative Reading Routine ■ Fluency Reading Routine	■ Children select any books they have read today or on another day. They read with a partner. Ms. Barbizon moves from pair to pair to note fluency and application of skills.
11:35	– Discuss what was learned today. Make a list on the board.		■ Ms. Barbizon concludes the literacy block by having children talk about what they learned. For example, children might say, "I learned a new word" or "I learned to read better." This helps children see the value of the literacy block.

You have focused on the important components of a beginning literacy program. You have learned a variety of routines to use within this program. Now let's focus on a specific literacy lesson that can be used in the program.

Standards-Based Literacy Lessons

A Standards-Based Lesson Using *No, No Titus!*

Standards Used in the Plan

- Sample standards are the First Grade Reading Standards from the Oregon Department of Education.
- The website at which you can find these standards is **http://www.ode.state.or.us/ teachlearn/real/standards/Default.aspx.** In this lesson, some Oregon indicators are addressed during the introductory activities and some during the reading and responding activities. We tell you how each indicator we included in our sample can be assessed.
- Remember to look at your own state standards to see how they compare to these standards at this grade level.

Reading

Concepts of Print: Analyze words, recognize words, and learn to read grade-level text fluently across the subject areas.

First Grade

EL.01.RE.02 Match oral words to printed words. (4 Resources)
Phonemic Awareness: Analyze words, recognize words, and learn to read grade-level text fluently across the subject areas.

First Grade

EL.01.RE.08 Orally blend two to four spoken phonemes (sounds) into recognizable words (e.g., /c/a/t/ = cat; /f/l/a/t/ = flat).
Decoding and Word Recognition: Analyze words, recognize words, and learn to read grade-level text fluently across the subject areas.

First Grade

EL.01.RE.12 Use letter-sound correspondence knowledge to sound out unknown words.
EL.01.RE.14 Read compound words and contractions.
EL.01.RE.17 Read common irregular sight words accurately and fluently (e.g., *the*, *have*, *said*, *come*, *give*, *of*).
EL.01.RE.18 Read aloud grade-level text with accuracy and comprehension in a manner that sounds like natural speech, using cues of punctuation to assist.
EL.01.RE.20 Read or demonstrate progress toward reading at an independent and instructional reading level appropriate to grade level. (4 Resources)

Listen to and Read Informational and Narrative Text: Listen to, read, and understand a wide variety of informational and narrative text across the subject areas at school and on own, applying comprehension strategies as needed.

First Grade

EL.01.RE.22 Demonstrate listening comprehension of more complex text through discussions. (5 Resources)

EL.01.RE.24 Notice when difficulties are encountered in understanding text. (5 Resources)

Vocabulary

First Grade

EL.01.RE.25 Understand, learn, and use new vocabulary that is introduced and taught directly through orally read stories and informational text as well as student-read stories and informational text.

EL.01.RE.26 Develop vocabulary by listening to and discussing both familiar and conceptually challenging selections read aloud.

EL.01.RE.30 Locate the title, name of author, name of illustrator, and table of contents.

EL.01.RE.33 Obtain information from print illustrations.

 ## No, No Titus!

1. Recall what you already know about the Shared Reading Routine. Discuss the chapter with a peer to clarify concepts.
2. Read the text and study the art of *No, No, Titus!* beginning on page 224.
3. Read the Teacher Preparation section beginning on this page, which explains the decision-making process of planning this lesson.

While Reading the Plan

1. Notice how the Shared Reading Routine is carried out.
2. Consider any changes you might have made had you written the lesson. Be ready to explain your thinking.
3. Read the Multilevel Notes to see how the teacher accommodates differences when everyone is reading the same text.

Teacher Preparation

This plan was developed for a first-grade class of twenty-two students in an urban setting. English is the second language for thirteen of these children, in whose homes several different languages are spoken. Two children have not yet begun speaking English at all, though they are beginning to understand some. The other eleven are at varying stages of acquiring oral English. The following outlines the steps used to plan the lesson and gives a rationale for each.

Unit Activities Prior to Reading the Book *No, No, Titus!*

1. The class is learning about farms and farm life as part of a larger unit about "work." The children have shared what they know about what foods are produced on farms, how the work is done, the animals, and how life on a farm differs from what they know in their urban setting.
2. The librarian has provided picture books, pictures, poems, and computer programs for children to share.

continued

3. I have identified a number of high-frequency words in the book: the words *said, the, a, to, be, what, was,* and *do* are on the first page.
4. Children have seen pictures of each animal, person, and vehicle in the book. They have learned the associated "noise" for each: bus, HONK-HONK; tractor, VROOM-VROOM; cow, MOO-MOO. . . and so forth. We have played a rhythm game that involved children taking turns wearing a mask indicating what vehicle or animal they are. As each is named, the child stands and all clap and say the appropriate "noise" words.

Major Outcomes and Standards Developed in This Lesson

You read earlier some Oregon state benchmarks and indicators met in this lesson.

1. Decoding and word recognition: reads common sight words (words that are often seen and heard).
2. Decoding and word recognition: uses initial consonant sounds (*t, s, b*) to read words.
3. Comprehension: confirms predictions after reading a given text.
4. Comprehension: uses details of a pattern story to understand farm life.
5. Literary response: increases knowledge about farm life; shares knowledge with peers and others; demonstrates understanding of story through discussion and writing of new text.

About This Lesson

1. The sample lesson that follows for *No, No, Titus!* uses the Shared Reading Routine.
2. The lesson includes ways to reread the book to practice known skills.
3. The first (and possibly second) reading of *No, No, Titus!* will be completed in one day.

As long as the group is interested, further rereadings can be carried out on several subsequent days to build fluency, reinforce known skills, and deepen understanding.

Standards-Based
Literacy
Lessons
continued

"Welcome to your new home, Titus," said the farmer.
"This farm needs a good dog!"
Titus wagged his tail. He wanted to be a good dog.
But what was a good dog supposed to do?

The farm was big and everyone was busy.

The school bus came down the road.
"HONK, HONK," went the school bus.
"WOOF, WOOF," barked Titus.
"No, no," said the children. "Dogs don't go to school!"

The farmer was plowing the fields.
"VROOM, VROOM," went the tractor.
"WOOF, WOOF," barked Titus.
"No, no," said the farmer. "Dogs don't drive tractors!"

The farmer's wife was milking.
"MOO, MOO," went the cow.
"WOOF, WOOF," barked Titus.
"No, no," said the cow. "Dogs don't give milk!"

The cat was chasing mice.
"MEOW, MEOW," went the cat.
"WOOF, WOOF," barked Titus.
"No, no," said the cat. "Dogs don't chase mice."

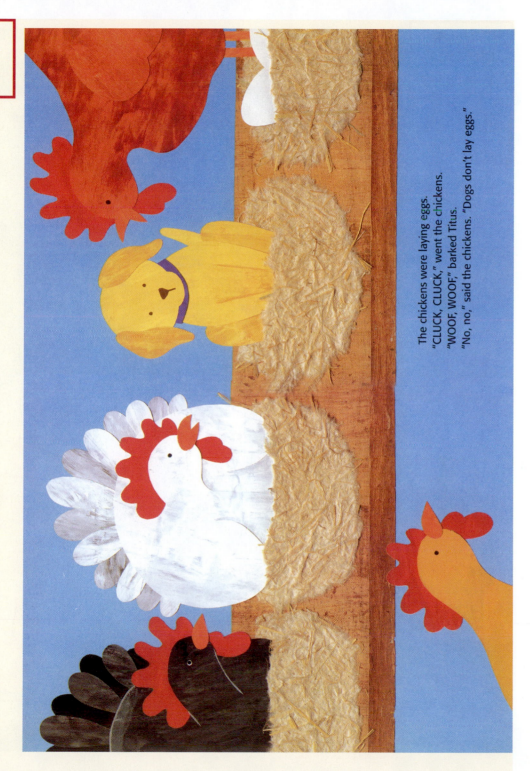

The chickens were laying eggs.
"CLUCK, CLUCK," went the chickens.
"WOOF, WOOF," barked Titus.
"No, no," said the chickens. "Dogs don't lay eggs."

Titus wanted to be a good farm dog.
But if dogs don't go to school, or drive tractors,
or give milk, or catch mice, or lay eggs . . .
what was Titus supposed to do?
He crawled into his doghouse and went to sleep.

Pitter, patter, pitter, patter.
Something was going to the chicken coop!
"WOOF, WOOF!" barked Titus.

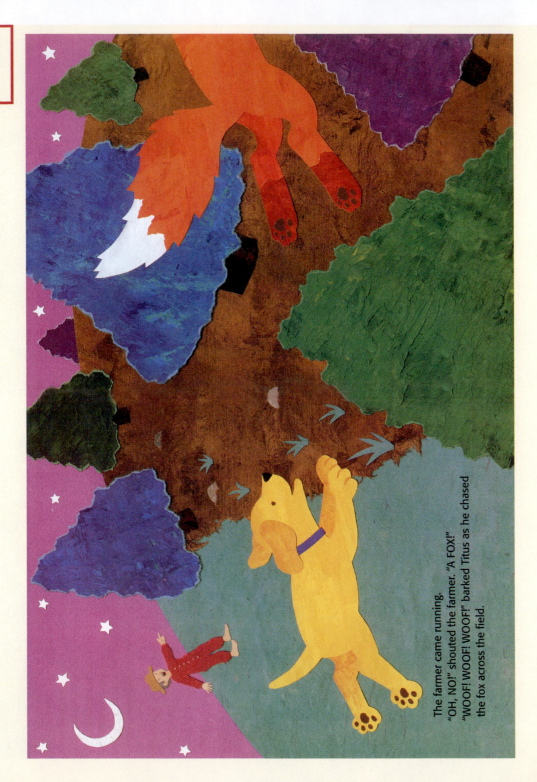

The farmer came running.
"OH, NO!" shouted the farmer. "A FOX!"
"WOOF! WOOF! WOOF!" barked Titus as he chased
the fox across the field.

**Standards-Based
Literacy
Lessons**

continued

"YIP, YIP, YIP, YIP," cried the fox, and it disappeared into the forest.

"HOORAY! HOORAY!" cheered the farmer, his wife, the children, and all the animals.
"What a good watchdog!"
"WOOF, WOOF!" barked Titus. "WOOF! WOOF! WOOF!"

✳ Introducing *No, No, Titus!*

Activity	Procedures, Comments and Multilevel Notes
Song; opening activity	1. Teach children the song *Old MacDonald Had a Farm* to use as a framework.
	2. Display and teach the following words and sounds from the book. Sounds should be shown in capital letters as in the book, but you might also show them in lowercase letters: *tractor* (VROOM-VROOM), *bus* (HONK-HONK), *dog/Titus* (WOOF-WOOF), *cow* (MOO-MOO), *cat* (MEOW-MEOW), *fox* (YIP-YIP-YIP), *farmer, wife, and children* (HOORAY-HOORAY). Sing the song together, pointing to words in random order.
	3. Review what the children remember from what they know about farms and the role of each of the people and animals on a farm.
	Comment: *Motivates, activates prior knowledge, stimulates oral language.*
Present the book and make predictions	1. Show the big book; read the title, author, and illustrator. Discuss the role of the author and the illustrator.
	2. Focus attention on the cover art, and ask volunteers for comments related to the pictures or the print.
	Comment: *Accept all comments; these could relate to the people or animals, colors, facial expressions, or the print. Some children may note familiar letters and say the sounds.*
	Multilevel Note: *Children who speak other languages may name the people, animals, and colors in their languages.*
	3. Reread the title and ask for predictions. Record the predictions, and tell students they will think about these predictions again later.
	Comment: *When children make predictions, they give themselves a purpose for reading.*
	4. Show the first two-page "spread." Have children tell what they think is happening. Read aloud the page ending with, "But what was a good dog supposed to do?" Invite children to change their predictions based on what they now know about the story.
	Comment: *Revising predictions with new information is a valuable thinking skill. You may want to lead children to "think like an author" at this point. Ask them to consider what story they would write with this title and this beginning.*

Standards-Based Literacy Lessons

continued

> **Assessment Note:** Assess the following Oregon standards while introducing *No, No, Titus!*:
> While showing the big book:
> - EL.01.RE.30
> - EL.01.RE.33
> While discussing the first two-page "spread" with children:
> - EL.01.RE.25
> - EL.01.RE.26
> - EL.01.RE.33

 ## Reading and Responding to *No, No, Titus!*

Activity	Procedures, Comments, and Multilevel Notes
Read the story aloud to children	1. Position the big book so everyone can see. Read each page aloud, sweeping your hand or a pointer under the words. Watch the children's faces for signs that they want to stop and talk about something. Otherwise, read straight through for pleasure. **Comment:** *This method of reading aloud to children models fluent reading.* 2. Reread the story, inviting children to join you. Hesitate before reading the "noises" so children can chime in. 3. Return to the predictions and compare them to the story. 4. Return to the text and ask differentiated questions of individual children to focus them on oral language, phonic skills, vocabulary, or comprehension. **Multilevel Note:** *Such questions allow you to include children at all literacy stages. Following are some examples of such questions: Find a word on this page that begins with the same sound as your name. Come up and point to a word that begins with the sound /d/. What parts of this story could be real? What couldn't? Which jobs on the farm have to be learned? Which are done naturally? Give a word that rhymes with dog.*
Respond to the story; collaborate on a new story **Subsequent rereadings**	1. Use *No, No, Titus!* as a framework, and help children dictate a new story. Make copies of the collaboration for each student. **Comment:** *The following are some possible ways to use subsequent rereadings to build fluency, construct meaning, reinforce skills, build oral language, and relate to literature.*

Standards-Based **Literacy** **Lessons** *continued*	**Activity**	**Procedures, Comments, and Multilevel Notes** (continued)

Procedures, Comments, and Multilevel Notes (continued)

1. Help children summarize or retell the story. Record the events as they recall them, and then compare to the book as you reread.

2. Distribute copies of the book to partners, and have pairs of children reread the story together.

   Comment: *Circulate as partners read to assess, coach, and guide children to use their skills.*

   Multilevel Note: *Sometimes one child may read aloud to a partner, pointing to the words and pausing to let the other child fill in the next word or attempt to decode a word.*

3. Encourage children to reread the version the class wrote independently or with a partner.

4. If children keep individual journals, encourage a written or picture response to the book.

   Multilevel Note: *All children, regardless of background or ability, can respond in some way.*

Assessment Note: Assess the following Oregon standards while reading and responding to *No, No, Titus!*:

While reading the story aloud:
- EL.01.RE.02

While comparing the children's predictions to the story:
- EL.01.RE.25
- EL.01.RE.26

While asking differentiated questions of individual children:
- EL.01.RE.08
- EL.01.RE.14
- EL.01.RE.17

As children summarize the story:
- EL.01.RE.22

As children read the story with a partner:
- EL.01.RE.08
- EL.01.RE.14
- EL.01.RE.20
- EL.01.RE.24

After Reading the Plan

1. With a partner, talk about other ways you could have planned this lesson.
2. Use one or more routines to plan a lesson for a different book.
3. Observe a primary teacher (K–2) who uses the Shared Reading Routine. Make notes about the teacher and the children. Make an appointment with the teacher to discuss your observations. Be prepared to share your observations with your peers.

Beginning Literacy: Key Points

To review the Key Points, see the ACE practice tests at the Student Website.

- The two big jobs of learning to read are decoding and comprehension, with decoding receiving the most emphasis at the beginning stage.

- Most words beginnings readers meet in print are already in their oral language.

- Six elements are necessary for independence in decoding: oral language, phonemic awareness, concepts of print, letter-sound associations (phonics/structure), analogy, and a way to think about words.

- Comprehensive balanced beginning literacy instruction is carried out through routines for decoding, reading, and comprehension. The fourteen routines presented in this chapter are listed in the How Do I Teach? box.

- Some routines will be used within any literacy lesson. An example was the first-grade lesson for *No, No, Titus!*

How Do I Teach?

Phonemic Awareness Routine, p. 194
Explicit Phonics Routine, p. 197
Analogy Routine, p. 201
Making Words Routine, p. 202
Word Wall Routine, p. 203
Decodable High-Frequency Words Routine, p. 205

Irregular and Phonetically Unpredictable High-Frequency Words Routine, p. 207
Decodable Text Reading Routine, p. 207
Fluency Reading Routine, p. 208
Read-Aloud Routine, p. 209

Shared Reading Routine, p. 211
Observational Guided Reading Routine, p. 214
Cooperative Reading Routine, p. 215
Explicit Comprehension Strategy Routine, p. 215

Video Case in This Chapter

- **Elementary Reading Instruction: A Balanced Literacy Program**

For Additional Reading

Barton, J., & Sawyer, D. M. (2003–2004). Our students *are* reading for this: Comprehension instruction in the elementary school. *The Reading Teacher, 57*(4), 334–347.

Bear, D. R., Invernizzi, M., Templeton, S., & Templeton, F. (2008). *Words their way: Word study for phonics, vocabulary, and spelling instruction* (4th ed.). Englewood Cliffs, NJ: Prentice Hall.

Bradley, B. A., & Jones, J. (2007). Sharing alphabet books in early childhood classrooms. *The Reading Teacher, 60*(5), 452–463.

Brown, K. J. (2003). What do I say when they get stuck on a word? Aligning teachers' prompts with students' development. *The Reading Teacher, 56*(8), 720–733.

Clark, K. F. (2004). What can I say besides "sound it out"? Coaching word recognition in beginning reading. *The Reading Teacher, 57*(5), 440–449.

Cole, A. D. (2006). Scaffolding beginning readers: Micro and macro cues teachers use during student oral reading. *The Reading Teacher, 59*(5), 450–459.

Cunningham, P. M. (2005). *Phonics they use: Words for reading and writing* (4th ed.). Boston: Pearson/Allyn & Bacon.

Fountas, I. C., & Pinnell, G. S. (1996). *Guided reading: Good first teaching for all children.* Portsmouth, NH: Heinemann.

Gambrell, L. B. (2004). Exploring the connection between oral language and early reading. *The Reading Teacher, 57*(5), 490–492.

Gill, S. R. (2006). Teaching rimes with shared reading. *The Reading Teacher, 60*(2), 191–193.

Gonzalez-Bueno, M. (2003). Literacy activities for Spanish-English bilingual children. *The Reading Teacher, 57*(2), 189–192.

Kelley, M., & Clausen-Grace, N. (2006). R[5]: The Sustained Silent Reading makeover that transformed readers. *The Reading Teacher, 60*(2), 148–156.

Meier, T. (2003). "What can't she remember that?" The importance of storybook reading in multilingual, multicultural classrooms. *The Reading Teacher, 57*(3), 242–252.

Mesmer, H. A. E., & Griffith, P. L. (2005/2006). Everybody's selling it—But just what is explicit, systematic phonics instruction? *The Reading Teacher, 59*(4), 366–376.

Palmer, R. G., & Stewart, R. A. (2003). Nonfiction trade book use in primary grades. *The Reading Teacher, 57*(1), 38–48.

Rasinski, T. (2006). Reading fluency instruction: Moving beyond accuracy, automaticity, and prosody. *The Reading Teacher, 59*(7), 704–706.

Richards, J. C., & Anderson, N. A. (2003). How do you know? A strategy to help emergent readers make inferences. *The Reading Teacher, 57*(3), 290–293.

Villaume, S. K., & Brabham, E. G. (2003). Phonics instruction: Beyond the debate. *The Reading Teacher, 56*(5), 478–482.

Wasburn-Moses, L. (2006). 25 best Internet sources for teaching reading. *The Reading Teacher, 60*(1), 70–75.

Wright, G., Sherman, R., & Jones, T. B. (2004). Are silent reading behaviors of first graders really silent? *The Reading Teacher, 57*(5), 546–553.

Websites

Visit the following websites to gain more information about beginning reading instruction.

Teaching Word-Identification Skills and Strategies: A Balanced Approach
http://www.eduplace.com/rdg/res/teach/

National Association for the Education of Young Children
The National Association for the Education of Young Children (NAEYC) is the nation's largest and most influential organization of early childhood educators and others dedicated to improving the quality of programs for children from birth through third grade.
http://www.naeyc.org
Enter "Beginning reading software" into a search engine to find websites that can lead you to products designed for helping children during beginning reading instruction. Here are a few companies that publish such material.
http://www.learningco.com
http://www.hmco.com
http://teacher.scholastic.com/wiggleworks/index.htm
http://www.steckvaughn.harcourtachieve.com

Intermediate Grades and Middle School: Decoding, Vocabulary, and Meaning

6

Terms
YOU NEED TO KNOW

- base words
- context
- direct teaching
- hierarchical array
- inflectional endings
- linear array
- prefixes
- root words
- semantic feature analysis
- suffixes
- Tier One words
- Tier Two words
- Tier Three words
- word bank (word file, word book)

*L*et's sit in the back of the room and enjoy an interlude in Ms. Li's sixth-grade class. Students have just returned from lunch.

Ms. Li grins and pulls out several books that the students obviously recognize. They turn and high-five each other. They clearly expect to enjoy themselves.

Ms. Li asks if anyone has a favorite poem he or she would like her to read. Several call out together, "Never Mince Words with a Shark." Ms. Li opens The New Kid on the Block *(Prelutsky, 1984) and reads the poem with pleasure, her class chiming in on the last line of each verse. Ms. Li then reads a couple of her own favorites: "What Is the Matter with 'P'?" (*Words, Words, Words, *O'Neill, 1966) and "Apology" (*If I Were in Charge of the World, *Viorst, 1981).*

Finally, she pulls out The Annotated Alice *(Carroll, 1960) and reads the first stanza of "Jabberwocky." Ms. Li displays the first stanza, tells students to focus on just the sounds, and has them read it aloud with her. Students then identify words they didn't understand (brillig, slithy, mimsy), and Ms. Li reads aloud the annotations about each made-up word in the first stanza. Afterward, they reread the stanza together.*

Most students enjoy "Jabberwocky," but some have puzzled looks on their faces, and one says, "That's silly!" Ms. Li allows a free discussion about word play, including making up words.

Ms. Li tells the students to get into their discussion groups. She directs them to select, read aloud, and discuss pieces of poetry from several different anthologies. As the groups work, she calls a small group of students to the reading area for a lesson on the strategy of decoding longer words. She has determined from her observations that these students need this instruction.

After she completes her lesson, Ms. Li closes the reading period with a promise to read more poetry the next day. Several students want to know about the rest of the words in "Jabberwocky," and Ms. Li gives them the annotated book for independent perusal.

The HM TeacherPrepSPACE Student Website offers many helpful resources, such as self-quizzes, glossary flashcards, lesson plan templates, and more.

This short visit to Ms. Li's classroom reflects the varying needs of upper elementary and middle school students. Though this was not a *vocabulary* lesson, it served two valuable purposes: to share pleasure in language—to increase awareness of words. The student who found "Jabberwocky" silly may relish the language in a different poem on another day. Ms. Li shares and values all kinds of poetry. She encourages students to share poems they have found and to compile personal anthologies of favorites. Ms. Li also includes the direct instruction students need to continue their growth in decoding.

In this chapter, we look at strategies and techniques for developing decoding, vocabulary, and meaning for upper elementary and middle school students. We will focus most heavily on vocabulary strategies, because the strategies and routines suggested for decoding at the beginning literacy levels (Chapter 5) and the strategies and routines suggested for constructing meaning (Chapter 4) will continue to be used at the upper elementary and middle school levels.

Standards at the Upper Elementary and Middle School Levels

See Chapter 5 for several routines for decoding.

Look at a copy of your state standards. Note that at the upper elementary and middle school levels, the same categories of standards continue: decoding, vocabulary, meaning, strategy use, and reading across subject matter, but they become increasingly sophisticated.

Decoding Needs of Upper Elementary and Middle School Students

See Chapter 9, "Helping Struggling Readers," for helping students who have not yet mastered basic decoding skills.

Most students will have mastered the basic decoding strategies and skills by the end of second or third grade. The major focus of decoding instruction, once students have mastered the basic skills, is on helping students to gain more independence as they meet an increasing number of words that are not in their oral vocabularies. This includes applying the decoding skills and strategies they have learned, learning structural analysis, and learning to use the dictionary effectively. Recall that Ms. Li in our opening scenario taught a small group of students the strategy for decoding longer words. Teaching structural analysis and using the dictionary are discussed later in this chapter.

Vocabulary Development

The goal of vocabulary development is to help students become independent learners who know how to use strategies for inferring or learning the meaning of unknown words when they encounter them (Bear et al., 2008). Thus, students increase the number of words that are familiar as they read and the words that they can use when they speak and write.

As readers develop vocabulary, they learn two aspects about words: recognition and meaning (Chall, 1987). These two aspects, however, *are not* separate from each other. Children's *recognition vocabulary* consists of that body of words they are able to pronounce or read orally; this receives the most attention for beginning readers. Children's *meaning vocabulary* is that body of words whose meanings they understand and can use. *Recognition and meaning vocabularies develop simultaneously as students learn to read and write.*

Students' recognition vocabulary ultimately becomes sight vocabulary, or words they are able to read instantly and use in constructing meaning. Beginning readers and writers rapidly build such vocabularies through reading and writing experiences.

What We Know About Meaning Vocabulary and Constructing Meaning

Vocabulary reflects an individual's prior knowledge and concepts in a particular area. For example, a person who is knowledgeable about music understands and uses the words *meter, clef,* and *timbre* in ways that reflect musical knowledge, and an avid gardener knows and uses terms such as *perennial, deciduous,* and *Gaillardia.*

The study of vocabulary has interested researchers and educators for many years (Beck & McKeown, 1991). Research long ago established a strong relationship between the knowledge of word meanings (vocabulary) and reading comprehension (Anderson & Freebody, 1981; Davis, 1971; Johnston, 1981). In the past, the strength of this relationship led educators to recommend that students be taught crucial word meanings before reading selections (Tierney & Cunningham, 1984). Later researchers challenged the wisdom of this procedure and others related to teaching vocabulary to improve comprehension (Nagy, 1988).

Improving an individual's ability to construct meaning involves a great deal more than just teaching a few words before a selection is read. We will address two significant issues to help you more fully understand the strong relationship between vocabulary knowledge and comprehension. First, how do learners acquire vocabulary knowledge? Second, does direct instruction in vocabulary lead to improved comprehension?

How Learners Acquire Vocabulary Knowledge

Studies of the size of children's vocabularies have given varying estimates for various grade levels (Loban, 1963; Lorge & Chall, 1963; Nagy & Anderson, 1984; Seashore, 1947). The discrepancies may have arisen because researchers used different definitions for what constituted a word, different concepts of what it means to know a word, and different bodies of words to represent English (Beck & McKeown, 1991). In light of these problems, researchers have concluded that the early estimates of vocabulary size are much too low (Nagy & Anderson, 1984). A reasonable estimate based on research places the *average* high school senior's vocabulary at approximately forty thousand words (Nagy & Herman, 1987). When the figures on vocabulary size are compared from year to year, it appears that students must learn twenty-seven hundred to three thousand new words per year (Beck & McKeown, 1991; Nagy & Herman, 1987), or approximately seven new words per day, to achieve this forty thousand average by the time they are seniors in high school.

The question, then, is: How do students acquire this astounding vocabulary? There are several plausible answers: through reading and/or listening to a wide variety of texts and other media and/or through direct instruction in word meanings. Extensive research on both of these points of view (Beck & McKeown, 1991; Blachowicz & Fisher, 2000; McKeown & Curtis, 1987; Nagy, 1988) has led to four major positions on how students acquire vocabulary (Beck & McKeown, 1991). Given the strength of the research supporting these four positions and our own experiences with children, we must consider all four as viable ways for students to acquire vocabulary.

Four Major Positions on How Students Acquire Vocabulary

1. Students learn some words from direct instruction in vocabulary (Beck, McKeown, & Kucan, 2002; Beck, McKeown, & Omanson, 1987; Graves, 1986, 1987; Stahl & Fairbanks, 1986; Stahl & Nagy, 2006).

2. Students develop some vocabulary knowledge through wide reading (Fielding, Wilson, & Anderson, 1986; Nagy & Herman, 1987; Stahl & Nagy, 2006).

3. Students learn some vocabulary from context but need instruction about context to use it effectively (Jenkins, Stein, & Wysocki, 1984; Stahl & Nagy, 2006; Sternberg, 1987).

4. Students are often hindered as much as they are helped by context. Therefore, learning vocabulary from context must be viewed as only a small part of the way students develop an extensive vocabulary. Students should be encouraged to use the dictionary as an aid in acquiring word meanings (Schatz & Baldwin, 1986; Stahl & Nagy, 2006).

The components of the Comprehensive Balanced Literacy Program are described in Chapter 2.

The research supporting wide reading as a means of improving both vocabulary and overall reading is very powerful and must be taken seriously. This is part of the rationale for having an independent reading and writing component in the literacy program. *But* while students are reading widely, they need to become independent in inferring word meanings; therefore, helping them develop an independent strategy for doing this through the use of context, the dictionary, and structural analysis will serve them well. Finally, *some students under some circumstances* profit from the direct teaching of vocabulary. We need to examine carefully what we know about direct teaching of vocabulary to determine how and when we should do it.

Direct Vocabulary Instruction and Constructing Meaning

It has been a long-standing practice to preteach words that are perceived to be critical for understanding a selection. This practice has been justified on the basis of research that shows a strong correlation between the knowledge of word meanings and comprehension. There are two important questions to consider when thinking about the **direct teaching** of vocabulary: (1) Does it improve comprehension? and (2) If direct teaching is used, how and when should it be done?

Direct Vocabulary Teaching and Improved Comprehension

The goal of teaching vocabulary is to improve students' overall comprehension. Early studies in this area had mixed results: some found that direct teaching did improve overall comprehension, whereas others found that it improved knowledge only of the specific words taught and had little or no effect on overall comprehension (Jenkins & Pany, 1981; Mezynski, 1983). Still other studies found that the direct teaching of selected words results in small but significant improvements in comprehension (Beck, McKeown, & Kucan, 2002; McKeown, Beck, Omanson, & Pople, 1985; Stahl, 1983; Stahl & Fairbanks, 1986; Weiss, Mangrum, & Liabre, 1986; Wixson, 1986). The determining factors seem to have been how the words were taught.

How and When Direct Teaching Is Effective

Direct teaching of vocabulary refers to activities in which information about the meanings of words is made directly available to students. This may range from strong teacher-led lessons to weaker forms of instruction, such as having students look up words in a dictionary (Beck & McKeown, 1991). In several studies, effective instruction appears to have had several important qualities:

1. *Only a few words central to the content of the story or informational text were taught* (Beck, Perfetti, & McKeown, 1982; Wixson, 1986). In other words, the random teaching of any unknown word does not help students improve their comprehension. The words must be key-concept words.

2. *Words were taught in meaningful contexts that conveyed the particular meanings relevant to the text* (Gipe, 1978/1979; Nagy & Herman, 1987). Because words have multiple meanings, teaching a meaning that does not fit the material to be read is fruitless for students and may even hinder overall comprehension.

3. *The teaching of vocabulary was integrated with the activation and development of prior knowledge.* Vocabulary is a specialized version of prior knowledge (Nagy & Herman, 1987). In all studies that succeeded in improving comprehension by teaching vocabulary, the words taught were in some way related to the students' prior knowledge.

4. *Teachers taught words thoroughly by offering students rich and varied information about them* (Beck et al., 1987; Nagy & Herman, 1987; Stahl & Fairbanks, 1986). Simply presenting definitions is not sufficient to teach students words; the words must be related to one another and to students' experiences. When possible, they were grouped into topical or semantic categories (Stevens, 1982).

5. *Students were exposed to a word many times* (Nagy & Herman, 1987). Knowledge of word meanings is gained in increments through many experiences. Therefore, words must be used in a variety of situations, such as writing and reading, to help students achieve ownership of them.

6. *Students were actively involved in the process of learning the words* (Beck et al., 1987; Nagy & Herman, 1987). Students were not passive learners who were simply being told information or definitions. They verbalized what they had learned and related it to their own lives.

Although research reveals these consistent characteristics of effective teaching, *it does not show that there is any one best method for achieving these qualities* (Beck & McKeown, 1991). Rather, a variety of techniques should be used for such instruction.

Another question about direct vocabulary teaching is when to provide it: before reading, during reading, or after reading. Researchers recommend teaching

A middle school teacher teaches vocabulary.
© Bill Aron/Photo Edit

vocabulary before, during, and/or after reading depending on the text to be read and the students involved (Beck, McKeown, McCaslin, & Burkes, 1979).

Many researchers have looked at the effects of preteaching vocabulary on students' overall comprehension (McKeown et al., 1985; Stahl, 1983; Weiss et al., 1986; Wixson, 1986). Although they all obtained positive results, they did not compare their preteaching with the effects of vocabulary instruction provided during or after reading instruction. As Tierney and Cunningham (1984) state, "These conclusions lead us to question the practice of cursorily introducing new word meanings before having students read. This practice is probably only justified when just one or two crucial words are taught at some depth" (p. 612).

Conditions for Direct Teaching of Vocabulary

Direct teaching of vocabulary is likely to lead to improved comprehension *only* when certain conditions are met (Beck, McKeown, & Kucan, 2002; Snow, Burns, & Griffin, 1998; Stahl & Fairbanks, 1986). The teacher can use the few words that are taught to model the process of learning word meanings. Direct teaching of vocabulary-related skills, such as the use of context clues, prefixes, suffixes, base words, and the dictionary, should occupy a small proportion of instructional time; incidental teaching at point of use or need may be of more value.

Conditions for Direct Teaching of Vocabulary

- A *few* key words are thoroughly taught in meaningful context.

- Words are related to students' prior knowledge in ways that actively involve them in learning.

- Students are given multiple exposures to the words.

Elements of Effective Vocabulary Development

Vocabulary knowledge should be considered part of prior knowledge. Students who have prior knowledge about a topic usually have the vocabulary to talk about that knowledge. They know the words for the concepts, although some, such as English Language Learners, may have the prior knowledge but lack the words to express that knowledge. Vocabulary development as described in this chapter will stimulate growth in the vocabulary of all students. You will decide which students need which kind of support.

As a teacher, you are responsible for implementing the literacy program in your classroom. Effective vocabulary development within that same program includes three important elements (Blachowicz & Fisher, 2000). In the following pages, you will learn about each:

- *Awareness of words.* This refers to students' self-awareness and motivation to learn words. We present activities that develop awareness of words.

- *Wide reading and extensive writing.* This refers to reading and writing that students choose to do; that is, it is self-selected. We suggest ways to support this in and out of the classroom.

- *Independent strategies that lead to vocabulary learning.* This refers to strategies that initially may need to be taught but eventually become part of students' ability to independently determine word meaning and increase vocabulary.

Awareness of Words

Considering the enormous number of words students encounter and need to learn, it is obvious that not all of them can be taught. Therefore, we must make students aware of learning words and create an intrinsic motivation and interest, so that they will learn words independently. Teachers, peers, books, magazines, and electronic books are excellent catalysts for this motivation and interest.

Being aware of and interested in words helps students develop ownership of them. This happens when students see how a word relates to their overall backgrounds (Beck, 1984). Students make connections; they develop networks of words and their relationships through repeated experiences with the words in their reading and writing and through activities specifically designed to help them build relationships among words. Thus, while first encounters with a word may help students learn its meaning, it is repeated use that develops ownership. As readers develop ownership of words, they relate them to their existing schemata and develop new schemata, thus cementing the ownership.

Many different types of activities help to promote awareness of words. The following suggestions are integral parts of reading and writing or extensions of reading and writing.

Noting Words in Journals

For more information on the use of journals, see Chapter 7.

As students keep journals, have them make personal lists of words that interest them or those they would like to discuss with a group, a peer, or you. Direct students to choose words that interest or puzzle them rather than having them simply identify all the words they do not know. This places the focus of such activities on what students can do, and makes it a positive learning experience. A related strategy, self-collection, is discussed later in this chapter.

Reading Aloud to Students

Listening to someone read aloud is an excellent way for students to become aware of words and expand their oral vocabulary, which is the foundation for all other vocabulary learning. As you are reading aloud a book such as *Anastasia Krupnik* (Lowry, 1979), stop periodically and discuss words such as *Hubbard Squash, ostentatious,* and others that might be interesting, unusual, or fun for children to think about. Books that are especially written to focus on certain types of words can be read aloud before students read them independently. Some examples are *Delivery Van: Words for Town and Country* (Maestro & Maestro, 1990), *Taxi: A Book of City Words* (Maestro & Maestro, 1989), *The Weighty Word Book* (Levitt, Burger, & Guralnick, 1985), and *Murfles and Wink-a-Peeps* (Sperling, 1985). For your own reference, you might want to have available a book about word histories, such as *Word Mysteries and Histories* (Editors of the American Heritage Dictionary, 2006), or other books about words, such as *Miss Alainious* (Frasier, 2000) and *Word Wizard* (Falwell, 1998).

Discussion Groups

See Chapter 7 for information about literature discussions.

After students have read a book, encourage them to respond to it and talk about words of interest. When students have read different books, they'll enjoy sharing funny or unusual words from what they have read. This motivates others to want to read the same book.

Word Banks, Word Files, and Word Books

In primary grades, students write words and sentences on coin-shaped cards and deposit them into banks made of plastic bottles or other containers and can "withdraw" them for review.

Devices such as word banks, word files, and word books are the students' personal files of words they have learned or want to learn. The words can come from books students have already read, from areas of study such as science, from interest areas, from writing, and from other sources, such as newspapers or the Internet. The student writes each word on a card or in a word book, along with a sentence using it and relating it to prior knowledge. **Word banks** (**word files** or **word books**) can be created in a word-processing program and saved on students' personal backup files. For example, a student might write the following sentence for the word *periodic:* "In my class, we have *periodic* tests in math two times a month."

Always encourage students to use the banked words in their writing.

Writing

Writing makes students aware of words and promotes ownership. Through shared writing and minilessons, you can help students be conscious of using a variety of words and using more descriptive words. When students use new words in their writing, you can be sure they have started to take ownership of them.

Word Expansion Activities

After several students have read the same book or worked together in a unit on the same topic, they can use such activities as word maps, semantic maps, or **semantic feature analysis** to play with the words that interest them. These activities are discussed later in this chapter.

Bulletin Boards or Word Walls

Bulletin boards that students develop to display words of interest or words on a particular topic, or word walls with lists of these words, also promote awareness and ownership. Students can then be encouraged to use the words from the bulletin board or word wall in their writing.

Electronic Books and Software

See Chapter 8 on writing.

If you have access to writing programs on CD-ROMs and software for student writing, take advantage of the ways they support literacy development.

These activities all stem from students' listening, reading, and writing. Words are not studied in isolation from meaningful contexts. The focus of these experiences is always relating new knowledge to old, constantly expanding students' schemata. The benefits of vocabulary awareness and ownership activities are far-reaching; they promote independence in word learning and motivate students to want to learn more about words.

Wide Reading and Extensive Writing

Increasing the volume of students' reading is an important part of vocabulary development (Nagy, 1988) but it is not adequate to rely solely on this part of the literacy program for vocabulary development (Beck, McKeown, & Kucan, 2002). Writing in conjunction with reading and writing alone both engages students in much more thoughtful learning and improves their ability to construct meaning (Tierney & Shanahan, 1991). Therefore, it is critical to promote wide, independent reading and self-initiated writing. Reading provides models of rich language that help students learn many new words, and writing provides an authentic reason for students to use those words and develop ownership of them. Because these two processes are so closely related and interrelated, they are mutually supportive.

Students *must* be encouraged to read self-selected books and do self-initiated writing every day. This should be a significant component of the literacy program, and not something done only during "extra time" or outside class. Some researchers suggest that *in-school independent reading time may be even more important to improving students' ability to construct meaning than out-of-school reading time* (Taylor, Frye, & Maruyama, 1990).

In-school reading and writing are not sufficient, however; teachers must support and encourage wide reading and writing at home as well. Students can keep book journals, chart books read at home, share writing done at home, and have informal book chats with each other. Teachers should share some of their own reading and writing that they do outside school. As awareness of words increases, the potential for developing vocabulary through independent reading and writing also increases.

In addition to the ideas suggested in Chapter 2, try the following activities.

Book Displays

Have exciting and colorful displays of your favorite books and new books. Take a few minutes to read or tell a little about the book, just enough to get students hooked on reading it. Encourage students to place books they have read in the display and comment briefly. This transfers much of the ownership for learning to the students and makes them active participants.

Discussions of Interesting Words

Occasionally, invite students (or parents, other adults from students' homes, school staff, and so forth) to talk about interesting or humorous words from books they have read or things they have written or heard. By sharing the sentence in which a word appears and telling others what they think it means, students learn to apply all aspects of vocabulary learning to independent reading and writing. Such words can be placed on a class word wall for all students to use.

Instructional Strategies That Lead to Independent Vocabulary Learning

While most vocabulary develops through wide reading and extensive writing, certain strategies and techniques can be taught to enhance that development—for example: how to infer word meaning from context and what to do when context isn't sufficient. Additional activities and strategies can deepen and expand students' understanding of words. These strategies move students toward becoming responsible for their own vocabulary learning.

The next pages discuss how to choose which words to teach and when to teach them, as well as which strategies to teach and how to teach them.

Guidelines for Effective Vocabulary Instruction

All of the strategies for vocabulary instruction suggested here meet the research guidelines discussed earlier in this chapter. As the teacher, you must continually decide which words to teach, when to teach them, and which strategies to use for teaching.

Selecting Words to Teach

When selecting the words you will focus on during a literacy lesson, you must consider both the text and your students. You want to select words that are important to the understanding of the selection. These are known as key-concept words. You also want to select words that enhance students' vocabulary growth. Beck, McKeown, and Kucan (2002) suggest from their research that words be selected in tiers:

- Tier One Words—Words in this tier are basic words like *clock, baby, happy,* and so on. These words rarely require attention to their meanings.
- Tier Two Words—These are words that are of high frequency for mature language users and are found across a variety of areas or domains. Examples of Tier Two words include *merchant, fortunate,* and *perform.* This is the category of words that are most useful for teaching because students will encounter them in so many situations.
- Tier Three Words—The words in this category have a low frequency of use and are usually specific to a particular content area. Examples include *isotope* and *peninsula.* You would teach Tier Three words in a specific content lesson such as social studies or science. Sometimes the key-concept words include Tier One, Tier Two, and Tier Three words.

The process for selecting vocabulary is similar to that suggested in Chapter 3 for identifying prior knowledge. Figure 6.1 summarizes the decisions involved in vocabulary teaching. The first five decisions are discussed next; the remaining two

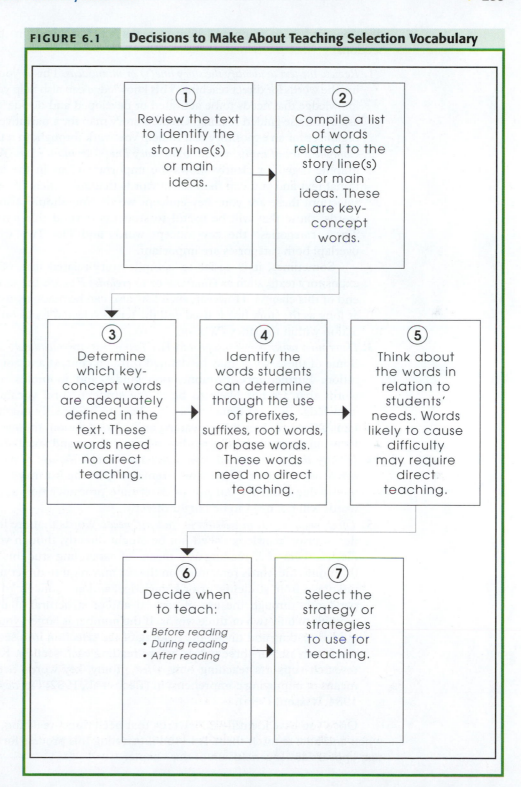

FIGURE 6.1   Decisions to Make About Teaching Selection Vocabulary

1. Review the text to identify the story line(s) or main ideas.

2. Compile a list of words related to the story line(s) or main ideas. These are key-concept words.

3. Determine which key-concept words are adequately defined in the text. These words need no direct teaching.

4. Identify the words students can determine through the use of prefixes, suffixes, root words, or base words. These words need no direct teaching.

5. Think about the words in relation to students' needs. Words likely to cause difficulty may require direct teaching.

6. Decide when to teach:
   - Before reading
   - During reading
   - After reading

7. Select the strategy or strategies to use for teaching.

decisions (when to teach and how to teach) are discussed in the following two sections:

1. *Review the text to identify the story line(s) or main ideas.* This is your basis for selecting the words for direct teaching. This knowledge can also help you select the prior knowledge that needs to be activated or developed and decide what questions to ask if you use guided reading. Create a story map for a narrative text or a graphic organizer for an expository text to help you work throughout a thematic unit.

2. *Compile a list of words related to the story line(s) or main ideas.* Your story map or graphic organizer clearly shows the important ideas in the story or informational text and you can then select words that are critical to understanding the selection; these are your key-concept words. You should also select Tier Two words, those that will be useful to students beyond this particular selection. These categories—the key-concept words and Tier Two words—sometimes overlap; both categories are important.

   Sometimes, it is easier to compile story-related lists of words by using expository texts, such as *Gladiator* or *Everglades Forever,* the sample lesson at the end of this chapter. However, such lists also can be made by using narrative text as long as the story line is used and the terms selected focus on the problem and action within the story (Wixson, 1986).

3. *Determine which key-concept and Tier Two words are adequately defined in the text.* Some of these words may be defined through context and some by direct definition. Furthermore, pronunciation guides and footnotes may be given for words that are not likely to be in the students' oral vocabularies and prior knowledge. A word usually does not have to be directly taught if the text contains adequate clues to its meaning and pronunciation, though you may want to focus on such words after reading as a way to expand vocabulary.

4. *Identify the words students can determine through the use of prefixes, suffixes, root words, or base words.* Some words remaining on the list may have structural elements that students can use to determine pronunciation and meaning. Such words will not need to be taught directly.

5. *Think about words in relation to students' needs.* Words that are likely to be in students' prior knowledge need not be taught directly, though you might want to discuss them after reading as a means of expanding students' vocabularies. At this point, the words remaining on the list may require direct teaching. They are unknown from students' prior knowledge, and are unlikely to be learned independently through the use of context and/or structural analysis. This should amount to only two or three words. If the number is larger, you may want to use guided reading and divide the reading of the selection into sections so that you teach only two or three words before reading each section. Keep in mind that research supports teaching only a *few,* if any, key words before reading as a means of improving comprehension (Beck et al., 1982; Tierney & Cunningham, 1984; Wixson, 1986).

Once you have identified the words that need direct teaching, you must decide when and how to teach them. A lesson illustrating this process for an informational text appears at the conclusion of this chapter.

When to Teach Vocabulary

Whether to develop vocabulary before, during, or after reading depends on a number of factors (Step 6 in Figure 6.1). Some students may need vocabulary support throughout their reading, and others may need no support. Let's look at the conditions under which vocabulary should be taught before, during, and after reading.

Before Reading

Provide vocabulary instruction before reading in the following situations:

- Students are experiencing difficulty in constructing meaning and seem to have limited prior knowledge of any kind, including vocabulary. They might be English Language Learners, students with learning disabilities, or students who are generally experiencing difficulty with comprehension.

- The text to be read contains words that are *clearly* a part of the prior knowledge students need to understand the text and you are confident students do not know these terms.

- The text has unusually difficult concepts. Even though your students do not normally need vocabulary support before reading, they may benefit from it in these situations. For example, suppose your third graders really want to read *The Mouse Rap* (Myers, 1990), which is developmentally somewhat above their age level. Before reading the book, you introduce some of the words and concepts that you think are beyond their knowledge and experience.

- Students have previewed the text they are going to read and have identified words they believe they need to know to understand the text. Sometimes this is a good way to identify words that students really do need to know. A word that is giving them difficulty, even one that is unimportant to understanding the text, may interfere with students' overall meaning construction. Through direct teaching before reading, you can help them see that knowing this word (or every word) is not important to their overall understanding of a text. Exercise caution when teaching vocabulary before reading based on student self-selection, however, because you could end up devoting too much time to words that are not important to understanding the material or have little value in general vocabulary use in students' future.

During Reading

Vocabulary instruction during reading is usually recommended only for students who need overall teacher support through guided reading. These students are likely to be experiencing difficulty in constructing meaning, or to be reading a text that has particularly difficult concepts. When you use guided reading, it may be more appropriate to deal with words and concepts at the beginning or end of each segment of reading. Vocabulary support during reading has the advantage of giving students immediate opportunities to use the words.

TABLE 6.1	When to Provide Direct Vocabulary Instruction		
Factors to Consider	**Vocabulary Instruction**		
	Before Reading	**During Reading**	**After Reading**
Student considerations	*Any* students are experiencing difficulty constructing meaning. Students have previewed text and identified words they want to know.	Students are receiving guided reading support.	Students have identified words of interest or that cause difficulty. Students need to expand their vocabularies.
Text considerations	Text has words that are definitely keys to understanding. Text has unusually difficult concepts. Text contains many Tier Two words.	Text has words that are keys to understanding the text and are likely to cause students difficulty in constructing meaning. Text contains Tier Two words and some Tier Three words that require instruction.	Text has good opportunities for expanding vocabularies with Tier Two words and Tier Three words.

After Reading

Vocabulary instruction after reading has two primary purposes: (1) to help students clarify the meanings of any words that were of interest to them during reading or that caused them difficulty and (2) to expand students' vocabularies by having them focus on interesting words that are related to the text they have read. For example, you might use *Johnny Tremain* (Forbes, 1971) to help upper elementary students see how an author uses rich, descriptive language. This is a good way to expand vocabulary and relate descriptive language to writing.

Base decisions about when to provide vocabulary instruction and support on students' needs and the nature of the text; *sometimes no instruction will be necessary*. Table 6.1 summarizes these considerations in relation to the appropriate times to teach vocabulary.

Strategies for Teaching Vocabulary

The final decision you must make is *how* to teach vocabulary directly (Step 7 in Figure 6.1). There is no one best method; however, the procedures must help students improve their ability to construct meaning, and not just learn isolated words. The strategies and techniques for supporting vocabulary development presented here all help students relate new knowledge to old knowledge, actively involve students in the process of learning, help students thoroughly learn words, and support students in the process of learning to use their own strategies for independently inferring word meanings. *The ultimate goal of all vocabulary development is to help students become independent learners who have strategies for inferring the meanings of unknown words when they encounter them in reading;* furthermore, these students will have extensive vocabulary knowledge that they are able to use in constructing meaning through both reading and writing and across the curriculum. (Read the "Educators Speak" feature on page 260 to see how one teacher addresses vocabulary across the curriculum.)

Table 6.2 presents an overview of strategies you can use in your literacy lessons to help students gain independence in vocabulary learning. They should *not* be used to develop isolated vocabulary lessons apart from reading and writing.

TABLE 6.2   Overview of Vocabulary Strategies That Promote Student Independence

Strategy	Purpose	When to Use	Comments
Inferring meaning from context	Help students learn independent strategy	During reading All texts	Must be taught before it can be used independently
Concept of definition (word maps)	Help students become independent word learners by teaching elements of a good definition	Before or after reading Expository texts	Good support strategy for independently inferring word meanings
Semantic mapping	Integrate prior knowledge and vocabulary learning	Before or after reading All texts	Develops in-depth word knowledge
Semantic feature analysis	Develop word knowledge by comparing words	Before or after reading Expository text and some narratives	Often more effective after reading
Hierarchical and linear arrays	Develop word relationships	After reading All texts	Encourages students to compare and contrast words
Preview in context	Use text context to develop word meanings	Before reading All texts	Must have text with good context clues
Contextual redefinition	Use context to determine word meaning	Before reading All texts	Useful when texts do not provide strong context clues
Vocabulary self-collection	Help students learn self-selected words	After reading All texts	Makes students responsible for own vocabulary learning
Structural analysis	Help students infer meaning independently	During reading All texts	Needs specific lessons before independent use
Dictionary/ Thesaurus	Help students infer meaning independently	During and after reading All texts	A lifelong skill; needs to be taught

Vocabulary Instruction Across the Curriculum

"Vocabulary in the content areas can be taught in a variety of ways. It is usually taught with a particular unit of study where many concepts are also being presented and developed. Most vocabulary words are teacher selected, while others are taught as the need arises.

One way to teach vocabulary is with a direct example of the word. For example, when studying the parts of a flower, show students the item represented by the vocabulary word. Students are given opportunities to label samples. After some experience with the words, students can also be asked to role-play as the teacher and teach the words to someone in their group or another group.

To provide more practice, students can be asked to sort the words into categories. The categories are meaning based and can vary by student. Students must be able to rationalize why they grouped the words in a particular way.

Looking at the affixes and base/root words can help students assign meaning to words and to see the relationships between words. For example, the root *chron,* meaning time, can be used with the teaching of *chronology, synchronize,* and *chronicle.* This often allows students to build on prior knowledge and connect known information to new information.

Many children benefit from adding kinesthetic activities to learning, as it stimulates different parts of the brain and can enhance learning. Charades or some kind of acting out of vocabulary words creates a learning opportunity for the actor as well as the viewer.

Word walls keep the words visible and allow for a quick review. "Find a word that means . . . Find two words that relate to . . ." Word walls allow the multiple exposures so often needed by students to ensure learning.

Vocabulary learning requires repeated exposures in different settings. Direct telling/teaching, modeling, restating, dramatizing, categorizing, and seeing relationships to other words can enhance vocabulary instruction. "

—Barbara "Bobbie" Lee, Reading Specialist
Horizon Elementary School
Sterling, Virginia

Independently Inferring Word Meanings from Context

A necessary part of effective vocabulary development is teaching students a strategy for independently inferring word meanings (Calfee & Drum, 1986; Graves, 1987; Paris et al., 1983). If students are reading extensively and come to an unknown word, they need a plan for trying to determine its meaning. Getting students to use such a strategy is well worth the time and effort.

The student strategy presented here is based on the suggestions of Calfee and Drum (1986) and Graves (1987) and on our own experiences with students. You will need to adjust the steps to meet the varying grade levels of your students. Teach the following steps to students:

1. When you come to a word you do not know, read to the end of the sentence or paragraph to decide if the word is important to your understanding. If it is *not* important, continue reading.
2. If the word *is* important, look for **base words, root words, prefixes,** or **suffixes** you recognize.
3. English Language Learners: think whether there is a word in your language that looks like the word you don't know.
4. Use what you know about phonics to try to pronounce the word. Is it a word you have heard before?
5. Reread the sentence or paragraph containing the word. Try using **context** to infer the meaning.
6. If you still don't know the word, use the dictionary or ask someone for help.
7. Once you think you know the meaning, reread the text to be sure it makes sense.

See Chapter 4, Figure 4.4 for a strategy poster you might use with primary-grade children.

Teach these steps in accordance with your students' level of maturity in reading. Figure 6.2 shows a strategy poster that you could use with intermediate or higher grades. Students may need guidance in learning to determine which words are not important. When students are learning this strategy, they should help in verbalizing the statements that go on the strategy poster; in this way, the strategy becomes theirs. Then, remind them to refer to the poster and use the strategy as they read.

Concept of Definition Procedure (Word Maps)

Description Schwartz and Raphael (1985) describe a strategy known as the *concept of definition procedure,* more commonly called a *word map* strategy. The purpose of the procedure is to help students in the intermediate grades and above gain control of the vocabulary acquisition process by teaching them the type of information that makes up a good definition and teaching them how to use context clues and background knowledge to increase their understanding of words. A word map helps students visually depict the elements of a given concept. Each concept is composed of three types of information:

1. Class: *What is it?*
2. Properties that distinguish the concept from others: *What is it like?*
3. Examples of the concept: *What are some examples?*

Figure 6.3 shows a completed word map for the concept *ice cream.*

Procedures Schwartz and Raphael (1985) suggest that this strategy can be taught in four lessons. The following procedures are adapted from their guidelines.

INFERRING WORD MEANINGS

When I come to an unknown word

Read to the end of the sentence to see if it is important

NOT IMPORTANT TO MY UNDERSTANDING

Read on

Continue to ask,
"Does this make sense to me?"

IMPORTANT TO MY UNDERSTANDING

①  First, I'll look for base words, prefixes, or suffixes I know.

②  If I still don't know it, I'll try phonics. Does it sound familiar?

③  Next, I'll try the context.

④  I'll look in the dictionary or ask someone.

⑤ **READ AND CHECK THE MEANING**

| FIGURE 6.3 | **Completed Word Map for *Ice Cream*** |

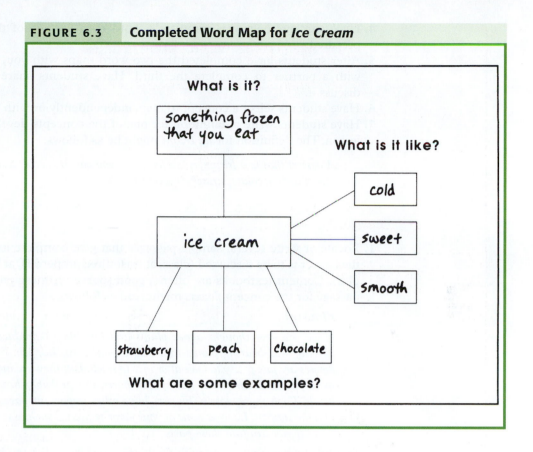

Lesson 1

1. Select three or more concepts children already know, and develop a list of information about each; include class, at least three properties, and at least three examples. Here is a sample list for *ice cream:*

   ice cream

chocolate	frozen
cold	sweet
dessert	peach
strawberry	smooth

2. Discuss the importance of being able to accurately determine word meanings to better comprehend texts. Tell students that the strategy they will be learning during the next four lessons will help them determine whether they really know the meaning of a word.

3. Present students with the structure of a word map. Tell them that this map is a picture of the three things that let us know when we really understand a word: class (what it is), properties (what it is like), and examples. Go over each part with them.

4. Have students help you complete a word map for two of the concepts you prepared.
5. After students have completed the two word maps with you, have them work with a partner to complete the third. Have students share their work and discuss it.
6. Have students select a concept to map, independently or with a partner.
7. Have students write a definition for one of the concepts developed during the lesson. The definition for *ice cream* might be as follows:

> *A dessert that is a frozen, sweet food that you eat. It is cold. Some examples of ice cream are chocolate, strawberry, and peach.*

Lesson 2

1. Locate or write several sample passages that give complete information about the concepts to be discussed (class, at least three properties, at least three examples). Content textbooks are often a good source for these passages. A sample passage for the concept *flowers* might read as follows:

> **Flowers**
>
> *Have you ever thought about plants and how they reproduce? Flowers are the parts of seed-bearing plants that help to make this happen. You may think that flowers are just pretty to look at or nice to smell. But they are important to making more plants. Each flower has special parts. You probably have noticed only the petals. Look more closely. Flowers have other important parts, such as the pistil and the stamen. Look at some of your favorite flowers such as a tulip, rose, or daisy to see if you can find these parts.*

2. Present the passages along with the blank word map. Tell students to read each passage and complete the word map.
3. Have students give oral or written definitions for the concepts presented.
4. Once students seem to understand the concept of the word map, tell them it is not necessary to limit properties and examples to three items.

Lesson 3

1. Write or locate several passages that are less complete in their definitions than those used in lesson 2.
2. Direct students to read the passages and complete the word maps for this lesson, as they did in lesson 2. If they do not see that the information provided in the passages is incomplete, help them see this by asking such questions as, "Does the passage tell you what _____ is like?" or "Does the passage give any examples of _____?"
3. Have students use other sources and their own prior knowledge to complete the word maps.
4. Guide students to the conclusion that texts do not always give complete definitions.

Lesson 4

1. Write or locate several more passages with incomplete contextual information for several concepts. For each concept, write incomplete definitions, leaving out one or more parts of the definition developed through the use of the word map. An incomplete definition might read as follows:

   A musician is a person who plays an instrument. A musician is very talented.

2. Tell students that the purpose of this lesson is for them to use what they have learned from developing word maps to decide whether some definitions are complete or incomplete.
3. Have students read the passages and evaluate the definitions for their completeness. Tell them to write the information that is missing from the definitions.
4. Conclude the lesson by discussing with students how they were able to tell the definitions were incomplete. Discuss how they should use this type of thinking any time they are reading and come to words they don't know.

It may be necessary to repeat one or more of these lessons several times for review purposes before students can use this procedure independently.

When to Use Research on the concept of definition procedure has been conducted using fourth and eighth graders. It appears to work best with students in the intermediate and higher grades and with expository texts. Maria (1990) also reports that it is effective with at-risk (hard-to-teach) students in the upper elementary grades. This strategy can be used in four lessons throughout a thematic unit to help students develop the understanding needed to apply the concepts in later units. The four lessons are likely to be more meaningful if they take place after the reading of selections.

You may also use the word map as a way to thoroughly develop the meanings of several related words before or after the reading of a selection or at the beginning of a particular theme. For example, if you are beginning a thematic unit on space travel, you might use the word map activity to develop concepts such as *astronaut, space shuttle, rocket,* and *pilot.* When developing closely related terms, include questioning such as that used in the rich vocabulary instruction program reported by Beck and her colleagues (Beck, McCaslin, & McKeown, 1980; Beck, McKeown, & Omanson, 1987; Beck, Omanson, & McKeown, 1982). Probe relationships by asking such questions as, "Is an astronaut the same as a *pilot?*" and "Do pilots *fly* rockets?"

Assessment Value You can learn two things about your students as they learn and use this strategy: their ability to determine unknown word meanings, and their prior knowledge of the concepts being developed. Schwartz and Raphael (1985) report that students who have been taught this strategy are more aware of what to do to figure out the meaning of a new word. When asked how to do this, students "indicated they would ask themselves questions and think about what they already knew. In contrast, the students without this instruction tended to answer, 'I would look it up'" (pp. 162–163).

You can determine students' knowledge and understanding of the particular concepts being developed through their responses to the structured portions of the lessons, and through their answers when they generate their own words for word maps and definitions. If you are using the word map concept to develop related terms, you can tell by the responses students give to your probing questions whether they really understand the terms.

Comments The concept of definition procedure is excellent for preparing students to use the strategy for independently inferring word meanings. This procedure helps students develop a concept of what they must know to understand a word and begin to think about the sources within the text that might help them define a word; that is, this strategy promotes the integration of existing prior knowledge with new knowledge. It requires heavy initial teacher support and guidance, however, and it does not work with all words; for example, it works with nouns but not with verbs.

Since many words have similar properties, Schwartz (1988) has expanded the word map concept to include the idea of comparisons. In one such revised version, the teacher and students place a word similar to the main concept in a comparison box and discuss how this word and the main word have common properties. This procedure helps students become more precise in thinking about the properties they identify for the main concept and also helps them to further integrate knowledge within their schemata.

Be careful, however, that making word maps does not become the goal of the activity, which *must always remain the development of vocabulary knowledge to improve the construction of meaning* and independence in word learning.

Semantic Mapping

Semantic mapping, discussed in Chapter 3 as an excellent strategy for activating and developing prior knowledge, is similar to the word map used in the concept of definition procedure. It can be used before reading and then expanded after reading to integrate students' new knowledge into their prior knowledge. It is a good way to develop in-depth word knowledge.

Semantic mapping is a time-consuming procedure. Therefore, when you use it before reading, you must be certain you have selected key-concept words. It is often better to use it after reading to expand vocabulary and pull together concepts students already possess. Semantic mapping has many variations and uses; it is a good way to brainstorm for writing.

See Chapter 8 on writing.

Semantic Feature Analysis

Description When using semantic feature analysis, students develop vocabulary and learn important concepts by looking at how related words differ and how they are alike (Johnson & Pearson, 1984). Figure 6.4 shows how some fourth-grade students set up a semantic feature analysis grid to compare vegetables after completing

FIGURE 6.4	Semantic Feature Analysis Grid			
VEGETABLES	GREEN	HAVE PEELINGS	EAT RAW	SEEDS
Potatoes	−	−	+	?
Carrots	−	+	+	−
Tomatoes	− +	+	− +	+
Broccoli	+	?	+	−
Squash	+ −	+	+	+
Cabbage	+	−	+	−

observations made during a plant unit. They then discussed each word, indicating what they knew about the word in relation to each characteristic.

Procedures Use the following procedures to develop semantic feature grids:

1. Select a category or class of words (such as vegetables).
2. List items that fall into this category down the left side of the grid.
3. List features that some of the items have in common across the top of the grid. Sometimes you can ask students to do this.
4. Have students put pluses (+), minuses (−), and question marks (?) in the squares of the grid to indicate whether the items in the category have the feature under consideration. Discuss each item, making sure students understand that some items are sometimes characterized by a feature and sometimes are not. For example, for the grid in Figure 6.4, be sure students understand that the tomato can be both green and red but is usually cooked when green.
5. Add additional words and features to the grid.
6. Complete the grid and discuss each word.

Repeat the process several times, using different categories and moving from the concrete to the abstract. Encourage students to look regularly for new words to add to the grids. Students can keep grid sheets in folders or notebooks, and add to them throughout the year.

After completing a semantic feature grid, students should examine the pattern of pluses and minuses to determine how the words are alike and how they differ. Question marks should serve as a basis for further research to clarify their understanding of the words. This strategy will help students expand their vocabularies as well as refine the meanings of words they already know.

When to Use Semantic feature analysis may be used before or after reading to develop vocabulary, but it is often more effectively used after reading as a means of expanding vocabulary. It is a helpful way to chart new knowledge during a unit of study. It is usually most helpful with expository texts but may also be used with some narrative texts. Finally, it is an excellent way for students to develop understanding in various content areas.

In addition to developing vocabulary, semantic feature analysis is very effective for reinforcing vocabulary and related concepts in content textbooks (Stieglitz & Stieglitz, 1981). Students at all levels can use it to review chapters before tests or pull together concepts in concluding a thematic unit. For younger students, semantic feature grids using very simple categories and features can serve as oral language activities.

Assessment Value As students develop semantic feature grids, you will be able to assess their prior knowledge in relation to the categories and words being discussed. Students' responses will help you assess their understandings of word relationships, as well as their thinking abilities.

Comments Semantic feature analysis is one of the strategies that concentrate on helping students build relationships among concepts. Although both the concept of definition procedure and semantic mapping also do this, they are not as effective. The strength of semantic feature analysis comes when students are actively involved in constructing the grids and discussing them. This fosters active participation in the process of learning.

Nagy (1988) suggests that the Venn diagram is another way to apply semantic feature analysis in the classroom. Figure 6.5 presents a blank Venn diagram. In these

FIGURE 6.5   Blank Venn Diagram

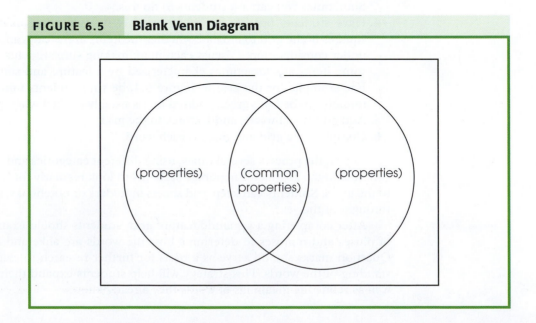

diagrams, two things are compared: the unique properties of each item are listed along the sides of the circles, and the properties common to both are listed in the intersection.

Hierarchical and Linear Arrays

Description Words sometimes have hierarchical relationships, for example, the names of scientific organisms (Nagy, 1988). A **hierarchical array** such as that in Figure 6.6 can help students understand these relationships. The exact structure of the array will depend on the concepts being analyzed.

FIGURE 6.6　**Hierarchical Array**

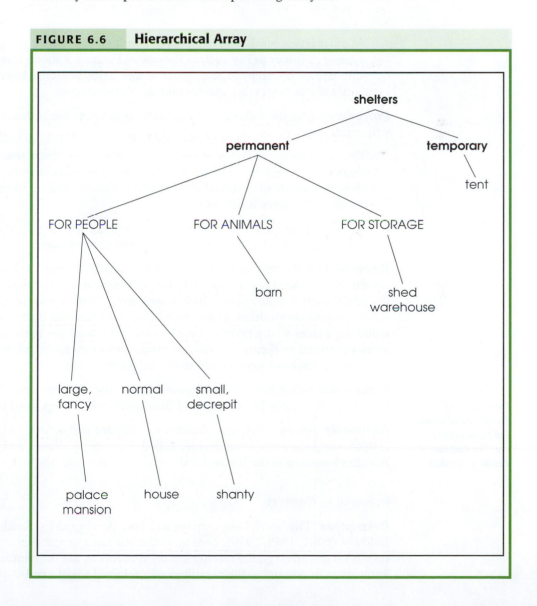

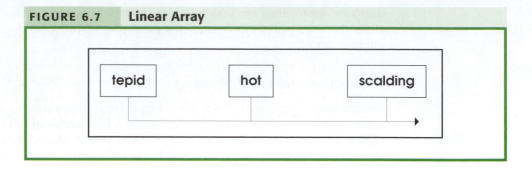

FIGURE 6.7   **Linear Array**

At other times, words have a linear relationship, for example: *good, better, best; tepid, hot, scalding*. A **linear array** such as the one in Figure 6.7 shows this relationship.

The use of hierarchical and linear arrays helps students learn to think independently about word relationships and develop concepts.

Procedures   Use the following procedures to develop hierarchical or linear arrays with students:

1. Select a concept or group of words from literature or from students' writing.
2. Begin by showing students the type of array they will construct.
3. Guide students in constructing the array. Discuss the relationship among the words as the array is developed.

After students have had considerable experience with arrays, they can select the words for study and decide on the type of array they will use.

When to Use   Arrays are best used after reading to help students expand their vocabularies. The visual aspect of arrays can help at-risk learners or English Language Learners see the relationships among words more concretely. You can also use arrays to activate students' prior knowledge; for example, if students are going to study the places where people live, you can begin with the basic framework of the array presented in Figure 6.6 and ask students to generate the information. As the unit progresses, students can add to or change the array.

Assessment Value   Students' responses during the development of arrays will help you assess their prior knowledge and their ability to develop word relationships.

For a detailed discussion of arrays, see Nagy (1988) in the "For Additional Reading" section.

Comments   Arrays encourage students to compare and contrast words. Blachowicz (1986) suggests several variations, called *semantic gradients* and *concept ladders*. Another variation of the hierarchical array is the *thinking tree*.

Preview in Context

Description   The preview-in-context strategy, developed by Readence, Bean, and Baldwin (1981, 1985, 1989), does just what the term says: it previews words in context. With this strategy, the teacher guides students to use the context and their prior knowledge to determine the meanings of a selected set of words.

Procedures Use the following four steps for this strategy:

1. *Prepare.* Select the words to be taught following the procedures suggested earlier in this chapter (refer to Figure 6.1). These should be key-concept words including Tier Two and Tier Three words; *you should teach no more than two or three at one time.* Identify passages within the text that contain strong context clues for the word. For example, we will focus on teaching *decay* and use the following passage from *Mummies, Tombs, and Treasure* (Perl, 1987):

   > *Without preservation, dead animal matter usually decays very quickly. This is true of plant matter, too. A dead bird or cat, a piece of rotting fruit, can show the stages of decay. Decay is caused by bacteria. (p. 2)*

2. *Establish the context.* Present the word and the context to students; read aloud the passage as students follow along. Then have students reread it silently.

3. *Specify the word meaning.* Now lead students toward a definition of the word under study. By asking them questions, you encourage them to use their prior knowledge and clues in the text to arrive at a meaning for the word. An example of this type of questioning follows:

   Teacher: *What does this text tell you about the word* decay?
   Student: *That dead animals decay.*
   Teacher: *What happens to them when they decay?*
   Student: *They rot.*
   Teacher: *How could you tell from this text that* decay *means "to rot"?*
   Student: *By what it says about rotting fruit.*

4. *Expand the word meaning.* After students have a basic understanding of the word, try to deepen their understanding by discussing synonyms, antonyms, other contexts, or other examples where the word might be used. This helps expand students' knowledge of the word. If students have access to a dictionary or a thesaurus, they can use it. The discussion might go as follows:

   Teacher: *Can you think of other things that decay?*
   Student: *Teeth. I get cavities sometimes.*
   Teacher: *How do we prevent decay?*
   Student: *Put something on things that keep them from decaying.*
   Teacher: *Like what?*
   Student: *Fluoride keeps your teeth from decaying.*
   Teacher: *What about dead things? How do we keep them from decaying?*
   Student: *You embalm dead people.*
   Teacher: *So the fluid used for embalming preserves things or keeps them from decaying. Can you think of words that mean the same thing as decay?*
   Student 1: Rot.
   Student 2: Spoil.

After you teach the words, encourage students to place them in their word banks or journals.

When to Use Use preview in context before reading, but *only* when the context for the word is strong. It is appropriate for all grade levels but not for students who have limited prior knowledge.

Assessment Value As students respond in the discussions, you will be able to assess the extent of their prior knowledge and their ability to use context clues.

Comments The preview-in-context strategy is simple and easy to use. However, it is often difficult to identify contexts that contain enough clues to help students infer word meanings. Nagy (1988) points out that "context may look quite helpful if one already knows what the word means, but it seldom supplies adequate information for the person who has no other knowledge about the meaning of the word" (p. 7).

The strength of this strategy comes through the intensive discussion between the teacher and students, which deepens students' understanding. Therefore, it is important to skillfully direct the discussion.

Contextual Redefinition

Description Since texts frequently do not provide sufficient context for students to determine the meaning of an unknown word (Schatz & Baldwin, 1986), contextual redefinition helps students use context more effectively by presenting them with *sufficient context* before reading and showing them how to use the clues to *make informed guesses* about a word's meaning (Cunningham, Cunningham, & Arthur, 1981).

Procedures The following five-step procedure for using contextual redefinition is adapted from Tierney, Readence, and Dishner (1990):

1. *Select unfamiliar words.* Using the procedures suggested earlier in this chapter, select two or three words to preteach. This example will use *hippophagy* and *carapace.*

2. *Write a sample.* Write one or more sentences that provide sufficient clues to teach the meaning of the word. Try to use different types of context clues, such as direct definition, synonyms, and comparison and contrast. If the text has sufficient context clues for the word in question, use it. Here are two samples:

    > *The drought had been so long and severe that the cattle had died. Only the horses survived. Yet the natives were so hungry, they had to resort to hippophagy to avoid starvation.*

    > *Without its carapace, a turtle has no protection and is subject to certain death from its enemies or the elements.*

3. *Present the words in isolation.* Using the whiteboard or overhead projector, present the words in isolation and ask students to pronounce them, or pronounce the words for them. Then encourage students to provide a definition for each word. Wild guesses may occur; this is part of the learning process. Encourage students to come to a consensus about the meaning of each word.

4. *Present the words in context.* Using the contexts prepared for the lesson, present each word and have students read the contexts aloud, or read the contexts for

them. As students discuss each word, have them come to a consensus about its meaning. Encourage guessing from the clues; in this way, at-risk students are able to participate. To help students become more attuned to the value of context, ask them to discuss the differences between trying to define the words in context and in isolation.

5. *Use a dictionary for verification.* Discuss the dictionary definition, and compare it to the one developed by the students.

When to Use Use the contextual redefinition strategy to teach totally *new* words before reading. It is appropriate for all students who possess some skill in using the dictionary and is especially useful when the text does not provide context that will help students infer the meanings of the words selected for preteaching. Students who are having difficulty learning to construct meaning and English Language Learners may benefit from this strategy.

Assessment Value You can assess students' prior knowledge from their responses in guessing definitions in isolation and in context. The use of the context samples lets you know how well students are able to use context. Finally, dictionary verification gives you opportunities to see how effectively students use the dictionary.

Comments Despite questions about the value of using context sentences to teach vocabulary, when the words to be pretaught are *carefully selected, kept to a minimum of two or three,* and *thoroughly taught,* preteaching to improve comprehension may have value (Tierney & Cunningham, 1984; Wixson, 1986). The keys to effectively using contextual redefinition are careful word selection and thorough discussion of the words, along with repeated encounters with the words through reading and writing to develop ownership of them.

Vocabulary Self-Collection

Description Vocabulary self-collection places the responsibility for learning words on the students (Haggard, 1982, 1986). After a reading experience, students select a word they think the entire class should study. They are also encouraged to select additional words for their own personal study. This strategy has the advantages of being interactive and being based on authentic reading experiences.

Procedures The following procedures are based on Haggard's suggestions (1986):

1. *Select words for study.* After students have read a story or an informational text, ask them to review it and select one word for class study. They may do this as individuals, partners, or teams. You should also select one word for study so that you are an active learning partner and gain some influence in the process. Encourage students to select words that seem important or interesting.

2. *Compile and define the words.* Ask each student or group to provide the word selected for study and the definition (determined from context) of the word. List each word and the definition on the whiteboard or overhead; include your own word as well. Use the dictionary to verify or complete definitions as needed, and encourage all students to participate in this process. With the students, agree on a final list of words and definitions.

3. *Finalize the list.* With the students, review the list to eliminate duplications, words that seem unrelated to the story or topic of study, and words that students simply do not want to study. Agree on a reasonable number (three to five) for the final list, and have students put the words and definitions in their vocabulary notebooks or journals. Some may choose to record words eliminated from the class list in their personal lists. When students write the words in their journals, ask them to write a sentence demonstrating the use of the word in their own lives or showing their understanding of it.

4. *Use and extend the words.* Encourage students to use the words in their writing and to look for them in other books they read. Plan activities that reinforce the words, such as semantic maps, semantic feature analysis, and arrays.

These procedures are based on teaching vocabulary development after reading, but you can adapt them for use before reading by having students preview the text and select for study words that they think will be important.

When to Use   You may use this strategy with both narrative and expository texts and with all students at any grade level. If students do not have sufficient skill to use the dictionary, you will need to provide the definitions.

Assessment Value   This strategy gives you many opportunities to assess students' word knowledge. When students select words for study and give definitions from context, you can assess their use of context clues. As they participate in expanding definitions given by other students, you can determine the extent of their prior knowledge.

Comments   Vocabulary self-collection is easy to implement, interactive, based on authentic reading experiences, and versatile. It supports the concept that children learn to read and write by reading and writing. By selecting their own words, students become active participants in their own learning and see the classroom as a community of learners. When the teacher participates, students and teacher become partners in learning. Some teachers may worry that students will not select important words, but there is no guarantee that students will learn words the teacher selects any more readily than they will learn self-selected words. This strategy respects the students as learners and incorporates all of the ideas about authentic learning that are stressed throughout this text.

Structural Analysis as an Aid to Decoding and Independence

Structural elements within the word may help students determine or infer a word's meaning. Students may learn about structural elements through reading and writing, but sometimes they require the teacher's support through direct vocabulary teaching strategies or through minilessons. However, direct teaching of structural elements is of limited value and should be done only under certain circumstances.

Structural analysis is the study of meaningful word parts. It may help students as they learn to recognize words (pronunciation) and as they determine the meanings of words. The following elements are usually considered part of structural analysis:

■ *Base words:* Meaningful linguistic units that can stand alone and contain no smaller meaningful parts; also called *free morphemes* (re*sell: sell* is the base word).

- ■ ***Root words:*** Words from which other words are derived. Usually the derivational word is from another language and is a bound morpheme; that is, it cannot stand alone (*scribble* comes from the Latin root *scribere,* meaning "to write"). Teachers frequently use the terms *base word* and root word synonymously, but they are not the same.

- ■ ***Prefixes:*** Units of meaning that can be added to the beginnings of base words or root words to change their meanings. These are bound morphemes and cannot stand alone (*un*happy: *un-* is the prefix meaning "not").

- ■ ***Suffixes:*** Units of meaning that can be added to the ends of base or root words to change their meanings. These are bound morphemes (tear*ful: -ful* is the suffix meaning "full of").

- ■ ***Inflectional endings:*** Word parts that can be added to the ends of root or base words to change their case, gender, number, tense, or form; these are bound morphemes (boy*'s:* possessive case; stewardess [*now virtually obsolete*]: gender; trees: number; walk*ed:* tense; funni*est:* form). Sometimes **inflectional endings** are called *suffixes.*

- ■ ***Compound words:*** Two or more base words that have been combined to form a new word with a meaning that is related to each base word (*run* + way = *runway*).

- ■ ***Contractions:*** Shortened forms of two words in which a letter or letters have been replaced by an apostrophe (*do* + *not* = *don't; there* + *is* = *there's*).

Students will become familiar with compound words and contractions through their reading and writing experiences, and for most students simply showing them what these are as reading and writing take place is usually sufficient. Some students, such as ELLs, may need more directed support using the minilesson, but even when this is required, the lesson *always goes back to the literature* to help students see how the compound or contraction was used in context. For example, if your students have just completed reading *Aunt Flossie's Hats (and Crab Cakes Later)* (Howard, 1991), and you noticed they were having trouble figuring out compound words or contractions, you can use this story as the basis for a minilesson involving the following steps:

1. Go back to the story to identify a compound word or contraction. Read the section containing it aloud to students as they follow along. Ask them if they notice anything special about the compound word or contraction.
2. Define *compound* or *contraction.* Point out another example; then point out words that are not examples.
3. Direct students to read a page containing another example. Ask them to find the compound word or contraction.
4. Make a chart of other examples that students find.
5. Conclude the lesson by discussing with students how they should use this new knowledge in reading and writing.
6. As students read and write, you may need to do periodic reviews.

Aunt Flossie's Hats (and Crab Cakes Later) is particularly good for this experience, because it contains numerous examples of both compounds and contractions such as *afternoons, hatboxes, here's,* and *she's.* Reading material for students in intermediate and higher grades will contain increasing examples of compound words and contractions frequently used in dialogue.

Knowledge of the remaining elements of structural analysis also develops through reading and writing. The addition of prefixes and suffixes to words accounts for a large number of words for students in grade 4 and above (Nagy & Anderson, 1984). However, the prefixes and suffixes encountered have variant meanings, which makes it difficult for students to see a pattern (Graves, 1987). If you have to provide a minilesson, it is important to know which prefixes and suffixes to focus on and how to construct your lesson (for guidelines, see Graves, 1987; Nagy & Anderson, 1984; White, Sowell, & Yanagihara, 1989).

White, Sowell, and Yanagihara (1989) determined, on the basis of frequency of occurrence, that there are nine prefixes and ten suffixes of sufficient use to students to merit instruction (see the table on page 514 in the Handbook Resource). They also determined that knowing the prefixes listed would account for 76 percent of prefixed words, and knowing the suffixes would account for 85 percent of suffixed words. Graves (1987) reported that knowing just four prefixes (*un-*, *in-*[not], *dis-*, and *non-*) would account for nearly 50 percent of all prefixed words. Therefore, in planning minilesson support focusing on word parts, you should give greatest attention to these nine prefixes and ten suffixes.

In addition to knowing which prefixes and suffixes are the most beneficial for students, you must be aware of some of the pitfalls of using prefixes as an aid to word meaning (White et al., 1989):

- Prefixes are not consistent in their meanings; for example, *un-*, *dis-*, *re-*, and *in-* each have two meanings.
- False analysis with prefixes often occurs. For example, removing *in* from *intrigue* leaves no recognizable base word. The prefixes *re-*, *in-*, and *dis-* have a particularly high risk of false analysis.
- Looking only at word parts may mislead the reader in determining the word's true meaning. For example, *unassuming* means "modest" instead of "not supposing."

If you are aware of these possible pitfalls and know how often the affixes occur, you can plan minilessons that will help students who have the need for such support. The suggestions that follow are adapted from White et al. (1989) and are for suffixes. Similar steps would be used to teach prefixes.

Minilessons Using Suffixes Suffixes (and inflectional endings) tend to have abstract meanings. Therefore, instruction should focus on removing the suffix and identifying the base word. The following lessons are recommended:

- *Lesson 1:* Teach the concept of suffixes (and inflectional endings).
- *Lesson 2:* Teach -*s*/*es*, -*ed*, and -*ing* with no spelling changes. Show students the suffixed word, and have them identify the suffix and define the base word (examples: *boxes, talking, lasted*).
- *Lessons 3–5:* Focus on three major spelling changes that occur using suffixes:

Consonant doubling: *begged, thinner, funny*
Change from *y* to *i*: *flies, worried, reliable*
Deleted silent *e*: *saved, rider, believable*

Follow the same pattern as suggested for lesson 2, but discuss the spelling change that has occurred. The suffixes used should be drawn from the list suggested in the table on page 514.

- *Lesson 6:* Suffixes that change the part of speech: *-ly, -er, -ion, -able, -al, -y,* and *-ness.* Again, follow the same pattern used with the other lessons. More than one lesson might be needed for this category of suffixes.

The exact grade levels for teaching prefixes and suffixes depend on students' needs. It is recommended, however, that all instruction should be completed by the end of grade 5.

White et al. (1989) report favorable results with students who were taught lessons similar to those just described. They stress that "the goal of prefix and suffix instruction is *use* of word-part clues to derive the meaning of unfamiliar words" (p. 307). They believe that a "reasonable" amount of direct teaching helps students learn to use an independent strategy for inferring word meanings.

The Dictionary and Thesaurus as Aids to Decoding and Independence

Two final areas of knowledge students must have to use the strategy for independently inferring word meanings and achieving independence in vocabulary learning are using the dictionary and using the thesaurus (Graves, 1987). The dictionary is an aid for reading, writing, and spelling; the thesaurus is more valuable for writing.

Using a Dictionary The dictionary is an invaluable tool for determining both the pronunciations and meanings of words. It is especially useful when students have tried all other skills and still have not determined the meaning or pronunciation of an unknown word. Unfortunately, students are often turned off by the way they are exposed to the dictionary. Therefore, keep the following "don'ts" and these very important and positive "dos" in mind:

Don'ts	*Do's*
■ ***Don't*** give students lists of isolated words to look up and define. Words out of context have no meaning, and students will not know which definition to select. This activity is boring and is not good instruction.	■ ***Do*** show students that you, the teacher, often turn to the dictionary to check the spellings, pronunciations, and meanings of words.
■ ***Don't*** use the dictionary as a means of punishment by having students copy pages. Who would ever want to see a dictionary again after that?	■ ***Do*** teach students how to use a dictionary.
■ ***Don't*** require that words on the spelling list be looked up in the dictionary and defined. This is a deadly, useless activity.	■ ***Do*** show students how to make use of a dictionary in their reading and writing.
■ ***Don't*** teach phonetic respelling, except as a way to determine the pronunciations of words in the dictionary.	■ ***Do*** show students how to use a dictionary in all content areas.

TABLE 6.3	Sequence for Teaching Use of the Dictionary

1. Use picture dictionaries to introduce the concept of the dictionary in kindergarten and first grade. Have students learn to locate words in the dictionaries, and teach them to make picture dictionaries of their own.

2. As soon as students have some knowledge of the alphabet, teach them how words are arranged in the dictionary. Give them practice in locating words.

3. Show students how words in the first half of the alphabet fall in the first half of the dictionary and words in the second half fall in the second half. Point out that this knowledge can help students save time by eliminating the need to sift through lots of extra pages.

4. Introduce the concept of phonetic respelling in relation to the pronunciation key, and show students how this key can help them figure out pronunciations.

5. Teach students to locate the meanings of words by using guide words; point out that the dictionary lists more than one meaning for many words.

6. Finish teaching students how to locate words alphabetically, showing them how words are alphabetized not just through the first letter but also through the second, third, fourth, and subsequent letters.

7. Have students learn to select the correct dictionary definitions for multiple-meaning words that are presented in written context.

8. Teach the special symbols used in dictionaries, such as *n* for noun, *v* for verb, and *sing.* for singular.

9. Show students all the other types of information they can find in the dictionary, including lists of synonyms, an atlas, and geographic listings.

10. Provide students with experiences using many different dictionaries and glossaries.

Dictionary use must be taught in a manner that will leave students with positive attitudes. Instruction should begin in kindergarten and continue through the grades until students know and understand the components of the dictionary and can use them effectively. The sequence in Table 6.3 should guide the teaching, which should be developed through meaningful experiences, not isolated skill lessons.

Once students have learned the basics of using the dictionary, it can become a part of their strategy for independently inferring word meanings.

Using a Thesaurus A thesaurus such as *Roget's Thesaurus* (2005) is a dictionary of synonyms and antonyms and is useful for helping readers and writers locate synonyms and antonyms, as well as providing subtle shades of meaning for words. Teachers can introduce elementary-grade students to a thesaurus appropriate to their level. The media specialist in your school can tell you what's available in your building.

It may be easier to learn to use a thesaurus than a dictionary. Once students know how to alphabetize and have learned the concepts of synonyms and antonyms, the rest is quite easy. They must be taught how the thesaurus is organized, how to locate a word, and how to read the synonym or antonym entries. Show students how writers use the thesaurus to locate alternate words to avoid repetition and enliven writing.

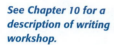

Metacognition: Helping Students Become Strategic Learners

Watch the video clip, study the artifacts in the case, and reflect on the following questions:

1. This chapter presents a list of effective strategies related to teaching vocabulary. Which of these effective vocabulary strategies can you identify within the Video Case?

2. In your own words, describe how the teacher in this Video Case gets her students actively involved in learning and defining new words.

See Chapter 10 for a description of writing workshop.

After students have learned to use the thesaurus, encourage them to use it as a means of improving their writing. One effective way to do this is through mini-lessons during the writing workshop, in which you demonstrate the use of the thesaurus in a group-written story.

The strategies just discussed help students become independent vocabulary learners and constructors of meaning. All require continual integration of new knowledge with old knowledge. Of course, no one strategy alone can meet the needs of all students and all learning situations. When used *judiciously* in combination with wide reading and extensive writing, these strategies should give students the experiences they need to develop strong vocabularies and improve their meaning construction.

A Standards-Based Lesson Using *Everglades Forever: Restoring America's Great Wetland*

Everglades Forever: Restoring America's Great Wetland is an informational (expository) text by Trish Marx and Cindy Karp (Lee & Low Books Inc., 2004) that provides an exciting introduction to America's great wetland.

Standards Used in the Plan

- Sample standards are from the Texas Essential Knowledge and Skills (TEKS) for English Language Arts and Reading for grade 5.
- The website at which you can find these standards is **http://www.tea.state.tx.us/teks/**.
- In this lesson, some Texas indicators are addressed during the introductory activities, some during the reading and responding activities, and some during the extending activities. We tell you how each indicator we included in our sample can be assessed.
- Remember to look at your own state standards to see how they compare to these standards at this grade level.

continued

English Language Arts and Reading, Grade 5

b. Knowledge and skills.

9. Reading/vocabulary development. The student acquires an extensive vocabulary through reading and systematic word study. The student is expected to:

  B. draw on experiences to bring meanings to words in context such as interpreting figurative language and multiple-meaning words (4–5);

  D. determine meanings of derivatives by applying knowledge of the meanings of root words such as like, pay, or happy and affixes such as dis-, pre-, and un- (4–8); and

  E. study word meanings systematically such as across curricular content areas and through current events (4–8).

10. Reading/comprehension. The student comprehends selections using a variety of strategies. The student is expected to:

  A. use his/her own knowledge and experience to comprehend (4–8);

  B. establish and adjust purposes for reading such as reading to find out, to understand, to interpret, to enjoy, and to solve problems (4–8);

  C. monitor his/her own comprehension and make modifications when understanding breaks down such as by rereading a portion aloud, using reference aids, searching for clues, and asking questions (4–8);

  D. describe mental images that text descriptions evoke (4–8);

  E. use the text's structure or progression of ideas such as cause and effect or chronology to locate and recall information (4–8);

  F. paraphrase and summarize text to recall, inform, or organize ideas (4–8);

  G. draw inferences such as conclusions or generalizations and support them with text evidence and experience (4–8);

  H. find similarities and differences across texts such as in treatment, scope, or organization (4–8);

  I. distinguish fact and opinion in various texts (4–8);

  J. answer different types and levels of questions such as open-ended, literal, and interpretative as well as test-like questions such as multiple choice, true-false, and short-answer (4–8); and

  K. represent text information in different ways such as in outline, timeline, or graphic organizer (4–8).

13. Reading/inquiry/research. The student inquires and conducts research using a variety of sources. The student is expected to:

  A. form and revise questions for investigations, including questions arising from interest and units of study (4–5);

  B. use text organizers, including headings, graphic features, and tables of contents, to locate and organize information (4–8);

  C. use multiple sources, including electronic texts, experts, and print resources, to locate information relevant to research questions (4–8);

  D. interpret and use graphic sources of information such as maps, graphs, timelines, tables, or diagrams to address research questions (4–5);

  E. summarize and organize information from multiple sources by taking notes, outlining ideas, and making charts (4–8);

    F. produce research projects and reports in effective formats using visuals to support meaning as appropriate (4–5);

    G. draw conclusions from information gathered from multiple sources (4–8); and

    H. use compiled information and knowledge to raise additional, unanswered questions (3–8).

21. Writing/inquiry/research. The student uses writing as a tool for learning and research. The student is expected to:

    A. frame questions to direct research (4–8);

    B. organize prior knowledge about a topic in a variety of ways such as by producing a graphic organizer (4–8);

    C. take notes from relevant and authoritative sources such as guest speakers, periodicals, or online searches (4–8);

    D. summarize and organize ideas gained from multiple sources in useful ways such as outlines, conceptual maps, learning logs, and timelines (4–8);

    E. present information in various forms using available technology (4–8); and

    F. evaluate his/her own research and raise new questions for further investigation (4–8).

Before Reading the Plan

1. Recall with a peer what you know about activating prior knowledge, vocabulary development, and modes of reading. These concepts are your prior knowledge for reading and evaluating this literacy lesson.

2. Read the text and study the photographs, maps, author's notes, and glossary of *Everglades Forever* on the following pages.

3. Read the Teacher Preparation section that explains the decision-making process used in planning this lesson.

While Reading the Plan

1. Notice how prior knowledge is activated and how vocabulary is developed. Also note mode(s) of reading.

2. Note that vocabulary to be developed includes key-concept words, some Tier Two words, and some Tier Three words.

3. Note mode(s) of reading.

4. Read the Multilevel Notes to see how the teacher is accommodating different reading abilities when all students in the class are reading the same text.

5. Think about changes you might make in the lesson, and be ready to discuss your ideas.

Teacher Preparation

This plan was developed for a fifth-grade class of twenty-eight students. The class includes some ELLs, some students who attend special classes for learning problems, some children who come from affluent families, and others who are on free lunch. In other words, it is a typical class with a range of backgrounds. The entire class will read *Everglades Forever* as part of a larger unit of study in which they read other informational books about endangered parts of our environment. The following section outlines the steps used to plan the lesson and gives a rationale for each.

continued

Unit Activities Prior to Reading the Book *Everglades Forever*

1. The class is starting a unit of study on the environment. They are using a K-W-L chart to discuss what they know about the environment and what they want to know.
2. The media specialist has helped us locate many books and computer-supported media for independent use during the unit. Students have been encouraged to bring books from home for the duration of the unit.

Specific Outcomes Developed in This Lesson

The following outcomes are generic, in that they fit virtually any state's standards. You saw the standards from Texas [TEKS], which can be developed in this lesson.

1. Vocabulary: Learning specific Tier Two and Tier Three words that are key-concept words for the text
2. Constructing meaning: Using K-W-L, generating questions, summarizing
3. Study Skills: Conducting research
4. Writing: Report writing

About This Lesson

1. Prior knowledge (including some vocabulary) will be activated by using a K-W-L chart. This activity will help students set purposes for reading the text.
2. The following words will be developed: Tier Two: *unique, p. 5* and *danger, p. 5; environment, p. 5;* Tier Three: *sloughs, p. 5.* Although several other words may be unfamiliar to students, students should be able to use independent strategies to infer meaning from context or use the glossary.
3. Students will choose words for the self-collection strategy as they read.
4. Students will choose which mode they prefer for reading: cooperative or independent.

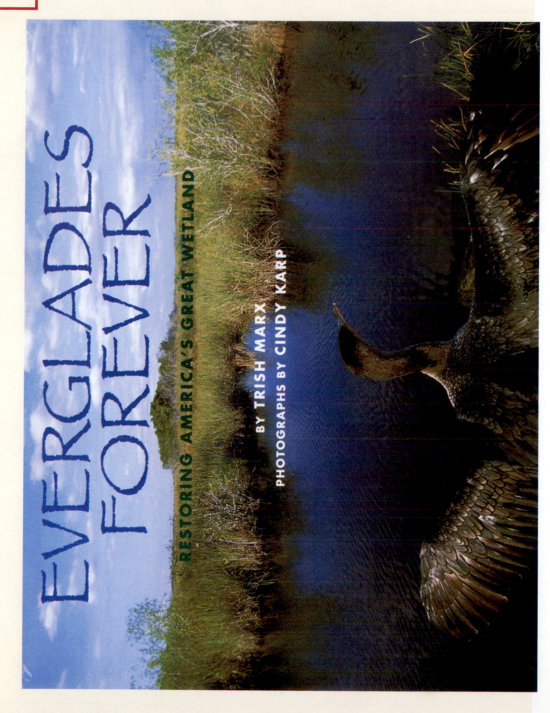

EVERGLADES FOREVER

RESTORING AMERICA'S GREAT WETLAND

BY TRISH MARX

PHOTOGRAPHS BY CINDY KARP

AVOCADO ELEMENTARY SCHOOL

*"In the whole world, there is only one Everglades,"
Ms. Stone told her fifth-grade class at Avocado
Elementary School.*

The Everglades is a wide, shallow, slow-moving river that spreads like a sheet over southern Florida. As the water makes its way to the ocean, it forms a wetland wilderness of prairies and sloughs, tree islands and pine forests, dense stands of cypress trees and brackish ocean inlets. This barely moving water is the life force of the Everglades, and most of it comes in the form of rain that falls during the wet season. Each wet and dry season renews the cycle and mix of plant and animal life that is special to the Everglades.

Ms. Stone's class was studying the Everglades because they live in Homestead, Florida, a town

perched on the eastern edge of this unique natural environment. The plants, animals, water, and weather of the Everglades form an ecosystem, a community that supports life, found nowhere else on Earth. In recognition of the special significance it holds in the world, Everglades National Park has been designated an International Biosphere Reserve, a World Heritage Site, and a Wetland of International Importance.

"The Everglades is in danger," Ms. Stone continued, "and it has been for many years." Today the Everglades is only half as big as it was one hundred years ago. Much of the land has been drained of water and used to develop farms and towns, and some of the water is polluted with chemicals and other substances from this development. All this changes the kinds of plants and animals that can live in the Everglades.

Ms. Stone opened a book of paintings by the famous naturalist John James Audubon. In the early 1800s, Audubon painted many of the birds in the Everglades. He said the sky used to be dark for minutes at a time with the flocks flying overhead.

The children looked out the window. It was hard to imagine that many birds. The Everglades now has only one tenth the number of birds it had two hundred years ago, and some species are endangered. In 1947 part of the Everglades became a national park to protect endangered birds and the thousands of other kinds of animals and plants that live there. Now that part is in serious danger too, because the amount, makeup, and distribution of water flowing into it from other parts of Florida have changed.

6

Map labels:

FLORIDA

Kissimmee River

Lake Okeechobee

EVERGLADES AGRICULTURAL AREA

WATER CONSERVATION AREAS

BIG CYPRESS NATIONAL PRESERVE

Miami

Homestead

Miccosukee Reservation

Shark Valley

Everglades National Park

Pinelands

Royal Palm Anhinga Trail

Atlantic Ocean

Florida Bay

Gulf of Mexico

N

0   10   20 miles

7

Ms. Stone showed the class a large map of southern Florida, including the part of the ocean called Florida Bay.

"This is Everglades National Park," Ms. Stone said, indicating the tip of Florida. She also pointed out a large lake, Lake Okeechobee. The Everglades began thousands of years ago in the Kissimmee River Basin, just north of Lake Okeechobee. The water flowed from the basin into the lake and then started a long, slow journey to the ocean. But in the last one hundred years, that journey has been interrupted.

What happened? the class wanted to know. Why have there been so many changes in the Everglades?

Ms. Stone and her students decided that a few of the children might visit the Everglades, find out more about these changes, and then report back to the class. This would help the students better understand the Everglades and prepare for their field trip to the national park that was coming up in a few weeks.

Four students—Tiler, Conrado, Robert, and Vedantee—volunteered to visit the Everglades. Robert's dad agreed to take them on a weekend trip. They planned to go to the northern part of Everglades National Park and the Miccosukee Reservation, which is located at the boundary of the park.

37

AUTHOR'S NOTE

Cindy Karp lives in Florida and has spent many days in the Everglades. I had been there only once, years ago, but I remember being moved by the mystery of *all that water.* As a child I had looked through a microscope at water from the streams and ponds of Minnesota. The water teemed with life. *Imagine all the life in the water of the Everglades,* I thought.

When Cindy suggested our next book be about the plan to restore the Everglades, I knew this would be an important and fascinating project. If we could involve some local children in the story of the Everglades and the efforts to restore it, we might help all children understand and appreciate what the Everglades means to the world.

At Avocado Elementary School in Homestead, Florida, we found Jacquelyn (Jackie) Stone and her fifth-grade class. Here was a teacher who was passionate about the Everglades and a class of charming, bright, questioning children who studied the Everglades as part of their regular curriculum. Ms. Stone has been teaching the Everglades to children for more than twenty years. "We always do an Everglades unit. I show videos, we read books, and we do an experiment with sponges that shows

the effects of water distribution. At the end we go on a field trip, and sometimes we have gone camping and slough slogging (wading through the Everglades)," she said.

Cindy and I were invited to explore the Everglades with the class, and Cindy visited the school for the experiment and other Everglades studies. There she saw a mural painted by some of the students. It represented the school's investment in the Everglades, both as an important subject to learn about and as a beautiful and mysterious inspiration for art.

"By teaching the Everglades, I am giving these children the responsibility, the legacy, to make sure the Everglades remains," said Ms. Stone. "I tell them I am leaving the Everglades to them."

Trish Marx, 2004

continued

FURTHER READING

Doherty, Kieran. *Marjory Stoneman Douglas: Guardian of the 'Glades.* Twenty-First Century Books, 2002.

Douglas, Marjory Stoneman. *Alligator Crossing,* illustrated by Trudy H. Nicholson. Milkweed, reissued 2003.

Fazio, Wende. *Everglades National Park.* Children's Press, 1999.

George, Jean Craighead. *Everglades,* illustrated by Wendell Minor. HarperCollins, 1995.

Graf, Mike and David Szymanski. *Everglades National Park.* Bridgestone Books, 2003.

Stewart, Melissa. *Life in a Wetland,* photographed by Stephen K. Maka. Lerner, 2003.

Yolen, Jane. *Welcome to the River of Grass,* illustrated by Laura Regan. Putnam, 2001.

WEB SITES OF INTEREST

audubonofflorida.org

avocado.dadeschools.net

everglades.fiu.edu/index.htm

everglades.national-park.com

everglades.org

evergladesplan.org

florida-everglades.com

miamisci.org/ecolinks/everglades

nps.gov/ever/home.htm

39

GLOSSARY

adapt to adjust to different conditions, such as changes in the environment

alga (*pl.* **algae**) (AL-ga, *pl.* AL-jee) single-celled water plant that can make its own food; sometimes they form mats, as in periphyton

aquifer (AK-wa-fer) underground rock formation that contains or can contain water

blueprint detailed plan or outline for action

brackish slightly salty; a mix of freshwater and salty ocean water

dike bank of earth and stone used to control or hold back water

ecosystem (EK-oh-sis-tem or EE-koh-sis-tem) community of organisms and its environment functioning together

elevation height to which something is raised above sea level or the surface of the ground

endangered faced with the danger of becoming extinct and disappearing from Earth

food web diverse relationships of organisms linked through their food; often the smaller is eaten by the larger, which in turn is eaten by a still larger one

fungus (*pl.* **fungi**) (FUNG-ges, *pl.* FUN-jie) living organism without flowers, leaves, or chlorophyll which gets nourishment from dead or living organic matter

habitat place where a plant or an animal naturally lives and grows

hammock land rising out of a wetland, usually containing rich soil and hardwood trees

invertebrate (in-VER-te-brit) animal without a backbone

levee (LEV-ee) wall or bank built to prevent a river from overflowing

lichen (LIE-ken) plant consisting of a fungus and an alga growing together as one plant

marine found in or produced by the sea

marsh soft, wet, low-lying land, often with grasses and cattails growing in it; swamp

migrate to move from one region or climate to another, usually at certain set times

periphyton (pe–RIF–i–ton, *common usage:* per-ee-FIE-ton) loose association of microscopic organisms such as algae and fungi that live attached to underwater surfaces

phosphorus (FOS-fer-es) chemical element used in fertilizers; also a necessary component of plant and animal life

pollutant something that contaminates something else

pollution act or result of a pollutant contaminating something

porous (POUR-us) full of tiny holes through which water can pass

prairie (PRER-ee) relatively level grassland or meadow that may be covered with water

slough (slew) area of soft, muddy ground, such as a swamp or marsh

species (SPEE-shez) group of plants or animals with related characteristics; organisms of a species can breed only with each other

swamp wet, soft land often flooded at regular intervals; marsh

tannic acid (TAN-ik AS-id) chemical formed from bark and other vegetable matter

thermoregulate (thur-mo-REG-ye-late) to regulate body temperature; maintain a constant internal body temperature

wetland low land containing a great deal of moisture with wet, spongy soil

 **Introducing *Everglades Forever***

Activity	Procedures, Comments, and Multilevel Notes
Activate prior knowledge and vocabulary; K-W-L	1. Tell students they are going to read a book entitled *Everglades Forever*. Display the K-W-L chart that asks students to talk about what they know about the Everglades and what they want to know about the Everglades. Discuss as a group. Then have each student complete the first two columns of their own copy of the chart.
	Multilevel Note: *Students may work with a partner.*
Present the book	2. Distribute books to students. Read the title aloud, and then allow a few minutes for students to leaf through the book and look at the photographs and map in the first chapter. Ask students to review their K-W-L charts to see if they want to add or change any of the things they listed. Ask individual students to share what they know and what they want to know.
	Multilevel Note: *All students, regardless of ability, can participate.*
Vocabulary strategy: preview in context	3. Write each Tier Two word on the whiteboard. Pronounce the word, tell students what page it can be found on—for example, this word is *unique;* it is on page 5. Find the word and read the context to tell what it means. Continue in the same manner with all Tier Two and Tier Three words. Discuss words as needed.
Using the glossary	Tell students that they should use the glossary if they encounter any words they do not know as they read.

 Reading and Responding to *Everglades Forever*

Activity	Procedures, Comments, and Multilevel Notes
Review K-W-L charts	Have students review their K-W-L charts to see if they want to make any changes or additions.
	Comment: *This activity reinforces for students that with additional information about a text, one's questions may change.*
Vocabulary; self-collection strategy	Remind students about the strategy of self-collection, which they already have been taught.
	Comment: *This strategy leads to a deeper study of words following reading.*
	Multilevel Note: *This is a powerful tool for students at all levels.*

Standards-Based
Literacy Lessons

continued

Activity	Procedures, Comments, and Multilevel Notes (continued)
Read the text	1. Review modes of reading from which students may choose.
	2. Allow students to choose their preferred mode.
	3. Have students read the first chapter of the text.
	Multilevel Note: *Partner or independent reading is a likely choice for most students. Of course, if there is a need in your class, you could do a guided reading with some or all of the students to meet the needs of students for whom the text may be too difficult.*
Return to K-W-L chart	After reading, have students return to their K-W-L charts and see if any of their questions were answered. Discuss students' responses.
Model summarize	Ask students to model a summary for the first chapter of *Everglades Forever*. If assistance is needed, provide a model for them. Ask different students to share their summary models.
Vocabulary; self-collection strategy	Complete the self-collection strategy steps (page 273).
	Comment: *When revisiting vocabulary in a text, you have opportunities to reinforce other strategies students have been learning. For example, if you had been teaching about inflected endings or suffixes, you might direct attention to examples of these in the text.*

Assessment Note: Assess the following Texas standards while reading and responding to *Everglades Forever*:
During reading:
  ■ Standard 10 (All strategies listed with Standard 10 are continuously used and assessed during reading.)
During review of K-W-L chart:
  ■ Standard 13b
During return to K-W-L chart:
  ■ Standard 13g
During model summarize:
  ■ Standard 21d
During vocabulary; self-collection strategy:
  ■ Standard 9d

Extending *Everglades Forever*

1. Students may add vocabulary words to their individual word books.
2. Tell students that while they are reading this text, they will learn to write reports. Suggest that they think about report topics as they continue to read this text. Ask several students to share possible ideas they have at this time.

**Standards-Based
Literacy
Lessons**

continued

> **Assessment Note:** Assess the following Texas standards during Extending Activities:
> - Standard 21a
> - Standard 21f

 After Reading the Plan

1. Review and discuss the plan with your peers. Focus on how prior knowledge was activated and vocabulary development was supported. Discuss how these two aspects of reading are linked.
2. Plan a different lesson for *Everglades Forever* using one or more other strategies for teaching vocabulary.

Intermediate Grades and Middle School: Decoding, Vocabulary, and Meaning: Key Points

To review the Key Points, see the ACE practice tests at the HM TeacherPrepSPACE Student Website.

- Standards continue to be important at the intermediate grades and middle school levels.
- At these levels, the main focus of students is the application and expansion of the basic decoding skills and strategies they have already developed.
- Students develop both recognition and meaning vocabularies. Meaning vocabulary is the major focus of this chapter.
- Effective vocabulary development includes helping students become aware of words, wide reading and extensive writing, and direct teaching of key words before reading.
- Words for teaching can be divided into key-concept words that include Tier One words, Tier Two words, and Tier Three words.

How Do I Teach?

Noting words in journals, p. 251
Reading aloud, p. 251
Discussion groups, p. 251
Word banks, word files, and word books, p. 252
Word walls or bulletin boards, p. 252

Inferring meaning from context, p. 260
Word maps, p. 261
Semantic mapping, p. 266
Semantic feature analysis, p. 266
Hierarchical and linear arrays, p. 269

Preview in context, p. 270
Contextual redefinition, p. 272
Vocabulary self-collection, p. 273
Structural analysis, p. 274
Dictionary & thesaurus, p. 277

294 ◆ Chapter 6 • Intermediate Grades and Middle School: Decoding, Vocabulary, and Meaning

Video Case in This Chapter

■ **Metacognition: Helping Students Become Strategic Learners**

For Additional Reading

Adams, T. L. (2003). Reading mathematics: More than words can say. *The Reading Teacher, 56*(8), 786–795.

Bear, D. R., Invernizzi, M., Templeton, S. R., & Johnston, F. (2008). *Words their way: Word study for phonics, vocabulary, and spelling instruction* (4th ed.). New York: Prentice Hall.

Beck, I. L., McKeown, M. G., & Kucan, L. (2002). *Bringing words to life: Robust vocabulary instruction.* New York: Guilford Press.

Block, C. C., & Mangieri, J. N. (Eds.). (2006). *The vocabulary enriched classroom: Practices for improving the reading performance of all students in grades 3 and up.* New York: Scholastic.

Hammerberg, D. D. (2004). Comprehension instruction for socioculturally diverse classrooms: A review of what we know. *The Reading Teacher, 57*(7), 648–658.

Jones, R. C., & Thomas, T. G. (2006). Leave no discipline behind. *The Reading Teacher, 60*(1), 58–64.

Jongsma, K. (2003). Beyond beginning learners. *The Reading Teacher, 56*(6), 550–553.

Nagy, W. E. (1988). *Teaching vocabulary to improve reading comprehension.* Newark, DE/Urbana, IL: IRA/NCTE.

Nilsen, A. P., & Nilsen, D. L. J. (2003). A new spin on teaching vocabulary: A source-based approach. *The Reading Teacher, 56*(5), 436–439.

Samblis, K. (2006). Think-Tac-Toe, a motivating method of increasing comprehension. *The Reading Teacher, 59*(7), 691–694.

Spencer, B. H., & Guillaume, A. M. (2006). Integrating curriculum through the learning cycle: Content-based reading and vocabulary instruction. *The Reading Teacher, 60*(3), 206–219.

Stahl, S. A., & Nagy, W. E. (2006). *Teaching word meanings.* Mahwah, NJ: Lawrence Erlbaum Associates.

Villano, T. L. (2005). Should social studies textbooks become history? A look at alternative methods to activate schema in the intermediate classroom. *The Reading Teacher, 59*(2), 122–130.

Wasburn-Moses, L. (2006). 25 best Internet sources for teaching reading. *The Reading Teacher, 60*(1), 70–75.

Websites

Use the Internet as a tool to keep up with the latest research in effective vocabulary development as well as ideas for lessons and activities. Here are a few:

The Clearinghouse on Reading, English, and Communication
This site is an information repository of the Indiana University School of Education.
http://reading.indiana.edu

The Face of Vocabulary Development

This article provides basic information about vocabulary development and links to many other sites. Also on this page are links to special features such as "Lesson of the Day" and "Game of the Week," which was "Secret Word" the day we looked. Or go directly to http://www.education-world.com to see all that is available there. If you enter "Special Theme Page" into their search engine, you will get a page on vocabulary games and activities.

http://www.education-world.com/a_curr/reading/ReadingCoach/ReadingCoach006.shtml

Literacy Matters

Literacy Matters is housed at the Education Development Center, Inc. (EDC, a nonprofit organization that conducts research and develops programs). At the URL provided here are links to many ideas related to developing vocabulary.

http://www.literacymatters.org/content/readandwrite/vocab.htm

Resources for Teaching Vocabulary

The ideas for vocabulary on this page are largely aimed at high school level but could be adapted for younger students. The site is designed to provide resources for home-schooled students, but the ideas apply to all.

http://www.redshift.com/~bonajo/vocabularyresources.htm

Puzzle Depot

Puzzle Depot challenges your brain with free puzzles, Shockwave and Flash games, crosswords, logic games, IQ tests, trivia games, and contests for prizes.

http://www.puzzledepot.com

Quia

This site allows teachers to create their own activities, puzzles, games, or quizzes online or access hundreds of activities created by other educators in all content areas.

http://www.quia.com

Responding and the Construction of Meaning

7

Terms
YOU NEED TO KNOW

- analysis
- creative response
- dialogue journals
- diaries
- double-entry journals
- generalization
- journals
- learning logs
- literature discussion group (or circle)
- personal response
- readers theater
- responding
- response charts
- response journals (reading journals, literature logs)
- retelling
- summary

The HM TeacherPrepSPACE Student Website offers many helpful resources, such as self-quizzes, glossary flashcards, lesson plan templates, and more.

We are looking in on a third-grade classroom, where many literacy activities are taking place. Melissa and several classmates are at their desks reading Mississippi Bridge *(Taylor, 1990). Melissa points out an illustration to a classmate. They chat for a few minutes and then return to their reading.*

Other students work with James and the Giant Peach *(Dahl, 1961). Some are reading the book, some are writing in their journals, and one very excited young man, Mark, is working on a project. I stop to talk to him.*

"This looks like an interesting project," I say. "Tell me about it."

Mark shows me the cover of his book. "Have you ever read it?" he asks.

"Yes, I have."

"Did you like it?"

"Yes! Did you?"

"I sure did! I loved when the peach started to roll away and the things that happened next. I'm making a movie box about my favorite parts in the book."

In another area of the room, Mrs. Eggars, the teacher, and a group of students are discussing How Many Days to America? *(Bunting, 1988). Joe says it would be really tough to leave everything you had and go off to a new country. Maria says, "Yes, but it would be better; they might have more things, and they wouldn't be afraid of the soldiers. I'd go."*

Mrs. Eggars adds, "You know, I don't know how I would feel. I've never had to leave my home like the people in our story. Do you know anyone who has ever had this kind of experience?"

Lisa says, "Our neighbors came from Vietnam."

The discussion continues in this manner.

Notice what we saw in this classroom:

- While Melissa and her classmates were reading, it was natural for them to stop and talk about the story. This shows that students are taking control of and monitoring their own reading.

- Other students were writing in journals about their books, and one student was working on a movie box, a series of pictures drawn on a roll of paper and shown as a movie by turning the roll through an opening in a box.

- Some students and the teacher were part of a discussion group. Each member participated in the discussion, no right or wrong answers were expected, and the teacher was an active participant.

The teacher's role in this class was essential. Mrs. Eggars had planned the experiences that allowed and encouraged children to read, respond, and monitor their own learning. At the same time she participated in groups, modeling for students and prompting them as needed. As all of the students in this class and their teacher show, active responding is an important element in learning to construct meaning and become literate (Hansen, 1987).

Responding: What It Means and Why It Is Important

Responding is what one does as a result of and/or as a part of reading, writing, or listening to any kind of text, fiction, poetry, drama, or nonfiction. The children in Mrs. Eggars' third-grade classroom responded in various ways during and after reading. You too do it all the time. You respond to a textbook chapter by discussing it with a peer, or you respond to a newspaper article on the homeless by finding out how to donate food to a local mission. Responding is a natural part of constructing meaning. (See the "Educators Speak" feature on page 323.)

When you respond to a piece of literature, or any kind of writing, you use prior knowledge to construct meaning. Therefore, each person's construction is individual and personal, the result of the transaction between the reader and the text (Rosenblatt, 1938/1976, 1978, 1991). Recall from your own college experience when you were asked to read a short story or poem and write your interpretation of it. Perhaps you received a "C" because your interpretation did not agree with that of your instructor. We know that many acceptable interpretations and responses are possible from reading a single piece of literature. Although there may be a generally accepted response, personal response varies greatly from student to student. Even within the generally accepted responses, different interpretations often occur. Therefore, as the teacher, you must be prepared to *expect, respect,* and *accept* a variety of responses from students (Martinez & Roser, 1991). These responses will help you decide what additional support your students need.

Responding is also valuable because it can serve as part of your assessment. Many literacy standards call for students to respond in different formats—learning logs, projects, and so forth.

For more discussion of using responses as a part of assessment, see Chapter 11.

Types of Responses

Responses to literature fall into two basic categories: personal and creative.

Personal responses are usually oral or written. Students may retell, generalize, and tell how they felt about what they read, their favorite part or character, or how what they read connects to their lives. For example, after reading *The Lion, the Witch, and the Wardrobe* (Lewis, 1950), a fifth-grade student wrote the personal response shown in Figure 7.1 in her dialogue journal. This student responded personally by relating the book to her own life and her parents, though her teacher may want to encourage deeper thinking. When students first begin responding their responses are much simpler. The second grader's response shown in Figure 7.2 simply naming his favorite story, *Skip to My Lou* (Westcott, 1989), shows that he needs support in responding. Later in the chapter, there is more about how teachers can support students' responses.

Creative responses are often expressed through activities such as art, music, drama, and dance. Students use what they have read in some creative way; of course, a creative response is personal also. The response shown in Figure 7.3 is a

FIGURE 7.1	Personal Response to *The Lion, the Witch, and the Wardrobe* (Lewis, 1950)

10-19

Dear Mrs. Fugler,

    I think *The Lion, The Witch, and The Wardrobe.* Was a very good book, and that you should read it some day in the class. It was a 186 pages long and has 11 chapters. Lucy in this story is kind of like me because I tell my parents but they don't believe me and I have to bother them and bother them just like Lucy did. Then they go and see for thier selfs and Then they believe her or Lucy.

                      Sincerely

                      Nichole B.

Dear Nichole,

    I enjoy that book myself. Are you going to read the rest of the series? yes I am

    You did a fine job of relating Lucy to yourself. You are ready to choose your next book.

                    Sincerely,

                    Mrs Fugler

two-sided poster that a student made after reading *Miss Nelson Is Missing* (Allard & Marshall, 1977).

    Creative responses may be prompted by the teacher, or they may be spontaneous on the part of the students. They may lead to good discussions. Keep in mind, however, that *it is not the number of activities that makes better readers; it is the amount of reading.*

FIGURE 7.2   **Personal Response to *Skip to My Lou* (Westcott, 1989)**

My favorite story is skip to my Lou darling!

Applebee (1978) suggests another way to look at responses: he describes four types of responses, each reflecting a different level of thought processes:

- **Retelling:** This is a simple recall of title, beginning and ending situations, and some dialogue, with no relative importance given to any of the events.
- **Summary:** Events are retold in order of importance. Summaries are usually shorter than retellings.
- **Analysis:** The response to the story is personal and subjective. For example, a student responding to *Annabelle Swift, Kindergartner* (Schwartz, 1988) might

FIGURE 7.3 **Creative Response to *Miss Nelson Is Missing* (Allard & Marshall, 1977)**

say, "This story is like what happened to me in kindergarten," and then relate a similar experience.

- ■ *Generalization:* This addresses the theme or meaning of the story. For example, a generalization of *Annabelle Swift, Kindergartner* (Schwartz, 1988) might focus on the idea that you should trust yourself and not depend on the advice of others.

Even younger children can often make limited generalizations or analyze a story to some degree (Many, 1991). Fourth graders can actively construct meaning by analyzing and evaluating literature (Kelly & Farnan, 1991).

Studies indicate that encouraging personal responses is important in helping students learn to construct meaning (Cullinan, Harwood, & Galda, 1983; Eeds, 1989; Galda, 1982, 1983; Gambrell, 1986; Hickman, 1983; Morrow, 1985; Purves, 1972). As Kelly (1990) says, "Allowing students to respond to what they read or heard from a read-aloud provided the framework for what Piaget referred to as the active involvement in learning through the construction of meaning. Readers deepen and extend their interpretations of literature when they respond to that literature in a variety of ways." As responses take place and are encouraged over time, students develop more complex responses that help them become more adept at constructing meaning.

English Language Learners (ELLs) can respond in their primary language, or draw pictures and label them, which keeps them involved (Freeman & Freeman,

See the "Websites" section at the end of the chapter for ideas of ways to share literature outside the classroom.

2001). Even if teachers can't read the response, it will be clear that the student did respond. Sometimes another student, an aide, or a parent can read these responses and react to them or help ELLs reframe them in English.

Students may enjoy posting their responses to literature on a website such as amazon.com. Here they can also read what others have said about books.

The Value of Responding

When all children are given opportunities to function in a response-centered classroom, they develop a sense of ownership, pride, and respect for learning.

- When all students respond to the same piece of literature, they know their responses will be valued and accepted as much as anyone else's.
- When both gifted students and at-risk students respond to the same piece of literature, each responds in a manner consistent with his or her functioning level.
- Students learn that the teacher values their responses, and they learn to value the responses of their peers.
- This type of respect leads to a sense of community and ownership.
- Responding helps students learn to monitor their own reading and writing. By being continually encouraged to think about and react to what they are reading and writing, students develop their metacognitive processes, which are important in constructing meaning (Palincsar & Brown, 1986; Paris et al., 1991).
- The goal of response activities is to get students to construct meaning by interacting with the text. Through this interaction, or transaction, students become better comprehenders.
- Responses help students learn skills and strategies. Look at the poster in Figure 7.3. This student obviously knows how to locate important information and character traits. She developed the use of these skills partly through reading and responding.

Responding and Standards

When students respond to what they read, they are engaged in activity that matches many standards. For example, a sample standard from IRA/NCTE (available online) states: "Students participate as knowledgeable, reflective, creative, and critical members of a variety of literacy communities." Clearly, any response to literature meets this standard. Individual states will have a similar standard. No matter where you teach, you will be planning instruction to meet standards. In fact, a written, oral, or other creative response to reading will undoubtedly meet other standards for students such as increasing the range of understanding, adjusting use of language, using strategies and different writing processes, applying knowledge of language structure and conventions, using one's first language to develop competency in English, and using spoken, written, and visual language to accomplish their own purposes.

A Classroom Atmosphere That Promotes Responding

Of course, you will create a literate environment and include extensive opportunities for students to read and write. (See the "Educators Speak" feature on page 323.) But the response-centered classroom has other characteristics as well.

As the teacher in such a classroom, you must believe that all students have reactions and feelings that are important and valid, and students must have this belief about one another and about you. A sense of community may begin with the physical arrangement of the room, but it also includes how you treat students. If they learn that you always expect "right" answers or reward only thinking that you agree with, they will treat one another in that manner and strive to give only expected responses. But if they learn that you accept many possible answers and interpretations of what they have read, they will become more tolerant and accepting of one another's ideas.

This classroom attitude of acceptance evolves partly out of the way you ask questions and respond to students' answers. In the past, teachers often just asked a series of questions to determine whether students comprehended what they read. For example, if students had read *The True Story of the 3 Little Pigs* (Scieszka, 1989), the teacher "checked" their comprehension by asking questions such as these: *Who told this story? What caused the wolf to go to the house of the first little pig? What happened at the house of the second little pig? What made the wolf angry at the third little pig's house? How did you feel about the wolf's story?*

Notice that only the last question begins to move students toward thinking more openly and relating what they have learned to their own experiences. Contrast these questions with the following:

1. What was different about this story and the one you already know about the three pigs?
2. Why do you suppose the wolf would choose to tell his story?
3. If you had been in the wolf's place, how would you have approached this situation?

These questions seek varied responses and let students know that it is entirely appropriate for each person to have a different response. A critical difference with this second group of questions is in the way you respond to the students. Suppose a student answers question 2 by telling you that the wolf probably told this story because he just wanted to tell another story, and you say or imply that the answer is wrong. That student and others who heard your response will get the message that you are looking for a certain "right" answer, despite what you say. But if you say, "That is certainly a possibility; let's hear some other thoughts," students will get a totally different message from you: your actions will match your words.

Sometimes it is appropriate to ask "mostly-right-answer" questions; for example, when students need support in understanding a story during teacher-guided reading. However, when you want to prompt children's responses to reading, you should ask more open-ended, suppositional questions and then show that you accept and value a variety of responses. Table 7.1 gives some examples of questions that suit this purpose. The questions in Group I specifically relate to the text being

TABLE 7.1	**Sample Open-Ended Questions That Promote Responses to Literature**

Group I

1. Where and when does the story take place? How do you know? If the story took place somewhere else or in a different time, how would it be changed?
2. What incident, problem, conflict, or situation does the author use to get the story started?
3. What does the author do to create suspense and make you want to read on to find out what happens?
4. Trace the main events of the story. Could you change their order or leave any of them out? Why or why not?
5. Think of a different ending to the story. How would the rest of the story have to be changed to fit the new ending?
6. Did the story end the way you expected it to? What clues did the author offer to prepare you to expect this ending? Did you recognize these clues as important to the story as you were first reading or hearing it?
7. Who is the main character of the story? What kind of person is the character? How did you know?
8. Are any characters changed during the story? If they are, how are they different? What changed them? Did it seem believable?
9. Some characters play small but important roles in a story. Name such a character. Why is this character necessary for the story?
10. Who is the teller of the story? How would the story change if someone else in the book or an outside narrator told the story?
11. Does the story as a whole create a certain mood or feeling? What is the mood? How is it created?
12. Did you have strong feelings as you read the story? What did the author do to make you feel strongly?
13. What are the main ideas behind the story? What makes you think of them as you read the story?
14. Is this story like any other story you have read or watched?
15. Think about the characters in the story. Are any of them the same type of character you have met in other stories?

Group II

1. What idea or ideas does this story make you think about? How does the author get you to think about this?
2. Do any particular feelings come across in this story? Does the story actually make you feel in a certain way, or does it make you think about what it's like to feel that way? How does the author do this?
3. Is there one character that you know more about than any of the others? Who is this character, and what kind of person is he or she? How does the author reveal the character to you?
4. Are there other characters important to the story? Who are they? Why are they important?
5. Is there anything that seems to make this particular author's work unique? If so, what?
6. Did you notice any particular patterns in the form of this book? If you are reading this book in more than one sitting, are there natural points at which to break off your reading? If so, what are these?
7. Were there clues that the author built into the story that helped you to anticipate the outcome? If so, what were they? Did you think these clues were important when you read them?
8. Does the story language seem natural for the intent of the story and for the various speakers?
9. Every writer creates a make-believe world and peoples it with characters. Even where the world is far different from your own, how does the author make the story seem possible or probable?
10. What questions would you ask if the author were here? Which would be the most important question? How might the author answer it?

Source: Group I: Reprinted by permission of the author and publisher from Sloan, Glenna Davis, *The Child as Critic: Teaching Literature in Elementary and Middle Schools*, 2d ed., pp. 104–106. (New York: Teachers College Press, 1984. ©1984 by Teachers College, Columbia University. All rights reserved.) Group II: From *Child and Story* by Kay Vandergrift. (©1980 Neal-Schuman Publishers. Reprinted with permission of the publisher.) Both cited by Harste, Short, and Burke (1988).

Video Case

Portfolio Assessment: Elementary Classroom

Watch the video clip, study the artifacts in the case, and reflect on the following questions:

1. Based on the Video Case, do you think Mr. Park has created a classroom environment that promotes responding? Cite specific examples from the Video Case and its accompanying materials to support your answer.

2. From the perspective of the classroom teacher, describe the benefits and challenges of using journals (and portfolios) as part of teaching methodology.

read; the questions in Group II encourage deeper thinking and more comparisons. Both groups of questions support divergent thinking.

Opportunities for response to literature will come primarily in two ways: through self-selected books and materials and through those that you assign. Students may be reading self-selected literature as a part of independent reading, or you may have reached a point where you encourage self-selected reading for instructional purposes.

See Chapter 2 for a detailed discussion of the literacy lesson.

Often the entire class will read the same piece of literature, although students of differing abilities will approach it differently: some will read independently, some cooperatively, and some supported through directed reading or read-alouds. The literature you have students read as an entire class will usually be the materials used for your literacy lessons, which are designed to promote responding. In all instances, students will respond to the literature according to their own abilities.

Procedures That Promote Responding to Literature

There are many ways to encourage and support students as they respond to literature, and each procedure has a special function. This section discusses four procedures: journals, response charts, literature discussion groups, and readers theater.

Journals

Journals are anything in which students record personal reflections about their reading and writing. Journals can range from a simple student-made booklet to a spiral notebook or binder with loose-leaf pages to a computer personal storage device.

See Chapter 10 for more about writing workshop.

Students who are involved in a writing workshop using process writing develop fluency and confidence in their writing, and using journals extends, reinforces, and supports these skills. Journals help tie together reading and writing, and give students opportunities to construct their own personal meanings (Atwell, 1998; Harste et al., 1988; Parsons, 2001; Tierney et al., 1990; Weaver, 1990a).

Journals can be divided into five basic categories: diaries, response journals, dialogue journals, double-entry journals, and learning logs. Except for diaries, all of these journal types can be diagnostic, in that they add to your assessment information about a student. Although their forms are similar, these journals have significant differences:

- ■ *Diaries* are private records of personal observations or random jottings, or a daily record of thoughts and feelings. These are usually not shared, and students do not usually use them for responding to a piece of literature.

- ■ *Response journals* are used by students to record their personal reactions to, questions about, and reflections on what they read, view, write, or hear. Response journals are sometimes called *reading journals* or *literature logs*. They might include lists of words students want to learn, goals for reading (such as number of pages to be completed), predictions made before and during reading, notes or comments made during reading, and reactions, thoughts, or feelings recorded after reading. If you just want students to keep track of their independent reading, you might not read these journals, but if you want them to respond to literature they have read or to pieces they have written, you probably will read them. Figure 7.4 shows a sample page from a fourth grader's response journal about *The Witch of Fourth Street and Other Stories* (Levoy, 1974).

- ■ *Dialogue journals* have the same basic purpose as response journals, except that the teacher (and sometimes a peer) reads and responds in writing to the student's responses. "The major characteristic that distinguishes Dialogue Journals from other forms is the importance given to communications between the student and the teacher" (Tierney et al., 1990, p. 97). The comments from others help the student construct meaning more effectively. Figure 7.5 presents a sample page from a dialogue journal about *Wait Till Helen Comes* (Hahn, 1986). Notice how the teacher's responses help the student think and construct meaning. E-mail is wonderful for this kind of journal. Students could share literature responses with friends anywhere in the world.

- ■ *Double-entry journals* have pages that are divided into two parts. On the left side of the page, students make notes, list predictions, and draw diagrams before and during reading. On the right side, they write a response to their reading. If the double-entry journal is also being treated as a dialogue journal, the teacher replies on the right-hand side of the page. These journals have been recommended for use with all students, including at-risk learners (Coley & Hoffman, 1990). Figure 7.6 shows a double-entry journal completed by a seventh grader reading *The Summer of the Swans* (Byars, 1970).

- ■ *Learning logs* are daily records of what students have learned (Harste et al., 1988; Thompson, 1990). Figure 7.7 shows a sample entry from a third grader's learning log; this is simply a daily account of what this student has learned, with little response to the book. Sometimes, however, the learning log focuses on the learning that has taken place in a particular content area, such as math, science, or social studies. Learning logs may be treated as simple response journals or as dialogue journals between the teacher and students.

FIGURE 7.4   **Page from a Fourth Grader's Response Journal**

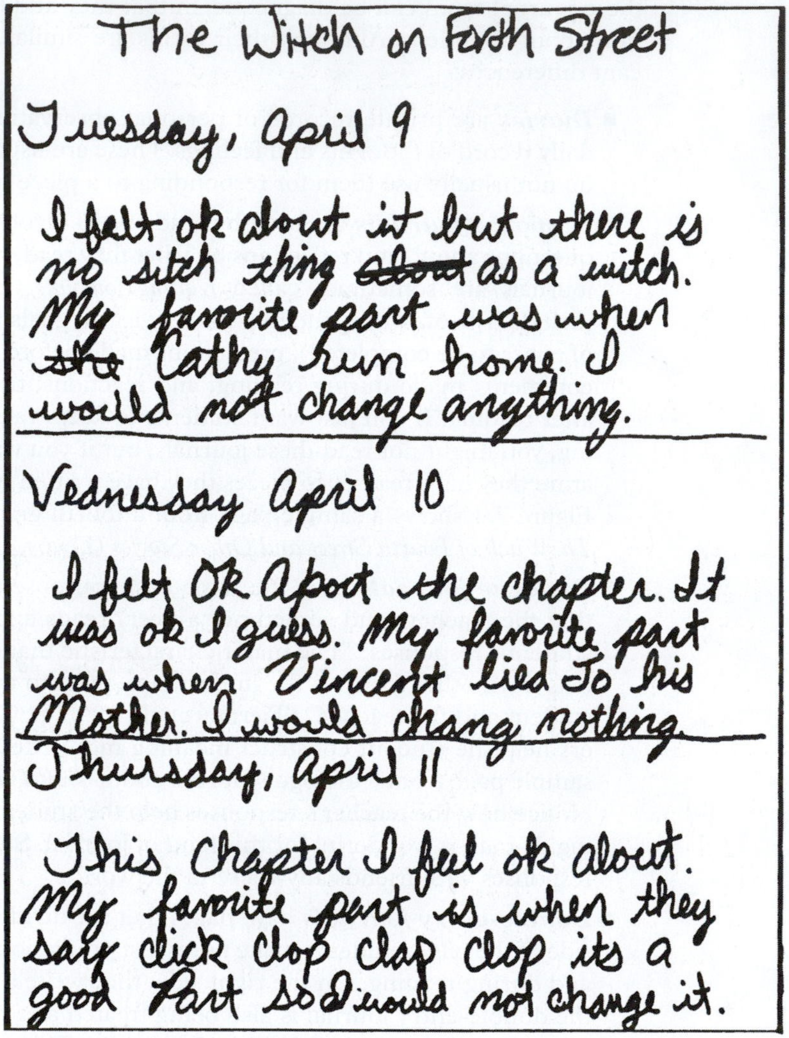

The Witch on Forth Street

Tuesday, April 9

I felt ok about it but there is no sitch thing ~~about~~ as a witch. My favorite part was when ~~the~~ Cathy run home. I would not change anything.

Wednesday April 10

I felt OK About the chapter. It was ok I guess. My favorite part was when Vincent lied to his Mother. I would chang nothing.

Thursday, April 11

This Chapter I feel ok about. My favorite part is when they say click clop clap clop its a good Part so I would not change it.

Deciding Which Journal Type to Use

Table 7.2 on page 312 summarizes the features of the five types of journals. You must decide which type, or combination of types, you want to use. The important thing is to know why you are having students keep a journal. Is it for:

- prompting students to reflect on their personal thoughts and feelings?
- encouraging students to keep a personal record of independent reading?
- encouraging students to respond to literature or their writing?
- carrying on a dialogue with students to help them learn to construct meaning?
- having students summarize what they have learned?

FIGURE 7.5   **Page from a Dialogue Journal**

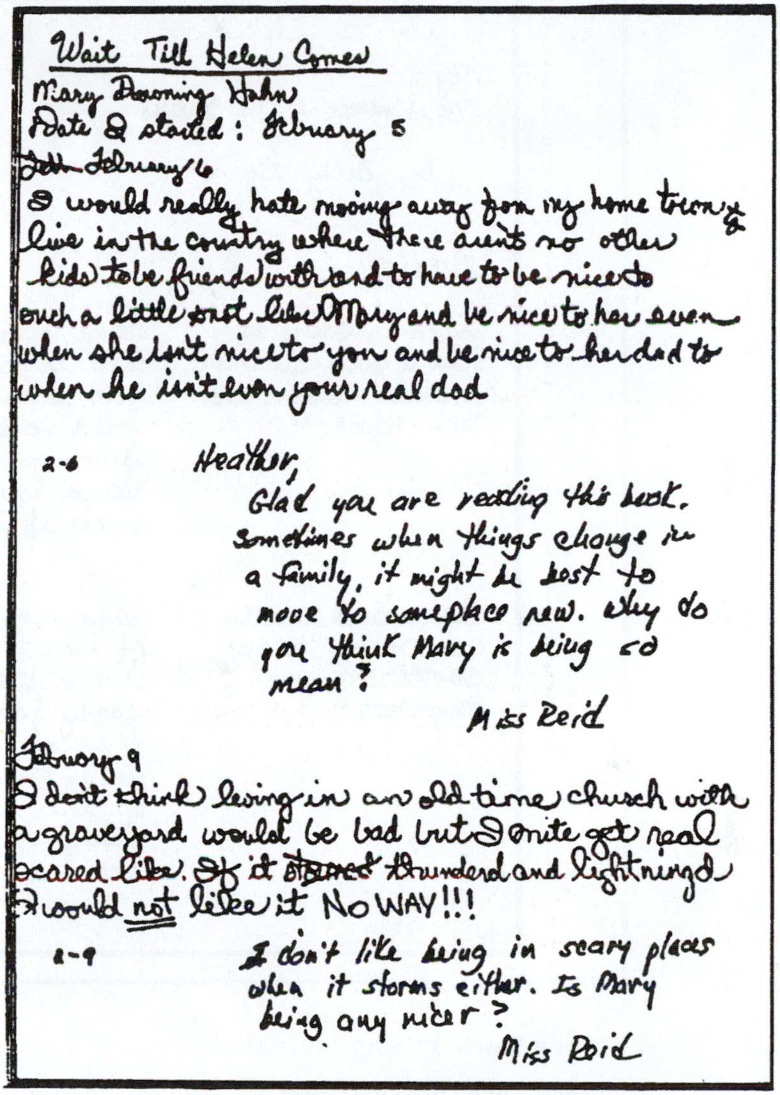

> Wait Till Helen Comes
> Mary Downing Hahn
> Date I started: February 5
> Feb. February 6
> I would really hate moving away from my home town to
> live in the country where there aren't no other
> kids to be friends with and to have to be nice to
> such a little snot like Mary and be nice to her even
> when she isn't nice to you and be nice to her dad to
> when he isn't even your real dad
>
> 2-6   Heather,
>   Glad you are reading this book.
>   sometimes when things change in
>   a family, it might be best to
>   move to someplace new. why do
>   you think Mary is being so
>   mean?
>   Miss Reid
>
> February 9
> I don't think living in an old time church with
> a graveyard would be bad but I mite get real
> scared like. If it started thundered and lightninged
> I would not like it NO WAY!!!
>
> 2-9   I don't like being in scary places
>   when it storms either. Is Mary
>   being any nicer?
>   Miss Reid

Once you have determined your purpose for using journals, you can decide on the type or combination of types you want to try. Remember that students do not have to write in their journals every day or after every piece of literature they read. Imposing such stringent requirements makes journal writing a laborious task and defeats its purpose. At first, you may have to nudge some students to write in their journals; however, as they become comfortable with the process, most will write readily.

May 8
The Summer of the Swans

by Betsy Byars

Predictions

Sara is going to have a good summer because swans are beautifull.	Sara is really bored. She is not having a good summer. It is hard to be a teenager. Summers are tough. Sara loves Charlie even if he is a pain.
Sara and Charlie are going to do something good together.	Sara has been sort of nice to Charlie. She is still feeling sorry for her self. I think she is really going to grow up this summer. Last summer I was a lot like Sara.

Getting Started Using Journals

Journals can be used with students at any grade level, though beginning learners are not expected to write as much as or use their journals in the same ways older students do. You should adapt the following procedures and suggestions to meet the needs of your students.

Begin by Making a Journal of Your Own with Some Entries in It Share your journal with your students, and discuss how all of you will keep journals in which you will write about what you have read. If you plan to read and respond to your students' journals, you should give them the opportunity to read and respond to yours too. It is important that you model this process for students as well as experience what they are going through.

FIGURE 7.7	Sample Entry from a Learning Log, Third Grade

> Jan. 28
>
> The Titanic
>
> I learned that the Titanic was a great ship. It is going on the first trip. A lots of people are on the ship. The ship hits a big iceberg. It starts to fill up with water. It is not supose to sink. People do not want to leave the ship. Music is playing. The ship sinks. Many people die. The safe ship was not safe. It was sad.

Explain the Idea of Journal Writing to Your Class Tell students that the purpose of journal writing is to encourage them to think about what they are reading and to share their thoughts. If you are going to respond to students' journals, point out that this is a way for you to talk to each of them and for them to talk to you.

Talk with Students About What Types of Entries They Might Make in Their Journals Tell students they may write about what they have read, draw about it, make notes indicating they have shared their book in some way with another person, or perhaps decide on some other idea of their own. The main thing is that they respond in some way to their reading. Encourage students to suggest how they might respond to a piece of literature, such as by telling about a character, writing about what they

TABLE 7.2	Types of Journals	
Journal Type	**Description**	**Features**
Diary	Private records of personal observations and thoughts	Not read by anyone unless student requests
Response journal (literature log or reading journal)	Reactions, questions, and reflections about what has been read	Sometimes a personal record and sometimes read by the teacher
Dialogue journal	A conversation between student and teacher about what has been read	Read by the teacher and sometimes peers; comments written by the reader
Double-entry journal	A split page on which students jot down ideas before and during reading on the left side and give reactions after reading on the right side	May or may not be read by the teacher or peers
Learning log	A listing of what has been learned	May be treated as a dialogue journal or as a response journal

would have done in a similar situation, or relating events to their own lives. Stress that there is no right or wrong way to respond. Obviously, responses will vary in quality, but your responses to their writing will help students improve.

Have Students Work in Cooperative Groups to Write Some Journal Entries
Cooperative groups support students as they begin journal writing without the need for models or samples. We have found that students tend to copy samples and be hampered by them. However, collaborative writing lets students see that they can create their own types of responses. Encourage students to share their responses with the class.

Talk with Students About the Format of Their Journals and How Often They Should Write in Them Give students a simple format (or several formats) for recording such information as the date of entry, book title, author, and copyright date. Then have them write whatever they want to say. Be sure the format or guidelines are not too rigid, or you may inhibit their responding. Help students evaluate and choose from among several formats and make modifications, if needed.

If others will read journal entries, students should strive to express their ideas so others can understand, but do not overemphasize legibility, spelling, or grammar at first. If students know their journal entries will not be evaluated for mechanics and spelling, they will be free from some of the concerns that might discourage writing. During writing workshop, students will learn about the common courtesy of writing and spelling to communicate with others.

See Chapter 10 for information about writing workshop.

Atwell (1998) tells how she uses a letter to introduce journal writing to her middle school students. A copy of a similar letter used by a third-grade teacher appears in Figure 7.8. You could adapt this idea for use at any grade level.

FIGURE 7.8   **Letter for Introducing Journals to Third Graders**

Michael D. Robinson   Third Grade Teacher

Dear Girls and Boys,   August

This year you will be using your Reading Journal to write me letters about the books you are reading. I will write letters back to you as I read your letters. This will be one of the ways we talk about your books. I will also tell you about the books I am reading.

As you write each letter, tell me about your book — how you feel about it, what you like and don't like, what it makes you think about, your favorite parts, etc.... Draw pictures if you want to. I may even draw some pictures for you!

These letters will help you and me decide how you are doing with your reading and writing. We will discuss them during conferences. Here are some things for you to remember:

- date all your letters
- be sure to give the title <u>and</u> author
- write at <u>least</u> two letters each week
- tape this letter in the front of your journal

I'm excited about getting your letters. We'll learn a lot about each other.

Happy Reading,
Mr. Robinson

Use a Response Chart or Some Other Device to Prompt and Support Students Who Need It Response charts are discussed later in this chapter. They are designed to help students think of ways to respond to their reading.

Plan with Students a System for Using and Storing Journals Choose a place for storing the journals alphabetically, such as in boxes, a file drawer, or a crate. Students can then find them easily. If journals are stored on an individual data back-up device, students may keep them in their desks or store them in a box next to the computers.

For more about journal use, see the "For Additional Reading" section at the end of this chapter.

During the Initial Stages of Journal Writing, Evaluate with Students How the Procedure Is Progressing Whenever students try something new or different, some details usually need to be worked out. Take time to talk about how things are going and identify ways to improve them.

What to Expect When Students Begin to Use Journals

Some students will embrace the use of journals from the start. Others may resist or have difficulties of one kind or another. With time and continued teacher support, all students can successfully use journals as one kind of response to literature. Here are some possible concerns:

"I Don't Know What to Do" This is a likely reaction from students who are insecure about their own literacy and are having difficulty constructing meaning. Most will become more comfortable with the process as they gain experience. Students may also react this way if they have had many past experiences in which only "right" answers were expected. Writing journal responses may be new for students. In a sense, these students are redefining reading for themselves, because they are learning that a text can have multiple interpretations. For these students, suggest some possible responses and use a response chart, discussed later in this chapter.

Concerns About Accuracy in Spelling and Usage Some students may be uncertain about the language or may have been in environments that stressed correctness. Keep reassuring them that you are not concerned about grammar and spelling in their journals; you are concerned only about their thinking and their reactions.

Retelling But Not Responding Some students may simply retell what they have read rather than responding personally. This is normal; students will progress beyond retelling as they gain more experience in responding. Your responses should consist of questions that focus attention beyond retelling. For example, you might write, "How would you have reacted in this situation?" or "What lesson do you think we can learn from this book?"

Some teachers encourage students to retell or summarize as one way to respond to literature and this can be an effective way to help children construct meaning (Gambrell, Pfeiffer, & Wilson, 1985; Marshall, 1983; Morrow, 1989b). Such responses are also easy for teachers to evaluate.

Retellings and evaluation of responses are discussed more in Chapter 11.

Getting in a Rut Some students immediately become comfortable with a particular mode of response and latch onto it, using it again and again. Your responses are important in moving these students forward. Asking a question such as, "Have you ever thought about the characters [or other aspects] in the stories you are reading?" will help them think of alternatives.

Anxiety About Teacher Opinion If you are using dialogue journals, some students may be anxious about what you will write in their journals and what you will think of their ideas. In these instances, you need to respond with positive, upbeat, non-judgmental comments that will allay these fears.

Journals are an excellent tool to use with all students. Barone (1990) notes that even young children begin responding by focusing on explicit story elements but soon become more interpretive, which indicates that they are working through the text they are reading, focusing on more than literal comprehension, and understanding the story more completely.

Responding to Students' Journals

In a response-centered classroom, both the students and the teacher are responsible for responding (Hansen, 1987). The students respond to their reading and writing and to one another's journals, including the teacher's. The teacher, in turn, responds to the students' journals, especially when dialogue journals are being used.

Teachers who want to use journals often raise two major questions: (1) "When do I find time to read all the journals?" and (2) "What exactly do I write in response to students' journal entries?" Both questions deserve serious consideration.

Finding Time to Read Journals You do not have to read every journal entry students make. A response journal that is an individual record for the student's own use does not require reading or responding by the teacher. Even if journals require you to respond, you do not have to do so every day for every entry. Dialogue journals require the most consistent form of response by the teacher because this is a major means of "talking" with students and helping them learn.

Finding the time to read journals is not nearly as difficult as it may seem at first, because journals will replace many papers that used to be assigned with a more meaningful learning task. One fourth-grade teacher said, "I read some of my students' journals during conference period if there is no one ready to talk with me. If there are any journals that I need to see on any day and haven't, I read them right after school. I rarely carry any of them home."

Some teachers use part of silent, or independent, reading time to read students' journals or any time when students are working independently. Others like to read journals just before or right after school. Your plan must fit your teaching style and needs.

How to Write Responses When you write responses in students' journals, keep in mind your goals.

You want to encourage students to continue to read and think about what they are reading, as well as to feel good about themselves and what they are writing. Some examples of encouraging types of responses appear below. Notice that each provides a different type of encouragement according to the situation. Although you will do more than encourage with your comments, *encouragement is your number one goal.*

Goals for Writing Responses to Journals

- Encourage students
- Guide students
- Refocus student responses
- Make helpful suggestions

Dear Jeri,

    You are doing a very good job telling about the characters in _Now One Foot, Now the Other_. Which character do you think is most important in this story? Why? I'm looking forward to your next entry.

              Mr. C

Source: Now One Foot, Now the Other (de Paola, 1980).

Dear Sam,

    The way you are retelling this story, I can tell that you are enjoying it !! Have you ever had an adventure like April's? If you have, why don't you compare your adventure to hers. Keep going! I can't wait to see what you think later in this book.

              Mr. C

Source: The Egypt Game (Snyder, 1976).

Sometimes you will find that more *guidance* is needed in helping the student see important points or the big message the author is trying to deliver. For example, Nichole (see Figure 7.1) did not address the big ideas in *The Lion, the Witch, and the Wardrobe* (Lewis, 1950) and would benefit from guidance. Suppose your third graders are all reading *Fly Away Home* (Bunting, 1991), and you notice that some students are not understanding why it is important for the father and little boy not to be noticed in the airport. (This story is about a homeless father and son who make their home in a large airport, moving from terminal to terminal to keep from getting caught.) One student wrote the following:

> The boy in this story did not talk to people. He was not a friend.

The teacher might respond as follows:

> I thought the little boy really wanted to be friends. He was friends with Mrs. Medina and her family. He just couldn't be friends with everyone in the airport. Look back through the book and see if you can find places that show why he can't be friends with everyone.

At other times, students will just need to be *refocused* in their journals and in their reading. If a student always responds by drawing a picture and labeling it "My Favorite Part," you might ask the student to try a different response. For example:

> Your pictures of favorite parts are great. For your next entry, draw three pictures that show the three main events in the next chapter. Write a sentence or two about each picture.

This type of response shows how instruction and the student's growth work together. It helps the student use drawing but begins to move her or him toward looking at important events in the story. Refocusing might also be needed when students get so caught up in minute story details that they miss the real message or story line.

See Chapter 11 for a discussion of using students' responses for assessment.

At other times, your responses may need to include various other kinds of *suggestions*—for other books to read, responses to try, or ideas to think about as reading continues. Your response in the journals and the students' responses to you are part of the running dialogue that lets you know how they are growing and gives you another way to guide them individually. Thus, the journal is both a teaching tool and a diagnostic tool.

When students read and respond to one another's journals, they learn from one another. These are sometimes called "buddy journals." It is best to delay using this type of journal until students have used dialogue journals with you, are comfortable with the procedure, and trust has been built between you. When you are ready, model appropriate responses, showing that the focus should not be on the mechanics of writing or on whether an idea is right or wrong, but rather reacting to each other's ideas and feelings.

Precautions When Using Journals

■ *Beware of overusing journals.* Sometimes teachers get so excited about journals that they use them in every subject area. Students become bored, and the journals lose their effectiveness.

■ *Don't require all students to write in their journals every day.* To get everyone to write, teachers often require a daily entry. This turns students off to journals. Allow students to use journals as a choice. (Some teachers do require a minimum number of entries each week, especially in middle school.)

■ *Make sure you know your reason for having students use journals.* Be confident about why you are using journals. Avoid using journals just for the sake of using them.

■ *Remember that journals are instructional tools.* Journals should replace less meaningful types of activities. They should not become more busy work that is added on to what students are already doing.

Response Charts

For students who need support in learning how to respond, you can use **response charts,** which give suggestions of ways to respond to a piece of literature. Figure 7.9 presents a response chart from a sixth-grade classroom. The teacher used it to get students back into journal writing at the beginning of the new school year. You and your students may develop a response chart together before or after reading.

FIGURE 7.9   Sample Response Chart from a Sixth-Grade Classroom

RESPONSE SUGGESTIONS

Before Reading

- List the title and author of the book in your journal. Give the date you started the book.

During Reading

- Note words of interest in your journal.
- Think about the story you are reading. Does it make sense? Write any questions you have in your journal.

After Reading (select one or more)

- Write a short summary of the story.
- Select your favorite character and describe his or her role in the story.
- Meet with a friend to talk about the story.
- *Other*—You decide what you would like to do.

While response charts are not necessary for every piece of literature students read, they have several uses:

- They accustom students to the concept of responding.
- They prime thinking and help students learn how to select their own modes of response.
- They support beginning learners or those experiencing difficulty in learning.
- They provide scaffolding for ELLs, who may have trouble with open-ended responses such as journals.
- They are appropriate when you observe that students do not clearly understand what they have read or are missing the point an author is trying to make.

You may note lack of understanding when reading students' written responses or listening to or observing their oral or other creative responses. For example, suppose some fifth graders read *The Scarebird* (Fleischman, 1987) and gave a skit based on it. If they portrayed Lonesome John as crazy instead of just lonely, you'd know they missed the point and needed support in identifying the story's problems. Therefore, you would model how to identify the problem in this story. For the next few stories students read, you might suggest one or two ways for them to respond that would focus their attention directly on identifying story problems, such as constructing a group story map or writing a paragraph describing the story problem.

See Chapter 3 for more about story maps.

Constructing Response Charts

Ultimately, you want students to be able to decide on their own modes of response. However, even the best readers may need some ideas from time to time. One way to meet individual needs is to suggest many types of responses and allow choices. Be sure that all choices are things students might naturally choose to do after reading a book; in other words, they should be authentic activities.

When making response charts, you need to consider two factors: the type of text being read and the needs of your students. Occasionally, the same response activity might work for both narrative and expository texts, but in most instances it will not. Student needs will range from missing the basic ideas, to an inability to be inferential and evaluative in their responses. In the first case, a structured response such as a story map might be helpful; in the second case, students might think about and be ready to discuss why, for instance, the main character behaved as he or she did.

All response charts should contain one option that says, "Other—You decide how you want to respond." When students effectively use the "other" option, it's a good sign that they no longer need response charts. Limit the number of options. A new response chart might have five options, whereas one you are adding to regularly might get only three new response options at one time.

Tables 7.3 and 7.4 list a selection of response options that should be helpful in constructing your own response charts for narrative and expository texts. They were developed from a variety of sources, including the works of Spritzer (1988) and Parsons (2001) and the ideas other teachers and we have found to be effective. As you work with your students, you will develop other options that are appropriate for them.

Two response options, discussion and readers theater, are explained in more detail later in this chapter.

Sometimes the response chart may include questions that cue students to respond in different ways. Parsons (2001) suggests that some students really need these aids to get them started and recommends the following questions for narrative texts:

- What surprised you about the section you read today? How does this change affect what might happen next in the story?

- What startling, unusual, or effective words, phrases, expressions, or images did you come across in your reading today that you would like to have explained or clarified? Which ones would you like to use in your own writing?

- How much do you personally agree or disagree with the way various characters think and act and the kinds of beliefs and values they hold? Where do you differ, and why?

- What issues in this story are similar to real-life issues that you've thought about or had some kind of experience with? How has the story clarified or confused or changed your views on any of these issues?

For expository texts, cuing questions also need to be open-ended. Some suggested questions for expository texts are:

- After reading this far in this text, what do you think you will learn about next?

- How would you feel if you were the scientist who made the discovery you just read about? Why?

TABLE 7.3	Response Options for Narrative Texts
Response Option	**Description**
Discussion	Talk about the story with others who have also read it (use questions from the response chart to structure your discussion).
Story mapping	Make a story map.
Rewriting	Rewrite a part of the story illustrating how you would have solved the problem.
Retelling	Retell the story to a friend or small group of friends.
Illustrating	Illustrate your favorite part or important scenes from the story. Write a sentence or two about each illustration.
Sharing	Tell a friend or classmate about the story you have read. Or read aloud your story to a friend, a classmate, or someone in a grade lower than yours.
Puppetry	Use puppets to share your story with other classmates or students in another class.
Posters	Make a poster to "sell" classmates on reading this book. Remember to make it exciting so they will want to "buy" it.
Other books by the author	Select another book by this author. Read and compare the two stories.
Book talk	Give a short (3–5 minute) book talk focusing on what you feel is most exciting about your book.
Dress-up	Dress like a character from your book and act out a favorite scene for your class.
Play/readers theater	Work with other students who have read the book to present a play or make a readers theater presentation.
Topical study	Use the topic of your story as the basis for an informational study. For example, a child who is reading *Nine-in-One Grr! Grr!* (Xiong & Spagnoli, 1989) might do a study about the Hmong people of Laos.
Mobile	Make a mobile of important characters or events in the story.
Movie	Work with others who have read the book to make a movie. Have a movie party to share your work with others.

- How do you feel the information in this text will be helpful in your life?
- How does the information you have just learned compare to what you already know about this topic?

You will find that you will develop your own bank of questions to use on response charts as you work with your students.

TABLE 7.4	Response Options for Expository Texts

Response Option	Description
Discussion	Talk about what you have read with others who have also read it. Use questions from the response chart to structure your discussion.
Graphic presentation	Share the important ideas you have learned through a graphic device, such as a chart, timeline, diagram, or graphic organizer. ① Important Idea — Support — Support — Support ① Important Idea — Support — Support — Support
Speech	Give a persuasive talk using the information you have gained about the topic of your book.
Display	Create a display related to the book you read.
Newspaper article	Write a newspaper article expressing your point of view about the book.
Book	Use the information from the book you read to make a book of your own on the topic. Include text, charts, illustrations, and diagrams if appropriate.
Debate	Have a debate with others who have read the book. Each group debating must take a different point of view.
Bibliography	Read other books on the same topic, and compile an annotated bibliography to share with others.
Written report	Write a report about your book focusing on what you learned and how it might be helpful in the world.
Map	Make a map to show important information you have learned. Focus on products, cities, recreation areas, and so forth.
Experiment	Use what you have learned to conduct an experiment. Write your results.
News report	Create a report using the information you and others have gained from their books. Write a script to accompany the visual report, including facts and opinions.

Technology Helps Children Respond to Literature and Connect to the World

" Kids engrossed in learning is the rule rather than the exception in this nearly 100-year-old red-brick elementary school that covers a city block inside one of America's poorest cities. Outside, litter lines the chain-link fences of the once elegant row houses, and police sirens are as frequent as birdsongs. Despite the differences between this community and mainstream America, our kids have one significant thing in common with kids in other districts, and that is simply that they *want* to learn.

Picture a group of children watching a herd of elephants thunder across a savanna. They can almost smell the dust they kick up as they head for safer ground. Children watch with wide eyes as adult elephants surround their babies to keep them safe from predators. No, these children are not on safari; they are at computers in the media center fascinated by the video clip in an online encyclopedia.

This particular second-grade class had read an elephant story in their classroom and written in their response journals. After collaborating with the classroom teacher, the kids and I were off and running. Collaboration is a wonderful way to continually integrate my program in the media center with the classroom teachers. I can address my media literacy objectives while I enhance classroom content.

Our first step was to use a graphic organizer, a K-W-L chart, to plot what we knew and what we didn't know. Then, we brainstormed how to find information and what materials we could use. Each group's challenge was to use one print source and one electronic source. By second grade, children are learning how to find materials, how to navigate software programs, and are beginning to perform simple Internet searches. I gave them a list of software programs, bookmarked websites (previewed in advance), and electronic encyclopedias, and taught them how to search our automated online catalogue of current library items.

I helped as needed, but independent work was encouraged. Once data were collected, the students' final charge was to make a creative presentation of their findings. Past projects include written reports, a digital photo diary with captions, a taped oral report, dioramas, dramatic skits, and murals, and soon we'll be adding the camcorder, scanners, and PowerPoint presentations.

As an information specialist, one of my major goals for my students (besides becoming lifelong readers) is that they will become independent locators, evaluators, and users of the wealth of information available today. I believe this will not only empower them, but it will improve their critical thinking skills. "

—Cynthia Sleeth, Media Specialist
Alfred E. Cramer Elementary School
Camden, New Jersey

Literature Discussion

See "Book Raps" in the "Websites" section at the end of the chapter about online book discussion groups.

Discussion is another procedure for promoting responses to literature. Whether it is called the literature circle (Harste et al., 1988), literature groups (Calkins, 1994; Weaver, 1994), or **literature discussion group (or circle),** the purpose is the same: to get students to read and respond to literature by talking with each other about what they have read. Remember that the term *literature* here refers to any text read: stories, poems, plays, biographies, historical fiction, memoir, nonfiction. Having students discuss what they have read is essential to developing their ability to construct meaning.

Children who have read the same book get together to discuss it and react to it. Initially, the teacher may start the discussion, but as students learn to function in the literature discussion group, they often take over this role. Sometimes a teacher may participate as an equal member of a group, rather than the discussion leader.

The procedures for using literature discussion groups have been described in detail by Harste et al. (1988). The guidelines given here are based on their ideas and our own experiences in working with children and teachers.

Guidelines for Using Literature Discussion Groups

Selecting Literature There are several options:

- one book read by the whole class
- multiple books chosen by students
- individual self-selection
- or, if several students are reading the same selection as part of their independent reading, these students may form a literature discussion group of their own.

Organizing Discussion Groups If everyone in the class is reading the same book, establish how many groups you will need to form in order to have three members in each; then have students quickly divide themselves into groups. Allowing students to select the discussion group they want to join gives them some control over their own learning and also helps to accommodate their individual needs. Students often sign up to be with their friends, which is fine. If behavior problems arise, you can adjust the groups, but this is usually not necessary.

See Chapter 10 for more about organizing.

If you are having students select from several different books, you can give a bit of information about each book as a teaser to spark interest and to help students make their choices. Then have students sign up for the book they want to read. If more than four or five students want to read the same book, form more than one group for that book.

The entire class need not be in literature groups at the same time. Those not involved may do independent reading or writing or other reading and writing activities.

Starting Discussion Groups Students begin by reading. If they are reading a short book or selection, they should read the entire piece before coming to the group. If they are reading a book with several chapters, they can meet at intervals and at the end of the book. Each time they meet, they can decide on reading goals to be completed before the next meeting and record these goals in their journals.

If you are working with beginning readers or students having problems reading, you can read the book aloud. So that there is no stigma in being part of the read-aloud group, announce that a certain book will be read aloud and invite all students to be part of this group. Most will want to be in the listening group from time to time. You also can provide a tape of the book.

Promoting Discussions In the initial stages of using literature discussion groups, you will need to model and demonstrate good questioning and discussion behaviors. You might model for the entire class using a small group. Then discuss with the class what happened and any problems they might see.

Each literature discussion group meeting will usually last from 5 to 10 minutes, depending on what is being discussed and the students' experience in this procedure. Since the primary focus of the discussion is to bring the students and the literature together and to allow students to construct their own meanings, the discussion must be open-ended.

As each group carries out its discussion, move from group to group to monitor what is taking place. You may need to remind students to refer to posted questions on a response chart. Sometimes, you may join the group and add to or stimulate the discussion with questions. For example, suppose a group is discussing *Regina's Big Mistake* (Moss, 1990) and you notice that the discussion seems to be lagging. You might join the group, saying, "You know, when I was in school, I often felt just like Regina. I was afraid of making mistakes. What problems like that have you had in school?" In this way, you become part of the group by modeling and prompting other things to think about.

Many teachers find that using a discussion chart such as the one in Figure 7.10 helps get the groups started and keeps the discussion moving. Present the chart to students and explain it. As students become more comfortable, they will start their own discussions, using the chart as a prompt. You may change the chart from time to time, and you can use some of the open-ended questions for cueing presented earlier in this chapter. After students have learned to work in groups, discontinue the use of charts.

FIGURE 7.10 | **Literature Discussion Chart**

LITERATURE DISCUSSIONS

1. Begin by telling the title and author of your book.
2. Talk about what you read.
   - What was your favorite part? Why?
   - How does this book relate to your life?
   - If you felt strongly about what happened to a character, what techniques did the author use to lead you to feel that way?
   - How important is the setting at this point?
   - What surprised you about the events in the story since last time the group discussed the story? Now what do you think will happen?
3. Make a list of things to discuss at your next meeting.

Concluding Literature Discussion Groups When students have completed a book, they can then decide whether they want to share it with the entire class or respond to it in some other way. The literature discussions may be sufficient response for most students. *It is neither necessary nor advisable for students to always complete additional activities. Only when they are really excited about a book should they be encouraged to respond further.*

Tips for Using Discussion Groups

There is no one correct way to use discussion groups; they are a flexible tool and should be used accordingly. At the beginning, proceed slowly and carefully. Teachers have found two ways to move themselves and their classes into literature discussion groups successfully.

One teacher starts her class by inviting students to help select a book for the entire class. She then introduces and explains the concept of literature discussion groups. After the groups are established, the class reads the book (or the first chapter in a longer book) and the teacher presents a literature discussion chart such as the one in Figure 7.10. She poses one open-ended question to get all the groups started. As they work, she moves from group to group to see what is taking place, joining groups as needed. She repeats this pattern several times using different books until she is comfortable that her students understand literature discussion and are working in the group effectively. Then she expands to two or more books, letting the children choose which books they will read.

A second procedure is to get one small group started, following the same basic procedure as that just described. When that group is working smoothly, you can add a second book and then a third book until all students are comfortable with the process.

Teachers may group students with the same first language for purposes of discussion. The students discuss the book in their first language and then, in English, report key ideas to the class or the teacher (Freeman & Freeman, 2001).

Regardless of the pattern you select, you will want to move slowly. When students have not had the experiences of such open discussions and have been accustomed to giving the teacher the "correct answer," they are often reluctant to talk. You may need to model open discussions several times before students accept the idea that there are no absolute or correct answers.

Readers Theater

Readers theater is a form of response in which children turn a story into a play. Sloyer (1982) describes readers theater this way:

> *Readers Theatre is an interpretive reading activity for all children in the classroom. Readers bring characters to life through their voices and gestures. Listeners are captivated by the vitalized stories and complete the activity by imagining the details of a scene or action. . . . Readers Theatre becomes an integrated language event centering upon oral interpretation of literature. The children adapt and present the material of their choice. A story, a poem, a scene from a play, even a song lyric, provide the ingredients for the script. As a thinking, reading, writing, speaking, and listening experience, Readers Theatre makes a unique contribution to our language arts curriculum. (p. 3)*

Fourth graders practice a Readers Theater presentation.
© Frank Siteman/
Photo Edit

This form of response allows all children to take part in the creative interpretation of a story. Even second-language or at-risk learners can succeed in this activity (Werthemer, 1974). Readers theater is also effective in helping students improve fluency (Rasinski, 2003).

For a detailed discussion of fluency, see Chapter 5.

The following procedures for using readers theater have been developed from numerous sources and from our own experiences in working with children and teachers (Coger & White, 1982; Harste et al., 1988; Sloyer, 1982).

Guidelines for Using Readers Theater

Selecting Literature As you begin using the readers theater, help students select stories with lots of dialogue, strong story lines, and suspense, humor, or surprise. Discuss with students the characteristics of a good piece to use.

Reading or Rereading the Literature After reading, students should discuss the story, focusing on the characters, setting, problem, action, and outcome. Many teachers have students develop a story map to help them decide what needs to be included in the script and what is not essential.

Developing a Script A good way to develop the script is through shared writing, using a chart or an overhead projector. This is also a good place to refer students to the story map. Talk about the things that can be left out, such as the word *said* and descriptions that are not essential to the story. Generate a list of story characters, and help students see how to identify the parts that must be read by a narrator. Figure 7.11 shows a partial script developed by some second graders and their teacher. Eventually, children will be able to develop a script on their own.

A Variety of Literature Connects with Diverse Students

"Author studies are the most enjoyable part of my second grade curriculum. On the first day of school, the children "meet" Kevin Henkes through *Wemberly Worried*. For several author studies, I have stuffed characters, puppets, or projects that add to their enjoyment. For example, by the end of the Henkes study, the class feels they know Lily of *Lily's Purple Plastic Purse*.

The *Arthur* series by Marc Brown is another big hit. As a culminating activity, the children write their own Arthur or D. W. adventure. When we have a story about a mouse in our basal reader, I declare one day Leo Lionni Day, and we read several of his stories with correlating art projects. *Frederick* and *Fish Is Fish* are their favorites.

Jack Prelutsky poetry promotes learning through humor. Several of his poems are about food, so they go with our Health chapter on food. Traesher's *Black Lagoon* series is fun when I replace the characters' names with my students' names. Tomi DePaola is another author I use year-round. The children learn to recognize his illustrations even when he is not the author.

The most encompassing study we do is on Jan Brett. I have almost two dozen of her books, and she provides such wonderful materials and such a great website that the children are convinced she is a personal friend of mine. Hedgie the Hedgehog, a character in most of her books, becomes our class pet. He, his backpack, and his journal spend weeks going home with my students, and they love sharing his writing with the class.

The school librarian can always tell whose books we're reading this week. When the book fairs come to our school, the first books the children grab are the authors they know. I also use literature in my social studies and science units; for example, Mem Fox books are terrific for learning about Australia. Jerry Polatta's alphabet books are a wonderful way to practice handwriting skills rather than mundane drill. The Laura Numeroff books such as *If You Give a Mouse a Cookie* are great to use if you want your children to write a cumulative story.

Patricia Pollaco is saved for the end of the year when the children are better prepared for the higher level thinking required. Also, our school requires all students to write a personal narrative for our Young Authors program. Pollaco stories are the perfect modeling tool; *My Rotten Red-Haired Older Brother* and *Betty's Doll* are good examples. When my students learn that Patricia has a learning disability and is now a famous author, it gives all of them more self-confidence no matter what their ability level.

The children write letters to every author we study. The responses are wonderful and reinforce their enthusiasm to read more. When my students return to visit, they often tell me that they learned to love books in my classroom. I guess that says it all."

—*Jan Richard, Second-Grade Teacher*
Mitchell Elementary School
Muncie, Indiana

FIGURE 7.11 **Partial Readers Theater Script for *Tye May and the Magic Brush* (Bang, 1981) Developed by Second Graders and Their Teacher**

TYE MAY AND THE MAGIC BRUSH

NARRATOR: Many years ago a cruel and greedy emperor ruled over China. His people were very poor. One of the poorest was Tye May. Her mother and father were dead and she lived alone. Every day she gathered firewood and cut reeds to sell in the marketplace. One day Tye May passed the school and saw the teacher painting. She knew right then what she wanted to do.

TYE MAY: "Please, sir, I would like to learn how to paint, but I have no money to buy a brush. Would you lend me one?"

TEACHER: (Angry) "Beggar girls don't paint. Get out of here!"

NARRATOR: But Tye May did not give up. She had an iron will. She drew pictures in the dirt when she collected wood. Her pictures looked real but she still didn't have a brush. One night when she was very tired she fell into a deep sleep.

WOMAN: "This is a magic brush. Use it carefully."

TYE MAY: "Thank you! Thank you!"

NARRATOR: The woman was gone and Tye May woke up.

See the "Websites" section for places to purchase scripts.

While it is possible to purchase readers theater scripts for many pieces of literature, one of the major values of using this activity comes from developing the script. Therefore, even if you decide to purchase some scripts, you should also have students develop some of their own to give them the experience of translating a story into a script. In either case, you will need multiple copies of the script.

Discussing Props Most readers theater is done with no props or costumes. Sometimes, simple props such as a yardstick for a sword or paper hats may be used. There is no scenery. Talk with students to identify the minimal props necessary.

Preparing and Rehearsing for the Presentation With students, choose who will read which part. If you are working with the whole class, you might divide the class into groups so that everyone can participate in this first production; each group could give its own performance of the same program. Guide students to make decisions about how and where to stand and make hand, body, or facial gestures to convey parts of the story to their audience. Give students time to rehearse their program.

Presenting the Program When students feel ready, let them perform for the class. After the performances, discuss what went well and what could be improved in the future. Focus on all aspects, from selecting the literature, to writing the script, to giving the program.

There is no one right way to use the readers theater in your class. Feel free to experiment, following your own ideas and those of your students.

Responding and the Construction of Meaning: Key Points

To review the Key Points, see the ACE practice tests at the HM TeacherPrepSPACE Student Website.

- Responding is an activity that occurs as a reaction to or as part of reading or listening.
- Responding to literature enhances the process of constructing meaning.
- Responses can be verbal or nonverbal.
- The atmosphere of the classroom sets the tone that promotes and supports students' responding activities.
- Journals, response charts, literature discussion groups, and readers theater are all procedures that promote responding to literature.
- Organizing and managing a response-centered literacy classroom is an important task for the teacher.

How Do I Teach?

Responses to Literature
Journals
- Diaries, p. 307
- Response journals, p. 307
- Dialogue, p. 307
- Double-entry, p. 307
- Learning logs, p. 307

Response Charts— Options for Response
Narrative text, p. 321
- Discussion
- Story mapping
- Rewriting
- Retelling

- Illustrating
- Sharing
- Puppetry
- Posters
- Other books by same author
- Book talk
- Dress-up
- Play or readers theater
- Topical study
- Mobile
- Movie

Expository text, p. 322
- Discussion
- Graphic presentation

- Speech
- Display
- Newspaper article
- Book
- Debate
- Bibliography
- Written report
- Map
- Experiment
- News Report

Literature Discussion Groups, p. 324
Readers Theater, p. 326

Video Case in This Chapter

■ **Portfolio Assessment: Elementary Classroom**

For Additional Reading

Brevig, L. (2006). Engaging in retrospective reflection. *The Reading Teacher, 59*(6), 522–530.

Cook, M. J. (2005). A journal for Corduroy: Responding to literature. *The Reading Teacher, 59*(3), 282–285.

Daniels, H. (2001). *Literature circles* (2nd ed.). Portland, ME: Stenhouse.

Daniels, H. (2001). *Looking into literature circles.* Portland, ME: Stenhouse. [Videotape.]

Evans, K. S. (2001). *Literature discussion groups in the intermediate grades.* Newark, DE: International Reading Association.

Ketch, A. (2005). Conversation: The comprehension connection. *The Reading Teacher, 59*(1), 8–13.

Labbo, L. D. (2005). Books and computer response activities that support literacy development. *The Reading Teacher, 59*(3), 288–292.

Long, T. W., & Gove, M. K. (2003/2004). How engagement strategies and literature circles promote critical response in a fourth-grade, urban classroom. *The Reading Teacher, 57*(4), 350–36l.

McMahon, S. I., Raphael, T. E., Goatley, V. J., & Pardo, L. S. (1997). *The book club connection.* Newark, DE: International Reading Association and New York: Teachers College Press.

Parsons, L. (2001). *Response journals revisited.* Portland, ME: Stenhouse.

Szymusiak, K., & Sibberson, F. (2001). *Beyond leveled books: Supporting transitional readers in grades 2–5.* Portland, ME: Stenhouse.

Wiseman, A. J., (2003). Collaboration, initiation, and rejection: The social construction of stories in a kindergarten class. *The Reading Teacher, 56*(8), 802–810.

Websites

Explore multimedia and hypermedia that support children in responding to literature. The following may also be helpful:

International Society for Technology in Education
http://www.iste.org

International Reading Association
The International Reading Association provides resources and links to a diverse array of topics and issues in reading.
http://www.reading.org

National Council of Teachers of English
The National Council of Teachers of English is devoted to improving the teaching and learning of English and the language arts at all levels of education.
http://www.ncte.org

Readers Theater

Following are a few websites that may be helpful as you work with students on readers theater:

- http://aaronshep.com/rt/index.html
- http://www.literacyconnections.com/ReadersTheater.html
- http://www.teachingheart.net/readerstheater.htm
- http://scriptsforschools.com
- http://www.readingonline.org/electronic/carrick

Book Raps

Book raps are discussions conducted by e-mail by students from around the world. Teachers or librarians can nominate a book for discussion by becoming a book rap coordinator. Current titles are listed on the book rap calendar. Some book raps may include author involvement, illustrators online, access to content area experts, and live chat sessions. Subject areas include English, study of society and environment, English as a Second Language, and science. The following site may offer useful information: **http://www.oz-teachernet.edu.au/projects/br/**

Literature Circles

Literature Circles
This resource supports conversation and idea sharing among people exploring student-led book discussion groups—a "best practice" strategy. Features include discussions, book recommendations and reviews, classroom management ideas, links to related sites and organizations, and news of relevant publications and events.
http://www.literaturecircles.com

Literature Circles Resource Center
Hosted by Seattle University and Katherine L. Schlick Noe, this site provides information and resources on literature groups, including book lists, guidelines, and other resources.
http://www.litcircles.org
Here are some additional sites related to responding:

- http://www.literacymatters.org/adlit/response/multimedia.htm—"Response Strategies Using Multimedia"
- http://www.learnnc.org/lessons/ReadWriteThink11212002678—"A journal for Corduroy: Responding to literature"
- http://www.ncte.org/profdev/online/rwt/topics/118595.htm—"Responding to Literature in the Middle Grades" (using technology)
- http://www.suite101.com/article.cfm/reading/38568/2—"Including Technology in Student Responses to Literature" (with other links embedded)
- http://www.readwritethink.org/lessons/lesson_view.asp?id=787—"Literary Scrapbooks Online: An Electronic Reader-Response Project"
- http://www.cal.org/caela/esl%5Fresources/digests/dialogue_journals.html— "Dialogue Journals: Interactive Writing to Develop Language and Literacy"
- http://www.kent.k12.wa.us/curriculum/writing/elem_writing/Bib/ learninglogs.htm—"Learning Logs"

Writing and the Construction of Meaning

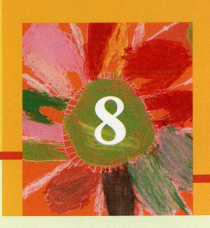

8

EDUCATORS SPEAK

A Mobile Lab and Individual Laptops Engage At-Risk Students in the Writing Process, p. 355
—*Caroline Goddard, Stafford, Virginia*

Terms
YOU NEED TO KNOW

- conventional writing phase
- clustering
- domain
- drafting
- invented spelling phase
- mode of writing
- picture writing
- planning/ previewing
- process writing
- proofreading/ editing
- publishing
- random letter phase
- revising
- scribble writing
- story frame
- traits

The HM TeacherPrepSPACE Student Website offers many helpful resources, such as self-quizzes, glossary flashcards, lesson plan templates, and more.

*R*ecently a third-grade teacher was asked, "What do you think it means to develop reading and writing together?" His answer was very clear:

> Children often read books that are related to the topics they are writing about. And, they often write about what they are reading. For example, a child in my last class was reading the personal narrative Little House in the Big Woods [Wilder, 1932]; it was very natural for her to extend personal narrative into her writing. Another boy was writing a story about dinosaurs. His writing experience became the catalyst for him to read books on dinosaurs. So you see, I can't just think of reading or writing. I think of a literacy experience or event. By giving my children support in the event they are experiencing, I am able to help them become better comprehenders; it doesn't really matter whether it is a reading focus or a writing focus. They use both of these things together.

In this chapter, we look at the relationships between writing and reading and how these processes develop together.

Why Writing and Reading Together?

Educators have supported integrating the language arts for many years (Durkin, 1989; Loban, 1963; Moffett & Wagner, 1983), and research has helped us understand how and why these processes develop together (Tierney & Shanahan, 1991). Several researchers have helped us to formulate a clearer (although not final) answer to the question, "Why writing and reading together?" (Dahl & Farnan, 1998; Pearson & Tierney, 1984; Shanahan, 1990; Tierney & Leys, 1984; Tierney & Shanahan, 1991). There are at least five major reasons for teaching writing and reading together:

- Both writing and reading are constructive processes.
- Reading and writing share similar processes and kinds of knowledge.
- Writing and reading, when taught together, improve achievement.
- Reading and writing together foster communication.
- Combining reading and writing develops critical thinking.

Let's discuss each of these reasons in more detail.

Both Writing and Reading Are Constructive Processes As Pearson and Tierney (1984) said, both readers and writers progress through four phases: planner, composer, editor, and monitor.

- *Planner:* Thoughtful readers plan reading with a purpose in mind; they think about the text and begin to activate or develop background relating to the topic. Writers go through a similar process. They have a purpose for writing and think about what they know or need to know before beginning to write.
- *Composer:* Next, readers begin to read and construct, or compose, meaning in light of their purposes and background, using cues in the text. A writer's task is

TABLE 8.1	Readers and Writers as Composers of Meaning	
Processes	**Readers**	**Writers**
Planner	Have purpose for reading	Have purpose for writing
	Generate background	Generate background
Composer	Read and compose meaning	Write and compose meaning
Editor	Reread, reflect, and revise meaning	Reread, reflect, and revise
Monitor	Finalize meaning	Finalize copy

to compose meaning so it can be conveyed to a reader, so the writer thinks about the topic or plot and develops it. While writers may have a general idea when they start to write, they really develop it only as they think more about it in the process of writing.

■ *Editor:* As the reading process continues, readers reread and change meaning as necessary. Writers do the same: they think about what they have written, reread it, and rewrite to make it clearer.

■ *Monitor:* Finally, readers reach a point where they are confident that the meaning they have composed, or constructed, is the best possibility at that time. Writers do the same in their final drafts.

Of course, readers and writers do not proceed through these stages one after another; they go back and forth between them as they perform the overall process (Dahl & Farnan, 1998; Graves, 1984; Murray, 1985; Pearson & Tierney, 1984). Table 8.1 summarizes the similarities between the reader and the writer as composers (or constructors) of meaning.

Proficient readers and writers may use the two processes simultaneously. Think about your own experiences in writing. As you write your ideas, you reread them to see whether they make sense and say what you mean to say. Often you turn to books or other sources to get more information to include or to clarify your meaning. The processes of proficient reading and writing not only function in similar ways but also tend to be used together.

Teaching students to write helps them construct meaning by making them more aware of how authors organize their ideas. As they learn to write and organize their own ideas, they will have a greater appreciation and understanding of how other authors do the same.

Writing and Reading Involve Similar Kinds of Knowledge and Processes Reading and writing should be taught together because they naturally develop together (Baghban, 1984; Bissex, 1980; Calkins, 1983; Sulzby & Teale, 1991), and they share many of the same processes and types of knowledge (Tierney & Shanahan, 1991). Researchers have consistently found reading and writing to be highly related (Applebee, 1977; Loban, 1963; Shanahan, 1988; Shanahan & Lomax, 1988), and they have been able to identify some specific similarities, such as the use of similar cognitive processes (Birnbaum, 1982; Langer, 1986; Martin, 1987).

Elementary Writing Instruction: Process Writing

Watch the video clip, study the artifacts in the case, and reflect on the following questions:

1. How does this Video Case support the text's statements about the importance of teaching reading and writing together?

2. Please describe the various steps of process writing that you can identify within the Video Case. Which parts of the process seem most important in developing students' writing skills?

Writing and Reading Improve Achievement Researchers have studied the effect of teaching reading and writing together on overall achievement. The classic U.S. Office of Education study of first-grade reading concluded that programs that incorporate writing are generally more effective in improving reading than those that do not (Bond & Dykstra, 1967). This conclusion continues to be supported. Research on the effects of teaching writing and reading together concludes that "studies have shown that writing led to improved reading achievement, reading led to better writing performance, and combined instruction in both led to improvements in both reading and writing" (Tierney & Shanahan, 1991, p. 258). Caution must be exercised, however. These studies show a correlation, not causation. We cannot say that simply providing instruction in one area will automatically lead to improvements in another area. All we know is that reading and writing together have benefits that neither taught alone will convey. By teaching them together, we help students recognize and understand the connections between the two processes.

Writing and Reading Promote Communication Reading and writing are processes that help us more effectively understand and communicate with one another. Through this communication, we are able to improve our world, prosper, and enjoy life. Since both communication and learning are social processes, developing reading and writing together has many social benefits.

Writing and Reading Together Develop Critical Thinking An underlying element of all literacy learning, and learning in general, is thinking. In combined writing and reading instruction, learners engage in a greater variety of experiences that lead to better reasoning and higher-level thinking than is achieved with either process alone (McGinley, 1988). Since thinking is a critical part of meaning construction, classrooms that actively foster meaning construction through reading and writing will produce better thinkers (Tierney & Shanahan, 1991).

For more discussion of the research on writing and reading, see the "For Additional Reading" section at the end of the chapter.

Let's return to the question posed at the beginning of this section: *Why writing and reading together?* Teaching reading and writing together fosters a broad perspective of literacy as a social process; it results in better achievement in both activities and leads to better thinking. Tierney and Shanahan (1991) conclude, "We believe strongly that in our society, at this point in history, reading and writing, to be understood and appreciated fully, should be viewed together, learned together, and used together" (p. 275).

Although some classrooms still focus on reading and writing as separate entities, research supports a view of reading and writing as a single entity called *literacy*. In the remainder of this chapter, we focus on how to build the reading-writing connection.

Standards and Writing

When you read any set of state standards, you will note that most deal with literacy as a comprehensive process that includes all kinds of language—listening, reading, speaking, and writing. Though some aspect of each may be taught separately, there is no question that the literacy processes must be integrated in order for students to become members of the literacy community.

As more demonstrations of grammar competency are demanded on high school tests, teaching grammar is showing up more in middle school and elementary standards. This is reflected in a return to an emphasis on grammar in some classrooms.

Many states now require students to demonstrate writing ability, which is judged by the use of rubrics. While you must help your students meet these particular standards, don't lose sight of the larger picture: writing as a component of literacy.

See more about rubrics in Chapter 11.

Ways to Think About Writing

We have discussed two types of texts (and writing), narrative and expository, and their relationship to meaning construction. Other ways to think about writing are domains, modes, and traits.

Domains

Writing can be seen in terms of broad categories, called **domains,** that somewhat parallel the types of texts students read. The four basic writing domains are sensory/descriptive, imaginative/narrative, practical/informative, and analytical/expository (McHugh, 1987). Each domain represents a specific purpose for writing. Because different languages may use different styles or patterns for various types of writing, teachers may need to help ELLs understand the patterns used in English.

Being aware of each domain and its purpose helps students clearly develop their own purposes for writing. Knowledge about domains also helps you plan a variety of literacy experiences. Table 8.2 summarizes the four domains of writing. As you will see, many projects may cut across several domains.

TABLE 8.2	Domains of Writing

- *Sensory/descriptive domain:* The sensory/descriptive domain focuses on describing something in such rich and clear detail that the reader or listener can almost see or feel it. Description also incorporates the feelings of the writer.
- *Imaginative/narrative domain:* The imaginative/narrative domain focuses on telling a real or imaginary story. In incorporating some aspects of the descriptive domain, the writer learns to use the elements of a story, including setting, problem, action, and outcome or resolution.
- *Practical/informative domain:* The practical/informative domain presents basic information clearly. The author provides the information without analyzing it.
- *Analytical/expository domain:* In the analytical/expository domain, the writer's primary purpose is to explain, analyze, and persuade. This most abstract form of writing uses elements of all of the other forms. The difference between a report written in this domain and one written in the practical/informative domain is that this report focuses more on *why.*

Modes

Modes of writing are described more thoroughly in Chapter 2.

We can also think in terms of **modes of writing.** The five modes are *independent writing, collaborative writing* (partners or a small group work together on a single writing product), *guided writing* (parallels guided reading), *shared writing* (group with the teacher; this parallels shared reading), and *write aloud* (teacher writes and verbalizes thinking aloud; students read and listen).

Figure 8.1 shows an example of a collaborative story written by a group of fourth graders. Any of the domains may be addressed in any mode, and the products or projects produced within one domain may also be developed in another domain. Table 8.3 identifies sample products that might be developed in each; notice how some products appear in several domains and modes and that many may be responses to reading.

Traits

See Northwest Regional Educational Laboratory in "Websites" for information about these traits.

Still another way of thinking about writing is based on identified **traits** or characteristics of all good writing, regardless of the age of the writer. The Six-Trait Analytical Assessment model from the Northwest Regional Educational Laboratory (NWREL) gives teachers a way to link instruction and assessment and makes evident that knowing what good writing looks like is essential for becoming a good writer. The NWREL model has spawned as many as fifty versions of the six-trait model. The six traits identified for grades 3 and up are *ideas, organization, voice, word choice, sentence fluency,* and *conventions.* There is a separate continuum of development to help teachers with writers in grades K–2. Complete information, which is continually evolving, is available at the NWREL website.

FIGURE 8.1 **Collaborative Story by a Group of Fourth Graders**

By Ryan
and Terry
Larry and Stacy Juarez

Once upon a time there were the martians. The first martian said, "Let's explore that planet. Of course, that planet was earth. When they landed, they saw a dog and a man. Suddenly..... the dog started to bark. He got very mad. And then the man saw the martians he was sccard and he ran. The martians were sccard, too... then Suddenly..., They both ran every which way and bumped into each other and fell to the ground. The martians was about to get up and run but...The dog caught the martions One had a lazer gun and shot the dog in the nose and then... The martions one got a gun. And shot the cat and the cat ran in the Haws.

| TABLE 8.3 | Domains and Modes of Writing with Sample Products or Projects |

Mode	Domain			
	Sensory/ Descriptive	Imaginative/ Narrative	Practical/ Informative	Analytical/ Expository
Independent writing	Diary Journal Letters Class notes Poems	Letters Short stories Poems	Lists Reports Letters Directions Class notes Invitations	Reports Letters to the editor Reviews Poems
Collaborative writing	Diary Journal Letters Poems	Letters Short stories Poems	Lists Reports Letters Directions Class notes Invitations	Reports Letters to the editor Reviews Poems
Guided writing	Any of the above	Any of the above	Any of the above	Any of the above
Shared writing	Diary Journal Letters Poems	Letters Short stories Poems	Lists Reports Letters Directions Class notes Invitations	Reports Letters to the editor Reviews Poems Poems
Write aloud	Any of the above	Any of the above	Any of the above	Any of the above

Activities That Connect Reading and Writing

Throughout your Comprehensive Balanced Literacy Program, you must continually help students make the connections between reading and writing, and think about how each carries over to the other. The following suggestions are a few ways to help students begin to make this explicit connection (Shanahan, 1988).

Reading Specific Types of Writing

Students need to use their writing as a springboard to reading, just as they use their reading as a springboard to writing. If you have a student who has written (or is writing) a mystery, encourage her or him to read some mysteries, such as *Encyclopedia Brown: Boy Detective* (Sobol, 1963) or *The Mysterious Disappearance of Leon (I Mean Noel)* (Raskin, 1971), to see how these authors developed their ideas.

Reading Student-Written Materials

As students begin to publish, they can read and enjoy one another's books. Student-written books should be displayed in both the classroom and the school library and be used as a part of the reading material for the literacy program. In many schools, student-written books are among those most frequently selected and checked out.

Developing a collection of student-written books is a simple procedure. Begin the school year by telling students that there will be a classroom library of their books and that throughout the year selected books will be placed in the school library. You and your students should develop criteria for selecting books—for example:

1. Well written (decide with students how to judge this)
2. Student's favorite topic or story
3. Topic others would most likely enjoy
4. Book student would like others to read

The student-written book collection for the library can be a schoolwide project. At the end of each school year, students may donate some of the books to the library, in which case copies should be made for the authors.

As student-written books are added to the school library, special announcements should be made through a school newspaper or a bulletin board display similar to that in Figure 8.2.

FIGURE 8.2 **Bulletin Board Publicizing Student Books in the School Library**

A special time may be designated for students to read the books written by their peers. Teachers can start with an hour every other week and increase the time to an hour or longer each week as more books are available. Students should use this time to read the books and talk about them in small groups or as a whole class. Be sure to focus on talking about the books, not evaluating them. In some classrooms, guidelines require making only positive comments about a classmate's book.

Having a time in the literacy program for students to read books written by their peers spotlights both reading and writing. It helps show students that these processes are related and also gives them an incentive to read and write.

Summaries

Students learn to make the connection between reading and writing by writing a summary of a text they have just read (Hill, 1991). This is a skill that must be taught. The following steps for summarizing expository texts are based on research by Brown and Day (1983):

1. Determine the topic of the paragraph or text.
2. Identify unnecessary information or trivia, and delete this information; it should not be included in the summary.
3. Look for information that is repeated; it should be included in the summary only once.
4. Note places where ideas or terms can be grouped together. For example, if the paragraph or text being summarized discusses travel by plane, ship, train, and car, all of these modes can be referred to as "transportation."
5. Identify a main-idea sentence for each paragraph, if possible. If no main-idea sentence exists, formulate one of your own.
6. Formulate your final summary, rechecking to be sure you have followed each guideline. Keep your summary short.

You should model writing a summary for students using procedures similar to those suggested for teaching the writing process, presented later in this chapter. Writing summaries after reading can be handled in creative ways—for example:

- Pretend to be a newspaper or TV reporter who must summarize what you have read. First, write a summary; then distribute it in newspaper form, or read as if on a TV news report.
- Maintain a log or journal that contains summaries of your favorite readings. (Students can also be instructed to write log entries for particular selections you assign.)

See Chapters 2 and 3 for more about story maps.

Summaries may also be written for narrative texts, in which case the same type of guidelines should be followed, focusing on the parts of a story map instead of main ideas.

Story Frames

A **story frame** is a basic outline that helps readers organize their ideas about a story they have read. It consists of a series of spaces hooked together by transition words;

each story frame usually follows a single line of thought or aspect of a selection. Story frames focus on story elements and are a good way to build the connection between reading and writing (Fowler, 1982). See Figure 8.3 for four examples of story frames: character frame, setting frame, plot frame, and character comparison frame.

After students read a selection, you can use a story frame as an oral discussion starter. Students fill in the slots in the frame, based on their reading; encourage them

---

FIGURE 8.3   Sample Story Frames

Character Frame

This story is about _____.

_____ is an important character.

_____ tried to _____.

The story ends when _____

_____.

Setting Frame

This story takes place _____

_____. I can tell this because the

author uses such words as _____

_____ to tell

where this story happens.

Plot Frame

This story begins when _____

_____. Next,

_____.

Then _____

_____. The story ends when

_____

_____.

Character Comparison Frame

_____ and _____ are

two characters in our story. _____ is

_____, whereas _____ is

_____. For instance, _____

tries to _____ and

_____ learns a lesson when _____

_____.

See Chapter 10 for ways to support writing as well as ways to organize and manage time and materials and keep track of student writing.

to express the ideas in their own words. When students have become familiar with story frames, they can use them in written activities after reading. Although story frames can be written for specific selections, some of the basic patterns can be used repeatedly.

Activities such as those just described are necessary but not sufficient for maintaining a reading and writing program.

Process Writing: A Way to Construct Meaning

Process writing (Calkins, 1994; Graves, 1983, 1991; Hillocks, 1987a, 1987b) is an approach to teaching writing that allows students to take charge of their own writing and learning; it applies to both narrative and expository writing. It has five steps: selecting the topic (sometimes called *planning* or *previewing*), drafting (sometimes called *composing*), revising, proofreading (sometimes called *editing*), and publishing.

A good way to help students become accustomed to using these steps is to display them on a classroom poster such as the one shown in Figure 8.4. We will discuss each of these steps in full.

As you introduce process writing, use write aloud, shared writing, and guided writing (Oczkus, 2007) to model, guide, and support each step until students take charge of their own writing. Although the need for modeling will diminish, you will always be a partner in learning with the students, interacting with them through individual and group conferences, discussing their writing ideas, having them share their writing, and providing minilesson support as needed. Through this continuing scaffolding, students will grow as writers and come to think of themselves as authors, a process that further develops their ability to construct meaning.

Process writing should begin in kindergarten, although students will be at various developmental phases in their writing. Some will be at the **picture-writing** phase, where they will simply draw a picture for their stories, as the student in Figure 8.5 has done. Other students will be at the **scribble-writing** phase, as shown in Figure 8.6. As students progress, they will move into the **random letter phase** depicted in Figure 8.7 and then into the **invented spelling phase** shown in Figure 8.8, in which they begin to associate some letters and sounds. Finally, they will reach the **conventional writing phase,** in which they will spell most words correctly.

For more discussion of spelling, see the "For Additional Reading" section at the conclusion of this chapter.

Beginning or less experienced writers are more likely to be at the picture, scribble, random letter, or invented spelling phases, and more experienced writers are usually closer to the conventional writing phase. In other words, it is normal to see some degree of invented spelling all the way through the elementary grades. Students' invented spelling will reflect their first language; for example, whereas English speakers usually begin with the use of consonants, Spanish-speaking children typically start with vowels (Freeman & Freeman, 1997). Teachers should be aware of these differences.

The following discussion focuses on one way to introduce process writing. Adjust your lessons to fit the grade level you teach. Begin with a brief discussion

FIGURE 8.4 **Poster for Process Writing**

FIGURE 8.4   Poster for Process Writing

FIGURE 8.5   **Picture-Writing Phase**

FIGURE 8.6   **Scribble-Writing Phase**

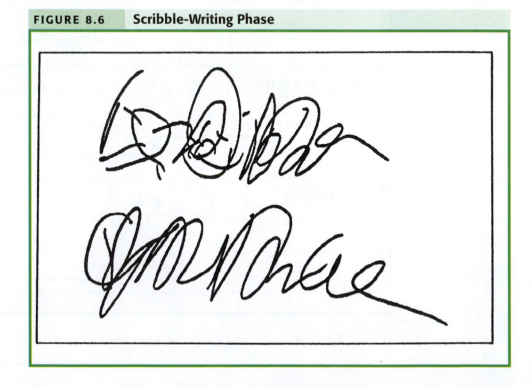

FIGURE 8.7   Random Letter Phase

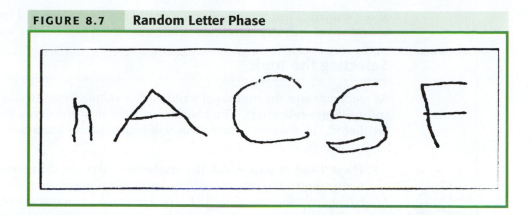

FIGURE 8.8   Invented Spelling Phase

about writing. Then show students a chart such as the one in Figure 8.4 and talk briefly about each step in process writing, using the name of the step.

Selecting the Topic

As students learn the process of writing, they should begin to *select their own topics* (**planning/previewing**). The teacher's role in this process is that of guide and facilitator. The following three steps will help students learn how to generate and select a topic:

1. **On a piece of paper, ask the students to list anything they might like to write about.** You may identify the particular domain or product you want them to produce; for example, "Think of some topics you could write a story about" would be appropriate if the focus is on the imaginative/narrative domain. As students are making their lists, model by making your own list, telling students what you are doing. After you have finished your list, move around the room to spot any students who are having trouble. Stop and ask these students such questions as, "What have you read that you would like to write about?" or "What topics are you thinking of?" Don't be critical or condescending; students must feel free to think for themselves and generate their own ideas.

   After a few minutes, stop the class and share your list of possible topics, commenting on your reasons for choosing them. Next, ask for volunteers to share their lists, encouraging students to comment on their own and one another's topics. Model positive comments with such remarks as, "Those are all exciting topics"; "I'd like to read a story about that"; "You have so many topics that you are going to have to really think about which one you want to write on."

   Be certain your comments are supportive and encouraging regardless of the length of a student's list. After several students have shared their lists, help them see that it doesn't matter whether their lists are long or short; all they need is one idea to begin writing.

2. **Have students review their lists to decide whether they want to add any topics.** You can model the process with your own list, perhaps by adding a topic similar to one a student has selected. This lets students know that it is all right for them to get ideas from others.

3. **Have students review their lists and select a topic for their first piece of writing.** Suggest that they consider the following points as they make their decisions: (a) Which topic is the most interesting to me? (b) Which topic do I feel I know the most about? and (c) Which topic do I think others might enjoy reading the most? Have students circle their choices. Then share your choice with the group and have volunteers do the same.

By following these steps, you will help students select their first topic for writing. It doesn't really matter what the topics are as long as the choices are the students' and the students want to write about them.

Students should keep their lists of possible topics in their writing folders and be encouraged to add to them. Assure them that they won't necessarily write on every topic. Their ideas will change; therefore, the lists can change.

See Chapter 3 for an explanation of brainstorming to activate prior knowledge.

Here are some other ways to help students select topics for writing:

- *Partners:* Have each student work with a partner to brainstorm and develop lists of possible topics. This is a particularly good strategy to use for the student who appears to have few ideas or doesn't want to write.

- *Clustering:* "**Clustering** is a nonlinear brainstorming process akin to free association" (Rico, 1983, p. 28). Working alone, with partners, or with the teacher, students start with a topic or idea that forms the core, or nucleus, for the cluster. They then add all of the things they can think of that are related to it and select the specific topic from the cluster they wish to write about or use the ideas to develop their writing. Figure 8.9 presents a cluster on animals developed by a second-grade teacher and his class to get ideas for writing.

FIGURE 8.9   **Cluster on Animals Developed by Second Graders**

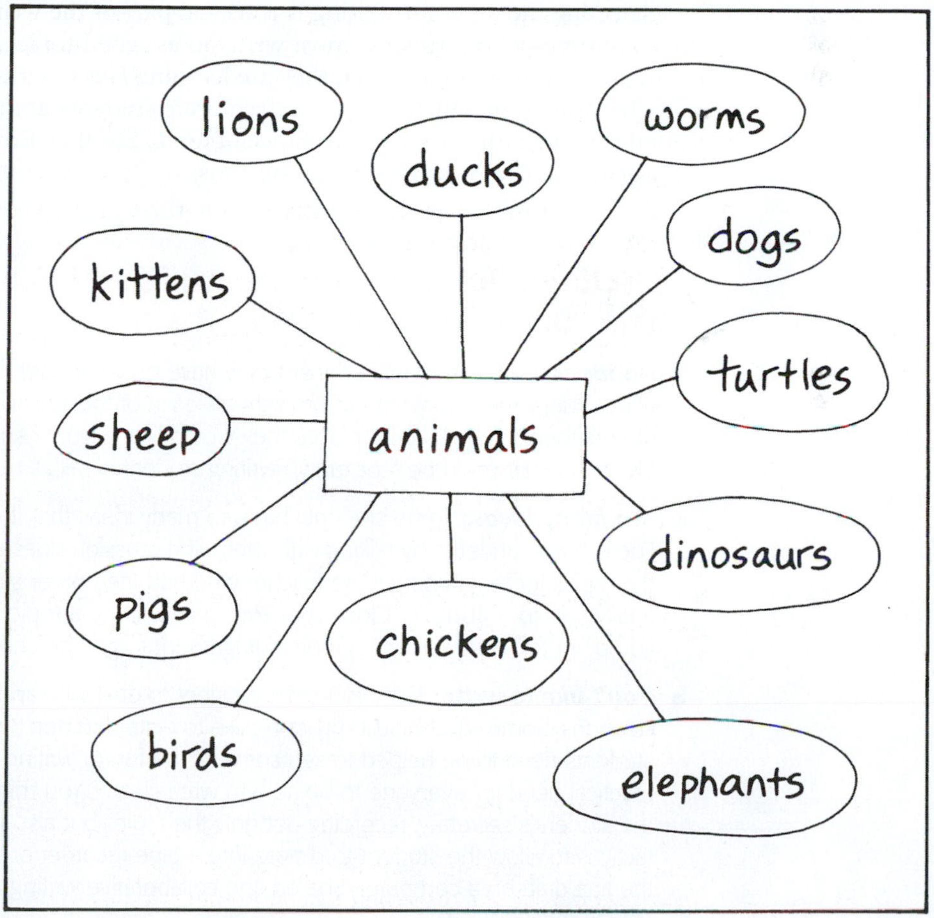

Teachers report that clustering is a successful technique to use with all students, including at-risk and second-language learners (Carr, 1987; Martinez, 1987; Pierce, 1987).

- *Looking for ideas away from school:* Encourage students to look for and jot down writing ideas on the way home from school, at home, or in places they visit.

- *Photography ideas:* Let students take photographs of possible topics. If possible, have them take pictures away from school, as well as bring photographs from home.

- *TV topics:* Encourage students to look for interesting topics as they watch TV shows.

- *The Internet:* Students may find a topic on the Internet that prompts them to write.

- *Reading:* Books or other reading may stimulate a desire to write about a topic.

Selecting the topic for writing is a critical part of the writing process. Although there are times when students must write on assigned topics, they must be allowed to choose their own topics when they are learning *how* to write. Even in classes such as social studies, in which reports are required, students are more likely to produce a good product if they have some choice of topic. See the "Educators Speak" feature on page 355 for what worked with one class.

Selecting a Topic: Problems Students Encounter and Suggestions for Overcoming Them

- *No ideas:* Some students will insist they have no ideas. Get these students to talk about things they enjoy away from school—each of these activities could be a topic. Or, ask them to think about places they would like to go, or something they would like to do. You could be "secretary," writing student ideas as they give them.

- *Too many ideas:* Some students have so many ideas that they can't choose one. Focus these students by talking with them. If discussion doesn't help, select one of the topics for the student. One teacher who had tried other strategies to no avail finally said to a student, "Close your eyes and point to a topic. Write about the one you point to." That was enough encouragement to get the child started.

- *Don't like to write:* This problem is tougher to deal with and there are no easy solutions. Some students simply don't like to write and don't want to write. These students need to be helped to see some of the fun of writing, as well as the very practical need for everyone to be able to write clearly. You might begin by serving as the student's secretary, recording not only the topics but also the first draft. Another tactic is to allow the student to dictate into a tape recorder or input ideas and write the first draft on a computer. Shared and collaborative writing are also good ways to get students started.

Teacher coaches students as they compose after teacher has modeled writing.
© Jupiter Images

Drafting

Once students have selected their topics, the teacher must show students how to write. **Drafting** has two stages, planning and composing, both of which should be modeled as students are learning to use process writing.

Planning

Good writers think about what they want to say and organize their ideas. They consider their purpose for writing and their audience. You should model this process using your own topic and the following steps:

1. **Tell the class your topic and what you want to write about it.** Mention your audience and purpose for writing, and allow students to ask questions. Next, on the whiteboard, overhead projector, or large sheets of paper, jot down some of your ideas. Group ideas that go together, but don't be concerned about organizing all of them at this point. Tell students that you now have a general plan of what you want to include in your writing and you know how you want to begin. Figure 8.10 shows the notes one teacher made while planning to write about her family's camping trip. If you are modeling expository writing, graphic organizers can help.

2. **Have students work in pairs, telling each other about their topics.** Afterward, have each student jot down some ideas or words about his or her topic on a sheet of paper. Have volunteers share their ideas and talk about what they want to include in their writing. Help students understand that this is a beginning plan and that it will probably change as they actually write.

FIGURE 8.10   Teacher's Notes for Planning Writing

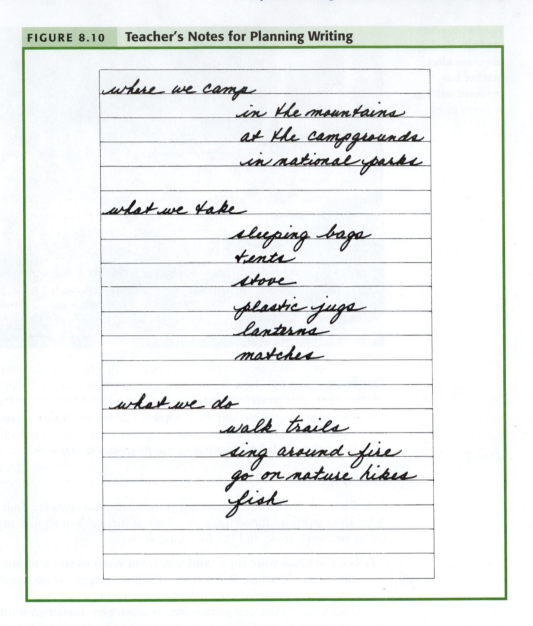

where we camp
        in the mountains
        at the campgrounds
        in national parks

what we take
        sleeping bags
        tents
        stove
        plastic jugs
        lanterns
        matches

what we do
        walk trails
        sing around fire
        go on nature hikes
        fish

Semantic mapping is discussed in Chapters 3 and 6.

As students' writing abilities mature, you can introduce outlining and include it in modeling expository writing. Students will find outlining useful for such activities as report writing. They may also use clustering or semantic mapping to help them organize their ideas.

Students will need less teacher-guided planning as they mature in their writing. However, students should be given enough modeling and support to see how planning is done and how it can help them. The more students write, the more automatically they will carry out the process. Planning for narrative writing may be less structured than in expository writing, but students need guidelines and modeling in both to help them move from having an idea to sitting down to write.

Composing

The second phase of drafting is composing. Students should be told to write on lined paper (unlined for beginners), using every other line to leave room for revisions. This practice helps them develop a positive attitude toward revision; it lets them know that changes are not only acceptable but are a sign of good writing.

You must model composing, because it is important that students see the teacher write. Beginning writers especially need to see the entire process of writing. With older, more mature writers the teacher and students can write independently and share their results later. For most students, the following procedure will be effective:

1. **Using the whiteboard, overhead projector, or large sheets of paper, begin to develop the topic you selected, discussing what you are doing as you go.** (You may also have technology in your classroom that allows you to compose on the computer and project your work onto a screen.) Note the mechanics of starting a sentence and paragraph, and show students how to organize ideas into sentences and paragraphs, asking them to suggest words or make changes in your writing. As you write, cross out and write in some words to show students how to make changes without erasing. Don't be afraid to tell students that you don't know what to say next and that you need some help. Figure 8.11 shows a sample of a teacher's draft for modeling the family camping trip story.

2. **After the initial teacher modeling, have students begin their own writing using their planning notes.** Move about the room offering guidance, assistance, and encouragement to those who need it. If a student is not writing, offer to be secretary for the first few sentences.

   If the writing is going smoothly, continue to move about the room offering assistance and support. A few minutes of talking about the topic or a few prompts from the teacher are often enough to keep students writing. Give students as much time to write as the schedule will allow and as much time as they can use productively. If little or nothing is being produced, it is probably best to resume modeling or to stop the writing.

   ELLs who are literate in their first language may benefit from doing brainstorming and initial drafting in their first language. This allows them to get ideas down quickly and serves as a basis for what they will later write in English.

   These students do not simply translate what they have written in their first language; instead, they use the draft as a source of ideas for their English writing.

3. **If you need to resume modeling, return to your story and continue to write, explaining as you go.** Continue to encourage students to help you. While you can note elements of good writing, do not overemphasize isolated mechanics at this point.

FIGURE 8.11 Teacher's Draft for Modeling Writing

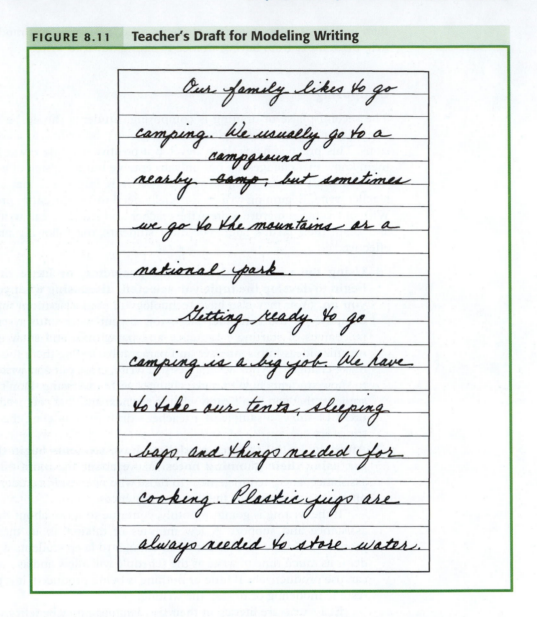

Composing is the phase of drafting in which students develop their topics. Usually they will have received enough direction up to this point that they can proceed with their own writing without additional instruction. Students should have uninterrupted writing time to develop their ideas. Modeling occurs for individuals as the teacher moves about the room offering assistance.

Students should concentrate on expressing their ideas freely and creatively, using whatever words are in their vocabularies, without concern about spelling. Encourage students to spell words the way they think they sound (invented spellings), reassuring them that spelling problems will be taken care of during revision

A Mobile Lab and Individual Laptops Engage At-Risk Students in the Writing Process

" The topic of writing can bring sighs and expressions of dread to some first graders. At such a young age, writing is a daunting task and one not enjoyed by all. Many first graders will say they don't have anything to write about or they have completed their piece in one attempt.

I have a class of at-risk readers this year. This class was developed to provide these students instruction at their level, with the aid of a reading specialist and a smaller class size. My first graders, who struggle with all areas of literacy development, don't like to write because it is difficult for them. One way I engage my students in the writing process is with computers.

Writer's workshop began during the first week of school, and was a real challenge for my students. I made them a part of the writing process with dictated stories. My school purchased a mobile (computer) lab, and I have a set of I-books, so each child is able to have a laptop during writing time. During September I typed the stories the students dictated, so they would have a story they had "written." The students could then listen to me read their story, and we could talk about the story elements included and those missing. We printed each story and students illustrated them. As the year progressed, the students wanted ownership of their writing and began to take risks and write their own stories. They were encouraged to use invented spelling, which we corrected during the editing process. They could save their story and add to it or change it. Since each child has his or her own laptop, they can move on at their pace. With this technology, there is the possibility of all students working to their potential.

Now that the year is half over, I have a class full of writers with many stories to their credit. The stories look wonderful and the students love to share each one they write. I also have the advantage of three other adults in the room to aid in the use of the laptops as well as a smaller class size. I think that all of these components—small class size, more adults, and individual laptops—have helped to create a proficient class of authors. "

—*Caroline Goddard, First-Grade Teacher*
Parkridge Elementary School
Stafford, Virginia

and/or proofreading/editing. For students who are overly concerned about spelling words correctly or are unable to use invented spelling, provide the correct spellings by writing the words in question on a sheet of paper or the whiteboard, or tell them to pretend they are alone on an island with no one to ask. Other techniques include having one student serve as a spelling helper or having a list of troublesome words on the board or a chart. *But nothing works as well to develop a sense of spelling as having students try to spell words the way they think they sound and then make corrections during revision and proofreading.*

The amount of time allowed for the composing phase depends on the students, their writing abilities, the nature of the piece being written, and the length of time allocated to writing in the classroom. Usually the composing phase will extend over several days or writing periods. Students can store their writing in their writing folders and return to it at the next writing period or when they have some extra time during the day. In the beginning stages, writing should not be assigned as homework, but should be done at school in order to provide supervision and assistance.

When students compose on a computer, they can save their drafts to disk. You should be aware that composing and revision often occur almost simultaneously when one is writing on a computer, so the revision stage may not be as clear.

Throughout the composing phase, you should continue to be available to help. If students get stuck, encourage them to ask you or a peer for suggestions. For example, if a student can't think of a good word to describe his or her old dog, you might give several possibilities or suggest using any word for the time being and planning to find the right word when revising. Asking questions and offering suggestions as the students are writing is an extension of modeling and also serves as a quick conference.

Revising

For more information, see Making Revision Matter (Angelillo, 2005) listed in "For Additional Reading."

Revising, the third stage in the writing process, is the step in which students look at their work to examine content—ideas, choice of words, and so forth. Revision may involve modeling by the teacher, conferences between student and teacher or student and student, and individual student work. Revising is not a natural step for students (Graves, 1984). Most beginning writers, especially kindergartners and first graders, are not ready for much revision; they think everything they have written is wonderful! Gradually, however, teachers must help students learn the importance of revision by systematically working through this stage with them.

You can model revision by using your own writing on an overhead or computer projection as an example. You and your students should first discuss what to look for when revising content:

- Have I expressed my ideas clearly so that my audience will understand what I am saying?
- Are there other ideas that I should add to my writing?
- Are there other words that I can use to make my writing more exciting and interesting?
- Are there better ways I can express my ideas?

The questions generated can be posted for students to think about as they work on their revisions. The items will vary according to the students' level and degree of sophistication.

After you and your students have developed guidelines for revision, use the write-aloud process to show how you would revise your piece. Check each of the points listed on the revision checklist you and your students developed and discuss problem areas, making changes with students' help. Throughout the revision step, you should stress the importance of clear expression so that others can understand

FIGURE 8.12 **Teacher's Story Used for Modeling Revision**

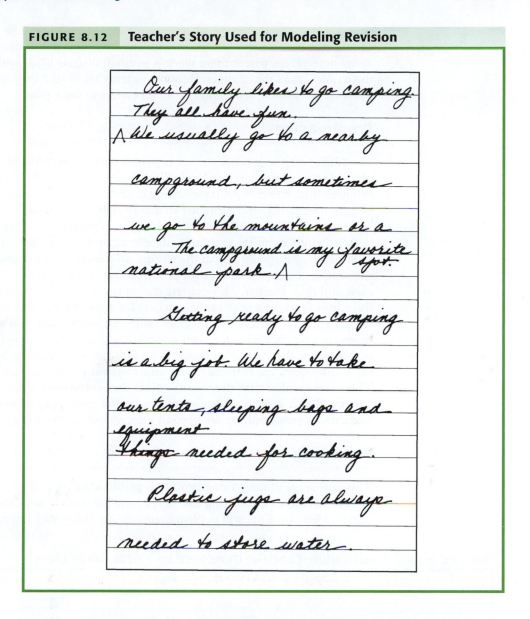

the writing. If, during revision, you notice spelling or usage that needs correction, circle it for attention during the next phase. During revision, the focus should remain on content. Figure 8.12 shows a copy of the teacher's story about the family camping trip after the teacher and students revised the content.

See Chapter 10 for a discussion of writing conferences.

Students are now ready to begin to work on their own revisions. At this point, they should begin to have revision conferences with one another and with you. During these conferences, students talk about their writing and look for places where they might make changes, with you and/or other students taking on the role of an editor who asks questions and points out areas for possible improvement. Many students will already know what some of these areas are. The teacher and peers should not become the "fixers" of students' writing; rather, they should help students note places where more work is needed, discuss ideas with students, and let the writers make the changes. Be sure students know that they do not have to make a change they don't agree with; writing belongs to the author.

Proofreading

The fourth step in process writing is **proofreading,** or **editing,** which should take place after students have made all the content changes they believe are necessary. In proofreading, students get their writing in order for the final copy, checking spelling, writing mechanics, and sentence structure. The teacher and students should work together to develop a list of things to look for in proofreading, and the list should be posted in the room so that students can refer to it as they work. In addition to spelling, the list should reflect the writing mechanics that were modeled throughout the writing. Figure 8.13 shows a proofreading checklist developed by a fifth-grade class and their teacher. This generic checklist can be used by the author (writer) or the editor (such as a peer or the teacher) for any domain of writing.

As you become more comfortable with process writing, you will want to develop more specific checklists for each domain, varying the items according to the level and sophistication of the students. If students are proofreading a document created on a computer, teach them to use and respond to spelling and grammar checks. They must realize that they are the final decision maker about whether a word is correct, that a computer cannot recognize homonyms as incorrect, and that such elements as paragraphing are beyond the capabilities of a computer to analyze.

Publishing

The final stage of the writing process is **publishing,** which has two steps: (1) making a final copy of the writing and (2) putting the writing in a form to be shared with others. Most students will publish their writing, but if they are not making progress

---

FIGURE 8.13   **Proofreading Checklist Developed by a Fifth-Grade Class**

	Author	*Editor*
1. Sentences and questions begin with capital letters.	☐	☐
2. Sentences and questions have the correct end marks.	☐	☐
3. Paragraphs are indented.	☐	☐
4. Possible misspellings have been circled and checked.	☐	☐

Author _____

Editor _____

with a piece, they may elect to drop it. This may occur at any point in the process. Indeed, not all writing should be published. The student, together with the teacher, should make this decision after considering both the quality of the writing and how the student feels about it. In a conference, you might ask the student such questions as, "How do you think others will feel about this piece of writing?" and, "Do you think it is a good idea to publish this one?"

See Chapter 11 for information about portfolios.

Sometimes it is appropriate for the teacher to say, "I don't think this is one of your best pieces of writing. Maybe you should just stop working on this piece or make a final copy for your file and start work on something new." Even writing that is not published may be placed in the literacy portfolio and used for later review.

If a student feels strongly that the piece should be published, it is probably best to proceed, but you must always weigh the consequences of having a student publish an inappropriate piece. Publishing authenticates the reason for writing, and gives students pride and enjoyment in their own work. The more students publish their writing, the more they will develop a sense of themselves as authors and grow in the writing process. If you have a few students who do not want to create final copies or publish, you should support and guide them until they experience the satisfaction of seeing their work published; this will motivate them to write more.

Producing Final Copy

After students have completed revising, editing, and proofreading, and have held their initial publishing conference with you, they are ready to make a final copy of their writing. In making their final copy, they should be encouraged to be as neat and accurate as possible. One way to get students to produce a good final copy is to use a computer with a word-processing program, since even very young children succeed with this approach.

You and your students should work together to develop a list of guidelines to follow in making final copies, and the list should be kept where students can refer to it easily. Points such as the following can be included, but each list must reflect the needs, abilities, and level of the students.

The manner in which the final copy is prepared will depend on whether it is to be published or simply filed.

Final Copy Guidelines

- Be neat.

- Indent each new paragraph.

- Keep margins at the top, bottom, and sides of the paper straight.

- Check punctuation.

- Check spelling.

- Reread your final copy to be sure it is correct.

Video Case

Parental Involvement in School Culture: A Literacy Project

Watch the video clip, study the artifacts in the case, and reflect on the following questions:

1. Explain in your own words why the publishing process is an important component of developing student literacy.

2. Look at the Classroom Artifacts that accompany this Video Case and share your reactions to the published student work. What are the most impressive aspects of the students' finished books? Have they effectively constructed meaning within their stories?

Ideas for Publishing

See the "Educators Speak" feature on page 355.

Publishing is a very important part of the writing process (Calkins, 1994; Graves, 1983). Students need this aspect of the writing process to help them develop a sense of the importance of their writing, an understanding of why one must learn to write, and a sense of their audience.

One way for students to publish their writing is in book form. Individual students can produce their own books, or several students can collaborate on a book. The excitement and pleasure on the faces of students after producing their first book are almost indescribable! Publishing also brings closure to the students' writing experience.

Books can be produced in many forms: construction paper covers over paper, folder books made from manila folders and paper, shape books cut to show the topic (for example, a snowman shape for a winter topic), or hardcover books made from cardboard and cloth.

Students can move from simple types of books to more complex forms as they become more practiced. They should be encouraged to include a cover page that presents their names, the illustrator's name, and the date. At the end of the book, they should place a page titled, "About the Author," on which they describe themselves and other books they have written. Also, when books are to be shared with classmates, it is a good idea to include a page in the back where students can indicate they have read the book and comment on how they felt about it.

There are many other ways for students to publish their writing without producing a book. Some of the following ideas broaden the concept of publishing to any form of sharing:

■ ***Bulletin boards:*** Use a catchy title and an attractive background for students to display final copies that have not been made into a book. The title might be "Great Writing from Great Kids," "Writing We Are Proud Of," "Great Writers Are Blossoming," "Award Winners," and so on. Sometimes you can attach a clothesline to the bulletin board on which students can hang their writing out for others to read.

■ ***Author's chair:*** A special chair may be labeled "Author's Chair" (Graves & Hansen, 1983). The student who has a piece of writing to share sits in the chair and reads it to the group, and a discussion of the writing follows. Usually the piece that is shared is the final copy.

■ *Class or school newspaper:* A class or school newspaper is an excellent way to create authentic reasons for students to write. Because of the nature of a newspaper, students can get experiences with many domains of writing and numerous products—articles, stories, letters to the editor, and so forth. The newspaper can have a staff, and students can publish it using a computer.

See later in this chapter and "Websites" at the end of this chapter for other ideas about online postings.

■ *Online postings:* Students may post writing for others to read. Some schools or classrooms have their own websites that parents can access.

■ *Computer data storage device:* Final copies may be published by inputting and saving them so that other students can read them on the class computer. Collections of class stories can be made for students to take home.

■ *Magazines of student-written works:* Students may choose to submit their writing to a print or online magazine that publishes student-written works.

The concept of the literature group or circle was introduced in Chapter 7.

■ *Writing circles:* In a writing circle, students get together to share and discuss their writing. Also referred to as RAGs, or Read Around Groups (Olson, 1987), the writing circle consists of five or six students who sit together to read and talk about (not critique) their writing. Several writing circles may be in operation at the same time. (They may also be used for selecting and discussing a topic, revising, and proofreading. To ensure that students know the real purpose of the circle, it might be better to use the title "Writing Circle" for sharing and "RAGs" when the circle is used for other purposes.)

It does not matter how children publish and share their writing as long as they *do* it, since it is through sharing that they develop their sense of authorship and show how they have constructed meaning by conveying their ideas to others. At any grade level, sharing is an essential part of constructing meaning through writing.

Sample Lesson Using the Shared Writing Routine

The following lesson is a sample of using the shared writing mode to teach both the mechanics of writing and the writing process.

PURPOSE	The Shared Writing Routine is used to model both the mechanics and the process of writing.
WHEN TO USE	This routine is used in the Learning to Write block of the literacy program.
DESCRIPTION/ PROCEDURES	In the Shared Writing Routine, children dictate a text, and the teacher adds his or her own ideas. By using modeling and writing together, you will systematically teach children how to write. Use the following procedures:

1. *Select a Topic*

■ Decide on the type of writing you want students to do—story, information, and so forth.

■ Tell students about the type of writing and define it.

Example:

"Boys and girls, we're going to learn to write a story today. Remember, a story has characters and a problem and there is a beginning, a middle, and an end."

■ Select a topic for the writing. Have children brainstorm with you and make a list of suggestions.

Example:

"What might we write about in our story?
–a boy who gets lost
–my new puppy's problem
–our zoo adventure

Raise your hand if you agree that the boy who gets lost will be our topic."

2. *Write Together*

■ After the topic has been selected, discuss how the type of writing might begin. Ask students to give ideas; you should feel free to add your own ideas. As students give ideas, begin to write using the overhead, large chart paper, or the chalkboard.

Example:

> A little boy named Roger got lost. He was walking in the woods. He meeted a talking bear. He met a talking tree.

■ When students give an incorrect usage, add a correct example soon after. Note the *meeted/met* example in the story. Continue the writing until you complete the piece.

3. *Revise*

■ On the same day or another day, use the piece you have written together to model ways to improve it. Ask students for ideas as well as giving your own.

■ As students give ideas and you add ideas, write them on the original piece so that everyone can see the additions. Sometimes you will want to share your thinking as to why you did something. This is modeling or thinking aloud for students.

Example:

> A little boy named Roger got lost. He was
> walking in the woods. He ~~meeted~~ met a talking
> bear. The bear was big. His teeth were
> long The boy met a talking tree. The bear
> and the tree helped him find his way home.

- You may combine revising and editing. Say, "I see one way we need to edit our story: we should change *meeted* to *met—He met a talking bear."*
- Many times you will add content or ideas to the story. Say: "To make our story interesting, we should tell some more about the bear."
- The process continues until the story is revised and edited.

Following the shared writing, children should write the same type of piece on their own or with a partner.

The Shared Writing Routine is an excellent way to teach children how to write. In the process, you can incorporate writing conventions such as spelling and grammar, which are discussed in the next section of this chapter.

Writing Conventions

We discussed the importance of writing in helping children learn to spell in Chapter 5. Writing is also important in helping students learn the various conventions of English.

Renewed emphasis on assessing student use of the conventions of writing as well as their thinking is leading to renewed attention to grammar and spelling lessons. We believe there is a place for isolated lessons in both areas, so long as students are shown the connection between the lessons and the real, meaningful writing they are doing.

Formal grammar teaching fell out of favor for awhile as teachers heeded such ideas as the following: "Why does grammar retain such glamour when research over the past ninety years reveals not only that students are hostile toward it, but that the study of grammar has no impact on writing quality?" and "the grammar sections of a textbook should be treated as a reference tool that might provide some insights into conventions of mechanics and usage" (Hillocks & Smith, 1991, p. 602). Current thinking reflects a balance of isolated lessons and integrated use.

The basic premise that children learn to read and write by reading and writing while receiving instruction as needed also applies to grammar, usage, and spelling. Minilessons held during conferences or in small groups are good ways to support students in learning mechanics, usage, and spelling, and these lessons can be built around a demonstrated need in students' writing (Rog, 2007). Figure 8.14 shows the steps for using students' writing as a basis for minilessons. This model is based on the work of Wilde (1990, 1996), Gentry (1996), and Gentry and Gillet (1992).

Figure 8.15 presents a sample spelling lesson, and Figure 8.16 shows a sample grammar lesson.

(*Text continues on page 371.*)

FIGURE 8.14   **Six Steps to Meaningful Teaching of Grammar and Spelling Based on Writing**

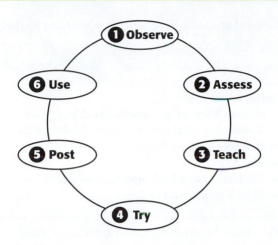

Each step is described below:

❶ **Observe**
- Examine students w riting.
- Identify strengths in spelling or grammar.
  AND
- Identify needs in spelling or grammar.

❷ **Assess**
- Have students write some words using the spelling pattern or grammar convention.
  OR
- Have students write a sentence using the grammar convention.
- Note how they do.

❸ **Teach**
- Teach a minilesson on the spelling pattern or grammar convention.
- Draw examples used in minilessons from literature being read.

❹ **Try**
- Have students write some words or a sentence or more using what they learned.
  OR
- Repeat the assessment used in Step 2.
- Compare to students' performance in Step 2, Assess.

❺ **Post**
- Write the grammar convention or spelling generalization or pattern on a chart with examples and post on the wall.
- For spelling patterns, add lists of words to the word wall.

❻ **Use**
- Encourage students to use the spelling pattern or grammar convention in their writing.
- Remind students to refer to wall postings as needed.

FIGURE 8.15 **Sample Spelling Lesson**

❶ **Observe**
- Several students have written sentences in their stories like the following:

  The dog had muddy feet. He jumped on the chair seet to get the met on the table.

  Major Strengths
  – Knows beginning consonants *d, m, f, j, s, t*
  – Knows high-frequency words *the, had, he, on, to, get*
  – Knows the double consonant pattern *dd*.

  Needs
  – Needs to learn long *e* pattern *ee* and *ea*.
  – Needs to learn *ed* ending.

  > ✪ Start by teaching a lesson on *ee, ea* words.

❷ **Assess**
- Ask students to write four words on their papers before you teach a minilesson—*beat* (My team will beat your team.), *keep, seat, tree*.

Examples of Students' Second Answers		
1	**2**	**3**
beat	*beat*	*beet*
keep	*ceep*	*keep*
seat	*seat*	*seet*
tree	*tree*	*tree*

❸ **Teach**
- Write the following list*of words on the board:

see	eat
three	meat
sleep	bead

  * (*Note:* Words should be taken from literature students are reading.)

- Have students underline what is the same in each column.

s<u>ee</u>	<u>ea</u>t
thr<u>ee</u>	m<u>ea</u>t
sl<u>ee</u>p	b<u>ea</u>d

(continued)

FIGURE 8.15   Sample Spelling Lesson (*continued*)

- Read aloud each list (or have the list read aloud).
- Ask what vowel sound you hear in each column of words (long *e*).
- Point out that long *e* may be spelled *ee* or *ea*.

❹ **Try** • Repeat the assessment used in Step 2.

Examples of Students' Second Answers		
1	2	3
beat	beat	beet
keep	ceep	keep
seat	seat	seet
tree	tree	tree

- Student 1 has the knowledge to spell words using *ea* and *ee*.
- Student 2 understands the *ea/ee* patterns but needs to work on the *k*.
- Student 3 understands the *ee* pattern but needs more work with *ea*.

❺ **Post** • Make a chart.

Spelling

The long **e** may be spelled **ee** or **ea** in words.

Examples: meat
          keep

- Add to the word wall.

Long *e*

ea	*ee*
sea	see
meat	tree
seal	sleep
meal	keep

- Continue to add other words over time.

❻ **Use** • Remind students to check the posting on the chart and the word wall to check their spelling as they write.
- Observe students' writing to see if they are using the *ee*, *ea* spelling patterns correctly.

FIGURE 8.16	**Sample Grammar Lesson**

❶ **Observe** • Several students have written sentences like the following:

Student 1

My dad drives a dodge ram truck. His name Harry. The truck is red.

Student 2

We went to california on a Vacation. We had fun and saw

the golden gate bridge.

Student 3

I live in kentucky near Barkley lake. I like to
fish and catch perch.

Major Strengths
   – Capitalizes beginning of sentences.
   – Uses correct end punctuation.
   – Uses nouns.

Needs
   – Does not know difference between common and proper nouns.
   – Does not capitalize nouns correctly.

✪ Teach a lesson on common and proper nouns.

❷ **Assess** • Dictate the following sentences to students:

Mr. Brown likes ice cream. His favorite brand is Blue
Bunny which really is nonfat yogurt.

(continued)

FIGURE 8.16   Sample Grammar *(continued)*

Examples of Students' Answers

1 Mr. Beaver likes ice cream. His favorite brand is Blue Bunny which really is nonfat yogurt.

2 Mr. Brown likes ice cream. His favorite brand is Blue Bunny which really is not fat Yogurt.

3 Mr. Brown likes ice cream. His favorite brand is Blue Bunny which really is Yogurt.

❸ **Teach**   • Write the following on the board:

- A <u>noun</u> is the name of a person, place, or thing.
- A <u>common noun</u> names any person, place, or thing.
- A <u>proper noun</u> is a particular person, place, or thing. Capitalize proper nouns.

• Have students open a book that the whole class is reading. Locate examples of common and proper nouns. Make a list of them.

Common Nouns	Proper Nouns
airplane	Boeing 747
ship	the Queen Elizabeth
submarine	Bob Marshall
mountain	Mt. Hood
book	Bridge to Terabithia

• Ask students what they notice about the two groups and how they are capitalized. (Point out if not given.)
• Note that little words like *to* in *Bridge to Terabithia* are not capitalized.

❹ **Try**   • Repeat the assessment used in Step 2.

(continued)

FIGURE 8.16   Sample Grammar (*continued*)

Examples of Students' Answers

1 Mr. Beaver likes ice cream.
His favorite brand is Blue
Bunny which really is nonfat yogurt.

---

2 Mr. Brown likes ice cream. His favorite brand is
Blue Bunny which really is not fat Yogurt.

---

3 Mr. Brown likes ice cream. His favorite brand is
Blue Bunny which really is Yogurt.

• All students have learned to differentiate between common and proper nouns. Students 2 and 3 need to focus on the word *nonfat*.

❺ **Post** • Make a chart for the wall about common and proper nouns. Add to the list over time.

Nouns
Names of persons, places, or things
dog, baby, house, automobile, airplane, Maple Tree, The White House, table, zoo, The Brookfield Zoo.

Common Nouns	**Proper Nouns**
Names of any person, place, or thing	Name of particular persons, places, or things. Capitalize proper nouns except for little words in the middle.
dog baby house automobile airplane table zoo	Maple Tree The White House The Brookfield Zoo

❻ **Use** • Remind students to check the posting and use what they have learned in their writing.
• Observe students to see if they are using common and proper nouns appropriately in their writing.

Using Technology to Support Writing and Reading

Technology grows at such a pace that it makes little sense to cite specific programs in a textbook. There are whole books devoted to the subject of using technology in teaching literacy. An excellent one is "Technology for Literacy Teaching and Learning" (Valmont, 2003).

We suggest that you use whatever professional resources you have to learn about software or online materials. Talk to friends who have used a program before ordering it for your students. Look for reviews. Have your students search online for material to help them write reports.

Remember that technology can never replace a teacher who understands the writing process and how students learn to write, and one who is always available to provide needed scaffolding and guidance and encouragement.

Keyboarding and word processing Research showed some time ago that the use of word processing leads students at all levels to write longer pieces and revise more (Dahl & Farnan, 1998). The teacher, of course, continues to play a critical role in the process through monitoring and coaching students as needed.

The quickest route to a program you might want is to enter what you are looking for into a search engine and go from there. For example, enter "keyboarding software for children." Following are some website addresses, correct at the time of this revision, that may lead you to some products to help students learn writing related skills:

http://www.childrenssoftware.com/ (This site reviews products.)
http://www.learningcompany.com
http://www.riverdeep.net
http://www.gamco.com
http://www.sunburst.com

Internet Following are two websites that are helpful to teachers of writing:

http://www.writingproject.org
This home page of the National Writing Project helps teachers stay abreast of research and new ideas on writing.

http://www.readwritethink.org
At this home page you can navigate to instructional resources or student resource.

Software Literacy Programs Enter "writing educational software" into a search engine and you may get more than eighty million hits, as we did. Because of the rapid changes in technology and materials, we suggest you rely on your media specialist and current professional journals to steer you to sites you want to explore further.

Writing and the Construction of Meaning: Key Points

To review the Key Points, see the ACE practice tests at the HM TeacherPrepSPACE Student Website.

Writing and reading should be taught together because:

- They both are constructive processes.
- They share similar types of knowledge and processes.
- They improve achievement in both areas.
- They foster communication.
- Together they produce outcomes that are not achievable by either alone.
- Writing can be classified by domains, modes, or traits.
- Various activities connect reading and writing.
- Process writing was developed as a major procedure for helping students learn to construct meaning through writing.
- Mechanics and the process of writing can be taught together.
- Writing conventions such as spelling and grammar can be taught through mini-lessons, which may be based on student writing.

How Do I Teach?

Writing and Constructing Meaning
Domains and Modes of Writing with Products and Projects, p. 340
Activities that Connect Reading and Writing
- Reading Specific Types of Writing, p. 340

- Reading Student-Written Materials, p. 340
- Summaries, p. 342
- Story Frames, p. 342
Process Writing, pp. 344–361

Sample Lessons
- Spelling Lesson, p. 366
- Grammar Lesson, p. 368

Video Cases in This Chapter

- **Elementary Writing Instruction: Process Writing**
- **Parental Involvement in School Culture: A Literacy Project**

For Additional Reading

Angelillo, J. (2005). *Making revision matter.* New York: Scholastic.
Calkins, L. M. (1994). *The art of teaching writing* (2nd ed.). Portsmouth, NH: Heinemann.

Dix, S. (2006). I'll do it my way: Three writers and their revision practices. *The Reading Teacher, 59*(6), 566–573.

Duke, N. K., Purcell-Gates, V., Hall, L. A., & Tower, C. (2006/2007). Authentic literacy activities for developing comprehension and writing. *The Reading Teacher, 60*(4), 344–355.

Dworin, J. E. (2006). The Family Stories Project: Using funds of knowledge for writing. *The Reading Teacher, 59*(6), 510–520.

Engel, T., & Streich, R. (2006). Yes, there *is* room for soup in the curriculum: Achieving accountability in a collaboratively planned writing program. *The Reading Teacher, 59*(7), 660–679.

Gammil, D. M. (2006). Learning the *write* way. *The Reading Teacher, 59*(8), 754–762.

Gentry, J. R. (2004). *The science of spelling: The explicit specifics that make great readers and writers (and spellers)*. Portsmouth, NH: Heinemann.

Graves, D. H. (1983). *Writing: Teachers and children at work*. Exeter, NH: Heinemann.

Graves, D. H. (2003). *Writing: Teachers and children at work* (20th anniv. ed.). Exeter, NH: Heinemann.

Helman, L. A. (2004). Building on the sound system of Spanish: Insights from the alphabetic spellings of English-language learners. *The Reading Teacher, 57*(5), 452–460.

Henk, W. A., Marinak, B. A., Moore, J. C., & Mallette, M. H. (2003/2004). The Writing Observation Framework: A guide for refining and validating writing instruction. *The Reading Teacher, 57*(4), 322–333.

Kern, D., Andre, S., Schilke, R., Barton, J., & McGuire, M. C. (2003). Less is more: Preparing students for state writing assessments. *The Reading Teacher, 56*(8), 816–826.

Knipper, K. J., & Duggan, T. J. (2006). Writing to learn across the curriculum: Tools for comprehension in content area classes. *The Reading Teacher, 59*(5), 462–470.

Leal, D. J. (2005/2006). The Word Writing CAFÉ: Assessing student writing for complexity, accuracy, and fluency. *The Reading Teacher, 59*(4), 340–350.

Oczkus, L. D. (2007). *Guided writing: Practical lessons, powerful results*. Portsmouth, NH: Heinemann.

Read, S. (2005). First and second graders writing informational text. *The Reading Teacher, 59*(1), 36–44.

Rog, L. J. (2007). *Marvelous minilessons for teaching beginning writing, K–3*. Newark, DE: International Reading Association.

Scala, M. C. (2001). *Working together: Reading and writing in inclusive classrooms*. Newark, DE: International Reading Association.

Strickland, D. S., Ganske, K., & Monroe, J. K. (2001). *Supporting struggling readers and writers*. Portland, ME: Stenhouse Publishers.

Valmont, W. J. (2003). *Technology for literacy teaching and learning*. Boston: Houghton Mifflin.

Van Leeuwen, C. A., & Gabriel, M. A. (2007). Beginning to write with word processing: Integrating writing process and technology in a primary classroom. *The Reading Teacher, 60*(5), 420–429.

Van Sluys, K., & Laman, T. T. (2006). Learning about language: Written conversations and elementary language learners. *The Reading Teacher, 60*(3), 222–233.

Websites

Digital Books

This website provides a printing template for publishing books on the Internet. It correlates with the book *Real e Publishing, Really Publishing!* by Mark Condon and Michael McGuffee (Heinemann, Portsmouth, NH, 2001). This book and its correlated website provide many sound suggestions for helping students of all ages create digital books.

http://www.realebooks.com

Online Publishing of Student Writing

Do a search for possible places to get student writing published online. For example, at one website (given below) we found links to the following:

Amazing Kids

Cyberkids—a magazine written by kids for kids ages 7–11

Cyberteens Home Page: Zeen, chat and contests

KidPub

MidLink Magazine

Parents and Children Together Online

Scriptito's Place Stone Soup—ages 8–13

The Virtual Refrigerator Door—artwork from kids ages 2–18

Young Writers' Clubhouse

http://www.emtech.net/student_publishing.htm

Writing Traits

The Northwest Regional Educational Laboratory website provides complete information about the initial and continuing development and revising of the 6 + 1 traits of writing.

http://www.nwrel.org

http://www.nwrel.org

Helping Struggling Readers

9

EDUCATORS SPEAK
Helping Struggling Readers, p. 396
—*Leslie Ericson-Alti, Rio Rancho, New Mexico*

Terms
YOU NEED TO KNOW

- acceleration
- frustration reading level
- independent reading level
- instructional reading level
- intervention
- jump-start
- more than adequate yearly progress
- reading intervention program
- remediation/ remedial reading
- struggling reader
- Tier I Intervention
- Tier II Intervention
- Tier III Intervention

*F*ranklin School is a K–6 elementary school with 728 students who come from a full range of economic levels. Most students ride a bus to school. There are seventeen different languages represented in the school. Today we are visiting Mr. Lazio in his first-grade classroom and Ms. Crystal in her sixth-grade class.

Mr. Lazio has just completed reading instruction for the morning. All twenty-one boys and girls in his class participated in the instructional activities. Mr. Lazio directs students to various centers, where they are to work on activities involving independent reading and writing, projects, or practicing needed skills. He reviews the directions chart posted at the front of the room and discusses with students what they should do if they encounter any problems.

Mr. Lazio then calls a group of seven students to the reading table, where he conducts a 30-minute reading lesson using two short books. Each student begins by silently rereading a book that he or she completed in a previous lesson. As the students read for 5 minutes, Mr. Lazio listens to one student read, coaching him as needed. This activity is followed by phonemic awareness and phonics instruction using three consonants and two short vowels. This activity lasts for about 10 minutes.

Next, Mr. Lazio introduces the new book for the day; we notice that the text has many words with the letter sounds that were just taught. Students first read the book silently. Then Mr. Lazio has students take turns reading sentences aloud; Mr. Lazio makes notes about how accurately each student reads. The lesson concludes with the group dictating a sentence about the book, which Mr. Lazio records on a chart.

Before we leave the room, Mr. Lazio tells us that the group we saw consisted of his most struggling readers. He gives them 30 minutes additional reading instruction four days a week.

Next we go to Ms. Crystal's room, just as six students are leaving for reading class. Ms. Crystal tells us that she has just finished her day's reading lessons and these students are going to Miss McMurray, the reading teacher, for additional reading instruction. Ms. Crystal suggests that we go with these students to see what they do in this extra reading time.

With a book begun on the previous day, Miss McMurray conducts a lesson using the teaching strategy known as reciprocal teaching (see Chapter 4). The students begin by summarizing their previous day's reading using a graphic organizer. Students then work with partners to complete a preview of the section of the book they will read today; they pose a question that they think will be answered in the text. Next, students read the text silently and then take turns with Miss McMurray modeling the four strategies of reciprocal teaching: question, summarize, clarify, and predict. The students conclude the lesson by writing about what they read and then discussing the process as well as their understanding of what they read.

As the students return to their class, we stay to talk with Miss McMurray. She tells us that these are some of Ms. Crystal's lowest readers. She notes that their reading has improved several levels over the last six months.

The HM TeacherPrepSPACE Student Website offers many helpful resources, such as self-quizzes, glossary flashcards, lesson plan templates, and more.

In the two classes we visited, we encountered **struggling readers:** students who were having difficulty learning to read. Think about what happened in each classroom:

- In both classrooms, the struggling readers received the same core reading instruction that the entire class received.

■ Mr. Lazio conducted the additional instruction that his group received in the classroom while other students worked at centers.

■ Ms. Crystal's struggling readers went to the reading teacher for additional reading instruction.

■ Mr. Lazio's group of struggling readers received additional instruction that focused on elements of fluency, phonemic awareness, and phonics. They read short texts that allowed them to apply immediately what they had been taught.

■ Miss McMurray used reciprocal teaching with Ms. Crystal's students, a strategy that works effectively to help older struggling readers accelerate their reading.

Both classrooms reflect effective ways to help struggling readers. In this chapter, we discuss the techniques used in Mr. Lazio's, Ms. Crystal's, and Miss McMurray's classrooms, as well as others. First let's explore who our struggling readers are.

Who Are Struggling Readers?

A struggling reader is any student who is having difficulty learning to read. The student may have difficulty with oral language, phonemic awareness, phonics, vocabulary, comprehension, motivation, or some other factor that prevents adequate yearly progress (Cooper, Chard, & Kiger, 2006). A student who is struggling with reading may exhibit difficulties in one or all of these areas. No two struggling readers are exactly the same.

Some struggling readers also cope with other difficulties, such as health, visual, or auditory problems, environmental issues, or background issues. For students with such complex reading problems, the reading specialist, psychologist, school nurse, or other specialist should be contacted for help in working out a plan. To determine whether a student has a complex reading problem requiring the services of one or more specialists, begin by doing a thorough diagnosis as described in this chapter and developing a treatment plan. Follow the diagnosis by trial teaching and ongoing assessment to determine whether the treatment plan is working. After four to six weeks, if the student's reading is not improving, seek the services of a reading or other learning specialist. If your district does not have a reading specialist, try to contact a local college or university to find out what services are available in your area.

For many years, the usual approach to struggling readers was to provide **remediation** or **remedial reading.** *Remediation* is the process of correcting a deficiency; teachers waited until the child had an established problem and then tried to correct it. This approach was not successful or effective (Allington & Walmsley, 1995; Snow, Burns, & Griffin, 1998) in helping struggling readers overcome their problems, primarily because it focused on weaknesses in skill areas rather than actual reading.

The accepted approach now is **intervention.** By definition, *intervention* is the act of coming into or between so as to hinder or alter an action. A **reading intervention program** is one that either prevents or stops failure by providing additional instructional time. With reading intervention, we don't wait for a problem to occur; instead, we recognize that a student is beginning to struggle and provide the necessary instruction to help him or her catch up.

All schools today are striving to help students achieve adequate yearly progress, generally defined as a month of growth for a month of instruction. Struggling readers, who may be two, three, four, or more years below level, will never catch up with just adequate yearly progress. These students must make **more than adequate yearly progress** in order to catch up and ultimately read on grade level. *Therefore, helping struggling readers requires* **acceleration** *of their reading, increasing the rate of growth so they will have more than a month's growth for a month of instruction.*

See Chapter 2 for more discussion of adequate yearly progress.

The Comprehensive Balanced Literacy Program, Standards, and Struggling Readers

For a detailed discussion of the Comprehensive Balanced Literacy Program, see Chapter 2.

The best way to deal with reading problems is to prevent them from occurring by providing good instruction. This is what this text and our model for a Comprehensive Balanced Literacy Program are all about. Our model consists of two main parts: core instruction and intervention.

Core Instruction

Core instruction has six blocks: (1) Daily Independent Reading, (2) Daily Independent Writing, (3) Reading: Learning Skills and Strategies, (4) Reading: Application of Skills and Strategies, (5) Writing: Learning to Write, and (6) Writing: Developmentally Appropriate Writing. These six blocks are provided for all students—those who are developing as we would expect as well as those who are struggling. The standards for your school or state guide the content of your program for all students. All students, those who are struggling and those who are not, are usually expected to meet the same standards.

Intervention: Three Tiers

Intervention, the second part and seventh block of the Comprehensive Balanced Literacy Program, is designed to help struggling readers make more than adequate yearly progress. The pyramid diagram in Figure 9.1 shows the way many school districts and state departments of education are thinking about intervention in relation

FIGURE 9.1   **Pyramid Diagram Showing the Relationship Between Core Instruction and Intervention**

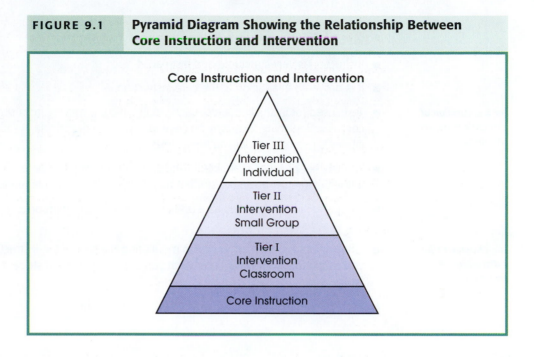

Core Instruction and Intervention

Tier III
Intervention
Individual

Tier II
Intervention
Small Group

Tier I
Intervention
Classroom

Core Instruction

to core instruction. Notice that Core Instruction forms the base of the pyramid and is the instruction provided to all students, including struggling readers and special education students.

Tier I Intervention is taught in the classroom and is directly related to the core instructional program that you are using. For example, if a struggling reader lacks background for a particular selection, you might provide a **jump-start** by doing a very structured, guided preview before introducing the selection to the whole group. Jump-start activities give struggling readers a head start with a learning task before they actually begin it with other students.

See Chapter 5 for more discussion on previews and picture walks.

Tier II Intervention is generally taught in small groups or individually either in or out of the classroom; it is designed to raise students' reading levels at a rate that is faster than would be expected (expected growth is one month's growth in one month's time) and thus lead to more than adequate yearly progress. The extra reading instruction that Mr. Lazio and Miss McMurray provided shows acceleration in action. Acceleration intervention is characterized by a number of critical features.

Tier III Intervention is designed for the struggling reader with the most severe needs. A reading specialist does a thorough diagnosis and usually provides the instruction, often on an individual basis.

Remember, both core instruction and intervention are developed using the same standards. Struggling readers need both core instruction and acceleration intervention to make more than adequate yearly progress.

Critical Features of Accelerated Intervention

■ Instruction is very structured and fast paced.

■ It is delivered in addition to the core instruction.

For a discussion of authentic texts, see Chapter 2.

■ Texts used for instruction are sequenced in difficulty, moving from simple to more complex. Beginning texts may be created and more decodable. As soon as possible, students move to reading authentic texts.

■ The teacher provides scaffolded instruction by providing lots of teacher modeling in the beginning, moving to student modeling and then to independence.

■ The instruction is delivered as a one-on-one tutorial program or as a small group of five to seven students.

See Chapter 11 for a discussion of assessment.

■ Ongoing assessment and progress monitoring is a part of the instruction. This lets you continuously know whether what you are trying for each student is really working.

■ Acceleration intervention is taught by a certified teacher.

Identifying Struggling Readers

As a classroom teacher your task is to evaluate each student's reading and determine which students are struggling and what instruction each one needs. To do this, you need to make the following decisions:

1. Determine how each student is reading in terms of various factors (see Figure 9.2).
2. Decide which students are struggling and need more than core instruction.
3. Plan the core instruction and intervention for the struggling readers in accordance with your program and available resources.
4. Carry out (or arrange for) the instruction, continually evaluating and revising in the light of student performance.

Figure 9.2 presents a reading evaluation checklist that will guide the decision-making process that you need to follow in order to identify your struggling readers and plan their instruction. As you look over the checklist, note the areas to be evaluated. Some of the information may be available from the students' cumulative records, although you will need to do further assessment and gathering of information. Always begin by using information that is already available.

In the following sections, we discuss each of the areas on the checklist presented in Figure 9.2. The remainder of the chapter then focuses on planning and carrying out core instruction and intervention with struggling readers.

FIGURE 9.2   **Reading Evaluation Checklist**

Reading Evaluation Checklist

Name _____   Date _____

Grade _____   Teacher _____

Area Being Evaluated	Findings/Comments
1. Reading Levels	Independent _____ Instructional _____ Frustration _____
2. Oral Language	Listening Level _____ General ability to use language: _____ _____ _____
3. Decoding	Phonemic Awareness: _____ Phonics: _____ Fluency: _____ _____
4. Comprehension	Background/Prior Knowledge: _____ _____ Strategies: _____ _____

(continued)

Reading Evaluation Checklist   *(continued)*

Area Being Evaluated	Findings/Comments
5. Related Factors	What other factors seem to be affecting this student's reading? _____ _____
6. Previous Program	What type of instruction has been provided for this student before? _____ _____

Instructional Plans

Core Instruction
Reading Level: _____

Materials: _____

_____

Skills: _____

_____

Intervention

_____

_____

Comments:

_____

_____

_____

Literacy Assessment: Administering an Informal Reading Inventory

Watch the video clip, study the artifacts in the case, and reflect on the following questions:

1. Carefully watch the Video Case and examine the Case Artifacts. What pieces of information indicate that Myrto is a struggling reader?

2. If you had an opportunity, what questions would you ask the literacy specialist, Joanna Pincus, about administering and scoring an IRI?

Reading Levels

For more information on determining reading levels, see Chapter 11 on informal reading inventories and Cooper and Kiger in "For Additional Reading."

First, you need to determine each student's reading levels: **independent, instructional,** or **frustration.** You can do this by using an informal reading inventory (IRI) or a running record with leveled texts. Alternatively, students can read from leveled texts, while you note both their decoding skills and comprehension. This information will help you decide what level of text to use for instruction, and what level the student can read independently. It will also help you plan all aspects of your instruction including fluency practice. If you are working with a nonreader, move on to the next area of concern, oral language.

Oral Language

Oral language (speaking and listening) is the foundation for learning to read. You need to assess each student's oral vocabulary, whether the student can express himself accurately and effectively, and how well the student listens with understanding. Observation in the classroom is the most efficient way to gather this information. Give each student an opportunity to talk by telling about him- or herself; note the vocabulary used and how the student uses language. You will not have a quantitative score, but your general observations will help you determine which students need more oral language development.

To determine the student's level of listening, use a series of graded (leveled) passages. Read aloud the passages and then ask questions orally. The highest grade level where the student can answer 75 percent of the questions correctly is considered this student's listening level, which suggests that the student has the language and comprehension to deal with text at this level. By comparing this score to the student's reading level, you can estimate how much growth this student is likely to make as long as there are no reading problems. Look at Example 9.1:

Example 9.1

Gilberto: Grade 2–Instructional Reading Level–1   Listening Level–4
Santiago: Grade 2–Instructional Reading Level–1   Listening Level–1

Gilberto's listening level is three grade levels higher than his reading level: clearly, he has the oral language base that should be sufficient for his reading to improve once he is given the appropriate instruction. Santiago's reading and listening levels are the same: he needs a strong oral language program as a part of his reading instruction, so both oral language and reading will continue to grow.

To give the listening test to a group of students or the entire class, convert the questions that accompany the passages to multiple-choice items. Then start reading aloud two passages below the students' actual grade placement and continue at least two levels above the students' grade placement. Use the same scoring criteria as discussed above.

For more about phonemic awareness, phonics, and structural analysis, refer to the Handbook Resource on page 503.

Decoding

For more about assessing a student's decoding needs, see Chapter 11 and Cooper and Kiger (2008) in "For Additional Reading."

You need to gather information about how the student uses phonemic awareness, phonics (including use of structural elements), and fluency. As you listen to each student read orally, note the student's miscues and analyze them to determine the student's ability to use phonics and structural analysis. For phonemic awareness, you can use informal observations (Cooper & Kiger, 2008) or a test such as the Yopp-Singer Test of Phoneme Segmentation (Yopp, 1995). For fluency assessment, you will need to take a 1-minute fluency check (Hasbrouck & Tindal, 1992).

Comprehension

You need to know whether a student has adequate background or prior knowledge for the reading task and can access it when needed. You also need to know the student's general level of comprehension as well as his or her ability to use the comprehension strategies discussed in Chapter 4—visualizing, making connections, monitoring, inferencing, identifying important information, generating and answering questions, summarizing and synthesizing, and evaluating. The specific strategies you assess will depend on the student's level. For example, for students at beginning reading levels, assess only a few strategies, such as identifying important information, inferencing (including predicting), and summarizing. The student's general level of comprehension can best be determined from the informal reading inventory and/or by using the process of retelling. Strategy use can best be determined by having the student read text appropriate to his or her level and then model (or show) the use of each strategy.

See Chapter 11 for information about retelling.

Related Factors

Many factors can affect how students learn to read; among these are home environment, vision, hearing, general health, interest, and attitude. If a student is affected by one of these, you need to be aware of it. Begin by checking the student's cumulative record to get as much information as possible. Then do the following as needed:

- Interview the student. Try to identify the student's feelings about learning to read and anything that may be causing him or her problems.
- Meet with the student's family or guardian to discuss the student's reading. Get their perceptions of how the student is performing. Discuss the student's general health.
- If you have a school nurse, request a vision and hearing screening. If no school nurse is available, explore options that are available within the community.
- Have the student complete an interest inventory or attitude survey, or both, to learn what really interests the student. This will help you in selecting materials for instruction and help you direct the student in selecting materials to be read independently.

See Chapter 11 for information on interest inventories.

Gathering this information will help you more fully understand the student's reading. Knowing about these factors will make it easier for you to plan instruction for the student and help you know how to relate to him or her. In some instances, you may need to seek outside help.

Previous Instructional Programs

Try to find out what type of instruction the student has had in the past. What seemed to help? What has not worked? Has the student received any intervention? What kind? Was it helpful? This information will help you decide how to approach this student in the classroom as well as make decisions about what other instruction and interventions you might try.

Completing the Information-Gathering Process

Once you have completed gathering as much information as possible in each of these six areas, use the checklist in Figure 9.2 to summarize what you have learned.

You will know which students are struggling. You will know their reading levels, have a picture of their oral language development, and know how they are doing in terms of phonemic awareness, phonics, fluency, overall comprehension, and using comprehension strategies. You should have a better understanding about any extenuating circumstances that may be influencing the student's learning to read. You may have some information about what types of instruction have been tried for this student and what worked and did not work.

You should now be able to plan the core instruction for your struggling readers. You should also be able to decide what tier of intervention is needed and plan how to provide that intervention depending on what is available in your school. Figure 9.3 shows what a completed checklist might look like.

Core Instruction for Struggling Readers

All the principles and guidelines for effective literacy instruction that are presented throughout this text also apply to struggling readers. All struggling readers, including students in special education, need high-quality classroom instruction. The intervention instruction that they might receive, whether provided by the classroom teacher or by another teacher, is *in addition to* the core instruction they receive in the classroom. (How to find time for intervention is discussed later in this chapter.)

For more information on instruction for struggling readers, see Cooper, Chard, and Kiger listed in "For Additional Reading."

Planning core instruction for struggling readers requires careful thought and continuous monitoring on your part as the teacher. However, it is very rewarding for both you and your students when you see the results. As you plan core instruction for struggling readers, there are four important factors to consider: strategies and skills to teach, level of texts to use, assessing student progress, and reading in content areas.

Strategies and Skills to Teach

You need two sets of strategies and skills in order to teach struggling readers:

1. The strategies and skills you determined from your diagnosis that the student is lacking.
2. The grade-level strategies and skills that you are required to teach.

The strategies and skills that you have determined the student is lacking, either because they were not taught or the student did not learn them, are taught during intervention, which we will discuss later in this chapter.

See Chapter 10 for information on flexible grouping.

Some of the grade level skills may be taught to the whole class including the struggling readers. However, most often, you will work with the struggling readers in a small group so you can adjust your instruction to their needs. Here are some ways to do that:

- Provide more modeling of the strategy or skill being taught.
- Break the skill or strategy instruction into shorter segments or more component parts.

FIGURE 9.3   Completed Reading Evaluation Checklist

Completed Reading Evaluation Checklist

Name Lisa R.   Date 9-8

Grade   4   Teacher   C. Spaulding

Area Being Evaluated	Findings/Comments
1. Reading Levels	Independent 1 Instructional 2-3 Frustration 4
2. Oral Language	Listening Level 6 General ability to use language: seems shy but has good oral language in social situations. Has lots of knowledge to share in groups.
3. Decoding	Phonemic Awareness: Passed all tests on district PA Test Phonics: Knows all basic phonic skills; unable to apply to longer words. Fluency: 97 words per minunte. Below expected progress.
4. Comprehension	Background/Prior Knowledge: Seems to have good background knowledge; often does not share. Strategies: Makes good predictions; does not monitor, summarize, or synthesize.

(continued)

Completed Reading Evaluation Checklist *(continued)*

Area Being Evaluated	Findings/Comments
5. Related Factors	What other factors seem to be affecting this student's reading? <u>Wears glasses, but has no other problems.</u>
6. Previous Program	What type of instruction has been provided for this student before? <u>Has been in special reading class for 2 years.</u>

Instructional Plans

Core Instruction
Reading Level: 3

Materials: Use grade level basal anthology & leveled books at 3rd grade level

Skills: Decoding longer words strategy; monitoring, summarizing, & synthesizing

Intervention
Talk with parents and special reading teacher about available options.

Comments:
Needs to have self-confidence developed. Work on fluency as part of reading program. Ask parents to consider a private tutor.

Home-School Communication: The Parent-Teacher Conference

Watch the video clip, study the artifacts in the case, and reflect on the following questions:

1. Based on reading the chapter and watching the Video Case, would you say that Julia is a struggling reader? Why or why not? What evidence can you find in the Video Case to support your argument?

2. If you were Julia's classroom teacher, what steps would you take to help her become a stronger reader? Use content from this chapter to help you devise your intervention plan.

- Give students more guided practice before allowing them to do independent practice.
- Provide more reteaching of strategies and skills as well as practice.
- Allow more time for reading of text that offers students the opportunity to apply the strategies and skills.

Instruction for struggling readers requires continuous monitoring. As you teach or reteach the skills and strategies, check continuously to see that students are applying them in texts they can read.

Level of Texts to Use

You will need two levels of text to use for each student—including struggling readers: the grade-level text and a text that is appropriate for each student's reading level. When struggling readers are reading from the grade-level text, they should work in a small group under your direction (not with an aide or volunteer). In this small group, you will vary the modes of reading to accommodate individual needs. You will need to provide more structured guided reading, sometimes even guiding the reading line by line. Sometimes you may alternate between the Teacher Read-Aloud mode and having the students read a short section independently. Sometimes you will use the Shared Reading mode. By changing the mode of reading, you scaffold support, moving from heavy teacher support to student independence. It is important for students to read at least some of the text successfully, though they may not read the entire text. This is how to ensure that struggling readers can succeed with grade-level text. Furthermore, they *know* they have been successful. Then when there is a whole-class discussion of the grade-level text, your struggling readers can participate with everyone else.

For more information on modes of reading, see Chapter 2.

The second text needed for each student is one that is appropriate to the student's instructional reading level. Students will work in a group with other students who are at a similar level. *Using this text, students will apply the grade-level skills they learned using text that they can read successfully.* Usually the mode of reading is silent guided reading, where students read a section to check their predictions or answer questions that they share with you during follow-up discussion. As soon as students can successfully read one level of text with a mode that provides strong support, move to more independent reading. When students can successfully read that text independently, advance them to the next higher level of text. With all readers, and especially struggling readers who need to make more than adequate yearly progress, the goal is to advance their levels as quickly as possible. Without this accelerated progress, struggling readers will remain forever behind.

The two levels of text used should represent a variety of types of literature. These texts should not only be the appropriate levels for the students but should also be motivating and interesting. Books such as *Owls* (Markle, 2004), *The Real Lucky Charm* (Richardson, 2005), *Incredible Sharks* (Simon, 2003), and *Spiders* (Editors of *Time* & Iorio, 2005) could be used with some students.

Assessing Student Progress

For more information on oral reading checks and fluency progress checks, see Chapter 11 of this text and books listed in "For Additional Reading."

For information on AIMSweb or DIBELS go to their respective websites: http://www.aimsweb.com and http://dibels.uoregon.edu/.

Continual assessment of progress for struggling readers is critical. You need to monitor their growth in knowledge of strategies and skills and their application of these strategies and skills as they read increasingly difficult texts.

Application of skills and strategies can be determined through the use of informal reading inventories and running records. Each student's level of progress should be reevaluated at least three or four times during the school year, and more often if you deem it appropriate. You can also determine student growth in strategy and skill knowledge and application by observing performance on daily work.

Another way to determine application of skills and strategies is through periodic oral reading samples and fluency progress checks. For struggling readers, fluency progress checks should be made every two to three weeks.

You can also use a published assessment system for monitoring student progress in literacy such as AIMSweb or DIBELS (Dynamic Indicators of Basic Early Literacy Skills).

Reading in Content Areas

See Chapter 4 for information on teaching strategies.

Another major concern about working with struggling readers is how to help them read in subject areas such as science and social studies. Readers in general often have difficulty adjusting the use of their reading strategies to informational texts, and struggling readers in particular have this problem. Therefore, it is essential that you teach all students how to use their reading strategies in both narrative and expository texts.

If struggling readers are unable to read the text adequately, how are they to learn the content? First, remember that not all learning in science, social studies, or other content areas occurs through reading. Many hands-on activities can and should take place to make learning more effective. Therefore, use as many types of activities as possible to make learning more effective for struggling readers.

Making Learning More Effective for Struggling Readers

- **Focus on pictures and illustrations.** When texts such as *Snakes* (Editors of *Time* & Rudy, 2005) and *Titanic* (Sherrow, 2001) contain pictures, illustrations, or graphics that convey some of the content, guide students in examining them for information. This can be done in small groups of mixed ability levels and including ELLs.

- **Experiments.** Experiments in science allow readers to draw conclusions from the results. Help students read directions by printing them on charts or cards, broken down into simple steps.

- **Role playing.** Set up role-playing situations where students act out events. Follow each role-playing scene with discussions where conclusions are drawn and group summaries are written.

- **Media.** Use a variety of media to support learning. Videos, audiotapes, CD-ROMs, and DVDs can help struggling readers learn the content you want them to learn.

For information on guided reading, see Chapter 2.

See Chapters 3, 5, and 6 for information on prior knowledge, vocabulary, and introducing text.

To help struggling readers improve their reading of content material, use what you have learned about the guided reading mode to assist them. Make the guided reading very structured by breaking the text into small chunks of paragraphs or even sentences. Before beginning the guided reading, introduce the key vocabulary for each section. Use a picture walk or structured preview to introduce key concept words. Keep focused on two objectives: helping students learn content and helping students learn to read content material.

You may also locate reading material on the subject that may be easier for struggling readers. Such material may cover the important concepts of the topic but include less extraneous information and fewer details.

Tiers of Intervention for Struggling Readers

Intervention is additional instruction that prevents or stops reading failure. Research has clearly demonstrated that some students will never achieve complete success in reading without instructional support that is given in addition to the core instruction provided in the classroom (Snow, Burns, & Griffin, 1998). We have discussed how to adjust core instruction for struggling readers. Here we discuss when to provide intervention and give the characteristics of effective intervention programs, along with descriptions of some existing programs.

When to Provide Intervention

Intervention may be provided in a number of ways:

- **In the classroom as a small group taught by you or another teacher who comes into the room. Tier I intervention is almost always provided in the classroom as an individual activity or small group activity as a part of core instruction.** If you provide small group Tier II intervention in addition to the core instruction, the challenge you face is finding the time to do it. If another teacher comes into the room to conduct a small intervention group, the question becomes, "What does the student miss?" The best answer we can give is that the student should never miss the core instruction in reading and language arts or math. (We discuss the time issue in more detail later in this chapter.)

- **As a pullout program for Tier II or Tier III intervention.** Struggling readers leave the classroom for instruction provided by another teacher, usually a reading specialist. The students who attend these programs should never miss the core reading or language arts instruction or math. Pullout programs are easier than in-class programs for you as the classroom teacher to manage.

- **Extended-day programs for Tier I, Tier II, or Tier III intervention.** Extended-day programs take place before or after the time for the regular school day. The advantage of this type of intervention program is that students do not miss any of the regular instructional day. You have to consider whether students are too tired or too involved in other activities to attend an instructional program before or after school.

- **Summer school.** The primary issue that must be considered here is whether the period of time is long enough to make a significant difference in the student's learning.

Characteristics of Effective Intervention Programs

Considerable research has been conducted on various types of intervention programs (Hiebert & Taylor, 1994; Pikulski, 1994; Snow, Burns, & Griffin, 1998). Successful programs share the following characteristics:

- **Small groups or individual instruction.** The most successful programs are either individual or small groups of five to seven students.

- **Structured, fast-paced lessons.** A lesson plan that is very structured and fast paced is followed. The same pattern of instruction is followed every day. Usually the lessons are 30 to 40 minutes in length, and are taught daily.

- **Skills systematically taught in the context of reading.** Skills are taught prior to reading texts, where the students immediately apply them. Sometimes skills and strategies are modeled within the actual context of reading.

- **Texts leveled and sequenced in difficulty.** The texts that students read are leveled and sequenced in difficulty, moving from simple to complex. This is part of the scaffolding process, which moves from heavy teacher support to student independence.

- **Lessons taught by a certified teacher.** The intervention lessons are taught by a certified teacher, not a paraprofessional. Paraprofessionals, aides, or volunteers can be used for other activities, such as listening to a student read or for individual or small-group discussions.

Many schools develop their own intervention programs based on these characteristics. Some intervention plans have been published. A few of these follow with brief descriptions and references for further reading. For more information on any of these programs enter the complete boldfaced title into a search engine

Published Intervention Plans

Early Intervention in Reading (EIR): A small-group intervention model for first-grade children. The research from this model served as the basis for the published program *Early Success* (Taylor, Pikulski, & Cooper, 2003). *Early Success* is designed for first- and second-grade children.

Taylor, B. M., Frye, B. J., Short, R., & Shearer, B. (1992). Classroom teachers prevent reading failure among low-achieving first-grade students. *The Reading Teacher, 45,* 592–597.

Reading Recovery: A one-on-one tutorial program for first-grade children. This model was developed in New Zealand and brought to the United States through Ohio State University.

Clay, M. M. (1985). *The early detection of reading difficulties* (3rd ed.). Portsmouth, NH: Heinemann.

Pinnell, G. S., Fried, M. D., & Estice, R. M. (1990). Reading recovery: Learning how to make a difference. *The Reading Teacher, 43,* 282–295.

Facilitating Reading for Optimum Growth (FROG): A small-group intervention program for first- and second-grade children.

Allington, R. L., & Walmsley, S. A. (Eds.). (1995). *No quick fix: Rethinking literacy programs in America's elementary schools.* New York: Teachers College Press.

Project SUCCESS/Soar to Success: Originally a small-group intervention program using reciprocal teaching, scaffolding, and graphic organizers to help struggling readers in grades 3–6 accelerate their reading. SOAR TO SUCCESS is now available K–6.

Cooper, J. D., Boschken, I., McWilliams, J., & Pistochini, L. (2001). *Soar to Success: The intermediate intervention program, levels 3–6.* Boston: Houghton Mifflin.

Cooper, J. D., Boschken, I., McWilliams, J., & Pistochini, L. (2000). A study of the effectiveness of an intervention program designed to accelerate reading for struggling readers in the upper grades. In T. Shanahan & F. V. Rodriguez-Brown (Eds.), *49th Yearbook of the National Reading Conference* (pp. 477–486). Chicago: National Reading Conference.

A fourth-grade teacher conducts an intervention group.
© Michael Newman/PhotoEdit

on your computer. Although the research on the effectiveness of these programs is inconclusive at this time, they are widely used, and there is much anecdotal evidence in support of their success. It is important that you select the intervention program that meets the students' needs and continually collect data on its effectiveness.

 ## Finding Time to Provide the Appropriate Tier of Intervention for Struggling Readers

There are two major questions that every classroom teacher must address: "How do I find time to work with my struggling readers during core instruction?" and "How and when do I provide intervention?" There are no easy answers to these questions. See the "Educators Speak" feature to see how one district approaches this issue (page 396).

During Core Instruction

Sometimes you may have only one struggling reader who needs special instruction. Other times you may have two, three, or more students, each at a different level. The first thing you will need to decide is what tier of intervention each student needs. Tier I and Tier II intervention can be provided in the classroom. It is most unlikely that Tier III intervention can be delivered in the classroom because it is too individualized and requires a specialist. Finding enough time to meet the needs of every student during core instruction is never easy but can be done provided you keep several key points in mind:

See Chapter 10 for information on classroom routines.

- Carefully plan each day, keeping in mind that effective management requires a schedule where you use routines and have a system to your day.

- You don't need to meet with every group every day. For many students, it is fine to meet three times a week and give them longer periods of time to work independently. But for struggling readers, frequent meetings for shorter periods of time work best.

- Always have a sufficient number of constructive, independent activities for students to turn to when they finish their assigned work and you are working with an individual or another group.

- Establish patterns and routines of working for your students. Rehearse these, and review them periodically.

- Identify times when you can meet with an individual or small group for short periods of instruction. This might be right before or after lunch, in the morning while students are arriving, or between special classes.

With these points in mind, you will be able to find time to provide your struggling readers core instruction that has been adjusted to meet their individual needs.

Intervention

The important issues to address for readers requiring intervention are which level, or Tier of intervention, do they need and where will it be provided: in the classroom or out of the classroom. You have read about the different ways intervention may be provided.

If you have no outside assistance, you must work out a plan that will allow you to provide the intervention to a small group within the classroom. You can do this by having a special block of 30 to 40 minutes that you call something like "Special Time." During this period, you work with your intervention group; students who do not need intervention do a variety of constructive activities that provide them enrichment, give them practice in an area of special need, or allow them time to complete work or do a special project. Conducting an intervention group within the classroom is not easy, but with careful planning and establishment of routines it can work.

Educators
Speak

Helping Struggling Readers

"My school district is committed to ensuring that every student is a successful reader by the end of third grade. Each school within the district is required to submit a strategic plan that details how that goal will be met. By using a variety of assessments and careful analysis of the test results, teachers can confidently identify students who are experiencing difficulties in core subject areas. The district has allocated monies to train staff and implement several intervention programs that provide a safety net for our lowest-performing students and are meant to supplement classroom literacy practices, not replace them.

My instructional time is divided between two programs: Reading Recovery and Literacy. Reading Recovery was developed by New Zealand educator and psychologist Marie Clay. Because students who struggle with reading and writing in first grade are likely to continue to struggle in subsequent grades, intensive one-to-one instruction is needed to accelerate their progress to meet the average of their grade-level peers. Reading Recovery involves daily individual 30-minute lessons with a highly trained teacher. Each Reading Recovery lesson includes the following components:

- Rereading two or more familiar books.
- Rereading a book introduced the day before and taking a running record.
- Analysis of the running records directs the focus for the next day's lesson.
- Letter identification and/or word making and breaking.
- Composing and writing a sentence.
- Cutting up that sentence to rearrange and reread.
- New book introduction.

After a full course of lessons, most Reading Recovery students have internalized effective reading strategies and no longer need substantial assistance to continue making progress in the regular classroom. Those who still need help are considered for additional assessments and other instructional options.

The primary-aged Literacy Program is a pullout program for first- and second-grade students not reading on grade level. Students are selected based on teacher recommendations and assessment test scores. Groups are leveled to accommodate students' specific needs. Each group meets four to five times per week for an average of 30 to 45 minutes.
Daily lessons include:

- Sight word review.
- Familiar reading.
- Taking a running record once a week on each student. Information gained is used to determine a student's current reading level and address specific needs.
- Guided reading instruction focusing on developing independent reading strategies.
- Interactive and independent writing activities.
- Skills practice to strengthen students' decoding skills.

(continued)

Data collected over time show that the majority of students have benefited from their involvement in the programs and gone on to succeed in the classroom.

—Leslie Ericson-Alti, Reading Recovery and Literacy Teacher
Rio Rancho Public Schools
Rio Rancho, New Mexico

If your struggling readers participate in a pullout program, they must not be required to make up work they have missed while out of the room. In order for pullout programs to work, coordination with other classroom teachers and special teachers is necessary. You should find some of the following suggestions helpful:

- **Meet with your grade-level colleagues.** Meet and talk with other teachers about when they have core instruction. Try to arrange times so that everyone in a given grade level is having it at about the same time of day. This will make it possible for students from a given grade level who need intervention to be pulled from several classrooms at the same time.

- **Involve the principal in planning.** Talk with the principal about the importance of scheduling special classes such as art, music, and computer lab so that students who are pulled out for intervention don't miss them.

- **Plan classroom activities that intervention students can miss.** Most basic curriculum instruction should not take place while intervention students are out of the class. Instead, if you have a time when students do special projects or independent work, schedule intervention at this time.

- **Make sure that intervention students do not miss creative, fun activities.** Intervention students must be able to participate in creative or fun types of activities. Therefore, try not to have struggling readers always miss these activities.

- **Consider how and when you teach science, social studies, health, and other subjects.** Struggling readers should not miss content-area instruction. However, if their reading level is so low that they cannot participate successfully in content-area instruction, consider having them miss a subject area for a given period of time in order to provide intervention. Alternate the subject areas missed. At middle school and junior high levels, intervention can be substituted for a class or study hall.

Obviously, there is no one right answer about how to find time to teach struggling readers. Every school has different circumstances and factors to consider. We do know that it is possible to work out plans that make it possible to provide struggling readers their core instruction and the intervention they need in order to make more than adequate yearly progress.

Helping Struggling Readers: Key Points

To review the Key Points, see the ACE practice tests at the HM TeacherPrepSPACE Student Website.

- Struggling readers are students experiencing difficulty learning to read.
- Help for struggling readers has moved from a remediation concept to an intervention concept.
- Intervention is instructional time in addition to core instruction; it is designed to prevent or stop reading failure and/or accelerate learning to help struggling readers make more than adequate yearly progress.
- Intervention can be thought of in tiers. Tier I intervention is delivered in the classroom as a part of core instruction. Tier II intervention may be delivered in or out of the classroom in small groups or individually. Tier III intervention is highly individualized based on a thorough diagnosis.
- Continuous monitoring and adjustment of core instruction is needed in order to provide help for struggling readers.
- Instruction for struggling readers must be based on each student's reading levels, oral language, decoding, comprehension, related factors, and previous instructional programs.
- Intervention must be provided by a certified teacher and can be individual or small-group, pullout, extended-day, or summer school.
- Lessons are structured and fast paced, taught within the context of reading and using texts that are sequenced in difficulty.
- Numerous developed and published programs can help schools meet the needs of their struggling readers.

How Do I Teach?

Instructional Strategies and Concepts for Helping Struggling Readers

This chapter presents the processes and guidelines for helping you plan which tier of intervention your students need.

Tier I Intervention—Classroom
Tier II Intervention—Small Group
Tier III Intervention—Individual

The instructional strategies that would be appropriate are the ones which have been presented throughout this text.

Video Cases in This Chapter

- **Literacy Assessment: Administering an Informal Reading Inventory**
- **Home-School Communication: The Parent-Teacher Conference**

For Additional Reading

Allington, R. L. (2005). *What really matters for struggling readers: Research-based program*s (2nd ed.). Boston: Allyn & Bacon.

Arthaud, T. J., & Goracke, T. (2006). Implementing a structured story web and outline strategy to assist struggling readers. *The Reading Teacher, 59*(6), 581–586.

Carrier, K. A., & Tatum, A. W. (2006). Creating sentence walls to help English-language learners develop content literacy. *The Reading Teacher, 60*(3), 285–288.

Cooper, J. D., Chard, D. J., & Kiger, N. D. (2006). *The struggling reader: Interventions that work*. New York: Scholastic.

Cooper, J. D., & Kiger, N. D. (2008). *Literacy assessment: Helping teachers plan instruction* (3rd ed.). Boston: Houghton Mifflin.

Cunningham, P. (2005). "If they don't read much, how they ever gonna get good?" *The Reading Teacher, 59*(1), 88–90.

Cunningham, P. (2006). What if they can *say* the words but don't know what they mean? *The Reading Teacher, 59*(7), 708–711.

Cunningham, P. M. (2006/2007). High-poverty schools that beat the odds. *The Reading Teacher, 60*(4), 382–385.

Ganske, K., Monroe, J. K., & Strickland, D. S. (2003). Questions teachers ask about struggling readers and writers. *The Reading Teacher, 57*(2), 118–128.

Pikulski, J. J. (1994). Preventing reading failure: A review of five effective programs. *The Reading Teacher, 48*(1), 30–39.

Smith, L. A. (2006). Think-Aloud Mysteries: Using structured, sentence-by-sentence text passages to teach comprehension strategies. *The Reading Teacher, 59*(8), 764–773.

Valencia, S. W., & Buly, M. R. (2004). Behind test scores: What struggling readers really need. *The Reading Teacher, 57*(6), 520–531.

Websites

CIERA's Building Comprehension in Struggling Readers
Useful resources and guidance from the Center for the Improvement of Early Reading Achievement (CIERA); a national center for research on early reading, representing a consortium of educators.
http://www.ciera.org/library/presos/2001/birdyshaw/01LAcompr/01lacdby.pdf

Gail Lovely's Strategies for Struggling Readers
A comprehensive clearinghouse of links to resources for educators dealing with struggling readers.
http://www.gaillovely.com/struggling%20readers%20resources.htm

The International Reading Association's Focus on Struggling Readers and Writers
Resources, position statements, journal articles, and professional development links for educators who are working with struggling readers and writers.
http://www.reading.org/resources/issues/focus_struggling.html

Reading Rockets
Strategies, lessons, and activities designed to help young children learn to read and resources to those who work with struggling readers.
http://www.readingrockets.org/helping

What Does It Mean to Be a Struggling Reader? (Wisconsin LEARNS)
http://wilearns.state.wi.us/apps/default.asp?cid=21

Essential Reading Strategies for the Struggling Reader: Activities for an Accelerated Reading Program
http://www.tea.state.tx.us/reading/products/essential.pdf

Adaptations for Struggling Readers in the Content Areas
http://www.ed.gov/teachers/how/tools/initiative/summerworkshop/dickson-adaptations/edlite-slide001.html

Internet Resources to Assist Teachers with Struggling Readers
http://www.readingonline.org/electronic/elec_index.asp?HREF=/electronic/webwatch/struggling/index.html

Developing a Management System for a Comprehensive Balanced Literacy Classroom

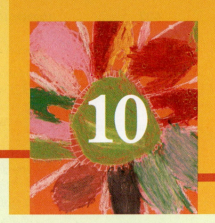

10

EDUCATORS SPEAK

Terms
YOU NEED TO KNOW

- conferences
- peer conferences
- Reading Workshop
- Writing Workshop

A short visit to Mrs. Dopheide's second-grade class on Monday morning will show how she has met the challenge of organizing and managing her balanced literacy classroom.

As we enter the room, the last student is sharing something she wrote over the weekend; she is reading aloud her note to a friend who has moved to another state. Each Monday morning, Mrs. Dopheide takes about 15 minutes for boys and girls to share reading and writing experiences they have had at home. She tells us that this activity builds good relationships with the home and helps the children see how much they use reading and writing in their lives.

"Boys and girls, let's talk for a few minutes about what we will be doing this week," Mrs. Dopheide says. She points to a chart entitled "Our Weekly Plans" (Figure 10.1) and continues, "We are all going to read a wonderful new book, Too Many Tamales *(Soto, 1993), which goes*

FIGURE 10.1   Weekly Class Plan

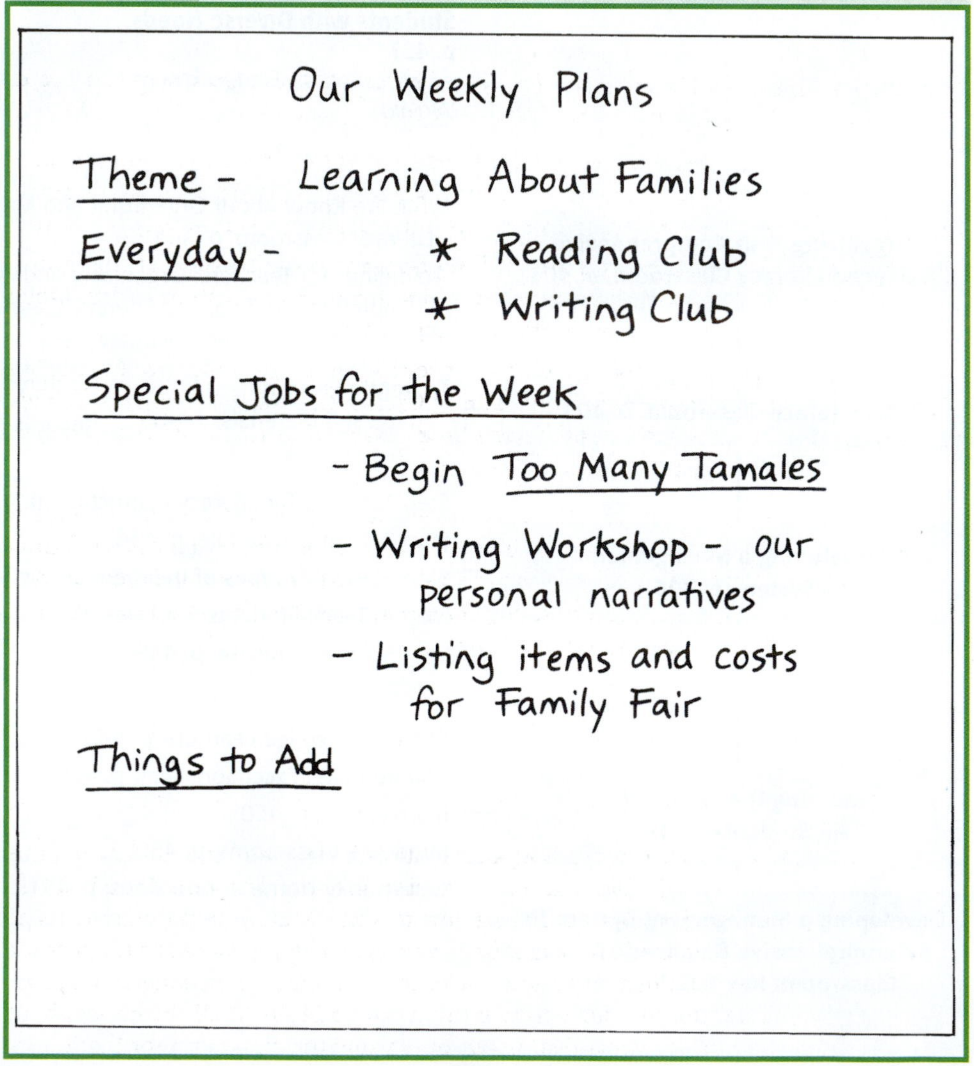

Our Weekly Plans

Theme – Learning About Families

Everyday – * Reading Club
             * Writing Club

Special Jobs for the Week

       – Begin Too Many Tamales

       – Writing Workshop – our
         personal narratives

       – Listing items and costs
         for Family Fair

Things to Add

with our Family theme. Of course, in Writing Workshop we will continue work on our personal narratives for our Families book. And—we have to start planning for our family fair. Can you think of any other things we need to do this week?"

"What about conference time? I need to talk with you about my new book," says Larry.

"Yeah, me too," adds Rosie.

"Aren't we having Reading Workshop this week?" asks Sonja.

"Yes, we are," replies Mrs. Dopheide.

"What new books do you have for us?" asks Eric.

"It's a surprise; you'll have to wait until Wednesday when we start our Reading Workshop."

"Oh, come on," groans nearly everyone.

Mrs. Dopheide adds children's suggestions to the chart and then says, "Now, time for Writing Club." She shows children the day's schedule and they begin Writing Club, the block for independent writing.

The HM TeacherPrepSPACE Student Website offers many helpful resources, such as self-quizzes, glossary flashcards, lesson plan templates, and more.

From this brief visit to Mrs. Dopheide's class, you can see that she organizes and manages a comprehensive literacy classroom in several ways:

■ By inviting volunteers to share their reading and writing experiences from the weekend, she demonstrates the importance of literacy at home and brings students' homes into the classroom community of learners.

■ Children are an integral part of the process of planning. By sharing her plans with the class and asking for their suggestions, Mrs. Dopheide makes everyone feel part of the learning process.

■ Mrs. Dopheide uses several organizational frameworks and concepts to organize her class: Reading Club (independent reading), Writing Club (independent writing), **Writing Workshop, Reading Workshop,** books for the whole class, **conferences,** and others.

A comprehensive balanced literacy classroom requires a variety of organizational structures. In this chapter you will learn about frameworks, organizational techniques, and procedures that will help you organize and manage a comprehensive balanced literacy classroom. All of these are based on our knowledge of *how children and young adults develop literacy.*

Organizing Your Comprehensive Balanced Literacy Classroom

Recall the reading and writing instruction you had when you were in elementary school. Did you have reading groups? Did you spend much time writing, or did anyone even teach you how to write? Were you in the same reading group all the time? Was English or language arts instruction generally taught from an English textbook, with units on various parts of speech or writing conventions such as punctuation, with little time for actual writing? In addition to all we know about literacy learning, we know a great deal about organizing the classroom for literacy instruction.

What We Know About Organizing and Managing the Literacy Classroom

For years, most elementary teachers divided their classes into three reading groups (Barr & Dreeben, 1991). Sometimes classes were tracked; that is, all students at one ability level were assigned to one teacher for all or part of the day. Both of these patterns of instruction were generally referred to as *ability grouping* or *tracking* (Cunningham & Allington, 2007). This concept of organizing for instruction came under considerable criticism (Allington, 1983; Dawson, 1987; Harp, 1989; Hiebert, 1983; Slavin, 1986; Sorensen & Hallinan, 1986), as research showed that ability groupings do not lead to success or prevent failure for students (Allington & Walmsley, 1995). Therefore, other types of organization are needed.

For descriptions of intervention programs, see Chapter 9.

For many years, teachers thought that students who were having difficulty learning, including ELLs, might be unable to learn to read and write at all. Different programs were tried, but none of them worked effectively (Allington & Walmsley, 1995; Cunningham & Allington, 2007). Now, effective programs such as Reading Recovery (Clay, 1985; DeFord, Lyons, & Pinnell, 1991) and small-group intervention plans (Hiebert & Taylor, 1994) have demonstrated that nearly *all* children can learn to read and write.

A related issue is the pace of instruction. As we have said, students who are having difficulty learning need instruction that is paced *faster* to help them catch up. In fact, we believe that *all* students need instruction that is appropriately fast paced. When instruction is paced too slowly, many students lose interest and fail to learn.

While students who are having difficulty learning often need extra support from intervention models, the key to having successful literacy programs for *all* students is to create classroom instruction that is oriented toward success for all students.

We need to know how to organize classrooms that prevent failure and promote success. To accomplish this, we need to organize classrooms based on what we know about how children and young adults learn.

Guidelines for Teachers: Organizing and Managing a Comprehensive Balanced Literacy Classroom

Guidelines for these literacy blocks were provided in Chapter 2.

Regardless of the grade level you teach, you will find it easier to organize and manage a literacy-centered classroom that promotes success if you consider the following eleven guidelines. These guidelines are based on the blocks for core instruction that are suggested in the model in Chapter 2. Recall that the six blocks for core instruction are:

- Daily Independent Reading
- Daily Independent Writing
- Reading: Learning Skills and Strategies
- Reading: Application of Skills and Strategies
- Writing: Learning to Write
- Writing: Developmentally Appropriate Writing

1. *Provide an exciting classroom environment that supports many literacy activities.*

Chapter 11 gives suggestions for determining students' interests and strengths.

See Chapter 11 for a discussion of the use of portfolios.

2. *Provide daily times for independent reading and writing.*
3. *Base your organization on students' interests and literacy strengths.*
4. *Make students part of the decision-making process.* Let students set goals for themselves and help to set goals for the class. Students should be given choices about what they read, how they read, and how they respond and share. They should also be given choices about what they write, how they write, and how they publish and share. Choices encourage students to take ownership of their own learning. Teachers may guide students to make thoughtful choices.
5. *Provide blocks of time for direct or explicit instruction as needed.* A well-designed Comprehensive Balanced Literacy Program includes both direct and indirect instruction. Use small groups for directly teaching skills and strategies.
6. *Provide blocks of time when all students can be successful at reading and writing.* Everyone should have the opportunity to experience or read the same text and do the same type of writing. This builds self-esteem and lets all students know they can do some of the same tasks as others.
7. *Provide blocks of times when all students have the opportunity to receive instruction with books at their instructional reading levels.*
8. *Provide blocks of time when students receive instructional support as they write on products and topics of their own choosing.*
9. *Keep in contact with students' homes.* Have activities that encourage home-school cooperation. These might include home read-aloud programs and writing.
10. *Keep the pace of instruction appropriately fast for all students.* Instruction needs to be delivered at a pace that holds students' attention. Remember, the number of activities doesn't affect how well students read and write; the amount of actual reading and writing they do is what matters.
11. *Be flexible.* Try different organizational techniques and procedures. Don't latch on to one procedure and use it all the time, or you will risk losing sight of students' needs. Remember that a variety of patterns will be needed to accommodate students' needs.

Nothing can make classroom organization and management foolproof. However, keeping these eleven guidelines in mind can help you make good decisions and develop a success-oriented classroom that runs smoothly.

The Literacy Classroom

Effective organization and management are dependent on careful, ongoing planning (Morrow, 2003). As you begin to plan your classroom, consider these three factors: a literate environment (space and materials), conferences, and recordkeeping.

A Literate Environment: Space and Materials

A literate classroom environment is rich in language and print. Such an environment stimulates learning and promotes the concept of the class as a community of people who are learning together. It is basic to every classroom at every grade level and provides part of the motivation for all learners to want to construct meaning. You need to think about how to make the best use of the available space. Limited space need not be a deterrent to creating a literate environment.

The literate environment should include various areas or centers, each with a specific focus. The contents, organization, and arrangement of these areas will vary from classroom to classroom and from grade level to grade level. *These special areas must be readily accessible to the children.*

Classroom Areas or Centers

- a library area,
- a writing and publishing area,
- a listening, speaking, and viewing area,
- a sharing area,
- a creative arts area,
- a group meeting area, and
- a display area

The main goal is the same for every teacher: to make sure the room arrangement promotes and supports the community of literacy learners and contributes to an exciting, literacy-centered atmosphere. Use the following steps to organize your classroom space:

1. Take inventory of what is available: for example, desks, tables, bulletin boards, bookcases, storage areas, electrical outlets, a water source, chalkboards, computers, tape, DVD or video players, an overhead screen. Think about which are fixed in place and which are movable.

2. Think about what you want: centers or areas, small- and large-group instructional areas, bulletin boards students can use, storage areas for student work, a place for teacher materials, and space to store extra materials. Take time to look around, and consider how you want to arrange your room.

3. Sketch the layout and begin making plans. Here are some tips to keep in mind:

   - Pushing desks together promotes conversation and interaction, an important goal of a literacy-centered classroom.
   - Some students cannot work with others around, so they need space where they can work alone.
   - Use movable bookshelves to section off private areas.
   - Art and science areas need access to water.
   - The teacher's desk or work table is often best placed off to the side, where the teacher can also hold conferences with students.
   - Areas where students are likely to be talking together should be away from an instructional area where you will be meeting with small groups.
   - Centers or areas requiring electrical equipment or computers need to be placed near outlets.

A sixth-grade classroom has special work areas even with limited space.
© Felicia Martinez/Photo Edit

4. Once you have a plan in mind, begin to arrange the room. If you have time before students arrive at the beginning of the school year, live with the arrangement as you do other things.

5. After students arrive, try out the arrangement for several days. If certain areas aren't working, change them.

Library Area

The major purpose of the library area is to promote and support independent reading. It should include many books of varying levels and interests, books on tapes, books on CD-ROMs, magazines, newspapers, brochures, and posters, all organized and displayed attractively. To promote the concept of the children as both readers and writers, this area should also include books that have been "published" by the students themselves.

Include books by past and current award winners appropriate to your grade. For example, in a fifth or sixth grade, you might include *So You Want to Be President?* by Judith St. George (2000), illustrated by David Small, which won the Caldecott Medal for 2001; and *A Year Down Yonder* by Richard Peck (2000), which won the 2001 Newbery Medal; or *Copper Sun* by Sharon Draper (2006), which won the Coretta Scott King Award for 2007; or *Esperanza Rising* by Pam Munoz Ryan (2002), which won the Belpre Award. Change or add to the collection of books in the library area frequently. Books may be borrowed from the school library, local library, or bookmobile; brought in by the children; or donated by parents or community groups.

Provide appropriate seating such as a rocker, beanbag chairs, a bathtub with pillows, or tables and chairs. There should also be a bulletin board where you might display book jackets or children might display an advertisement for their favorite book. For example, a child who has just finished reading *El Chino* (Say, 1990), a book about the first Chinese bullfighter, might want to make a poster to advertise and "sell" the book to other children.

Personnel in your central library can help. Work with a librarian, media specialist, or other type of support person as you create your classroom library area. The school library is an extension of the classroom library, since both it and the librarian are valuable resources. The librarian can help you select books and plan units, and the school library should become a place where students can come and go freely to select books and other resources.

For emergent, or beginning, readers, have lots of little, easy-to-read books. Many teachers organize these books in baskets, boxes, or barrels that are color-coded for difficulty. For example, the easiest "Basket of Books" might be yellow, with each book having a yellow dot; red might be average; and green might be more challenging. This coding helps students select books, but students can move from one color to the next color when they feel ready. The books in the baskets can be trade books or may come from the many collections of books for emergent readers published by such companies as Houghton Mifflin, Harcourt Achieve/Rigby, and McGraw Hill/Wright Group.

The "thumbs-up" test is described on page 27 in Chapter 2.

As readers become more mature, teach them how to select books for themselves. One way is the *thumbs-up test*. Of course, if a student really wants to read a book with five or more unfamiliar words on a page, encourage and then support the effort. Strong interest goes a long way in overcoming word recognition difficulty.

Have a simple checkout system: a card with the book title and a place for students to write their names will work. Let students take turns being the librarian to help develop responsibility and provide an opportunity for students to learn more about "real-world" literacy.

If you have older ELLs, provide books for them. Some picture books with limited text may be appropriate so long as the pictures are not too primary. Other books might include those with side-by-side text in English and another language.

Instructional Materials

You will need class sets of books, sets of decodable texts for the beginning literacy program, multiple copies of single titles, and a variety of single titles. If you are using a published reading or language arts program, an anthology may be used as your class set of books, but this is not enough. You also need sets of trade books covering a wide range of interests and difficulty levels.

Class sets or multiple copies of trade books may be stored in a central location within the school to facilitate wider use. Rolling carts make it easier to move sets of books in and out of classrooms. Teachers at each grade level then agree that certain pieces of literature are core at that grade level. For example, fourth-grade teachers might agree that *Big Boy* (Mollel, 1995) would be a core piece for their grade. Choosing core books means students won't be required to read a book that they've already read in a prior year.

Writing and Publishing Area

Every classroom needs a writing and publishing area or center, where you promote writing and display some of the children's writing. Furnish it with:

- Tables and chairs
- Paper (unlined for beginners)
- Pencils, pens, markers, crayons
- Supplies for publishing books: scissors, tape and glue, construction paper and cardboard, wallpaper sample books, yarn, brads, and staplers
- A computer (or typewriter)
- A place to display writing
- A storage area for writing folders, computer disks, or other storage devices

For a discussion of the use of word processing in writing and other topics about educational technology, see Grabe (2006) in the "For Additional Reading" section.

You can learn about new software from magazines such as *Learning and Leading with Technology* (formerly *The Computing Teacher,* International Society for Technology in Education, http://www.iste.org/).

The writing center can be the place where students write, meet for conferences with peers or the teacher, or do the final work on a piece of writing they wish to publish. Having this area or center in your classroom gives significance to writing.

In their writing folders students can keep such items as a list of possible topics for writing (see Figure 10.2 for a sample form), pieces of writing in progress, and a

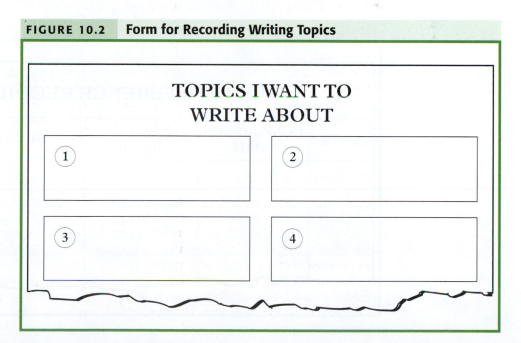

FIGURE 10.2   Form for Recording Writing Topics

TOPICS I WANT TO
WRITE ABOUT

1

2

3

4

FIGURE 10.3   **Form for Recording Completed Writing Projects**

WRITING RECORD

Name _____

P=Published

Date Started	Type of Writing	Title of Piece	Date Completed or Dropped

list of pieces of completed writing (see Figure 10.3 for a sample form). Students may also choose to keep a list of words from their own writing that cause them spelling problems; many teachers encourage students to do this.

Some teachers encourage students to keep a record of conferences with classmates, or peers. This helps students prepare for teacher conferences. (See Figure 10.4 for a sample form.) The writing folder is basically the student's working folder. The student brings it to conferences with the teacher, but it is primarily for the student's use.

FIGURE 10.4   **Peer Conference Record**

PEER CONFERENCE RECORD

DATE	CONFERENCE WITH	WRITING PIECE	SUGGESTIONS

FIGURE 10.5 **Goal Sheet from a Sixth Grader's Writing Folder**

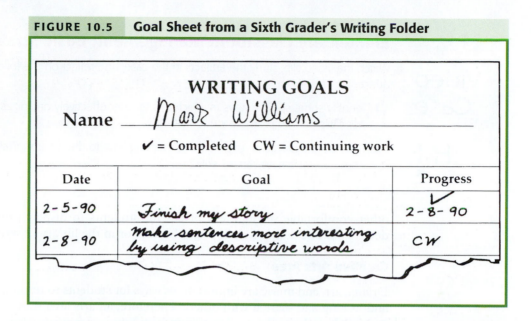

WRITING GOALS

Name *Mark Williams*

✔ = Completed   CW = Continuing work

Date	Goal	Progress
2-5-90	*Finish my story*	✔ 2-8-90
2-8-90	*Make sentences more interesting by using descriptive words*	CW

In their writing folder, students may also keep a list of goals established with the teacher during a conference. These may range from general goals such as, "Complete my story," or, "Try a different ending" to goals that are very specific, such as, "Make more use of descriptive words," or, "Pay attention to capital letters and periods." After goals are met, the student and the teacher discuss the progress made and establish new goals. Figure 10.5 shows a goal sheet from a sixth grader's writing folder.

Keep writing folders simple at first. Many students have difficulty keeping records and need help in learning their importance (Graves, 1991). Don't have students put in so many pieces that the folders lose their real purpose: as *a place to keep writing in progress.*

Listening, Speaking, and Viewing Area

This area should contain a listening post with headphones, a tape recorder, and/or a CD player. There should be tapes or CDs of books and stories for listening, as well as blanks for students to record their own stories. For viewing, the area may have filmstrip viewers, video players and recorders, and computers that allow students to practice literacy skills with electronic books and other instructional technology. See the Educators Speak feature on page 427 for an illustration of how one teacher enhanced a sixth-grade literacy block.

Sharing Area

See Chapter 8 for a description of the author's chair.

An important part of learning to construct meaning is sharing what you have read or written and approximating authentic reading and writing experiences; children need a special place for this activity. This area should include tables and chairs or

Video Case

Elementary Classroom Management: Basic Strategies

Watch the video clip, study the artifacts in the case, and reflect on the following questions:

1. Identify some specific ways in which this teacher effectively organizes and sets up her classroom to promote student literacy.

2. How does this teacher use morning meeting time to discuss important classroom issues and promote literacy skills?

other comfortable seating, and places for students to display products they have developed. The author's chair might be here or in the library or writing area.

Creative Arts Area

Drama, art, and music are important as ways for students to respond to their reading and writing and share it with others. Therefore, an arts area should include puppets and items students can use for costumes and props for giving plays, retelling stories, or doing readers theater.

A portion of this area might have materials for painting, drawing, paper sculpture, or other art activities. If space is available, develop a separate area for just for art. Also make available simple musical instruments, such as recorders, autoharps, or xylophones. Using music with pieces of literature such as *Ben's Trumpet* (Isadora, 1979) or *Song and Dance Man* (Ackerman, 1988) is appropriate at many grade levels (Lamme, 1990). You don't have to be musically inclined to help students engage in these activities.

Group Meeting Area

You need a place to meet with small groups for discussion and instruction. This area might contain a whiteboard, easel and chart paper, an overhead projector, and other materials you will need for teaching, such as books and charts.

Display Area

To help to motivate students and expand their backgrounds, display items related to topics of study such as art pieces, photographs, and posters. The display area should be changed frequently and include material brought in by students. For example, a class that is reading or listening to *Where the Red Fern Grows* (Rawls, 1961) might create a display of photographs of pets that have meant a great deal to them, just as Old Dan and Little Ann were important to Billy.

A literate environment is both motivating and a vital part of developing oral language, expanding prior knowledge, and creating an atmosphere that promotes opportunities for authentic reading and writing experiences that children share with all members of the classroom community. Figure 10.6 presents a checklist for evaluating the literate environment in your classroom.

FIGURE 10.6   **A Checklist for Evaluating the Classroom Literate Environment**

	Yes	No	Needs Work
1. Do I have the following areas or combinations of areas in my classroom?			
• Library area			
• Writing and publishing area			
• Listening, speaking, and viewing area			
• Sharing area			
• Creative arts area			
• Group meeting area			
• Display area			
2. Do I change or improve areas within reasonable time frames?			
3. Do students utilize certain areas more than others?			

Which ones? _____

_____

4. Areas that I need to add:

_____

_____

5. Areas that I need to improve or change:

_____

_____

Conferences

Conferences may take place between two students or between the teacher and student(s). During a reading conference, the focus is on reading material, and during a writing conference, the focus is on a piece of student writing. Conferences play an important role in all aspects of literacy learning (Calkins, 1994; Graves, 1983, 1991). Graves (1991) maintains that "the conference—the listening stance—is the heart of good teaching" (p. 89).

Conferences may be formal, planned events or informal ones that occur at odd times during the day—in the hallway, in the lunchroom, on the playground, or during any part of the daily classroom routine. Some educators refer to informal conferences as *miniconferences* or *on-the-spot conferences*. These conferences are simply times when you stop to chat and listen carefully to students. Good teachers do this all the time.

During informal miniconferences, you might ask children such questions as, "What are you reading?" "How do you like this book?" or, "What writing piece are you working on now?" For example, Mrs. Laird, a fourth-grade teacher, stopped by the desk of one student:

Mrs. Laird: *What have you been reading lately?*
    Mark: *I'm still reading the same book I got last week.*
Mrs. Laird: *How do you like it?*
    Mark: *I don't.*
Mrs. Laird: *Why don't you stop reading this book and select another one?*
    Mark: *I don't know.*
Mrs. Laird: *Don't you like dinosaurs?*
    Mark: *Yes!*
Mrs. Laird: *I saw a great dinosaur book in the reading center this morning. You'll love it! It's called* Tyrannosaurus Was a Beast *(Prelutsky, 1988). Try that one.*

In this brief discussion, Mrs. Laird learned that Mark was bogged down with a book he didn't like and directed him to a book in an area of his interest. Although informal conferences may last only a minute or two, they yield valuable information and enable the teacher to provide on-the-spot support.

After this brief encounter, Mrs. Laird wrote a note about this miniconference on the student's page in her notebook. (Some teachers keep notes on a computer.) Sometimes she relies on memory and makes notes later. It is not always necessary to make notes about a miniconference; this particular one revealed information that the teacher wanted to record. Some teachers carry sticky pads to write on and date; later they stick them on the students' pages in their notebook.

Purposes of Formal Teacher-Student Conferences

Formal literacy conferences may have several purposes:

1. *Sharing and discussing a book.* The teacher and the student talk about a book the student is reading or has completed, and the student may read aloud favorite parts. The teacher might share thoughts or feelings about the book, or make suggestions for other books for the student to read. If the students are keeping journals, responses might be shared and discussed, or questions about the book or words of concern to the student might be reviewed.

2. *For the teacher and student to discuss some aspect of the student's writing* and for the teacher to *ask probing or guiding questions* that will help the student formulate ideas. This is a time for modeling and coaching to help students develop their writing.

3. *Provide a minilesson on a particular strategy or skill* that seems to be causing the student difficulty. During this conference, the teacher uses the minilesson concept and models the particular strategy or skill needed.

4. *Assess student progress.* As students share their responses to a piece of literature, the teacher can tell how well they comprehend or construct meaning. Oral reading gives clues to the students' decoding abilities, and written responses in journals provide evidence about spelling, grammar and usage, and comprehension.

One conference might have several purposes. For example, students might be sharing a book at the same time the teacher is assessing progress. In fact, a single conference should serve as many purposes as possible. The following suggestions should be helpful in planning conferences:

- **When you begin to use conferences, explain their purpose and procedures to students.** Role-play several conferences to establish routines and guidelines for behavior.

- **Keep conferences short and focused.** If students don't need a conference, don't have one. Their time is better spent reading or writing.

- **Maintain a positive, interactive environment.** Use probing questions and statements that encourage students to think about and talk about their writing.

- **From time to time, have group conferences during which you talk with several students about their writing.** This is an especially useful procedure if students are doing similar types of writing or appear to have similar needs for support.

- **In writing conferences with ELLs (as with all other writers), it is important to start by discussing the content of the piece.** Don't focus on the mechanics first, even though the writing may show many second-language errors. When you do talk about the mechanical aspects of writing, limit the focus to only one or two types of errors so as not to overwhelm ELLs.

- **Keep a simple record sheet for each student.** Figure 10.7 shows a sheet you can use for writing. This will tell you what students are doing and what their needs are.

FIGURE 10.7 **Record Sheet for Keeping Track of Students' Writing**

Name _____ Grade _____

Date	Writing Piece	Suggestions	Minilesson Needs	Goals/Comments

FIGURE 10.8   **Conference Sign-up Chart**

READING CONFERENCES

	Student Requested	Teacher Requested
Monday	Leo Susan Lisa Joan Jeff	
Wednesday	Terri Frank Joey Sid	Tim Mike
Friday		Sara Mary Anne Bill

Scheduling Conferences

Literacy conferences seldom last more than 5 to 10 minutes. It is best to keep conferences as short as possible and focused on your purpose.

Students should sign up for a conference on a sign-up sheet or a section of the chalkboard at least once a week. (Sometimes you will initiate a request to see a student.) Figure 10.8 shows a conference sign-up chart that a second-grade teacher uses. No one requested a conference on Friday, so the teacher had time to meet with students she had not seen recently. A good rule of thumb is to have a conference with each student at least once a week for first, second, and third graders and once every other week for fourth grade and above. However, students' needs should be the major determining factor in establishing the frequency of conferences.

Each teacher must work out the best time during the daily schedule to hold conferences. Some prefer to schedule a few each day, and others schedule on designated days, such as Monday, Wednesday, and Friday.

FIGURE 10.9   **Chart Showing Students What to Do While the Teacher Is in Conference**

THINGS TO DO DURING
CONFERENCES

- Read your book or selection
- Write in your journal
- Work on your writing project
- Meet with a Literature Circle
- OTHER— You decide on something
          worthwhile to do
- Work in the Listening Center
- Prepare for your conference

Preparing for Conferences

Both you and the students must be prepared and students must understand how and why conferences take place. The best way to do this is to role-play and model a conference period so that students see how they work.

When teachers begin to use conferences, they are often concerned about what the rest of the class does while one or two children are in conference. A chart, such as the one shown in Figure 10.9, lists options that other students have during the conference period. Once students become comfortable with conference times, a chart is usually not needed.

Students have to prepare for a conference. Figure 10.10 shows a chart that many teachers find helpful. After a week or so of conferencing, *you and the class* should evaluate how the conferences are going and make adjustments as needed.

Finally, you too must prepare for the conferences. A loose-leaf notebook with a section for each student is helpful. On the first page, write the student's name, age, and grade, and also list the student's interests and any pertinent information about his or her reading and writing strengths. One of these pages might look like Figure 10.11. Following the opening page, you will need blank pages on which to

FIGURE 10.10 **Chart for Helping Students Prepare for a Conference**

BEFORE YOUR READING CONFERENCE

(1) Have your book.

(2) Be sure your journal is up to date.

(3) Make a list of things you want to discuss. Put them in your journal.

record observations and comments from the conference, and goals you and the student agree should be accomplished before the next conference. Keep the page simple, such as that shown in Figure 10.12.

See Table 7.1 in Chapter 7 for lists of open-ended questions.

Have some ideas about questions or statements you might use to prompt students to discuss the book they are currently reading. In addition, individual conferences should explore four areas with students: personal involvement of the child with the book, ability to read and understand, sheer mechanical reading ability, and oral reading. Hundreds of questions can be asked in each of these areas. Here are some samples.

1. Area of personal involvement

Teacher: *Why did you choose this story? Do you know anyone else in this class who would like it also?*
Why do you think you are more interested in this kind of story than others in this class are?
Would you like to be this character? Why?

FIGURE 10.11 Partial Teacher's Notebook Page for Each Student

Name *Lisa Smith*   Age *8* Grade *3*

Interests: *horses, roller skating, making clay figures*

Reading Strengths	Writing Strengths
– *Rereads when things aren't clear* – *Always previews her book*	– *Loves to write* – *Uses descriptive words*

OTHER OBSERVATIONS

2. Area of critical reading or general comprehension

Teacher: *What kind of a story is this? Real?*

or

> *Could this story have happened? Why? Or why not?*
> *Tell me the story rapidly.*
> *If this character did so and so, would you think he would get in trouble?*
> *At the time this story was supposed to have happened, what was going on in our country that was very important?*

3. Area of mechanical skills

Teacher: *What words did you have trouble with?*

or

> *Here are two words that look very much alike. Tell me how you know the difference.*

or

> *Let me point to several words in your story. Tell me what they are and what they mean.*

FIGURE 10.12 Sample Conference Page from Notebook

Date	Comments	Goals for Next Conference
9/7	Terri had finished reading _Jam_. She loved the story and said her uncle was like Mr. Castle. She thought it was OK for dads to stay home. No problems with vocabulary or comprehension. Excellent oral reading. Needs to select more challenging book.	1. Select a more challenging book. 2. Use different responses in journal other than drawing.

4. Area of oral reading

> Teacher: _Which part of the book have you chosen to read aloud to me?_
> _Make your voice go up and down._
> _Make your voice spooky, or scary, or sad, or mean, or whatever the story calls for._ (Veatch, 1978, p. 69)

The questions you ask during a writing conference should help students reflect on their writing (think about it critically), expand their writing, and select ways to improve their writing.

Following are some examples:

Reflecting About Their Writing

- What is the most interesting part of your piece and why?
- How did you want your reader to feel as they read?
- Here's what I think you were saying. . . . Did I get the right idea?

Expanding Their Thinking to Encourage Revision

- You talked about some things that aren't in your writing. Would you like to include them?
- I'd like to know a little more about . . . ? Can you work it in?
- Could you add something to make the reader feel more . . . ?

Improving Their Writing

See Chapter 11 for ideas on assessment that can easily be incorporated into conference sessions.

- Which parts could be combined to make your writing more organized?
- Did you and your partner talk about titles? Which did you decide on? Why?
- The first sentence needs to grab the reader. Do you want to revise yours?
- The ending sticks with the reader. Does your ending have the most important idea or feeling?
- Compare your ending to the beginning. Did you just repeat the same thing? Could you say it better?
- Look at your sentence beginnings. Do they vary?
- This sentence is complicated. Could you break it into two sentences?
- Here are several short sentences in a row. Could they be combined? How?
- Tell me which sentences you think are strongest. Why?
- Find some places where you could change particular words to show instead of tell.

Conducting Conferences

During literacy conferences, you will talk with students about their independent reading and writing. Books you have assigned for the whole class to read are usually dealt with through literature groups or whole-class discussions.

The conference time should be a relaxed, pleasant experience. You can let the conference evolve naturally, but it is a good idea to have a plan. You also need a plan for writing conferences. If the student asked for the conference, begin by having the student tell what he or she wants to discuss and proceed from there. See the box titled "Sample Plans for Reading and Writing Conferences" on page 422 for some possible sequences for reading and writing conferences.

Every conference will be different, but having a plan is helpful in the beginning. As you and your students have more conferences, you will devise a plan that works best for you.

You can have a reading conference even if you have not read the book yourself. Just tell students if you don't know the book they are reading; they will enjoy sharing something new with you. You can talk about any book by using very general questions.

Sometimes it is helpful to have a conference with two students at the same time. This works well when you have assigned a book for the entire class or when two students have read the same book or books that are closely related in topic, genre, or theme. With two students, you can encourage higher-level thinking by comparing and contrasting books.

Sample Plans for Reading and Writing Conferences

Reading Conference	Writing Conference
1. What would you like to focus on?	**1.** *Opening:* The student reads his or her draft. You listen or read along as the student reads.
2. Tell me about your book.	**2.** *Discussion:* Talk about the content and sequence of ideas, unless the student has some other specific purpose. Ask questions that prompt the student to talk about the piece of writing.
3. What have you written in your response journal that you would like to share?	**3.** *Closing:* Help the student focus attention on one thing to do to improve the writing. This will help the student realize quick success (Calkins, 1994).
4. Read aloud the part that you liked best.	
5. Let's talk about what you think your goals should be for next time.	

General Questions for Talking About Narrative and Expository Texts

Narrative Texts	Expository Texts
■ Tell me about your book.	■ What is the topic of your book?
■ Who are the characters?	■ What are the big ideas the author tells you?
■ Where does it take place?	■ Find something to read aloud that supports one of the author's big ideas.
■ What happened?	
■ How did the story end?	

Peer Conferences

Peer conferences provide a way for students to have a conversation with someone about their writing or reading (Dahl, 1988). Peer conferences are often held in preparation for a teacher conference.

FIGURE 10.13 Peer Conference Guidelines from a Third-Grade Class

Our Peer Conference Guidelines

- *Remember that your friend's writing is his/her own work. Don't try to rewrite it.*
- *Let the writer read the piece of writing aloud.*
- *Talk about the things you like.*
- *Ask questions about things you don't understand.*
- *Make one or two suggestions for improving the writing.*
- *If you are proofreading, also read it silently.*

Peer conferences work well with ELLs when teachers can pair students who have the same first language. The students confer in their first language and then prepare for their teacher conference, which will be in English.

Be sure students know what is expected of them and what they should do during the peer conference. Teacher conferences may serve as models for peer conferences. It is also a good idea to role-play peer conferences and talk with students about how to improve them. An effective way to get started is to develop with the class a set of guidelines to follow. Figure 10.13 shows guidelines for peer writing conferences developed by a third-grade class. Similar guidelines can be developed for reading. Adjust the guidelines for your grade level.

Evaluating Conferences

As you work with conferences, you and your students should take time to evaluate them, using questions like these:

1. How are our conferences working?
2. What is especially good about our conferences?
3. What problems do we have?
4. What can we do to improve our conferences?

If your students are new to conferences, you will probably need to evaluate them several times early in the year until they are running smoothly.

You must also evaluate your own skill in conducting conferences. The more experience you have, the better you will be at this activity. Here is a list of questions to ask yourself:

1. How are my conferences going overall?
2. Are they too long or too brief?
3. Am I asking questions that prompt children to think?
4. Is the conference truly a discussion, or am I testing?
5. Am I getting helpful information about my students' abilities to use reading and writing?
6. Are the other students in the class engaged in productive activities while I am conferencing?

A good way to evaluate yourself is to tape-record one or two conferences. As you listen to the tapes, you will see ways to improve and think of other questions to ask yourself.

Records

Keeping your classroom running smoothly depends on keeping careful records of what is happening and what individual students are doing in a way that suits your circumstances. Following are some options to consider. If you decide to keep records on your computer, you will want to include the same kinds of information.

Teacher Notebook or Portfolio

The teacher notebook or portfolio is an excellent way to organize a lot of information in one place. Use a large three-ring binder with dividers. Here are some possible sections:

- *Theme plans:* This section contains a simple outline plan for the theme you are covering. It may also include information about completed and future themes.
- *Schedules and lesson plans:* Daily or weekly schedules and lesson plans can be kept here. Some teachers like to keep lesson plans separate from this notebook, whereas others like to include as much information as possible in one place.
- *Book lists:* Keep lists here of books you want for a particular theme, want to order through the librarian, or want to purchase with available funds. The title, author, publisher, and ISBN number are all you need to obtain the book when the time comes. Lists can also be located in professional journals and on various websites.
- *Student information:* This section contains a separate tab for each student and includes copies of forms such as those shown in Figures 10.14 and 10.15 to record pertinent observations and conference information. A page such as the one in Figure 10.16 is for parent conferences.

Other Ways to Keep Records

Not all teachers like the teacher notebook or portfolio concept, especially for student records. Some teachers keep separate folders or notebooks for each student or

FIGURE 10.14 Student Data Sheet for Teacher Notebook

Name ________________________________ Birthdate ______________ Age ______

Address ________________________________ Telephone ________________

Parent(s)/Guardian ________________________________

Reading Data

Writing Data

Listening, Speaking, and Viewing Data

FIGURE 10.15 Sheet for Recording Observations and Student Conference Results

Name ________________________________ **Grade** ______________

Date	Observation	Date	Observation

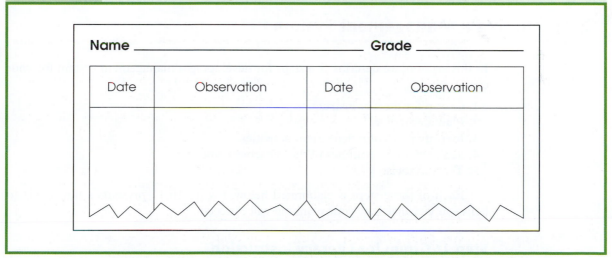

use 5 × 8 notecards. The same types of information described above would be kept here.

Portfolios are discussed in Chapter 11.

Some teachers rely on the student portfolio concept. You may keep records on a computer, devising your own method of recording information to build a cumulative record of each student's literacy growth as well as plans, schedules, and book lists.

FIGURE 10.16 **Sheet for Recording Observations and Parent Conference Results**

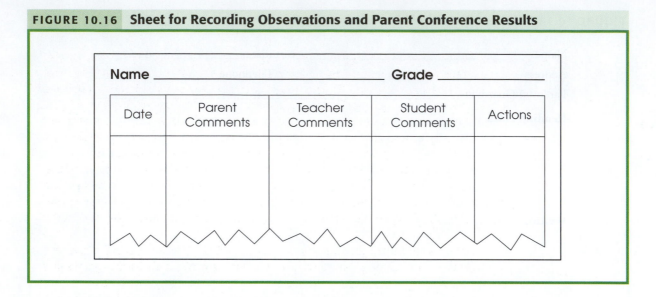

The important point is that there is more than one way to keep records. You should choose the method that best helps you monitor and adjust your classroom organization.

Developing a Management System

In this section, we describe five steps for developing a management system for your classroom:

1. Group for literacy instruction,
2. Plan a schedule,
3. Identify types of independent activities,
4. Teach students routines of the classroom, and
5. Try and revise

Each of these steps is elaborated below. Figure 10.17 presents a flow chart to help you visualize how your planning will proceed.

Step 1: Group for Literacy Instruction

During much of the day, students will be grouped in various ways for various purposes. First, we discuss the concept of flexible grouping and give examples of such groups. Then we present five frameworks for grouping for literacy instruction: three for reading (core books/anthologies, leveled books, and Reading Workshop) and two for writing (teacher-modeled writing and Writing Workshop).

Sixth-Grade Literacy Block Enhanced with Computers

"Meeting the individual needs of thirty-four sixth-grade students can be a daunting task. One thing that helps me is a 45-minute block of time each day when every student is reading at his or her level. During this time I work in a small group with my most critical students. Technology is extremely beneficial during this time. My students do extensive research projects that are often related to our social studies curriculum such as an ancient civilization that we are studying. They use the computers to conduct research, practice word processing skills, and turn their research into slide show presentations to share with the rest of the class.

Computers give students access to information that otherwise would not be available. They are developing critical thinking skills as they locate the necessary information, pull out relevant facts, and sift through extraneous information. The reading strategies of summarizing, clarifying, and questioning that have been ingrained in these students are now used at a much higher level.

Word processing skills may not seem to tie into literacy, but if students are quick and accurate with keyboarding skills, it will help them throughout their education. The less they have to concentrate on where the keys are, the more attention they can pay to the content of what they are writing. Allowing access to computers during research time gives students the practice and application they need.

After students have completed their research and typed a paper, they share what they learned with the class through a presentation in the form of a slide show on the computer. For this, they need to again gauge the importance of the information they have found and whittle it down to the main details. They also must think about the sequencing of events.

As students complete these projects independently, while I am working with a small group, they apply several reading and writing strategies as well as improve a variety of technology skills that are a necessity in today's world."

—Jill Baker, Sixth-Grade Teacher
Grand Oaks Elementary School
Citrus Heights, California

Chapter 7 provides information on literature discussion groups.

An important teaching and organizational strategy is using *flexible groups*. As the name implies, these are groups that exist temporarily for a particular purpose and change frequently, sometimes as often as every day or two. They may consist of two, three, or more students working together, depending on the purpose. For example, literature discussion groups are usually most successful when they contain three to five students, which allows for interaction and ensures that everyone gets to participate. The rule of thumb is to keep the group small enough to accomplish the intended purpose:

■ Use *interest groups* any time you want students with similar interests to discuss something, complete a project, or have a lesson. For example, if several students have strong interests in electricity, you could group them to teach them an experiment, or to complete a project.

FIGURE 10.17   A Management System Flow Chart

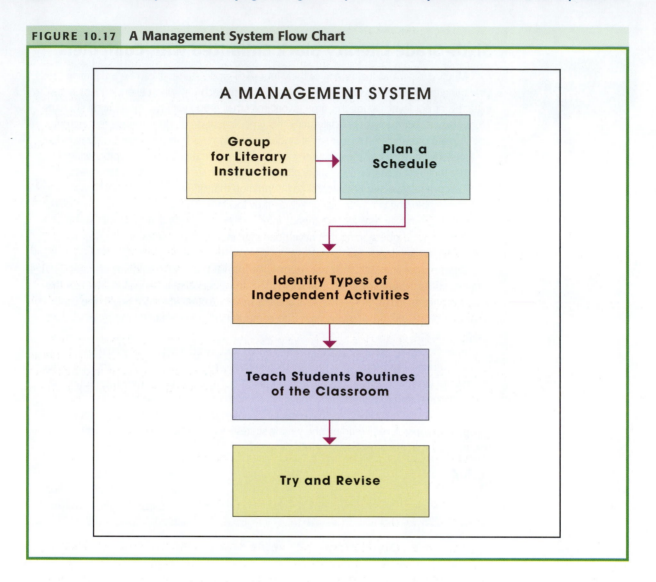

■ *Strengths and needs groups* build on students' strengths or help them learn something they need. For example, after students have read and discussed the book *Pelicans* (Patent, 1992), you might bring together those who had trouble identifying the main ideas for a minilesson. Or, you might have a support-in-advance activity, to build background knowledge by mixing students who have some background with those who have little background in a topic.

Support-in-advance is described more fully later in this chapter.

■ *Minilesson groups* are for lessons that certain students need. Many times they will be used for direct instruction of a specific skill or strategy. However, remember that minilessons are not always based on need and are not always taught to a small group. Some are taught simply because there is something you want a group or the class to learn. For example, at the beginning of the year you may

See Chapter 4 for a detailed discussion of the minilesson and sample lessons.

teach a minilesson to the whole class on how to select books that are appropriate for their reading levels. Some minilessons may be taught several times throughout the year. For example, you may need to teach a minilesson on adjectives every time some students are writing a description.

- *Discussion groups* often follow the reading of part or all of a book. These groups may be formed by student choice, teacher assignment, or a combination of the two. Discussion groups may also be formed for students to share their writing and to get peer reactions. In one sixth-grade class, students read aloud and talked about mysteries they had written.

- *Project groups* may be formed for long- or short-term projects related to any aspect of the curriculum. For example, a first-grade class may work on a mural about seasons throughout the year; different groups are responsible for different seasons. Often project groups are composed of students with differing abilities and needs.

- *Modeling groups* may be used any time students need more modeling of reading, writing, or any skills or strategies. Students, the teacher, or another adult may provide the model. For example, struggling fourth graders might prepare a book to read aloud to first graders. The first graders get good models, and the fourth graders build their confidence and skill.

The important thing to keep in mind about the various types of groups is that they are *flexible;* they are always changing based on students' strengths, needs, interests, and purposes for learning. Flexible grouping is an important concept that helps you use the three Frameworks for Reading Instruction discussed in the following sections.

Frameworks for Reading Instruction

Three frameworks will help you plan reading instruction:

- Core Books/Anthologies Framework
- Guided Reading with Leveled Books Framework
- Reading Workshop

Using the Core Books/Anthologies Framework This framework is designed to help you accomplish what needs to be done in the Reading: Learning Skills and Strategies block of the Comprehensive Balanced Literacy Program. This block is often referred to as *whole-class instruction*, but a better name is *core book/anthology with flexible groups,* because the only aspect of it that is whole class is that everyone has experience reading the same text. Figure 10.18 shows how it operates.

Description

Everyone in the class will read the same piece of text. This could be the grade-level anthology or a trade book (the core book) such as *Head for the Hills!* (Walker, 1993). Each student needs a copy of the book being read.

Begin by activating prior knowledge and developing background and vocabulary for the piece of literature. For students with limited prior knowledge provide a preview or develop key concepts to give them a stronger base for what the whole class will read. This concept is known as *support in advance* or *jump-starting* and may

Prior knowledge is discussed in Chapter 3.

FIGURE 10.18 Core Book/Anthology with Flexible Groups

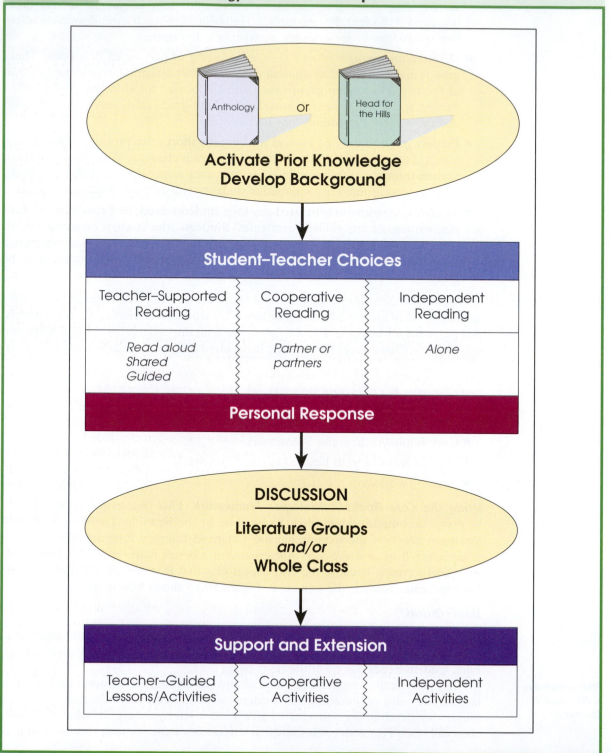

be provided by the classroom teacher or a support teacher such as a Title I teacher. Then, when the whole class begins the book, a different prior-knowledge activity is used; the students who were given support in advance are now able to function more successfully with the whole class.

Modes of reading are discussed in Chapter 2.

After prior knowledge has been activated and developed, students are ready to read. You accommodate individual differences by using different modes of reading. Usually, you assign the mode of reading for each student. You may sometimes give students choices about how they read, but remember that when less able readers are given choices, they often choose a mode that allows them to "hide" because they don't want to reveal that they need help.

You may give the students two or three choices, for example: "Today you may read the first two chapters independently or come to the table and read the chapters with me." If students are not making good choices, guide them to better decisions. A critical element in making this pattern of instruction work is varying the modes of reading to accommodate individual needs. Kindergarten and first-grade teachers are likely to conduct most of their initial readings as teacher-supported reading.

After students have read the piece of literature, they should make a personal response to what they have read, often by writing. Personal response is followed by discussion, during which you should use the literature discussion group concept, giving students the option to decide with whom they will discuss what they have read. The literature discussion groups may be followed by whole-class discussion to pull together the ideas of various groups. During the discussion groups, pay close attention to how students respond in order to plan the support and extension activities that students need. For example, if during response you notice that some students reading *Head for the Hills!* missed important details, you might plan a minilesson on identifying significant details using the chapters students have read.

For more information on observing students during responses, see Chapter 11.

The final step in the core book/anthology framework is providing support and extension, where you teach skills and strategies and do other activities that extend students' reading. Support and extension activities may consist of teacher-guided lessons or activities, cooperative activities, or independent activities, depending on what you believe is needed to thoroughly develop the students' abilities to construct meaning. For example, after reading the first two chapters in *Head for the Hills!* you may teach a needed skill lesson and defer other activities for when the book is completed. In addition to minilessons, support and extension activities may include creative responses such as art or vocabulary activities such as word maps or word webs.

An important issue is how much time this framework requires. Obviously, the answer depends on the text and the students. However, the following guidelines should help you:

- Prior knowledge should be activated quickly. Support in advance is likely to be completed on a day prior to beginning the literature with the whole class. Therefore, the whole-class prior-knowledge activity should last no longer than 10 to 15 minutes. After students start reading, if they need more prior-knowledge support, provide it quickly. *Remember, students want to read!* Don't wear out the book with too much prior-knowledge work.

- The amount of time allotted to reading each day will vary with the book and the grade level. It may range from 15 to 30 minutes.

■ Discussion groups should be kept short to keep students focused and on task. In kindergarten and first grade, these discussions may last only a matter of seconds. Beyond these levels, 5 to 10 minutes is usually long enough.

■ The amount of time for support and extension activities depends on the nature of the activities. Minilessons may last only 5 to 10 minutes, whereas other types of activities may last longer.

Be sure to keep the pace of instruction *appropriately fast.* The pace depends on students' strengths and needs. Keep students reading and don't spend too long on one book by doing too many activities. A chapter or two in a book such as *Head for the Hills!* should take one or two blocks of class time. More will be said about time in the section on scheduling.

Benefits of the Core Books/Anthologies Framework

This framework offers many benefits. First, it puts everyone in the class on a level playing field. All students are confident that they are able to read the same books everyone else in the class can read; this reduces the stigma that has been attached to ability grouping.

Second, it provides a way to teach key skills and strategies. Students then apply these when they read leveled books.

Third, this framework promotes and supports discussion involving *all* students. This is very important in helping students construct meaning.

A final benefit is flexibility; this framework is not linear. You may start by activating prior knowledge, having students read, and then having them discuss. You may reserve the support and extension for later. The next day you may continue with reading and no further activation of prior knowledge. Another option is to teach a skill or strategy before the selection is read; reading then provides immediate practice and application.

Problems to Avoid

See Chapter 2 on leveling books.

Although this is a strong framework for promoting success, it can have problems and pitfalls if the plan is misused. First, this plan *must be balanced* with the leveled books framework described in the next section. *All students must be given instruction with books that are appropriate for their reading levels.*

Second, although all students are reading the same book, the plan will fail if all students are treated the same. In other words, you must vary the modes of reading, the discussion groups, and the support and extension activities. You can't expect the whole class to read the book independently, answer questions, and complete the same activity. *Choice for students is critical to truly accommodate individual needs.*

Using the Guided Reading with Leveled Books Framework The Guided Reading with Leveled Books Framework helps you accomplish what needs to take place during the Reading: Application of Skills and Strategies block of the Comprehensive Balanced Literacy Program. In this block, all students will read books that are appropriate for their reading ability. Figure 10.19 shows how this framework operates when you have three groups reading at different levels.

FIGURE 10.19 **Guided Reading with Leveled Books Routine**

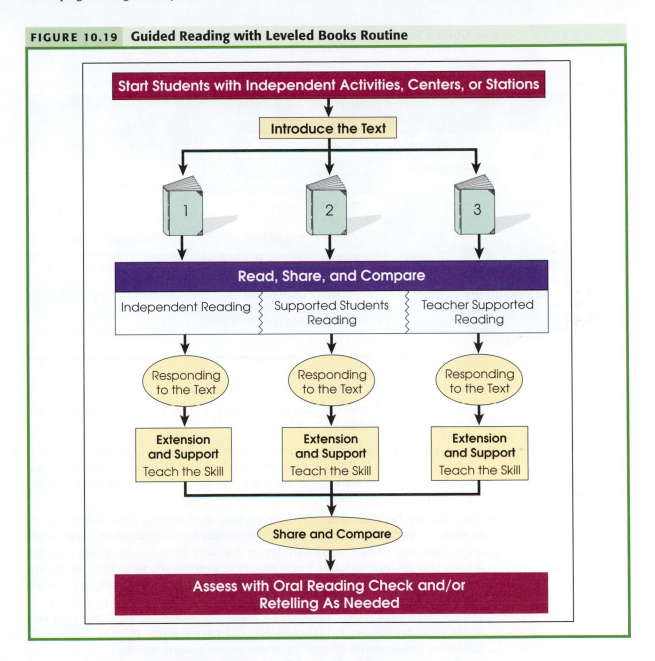

Description

The basic plan for teaching a lesson for the leveled books is:

- Introduce the Text
- Read
- Respond

FIGURE 10.20 **Sample Guided Reading Plan: Three Groups**

Min.	Group A	Group B	Group C
5	Start all students on independent activities, centers, stations		
10	*Independent activities		Introduce the text
15	*Continue independent activities	Introduce the text	Independently read the text
20	Introduce the text	Read text with partners	
35	Read text with teacher—discuss	Respond to text	Respond to text
45	Respond to text—individually	Discuss/teach skill	*Independent activities
55	*Independent activities	*Independent activities	Discuss with teacher
60	Share books read in mixed groups		

Figure 10.19 shows how the plan flows as well as other activities that take place. The basic framework operates like this:

See "For Additional Reading" for many good ideas for these types of activities.

- You begin this framework by getting students started on independent activities, learning centers, or learning stations that provide reinforcement for reading and language arts. These activities provide students meaningful work while you are teaching one group at a time.

- The class has been divided into three groups, each reading a book appropriate to students' independent or instructional reading level. Remember, these books are for application of skills and strategies that have been taught. While students are working on their independent activities or centers, you introduce the appropriate book to one group at a time. Figure 10.20 shows you how to schedule work with the three groups for one hour. The shaded areas show where you are working with each group. Each group reads the book independently, cooperatively, or under teacher guidance. When you have a group reading under your guidance, you stay with that group and conduct guided reading.

  After you introduce the book for one group, you move on to another group, leaving the first group to read the text on their own.

- After each group has read their book, they complete some type of response activity. Then you have the groups do extension and support or teach a skill as needed. You meet with groups for discussion.

- At the end of each day, you have students meet in mixed level groups for just a few minutes to share and talk about what they read that day. Students enjoy this

Students and their teacher during a guided reading group.
© Elizabeth Crews/The Image Works

activity because it gives them a chance to see and hear about what everyone is reading. This helps to motivate them to want to read other books.

■ Periodically you assess students using some type of oral reading check and/or a retelling.

Benefits of the Guided Reading with Leveled Books Framework

This framework provides all students the opportunity to apply the strategies and skills they learned while reading the core book or anthology in books that are appropriate to their reading ability.

Problems to Avoid

Teachers report that the biggest problem with this framework is management: it is difficult to have many groups going at one time. We suggest that most teachers can effectively manage three groups and many may want to start with just two groups.

Finally, you and your school will need to build collections of books with multiple copies at a wide range of levels. Centralized book collections facilitate the developmentally appropriate books process.

Using the Reading Workshop Framework   The Reading Workshop is a third framework you can use to organize and manage the literacy-centered classroom. Atwell (1998) introduced the concept of the Reading Workshop as a time when the entire class is engaged in reading, responding, and sharing books with the teacher and with peers. Our discussion incorporates ideas from many variations of Reading Workshop.

Description

The Reading Workshop consists of five main components: teacher sharing time (the teacher reads aloud), minilessons, state-of-the-class conference (a management technique), reading and responding (activities here can vary, but self- selected reading is always included), and student sharing time. These are outlined in Figure 10.21, along with suggested times.

Teacher Sharing Time. The teacher reads aloud or discusses a book to motivate or excite students about literature. For example, you might use a short story such as *Hemi's Pet* (de Hamel, 1985) to introduce students to a series of books on pets or one of Jack Prelutsky's poems from *Tyrannosaurus Was a Beast* (Prelutsky, 1988) to excite children about the study of dinosaurs. This sharing takes from 5 to 10 minutes and serves to warm up the class.

You can use this sharing time to lead into a minilesson.

Minilesson. This is a strategy or a skill lesson based on students' responses to reading or to provide prereading support for a piece of literature. The lesson uses direct instruction and incorporates the skill or strategy within the context of something students have already read or listened to. It may be done with the whole class or a small group.

Minilessons may be drawn from teachers' resource books or developed by the teacher and should be taught only if a real need exists.

State-of-the-Class Conference. During this brief period (5 minutes or less), you will take stock of what students are doing or planning to do during the remainder of the day's workshop. Reutzel and Cooter (1991) suggest using a chart similar to that shown in Figure 10.22 to keep track of what each student is doing. Eventually, the students can complete the chart themselves, and a large version can be posted each week. When students announce what they will be doing, they commit themselves to a particular task.

The chart helps you know which students may need a conference or other teacher support. For example, if you notice that a student has been reading the same

FIGURE 10.21	**Reading Workshop Plan**

- **Teacher Sharing Time** (5–10 minutes)
  A time when the teacher shares some literature to spark students inte rests and motivate them for independent reading.

- **Minilessons** (5–10 minutes)
  A teacher-directed lesson focusing on prereading activities that activate and develop prior knowledge for a particular piece of literature or a skill or strategy needed.

- **State-of-Class Conference** (3–5 minutes)
  Each student tells the teacher and the rest of the class what he or she is doing that day. The teacher records on the state-of-the class chart. This lets the teacher determine needs for conferences, etc.

- **Reading and Responding** (40–60 minutes)
  Alternative A
  During this time, students engage in several possible activities:
    - Self-selected reading (10–20 minutes)
    - Literature groups (20–30 minutes)
    - Conferences with the teacher (20 minutes)
  Alternative B
  A variation of this plan requiring 60 minutes is often used.
    - Whole-class reading and responding (10–20 minutes)
    - Self-selected reading and responding (10–20 minutes)
    - Literature groups (10–20 minutes)
    - Conferences with the teacher, held during teacher-assigned reading or only on selected days (10 minutes)

- **Student Sharing Time** (5–10 minutes)
  Students share what they are doing or have done. This may be done in sharing circles or as a whole class. The teacher may comment about activities or commend students who participated in conferences.

book for several days with no response activity, you may need a meeting to find out what progress has been made and to set new goals or change existing ones.

Reading and Responding. This is the heart of the Reading Workshop. There are two alternatives for using this time. Alternative A has three basic types of activities: self-selected reading, literature responses, and individual reading conferences. Usually this portion of the workshop lasts from about 40 to 60 minutes, depending on the age level of your students:

- *Self-selected reading* usually lasts from 10 to 20 minutes, depending on the grade level. Students read independently or with a partner, and you read part of the time to serve as a model. You should also circulate to hold individual miniconferences,

FIGURE 10.22   Reading State-of-the-Class Chart

STATE-OF-THE-CLASS

Name	M	Tu	W	Th	F
Ann	SSR	J			
Beth	LG-D	SSR			
Bill	SSR	LG-D			
Carl	J	SSR			
Cathy	LG-DNR	SSR			
Darin	R	SSR			
David	SSR	SSR			

CODE   SSR - Self-Selected Reading   LG - Literature Group Meeting
         J   - Journal   D   - Discussing
         R   - Response Activity   G   - Setting Goals
         RK   - Record Keeping   DNR - Determining New
                                                              Response

keep students motivated and encouraged, and do on-the-spot, incidental teaching. During this time, students may make entries in their journals.

■ *Literature responses* can include activities such as writing in journals or meeting with a literature group. You continue to circulate and confer with individuals, or you sit with a literature group to participate or serve as a recorder. Some students may continue their silent reading. If students have not chosen to meet with a literature group, they should be encouraged to respond in some other way, such as by sharing with a friend or completing a project.

■ *Individual reading conferences* with students who are not in literature groups make up the last 10 to 20 minutes of the period. Usually two or three conferences are held each day.

If you want the whole class or a selected group of students to read the same book, use alternative B, in which you assign a book and provide activities for a literacy lesson. You also include time for self-selected reading. If you are keeping a chart such as Figure 10.22, you can adjust the code to RT—Reading Time, SS—Self-Selected, and AR—Assigned Reading. Adjust the times for the other activities according to students' needs.

Some teachers move into the Reading Workshop gradually, scheduling two days for the workshop and the remaining days for other reading activities before making Reading Workshop their full program.

If your school uses a literature anthology, you can use the anthology for students to select what they want to read or combine the reading workshop framework with the core-book/anthology framework discussed earlier. Lessons in the teacher's resources that accompany an anthology may be used selectively for minilessons. This pattern is alternative B suggested in Figure 10.21.

Student Sharing Time. During the last 5 to 10 minutes of the Reading Workshop, students share books they have read and report on response activities. During this time, students may ask one another for ideas to improve what they are doing. Some teachers divide the class into small sharing groups (three to five students) for greater student involvement. The teachers circulate, commenting or just observing. More time may be scheduled when required for a special activity or project. Sharing time "advertises" the excitement of literacy learning and helps to promote the class as a community of readers.

Benefits of the Reading Workshop

The Reading Workshop provides one effective framework for systematically developing the reading block in your literacy classroom. If you use alternative B as outlined in Figure 10.21, you are also able to incorporate both of the other reading frameworks we have described: instruction with core-books/anthology and guided reading with leveled books.

Problems to Avoid

If you use the Reading Workshop as a totally self-selected reading block (alternative A), you may overlook the need for more instruction and in-depth discussion that comes when all students experience the same book or self-select from a controlled set of books. Alternative B avoids this problem.

Also, be sure to teach students how the format works and monitor it closely as you begin.

Writing Frameworks

See Figure 2.1 in Chapter 2.

A classroom that promotes and supports writing must have identified times for this activity. Our model of a Comprehensive Balanced Literacy Program provides three such blocks of time. On the basis of his research, Graves (1991) recommends that children write 35 to 40 minutes per day for a minimum of four days a week. If you really believe children and young adults learn to read and write by reading and writing, there is no way to accept anything less than a plan that calls for *writing every day*.

The time provided must be time when students actually write, beyond the time used for minilessons and other modeling or demonstrations of writing. The two writing frameworks we describe are Teacher-Modeled Writing and Writing Workshop. Both are effective ways to provide time for actual writing and necessary instruction.

See Chapter 8 for a discussion of modes of writing as well as domains.

Teacher-Modeled Writing Framework The teacher-modeled writing framework is an effective way to model writing using the shared writing mode discussed earlier in this text.

Description

This framework begins by having the whole class (or a large group) work with the teacher to develop a common piece (the Writing: Learning to Write block). The teacher or students may actually write the text. At another time, the teacher conducts a minilesson using the group-written piece to revise and improve the particular type of writing. The teacher elicits ideas from the students and models various elements to help students see how to write in the domain or product being modeled. Depending on their needs, students move to either supported writing (Writing: Developmentally Appropriate Writing block) or independent writing; students who first do supported writing will later move on to independent writing.

Benefits of Teacher-Modeled Writing

This framework provides a reliable way for you to model writing for your students. By having students move from shared to guided, collaborative and cooperative, and independent writing, you scaffold instruction and gradually release responsibility to students. Modeling writing is especially important for ELLs, in that such scaffolded instruction makes the input comprehensible.

In addition, this framework can be easily combined with the Writing Workshop, the next framework discussed. By combining the two frameworks, you achieve a balance of modeled writing and developmentally appropriate writing.

Problems to Avoid

The biggest problem in this framework is pacing. Too little or too much modeling can cause problems for students. Once students know how to write in the particular domain or for the particular product, the only way for them to develop and mature is by *writing*. Even during independent writing, you continue to model and support students through conferencing.

Writing Workshop Framework The Writing Workshop, which is similar to the Reading Workshop, has been recommended by numerous researchers and writing specialists (Atwell, 1998; Calkins, 1994; Hansen, 1987). It is a flexible plan that places students and teacher in a partnership for learning.

Description

The Writing Workshop consists of four basic parts: minilessons, state-of-the-class conferences, writing and conferring, and group sharing. Each part flows into the next to make up the block of time allocated for writing. The ideas and suggestions given here are based on the work of Atwell (1998), Calkins (1994), and Hansen (1987) and our own experiences in working with students and teachers.

Minilessons

The minilesson is done with the whole class and usually lasts from 5 to 10 minutes. The content is determined by student needs as evidenced during a previous Writing Workshop.

Since the minilesson content is based in part on student needs, the topics covered may range from how to select a topic to how to write a business letter.

Possible Topics for Minilessons

- Writing Workshop procedures
- Writing opening paragraphs
- Punctuating items in a series
- Words to show characteristics
- Selecting topics
- Writing a friendly letter

- Humor in literature
- Correct paragraph form
- Outlining
- Writing description
- Punctuating dialogue

There are many more possible topics. On some days, no minilesson is needed; this time may be used for more sharing or writing.

State-of-the-Class Conference. The state-of-the-class conference functions for writing the way it did for reading—it helps to ensure that you know exactly what all students are doing. You may construct a chart and codes similar to the ones for reading in Figure 10.22. After the minilesson, take 5 minutes to ask students to identify what they will be doing during the day's workshop. Teachers often say that this gives them the control they feel they need but still encourages student independence.

Writing and Conferring. The writing and conferring block is the core of the Writing Workshop and usually lasts from 30 to 40 minutes, depending on the grade level. Since students will be at various stages in developing their writing piece, what you do depends on their needs. Here are some activities that might occur during this time:

- You may be working on some writing of your own, thus modeling adult writing and expressing that you value this activity. At other times you will be circulating, talking with individual students, reading portions of their writing, prompting and encouraging them, and offering whatever support they need. These brief encounters may be viewed as miniconferences or just times to talk with, guide, and support students. During this time, you will gain information that will help you plan minilessons and assess students' progress. You will want to make notes for future use in planning or for insertion into your notebook page for each student.

- Students may be holding a peer conference, working on revision, editing, planning a new piece, or just getting topics for writing. You might stop to visit, but remember that these are *peer* conferences. You will have a time to meet with students later.

- You will hold formal group and individual conferences with students. Using a sign-up chart or an area of the chalkboard, students should sign up in advance of conference time to meet with you, either at the beginning of each day's Writing Workshop or the day before you announce you will hold conferences.

Group Sharing. Group sharing is just like an individual or peer conference, except that the whole group reacts to a piece of writing. This portion of the Writing Workshop usually lasts 5 minutes or longer, depending on your schedule and what needs to take place. During this time, you might incorporate the concept of the author's chair.

Group sharing is not a show-and-tell time; it is a time for students to talk about their writing with peers and get reactions, as well as a time to celebrate their successes by sharing finished products. Sharing promotes the classroom as a community of writers, a place where writers discover how well they have constructed meaning. For example, if a student gives a report on dinosaurs, other students might ask questions about things they don't understand or think are incorrect, or even suggest another book on dinosaurs that the author should read before finishing the piece.

Some teachers divide the class into two or three sharing groups so that more individuals can share at one time. Don't skip sharing time or cut it short: it provides enormous benefits:

- It provides students with authentic reasons for writing and gives them the audience writers need.

- It brings closure to the construction of meaning by having both readers and writers discover whether they have successfully accomplished their purpose.

- It helps students grow in both their writing and reading by getting feedback from peers and having to respond to that feedback.

- It is another point in the development of literacy where reading and writing are integrated into one process within the community of learners.

Benefits of the Writing Workshop

The Writing Workshop is a flexible, manageable framework that allows you to meet individual needs. It can be combined with the teacher-modeled writing framework to provide balanced writing instruction. The teacher-modeled writing piece can be inserted into the minilesson slot of the Writing Workshop, thereby giving you a way to model writing while at the same time having students write independently. You might do one shared piece each week or follow a regular cycle, using the remaining time to have students do guided, collaborative or cooperative, or independent writing.

Problems to Avoid

It takes time to move effectively into the Writing Workshop framework. Therefore, you need to develop a systematic plan for its use and try it out gradually. It is especially important to share the framework with students, discussing each section. As you work with students in the Writing Workshop, periodically evaluate how its components are working. Teachers at various grade levels have found the following procedures helpful as they begin using the Writing Workshop:

1. *Familiarize yourself with the Writing Workshop plan.* Think about how you will use it in your classroom.
2. *Think through procedures you will use.* The state-of-the-class chart, conference scheduling, and simple recordkeeping for your conferences are enough to get started. Gradually add other procedures you have learned from this text and other sources.
3. *Talk with your students about the workshop.* Make a chart showing the parts of the plan, and use it as a guide for you and your students.
4. *Designate a day to begin.* This may take place at the beginning of the year or at any point during the year. Students may have pieces of writing in progress, or you may want everyone to start with a new piece of writing. Teachers find both approaches successful.
5. *Use your first few minilessons to establish basic routines.* After the first day, you will know what types of support your students need with procedures and routines. (There really aren't many to be concerned about.)
6. *Evaluate what is happening with your students.* Talk about the Writing Workshop. Ask students for suggestions to make it better.
7. *Trust your judgment.* You are a professional and know how to make decisions. If something feels right, do it; if it feels wrong, don't do it. However, give new ideas time to work; don't just drop something after one attempt.

Once you become comfortable with both Reading and Writing Workshops, you can integrate them into a literacy workshop. Such a plan would be similar to the concept of integrated language arts that many teachers have tried to achieve in their classrooms (Templeton, 1997).

Now that you are familiar with the five frameworks for organizing and managing a success-centered literacy classroom, we will focus on how to plan daily routines and schedules using these frameworks, along with time for independent reading and writing.

Step 2: Plan a Schedule

Every type of program requires a daily plan that will help you manage the instruction and activities of your classroom. There is *no one right schedule* that works for all teachers. However, having a system for thinking about your schedule makes planning easier and more efficient. Researchers have found that blocking leads to improved student achievement and more effective and efficient use of student and teacher time (Cunningham, Hall, & Defee, 1998). See the "Educators Speak" feature on page 451 to see how one teacher used parallel block scheduling to help students with diverse needs.

A Blocked Plan for Scheduling

See page 27 to review the Model for a Comprehensive Balanced Literacy Program.

We presented a model for a Comprehensive Balanced Literacy Program in Chapter 2, and have consistently referred to this model throughout this text. This model balances the essential components of a literacy program in seven blocks; six of these are necessary for all students, and an additional intervention block may be necessary for some students. Each block is given varying amounts of time, depending on what needs to be done.

Thinking about your literacy program schedule in blocks does the following:

- It gives you a way to organize and plan systematic daily instruction.
- It keeps you from skipping things because each block is generally included every day.
- It allows you to effectively plan for and use any support staff you may have (aides, reading specialists, resource teachers, and volunteers).
- It helps students participate more fully because they know what is to come and what to expect each day.

Amount of Time Required A daily blocked plan will work from kindergarten through grade 8. Although research does not specify exactly how much time should be devoted to literacy instruction in general or to each block, we suggest that the times presented in Table 10.1 are the minimum needed at each grade level to have an effective literacy program. As you will see when you read the sample schedules, the blocks may be separated by breaks, other subjects, or lunch. When combined, they add up to the recommended total amount of time.

How do the suggested times stack up against what you know about the amount of time teachers usually have for literacy instruction? If you find yourself saying, "I [or teachers I know] usually have more time," *great*. If you find yourself saying, "No way. I [or teachers I know] don't have this much time," you need to rethink your schedule. Remember, it *takes time* to provide quality literacy instruction that prevents student failure.

TABLE 10.1	Minimum Amounts of Time for a Daily Blocked Literacy Schedule
Grade Levels	**Minimum Times**
Kindergarten	3 hours[a]
Grades 1–2	2–3 hours
Grades 3–5	1 1/2–2 hours
Grades 6–8	1–2 hours

[a]Most half-day kindergartens don't have this much time.

FIGURE 10.23 **Ms. Barnett's Kindergarten Schedule**

Ms. Barnett's Kindergarten Schedule	
8:30	Arrival and Sign-in independent Writing
8:45	Warm-up/Daily News/Morning Message
9:00	Reading: Learning Skills and Strategies
9:15	Reading: Application of Skills and Strategies
9:30	Independent Reading
9:40	Center Time (math, science, social studies)
10:00	Break/Recess/Specials art, music, computer lab)
10:30	Writing (blocks alternate as needed) Writing: Learning to Write Writing: Developmentally Appropriate Writing
11:10	Sharing
11:30	Dismiss

Sample Schedules Incorporating Frameworks

As you plan your daily schedule, you will want to include some of the frameworks we have discussed. A look at some sample schedules from several teachers will help you see how to incorporate the frameworks into your blocked schedule and get in all the necessary components of a Comprehensive Balanced Literacy Program. Figures 10.23, 10.24, 10.25, and 10.26 present sample schedules from four teachers. Study the schedules with the following points in mind:

- Does each teacher plan for all blocks? How do they vary the way it is done?
- How do these teachers' time allotments compare to the times given in Table 10.1?
- How does each teacher start the day? What is the teacher's purpose with this type of activity?

Step 3: Identify Types of Independent Activities

When you have planned for grouping your students and worked out your schedules, your next thought may be, "But what do the other students do while I'm working with a small group?" The answer to that question lies with the concept of *independent activities*. As the name suggests, these are activities students can engage in

FIGURE 10.24   Mr. Lopez's First-Grade Schedule

Mr. Lopez's First-Grade Schedule

8:45	Opening exercise/Morning Message
9:00	Reading blocks
	Independent Reading
	Reading: Application of Skills and Strategies
	Specially written texts/Leveled texts
	Reading: Learning Skills and Strategies
	Core Book/anthology
	Instruction in decoding skills
	Construction of meaning
10:15	Break
10:30	Writing blocks
	Independent Writing
	Writing: Learning to Write
	Writing: Developmentally Appropriate Writing
11:15	Morning share and lunch
11:45	Math
12:20	Specials (art/music/PE)
1:10	Teacher read-aloud
1:25	Science/social studies/health
1:50	Projects/response activities
2:20	Clean up/closing activities
2:30	Dismiss

without supervision. Students may work alone, with a partner, or in a small group. Some of these activities, such as independent reading or writing, may be part of your blocked schedule; for example, during the block of time allotted to independent reading, you may be teaching a minilesson to a small group.

The following are a few such independent activities. As the year progresses, you and your students will be able to add to this list:

- Independent reading
- Independent writing
- Response to a book

(*text continues on page 448*)

FIGURE 10.25   Ms. Sanders's Fifth-Grade Schedule

Ms. Sander's Fifth-Grade Schedule

8:30	Arrival/journal writing
8:45	Writing blocks
	Daily Independent Writing
	Writing: Learning to Write/Developmentally Appropriate Writing
9:30	Reading blocks
	Reading: Learning Skills and Strategies (core book/anthology)
	Reading: Application of Skills and Strategies (leveled books)
10:30	Break
10:45	Specials (art, music, PE, computer lab)
11:30	Lunch
12:00	Independent Reading block
12:30	Math
1:45	Social studies/science
2:30	Clean up and end of day activities
2:40	Teacher read-aloud
3:00	Dismiss

FIGURE 10.26   Mr. Burgess's Eighth-Grade Schedule (60-minute period)

Writing Workshop—M-T-W (Writing/Language—Word Work)
Reading Workshop—Th-F (Reading—Word Work)

Upon arrival	• State-of-class check
5 minutes	• Group sharing
10 minutes	• Minilesson
30 minutes	• Read/Write/Confer
10 minutes	• Partner/Class share
5 minutes	• Goal setting/Close

- Vocabulary game
- Computer work
- Audiotapes
- Map activities
- Projects
- Learning centers

You may want to limit which independent activities you want students to engage in at certain times. Activities written on individual strips of tag board to post on a bulletin board or affix with magnets will make it easy to mix and match and add and delete activities. Some teachers keep a comprehensive list posted, but clip a clothespin next to those from which students can choose on a given day.

Step 4: Teach Students Routines of the Classroom

In order to manage your classroom effectively, you must develop routines with your students. There are three critical steps in the process of developing management routines:

1. **Develop a daily schedule.** We have discussed this earlier. Review now if you need to do so.
2. **Identify independent activities for students to do.** We have already suggested what these activities might include. Students need to know what to do when they have completed any of their work and are not working with you. The list of possible activities should be posted where students can easily refer to them, and they should be changed frequently. Teach students how to engage in these activities without disturbing each other or the group that is working with you.
3. **Develop and discuss routines with students.** To help students feel comfortable working in groups and working independently, you need to develop routines within the classroom. Many teachers have found the following steps effective:

   - Develop with students a set of classroom guidelines for general behavior. Post these where they can be easily seen (see Figure 10.27).
   - Appoint one or two students as monitors each week. Students can go to these persons with questions if you are busy with a group.
   - Present and post your daily schedule for students to see. Discuss what will be happening throughout each day.
   - Role-play the schedule and procedures with students. Create situations where problems are likely to arise (e.g., need to go to the restroom, student doesn't know a word). Discuss and evaluate the role-playing. This may need to be done frequently at the beginning of the year. Allow room for new guidelines to be added.

FIGURE 10.27 **Classroom Behavior Chart**

During work times we will . . .

* Work quietly

* Go to our weekly monitors for help if Miss Janes is busy.

* Select an independent activity to do when my work is finished

Step 5: Try and Revise

Try your plans, and revise them as needed. After using your schedule and routines for a few days, discuss with students how things are going. Ask for suggestions for improving or changing the schedule or any routines. Talk about how monitors are being used.

Although a management plan is essential, no plan should be written in stone. In fact, the beauty of the plan is that it can and should be modified. What might have seemed essential at the beginning of the school year may not be necessary as classroom routines become second nature and students have grown in their ability to work independently.

Meeting the Needs of All Students

The four classrooms and schedules just reviewed show you a variety of ways teachers plan a schedule. There are, however, five special considerations you must also address in scheduling: ELLs, children with exceptionalities, intervention, multi-age classrooms, and community-home connections.

English Language Learners

All four of the teachers reviewed in the previous section have students who are ELLs. Although these students may require more patience and extra support, they participate in the same literacy learning experiences as other students. Routines are especially

Video Case

Inclusion: Grouping Strategies for Inclusive Classrooms

Watch the video clip, study the artifacts in the case, and reflect on the following questions:

1. Describe some of the strategies that the classroom teacher and inclusion specialist in this Video Case use to meet the needs of their diverse student population.

2. This chapter stresses the importance of meeting the needs of all students in your future classroom. How can a classroom teacher be more prepared to meet diverse learning needs? Can you identify some potential resources to call upon?

important for ELLs, because a routine makes the classroom day predictable. Once such learners know the routines, they can focus more fully on learning activities. The ideas presented throughout this text work effectively with ELLs.

Children with Exceptionalities

Our four teachers all have students who are classified as exceptional. Some have been included in the regular classroom from special education, some are gifted and talented, and others have learning disabilities. In all cases, the teachers used flexible grouping along with the various frameworks and a variety of teaching strategies to meet the needs of all students.

Intervention

See Chapter 9 for information about working with struggling readers and programs designed to meet this need.

Intervention is additional instruction (usually in reading) that prevents or stops reading failure. Research has clearly demonstrated that some students will never achieve complete success in reading without instructional support that is given *in addition to the balanced classroom program* that everyone receives (Snow, Burns, & Griffin, 1998).

Multi-Age Classrooms

Some schools incorporate the multi-age concept, whereby several ages are placed in the same class. These classes are sometimes called "families." Within each family, students usually study a common theme. Within any theme, the teacher can use the five frameworks described in this chapter to organize and manage instruction.

Frameworks such as the guided reading with leveled books, Reading Workshop, and Writing Workshop are very effective in organizing the multi-age classroom. If you review the schedules of the first three teachers presented in the previous section, you can easily see that they could also be used for a multi-age class. The biggest mistake often made in multi-age classes is treating each age as a separate group. This is contrary to the theory and research behind the multi-age concept.

Parallel Block Scheduling Helps Students with Diverse Needs

"The students in my first-grade class come from varied backgrounds and the range of instructional needs is wide. At the beginning of each year, some students do not yet have the concept of a word, while others may be reading on a second-grade level. I meet this range of needs by using small, homogeneous groups. This year, parallel block scheduling was introduced in grades 1 and 2. Each grade level consists of five teachers, but only four homerooms. The fifth teacher is a content specialist in either science or social studies. My homeroom is divided so that reading and math groups have low student-to-teacher ratios, so instruction is more effective. The rest of the class goes to the science or social studies extension room. After approximately 50 minutes, the groups rotate.

My reading block consists of guided reading and word study. Small groups meet with me by using a procedure known as *circle, center, seat rotation*, which allows all students to work on activities at their targeted, instructional level. A weekly schedule for word study instruction is consistent throughout the year and includes activities for each day of the week—for example:

Monday: Introduce new words, cut out and sort words, and keep in our word study notebooks.
Tuesday: Sort words and draw and label or write a sentence for one word from each category.
Wednesday: Word hunt for words that follow the same patterns in books we are reading.
Thursday: Buddy speed sort and games.
Friday: Spell check.

Groups meet with me during *circle time* and I conduct guided reading with instructional text, as well as word study. I monitor progress by observation, spell checks, and running records, which allows for flexible grouping. For example, when Jenny had trouble on specific word features, I moved her to another group, where she experienced success and progress.

While this small group works with me, the remainder of the class is divided into *seat and center time*. Students at their seats work on word study and writing activities. Students at centers work on activities related to literacy.

My schedule allows me to manage groups of students with diverse educational needs, and all students make progress when their individual needs are met. It sure has made a difference in my classroom!"

—*Kelly L. Andrus, First-Grade Teacher*
Parkside Elementary School
Fredericksburg, Virginia

Community-Home Connections

Our four teachers maintain close ties with students' homes and communities. They draw on community resources, have students share at home books they have read and pieces they have written in school, and maintain constant communications with families through conferences and newsletters. Teachers can use paraprofessionals and bilingual parents to help develop good connections with the homes of ELLs. A continuous connection with students' homes is critical to the effective literacy classroom.

Developing a Management System for a Comprehensive Balanced Literacy Classroom: Key Points

To review the Key Points, see the ACE practice tests at the HM TeacherPrepSPACE Student Website.

- Guidelines based on how children learn help teachers organize and manage a classroom.
- A literate classroom involves the use of space and materials.
- A literate classroom involves conferences and recordkeeping.
- The first step leading to a successful management system involves flexible grouping, using groups in different ways for different purposes.
- Part of the concept of grouping is using frameworks for reading and writing instruction.
- Three reading frameworks are: core books/anthologies, guided reading with leveled books, and Reading Workshop.
- Two writing frameworks are: teacher-modeled writing and Writing Workshop.
- The second step is scheduling literacy blocks.
- The third step is planning for independent activities.
- The fourth step is teaching and practicing classroom routines.
- The last step is trying out a plan and revising as needed.
- Special attention must be paid to the needs of English Language Learners, children with exceptionalities, intervention programs, multi-age classrooms, and maintaining the connection between school and community/home.

How Do I Teach?

Strategies and Routines to Help You Manage the Comprehensive Balanced Literacy Classroom

Video Cases in This Chapter

- **Elementary Classroom Management: Basic Strategies**
- **Inclusion: Grouping Strategies for Inclusive Classrooms**

For Additional Reading

Cooper, J. D., Boschken, I., McWilliams, J., & Pistochini, L. (2000). A study of the effectiveness of an intervention program designed to accelerate reading for struggling readers in the upper grades. In T. Shanahan & F. V. Rodriguez-Brown (Eds.), *49th Yearbook of the National Reading Conference* (pp. 477–486). Chicago: National Reading Conference.

Cunningham, P., & Allington, R. L. (2007). *Classrooms that work: They can all read and write* (4th ed.). Boston: Allyn & Bacon.

Grabe, M. (2006). *Integrated technology for meaningful learning* (5th ed.). Boston: Houghton Mifflin.

Jones, J. A. (2006). Student-involved classroom libraries. *The Reading Teacher, 59*(6), 576–580.

Morrow, L. M. (2003). *Organizing and managing the language arts block: A professional development guide*. New York: Guilford Press.

National Council of Teachers of English. (2001). *Language Arts* (entire issue focuses on organizing for literacy instruction), vol. 79, no. 2. Champaign-Urbana, IL: National Council of Teachers of English.

Pikulski, J. J. (1994). Preventing reading failure: A review of five effective programs. *The Reading Teacher, 48*(1), 30–39.

Solvie, P. A. (2004). The digital whiteboard: A tool in early literacy instruction. *The Reading Teacher, 57*(5), 484–487.

Vardell, S. M., Hadaway, N. L., & Young, T. A. (2006). Matching books and readers: Selecting literature for English learners. *The Reading Teacher, 59*(8), 734–741.

Websites

Center for Applied Special Technology (CAST)

CAST is a nonprofit organization whose mission is to expand opportunities for individuals with disabilities through the development of innovative uses of technology. This site has publications, sample software programs, and interactive teaching strategies.

http://www.cast.org

Council for Exceptional Children

This site includes information about the organization special interest groups, publications, professional standards and accreditation, training and events, public policy, and legislative information.

http://www.cec.sped.org

Inclusion Literature

This article from the *ALAN Review* covers children's and adolescent literature that is written by parents and teachers and is related to inclusion issues such as self-esteem and individuality.

http://scholar.lib.vt.edu/ejournals/ALAN/spring98/andrews.html

Learning to Read/Reading to Learn Campaign

This site, sponsored by the National Center to Improve the Tools of Educators at the University of Oregon, presents research results on the literacy skills and understandings that children must acquire to learn to read.

http://idea.uoregon.edu/~ncite/programs/read.html

National Institute on Child Health and Human Development: Publications

This website provides a list of publications available from the National Institute on Child Health and Human Development.

http://www.nichd.nih.gov

National Institute on Early Childhood Development and Education

This site focuses on research and resources for families, educators, communities, and policymakers in an effort to assist all children, regardless of societal, economic, family, linguistic, and/or disability conditions.

http://www.ed.gov/offices/OERI/ECI/

Search the web for yourself by entering a topic such as "Classroom Management" or "Reading Workshop" into your search engine. And explore some of these sites:

- http://www.netc.org/focus/challenges/literacy.php—Links to other sites related to literacy and technology.
- http://www.internet4classrooms.com/classroom_organization.htm—Provides links to many sites related to classroom management.
- http://wilearns.state.wi.us/apps/default.asp—Wisconsin state site; look for links to topics such as peer conferences.
- http://www.readingrockets.org/article/c64/—This article about Differentiated Instruction provides links to other articles. While at this site, look for other pertinent topics.
- http://www.busyteacherscafe.com/literacy_centers/main.htm—Loaded with ideas for managing literacy centers, including charts and advice.

Assessment and Evaluation in the Comprehensive Balanced Literacy Classroom

11

Terms
YOU NEED TO KNOW

- authentic assessment
- checklist
- cold read
- fluency check
- formal assessment
- grade score/grade equivalent
- informal assessment
- informal reading inventory (IRI)
- interest inventory
- miscue
- miscue analysis
- observation
- percentile
- performance assessment
- process interview
- rubric
- running record
- standard score
- standardized test

The HM TeacherPrepSPACE Student Website offers many helpful resources, such as self-quizzes, glossary flashcards, lesson plan templates, and more.

*M*r. Ryan is concerned about his second graders' progress in learning to construct meaning. Let's look at some of the classroom activities he uses to assess literacy growth.

As we enter the classroom, we see four literature discussion groups, each group discussing the same book, Ira Says Goodbye *(Waber, 1988)*. Discussion points are listed on the chalkboard:

1. *Why Reggie acted as he did*
2. *Your favorite part*
3. *How you would feel*

Mr. Ryan is seated with one of the groups, listening. At one point he joins in by saying, "When my best friend moved away, I wouldn't talk to anyone about it. How would you act if you had been in Ira's place, Lisette?"

Then Mr. Ryan moves from group to group, carrying a clipboard and a pad of sticky notes. He jots observations on the sticky notes and puts them on the clipboard.

After the literature groups, students do self-selected, independent reading, Some students then go to a box marked "Reading and Writing Portfolios" and record the book they just read.

At the end of the day, Mr. Ryan looks over the notes he has placed on the clipboard during the day. He has a notebook with a section for each student, and he places some of the sticky notes on students' pages, reading and discarding others. Then he quickly looks through the portfolios to see how much independent reading students have done and whether they have added any other pieces of writing to their portfolios.

From his notes, Mr. Ryan can tell that several students did not understand the story Ira Says Goodbye; *he lists their names so he can form a group in which he will teach the skill of noting details using a story map in a text students have read. From his examination of the portfolios, Mr. Ryan sees that all students except one are doing a lot of independent reading, so he makes a note to have a conference with her soon.*

Think about this classroom in terms of assessment, and list all the places where you thought assessment was taking place. Then compare your list to the following discussion. Mr. Ryan obviously believes that children learn to read and write by reading and writing, and assessment is an integral part of his instructional activities. Look at all the places where this is evident:

- Mr. Ryan participated in the literature groups, so he was able to observe students' responses to *Ira Says Goodbye*.

- Mr. Ryan made notes as he observed various aspects of students' reading. Later he reviewed those notes and kept some for planning future instructional activities.

- Mr. Ryan used his observations to determine skills that should be taught.

- Students participated in their own assessment by recording books in their reading and writing portfolios that they had completed during independent reading time.

- At the end of the day, Mr. Ryan reviewed his notes and students' portfolios to assess their progress and plan future activities.

■ Mr. Ryan assessed students against their previous performances, comparing current work to work already in their portfolios.

Although this was only a small part of the overall assessment plan in Mr. Ryan's room, we begin to get a picture of how he views and approaches assessment. In this chapter, we examine some basic ideas about how to develop assessments that are in line with the overall concept of the comprehensive balanced literacy program stressed throughout this text. We will focus on the classroom, giving only minor attention to the overall school literacy program. *The material in this chapter should be viewed as a basic framework for thinking about assessment in the comprehensive balanced literacy classroom.*

A Current View of Assessment

Practices in literacy assessment should reflect what we know about literacy, as was true in Mr. Ryan's classroom. While other kinds of assessment are likely required by his school system or state, he finds that daily interactions with students and careful attention to what they are doing as they read and write provide the most valid information for making instructional decisions.

Assessment and Evaluation

Although the terms *assessment* and *evaluation* are often used interchangeably within the field of education and especially within the field of literacy, they really represent different aspects of related processes (Bertrand, 1991). See the "Educators Speak" feature on page 462 for one way a curriculum support specialist helps teachers understand assessment. *Assessment* is the process of gathering information about a student's performance and *evaluation* is the process of making a judgment based on that information to determine how well the student is achieving or has achieved what is expected. For example, asking a student to retell a story is *assessment*; you are asking that student to respond. Then, when you judge the accuracy of the retelling and give it a score or a grade, or make an instructional decision based on it, you are *evaluating* the response.

Years ago assessment was simple; teachers gave a test and expected students to achieve a certain score. If they achieved that score, it was assumed they knew whatever the test was supposed to measure. If they did not, teachers simply retaught what the test was claimed to measure and then retested the students. However, teachers often had students who could pass the skills tests, but could not read or write—or could read and write but not pass the skills tests; the old way clearly did not reflect the full processes of reading and writing.

In the comprehensive balanced literacy classroom, procedures for assessment and evaluation must go together: one has no value without the other. A beginning step in planning for assessment in your classroom is to think about why you are assessing students.

The Role of Standards

We have addressed standards throughout this text; later in this chapter, we will talk about using standards to guide assessment. Standards state what students are expected to know or be able to do; often they specify achievement at various grade levels. These standards are often established at the state level. You, as a classroom teacher, must assess how well your students meet such standards. Some states spell out exactly what information each teacher must gather, what instrument should be used to gather the information, and how it is to be recorded. Each teacher must document that the required assessment is being carried out with each student. Your local school administrators must ensure that your school meets the state standards, though there may be local adaptations. Each school system disseminates assessment information to individual schools and individual teachers. These are assessments about which you will have no choice; they may include standardized tests as well as informal tests.

Teachers need to assess students—of that there can be no doubt. Teachers need to know how their students are doing; students also need to know how they are doing; families and the community need to know how students are doing. Ideally, such assessment would be a perfect match with what has been taught, would be free of cultural bias, and would lead directly to instructional decisions. It may seem that imposing standards-based assessment on classroom teachers would preclude this sort of ideal assessment, but it does not. All the techniques provided in this chapter will help you assess how well your students are meeting standards, as well as help you make instructional decisions.

A Framework for Assessment

As you begin to think about assessment in your classroom, you will need to understand a number of concepts and terms. Table 11.1 presents a selected list of these terms and their definitions. Most of them are discussed in more detail throughout this chapter. You may want to review these terms before reading further.

Assessment may be considered in terms of two broad categories: informal and formal. **Informal assessment** uses observations and other nonstandardized procedures; **formal assessment** uses standardized procedures or procedures carried out under controlled conditions (Harris & Hodges, 1995). Examples of informal assessments are the use of checklists, observations, and performance assessments or tasks. Informal assessments are clearly and easily incorporated into instruction. Formal assessments include state tests, standardized achievement tests, or tests accompanying a published program. Although these types of assessment are not embedded in instruction, they *must reflect the instruction* to be of value in assessing students' literacy development. The standardized achievement test is most useful in evaluating overall program growth; it is less useful for evaluating individual student progress or determining instructional needs.

TABLE 11.1	Assessment Terminology
Term	**Description**
Authentic assessment	Assessment activities that reflect literacy in the community, the workplace, and the instructional activities of the classroom. *Example:* Students write a letter to the editor about an environmental problem; the letter may be used to assess and evaluate students' writing abilities and skills. (See also *performance assessment.*)
Benchmarks (standards)	Statements of expectations of what students are to learn, usually given grade by grade or age by age. *Example:* First graders will orally read age/grade-appropriate text with 90 percent accuracy.
Checklist	A form that lists targeted behaviors as indicators of achievement, knowledge, or skill. *Example:* An oral language checklist that a kindergarten teacher might use.
Formal assessment	A test or task using procedures that are carried out under controlled conditions. *Example:* A state-level competency test.
Grade score/grade equivalent	A score transformed from a raw score on a standard test that is the equivalent earned by an average student in the norming group; these scores are not recommended for use because they may be misleading. *Example:* A grade 3 student scores 7.1 on a reading comprehension test but was never tested on passages at the grade 7 level.
Informal assessment	Observations or other nonstandardized procedures. *Example:* A teacher-made checklist.
Informal reading inventory (IRI)	A series of graded passages used to determine students' levels of reading and strengths and needs in decoding and comprehension. (See also *miscue* and *running record.*) *Example:* Most published reading series have passages that correlate with their materials.

Miscue	An oral reading response that differs from the text; may be analyzed to assess a student's reading development. (See also *informal reading inventory* and *running record.*) *Example:* A student reads the following sentence with the miscues noted:
	
	       pony
	 The horse/galloped so
	    (1)
	 fast that the man was thrown
	        ark night
	 through the air/at lightning/
	      (2) (3)
	   sky
	 speed/.
	   (4)

(continued)

TABLE 11.1	**Assessment Terminology** *(continued)*
	Miscue 1 does not change meaning; miscues 2, 3, and 4 do change meaning and should be analyzed further.
Percentile	A score on a scale of 100 showing the percentage of a distribution that is equal to or below it. *Example:* A score at the 70th percentile is equal to or better than 70 percent of the scores of others on whom the test was normed.
Performance assessment	A task that requires the student to demonstrate his or her level of knowledge and skill by making a response such as that required in instruction or the real world. (See also *authentic assessment.*) *Example:* A student is asked to construct a model of a catapult. The task requires the student to demonstrate such abilities as reading, following directions, and so forth.
Reflection	The process by which students and/or the teacher look back at what they have learned, discussing how it has helped them, where they might use it, and what they might concentrate on next. *Example:* After students have read a text with emphasis on certain strategies, they discuss with the teacher and peers how the strategies helped them construct meaning.
Rubric	A set of guidelines or acceptable responses for the completion of a task. *Example:* A rubric for assessing the writing quality of a story would include being able to identify the story elements (setting, character[s], problem, action, outcome) and a 4-point scale in which 4 is high, 3 is average, 2 is low, 1 is inadequate, and 0 indicates insufficient material.
Running record	A written record of a student's oral reading in which a blank sheet of paper rather than a copy of the actual text is used in coding. *Example:* A first-grade teacher has a student read aloud a previously read book, noting the correct and incorrect words.
Standard score	A score that tells how far an individual is from the average score (mean) on a test in terms of the standard deviation. Standard scores are most commonly used on standardized tests. *Example:* A student scores 60 on a test; the standard deviation is 5, and the average (mean) score is 55. This student is one standard deviation above average.
Standardized test	A test given under specified conditions allowing comparisons to be made; a set of norms or average scores are given to allow comparisons. *Examples: Metropolitan Achievement Tests; Iowa Test of Basic Skills*

Over the years, criticisms have been leveled at **standardized tests.** Although written a number of years ago (Tyler & White in Farr and Carey, 1986, p. 11), the following are still legitimate concerns:

- Tests do not reflect the full range of student cultural backgrounds and thus lead to decisions that are often unfair to minority students.
- Standardized tests have only limited value for holding teachers, schools, and school systems accountable for the quality of education.
- Tests impose a limiting effect on classroom teaching.
- Tests are too narrow in scope to provide fair evaluation of new approaches to teaching.

Current assessment is coming closer to reflecting current knowledge about literacy learning and effective literacy instruction. Efforts are being made to address the following:

- making sure assessment focuses on the standards being covered,
- not just testing isolated skills,
- using full-length authentic texts to construct meaning,
- accounting for prior knowledge,
- including samples of student work, and
- incorporating student self-assessment.

We must be able to demonstrate that our programs are successfully helping students develop literacy, especially as we try new instructional techniques. Failure to show that programs are working could result in a return to practices that are not as effective.

Principles to Guide Effective Assessment

As you begin to plan for informal and formal assessment in your classroom, you should consider the following eight principles. These ideas and principles are as valid today as ever. Numerous researchers and educators have developed guidelines for comprehensive literacy assessment (Farr & Tone, 1994; Valencia, 1990a, 1990b; Valencia, Hiebert, & Afflerbach, 1994). The following principles are based in part on their ideas and on our personal interpretations of this research while working with teachers.

1. *Assessment should be an ongoing process.* Literacy assessment is not a test given at the end of a lesson or unit of study, separate from the ongoing daily activities of instruction. Instead, assessment takes place every time a student reads, writes, speaks, listens, or views something.
2. *Effective assessment is an integral part of instruction.* The best forms of assessment are the routine daily activities of instruction, which tell us exactly how students are performing. By comparing the work of each student over time,

Helping Teachers Understand Assessment

Dealing with teachers and assessment is probably the most challenging part of my job. My charge is to be sure teachers are using the information they have about student performance to make informed educational decisions about placement in materials for guided readings and other interventions.

Miami-Dade County Public Schools (M-DCPS) divides assessment into three categories: Screening/Diagnostic, Progress Monitoring, and Outcome. I work with all elementary teachers to help them understand each category and how it relates to instructional procedures. Emphasis is given to baseline data (collected from the previous year's outcome measures) as a starting point. Students who fall below standard or are judged as being at "high risk" of failure are tracked for immediate, intensive intervention based on these data as well as a diagnostic measure given so that instruction can be targeted. A true challenge is to get teachers to use the progress monitoring instruments as teaching tools and not just a way to collect and report information. I try to help teachers see these assessments as valuable parts of the instructional-assessment cycle.

M-DCPS is committed to data-driven decision making and has provided classroom teachers, reading leaders, and administrators with electronic templates that manage both individual student data and whole-class data. These templates allow us to view data in a way that promotes analysis and discussion. My job is helping teachers look at these vast amounts of data and look for trends in their classrooms and students who need more support through intervention.

Helping teachers see trends involves looking at whole-class data. We work collaboratively and ask, "What does this mean? How should this information be affecting instruction?" If teachers are unable to make connections, I work individually to help them see the holes that exist in achievement and hope they make the connection that a lack of instruction usually leads to a drop in achievement. Looking at these holes and then looking at what needs to happen in the classroom that is now missing is the key to helping teachers use this data effectively.

Teachers are now seeing the power of informed teaching based on a collection and analysis of data. My goal is for teachers to see that assessment is not done just for the state or district but rather for the benefit of teachers and ultimately their students.

—*Michael D. Robinson, Curriculum Support Specialist*
Miami-Dade County Public School
Division of Language Arts/Reading
Miami, Florida

we can determine patterns of growth. When a student writes a story about her trip to visit friends, you can assess her ability to organize ideas, express herself, and use the various conventions of language. Overall, you get a picture of how effectively she constructs meaning through writing. We have heard many teachers say, "There was no reason to give that test. I already knew what my kids could do from their daily activities." In other words, we must learn to trust our judgments as we make them from evidence gathered during instruction.

3. *Assessment must be authentic, reflecting "real" reading and writing.* For years, we have asked teachers, "If you want to know how well children read and write, what do you need to have them do?" They all say the same thing: "Have them read and write." For example, when a student reads Roald Dahl's book *Esio Trot* (1990) and writes a response to it, you can assess his or her ability to construct meaning. Assessment must reflect and honor the "wholeness" of language (Harp, 1991). Some effective readers and writers don't do well on a test of an isolated piece of the process.

4. *Assessment should be a collaborative, reflective process.* It is not something the teacher does to the students. We know learning is a collaborative process; we learn alongside and with our students and our peers (Collins, Brown, & Newman, 1987). If this is true for learning, it is also true for assessment. As students collaborate with their teacher on assessment, they reflect and ask themselves, "How have I done?" "What can I do to improve?" "How can I use what I have learned?" Thus, students should help you assess and evaluate their own progress in literacy. One of us learned this the hard way many years ago from a fifth-grade student named Paul. Paul was an excellent student. He could read and critically discuss anything put in his hands. However, he wasn't a good oral reader. Even when I placed him in a lower-level book group, he still couldn't read aloud. Finally, I asked Paul what he thought his problem was. He was not only very intelligent but also very outspoken. He said, "I don't have a problem. When are you going to learn that I don't like to read out loud?" Needless to say, I learned pretty fast! It turned out that Paul could construct meaning better than any other fifth grader I had that year.

   Students should sometimes help select *what* they want evaluated. This joint effort should also involve parents and other caregivers (Dillon, 1990). When students, teacher, and families collaborate on evaluation, the responsibility is shared, as it should be.

5. *Effective assessment is multidimensional.* Quality assessment should be based on several different tasks, such as samples of writing, student retellings, records of independent reading, self-evaluations, and checklists. Although these techniques are informal, we must still know that they are trustworthy (Valencia, 1990a); looking at multiple tasks can show a consistent pattern of performance. Cambourne and Turbill (1990) argue that data generated from multiple sources using teacher observations and judgments are just as trustworthy and "scientific" as those generated by what have been called "measurement-based" approaches to assessment. Trust your own intuition based on your knowledge and observations about students.

6. *Assessment should be developmentally and culturally appropriate.* Children develop literacy by "trying out" their reading and writing and making approximations. Therefore, tests or procedures that require absolute mastery at a given level or complete mastery of a given set of words before moving to a new book are *completely contrary* to how we know children learn. We must select assessment tasks that respect children's developmental levels of learning.

   At the same time, we must consider the cultural diversity of our classrooms. Children from different cultures have not only different language bases but also different patterns and styles of learning (Au, 1993; Garcia, 1994). We must take these into consideration as we plan assessment procedures.

7. ***Effective assessment identifies students' strengths.*** Children learn to construct meaning by doing what they already know how to do and by getting support in gaining new strategies and techniques. Effective assessment therefore must help us identify what students do well. We should not just test to learn about weaknesses; this is contrary to how students acquire language and contrary to how they learn to construct meaning.

8. ***Assessment must be based on what we know about how students learn to read and write.*** This entire text has focused on how students learn to read and write and construct meaning. We know the two processes are similar but different. We also know they develop together and produce benefits that are attainable by neither one alone (Tierney & Shanahan, 1991). And we know that reading and writing are both constructive processes. As we plan assessment tasks, we must keep this knowledge in mind, incorporating new knowledge as it becomes available.

In the remainder of this chapter, we focus on ideas and techniques for applying these eight principles to the comprehensive balanced literacy classroom.

Using Standards to Guide Assessment

Assessment must be based on goals (Armbruster & Osborn, 2003). What do we want students to do? How will we know if they are learning to do it? This simple view of assessment has not changed over the years. What has changed is that school systems now have standards or benchmarks that dictate exactly what students should do, as well as how to know if they are learning to do it. Each teacher must become familiar with these literacy standards and use them to guide assessment. We have shown throughout this text that though the wording of standards varies from one state to another, the essence is the same.

For a detailed look at how to use standards and benchmarks to plan instruction, see Cooper and Kiger (2008) listed in the "For Additional Reading" section at the end of the chapter.

It is likely that most activity in your classroom can be linked to one or more literacy standards. In fact, the routine daily activities of reading and writing also serve as assessment activities. Although this ongoing, daily assessment may not be sufficient to demonstrate that your students have reached the mandated standards, the standards can guide your daily assessment decisions. Ongoing, daily assessment helps us determine whether students are making adequate yearly progress or, for struggling readers, more than adequate yearly progress.

Organizing Assessment Information for Instructional Use

The primary reason for assessing student literacy is to help you plan the instructional activities and experiences that will help students continue to grow. Instruction *is* assessment; in other words, every instructional activity is an assessment activity. By looking at how students perform during instruction, you get a sense of what they are learning and using in terms of reading, writing, speaking, listening, thinking, and viewing. In fact, your observations during instruction may be your best assessment tools.

Three guiding principles will help you use assessment information for instructional purposes:

1. *Organize.* For the information to be helpful in planning instruction, it must be organized. It doesn't matter how you organize it. It only matters that you *do organize it*.
2. *Review.* You must review the information on a regular basis—daily or weekly. This means that you are constantly looking at how students are performing and deciding what needs to happen next. This is what Cooper and Kiger (2008) call assessment-based literacy instruction.
3. *Update.* Updating information is part of the reviewing process. As you continuously review how students are performing, you should also add new information and revise what you have. We may think we will remember what students have done, but it is easy to forget, especially when dealing with large numbers of students.

We present four alternatives for organizing assessment information: portfolios, computers, file cards or binders, and folders. The next section discusses several assessment techniques. You should select the organizational procedure and techniques that will work best for you.

Four Alternatives for Organizing Assessment Information

1. **Some schools use the portfolio concept for organizing all assessment data.** Portfolios are collections of an individual student's work gathered over time, with the primary purpose of presenting a picture of performance and progress. A master version of the portfolio may be passed on each year from teacher to teacher. Individual teachers may keep more specific daily instructional information in one of the other forms described in the following sections.

2. **Computers offer other ways to organize information for quick retrieval and use.** You will want to learn about the options available in your school or district. You may also devise your own ways to organize information for your own instructional use.

3. **File cards or binders help some teachers keep records of students' performance.** The teacher can easily refer to these on a daily basis.

4. **Teachers have used folders of work for years to keep track of how each student is performing.** This is much like using a portfolio. Like the portfolio, this technique must have an organizational structure to be effective. This is usually done using some type of checklist.

Assessment Techniques

Assessment is a dynamic and interactive process that is an integral part of instruction. You can use many different assessment techniques. Some blend naturally into instruction; others are a somewhat more formal way to assess student progress.

The overall goal of literacy learning is meaning construction, and the techniques we suggest deal with the process as a whole or with an important aspect of the process. Most can be used on the basis of the information given here; references are given for those that require more study. As you read about these techniques, think about those that will be most helpful to you in your classroom and those you need to learn more about. *You do not need to use them all.*

Observation

Observation is the process of observing students as they perform authentic literacy tasks or looking at the results of those tasks. It is a powerful and reliable part of your assessment and evaluation process. Observations must be based on what you know about how children learn to read and write. Therefore, you need to understand what responses are expected and typical, and what responses might indicate a need for more or different support. For example, the first grader who writes a sentence about his *dg* is not misspelling the word *dog;* rather, he is making an approximation that shows he is learning the spelling pattern in the word *dog*. This student would benefit from shared reading experiences with natural, repetitive language and words following the type of spelling pattern in the word *dog*, as well as opportunities to continue writing his own stories.

As a teacher, you must develop the habit of always looking, thinking, and asking, "What does this mean?" Opportunities to observe students are unlimited and include the following:

- Listening to a student read aloud
- Watching students give a play
- Reading and noting how a student has written a response to a story
- Analyzing a student's written report
- Listening to and studying what students say as they give oral reports
- Listening to conversation between two students waiting in line for lunch

Keep in mind that one observation is not sufficient: you must look at several observations over time, watching for patterns of performance. From these patterns, you can assess and evaluate students' ability to construct meaning. As you gain more experience, you will become more and more comfortable. You will soon realize that instruction and assessment are really one ongoing process.

Many techniques can be combined with observation, or used in addition to observation to help you become an effective observer. Figure 11.1 shows some sample

FIGURE 11.1 **Observation Notes from Mrs. Ehrman's Third-Grade Class**

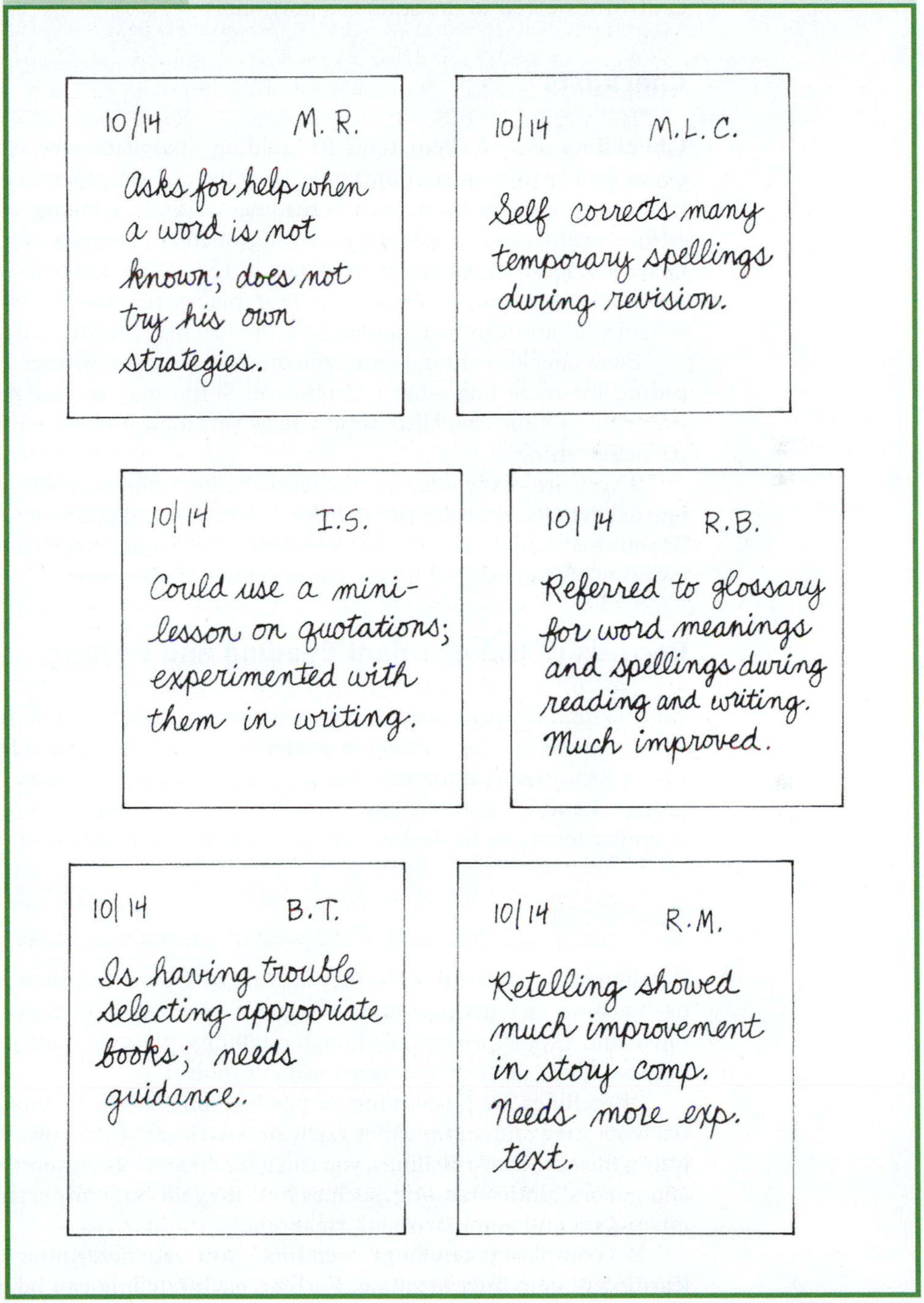

10/14   M. R.

Asks for help when a word is not known; does not try his own strategies.

10/14   M.L.C.

Self corrects many temporary spellings during revision.

10/14   I.S.

Could use a mini-lesson on quotations; experimented with them in writing.

10/14   R.B.

Referred to glossary for word meanings and spellings during reading and writing. Much improved.

10/14   B.T.

Is having trouble selecting appropriate books; needs guidance.

10/14   R.M.

Retelling showed much improvement in story comp. Needs more exp. text.

observation notes made by Mrs. Ehrman in her third-grade class. She used sticky notes and put the student's initials and the date on each. The notes could then be easily transferred to the student's portfolio.

Checklists

Checklists are excellent tools for guiding observation of various aspects of students' ability to construct meaning. They may be developed in general areas related to meaning construction, such as reading, writing, speaking, listening, and viewing, or for specific aspects of literacy learning, such as concepts of print or story retelling. General checklists, such as that shown in Figure 11.2, may be placed in the literacy portfolio. The sample shown has four places to record observations during the school year and can be completed by the teacher, the student, or both.

Each checklist should name the qualities or traits you are looking for and a procedure for recording what you observe. Some may be designed to record growth over time. Other checklists simply help you look for the presence or absence of a particular thing.

There are many sources of checklists, including curriculum guides, textbooks, journal articles, and the Internet. You can take an existing checklist and adapt it to fit your needs, or you can construct your own. Some checklists can be developed for group observations and others for individual observations.

Records of Independent Reading and Writing

An essential aspect of meaning construction is self-selected, independent reading and writing. Records may be kept in student journals or learning logs, but it is useful to have a form that summarizes this information in the student's literacy portfolio. Figures 11.3 and 11.4 present two forms students can use to record independent reading. A similar form can be devised for summarizing the progress of writing projects.

Retellings

Retellings are powerful tools; they are one of the most authentic techniques you can use for both instructional and assessment purposes and can be used with both narrative and expository text. Although retellings integrate instruction and assessment, here we focus on their use as assessment tools.

"Retellings are postreading or postlistening recalls in which readers or listeners tell what they remember either orally or in writing" (Morrow, 1989b, p. 40). By analyzing the students' retellings, you can gain insights into their thinking, organization, and general understanding, such as how they identify important information, make inferences, and summarize information.

By comparing retellings over time, you can determine students' progress in learning to construct meaning. Further, each retelling can be used diagnostically to help you develop support activities.

FIGURE 11.2   **Checklist for Meaning Construction**

Construction of Meaning

Name _____

Date	1	2	3	4
Retells stories and text accurately				
Gives responses to stories and text that show understanding				
Conveys meaning through written stories and reports				
Conveys meaning through spoken language				
Comments:				

CODE:
+ = very effectively
∨ = effectively
− = needs improvement
NO = Not Observed

FIGURE 11.3   **Independent Reading Record**

Name _____

Date Completed	Title and Author	Comments

The following guidelines for using retelling as an assessment tool are based on Morrow (1989b), and on our own experiences in working with children and teachers.

Guidelines for Using Retellings for Assessment

Selecting the Text Select the story or informational text that students are to read, or have students make the selection. If you are comparing retellings over time, use the same type of texts each time; for example, compare narrative with narrative and expository with expository. Be sure the conceptual difficulty is not drastically different from one assessment to the next. In other words, don't compare retellings from a simple text such as *Cranberries* (Jaspersohn, 1991) with a more complex text such as *Franklin Delano Roosevelt* (Freedman, 1990).

Preparing the Text Read the text yourself. With stories, identify the setting (place and time if important), characters, problem, action (events leading to outcome), and outcome or resolution. For informational texts, identify the topic, purpose, and main ideas. List this information on a sheet of paper.

Reading and Retelling the Text Have the student read the text silently. (If you are using this as a listening experience, read the text to the students.) This should be treated as a routine instructional activity. Immediately following the reading, ask the student to retell the story or text. Do not prompt initial retellings, except for generic prompts such as, "Tell me more," or, "Keep going; you're doing a nice job."

As students give their retellings, check off the ideas given on the paper you prepared earlier. After they have completed their unprompted retellings, you may then prompt them with questions about specific parts that they did not include.

FIGURE 11.4 **Independent Reading Record**

INDEPENDENT READING RECORD

BOOKS THAT CARRY ME AWAY

Summarizing and Evaluating the Retelling Figures 11.5 and 11.6 present forms you can use for summarizing each student's retelling. Each retelling has a possible score of 10, and the guidelines for scoring each retelling are basically the same. One point is given for correct responses, and exceptions to this rule are given on the summary sheets. In scoring retellings, use your own judgment and your observations.

FIGURE 11.5   Retelling Summary Sheet for Narrative Text

Story Retelling Summary Sheet

Name _____   Date _____

Title _____

Student selected _____   Teacher selected _____

	Scores	
	Unprompted	*Prompted*

Setting:
   Begins with introduction (1 pt.)   _____   _____

   Gives time and place (1 pt.)   _____   _____

Characters:
   Names main character (1 pt.)   _____   _____

   Identifies other characters (1 pt.)   _____   _____

      Gives names _____
      Gives number _____
      Actual number _____
      Number given _____

Problem:
   Identifies primary story problem (1 pt.)   _____   _____

Action:
   Recalls major events (1 pt.)   _____   _____

Outcome:
   Identifies how problem was solved (1 pt.)   _____   _____

   Gives story ending (1 pt.)   _____   _____

Sequence:
   Retells story in order (2 pts. = correct;   _____   _____
   1 pt. = partial, 0 = no evidence of sequence)

                        TOTAL SCORE   _____   _____
                        (10 pts. possible)

Observations/comments:

Analysis:

Source: Adapted from L. M. Morrow, Using story retelling to develop comprehension, in K. D. Muth, ed., *Children's comprehension of text: Research into practice,* pp. 37–58. Copyright © 1989 International Reading Association. Used with permission.

FIGURE 11.6   Retelling Summary Sheet for Informational Text

Informational Text Retelling Summary Sheet

Name _____ Date _____

Title _____

Student selected _____ Teacher selected _____

	Scores	
	Unprompted	*Prompted*

Introduction:
   Identifies topic (1 pt.)   _____   _____

   Gives some purpose or focus (1 pt.)   _____   _____

Main Ideas:
        Number given _____
        Actual number _____
        (6 pts. = all correct; 4 pts. = 2/3 correct;
        2 pts. = 1/3 correct; 0 pts. = none correct)

Shows logical understanding of how ideas are
related; explains ideas   _____   _____
        (2 pts. = relates all ideas; 1 pt. = relates
        some ideas; 0 pts. = shows no relationship of ideas)

                                    TOTAL SCORE   _____   _____
                                    (10 pts. possible)

Observations/comments:

Analysis:

After scoring each retelling, examine it to determine whether the student understands the story or text, has ideas well organized, or has used various strategies. Then discuss and review the retelling with the student. This information will help you develop instructional experiences.

Responses to Literature

Responses to literature were discussed in Chapter 7.

The way a student responds to literature may help indicate how the student has constructed meaning. For example, the student who always says or writes, "I liked it," "It was funny," or, "The best part was _____," may not understand what was read, or perhaps has not learned to respond to literature and needs more support and prompting from the teacher. The student who gave the following response to *Where the Red Fern Grows* (Rawls, 1974) demonstrated in her journal that she had constructed appropriate meaning from this book:

> Billy's love for his dogs is like my love for my cat Prince. I had to work hard to get Prince. I love him so much. Billy learned how important love was. I did to. Everybody needs somebody to love.

As you encourage students to respond to literature, you will need some criteria for evaluating those responses. The following questions should be helpful:

1. Does the response show that the student knows the story line (narrative) or main ideas (expository) of the text?
2. Did the student simply retell the text or relate it to his or her own experiences?
3. Does the response show that the student is thinking clearly and logically?
4. Does the response show that the student is using any skills or strategies?

How would you evaluate the response given to *Where the Red Fern Grows* using these questions?

Teachers can encourage English Language Learners (ELLs) to respond in their first language. Aides, family members, or other bilingual students can read the response. Such first-language responses can be added to the students' portfolios (Freeman & Freeman, 2001).

Many teachers use a simple form, such as the one in Figure 11.7, to evaluate students' responses to literature. They then attach the evaluations to the response and place it in the portfolio.

Student Self-Evaluations

Student self-evaluations have been recommended as a vital part of assessing and evaluating meaning construction (Flood & Lapp, 1989; Tierney, Carter, & Desai, 1991). You can promote these evaluations by asking students to write in their journals about the progress they are making in reading and writing. Self-evaluation can be prompted by such questions as the following:

■ How do you feel you are doing in reading/writing?
■ What are your strengths in reading/writing?

FIGURE 11.7   Form for Evaluating Responses to Literature

Constructing Meaning Evaluation

Name _____ Date _____

Title _____

Circle one:

+	√	0
Shows thorough understanding	Shows some understanding	Needs support in developing understanding

Comments:

- What do you enjoy the most about reading/writing?
- What do you feel you need to do to improve your reading/writing?

Another way to encourage students to evaluate their construction of meaning is by giving them a form such as the one in Figure 11.8 to help them evaluate their understanding of what they read. The form can be used periodically and placed in the literacy portfolio. Similar types of self-evaluation forms may also be completed for writing.

Self-evaluation helps students learn to monitor their own reading and writing. A checklist such as the one in Figure 11.9 can be used to evaluate the use of various strategies. As always, you should model the process before expecting students to do it on their own. This type of checklist can be written to include only those strategies students have learned.

Process Interviews

Learning about students' metacognition, or how they "think about their reading," will help you help them learn to construct meaning. To assess students' thinking about their reading, Paratore and Indrisano (1987) developed a procedure known as

FIGURE 11.8   Form for Self-Evaluation of Reading

Self-Evaluation of Reading

Name_____ Date_____

Book read_____

Mark the scale below:

```
├─────────────────────┼─────────────────────┼─────────────────────┤
```

I feel that   I dont
I thoroughly   feel that
understood   I understood
this book.   this book.

Why I marked the scale as I did:

_____

_____

_____

_____

the **process interview,** sometimes called a *reading interview.* It consists of the following seven questions:

1. *How do you choose something to read?*
2. *How do you get ready to read?*
3. *When you come to a word you cant read, what do you do?*
4. *When you have a question you can't answer, what do you do?*
5. *What do you do to help remember what you've read?*
6. *How do you check your reading?*
7. *If a young child asked you how to read, what would you tell him or her to do?*
   (Paratore & Indrisano, 1987, p. 782)

After a student orally answers the questions and you record the responses, you analyze them to determine what type of support the student needs. For example, a student who answers question 6 even after prompting by saying that she "looks for pictures" does not have good monitoring strategies. It might be helpful to teach this student to use a strategy such as stop and think, focusing on rereading, reading ahead, and other techniques for monitoring reading.

A process interview for writing would follow a pattern similar to that used for reading. Since this is an informal procedure, questions for either interview can be rephrased or changed to ensure that students understand them. Interviews of this type can be conducted with students of all ages as long as the questions are worded appropriately.

| FIGURE 11.9 | **Student Self-Monitoring Checklist** |

THINKING ABOUT MY READING

HOW DID I DO?

BEFORE READING

- Did I preview the text?
- Did I make predictions?

DURING READING

- Did I STOP AND THINK about what I was reading?
- Did I change my predictions?

AFTER READING

- Did I think back about my predictions?
- Did I summarize in my head?

To improve my reading, I need to: _____
_____
_____

Teacher-Selected Reading Samples

Materials used for assessment should be books and texts that students read every day. Select whatever piece of text you want students to read, and introduce the material as you would for a literacy lesson. Have students read the text silently, and then ask them to complete a task appropriate to their ability level that will show you how effectively they have constructed meaning. These tasks could include:

- Completing a story map
- Listing the most important or main ideas
- Writing a summary (this should be reserved for upper elementary and middle school)

- Answering questions that focus on the story elements
- Answering questions that draw out the main ideas

All except the summary can be scored by the percentage of items correct. The summary has to be scored more holistically by giving it a rating such as the following:

1 = All major ideas included
2 = Most major ideas included
3 = Many major ideas missing

Samples of reading can be taken over time, and compared to determine student progress.

Fluency Checks and Application of Decoding Skills

See Chapter 2 for a complete discussion of fluency.

Teacher-selected or student-selected samples may be chosen for oral reading fluency checks. Students may practice their passages or they may read them without practice which is often referred to as a **"cold read."** A "cold read" allows the teacher to see how well a student actually applies skills and strategies in new text. Students may read the passages aloud into a tape recorder or to the teacher. Usually they are timed for one minute. They are evaluated using the appropriate norms (Hasbrouck & Tindall, 2006). The teacher does **fluency checks** at regular intervals and compares them to show student development in decoding and growth in fluency. This procedure allows a teacher to compare a student's performances over time. (The fluency check differs from miscue analysis, which is discussed later in this chapter, because in miscue analysis, students do not prepare their passages.)

You can analyze students' ability to decode words by looking at the patterns of responses on these taped passages. Many teachers make the tape recordings a part of the students' portfolios, so students can compare passages and determine their own growth in decoding; the tapes can also be used during conferences to help families see the progress their children are making. Figure 11.10 shows a passage a second grader read from *Fix-It* (McPhail, 1984). The teacher's markings and notes show what the student read and how the teacher judged the student's decoding abilities.

FIGURE 11.10 **Second-Grader's Marked Oral Passage**

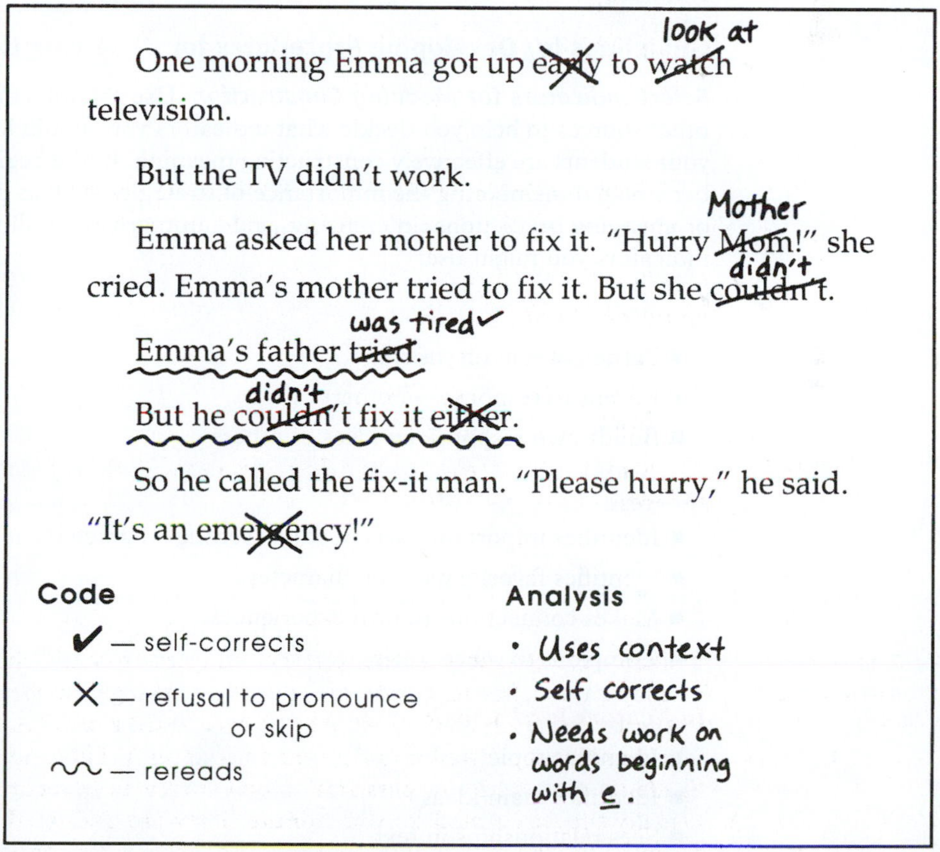

One morning Emma got up ~~early~~ to ~~watch~~ *look at* television.

But the TV didn't work.

Emma asked her mother to fix it. "Hurry ~~Mom~~ *Mother*!" she cried. Emma's mother tried to fix it. But she ~~couldn't~~ *didn't*.

Emma's father ~~tried~~ *was tired* ✔.

But he ~~couldn't~~ *didn't* fix it ~~either~~.

So he called the fix-it man. "Please hurry," he said. "It's an eme~~r~~gency!"

Code

✔ — self-corrects

✗ — refusal to pronounce or skip

∿ — rereads

Analysis

• Uses context
• Self corrects
• Needs work on words beginning with <u>e</u>.

Literature Groups

See Chapter 7 for a discussion of using literature groups as a response.

The literature group presents a good opportunity to observe students' ability to construct meaning and react personally in an authentic literacy experience. Wood's (1988) procedure for assessing and evaluating comprehension during a group discussion involves looking at nine behaviors related to meaning construction as students discuss what they have read: making predictions, participating in discussion, answering questions on a variety of levels, determining word meaning through context, reading smoothly and fluently, retelling selections in own words, comprehending after silent reading, reading between the lines, and having a broad background knowledge. A grid is used to record students' responses using a simple code: Often = +, Sometimes = S, Seldom = −, and Not Observed = N.

Using the literature group to assess and evaluate meaning construction may work best when teachers develop (or adapt from some other source) their own specific procedures and indicators. The following general guidelines should help you accomplish this purpose.

Guidelines for Developing Procedures for Observing Literature Groups

Select Indicators for Meaning Construction Use the information in this text and other sources to help you decide what indicators you should look for to tell you that your students are effectively constructing meaning. In the beginning, keep the number small, remembering the importance of strategies such as predicting, confirming or changing predictions, inferencing, and summarizing. Following are examples of indicators you might use:

General Indicators

- Participates in discussion
- Listens to responses of others
- Builds own response on ideas of others

Indicators for Narrative Texts

- Identifies important parts of story (setting, characters, and so forth)
- Identifies favorite parts or characters
- Makes connections to own experiences
- Compares to other stories

Indicators for Expository Texts

- Identifies topic
- Identifies main ideas
- Sees relationships in text
- Shows signs of using knowledge gained
- Connects information to own life or information from another source

FIGURE 11.11   **Grid for Observing Construction of Meaning During a literature Discussion Group**

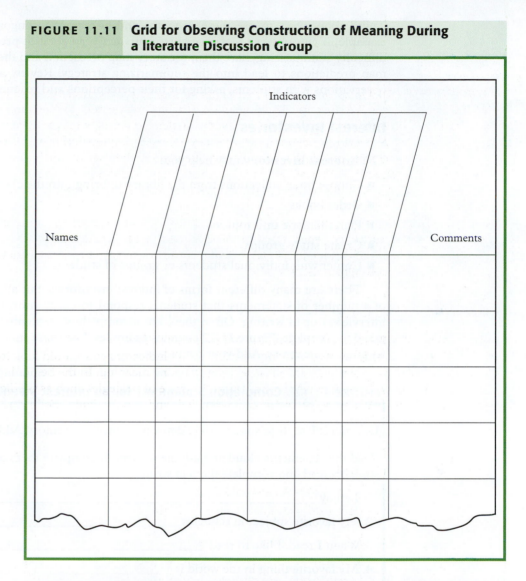

Develop a Procedure for Recording Information   You can use a simple grid such as the one in Figure 11.11 with a code similar to the one developed by Wood (1988), discussed earlier. This grid contains a space for comments or observations.

Designate a Time for Observation   Select a time to assess (it is not necessary to observe every literature group). You may either participate in the discussion or sit off to the side to observe. Teachers who become accustomed to this procedure report that they are always observing even when they are participating. This activity becomes a natural part of teaching.

Review the Data for Yourself and with Students   After you have completed your observation, study the data you have collected to identify your students' strengths.

Think about ways to use these strengths and also provide ongoing support. For example, if you observe that several students are very good at predicting but have difficulty summarizing, have them use story map prediction and then use their story map predictions to lead into the summarizing strategy. Review and discuss your observations with students, asking for their perceptions and reactions.

Interest Inventories

The **interest inventory** may help you:

- Choose book collections from the library to bring into the classroom
- Order books
- Plan thematic unit topics
- Create study groups
- Confer with individual students or groups of students

There are many different forms of interest inventories, but all generally consist of a number of statements that students respond to orally (during conferences or interviews) or in writing. Often these are incomplete statements that students are asked to complete; Figure 11.12 contains examples. Use these statements to develop an interest inventory. Add your own ideas.

FIGURE 11.12 **Completion Statements for an Interest Inventory**

Directions: Use these statements to develop an interest inventory. Add your own ideas.

Read the statements aloud and ask the student to complete them orally or have students read and complete them in writing.

1. I enjoy _____.
2. My favorite subject in school is _____.
3. When I read, I like to read _____.
4. My favorite thing in the world is _____.
5. I like to spend time _____.
6. My hobbies are _____.
7. I like to write about _____.
8. When I finish school, I want to be _____.
9. My favorite television shows are _____.
10. I would like to learn more about _____.
11. I would like to spend more time in school _____.

Scoring Writing Using Rubrics

Holistic scoring is a widely used procedure to assess and evaluate a student's ability to construct meaning through writing. It involves looking at a piece of writing in its entirety and assigning it a score, using a set of guidelines called a **rubric.** This process is generally used on assigned writing tasks rather than on self-initiated writing or written responses to literature. Holistic scoring assumes that all aspects of writing are related and must be viewed in their entirety.

When using the holistic procedure, the teacher reads the piece of writing and assigns it a score from 0 to 4. Although a detailed discussion of holistic scoring is beyond the scope of this text, the following scale (or rubric) from Millett (1986) may give you a sense of how this procedure is used:

0   *Papers in this category cannot be scored for one reason or another. Papers that are blank, that respond to an assignment different from the one given, that merely comment on the assignment ("This topic is silly"), that only copy or rephrase the assignment, or that are illegible would all be included in this category.*

1   *Papers in this category attempt to deal with the assignment, but they fail to do so adequately. These papers are too general, abrupt, or refer to the assignment only indirectly.*

2   *Papers in this category respond to the task set up in the assignment, but they do so in a way that is sketchy, inconsistent, and incomplete. There are gaps or other problems in the organization. Vocabulary may be too general and the paper lacking in the detail necessary to convey the purpose clearly and exactly. The reader has a basic idea of what the writer is trying to say but has to make many inferences.*

3   *Papers in this category fulfill the requirements of the assignment although the reader might encounter a little confusion from time to time. The paper is generally well organized so that the reader does not need to make a lot of inferences. These papers include sufficient details so that the reader understands the writer's message.*

4   *Papers that merit this highest score are well organized, complete, and explicit. These papers include all of the strengths of the 3 category, but they are more clearly and consistently presented. The reader grasps the writer's message easily without having to make inferences. The writer uses a varied and exact vocabulary that enhances as well as clarifies the message. (pp. 51–52)*

See Chapter 8 about the 6 +1 TRAIT™ model linking writing instruction and assessment; the model provides rubrics that correspond to each trait. See the NWREL website for further information.

Miscue Analysis

Miscue analysis is a procedure that lets the teacher "get a window on the reading process" (Goodman, 1965). A **miscue** is an oral response that is different from the text being read. For example, if the text reads, "Billy rode his horse around the ranch," and a child reads, "Billy rode his pony around the ranch," this miscue shows that the child has constructed the appropriate meaning for this sentence, even though she didn't say the exact words. Sometimes miscues are referred to as *unexpected responses* or *errors*.

Many years ago, Goodman (1965) concluded from his research that by studying a student's miscues from an oral reading sample, the teacher could determine the cues and strategies the student was using or not using in constructing meaning. This procedure attempts to look at the process of reading holistically.

See Goodman in "For Additional Reading" for more on miscue analysis, or search the Internet.

On the basis of Goodman's research, the reading miscue inventory (Goodman & Burke, 1972) was developed. Although this analysis is normally reserved for students who are having difficulty constructing meaning, the classroom reading miscue assessment (CRMA), a simplified version of miscue analysis (Rhodes & Shanklin, 1990), can be used with all students in a classroom. The CRMA takes from 10 to 15 minutes per student. Rhodes and Shanklin (1990) indicate that it "helps teachers gather important instructional information by providing a framework for observing students' oral reading and their ability to construct meaning" (p. 254). All of the variations of miscue analysis require additional study on your part as a teacher.

Informal Reading Inventories

The **informal reading inventory (IRI)** consists of a series of samples of text organized in increasing difficulty; students individually read the texts orally or silently. By studying their oral reading patterns and their responses to comprehension questions, the teacher can get a picture of how they analyze words in context (Walpole & McKenna, 2006), how they construct meaning, and what their approximate levels of reading are. IRIs usually consist of four types:

1. *Teacher constructed,* using materials from which students will be reading
2. *Publisher constructed* to match series of texts to be used for reading instruction
3. *Generic IRIs,* using samples of a variety of types of texts
4. *Group IRIs* that have been adapted from the individual IRI concept; these are usually teacher made

For an explanation of the procedures for using IRIs, see Cooper and Kiger (2008), listed in "For Additional Reading."

A major advantage of IRIs was that actual reading was used as the basis for seeing how well students could read. Their ability to analyze words was determined by looking at how they carried out this process in context. Now many IRIs also incorporate some of the concepts of miscue analysis to the analysis of oral reading. As you learn to use this widely used procedure, keep the following three questions in mind:

1. Does the reading of samples or portions of text give you the same picture of students' ability to construct meaning that the reading of complete texts does?
2. Can you identify precise levels of text and determine students' reading levels using these passages?
3. Are the procedures used to administer, score, and interpret the IRI consistent with what we know about how children develop literacy?

These questions should help you to be a more critical (evaluative) user of the IRI. The value of IRIs is enhanced when miscue analysis is used to analyze oral reading or when the running record (see the next section) concept is applied to the IRI.

Video Case

Assessment in the Elementary Grades: Formal and Informal Literacy Assessment

Watch the video clip, study the artifacts in the case, and reflect on the following questions:

1. This Video Case illustrates two very different assessment strategies—running records and student portfolios. Discuss the positive aspects of both assessment strategies, and their limitations.

2. Reflect on your own beliefs about assessment. Which forms of assessment do you think are most accurate and effective in measuring student performance?

Running Records

Another procedure for analyzing a student's reading is the **running record** (Clay, 1985), which is similar to miscue analysis. In this procedure, students read complete texts or samples of text. By looking at the students' responses, you are able to see their strengths and weaknesses in using various reading strategies and cueing systems. Running records are an important part of the assessment and evaluation used in the Reading Recovery Program in New Zealand and the United States (Clay, 1985; Pinnell, Fried, & Estice, 1990). They are also very useful for any classroom with beginning literacy learners.

See Chapter 5 on beginning literacy.

Teachers in kindergarten through third grade should find this technique useful in determining students' progress as they develop what Clay (1982) calls a "self-extending system," or independence in using reading strategies; the technique may also be used with any students who are developing beginning reading strategies. The following guidelines should be helpful:

1. Choose or have the child choose a book (or selection) she or he has read previously. For longer books, use a sample containing at least one hundred words.
2. Have the child read aloud the text. As the child reads, make a check mark on a blank sheet of paper for each word called correctly. (See Figure 11.13, which shows a sample running record taken by a first-grade teacher using the book *My Five Senses* [Miller, 1994].)
3. If the child makes miscues, mark as follows:

For a detailed discussion of running records, see Clay (1985), listed in the "For Additional Reading" section.

   ■ *Misreads word:* Write the word with the error above it (see Figure 11.13, [p. 2]).
   ■ *Omits word:* Write the word and circle it (p. 4).
   ■ *Self-corrects:* Write the word with SC above it (p. 2).
   ■ *Teacher tells word:* Write the word with T above it (p. 19).

4. To score, use the following formula:

$$\frac{\text{Total Words Read Correctly*}}{\text{Number of Words in Book/Sample}} \times 100 = \underline{\qquad}\%$$

   * Self-corrections are correct

5. Ninety percent accuracy or higher is considered good progress.
6. Look at the student's miscues to determine strategies used and those not used.

FIGURE 11.13 **Running Record Summary Sheet**

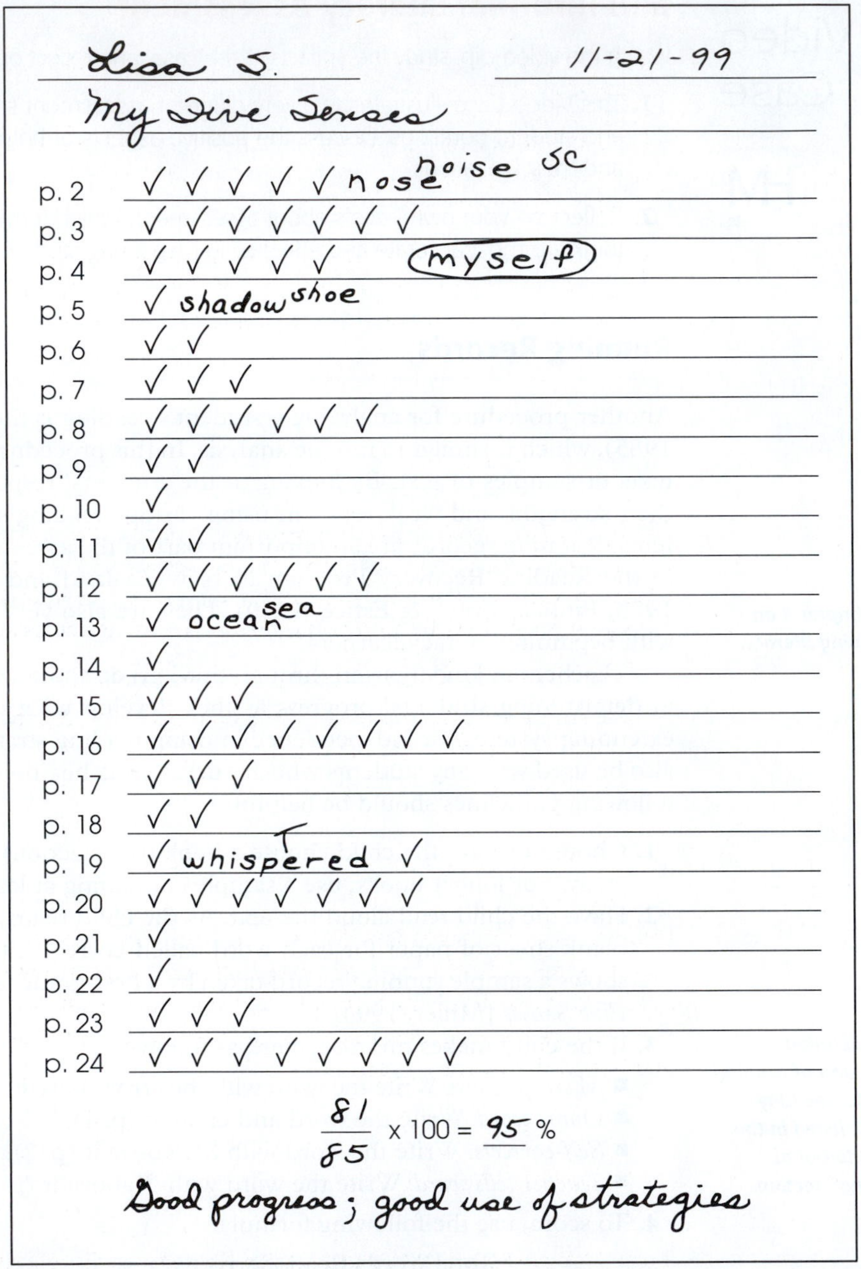

Lisa S.   11-21-99

My Five Senses

p. 2   ✓ ✓ ✓ ✓ ✓ nose^{noise} SC

p. 3   ✓ ✓ ✓ ✓ ✓ ✓

p. 4   ✓ ✓ ✓ ✓ ✓   (myself)

p. 5   ✓ shadow^{shoe}

p. 6   ✓ ✓

p. 7   ✓ ✓ ✓

p. 8   ✓ ✓ ✓ ✓ ✓ ✓

p. 9   ✓ ✓

p. 10 ✓

p. 11 ✓ ✓

p. 12 ✓ ✓ ✓ ✓ ✓

p. 13 ✓ ocean^{sea}

p. 14 ✓

p. 15 ✓ ✓ ✓

p. 16 ✓ ✓ ✓ ✓ ✓ ✓ ✓

p. 17 ✓ ✓ ✓

p. 18 ✓ ✓

p. 19 ✓ whispered ✓

p. 20 ✓ ✓ ✓ ✓ ✓ ✓ ✓

p. 21 ✓

p. 22 ✓

p. 23 ✓ ✓ ✓

p. 24 ✓ ✓ ✓ ✓ ✓ ✓ ✓ ✓

$$\frac{81}{85} \times 100 = \underline{95}\%$$

Good progress; good use of strategies

Video Case

Performance Assessment: Student Presentations in a High School English Class

Watch the video clip, study the artifacts in the case, and reflect on the following questions:

1. Based on watching this Video Case and reading the chapter, do you think that performance assessment is an effective way to measure student knowledge of a given topic? Explain your answer.

2. Develop your own grading rubric for assessing the student presentations within this Video Case. What are some of the elements that would be included in your grading rubric? Check the Case Artifacts for additional information that will help you create your rubric.

Performance Assessments

Performance assessments are tasks that require students to demonstrate their literacy knowledge and skills by making real-world responses. Performance assessments include tasks such as reports, posters, construction projects, and plays. Here are some guidelines to help you develop performance assessments:

- Identify the specific strategies, skills, and knowledge you want students to learn.
- Be sure the performance task selected actually requires the use of the strategies, skills, and knowledge identified.
- Develop a rubric for evaluating the task.

Assessment Procedures Accompanying Published Materials

Publishers of basal readers produce a variety of tests to accompany their materials and most include suggestions and procedures for authentic assessment and evaluation. If you use a published resource, remember what you have learned about effective literacy learning and assessment and select only those procedures that fit your needs and the needs of your students.

Making Decisions from Assessment Data

Table 11.2 summarizes the assessment techniques discussed in the previous section; it can serve as a reference guide for your use. Each technique can be used in the comprehensive balanced literacy classroom and reflects what we know about literacy learning and assessment at this time. As mentioned earlier, *no classroom needs all of these techniques all of the time*. You must become a selective user of the various techniques.

TABLE 11.2	Reference Guide to Assessment Techniques	
Technique	**Purpose**	**Comments**
Observation (p. 466)	Watch students' performance in authentic learning situations	An essential procedure for good classroom assessment and evaluation
Checklists (p. 468)	Guide observations	May be used to guide observations in many areas related to literacy learning
Records of independent reading and writing (p. 468)	Keep track of independent reading and writing	Should be used at all levels; gives insights about students' attitudes and habits
Retellings (p. 468)	Assess comprehension	One of the best procedures to assess construction of meaning
Responses to literature (p. 473)	Assess comprehension, levels of thinking, and use of strategies	Shows how students use what they have read and integrate ideas into their own experiences
Student self-evaluations (p. 474)	Determine students' perceptions of their own reading and writing	Helps students take ownership of learning
Process interviews (p. 475)	Gain insight into students' metacognition processes	Individual procedure that should be used selectively
Teacher-selected reading samples (p. 477)	Assess meaning construction Assess decoding, if done orally	Informal procedure; may be collected and compared over time
Fluency checks and application of decoding skills (p. 478)	Check decoding	Checks application of decoding in context
Literature groups (p. 480)	Assess meaning construction	Integrates instruction and assessment
Interest inventories (p. 482)	Determine students' interests	Provides a basis for planning learning activities
Scoring writing using rubrics (p. 483)	Evaluate meaning construction through writing	Provides a way of judging writing by looking at the entire piece
Miscue analysis (p. 483)	Assess decoding and use of strategies	Requires detailed training (see "For Additional Reading")
Informal reading inventories (p. 484)	Assess meaning construction and decoding	Requires detailed training (see "For Additional Reading"); use judiciously
Running records (p. 485)	Assess use of decoding strategies	Requires detailed training (see "For Additional Reading")
Performance assessments (p. 487)	Assess application of all strategies, skills, and knowledge	Makes assessment an integral part of instruction
Assessment procedures accompanying published materials (p. 487)	Varies according to publisher	Should be used selectively

Consider the following points as you decide which techniques to use:

The eight principles were explained in detail earlier in this chapter.

- ■ *How children develop literacy:* This is paramount to everything we have discussed in this text. Any assessment technique used should be in line with what we know about how children learn and develop literacy.

- ■ *Principles for effective assessment:* Continuously refer to these eight principles and ask yourself whether the techniques you are using are consistent with them.

- ■ *Trust your judgment:* Give a technique several trials before discarding it. Then if you still think it inappropriate, consider an alternative.

- ■ *Start small:* Select one or two techniques to use, and try them out. Add others if necessary.

- ■ *Evaluate techniques:* Ask yourself whether the techniques you use are assessing what you want to assess. *If they don't inform instruction and help you and your students improve literacy learning, they shouldn't be used.* Your colleagues may help you find alternatives.

Use assessment information gathered from students' literacy activities to make decisions about instruction for and with your students. The following scenarios illustrate how this works.

Possible Scenarios

- ■ As you observe a group of six students reading a little version of a big book, you notice that four of them have not developed fluency with the text. Therefore, you decide to reread the big book, using sentence strips and word cards to reconstruct the book in the pocket chart. You will also have children add words to the word wall.

- ■ During Writing Workshop, many students are still having trouble writing persuasive paragraphs. Therefore, tomorrow you will conduct a minilesson on persuasive writing using the shared writing technique. For those who need it, this will be followed by collaborative or cooperative writing to provide continued scaffolding.

- ■ After seven students retell a story they have read, you note that all have good understanding of story elements and concepts. You decide they are ready for more challenging chapter books.

The use of assessment and evaluation data as described in the preceding examples shows how assessment and instruction truly go hand in hand.

What to Do About Grading

The issue of grading continues to frustrate many teachers. Nearly all schools continue to give grades, which may or may not be a good match for the assessment plan they have implemented. Averages of numerical grades from worksheets, workbooks, and tests don't reflect what the students are doing in the classroom. So, many

Video
Case

Grading: Strategies and Approaches

Watch the video clip, study the artifacts in the case, and reflect on the following questions:

1. Do you agree with Mr. Turner's advice about developing your own personal grading system?

2. Critique Mr. Turner's grading policy. What are the pros and cons of his grading policy—from both the teacher and student perspective?

schools are rethinking their report card system. If letter grades must be given in a comprehensive balanced literacy classroom, evaluation must be viewed as being more subjective. Therefore, here are some factors to consider.

First, written descriptions (or rubrics) for each letter grade should be developed that vary by grade level and school and are based on the overall school objectives. The descriptions could include some of the benchmarks or standards discussed earlier. For example, an A at grade 3 might read as follows: "A = Reads many self-selected books with understanding. Is able to compare books and draw conclusions. Shows a thorough understanding of what has been read." These letter descriptions would guide the assessment.

Second, a rating scale might be used to evaluate written and oral responses to literature. For example, "A = Response indicates *thorough* understanding of what was read; B = Response shows some understanding of what was read"; and so forth.

Third, students should participate in their own grading. After discussing your grading criteria with them, you might ask them to determine their own grades and place their grades in their portfolios with written justification.

Use the principles for assessment discussed earlier in this chapter, along with your criteria for grading, to make this difficult task easier.

Assessment and Evaluation in the Comprehensive Literacy Classroom: Key Points

To review the Key Points, see the ACE practice tests at the HM TeacherPrepSPACE Student Website.

■ Eight principles for effective assessment were suggested:

1. Assessment should be an ongoing process.

2. Effective assessment is an integral part of instruction.

3. Assessment must be authentic, reflecting "real" reading and writing.

4. Assessment should be a collaborative, reflective process.

5. Effective assessment is multidimensional.

6. Assessment should be developmentally and culturally appropriate.

7. Effective assessment identifies students' strengths.

8. Assessment must be based on what we know about how students learn to read and write.

■ Standards can guide assessment.

■ Assessment information must be organized to be useful.

■ Assessment techniques should be used selectively.

■ Assessment should inform instruction.

How Do I Teach?

Assessment Techniques in This Chapter

The assessment techniques presented in this chapter are summarized in Table 11.2 on page 488.

Video Cases in This Chapter

■ **Assessment in the Elementary Grades: Formal and Informal Literacy Assessment**
■ **Performance Assessment: Student Presentations in a High School English Class**
■ **Grading: Strategies and Approaches**

For Additional Reading

Assaf, L. (2006). One reading specialist's response to high-stakes testing pressures. *The Reading Teacher, 60*(2), 158–167.

Clay, M. M. (1985). *The early detection of reading difficulties* (3rd ed.). Auckland, New Zealand: Heinemann.

Cobb, C. (2003/2004). Effective instruction begins with purposeful assessments. *The Reading Teacher, 57*(4), 386–388.

Cooper, J. D., & Kiger, N. D. (2008). *Literacy assessment: Helping teachers plan instruction* (3rd ed.). Boston: Houghton Mifflin.

Dewitz, P., & Dewitz, P. K. (2003). They can read the words, but they can't understand: Refining comprehension assessment. *The Reading Teacher, 56*(5), 422–435.

Dickinson, D. K., McCabe, A., & Sprague, K. (2003). Teacher Rating of Oral Language and Literacy (TROLL): Individualizing early literacy instruction with a standards-based rating tool. *The Reading Teacher, 56*(6), 554–563.

Fiene, J., & McMahon, S. (2007). Assessing comprehension: A classroom-based process. *The Reading Teacher, 60*(5), 406–417.

Flippo, R. F. (2003). *Assessing readers.* Portsmouth, NH: Heinemann.

Forbes, S., Poparad, M. A., & McBride, M. (2004). To err is human; to self-correct is to learn. *The Reading Teacher, 57*(6), 566–572.

Goodman, Y., Watson, D., & Burke, C. (2005). *Reading miscue inventory: From evaluation to instruction* (2nd ed.). New York: Richard C. Owen.

Hasbrouck, J. E., & Tindal, G. A. (2006). Oral reading fluency norms: A valuable assessment tool for reading teachers. *The Reading Teacher, 59*(7), 636–644.

Jimenez, R. T. (2004). More equitable literacy assessments for Latino students. *The Reading Teacher, 57*(6), 576–578.

Johnson, M. S., Kress, R. A., & Pikulski, J. J. (1987). *Informal reading inventories* (2nd ed.). Newark, DE: International Reading Association.

Johnston, P. (2003). Assessment conversations. *The Reading Teacher, 57*(1), 90–92.

Lenski, S. D., Ehlers-Zavala, F., Daniel, M. C., & Sun-Irminger, X. (2006). Assessing English-language learners in mainstream classrooms. *The Reading Teacher, 60*(1), 24–34.

McCabe, P. P. (2003). Enhancing self-efficacy for high-stakes reading tests. *The Reading Teacher, 57*(1), 12–20.

McKenna, M. C., & Walpole, S. (2005). How well does assessment inform our reading instruction? *The Reading Teacher, 59*(1), 84–86.

Mather, N., Sammons, J., & Schwartz, J. (2006). Adaptations of the Names Test: Easy-to-use phonics assessments. *The Reading Teacher, 60*(2), 114–122.

Popham, W. J. (2001). *The truth about testing.* Alexandria, VA: Association for Supervision and Curriculum.

Rogers, T., Winters, K. L., Bryan, G., Price, J. McCormick, F., House, L., Mezzarobba, D., & Sinclaire, C. (2006). Developing the IRIS: Toward situated and valid assessment measures in collaborative professional development and school reform in literacy. *The Reading Teacher, 59*(6), 544–553.

Valencia, S. W., & Buly, M. R. (2004). Behind test scores: What struggling readers really need. *The Reading Teacher, 57*(6), 520–531.

Walpole, S., & McKenna, M. C. (2006). The role of informal reading inventories in assessing word recognition. *The Reading Teacher, 59*(6), 592–594.

Websites

Learning to Read Resources
This site supplies links to many issues related to teaching and assessing literacy, including running records, readability calculators, and more.
http://www.toread.com

FairTest: National Center for Fair and Open Testing

The National Center for Fair and Open Testing (FairTest) is an advocacy organization working to end the abuses, misuses, and flaws of standardized testing and to ensure that evaluation of students and workers is fair, open, and educationally sound. The site provides survey information on state-by-state assessment practices for K–12, university, and employment tests. It also provides links to publications, articles, and fact sheets on standardized and alternative assessment.
http://www.fairtest.org

National Assessment of Educational Progress

The National Assessment of Educational Progress (NAEP) is mandated by Congress to provide objective data about the levels of knowledge, skills, and student performance at national, regional, and, on a trial basis, state levels. This site provides access to information and data about government-mandated, nationwide assessments at the national, regional, and state levels.
http://nces.ed.gov/nationsreportcard/

National Center for Research on Evaluation, Standards, and Student Testing (CRESST)

The National Center for Research on Evaluation, Standards, and Student Testing (CRESST) conducts research on important topics related to K–12 educational testing. This site provides publications, research reports, parents' guides, sample assessments, and a searchable database of alternative assessments in practice.
http://www.cse.ucla.edu

Toolkit98: Alternative Assessment

Toolkit98 contains items that can be used to construct authentic instruments to assess student achievement. This site contains chapters that provide background or foundation information on alternative assessments, and training activities designed to model effective teaching strategies.
http://www.nwrel.org/assessment/toolkit98

You can enter any of the topics or assessment tools from this chapter into a search engine. The following are just some of the many websites you might want to explore:

This site is called Authentic Assessment Toolbox. The tasks and rubrics were developed by the site developer's graduate students.
http://jonathan.mueller.faculty.noctrl.edu/toolbox/examples/authentictaskexamples.htm.

This is the Chicago Public Schools assessment page. Here you will find links to performance tasks, how to create rubrics and a rubrics bank.
http://intranet.cps.k12.il.us/Assessments/Ideas_and_Rubrics/ideas_and_rubrics.html

This is a free tool to help teachers develop rubrics.
http://rubistar.4teachers.org/index.php

EPILOGUE
Tickets to Far Away Places

Books are tickets to far away places,
Adventure and friends everywhere.
Best of all, you can travel the world,
Without ever leaving your chair!

—Author Unknown

This poem was given to us more than forty years ago by a wonderful elementary supervisor, Dr. Grace Champion, of the Louisville Public Schools in Kentucky. We believe that the message of this poem is what all teachers of literacy are trying to achieve. We want to make it possible for all students to have the ticket to travel the world without ever leaving their chairs—that is being able to successfully use their literacy skills.

We have read this poem to thousands of students and have used it in speeches when talking with thousands of teachers. Over the years the message has become clearer and clearer to us—**our goal is to teach every student to read and write.**

As we reflect on the seventh edition of *Literacy: Helping Students Construct Meaning,* we hope that in some small way we have helped every teacher who reads this text develop the skills they need to help their students to gain the **"tickets to far away places."**

J. David Cooper
Nancy D. Kiger

Good Books and Where to Find Them

The goal of teaching reading is to help students learn the strategies and skills necessary to read successfully so they can enjoy wonderful books, both narrative and expository. Even though students may begin learning to read with decodable texts, the goal is for them to move as quickly as possible into many other types of wonderful literature. This resource section presents resources that will help you keep up with new books, lists of recent major award-winning books (with links to websites to find the complete lists), and a list of wonderful literature cited in this text.

KEEPING UP WITH NEW BOOKS

In Chapter 2 we gave some websites that will help you keep up with new literature that is being published. We have found that the best way for teachers to keep up with newly published books is to sign up for a free newsletter. Here is how:

1. Go to http://www.publishersweekly.com.
2. Click Newsletters and then select Subscribe.
3. Click E-Mail Newsletters—Children's Bookshelf.
4. Complete the form.
5. Click Submit.

Once a week you will get all kinds of news about new children's and young adult literature—including information about recent prizes for literature such as the *LA Times* Book Prize, the Edgar Awards, the Ezra Jack Keats Book Award, the California Young Readers Medal, and so forth.

BOOK AWARDS

Following are bibliographies and the most recent winners of some of the most famous book awards available today.

The Pura Belpré Award Winners

(http://www.ala.org/ala/alsc/awardsscholarships/literaryawds/belpremedal/belprmedal.htm)
The Pura Belpré Award, established in 1996, is presented to a Latino/Latina writer and illustrator whose work best portrays, affirms, and celebrates the Latino cultural

experience in an outstanding work of literature for children and youth. It is co-sponsored by the Association for Library Service to Children (ALSC), a division of the American Library Association (ALA), and the National Association to Promote Library and Information Services to Latinos and the Spanish-Speaking (REFORMA), an ALA Affiliate.

2006 Winners
For Narrative

Viola Canales, ***The Tequila Worm*** (Wendy Lamb Books, a division of Random House, 2005)

Honor Books

Carmen T. Bernier-Grand, ***César: ¡Sí, Se Puede! Yes, We Can!*** Illustrated by David Diaz (Marshall Cavendish, 2004)

Pat Mora, ***Doña Flor: A Tall Tale About a Giant Woman with a Great Big Heart,*** Illustrated by Raul Colón (Alfred A. Knopf, a division of Random House, 2005)

Pam Muñoz Ryan, ***Becoming Naomi León*** (Scholastic Press, 2004)

For Illustration

Raul Colón, ***Doña Flor: A Tall Tale About a Giant Woman with a Great Big Heart,*** Written by Pat Mora (Alfred A. Knopf, a division of Random House, 2005)

Honor Books

Selected and illustrated by Lulu Delacre, ***Arrorró, Mi Niño: Latino Lullabies and Gentle Games*** (Lee & Low Books, Inc., 2004)

David Diaz, ***César: ¡Sí, Se Puede! Yes, We Can!*** Written by Carmen T. Bernier-Grand (Marshall Cavendish, 2004)

Rafael López, ***My Name Is Celia/ Me Llamo Celia: The Life of Celia Cruz/La Vida de Celia Cruz,*** Written by Monica Brown (Luna Rising, a bilingual imprint of Rising Moon, 2004)

Newbery Medal and Honor Books

(http://www.ala.org/ala/alsc/awardsscholarships/literaryawds/newberymedal/newberyhonors/newberymedal.htm)
The Newbery Medal was named for eighteenth-century British bookseller John Newbery. It is awarded annually by the Association for Library Service to Children, a division of the American Library Association, to the author of the most distinguished contribution to American literature for children.

2007 Medal Winner

Susan Patron, ***The Higher Power of Lucky,*** Illustrated by Matt Phelan (Simon & Schuster/Richard Jackson)

2007 Honor Books

Jennifer L. Holm, ***Penny from Heaven*** (Random House)

Kirby Larson, ***Hattie Big Sky*** (Delacorte Press)

Cynthia Lord, ***Rules*** (Scholastic)

Caldecott Medal Winners and Honor Books

(http://www.ala.org/ala/alsc/awardsscholarships/literaryawds/caldecottmedal/caldecottmedal.htm)

The Caldecott Medal was named in honor of nineteenth-century English illustrator Randolph Caldecott. It is awarded annually by the Association for Library Service to Children, a division of the American Library Association, to the artist of the most distinguished American picture book for children.

2007 Medal Winner

David Wiesner, *Flotsam* (Clarion)

2007 Honor Books

David McLimans, *Gone Wild: An Endangered Animal Alphabet* (Walker)

Kadir Nelson, Illustrator, *Moses: When Harriet Tubman Led Her People to Freedom,* Written by Carole Boston Weatherford (Hyperion/Jump at the Sun)

Coretta Scott King Book Award Winners

(http://www.ala.org/ala/emiert/corettascottkingbookaward/corettascott.htm)

The Coretta Scott King Book Awards, established in the late 1960s for authors and illustrators, is designed to encourage the artistic expression of the African American experience via literature and the graphic arts, including biographical, historical and social history treatments by African American authors and illustrators.

2007 Author Award Winner

Sharon Draper, *Copper Sun* (published by Simon & Schuster/Atheneum Books for Young Readers)

2007 Illustrator Award Winner

Kadir Nelson, Illustrator, *Moses: When Harriet Tubman Led Her People to Freedom,* Written by Carole Boston Weatherford. (Hyperion/Jump at the Sun)

2007 Author Honor Books

Nikki Grimes, *The Road to Paris* (G.P. Putnam's Sons, a division of Penguin Young Readers Group)

2007 Illustrator Honor Books

Christopher Myers, *Jazz,* Written by Walter Dean Myers (Holiday House, Inc.)

Benny Andrews, *Poetry for Young People: Langston Hughes,* Edited by David Roessel and Arnold Rampersad (Sterling Publishing Co., Inc.)

LITERATURE CITED IN THIS TEXT

Ackerman, K. (1988). *Song and dance man*. New York: Alfred A. Knopf.

Adler, D. A. (1986). *Martin Luther King, Jr.: Free at last*. New York: Holiday House.

Alexander, M. (1970). *Bobo's dream*. Boston: Houghton Mifflin.

Allard, H., & Marshall, J. (1977). *Miss Nelson is missing!* Boston: Houghton Mifflin.

Allard, H., & Marshall, J. (1978). *The Stupids have a ball.* Boston: Houghton Mifflin.

Apfel, N. H. (1991). *Voyager to the planets.* New York: Clarion.

Aylesworth, J. (1992). *Old black fly.* New York: Holt.

Bang, M. G. (1981). *Tye May and the magic brush.* New York: Greenwillow Books.

Baylor, B. (1976). *Hawk, I'm your brother.* New York: Charles Scribner's Sons.

Baylor, B. (1982). *The best town in the world.* New York: Charles Scribner's Sons.

Behrens, J. (1978). *Fiesta!* Chicago: Childrens Press.

Bennett, K. (2005). *Not Norman: A goldfish story.* Cambridge, MA: Candlewick Press.

Bredeson, C. (2006). *Great white sharks up close.* Berkeley Heights, NJ: Enslow Publishers, Inc.

Bunting, E. (1988). *How many days to America?* New York: Clarion.

Bunting, E. (1991). *Fly away home.* New York: Clarion.

Bunting, E. (2002). *Girls A to Z.* Honesdale, PA: Boyds Mills Press.

Burningham, J. (1970). *Mr. Gumpy's outing.* London: Henry Holt.

Byars, B. (1970). *The summer of the swans.* New York: Viking Penguin.

Carle, E. (1971). *Do you want to be my friend?* New York: HarperCollins.

Carle, E. (2002). *"Slowly, slowly, slowly," said the sloth.* New York: Philomel Books.

Carroll, L. (1960). *The annotated Alice by Lewis Carroll: illustrated by John Tenniel; with an introduction and notes by Martin Gardner.* New York: Random House.

Cherry, L. (1992). *A river ran wild: An environmental history.* New York: Gulliver Green.

Cummings, P. (1991). *Clean your room, Harvey Moon!* New York: Bradbury Press.

Dahl, R. (1961). *James and the giant peach.* New York: Viking Penguin.

Dahl, R. (1988). *Matilda.* London: Jonathon Cape.

Dahl, R. (1990). *Esio trot.* New York: Viking.

de Hamel, J. (1985). *Hemi's pet.* Auckland: Reed Methuen.

Demarest, C. L. (2006). *Hurricane hunters! Riders on the storm.* New York: Margaret K. McElderry Books.

de Paola, T. (1978). *The popcorn book.* New York: Holiday House.

de Paola, T. (1980). *Now one foot, now the other.* New York: G. P. Putnam.

de Paola, T. (1989). *The art lesson.* New York: G. P. Putnam.

Draper, S. (2006). *Copper sun.* New York: Atheneum Books for Young Readers.

Editors of TIME for Kids. (2005). *Snakes!* New York: Harper Collins Publishers.

Editors of TIME for Kids. (2005). *Spiders!* New York: Harper Collins Publishers.

Falwell, C. (1993). *Feast for 10.* Boston: Houghton Mifflin.

Falwell, C. (1998). *Word wizard,* New York: Clarion.

Fleischman, S. (1987). *The scarebird.* New York: Greenwillow Books.

Flournoy, V. (1985). *The patchwork quilt.* New York: Dial Books for Young Readers.

Forbes, E. (1971). *Johnny Tremain.* New York: Dell.

Fox, D., & Marks, C. (1987). *Go in and out the window: An illustrated songbook for young people.* New York: Henry Holt.

Fox, M. (1985). *Wilfrid Gordon McDonald Partridge.* New York: Kane/Miller.

Frazier, D. (2000). *Miss Alainious.* Orlando, FL: Harcourt.

Freedman, R. (1987). *Lincoln: A photobiography.* New York: Clarion.

Freedman, R. (1990). *Franklin Delano Roosevelt.* New York: Clarion.

Gerth, M. (2000). *Ten little ladybugs.* Los Angeles: Intervisual Books.

Gibbons, G. (1989). *Monarch butterfly.* New York: Holiday House.

Giff, P. R. (1980). *Today was a terrible day.* New York: Viking.

Giff, P. R. (1988). *Ronald Morgan goes to bat.* New York: Viking Kestrel.

Gilman, P. (1985). *Jillian Jiggs.* New York: Scholastic.

Gilman, P. (1988). *The wonderful pigs of Jillian Jiggs.* New York: Scholastic.

Graham, F. (illus.). (1987). *Roundabout cozy cottage.* New York: Grosset & Dunlap.

Guilfoile, E. (1957). *Nobody listens to Andrew.* Cleveland: Modern Curriculum Press.

Hahn, M. D. (1986). *Wait till Helen comes.* New York: Clarion.

Hamilton, V. (1990). *Cousins.* New York: Philomel.

Hatkoff, I., Hatkoff, C., & Kahumbu, P. (2007). *Owen & Mzee: The language of friendship.* New York: Scholastic Press.

Hodges, M. (1976). *Knight prisoner: The tale of Sir Thomas Malory and his King Arthur.* New York: Farrar, Straus and Giroux.

Howard, E. F. (1991). *Aunt Flossie's hats (and crab cakes later).* New York: Clarion.

Huck, C. (1989). *Princess Furball.* New York: Greenwillow Books.

Hutchins, P. (2002). *We're going on a picnic.* New York: HarperCollins.

Isadora, R. (1979). *Ben's trumpet.* New York: Greenwillow Books.

Jaspersohn, W. (1991). *Cranberries.* Boston: Houghton Mifflin.

Lamott, A. (1994). *Bird by bird.* New York: Doubleday and Company, Inc.

Landau, E. (2003). *Popcorn!* Watertown, MA: Charlesbridge.

Levitt, P. M., Burger, D. A., & Guralnick, E. S. (1985). *The weighty word book.* Longmont, CO: Bookmakers Guild.

Lewis, C. S. (1950). *The lion, the witch, and the wardrobe.* New York: Macmillan.

Lobel, A. (2000). *One lighthouse, one moon.* New York: Greenwillow.

Lowry, L. (1979). *Anastasia Krupnik.* Boston: Houghton Mifflin.

Lowry, L. (1989). *Number the stars.* Boston: Houghton Mifflin.

McCloskey, R. (1948). *Blueberries for Sal.* New York: Viking.

McPhail, D. (1984). *Fix-it.* New York: Dutton Children's Books, a Division of Penguin.

Macaulay, D. (1977). *Castle.* Boston: Houston Mifflin.

Maestro, B., & Maestro, G. (1989). *Taxi: A book of city words.* New York: Clarion.

Maestro, B., & Maestro, G. (1990). *Delivery van: Words for town and country.* New York: Clarion.

Markle, S. (2004). *Owls*. Minneapolis: Carolrhoda Books, Inc.

Markun, P. M. (1993). *The little painter of Sabana Grande*. New York: Bradbury Press.

Marshall, J. (1988). *Goldilocks and the three bears*. New York: Dial Books for Young Readers.

Martin, B., Jr. (1967). *Brown bear, brown bear*. New York: Henry Holt and Co.

Martin, J. (1998). *Snowflake Bentley*. Boston: Houghton Mifflin.

Marx, T. (2004). *Everglades forever: Restoring America's great wetland*. New York: Lee & Low Books, Inc.

Marzollo, J. (1990). *Pretend you're a cat*. New York: Dial Books for Young Readers.

Masurel, C. (1997). *No, No, Titus!* New York: North-South Books.

Miller, M. (1994). *My five senses*. New York: Simon & Schuster.

Mohr, N. (1979). *Felita*. New York: Dial Books for Young Readers.

Mollel, T. M. (1995). *Big boy*. New York: Clarion.

Mollel, T. M. (1997). *Ananse's feast: An Ashanti tale*. New York: Clarion.

Mora, P. (1997). *Tomás and the library lady*. New York: Alfred A. Knopf, a Division of Random House.

Moss, M. (1990). *Regina's big mistake*. Boston: Houghton Mifflin.

Murawski, D. A. (2004). *Spiders and their webs*. Washington, D. C.: National Geographic.

Murphy, J. (1990). *The boys' war*. New York: Clarion.

Myers, W. D. (1990). *The mouse rap*. New York: Harper & Row.

O'Neill, M. (1966). *Words, words, words*. New York: Doubleday & Company, Inc.

Park, B. (1987). *The kid in the red jacket*. New York: Random House.

Patent, D. H. (1992). *Pelicans*. New York: Clarion.

Paterson, K. (1977). *Bridge to Terabithia*. New York: HarperTrophy.

Peck, R. (2000). *A year down yonder*. New York: Dial Books for Young Readers.

Peek, M. (1985). *Mary wore her red dress and Henry wore his green sneakers*. New York: Clarion.

Perl, L. (1987). *Mummies, tombs, and treasure*. New York: Clarion.

Prelutsky, J. (1984). "Never mince words with a shark." In J. Prelutsky, *The new kid on the block* (p. 89). New York: Greenwillow Books.

Prelutsky, J. (1988). *Tyrannosaurus was a beast*. New York: Greenwillow Books.

Prelutsky, J. (2000). *It's raining pigs and noodles*. New York: Greenwillow Books.

Prelutsky, J. (2002). *The frog wore red suspenders*. New York: Greenwillow Books.

Raffi. (1980). *The Raffi singable songbook*. New York: Crown.

Raskin, E. (1971). *The mysterious disappearance of Leon (I mean Noel)*. New York: E. P. Dutton.

Rawls, W. (1961). *Where the red fern grows*. New York: Doubleday.

Richardson, C. K. (2005). *The real lucky charm*. New York: Puffin Books.

Richardson, C. K. (2005). *The real slam dunk*. New York: Puffin Books.

Robison, B. H. (1978). *Lurkers of the deep: Life within the ocean depths*. New York: David McKay.

Ryan, P. M. (2000). *Esperanza rising*. New York: Scholastic.

Sachar, L. (1989). *Wayside School is falling down*. New York: Lothrop, Lee & Shepard.

Sancha, S. (1983). *Luttrell Village: Country life in the Middle Ages*. New York: HarperCollins.

Say, A. (1990). *El Chino*. Boston: Houghton Mifflin.

Schwartz, A. (1988). *Annabelle Swift, kindergartner*. New York: Orchard Books.

Scieszka, J. (1989). *The true story of the 3 little pigs*. New York: Viking Kestrel.

Sendak, M. (1962). *Chicken soup with rice*. New York: Scholastic Inc.

Seuss, D. (1963a). *Dr. Seuss's ABC*. New York: Random House.

Seuss, D. (1963b). *Hop on Pop*. New York: Random House.

Seuss, D. (1974). *There's a wocket in my pocket*. New York: Random House.

Seymour, S. (2003). *Incredible sharks*. San Francisco: SeaStar Books.

Shaw, N. (1986). *Sheep in a jeep*. Boston: Houghton Mifflin.

Sherrow, V. (2001). *Titanic*. New York: Scholastic.

Simon, S. (2005). *Amazing bats*. San Francisco: SeaStar Books.

Simon, S. (2005). *Bridges*. San Francisco: SeaStar Books.

Small, D. (1985). *Imogene's antlers*. New York: Crown.

Snyder, Z. K. (1976). *The Egypt game*. New York: Atheneum.

Sobol, D. J. (1963). *Encyclopedia Brown: Boy detective*. New York: Lodestar Books.

Soto, G. (1993). *Too many tamales*. New York: G. P. Putnam's Sons.

Souza, D. M. (2007). *Look what whiskers can do*. Minneapolis: Lerner Publications Company.

Sperling, S. K. (1985). *Murfles and wink-a-peeps: Funny old words for kids*. New York: Clarkson N. Potter.

St. George, J. (2000). *So you want to be president?* New York: Philomel.

Steptoe, J. (1987). *Mufaro's beautiful daughters: An African tale*. New York: Scholastic Inc.

Taback, S. (2002). *This is the house that Jack built*. New York: Putnam.

Taylor, M. D. (1990). *Mississippi bridge*. New York: Dial Books for Young Readers.

Twain, M. (1987). *A Connecticut Yankee in King Arthur's court*. New York: Morrow.

Van Allsburg, C. (1984). *The mysteries of Harris Burdick*. Boston: Houghton Mifflin.

Van Allsburg, C. (1985). *The polar express*. Boston: Houghton Mifflin.

Viorst, J. (1981). *If I were in charge of the world*. New York: Atheneum.

Waber, B. (1988). *Ira says goodbye*. Boston: Houghton Mifflin.

Walker, P. R. (1993). *Head for the hills!* New York: Random House.

Watkins, R. (1997). *Gladiator*. Boston: Houghton Mifflin

Weeks, S. (1998). *Mrs. McNosh hangs up the wash*. New York: HarperCollins.

Westcott, N. B. (1988). *The lady with the alligator purse*. Boston: Little, Brown.

Westcott, N. B. (1989). *Skip to my Lou*. Boston: Little, Brown.

Wiesner, D. (1991). *Tuesday*. New York: Clarion.

Wiesner, D. (1999). *Sector 7*. New York: Clarion

Wilder, L. I. (1932). *Little house in the big woods*. New York: Harper.

Williams, S. (1990). *Mommy doesn't know my name*. Boston: Houghton Mifflin.

Williams, V. B. (1997). *Lucky song*. New York: Greenwillow Books.

Wright, S. (1988). *Age of chivalry*. New York: Watts.

Xiong, B. (told by), & Spagnoli, C. (adapted by). (1989). *Nine-in-one. Grr! Grr!* San Francisco: Children's Book Press.

Yep, L. (1989). *The rainbow people*. New York: Harper & Row.

Yolen, J. (1998). *Raising Yoder's barn*. Boston: Little, Brown.

Word Skills: Phonics and Structural Analysis for Teachers

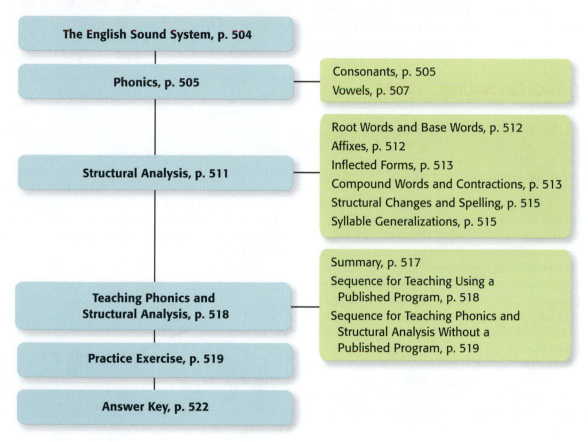

This handbook resource is designed to help you develop a basic knowledge about phonics and structural analysis. *It is not intended in any way to provide complete coverage of all the technical aspects of the structure of language and/or phonology.*

Read pages 504–519 using the embedded questions to guide your reading. After reading, complete the practice exercise on pages 519–522. Check your answers.

THE ENGLISH SOUND SYSTEM

What is the alphabetic principle?

English is an alphabetic language based on the alphabetic principle. This means that each speech sound of the language is represented by a graphic symbol.

What are phonemes and graphemes?

The smallest unit of speech sound in language is the *phoneme.* The symbols that represent phonemes are referred to as *graphemes.* The word *cat* has three phonemes—/c/ /ă/ /t/—represented by three graphemes. The word *deep* also has three phonemes—/d/ /ē/ /p/—even though the word has four letters—d-e-e-p. The middle phoneme is represented by two letters—*ee.*

Although English is an alphabetic language, it does not have one-to-one phoneme-grapheme correspondence. In other words, not all phonemes are represented by the same grapheme every time. For example, the /f/ phoneme can be represented by more than one grapheme, as shown in the following words:

/f/	*ph*one
	*f*ork
	pu*ff*
	rou*gh*

What is phonology?

Phonology is the study of speech sounds. *Phonological awareness* is the knowledge that words have separate parts. There are three ways to look at the parts of words:

syllables: *look* (one syllable)

onsets and rimes:
    look
    /l/ = onset
    /o͝ok/ = rime
    or
    brick
    /br/ = onset
    /ick/ = rime

phonemes: /l/ /o͝o/ /k/

What is phonemic awareness?

One part of phonological awareness is *phonemic awareness,* which is the awareness that spoken words are made up of speech sounds or phonemes. Think of the word for each of the following pictures and think of the number of phonemes the word has:

= 3 phonemes
/d/ /o/ /g/

= 3 phonemes
/h/ /ou/ /s/

---

*This section is adapted from J. D. Cooper, E. W. Warncke, & D. Shipman. (1988). *The What and How of Reading Instruction*, 2nd ed. Copyright © 1988. Reprinted by permission of Pearson Education Inc., Upper Saddle River, NJ.

What are segmenting and blending?

There are two major processes involved in phonemic awareness: segmenting and blending. *Segmenting* is the process of hearing a spoken word and being able to identify its phonemes; for example, *boat* has three phonemes—/b/ /ō/ /t/. *Blending* is the process of hearing the phonemes and being able to put them together (blend) to tell what the word is; for example, /s/ /ŏ/ /k/ is *sock*. Phonemic awareness is a prerequisite to learning phonics. Children are able to perform segmenting and blending tasks without being able to name the letters.

PHONICS

What is phonics?

Phonics is the study of the relationships between the speech sounds (phonemes) and the letters (graphemes) that represent them. Phonics is sometimes called *decoding*. It is the sounding out of unknown words. The amount of phonics instruction that individual learners need varies greatly.

Phonics produces *only* pronunciation, or an approximate pronunciation, of the unknown word. The pronounced word must be in the reader's oral language, to check both the accuracy of the decoding process and the meaning of the word in its contextual usage. For example,

Pitta are almost extinct because of acid rain.

Although readers may be able to say "pitta," they may not understand the above sentence. No real reading has taken place unless the author's meaning has been conveyed to the reader, even if the decoding was perfect! The reader may infer that "pitta" is plural because of the word *are* and a living thing because *extinct* is a term used with creatures. Therefore, some meaning has been conveyed. It is just not complete. (By the way, pitta are brightly colored birds found in southern Asian and Australian forests.)

Consonants

What is a consonant?

There are two basic categories of sounds in English: consonants and vowels. A *consonant* is a speech sound (phoneme) in which the flow of breath is constricted or stopped by the tongue, teeth, lips, or some combination of these. The letters (graphemes) representing such speech sounds are also called consonants. Most single consonants are regular in sound in that they represent only one sound no matter where they appear in a word.

boy	ta*b*	ra*b*id (*b*s all sound alike)
dog	ha*d*	ra*d*ar (*d*s all sound alike)

What sounds are expected for *c* and *g*?

There are several notable exceptions to consistent single consonant sounds. Consonants *c* and *g* have hard and soft sounds. The grapheme *c* is expected to have its hard sound /k/ when it is followed by the vowels *a, o, u,* or by another consonant. The hard sound of *c* is the sound usually associated with the letter *k*.

cat   cot   cut   class   al*c*ove

The soft sound of *c* is the sound heard in *city*. The soft sound of *c* occurs when the *c* is followed by *e, i,* or *y*.

cell   cider   cycle

The hard and soft *g* generalization is not as consistent as the hard and soft *c* generalization. The grapheme *g* is expected to have its hard sound when it is followed by the vowels *a, o, u,* or another consonant. The hard sound of *g* is the guttural sound that is heard in the following words:

gate   got   gum   glad   rag

The soft sound of *g*—/j/—is expected when it is followed by the vowels *e, i,* or *y*. The soft sound of *g* is the sound usually associated with the letter *j,* as in the following words:

gentle   giant   gym

What sounds are associated with *s*?

The letter *s* has four different sounds. There is no generalization covering when the reader should expect each sound. The sounds represented by *s* are illustrated by:

see—/s/

sure—/sh/

has—/z/

treasure—/zh/

What are some other exceptions to consistent consonant sounds?

The following exceptions to consistent single consonant sounds are far less common than those noted above. They are presented here to illustrate that there are other exceptions and as a caution to teachers to think carefully before requiring learners to decode phonetically unpredictable words.

Grapheme	Phoneme	Word
f	/v/	o*f*
x	/ks/	e*x*it
x	/z/	*x*ylophone
qu	/k/	anti*qu*e
qu	/kw/	*qu*iz

What are consonant clusters, and what else may they be called?

Consonants may also appear in *clusters* in words; that is, more than one consonant may come together before a vowel or between vowels in a word. Some materials for reading instruction refer to all groups of consonants as consonant clusters. Other materials divide them into two categories: consonant digraphs and blends.

What are digraphs?

Consonant Digraphs   A consonant digraph is two consecutive consonants (in a word or syllable) that represent one speech sound. In other words, two graphemes represent just one phoneme. The word *digraph* means (*di*) two (*graph*) letters. In fact, the word *digraph* contains a digraph, *ph*. There are essentially three kinds of digraphs:

1. **New sound.** Some consonant digraphs represent a new sound that is unlike the sound of either of the single consonants or any other consonants. This type of consonant digraph may have more than one sound.

Digraph	Word	Phoneme
sh	*sh*ut	/sh/
th	*th*is	(voiced *th*)
	*th*in	(unvoiced *th*)
wh	*wh*en	/hw/
	*wh*o	/h/
ch	whi*ch*	/ch/
	*ch*asm	/k/
	*ch*ef	/sh/

2. **Either sound.** Some consonant digraphs represent the sound of one of the single consonants contained in the digraph.

Digraph	Word	Phoneme
ck	ki*ck*	/k/
kn	*kn*ot	/n/
wr	*wr*ite	/r/
gn	*gn*at	/n/
pn	*pn*eumatic	/n/
gh	*gh*ost	/g/

3. **Another sound.** Some consonant digraphs represent the sound of another grapheme.

Digraph	Word	Phoneme
gh	lau*gh*	/f/
ph	*ph*one	/f/

Other consonant clusters often referred to as digraphs include *nk* as in ba*nk*; *ng* as in si*ng*; and double consonants as in mi*tt*en, su*mm*er, and ru*dd*er.

What are consonant blends?

Consonant Blends   A consonant blend is two or three consonant sounds clustered together in a word or syllable, where all consonant sounds are heard. The phonemes merge in speech sounds. The reader produces a speech sound for each consonant seen. The word *blend* contains two blends: *bl* and *nd*. There are three major categories of blends:

1. Blends beginning with the letter *s*:

str	*str*ong	sc	*sc*ab	sn	*sn*ail
spl	*spl*ash	sk	ri*sk*	sp	wa*sp*
scr	*scr*eam	sl	*sl*ow	st	la*st*
spr	*spr*ing	sm	*sm*og	sw	*sw*an

2. Blends concluding with the letter *r*:

br	*br*oth	fr	*fr*esh	tr	*tr*out
cr	*cr*owd	gr	*gr*ass	spr	*spr*ay
dr	*dr*aft	pr	*pr*ove	str	*str*aw

3. Blends concluding with the letter *l*:

bl	*bl*ue	gl	*gl*ass	cl	*cl*ose
pl	*pl*ace	fl	*fl*ip	sl	*sl*ave

The *lp* in he*lp*, the *tw* in *tw*in, the *dw* in *dw*arf, and the *nd* in sa*nd* are all examples of other consonant blends. Remember, whenever each consonant in a cluster can be heard, the cluster is called a blend.

Why are consonant sounds important?

Consonant sounds are more consistent than vowel sounds. There is less deviation in the sounds of consonants, whether they are single or in clusters. Therefore, a few consonants, along with a vowel, are usually taught first so children can begin to build words.

Vowels

What is a vowel? What are the categories of vowel sounds?

A vowel is a speech sound in which the flow of breath is relatively unobstructed. The letters representing such sounds are also called vowels. The letters *a, e, i, o,* and *u* always function as vowels. The letter *y* is sometimes a consonant (as in *y*ell) and sometimes a vowel (as in b*y* and ma*y*). The letter *w* functions as a vowel in combination with another vowel (as in la*w*). The categories of vowel sounds are short vowels, long vowels, vowel digraphs, diphthongs, the schwa sound, exceptions to expected vowel sounds, and *y* and *w* functioning as vowels.

What are short vowels?

Short Vowel Sounds   Short vowel sounds are sometimes referred to as unglided. The five short vowel sounds are represented in the following words:

$$/ăt/ \quad /ĕd/ \quad /ĭt/ \quad /ŏx/ \quad /ŭp/$$

The breve (*brĕv*), or curved line over a vowel (ă), is the diacritical marking used to indicate the short vowel sound in phonetic respellings. Sometimes dictionaries make no mark for the short vowel sound.

Two other vowel sounds also referred to as short vowel sounds are the /aw/ sound as represented by the *a* in c*a*ll, the *ou* in c*ou*gh, the *au* in c*au*ght, and the *aw* in l*aw*; and the short *oo* sound /o͞o/ as in l*oo*k and g*oo*d.

What are long vowels?

Long Vowel Sounds   Long vowels are those in which the name of the letter is heard. These sounds are sometimes referred to as the glided sounds. There are five long vowel sounds in English, as represented in the following:

Word	Pronunciation
ate	/āt/
eat	/ēt/
ice	/īs/
open	/ō·pən/
use	/ūz/ v.
	/ūs/ n.

The macron /mā′-kron/, a straight line over the vowel (ā), is the diacritical mark used to indicate the long vowel sound in phonetic spellings. Another vowel of this type is the long oo sound /o͞o/, as heard in room and cool.

What are vowel digraphs?

Vowel Digraphs   Vowel digraphs, like consonant digraphs, occur when two adjacent vowels in a syllable represent one speech sound; that is, two vowel letters evoke only one phoneme and are therefore considered one grapheme. The most frequently occurring vowel digraphs are:

Vowel Digraph	Word	Vowel Phoneme
ee	seed	/ē/
oa	goat	/ō/
ea	seat	/ē/
ai	pain	/ā/
ay	day	/ā/

The most usual sound of these vowel digraphs is the long sound of the first vowel. However, there are exceptions—for example:

Vowel Digraph	Word	Vowel Phoneme
ea	break	/ā/
ea	bread	/ĕ/
ie	piece	/ē/
oa	broad	/aw/

What are diphthongs?

Diphthongs   Diphthongs, like consonant blends, consist of two vowels in one syllable where two sounds are heard. In some reading materials, diphthongs are called vowel blends. The most frequently occurring diphthongs are:

Diphthong	Example Word
oi	oil
oy	oyster
ou	house
ow	now

What vowel combinations can be either diphthong or digraph?

Two vowel combinations function sometimes as digraphs and sometimes as diphthongs: ou and ow. The ou in out is a diphthong; in brought, it is a vowel digraph. The ow in now is a diphthong; in show, it is a vowel digraph. When teaching the phonemes to be associated with these graphemes, it is necessary to teach that each has two distinct sounds.

ou

Digraph	Diphthong
cough /aw/	couch /ou/
through /o͞o/	
tough /ŭ/	

ow

Digraph	Diphthong
snow /ō/	cow /ou/

What is a schwa?

Schwa   The schwa sound of a vowel is known as the softened or indeterminate sound. It sounds like a short u and frequently occurs in the unstressed or unaccented syllable of a word. It may be spelled with any vowel or combination of vowels. The diacritical mark representing the schwa sound is often an upside down and backward *e* (ə).

Vowel	Example of Schwa Sound	
a	above	/ə•buv′/
e	craven	/krā′•vən/
i	beautiful	/byoo′•tə•fəl/
o	committee	/kə•mit′•ē/
u	cherub	/chĕr•əb/

The schwa sound may be represented sometimes by two vowels as shown with the *io* in the word port*io*n /pôr′•shən/.

What are the exceptions to expected vowel sounds?

Exceptions to Expected Vowel Sounds   Short vowel sounds are the most common vowel sounds in words. The short vowel is expected in a closed syllable, a syllable (or word) ending with one or more consonants. For example, *cat* and *at* are closed syllables; they end with a consonant. There are four standard exceptions to the expected short vowel sounds in a closed syllable.

1. When a vowel is followed by *r*, the vowel sound is not short; rather, it is called an *r*-controlled vowel.

ar	c*ar*	er	h*er*	ir	f*ir*
or	f*or*	ur	f*ur*		

   Notice that the *er, ir,* and *ur* all sound the same. The *ar* sounds like the letter name *r*, and the *or* sounds like the word *or*.

2. When the vowel *a* is followed by *l*, it usually represents the /*aw*/ phoneme.

   s*al*t (sôlt)
   t*al*k (tôk)
   b*al*l (bôl)

3. When the vowel grapheme *o* is followed by *lt* or *ld*, it has the long *o* phoneme.

   b*o*lt   g*o*ld

4. When the vowel grapheme *i* is followed by *gh*, *ld*, or *nd*, it usually has the long *i* phoneme (exception w˘ind).

   n*i*ght   s*i*gh   w*i*ld   m*i*nd

When do *y* or *w* serve as vowels?

Y as a Vowel   The letter *y* functions as a vowel when it represents either the short or long sounds of the letter *i* or is part of a digraph or diphthong. The short *i* sound of *y* is expected in a closed syllable.

   g*y*m   g*y*p   s*y*mbol

The long *i* sound of *y* is expected when it occurs alone in an open syllable, that is, one ending with a vowel, in this case *y*.

   m*y*   d*y*namic   p*y*thon

When *y* is preceded by the vowels *a* or *e*, it functions as the second vowel of a vowel digraph.

   d*ay*   th*ey*   k*ey*

When *y* is in the final position in words of two or more syllables, it usually represents the long *e* sound.

   part*y*   assembl*y*

Note: In some dialects, this final *y* sound is the short *i*. Some dictionaries mark its pronunciation both ways.

   There are two infrequent patterns in which *y* also represents a vowel: when *y* is preceded by *u* or followed by *e*.

   g*uy*   b*ye*

W as a Vowel The letter *w* functions as a vowel only when it is in combination with another vowel: as part of a digraph when preceded by *a, e,* or *o;* as part of a diphthong when preceded by *o* (sometimes).

W as Part of a Digraph

p*aw*

bl*ow*

gr*ew*

W as Part of a Diphthong

cl*ow*n

What generalizations govern vowel sounds?

Vowel Sound Generalizations There are no hard and fast rules for the expected vowel sounds, only generalizations. The generalizations are quite interrelated. Only those generalizations determined to be the most consistent and applicable are presented in this text (Bailey, 1967; Clymer, 1963/1996; Emans, 1967).

■ **The most common vowel sound generalization relates to the short vowel sound.** This sound is expected in a closed syllable, one ending with a consonant. This kind of syllable is sometimes referred to as the CVC pattern (C = Consonant, V = Vowel, C = Consonant). The consonants may be single or in clusters, and it is not mandatory to have a consonant in the initial position of such a syllable or short word. The following words follow the CVC pattern:

rag (CVC)

slot (CCVC)

wish (CVCC)

at (VC)

The CVC generalization is useful in pronouncing one-syllable words as well as the individual syllables of polysyllabic words. The following words all contain closed syllables with a short vowel sound:

hamlet   /hăm·lĭt/

fancy   /făn′·sē/

section   /sĕk′·shən/

■ **There are three generalizations for when to expect long vowel sounds.** The first is the sound expected in an open syllable, one that ends in a vowel. It is sometimes referred to as the CV pattern (C = Consonant, V = Vowel). There may or may not be a consonant before the vowel. The following words and syllables within words follow the CV pattern:

m*e*   /mē/

*o*pen   /ō·pən/

h*o*tel   /hō·tĕl′/

m*u*sic   /myo̅o̅′·zĭk/

The CV generalization is useful in pronouncing one-syllable words as well as individual syllables of polysyllabic words. The following words contain open syllables with long vowel sounds:

m*u*sic   /myo̅o̅′·zĭk/

prem*o*lar /prē·mō′·lər/

r*o*mance   /rō·măns′/

T*i*tanic   /tī·vtan′·ĭk/

m*e*ter   /mē′·tər/

■ **A long vowel sound is also expected with certain vowel digraphs.** When the vowel digraphs *ee, oa, ea, ai,* and *ay* are in the CVVC pattern, the first vowel often represents its long sound, and the second vowel is not sounded. The following words follow the CVVC pattern:

b*oa*t	s*ay*	str*ai*n	*ea*t	s*ee*
c*oa*st	del*ay*	p*ai*nt	tr*ea*t	sleep

■ **A long vowel sound is also expected in the CVCe (the *e* is usually shown in lowercase) pattern.** This is sometimes referred to as the final *e* pattern. The final *e* serves to indicate that the preceding vowel should probably represent the long sound. It occurs most frequently in one-syllable words. The following words follow the CVCe pattern:

ate   make   rebate   stroke   fine

Summary

What is the key to a reader using phonics effectively?

It is important to remember that when a reader uses phonics, it will have value only if the word to be decoded is in the reader's oral language. Once phonic generalizations have been applied to an unknown word, the reader has to test it against his or her oral vocabulary to determine whether the decoding process has resulted in a recognizable English word. In effect, the reader pronounces a sound(s) and asks: Is this a word I know? The reader also needs to use context clues to decide whether the decoded word makes sense in the sentence.

Phonics is one of several word recognition skills students need in order to learn to read. Phonics is not the goal of reading instruction. It serves as a means to an end: the construction of meaning. Some learners may have difficulty learning phonics; in this case, other word recognition skills such as context should be taught.

STRUCTURAL ANALYSIS

What is structural analysis?

Structural analysis is a word recognition skill in which knowledge of the meaningful parts of words aids in the identification of an unknown written word. A reader may use structural analysis as an aid to either the pronunciation of an unknown word or to understanding the meaning of an unknown word. Structural analysis may be considered both a word recognition and a comprehension skill. A mature reader may use structural analysis for both purposes simultaneously.

Structural analysis requires the reader to look at meaningful units or parts of words in order to decode a word or to decide what a word means. The following diagram shows the relationships among the parts of structural analysis that will be discussed in this section.

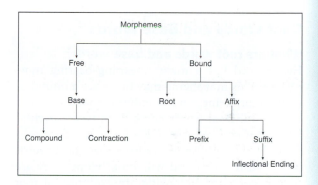

What are morphemes?

The meaningful structural parts of words are called *morphemes*. A morpheme is the smallest unit of meaning in a word. Any unit of meaning in a word is a morpheme.

Cat is a single morpheme.
Cats is two morphemes.

The *s* added to the word *cat* means more than one cat, so it is a second meaning unit added to the meaning unit *cat*.

What are the two types of morphemes?

There are two types of morphemes: bound morphemes and free morphemes. A bound morpheme must be attached to another morpheme in order to carry meaning. A free morpheme can stand alone, as a word, in the English language. The *s* in *cats* has no meaning unless it is attached to a word; it is a bound morpheme. The word *cat* can stand alone; it is a free morpheme. The following words illustrate bound and free morphemes.

Unhappy has two morphemes. (*un* is bound; *happy* is free)

Redoing has three morphemes. (*re* and *ing* are bound; *do* is free)

Disagreeable has three morphemes. (*dis* and *able* are bound; *agree* is free)

Desk has one morpheme. (it is free)

Root Words and Base Words

What are root words and base words?

Every word has a major meaning-bearing morpheme. This morpheme may be either a bound or a free morpheme, and is either a root word or a base word. Root words come from or are derived from another language and will not stand alone in English; they are bound morphemes. Base words are English words and will stand alone; they are free morphemes. Following are examples of root words/derived words:

Root Words/Derived Words

con*tain*	de*tain*	re*tain*
re*fer*	con*fer*	de*fer*
con*cede*	re*cede*	

Notice that *tain*, *fer*, and *cede* are the major meaning-bearing parts of these words, but are not English words. An English word is formed only when other bound morphemes are added to these roots. Each of the above words contains two bound morphemes. Following are examples of base words:

Base Words

girl	*girls*
comfort	un*comfort*able
mark	re*mark*ing

Notice that the base word remains a free morpheme even when one or more affixes have been added to it.

Affixes

What are affixes?

An affix is any morpheme attached to the main meaning-bearing part of a word. Affixes are prefixes, suffixes, and inflectional endings and are bound morphemes. An affix may either precede or follow the root or base word, or both. Base and root words may have more than one affix. Root words must have at least one affix.

What is a prefix?

A *prefix* is a bound morpheme added to the beginning of a word. Prefixes add to and change the meaning of the base or root word.

Prefix	Meaning	Example
dis	not	disable
	remove, to make not	disappear
	undo, reverse	disassemble
ex	out	exhale
	beyond	expand
re	back	revert
	again	remake

What is a suffix?

A *suffix* is a bound morpheme added to the end of a word. Suffixes add to and change the meaning of the base or root word.

Suffix	Meaning	Example
er	one who has to do with	laborer
	resident of	Southerner
	performs an action	worker
ness	condition of being	fullness
less	without	powerless
	beyond the range of	sightless

Words formed by the addition of prefixes or suffixes to base or root words are known as *derived words,* or derivatives. A different meaning has been derived, or obtained, from the meaning of the original root or base word.

Inflected Forms

What are inflectional endings?
Inflectional endings are a special set of suffixes. They, like other suffixes, are added to the end of a root or base word. Inflectional endings change the number, case, or gender when added to nouns; tense when added to verbs; and form when added to adjectives and adverbs.

Group

n.	Number: cat*s*	more than one
n.	Case: child*'s*	shows ownership
n.	Gender: host*ess*	changes to female
v.	Tense: help*ed*	past tense
adv./adj.	Form: tall*er*	compares two things

The most common inflectional endings are:

Nouns

- *Number* s and es when affixed to nouns to indicate plurality, as in *toys* and *dresses*.
- *Case* 's when attached to nouns to indicate possession, as in "John's ball is red."
- *Number and case* s' to indicate plurality and possession, as in "It is the girls' recess time."
- *Gender* ess when attached to nouns to indicate change of gender, as from *steward* to *stewardess*.

Verbs

- *Tense* ed and ing when attached to verbs to indicate, respectively, past tense and present participle, as in *walked* and *walking* and s to verbs to indicate agreement with third-person singular nouns, as in "Mary works."

Adjectives/Adverbs

- *Form* er and est when affixed to adjectives or adverbs to indicate, respectively, compara-

tive and superlative forms, as in *faster* and *fastest*.

When new words are formed by the addition of inflectional endings, they are called inflected forms of the words. The *er* in *taller* is an inflectional ending because it changes the form of the word, but *er* in *helper* is not an inflectional ending because it does not change the tense, case, number, form, or gender of the word. (The *er* in *helper* is a suffix; it changes the verb *help* into a noun—one who helps.)

It is possible for a word to be both derived and inflected. Any word that has had a prefix or suffix added to it is a derived form of that word. The addition of an inflectional ending produces the inflected form.

Independent is a derived form of *depend*. (prefix *in* + *depend* + suffix *ent*)

Unhappier is both derived and inflected. (prefix *un* [not] + *happy* [base word] + inflected ending *er* [comparative])

Compound Words and Contractions

What are compound words and contractions?
Two other types of words are formed by the combination of meaningful structural units, or morphemes: compound words and contractions. *Compound words* are a combination of two free morphemes. The meaning of the new word must retain elements of both meanings and pronunciation of the two previous morphemes in order to be classified as a compound word. *Dollhouse, racetrack*, and *bathroom* are compound words; *office, target*, and *together* are not compound words.

Contractions are formed by combining two free morphemes into a shortened form by the omission of one or more letters and the insertion of an apostrophe where those letters were omitted.

are + *not* form the contraction *aren't*

they + *are* form the contraction *they're*

he + *will* form the contraction *he'll*

PREFIXES AND SUFFIXES THAT MERIT INSTRUCTION

PREFIXES

[a]*un-* *dis-* [a]*in-, im-* [a]*non* *ir-*	Meaning "not": *unhappy* *disrespectful* *inactive* *impossible* *nonresistant* *irresponsible*
re-	Meaning "back" or "again": *revisit*
[a]*un-* *dis-*	Meaning "do the opposite of": *untie* *disassemble*
in-, im-	Meaning "in" or "into": *indoors*
en-, em-	Meaning "into" or "within": *entangle*
over-	Meaning "too much": *overdose*
mis-	Meaning "wrong": *misspell*

SUFFIXES

-s, -es	Plural: *girls* Tense: *jumps*
-ed	Tense: *jumped*
-ing	Tense: *jumping*
-ly	Meaning "like": *sisterly*
-er, -or	Meaning "one who performs a specialized action": *swimmer* Used to form comparative degree with adjectives: *darker*
-tion *-ion* *-ation* *-ition*	Meaning "action": *absorption*
-able *-ible*	Meaning "susceptible," "capable" Meaning "worth": *debatable*
-al, -ial	Meaning "of" or "relating to": *parental*
-y	Meaning "consisting of" or "inclined toward": *sleepy*
-ness	Meaning "state," "quality," "condition," or "degree": *brightness*

[a] Accounts for nearly 50 percent of all prefixed words (Graves, 1987).

Source: Based on White, Sowell, and Yanagihara (1989).

Without the use of context clues, confusion may arise with the use of 's with singular nouns. The word *boy's* could be the contracted form of *boy + is* or it may be a change of case and the possessive form of boy.

John's sister can't say what John's going to do.

In this sentence, the first *John's* is possessive, while the second one is the contracted form of *John is*.

Structural Changes and Spelling

What are the important structural changes in a word that influence spelling?

Structural analysis can be helpful, but sometimes beginning readers find the addition of a structural part to a known word confusing. The word may look so different that they are unable to recognize the derived word. This is especially true when a spelling change occurs in the base word.

The following generalizations should be taught to aid in the reader's recognition of base words and derived words as well as to aid in the spelling of such words.

1. When a word ends with *e*, the *e* is dropped before adding an inflectional ending that begins with a vowel.

   bake + ing becomes *baking*
   hope + ed becomes *hoped.*

2. When a word ends with a single vowel followed by a single consonant, that consonant is doubled before adding *ing* or *ed*.

   hop + ed becomes *hopped*
   begin + ing becomes *beginning*

3. When a word ends with *f* or *fe* (with a silent *e*), the *f* is usually changed to *v* before the ending is added.

   calf + es becomes *calves*
   wife + es becomes *wives*

4. When a word ends in *y* preceded by a consonant, the *y* is usually changed to *i* before endings are added, unless the ending begins with *i*.

   dry + ed becomes *dried*
   party + es becomes *parties*
   sorry + est becomes *sorriest*
   cry + ing becomes *crying*

5. When a word ends with *y* preceded by a vowel, no change is made in the base word before adding endings.

   boy + s becomes *boys*
   stay + ed or *ing* becomes *stayed* or *staying*

6. When the base word ends with *s, ss, ch, sh,* or *x,* the inflectional ending *es* is added rather than *s;* when the word ends in *f/fe,* change to *v* and add *es;* when the word ends in *y,* change to *i* and add *es.*

   focus becomes *focuses*
   mess becomes *messes*
   lunch becomes *lunches*
   dish becomes *dishes*
   box becomes *boxes*
   half becomes *halves*
   cry becomes *cries*

Syllable Generalizations

What is a syllable, and how does knowledge of syllables aid in word pronunciation?

A syllable is an oral language unit in which a vowel sound is heard. There are as many syllables in a word as there are vowel sounds. In word recognition, we don't worry about conventions of "correct" division of words; rather, we divide in order to deal with pronunciation of one syllable at a time. A syllable may or may not contain a consonant sound.

> a, my, ate, dog, boat (these are monosyllabic words)
>
> dis-con-tin-ue, re-lat-ed (these are polysyllabic words)

Knowledge governing vowel sounds (discussed earlier) applies whether to a one-syllable word or a polysyllabic word.

The primary reason for teaching or learning how to divide words into syllables for reading or decoding purposes is to give the reader clues to the possible pronunciation of vowel sounds in unknown words.

What are the generalizations concerning syllable division?

Generalizations for syllabic division of words give the reader possibilities to chunk an unfamiliar word so that he or she may decode it by applying phonic and structural analysis. (Syllabication is *not* used for dividing words in writing. The dictionary should be used for this purpose. Therefore, students must be taught to read phonetic respellings.) If the decoded word is in the reader's oral language, this serves as the reader's check on the accuracy of the generalizations that have been applied. Structural elements of the word are dealt with first; then phonic generalizations are applied as needed.

What are three structural generalizations for dividing words into syllables?

The first three generalizations for syllables deal with the structural parts of unknown words; that is, bases, roots, and affixes. Whenever readers are being taught to divide words into syllables, they should first look for meaningful chunks of the unknown word.

1. Almost all affixes form separate syllables. In the word *rewrite, re* is a separate syllable; in the word *useless, less* is a separate syllable. Exceptions to

this include the inflectional endings *'s, s,* and *ed* except when *ed* is preceded by *d* or *t.*

books is one syllable
Sue's is one syllable
chained is one syllable
wanted is two syllables
loaded is two syllables

2. The two words of a compound word form separate syllables, even if there are additional syllables in one or both of the words used to form the compound word.

Word	Morphemes	Syllables
cowboy	*cow + boy*	2 syllables
lumberjack	*lumber + jack*	2 + 1 = 3 syllables
policewoman	*police + woman*	2 + 2 = 4 syllables

3. The contracted form of two words sometimes produces just one syllable because it is a vowel that has been deleted to form the contraction. Sometimes it produces two syllables:

can't is one syllable
they'll is one syllable
couldn't is two syllables
wasn't is two syllables

The next five syllabication generalizations help readers apply phonic generalizations by dividing long words into syllables (chunking).

1. When two consonants occur between two vowels, the syllabic division is usually *between the two consonants.* (Do not divide consonant digraphs and blends; they are treated as single consonants.) This pattern is known as the VCCV-pattern. There may or may not be other consonants preceding or following this pattern.

bargain	bar-gain
circus	cir-cus
enter	en-ter
entertain	en-ter-tain

2. In the -VCCV- pattern, divide before or after the blend or digraph. (There is an exception: double consonants. Many experts treat double consonants as digraphs.)

letter   lett-er
graphic   graph-ic
doctrine   doc-trine

3. When one consonant occurs between two vowels, the syllabic division may put the consonant with either the first or second vowel. This is known as the -VCV- pattern. There may or may not be other consonants preceding or following this pattern.

 a. When the consonant goes with the first vowel, the first syllable is closed, and the first vowel sound is expected to be short (VC-V).

riv-er   ex-it   liz-ard

 b. When the consonant goes with the second vowel, the first syllable is open and the first vowel is expected to be long (V-CV).

ma-jor   ho-tel   ba-con

First, try the consonant with the first vowel, and check against oral language. If this seems incorrect, try the consonant with the second vowel.

There are a few words in our language with the -VCV- pattern that actually appear to divide both ways. These words are called *homographs* because they are spelled the same. However, they are two different words with different pronunciations and meanings. The contextual usage of the words and the reader's oral language are the only checks on the correct pronunciation. The words don't actually divide differently; the accent is placed differently.

record (rē-cord′ rĕ′-cord) Be sure to record record low temperatures.
present (prē-sent′ prĕ′-sent)

Will you present the present to our guest?

4. When a word ends in *le* preceded by a single consonant, the final syllable usually consists of the consonant plus the *le*.

cradle   cra-dle   (krā-dəl)
trifle   tri-fle   (trī-fəl)

If two consonants precede the *le*, usually divide after the second consonant to prevent splitting blends and digraphs.

rattle   ratt-le
ankle   ank-le

5. The vowel sound in an unstressed or unaccented syllable is often the schwa sound. Any vowel may have the schwa sound, which sounds like the short *u*.

com-mit′-tee   (kə•mĭt′•ē)
a-gain   (ə•gĕn′)
dem′-*on*-strate   (dem′•ən•strāt)

Summary

The division (or chunking) of unfamiliar words is guided by generalizations or possibilities, not by rules. These generalizations must be used in conjunction with each other and with phonics. Because many words in the English language are not phonetically regular, sometimes it is necessary to check the pronunciation of a word in the dictionary. Before requiring students to sound out words, teachers must be sure that the words follow accepted generalizations for their pronunciations. The following steps summarize how to apply generalizations for dividing words into syllables or chunks:

1. Separate affixes.
2. Follow generalizations to divide base or root words.
3. Apply phonic generalizations.
4. Try alternates if the first attempt doesn't result in an acceptable word for the context.

TEACHING PHONICS AND STRUCTURAL ANALYSIS

Is it important to teach phonics and structural analysis in a systematic way?

Yes. While some children may seem to acquire phonic and structural analysis skills either on their own or through incidental teaching, most do not. A systematic system ensures that no skills are overlooked and works best for most children.

Can I teach phonics and structural analysis as needed while children are reading meaningful text?

This kind of instruction, sometimes referred to as incidental instruction, may work for some children some of the time. It will not work for all children. Therefore, we recommend a systematic system of instruction.

Should all children be taught in the same way? That is, given that I should teach systematically, should I use the same system for all children?

Begin with the assumption that the chosen system will be successful for all children, but observe very carefully as you teach and as children begin to apply newly taught skills to reading meaningful text. If what you are doing is not bringing success for some children, be prepared to change the pace of instruction or look for a different system for those children.

Should children who are already reading fluently without having had phonics instruction be required to do such lessons anyhow?

Sometimes a child learns to decode words without formal instruction, apparently having learned intuitively. Remember that phonics analysis is a means to an end. Use your judgment about the need for such a child to participate in phonics lessons. Most such children have no need for the lessons.

Can I use the phonics component of my school's adopted published reading or language arts program?

Yes. In fact, following the phonics component of the published reading program you are using makes good sense. Absent this, a stand-alone published program may also be useful to you.

Sequence for Teaching Using a Published Program

Should I follow the sequence of phonics instruction in our published basal reading program or change the sequence?

Follow the sequence as given in the published program. It has been developed to fit well with what children are asked to read in their pupil books.

What if my school purchases and recommends using a stand-alone phonics program in addition to the basal program?

We recommend sticking to the sequence suggested by the basal reading program publisher because it logically works with material children will be reading. You can use lessons on particular skills from the stand-alone program to supplement the basal lessons when needed.

When should I supplement the published program?

If, after teaching the published program lessons, you find some or all children have not grasped the skill or are not able to apply the skill, you may need to reteach. Repeating the very same lesson may not be effective. Instead, locate (or create) another lesson for teaching the same skill. You should also adjust the pace of the lesson, the number of examples provided, and the amount of repetition to fit the needs of the children. This requires you to assess continually as you teach, being alert to signs that a child has become lost or failed to get what you are teaching.

Should I ever omit or change the sequence or content of the published program?

While we recommend systematic teaching, which means omitting nothing and not changing a well-developed sequence, there may be times when it is appropriate to do either or both. For example, if you have observed that your students are already using a skill, there is no need to spend time having them go through a lesson on that skill. If they will be reading something that lends itself to a lesson on a particular skill that is not next in the sequence, adjust the sequence to meet the needs of the students. If the children are engaged in writing and it seems sensible to you to teach a phonics lesson on the spot, then do so. Such as-needed incidental lessons should not, however, take the place of adherence to the systematic sequence of lessons.

Sequence for Teaching Phonics and Structural Analysis Without a Published Program

If our school doesn't have a structured series of phonics and structural analysis lessons within a reading program or as a stand-alone program, does the sequence I use matter?

Yes. There is a logical sequence for teaching phonics that forms the basis for most published programs. The sequence that makes sense is based on utility; that is, in what order can we expect children to find phonics elements easiest to learn and most helpful as they become literate? We teach phonics and structural elements in a sequence that helps children learn most easily, building on what is known as new elements are taught, and giving many opportunities to apply skills as they are learned.

What is an appropriate sequence for teaching phonic and structural analysis elements?

If you have state or local standards, the sequence you follow should reflect the one suggested in those standards. If the standards do not provide a sequence, we suggest that you look at the sequence for a published program. The following general guidelines should be helpful in developing an appropriate sequence for teaching phonics and structural analysis skills:

1. Teach and develop phonemic awareness skills.

2. Teach one short vowel and a few consonants that will make a word or words—for example, short *a* and the consonants *s, t,* and *m.* These letters can be used to make words.

3. Teach a few high-frequency words.

4. Continue teaching consonants and vowels until all have been taught.

5. Continue adding high-frequency words.

6. Teach other phonic elements, such as blends/clusters and digraphs.

7. Teach students a strategy that will assist them in applying the decoding skills being taught.

8. Teach structural elements such as endings, prefixes, and suffixes.

9. Continue teaching all phonic and structural elements until students are able to apply their knowledge independently while reading.

PRACTICE EXERCISE

Directions

This series of exercises is designed to help you practice and check the knowledge you gained from this resource. Complete each exercise; then check your answers with those on pages 522–523.

> **Part I**

Write the answer on the line for each question.

1. How many sounds do your hear in _____ ?

HANDBOOK RESOURCE

2. Write the word for these sounds:
   /h/ /ou/ /s/. _____

3. Identify the onset and rime in the following words:

	onset	rime
street	_____	_____
day	_____	_____
race	_____	_____

Part II

Classify the italicized letters in the following words as (a) diphthong, (b) vowel digraph, (c) consonant digraph, or (d) consonant blend. Write the correct letter in the blank to the left of each word.

_____	1. *bl*ack	_____	11. *gn*aw
_____	2. *oy*ster	_____	12. pa*il*
_____	3. *sh*ine	_____	13. *br*ought
_____	4. to*il*	_____	14. wre*ck*
_____	5. *br*ight	_____	15. to*w*
_____	6. *dw*indle	_____	16. thi*ng*
_____	7. *pn*eumatic	_____	17. *cr*aft
_____	8. g*oa*t	_____	18. n*ee*d
_____	9. *ea*se	_____	19. *str*ing
_____	10. h*ow*	_____	20. la*y*

Part III

From among the four words in each list, select the one that *does not* conform to the phonics generalization that the other three do. Write the letter of the exception on the line to the left. Then write the generalization to which the other words conform on the next line. If all words conform, choose "e," no exception. Example:

___*c*___   a. bait   b. sail   c. said   d. bail   e. no exception
_____*CVVC generalization - ai digraph*_____

___ **1.**   a. rate   b. line   c. mete   d. seem   e. no exception

___ **2.**   a. gin   b. gift   c. gym   d. gem   e. no exception

___ **3.**   a. cup   b. pin   c. slur   d. get   e. no exception

___ **4.**   a. eat   b. seat   c. coat   d. seem   e. no exception

___ **5.**   a. be   b. no   c. music   d. me   e. no exception

___ **6.**   a. fir   b. fur   c. order   d. me   e. no exception

Part IV

From column B, select the synonym, example, or definition that best fits the term in column A. Then write the letter of the synonym, example, or definition on the line to the left.

Column A

_____ 1. grapheme
_____ 2. morpheme
_____ 3. derived word
_____ 4. phoneme
_____ 5. digraph
_____ 6. compound
_____ 7. phonics
_____ 8. basic sight word
_____ 9. affixes
_____ 10. base word
_____ 11. possessive
_____ 12. diphthong
_____ 13. contraction
_____ 14. inflected word
_____ 15. phonemic awareness

Column B

a. *can't*
b. blended vowel sound
c. *inhospitable*
d. letter
e. clues provided by sentence meaning
f. speech sound
g. merging consecutive consonant sounds, each retaining its own identity
h. meaningful structural unit
i. *meaner*
j. two letters representing one phoneme
k. *tablecloth*
l. *women's*
m. study of phoneme-grapheme relationships
n. *an*
o. major meaning-bearing unit
p. prefixes, suffixes, inflectional endings
q. awareness of sounds in spoken words

Part V

Divide each of the following nonsense words in syllables, and mark the vowels with diacritical marks. Be ready to state your reasons for syllabication and for vowel sounds. Where two possibilities for division exist, give both.

1. ekon
2. roashing
3. whochment
4. sluppelgug
5. presilnapishment
6. drackle
7. mastle
8. kromsul
9. bleting

Part VI

Choose the best answer among the stated possibilities.

1. The study of the phoneme/grapheme relationship in English is called
   a. phonetics.
   b. phonics.
   c. linguistics.
   d. both a and b

2. The word pronounced by the use of phonics must be in the reader's oral language in order to
   a. check the accuracy of the pronunciation.
   b. check the accuracy of phonics rules.
   c. check the contextual meaning of a word.
   d. All of the above.

3. The sounds of *c* and *g* may be identified as
   a. hard and soft.
   b. short and long.
   c. hiss and guttural.
   d. None of the above.

4. Which of the following words contains a digraph?
   a. blind
   b. must
   c. kick
   d. gram

5. Which of the following words contains a consonant blend?
   a. wash
   b. letter
   c. ship
   d. stripe

6. The sounds of *s* may be
   a. c, st, sh, s
   b. s, sh, z, zh
   c. k, c, z, s
   d. gz, ks, s, c

7. In which of the following groups of words are all three exceptions to vowel generalizations?
   a. sir, cat, bake
   b. colt, see, out
   c. car, find, old
   d. vie, sigh, my

8. Which of the following words is probably correctly divided into syllables?
   a. mis-thez-ment
   b. bomn-y
   c. ci-mtor
   d. ba-tmle

9. Which of the following words contains a schwa?
   a. again
   b. cart
   c. book
   d. below

See the Answer Key to check your answers.

Answer Key

Part I

1. three
2. house
3. *str*   *eet*
     d   *ay*
     r   *ace*

Part II

1. d	8. b	15. b
2. a	9. b	16. c
3. c	10. a	17. d
4. a	11. c	18. b
5. d	12. b	19. d
6. d	13. b	20. b
7. c	14. c	

Part III

1. d—final *e* or CVCe generalization
2. b—soft *g* generalization or
 e—CVC generalization
3. c—CVC generalization
4. e—CVVC generalization
5. e—if only first syllable of music is considered;
 c—if second syllable is—open syllable generalization
6. d—r-controlled vowel sound

Part IV

1. d
2. h
3. c
4. f
5. j
6. k
7. m
8. n
9. p
10. o
11. l
12. b
13. a
14. i or l
15. q

Part V

1. ē•kŏon, ĕk•ən
2. rōash• ĭng
3. whŏch•mənt
4. slŭp•pĕl•gŭg, slŭpp•əl•gəg
5. prē•sĭl•năp• ĭsh•mĕnt, prē•sĭl•nā•pĭsh•mənt
6. drăck•əl
7. măs•təl, măst•le
8. krŏm•sŭl
9. blĕt•ing

Part VI

1. b
2. a
3. a
4. c
5. d
6. b
7. c
8. a
9. a

Glossary

acceleration   More than the expected rate of growth.

adequate yearly progress   The expected amount of growth a student should make in reading during one school year. A term used in various government-supported educational programs. Currently defined for each state by its state education agency.

alphabetic principle   The assumption that each speech sound has a corresponding graphic representation.

analogy   In decoding, using letter-sound relationships in known words to figure out the probable pronunciation of unfamiliar words.

analysis   As a form of response, telling how a story event relates to a personal event.

anticipation guide   A series of statements with which students agree or disagree prior to reading and to which they return after reading; used to activate prior knowledge and help students establish a purpose for reading.

application   Part of the follow-up to a minilesson in which students use a strategy in a totally new reading experience; this step supports the ability to transfer strategy use.

authentic assessment   Assessment activities that reflect literacy in the community, the workplace, and the classroom.

authentic literature   Narrative and expository text in its original form. Often referred to as real or trade book literature.

automaticity   Fluent processing of information that occurs with little effort. Doing something automatically.

background knowledge   (also background information, prior knowledge) What students already know, through learning and experience, about a topic or about a kind of text.

basal series or system   A set of texts and other materials produced by a given publisher for teaching literacy. Usually these series are for grades K–6 or K–8. They are often referred to as basal readers or basal programs and are usually called by the publisher's name.

base words   Meaningful linguistic units that can stand alone and contain no smaller meaningful parts; also called free morphemes.

benchmarks   Behaviors exhibited by students at certain stages of development. Sometimes used interchangeably with the term **standards**.

checklist   A form that lists targeted behaviors as indicators of achievement, knowledge, or skill.

cold read   Reading a passage aloud without prior silent reading or preparation. Sometimes used when checking fluency.

clustering   A way of brainstorming on paper; a topic is positioned centrally and concepts and ideas related to that topic are clustered around the center, or core.

comprehension   The part of reading that involves constructing meaning by interacting with text. Comprehension is one part of the reading process.

comprehensive balanced literacy instruction   A combination of teacher-directed instruction and student-centered activities.

Comprehensive Balanced Literacy Program   A plan for literacy instruction that includes the essential blocks of instruction that are supported by research.

concept development   Activating and/or developing student knowledge or background of ideas, understandings, or issues in material to be read.

concepts of print   Features of printed text; usually divided into four categories: *books, sentences, words,* and *letters.*

conference   A meeting between teacher and student or between students; teacher-student conferences may be held in order to share and discuss a book, discuss an aspect of writing, provide a mini-lesson, assess progress, or a combination of these purposes. A conference may be scheduled and structured or informal and unstructured.

context   In literacy, the setting in which a certain word occurs and which contributes to the inference of meaning; context can be a phrase, a sentence, a paragraph, a chapter, or an entire body of work.

conventional writing phase   The time when students will spell most words correctly, or conventionally.

core instruction   The part of the comprehensive literacy program that all students need.

corrective feedback   The process of helping a student overcome a mistake or error by asking leading questions or guiding him or her to achieve a correct response.

created text   Any text especially written to be decodable or to control high-frequency words, concepts, skills, strategies, and overall difficulties.

creative response   An individual or group response to literature that involves such things as art, music, or drama.

cueing systems   Sources of information that help in the identification of a word; these include phonics, structural elements of words, meaning, and language clues.

decodable text   A published or created text that is suitable for the application of previously taught phonics skills.

decoding   The process of translating written language into verbal speech sounds. Decoding is one part of reading.

diagnosis   Testing or assessment done to determine a student's strengths and weaknesses.

dialogue journals   Response journals in which another person (teacher or peer) reads and responds in writing to the student writing.

diaries   Private journals, not usually about something read; not intended to be read by others.

differentiated (differentiating) instruction   Instruction that is designed to accommodate a student's strengths, needs, and stage of development.

direct instruction   Explicit, teacher-led or teacher-modeled instruction.

direct teaching   Planning explicit lessons to teach specific words, information, concepts, or skills.

diversity   In education, having classrooms with students of various backgrounds, languages, needs, and conditions.

domain   A category of writing based on the purpose or type of writing.

double-entry journals   Journals in which a page is divided in half vertically: on the left side students record predictions, take notes, and draw before and during reading; on the right side students write a response after reading. Can also be used as a dialogue journal with the teacher responding on the right side.

drafting   The second part of process writing, with two parts: (1) planning what to write and how to write it, and (2) composing, or writing.

evaluating   A reading strategy using critical thinking to make judgments about what one has read and about one's own reading ability.

explicit instruction   Direct, teacher-led instruction. Involves teacher modeling, student practice with teacher guidance and feedback, and student application in a new situation. Term is used interchangeably with **direct instruction** or **direct teaching**.

explicit modeling   Directly showing and talking about what is to be learned.

expository text   Text that presents information and is organized in whatever way best suits the type of information being presented and the purpose for presenting it.

fluency In reading, the ability to read words of connected text smoothly and without significant word recognition problems. A fluency record is taken by keeping track of words read aloud correctly and those not read correctly. See **running record**.

fluency check Record of student reading aloud a prepared passage to show development in decoding.

formal assessment A test or task using procedures that are carried out under controlled conditions.

frustration reading level The level of material that is too difficult for a reader, even with good instructional support.

generalization A response that shows the student has grasped the theme or meaning of a story.

generating and answering questions Thinking of questions while reading that require integration of new information and then reading to answer those questions.

grade score/grade equivalent A score derived from a raw score on a standardized test that is the equivalent earned by an average student in the norming group.

grapheme A written or printed symbol representing a phoneme; for example *cat* has three phonemes /c/, /a/, /t/. A grapheme may be made up of more than one letter. For example, the word *goat* has three phonemes, but four letters—/g/, /o/, /t/. The letters "oa" stand for the long o phoneme.

graphic organizer Any visual representation that organizes information, such as a story map or semantic map; can be used when activating prior knowledge before reading or when reviewing or summarizing information after reading.

guided listening lesson A structure for planning a listening lesson around a text that has been read aloud to teach a particular strategy or skill. A guided listening lesson has three parts: introduce the text, listen and respond to the text, and extend the text.

guided practice The part of a minilesson in which students continue to use a strategy with teacher guidance, but without modeling.

hierarchical array Graphic display showing the relationship of concepts, often branching to show which concepts are part of some other concept.

high-frequency words The most commonly occurring words in the English language.

implicit modeling Modeling that is not directly stated.

independent reading level The level of material that a reader can read, with few word recognition problems and good comprehension, without instructional support.

inferencing Judging, concluding, or reasoning from given information.

inflectional endings Word parts that can be added to the endings of base or root words and that change the number, gender, tense, or form of the word; sometimes included in the term *suffixes*.

informal assessment Observations or other nonstandardized procedures.

informal reading inventory (IRI) A series of graded passages used to determine a student's reading level as well as strengths and needs in decoding and comprehension.

instructional reading level The level of material that a reader can read with instructional support.

interest inventory A series of statements to which students respond orally or in writing; meant to reveal a student's interests and/or attitudes.

intervention (see also **Tier I, Tier II, and Tier III Intervention**) An instructional program that prevents or stops failure by providing additional instructional time beyond the core instruction.

invented spelling phase In spelling development, the period when the child is associating letters and sounds but not yet using entirely conventional spelling.

journals Places where students record personal reflections, including those about their reading and writing.

jump-start Giving struggling readers a head start with a learning task before they actually begin the task with other students.

K-W-L A strategy for accessing prior knowledge and setting purposes for reading a given text, usually expository, and then recording what has been learned after reading; K = what I know, W = what I want to know, and L = what I have learned or still need to learn.

learning logs Daily records of what a student has learned; does not include a response. Logs can be focused on a particular area of learning.

linear array A kind of hierarchical array that shows a straight-line relationship of certain concepts, such as from highest to lowest, or coldest to hottest.

literacy Ability to listen, speak, read, write, and think. Viewing is a part of literacy that uses many of the skills and strategies involved in the other aspects of literacy.

literacy lesson A structure for planning a teacher-directed reading and writing lesson around a given piece of text. A literacy lesson has three parts: introducing the text, reading and responding to the text, and extending the text.

literature discussion group (or circle) An activity in which children who have read the same book discuss that book; can also be focused on a single author or theme. A teacher may be part of the group or circle initially in order to guide students; the goal is a group discussion without teacher guidance.

making connections A strategy where the reader connects what is read to his or her own experiences, to other texts, and to the world knowledge he or she has.

mapping A kind of graphic organizer; students show important information and the relationships among pieces of information by using a series of boxes, ovals, or lines.

metacognition Knowledge and control of one's own thinking and learning. In reading, metacognition refers to the reader being aware of when reading makes sense and adjusting his or her reading when comprehension fails.

minilesson or focus lesson A concise teacher-directed lesson that is designed to teach a specific strategy, skill, concept, or process.

miscue An oral reading response that differs in some way from the text.

miscue analysis Analyzing a student's reading miscues in order to infer which strategies a student is or is not using.

modeling The process of showing or demonstrating how to use or do something.

modes of reading Different ways in which a text can be read, moving from teacher-directed reading to student independent reading. Usually there are five modes of reading: independent reading, cooperative reading, guided reading, shared reading, and read-aloud.

modes of writing Different ways that writing can take place, moving from teacher-directed writing to student independence. Usually there are five modes of writing: independent writing, collaborative/cooperative writing, guided writing, shared writing, and write-aloud.

monitoring/clarifying A developmental process; while reading, knowing when meaning is lost and having a plan to overcome the problem.

more than adequate yearly progress More than a year's growth in a year's time.

narrative text Text that tells a story; it is usually organized in a sequential pattern and consists of story elements. See **story map**.

observation Looking at student performance of literacy tasks in order to note achievement and draw inferences on which to base instruction.

oral language Listening and speaking.

peer conference Conference between two students having to do with reading or writing.

percentile A score on a scale of 100 indicating the percentage of scores that occur at or below a given raw score; derived from those on whom the test was normed.

performance assessment A task that requires the student to demonstrate literacy knowledge or skill through "real-world" response; a form of authentic assessment.

personal response An oral or written response to something heard or read; it could involve, for example, retelling, generalizing, sharing favorite elements, or telling how a piece of literature relates to one's feelings or one's life.

phoneme The smallest unit of sound in speech; for example, the word *dog* has three phonemes and the word *goat* has three phonemes.

phonemic awareness The knowledge that words are composed of sounds (phonemes).

phonics The use of one's knowledge of the relationship between the letters and the sounds the letters represent to help in determining the pronunciation of a word.

picture walk A strategy to activate prior knowledge and develop concepts and vocabulary before reading; the teacher guides students through a text's pictures, illustrations, or graphics by asking questions to get students to respond.

picture writing A stage in writing development; the child draws a picture to tell a story.

planning/previewing Another term for "selecting the topic," this is the first step in process writing; during this step students decide what they want to write about.

predictable text A text with some type of repeated pattern that allows students to anticipate what is likely to come on subsequent pages.

prediction In reading, telling what one thinks will happen in a story or what information will be presented before actually reading the text.

prefixes Units of meaning that can be added to the beginning of base words or root words to change their meanings; these are bound morphemes and cannot stand alone.

preview and predict A strategy for accessing prior knowledge by previewing the text to be read and making predictions about it.

prior knowledge See **background knowledge**.

process interview In literacy, a series of questions designed to elicit how a student thinks about reading or writing; used to plan future teacher support.

process writing An approach to teaching writing that involves five steps: planning, drafting, revising, proofreading, and publishing.

project A task undertaken to achieve a certain goal; can be used before reading as students activate prior knowledge and after reading to display what has been learned.

proofreading/editing Terms often used interchangeably for the fourth part of process writing; students examine mechanics such as spelling, punctuation, grammar, and paragraphing and make corrections.

publishing The final stage in process writing, involving two steps; students make a final copy and put their writing in a form for sharing with others.

quick writing A strategy for activating prior knowledge by writing for three to five minutes about a topic or idea.

random letter phase In spelling development, the period when the child uses letters in writing that have little or no relationship to the sounds in words.

readers theater A response in which students turn a story into a play by writing the script and then reading (or performing) the play.

reading intervention program A program that either prevents or stops failure by providing additional instructional time.

reading workshop A framework to organize and manage reading in a literacy classroom; includes teacher sharing, minilessons, a state-of-the-class conference, self-selected reading and responding, and student sharing time.

reciprocal teaching An interactive process in which the teacher and students alternate modeling the use of strategies.

reflection Part of the follow-up to a minilesson in which students recall and talk about their use of strategies. Reflection is also part of assessment;

students and teachers discuss what has been learned, how the learning has helped, where it can be used, and what to concentrate on next.

remediation/remedial reading   The process of correcting a deficiency, particularly in reading.

responding   In literacy, what one does as a result of and/or as a part of reading, writing, or listening.

response charts   A way to present response options to students from which they can choose.

response journals/reading journals/literature logs   Record of students' personal reactions to, questions about, and reflections on something read, seen, listened to, or written.

retelling   Recall of something read, usually in the order in which it was presented, including key story elements, main ideas, or important details. See **summary**. As a method of assessment, retelling refers to using a student's unprompted recall of text to infer the student's construction of meaning.

revising   The third part of process writing, during which students examine their work in terms of such things as ideas, organization, word choice, flow, and voice and make changes to improve each of these.

rime   The vowel and any following consonants in a syllable. In the word *rime,* /ime/ is the rime.

role playing   Taking parts and acting out a situation; can be used to activate prior knowledge before or after reading to retell or summarize.

root words   Words, often from another language, from which other words are derived; roots are bound morphemes in that they cannot stand alone as a **base word** in English; sometimes *root* and *base* are used interchangeably.

routine   A pattern of instruction or classroom activity that is used over and over again.

rubric   A set of guidelines or acceptable responses for a given task.

running record   A written record of a student's oral reading, usually recorded on a blank sheet of paper.

scaffolding   The process of providing strong teacher support at the beginning of new learnings and gradually taking it away to allow the student to achieve independence.

schema theory   (pl. schemata) Theory that individuals develop a cognitive structure of knowledge in the mind to which new information and experiences are added as they occur.

scribble writing   A stage in spelling development; the child makes scribble marks on paper that are clearly attempts at writing and not a picture.

semantic feature analysis   Looking at related words (concepts) in terms of similarities, contrasts, or shared characteristics.

semantic mapping   A visual, or graphic, representation of a concept; when used before reading, it is a strategy for activating prior knowledge and developing vocabulary and concepts.

stages of literacy development   Various points in time in the development of the overall literacy process. There are five stages: early emergent literacy, emergent literacy, beginning reading and writing, almost fluent reading and writing, and fluent reading and writing.

standard score   A score that indicates how far an individual is from the average score (mean) on a test in terms of the standard deviation.

standardized test   A test given under specified conditions that allow comparisons to be made; norms or average scores are given to allow comparisons.

standards   Statements that express a degree or level of performance that is expected from students at certain times.

stop and think   A monitoring strategy; also known as a "fix-up" strategy.

story frame   A basic outline for a story with key information omitted; the student fills in the empty slots. A frame may focus on a particular story element or on the whole story.

story map   A graphic display of story elements (setting, character, problem, action or events, and solution); can be used to help students activate prior knowledge about narrative text structure before reading and to summarize a story after reading.

strategy   A plan to accomplish a particular goal.

structural analysis   Using meaningful parts of words such as prefixes, suffixes, inflectional endings, roots, and bases to identify words.

structured preview Guided preview of text that may include a graphic display of information; used to activate prior knowledge before reading.

struggling reader Any student who is having difficulty learning to read.

student modeling The part of a minilesson in which students take over the modeling process with the guidance of the teacher.

student-centered instruction Instruction designed so that students learn implicitly by participating in different activities or experiences.

suffixes Units of meaning that can be added to the ending of base or root words to change the meaning or the function; these are bound morphemes.

summarizing Pulling together the essential elements or main ideas of expository text; also, recapping the story elements of a narrative.

summary Based on something read, an oral or written statement of key story elements, theme, or main ideas. See **retelling**.

synthesizing Integrating new information into existing knowledge as one reads; this leads to a new perspective.

teaching The process of imparting knowledge, a skill, or a strategy to someone. It involves knowing how to model the skill, strategy, or process for students and tell when a student has learned what is being taught.

text structure The organization of informational text.

text walk Similar to a picture walk; refers to a procedure for activating prior knowledge in narrative and expository text that has few pictures, illustrations, or other graphic examples.

think-aloud A kind of explicit modeling in which the teacher shares his or her own thinking processes when performing a task.

Tier I Intervention Intervention instruction that is taught in the classroom and is directly related to the core instructional program that is being used.

Tier II Intervention Intervention provided by a certified teacher, either in small groups or individually, in additional to core instruction but related; it is designed to help students make more than adequate yearly progress.

Tier III Intervention Intervention designed for the struggling reader with the most severe needs. A reading or other learning specialist does a thorough diagnosis and usually provides the instruction, often on an individual basis. It is in addition to core instruction.

Tier One Words Words that are basic and rarely need attention to meaning.

Tier Two Words Words that are of high frequency for mature language users and are found across a variety of areas or domains. They are most useful for teaching because students will encounter them in so many situations.

Tier Three Words Words that have a low frequency of use and are usually specific to a particular content area. They should be taught only for specific reading needs.

traits Characteristics; e.g., the NWREL Six-Trait Analytical Assessment model links writing assessment with writing instruction.

visualizing Forming mental pictures while reading to connect the questions and knowledge in one's head with what one is reading.

vocabulary Words known by an individual; *recognition vocabulary* refers to words an individual can pronounce and understand when he or she encounters them in print; *meaning vocabulary* refers to words one knows the meaning of whether or not one can yet recognize them in print.

word bank (word file, word book) One's personal collection of words learned or words one would like to learn.

word wall A cumulative display of words related to a particular topic, to an interest, or to a structural or phonetic feature.

writing workshop A framework to organize and manage writing in a literacy classroom; includes minilessons, a state-of-the-class conference, writing and conferring, and group sharing.

References

Adams, M. J. (1990). *Beginning to read: Thinking and learning about print*. Cambridge, MA: The MIT Press.

Adams, T. L. (2003). Reading mathematics: More than words can say. *The Reading Teacher, 56*(8), 786–795.

AIMSweb. (n.d.). Evidence-based progress monitoring and improvement system. http://www.aimsweb.com

Alexander, P. A., & Jetton, T. L. (2000). Learning from text: A multidimensional and developmental perspective. In M. L. Kamil, P. B. Mosenthal, P. D. Pearson, & R. Barr (Eds.), *Handbook of reading research* (Vol. 3, pp. 285–310). Mahwah, NJ: Lawrence Erlbaum Associates.

Allington, R. L. (1977). If they don't read much, how they ever gonna get good? *Journal of Reading, 21,* 57–61.

Allington, R. L. (1983). The reading instruction provided readers of differing reading abilities. *Elementary School Journal, 83,* 548–559.

Allington, R. L. (1997). Overselling phonics. *Reading Today,* August/September, pp. 15–16.

Allington, R. L., & Walmsley, S. A. (Eds.). (1995). *No quick fix: Rethinking literacy programs in America's elementary schools*. New York: Teachers College Press.

Alvermann, D. E., Dillon, D. R., & O'Brien, D. G. (1987). *Using discussion to promote reading comprehension*. Newark, DE: International Reading Association.

Alvermann, D. E., & Hynd, C. R. (1987, December). *Overcoming misconceptions in science: An on-line study of prior knowledge activation*. Paper presented at the meeting of the National Reading Conference, St. Petersburg, FL.

Alvermann, D. E., & Moore, D. W. (1991). Secondary school reading. In R. Barr, M. L. Kamil, P. B. Mosenthal, & P. D. Pearson (Eds.), *Handbook of reading research* (Vol. 2, pp. 951–983). New York: Longman.

Alvermann, D. E., Smith, L. C., & Readence, J. E. (1985). Prior knowledge activation and the comprehension of compatible and incompatible text. *Reading Research Quarterly, 20,* 420–436.

Anderson, R. C., & Freebody, P. (1981). Vocabulary knowledge. In J. T. Guthrie (Ed.), *Comprehension and teaching: Research reviews*. Newark: International Reading Association.

Anderson, R. C., Hiebert, E. H., Scott, J. A., & Wilkinson, I. A. G. (1985). *Becoming a nation of readers: The report of the Commission on Reading*. Washington, DC: The National Institute of Education.

Anderson, R. C., & Pearson, P. D. (1984). A schema-theoretic view of basic processes in reading comprehension. In P. D. Pearson (Ed.), *Handbook of reading research* (pp. 255–291). New York: Longman.

Anderson, R. C., Reynolds, R. E., Schallert, D. L., & Goetz, E. T. (1977). Frameworks for comprehending discourse. *American Educational Research Journal, 14,* 367–381.

Angelillo, J. (2005). *Making revision matter*. New York: Scholastic.

Applebee, A. N. (1977). Writing and reading. *Journal of Reading, 20,* 534–537.

Applebee, A. N. (1978). *The child's concept of story: Ages two to seventeen*. Chicago: University of Chicago Press.

Applegate, M. D., Quinn, K. B., & Applegate, A. J. (2006). Profiles in comprehension. *The Reading Teacher, 60*(1), 48–57.

Armbruster, B. B., & Osborn, J. (2003). *Put reading first: The research building blocks for teaching children to read (K–3)* (2nd ed.). Ann Arbor: Center for the Improvement of Early Reading Achievement, University of Michigan.

Armento, B. J., Nash, G. B., Salter, C. L., & Wixson, K. (1991). *America will be*. Boston: Houghton Mifflin.

Arthaud, T. J., & Goracke, T. (2006). Implementing a structured story web and outline strategy to assist struggling readers. *The Reading Teacher, 59*(6), 581–586.

Assaf, L. (2006). One reading specialist's response to high-stakes testing pressures. *The Reading Teacher, 60*(2), 158–167.

Association for Supervision and Curriculum Development. (1995). *Educating everybody's children: Diverse teaching strategies for diverse learners*. Alexandria, VA: Author.

Atwell, N. (1998). *In the middle* (2nd ed.). Portsmouth, NH: Heinemann.

Au, K. H. (1991). Speech delivered at the Notre Dame Reading Conference, South Bend, IN, June 25, 1991, sponsored by Houghton Mifflin Company, Boston.

Au, K. H. (1993). *Literacy instruction in multicultural settings*. Fort Worth, TX: Harcourt, Brace.

Au, K. H., Carroll, J. H., & Scheu, J. A. (2001). *Balanced literacy instruction: A teacher's resource book* (2nd ed.). Norwood, MA: Christopher-Gordon Publishers.

Baghban, M. (1984). *Our daughter learns to read and write: A case study from birth to three*. Newark, DE: International Reading Association.

Ball, E. W., & Blachman, B. A. (1991). Does phoneme segmentation training make a difference in early word recognition and developmental spelling? *Reading Research Quarterly, 26,* 49–66.

Bandura, A. (1986). *Psychological modeling: Conflicting theories*. Chicago: Aldine-Atherton.

Barone, D. (1990). The written responses of young children: Beyond comprehension to story understanding. *New Advocate, 3,* 49–56.

Barr, R., & Dreeben, R. (1991). Grouping students for reading instruction. In R. Barr, M. L. Kamil, P. Mosenthal, & P. D. Pearson (Eds.), *Handbook of reading research* (Vol. 2, pp. 885–910). New York: Longman.

Barr, R., Kamil, M. L., Mosenthal, P., & Pearson, P. D. (1991). *Handbook of reading research* (Vol. 2). New York: Longman.

Barrera, R. B. (1983). Bilingual reading in the primary grades: Some questionable views and practices. In T. H. Escobedo (Ed.), *Early childhood bilingual education* (pp. 164–184). New York: Teachers College Press.

Bartlett, F. C. (1932). *Remembering*. Cambridge: Cambridge University Press.

Barton, J., & Sawyer, D. M. (2003–2004). Our students are reading for this: Comprehension instruction in the elementary school. *The Reading Teacher, 57*(4), 334–347.

Baumann, J. F. (1984). The effectiveness of a direct instruction paradigm for teaching main idea comprehension. *Reading Research Quarterly, 20*(1), 93–115.

Baumann, J. F. (1986). *Teaching main idea comprehension*. Newark, DE: International Reading Association.

Bear, D. R., Invernizzi, M., Templeton, S. R., & Johnston, F. (2008). *Words their way: Word study for phonics, vocabulary, and spelling instruction* (4th ed.). New York: Prentice Hall.

Beck, I., & McKeown, M. (1981). Developing questions that promote comprehension: The story map. *Language Arts, 58,* 913–918.

Beck, I., & McKeown, M. (1991). Conditions of vocabulary acquisition. In R. Barr, M. L. Kamil, P. Mosenthal, & P. D. Pearson (Eds.), *Handbook of reading research* (Vol. 2, pp. 789–814). New York: Longman.

Beck, I. L. (1984). Developing comprehension: The impact of the directed reading lesson. In R. C. Anderson, J. Osborn, & R. J. Tierney (Eds.), *Learning to read in American schools: Basal readers and content texts* (pp. 3–20). Hillsdale, NJ: Lawrence Erlbaum Associates.

Beck, I. L., McCaslin, M., & McKeown, M. (1980). *The rationale and design of a program to teach vocabulary to fourth-grade students*. Pittsburgh: University of Pittsburgh, Learning Research and Development Center.

Beck, I. L., McKeown, M. G., & Kucan, L. (2002). *Bringing words to life: Robust vocabulary instruction.* New York: Guilford Press.

Beck, I. L., McKeown, M. G., McCaslin, E. S., & Burkes, A. M. (1979). *Instructional dimension that may affect reading comprehension: Examples from two commercial reading programs.* Pittsburgh: University of Pittsburgh, Learning Research and Development Center.

Beck, I. L., McKeown, M. G., & Omanson, R. C. (1987). The effects and uses of diverse vocabulary instructional techniques. In M. G. McKeown & M. E. Curtis (Eds.), *The nature of vocabulary acquisition.* Hillsdale, NJ: Lawrence Erlbaum Associates.

Beck, I. L., Omanson, R. C., & McKeown, M. G. (1982). An instructional redesign of reading lessons: Effects on comprehension. *Reading Research Quarterly, 17*(4), 462–481.

Beck, I. L., Perfetti, C. A., & McKeown, M. G. (1982). Effects of long-term vocabulary instruction on lexical access and reading comprehension. *Journal of Educational Psychology, 74,* 506–521.

Bertrand, J. E. (1991). Student assessment and evaluation. In B. Harp (Ed.), *Assessment and evaluation in whole language programs* (pp. 17–33). Norwood, MA: Christopher-Gordon Publishers.

Biancarosa, G. & Snow, C. E. (2004). *Reading next—a vision for action and research in middle and high school literacy: A report to Carnegie Corporation of New York.* Washington, DC: Alliance for Excellent Education.

Birnbaum, J. C. (1982). The reading and composing behavior of selected fourth- and seventh-grade students. *Research in the Teaching of English, 16,* 241–260.

Bissex, G. L. (1980). *Gnys at wrk: A child learns to read and write.* Cambridge, MA: Harvard University Press.

Blachowicz, C. L. Z. (1986). Making connections: Alternatives to the vocabulary notebook. *Journal of Reading, 29,* 643–649.

Blachowicz, C. L. Z., & Fisher, P. (2000). Vocabulary instruction. In M. L. Kamil, P. B. Mosenthal, P. D. Pearson, & R. Barr (Eds.), *Handbook of reading research* (Vol. 3, pp. 503–523). Mahwah, NJ: Lawrence Erlbaum Associates.

Blair, T. R., Rupley, W. H., & Nichols, W. D. (2007). The effective teacher of reading: Considering the "what" and "how" of instruction. *The Reading Teacher, 60*(5), 432–438.

Block, C. C., & Mangieri, J. N. (Eds.). (2006). *The vocabulary enriched classroom: Practices for improving the reading performance of all students in grades 3 and up.* New York: Scholastic.

Bloomfield, L., & Barnhart, C. (1961). *Let's read: A linguistic approach.* Detroit: Wayne State University Press.

Bond, G. L., & Dykstra, R. (1967). The cooperative research program in first-grade reading instruction. *Reading Research Quarterly, 2* (entire issue).

Bradley, B. A., & Jones, J. (2007). Sharing alphabet books in early childhood classrooms. *The Reading Teacher, 60*(5), 452–463.

Brassell, D. (2006/2007). Inspiring young scientists with great books. *The Reading Teacher, 60*(4), 336–342.

Brevig, L. (2006). Engaging in Retrospective Reflection. *The Reading Teacher, 59*(6), 522–530.

Bridge, C., Winograd, P. N., & Haley, D. (1983). Using predictable materials vs. preprimers to teach beginning sight words. *The Reading Teacher, 36*(9), 884–891.

Broemmel, A. D. & Rearden, K. T. (2006). Should teachers use the Teachers' Choices books in science classes? *The Reading Teacher, 60*(3), 254–265.

Brown, A. L., & Day, J. D. (1983). Macrorules for summarizing texts: The development of expertise. *Journal of Verbal Learning and Verbal Behavior, 22*(1), 1–14.

Brown, J. S., Collins, A., & Duguid, P. (1989). Situated cognition and the culture of learning. *Educational Researcher, 18,* 32–42.

Brown, K. J. (2000). What kind of text—For whom and when? Textual scaffolding for beginning readers. *The Reading Teacher, 53*(4), 292–307.

Brown, K. J. (2003). What do I say when they get stuck on a word? Aligning teachers' prompts with students' development. *The Reading Teacher, 56*(8), 720–733.

Buehl, D. (2001). *Classroom strategies for interactive learning* (2nd ed.). Newark, DE: International Reading Association.

Burns, P. C., Roe, B. D., & Ross, E. P. (1988). *Teaching reading in today's elementary schools* (4th ed.). Boston: Houghton Mifflin.

Cain, K. (1996). Story knowledge and comprehension skills. In C. Cornoldi & J. Oakhill (Eds.), *Reading comprehension difficulties: Processes and interventions* (pp. 167–192). Mahwah, NJ: Lawrence Erlbaum Associates.

Calfee, R. C., & Drum, P. A. (1986). Research on teaching reading. In M. C. Wittrock (Ed.), *Handbook of research on teaching* (3rd ed., pp. 804–849). New York: Macmillan.

Calkins, L. M. (1983). *Lessons from a child on the teaching and learning of writing.* Exeter, NH: Heinemann.

Calkins, L. M. (1994). *The art of teaching writing* (new ed.). Portsmouth, NH: Heinemann.

Cambourne, B., & Turbill, J. (1990). Assessment in whole language classrooms: Theory into practice. *Elementary School Journal, 90,* 337–349.

Carnine, L., Carnine, D., & Gersten, R. (1984). Analysis of oral reading errors made by economically disadvantaged students taught with a synthetic phonics approach. *Reading Research Quarterly, 19,* 343–356.

Carr, M. (1987). Clustering with nonreaders/writers. In C. B. Olson (Ed.), *Practical ideas for teaching writing as a process* (pp. 20–21). Sacramento, CA: California State Department of Education.

Carrier, K. A., & Tatum, A. W. (2006). Creating sentence walls to help English-language learners develop content literacy. *The Reading Teacher, 60*(3), 285–288.

Cartwright, K. B. (2006). Fostering flexibility and comprehension in elementary students. *The Reading Teacher, 59*(7), 628–634.

Cazden, C. (1972). *Child language and education.* New York: Holt, Rinehart and Winston.

Center for the Study of Reading. (n.d.) *Suggestions for the classroom: Teachers and independent reading.* Urbana: University of Illinois Press, Center for the Study of Reading.

Chall, J. S. (1967). *Learning to read: The great debate.* New York: McGraw-Hill.

Chall, J. S. (1983). *Learning to read: The great debate* (rev. ed.). New York: McGraw-Hill.

Chall, J. S. (1987). Two vocabularies for reading: Recognition and meaning. In M. G. McKeown & M. E. Curtis (Eds.), *The nature of vocabulary acquisition* (pp. 7–17). Hillsdale, NJ: Lawrence Erlbaum Associates.

Chall, J. S. (2000). *The academic achievement challenge.* New York: The Guilford Press.

Chard, D., & Osborne, J. (n.d.). *Guidelines for examining phonics and word recognition instruction in early reading programs.* Austin, TX: Texas Center for Reading and Language Arts. (photocopy)

Chard, D. J., & Osborne, J. (1999). Phonics and word recognition instruction in early reading programs: Guidelines for accessibility. *Learning Disabilities Research and Practice, 14*(2), 107–117.

Chen, L. & Mora-Flores, E. (2006). *Balanced literacy for English language learners, K–2.* Portsmouth, NH: Heinemann.

Chomsky, N. (1965). *Aspects of the theory of syntax.* Cambridge, MA: MIT Press.

Clark, C. M. (1984). Teacher planning and reading comprehension. In G. G. Duffy, L. K. Roehler, & J. Mason (Eds.), *Comprehension instruction: Perspectives and suggestions* (pp. 58–70). New York: Longman.

Clark, K. F. (2004). What can I say besides "sound it out"? Coaching word recognition in beginning reading. *The Reading Teacher, 57*(5), 440–449.

Clark, M. M. (1976). *Young fluent readers.* London: Heinemann.

Clay, M. M. (1982). *Observing young readers: Selected papers.* Exeter, NH: Heinemann.

Clay, M. M. (1985). *The early detection of reading difficulties* (3rd ed.). Portsmouth, NH: Heinemann.

Clay, M. M. (1991). *Becoming literate: The construction of inner control.* Portsmouth, NH: Heinemann.

Cobb, C. (2003/2004). Effective instruction begins with purposeful assessments. *The Reading Teacher, 57*(4), 386–388.

Coger, L. E., & White, M. R. (1982). *Readers theatre handbook: A dramatic approach to literature.* Glenview, IL: Scott, Foresman.

Cole, A. D. (2006). Scaffolding beginning readers: Micro and macro cues teachers use during student oral reading. *The Reading Teacher, 59*(5), 450–459.

Coley, J. D., & Hoffman, D. M. (1990). Overcoming learned helplessness in at-risk readers. *Journal of Reading, 33,* 497–502.

Collins, A., Brown, J. S., & Newman, S. E. (1987). *Cognitive apprenticeship: Teaching the craft of reading, writing and mathematics.* Technical Report No. 403. Urbana: University of Illinois Press, Center for the Study of Reading.

Cook, M. J. (2005). A journal for Corduroy: Responding to literature. *The Reading Teacher, 59*(3), 282–285.

Cook-Gumprez, J. (Ed.). (1986). *The social construction of literacy.* Cambridge: Cambridge University Press.

Cooper, J. D. (1986). *Improving reading comprehension.* Boston: Houghton Mifflin.

Cooper, J. D., Boschken, I., McWilliams, J., & Pistochini, L. (2000). A study of the effectiveness of an intervention program designed to accelerate reading for struggling readers in upper grades. In T. Shanahan & F. V. Rodriguez-Brown (Eds.), *Forty-ninth Yearbook of the National Reading Conference* (pp. 477–486). Chicago: National Reading Conference.

Cooper, J. D., Boschken, I., McWilliams, J., & Pistochinni, L. (2001). *Soar to Success, 3–8.* Boston: Houghton Mifflin.

Cooper, J. D., Chard, D. J., & Kiger, N. D. (2006). *The struggling reader: Interventions that work.* New York: Scholastic.

Cooper, J. D., & Kiger, N. D. (2008). *Literacy assessment: Helping teachers plan instruction* (3rd ed.). Boston: Houghton Mifflin.

Cooper, J. D., Warncke, E., Shipman, D., & Ramstad, P. A. (1979). *The what and how of reading instruction.* Columbus: Charles E. Merrill.

Cortese, E. E. (2003–2004). The application of Question-Answer Relationship strategies to pictures. *The Reading Teacher, 57*(4), 374–380.

Cullinan, B., Harwood, K., & Galda, L. (1983). The reader and the story: Comprehension and response. *Journal of Research and Development in Education, 16,* 29–38.

Cummins, J. (1981). The role of primary language development in promoting educational success for language minority students. *Schooling and language minority students: A theoretical framework* (pp. 3–49). Los Angeles: Los Angeles Evaluation, Dissemination and Assessment Center, California State University.

Cunningham, J. W., Cunningham, P. M., & Arthur, S. U. (1981). *Middle and secondary school reading.* New York: Longman.

Cunningham, P. (2005). "If they don't read much, how they ever gonna get good?" *The Reading Teacher, 59*(1), 88–90.

Cunningham, P. (2006). What if they can *say* the words but don't know what they *mean? The Reading Teacher, 59*(7), 708–711.

Cunningham, P., & Allington, R. L. (2007). *Classrooms that work: They can all read and write* (4th ed.). Boston: Pearson/Allyn & Bacon.

Cunningham, P. A., Hall, D. P., & Defee, M. (1998). Nonability grouped, multilevel instruction: Eight years later. *The Reading Teacher, 5*(18), 652–664.

Cunningham, P. M. (2005). *Phonics they use: Words for reading and writing* (4th ed.). Boston: Pearson/Allyn & Bacon.

Cunningham, P. M. (2006/2007). High-poverty schools that beat the odds. *The Reading Teacher, 60*(4), 382–385.

Cunningham, P. M., & Cunningham, J. W. (1992). Making words: Enhancing the invented spelling-decoding connection. *The Reading Teacher, 46*(2), 106–115.

Dahl, K. L. (1988). Peer conferences as social contexts for learning about revision. In J. E. Readence & R. S. Baldwin (Eds.), *Dialogues in literacy research* (pp. 307–315), Thirty-seventh Yearbook of the National Reading Conference. Chicago: The National Reading Conference.

Dahl, K. L., & Farnan, N. (1998). *Children's writing: Perspectives from research.* Newark, DE;

International Reading Association; and Chicago, IL: National Reading Conference.

Daniels, H. (2001). *Literature circles* (2nd ed.). Portland, ME: Stenhouse.

Daniels, H. (2001). *Looking into literature circles.* Portland, ME: Stenhouse. [Videotape.]

Davey, B., & McBride, S. (1986). Effects of question generating training on reading comprehension. *Journal of Educational Psychology, 78*(4), 256–262.

Davis, F. (1971). Psychometric research in reading comprehension. In F. Davis (Ed.), *Literature of research in reading with emphasis on models.* Brunswick, NJ: Rutgers University Press.

Dawson, M. M. (1987). Beyond ability grouping: A review of ability grouping and its alternatives. *School Reading Review, 16,* 348–369.

DeFord, D. E., Lyons, C. A., & Pinnell, G. S. (1991). *Bridges to literacy: Learning from reading recovery.* Portsmouth, NH: Heinemann.

Dewitz, P., & Dewitz, P. K. (2003). They can read the words, but they can't understand: Refining comprehension assessment. *The Reading Teacher, 56*(5), 422–435.

Dickinson, D. K., McCabe, A., & Sprague, K. (2003). Teacher Rating of Oral Language and Literacy (TROLL): Individualizing early literacy instruction with a standards-based rating tool. *The Reading Teacher, 56*(6), 554–563.

Dillon, D. (1990). Editorial. *Language Arts, 67,* 237–239.

Dillon, J. T. (1984). Research on questioning and discussion. *Educational Leadership, 42,* 50–56.

Dix, S. (2006). I'll do it my way: Three writers and their revision practices. *The Reading Teacher, 59*(6), 566–573.

Dolch, E. W. (1936). A basic sight vocabulary. *Elementary School Journal, 36,* 456–460.

Dole, J. A., Duffy, G. G., Roehler, L. R., & Pearson, P. D. (1991). Moving from the old to the new: Research on reading comprehension instruction. *Review of Educational Research, 61,* 239–264.

Dole, J. A., & Smith, E. L. (1989). Prior knowledge and learning from science text: An instructional study. In the *Thirty-eighth Yearbook of the National Reading Conference, Cognitive and Social Perspectives for Literacy Research and Instruction* (pp. 345–352). Chicago: The National Reading Conference.

Donovan, H., & Ellis, M. (2005). Paired reading— More than an evening of entertainment. *The Reading Teacher, 59*(2), 174–182.

Dorr, R. A. (2006). Something old is new again: Revisiting language experience. *The Reading Teacher, 60*(2), 138–146.

Dressel, J. H. (1990). The effects of listening to and discussing different qualities of children's literature on the narrative writing of fifth graders. *Research in the Teaching of English, 24,* 397–414.

Driver, R., & Erickson, G. (1983). Theories in action: Some theoretical and empirical issues in the study of students' conceptual frameworks in science. *Studies in Science Education, 10,* 37–60.

Drucker, M. J. (2003). What reading teachers should know about ESL learners. *The Reading Teacher, 57*(1), 22–29.

Duffy, G. G. (1993). Rethinking strategy instruction: Four teachers' development and their low achievers' understandings. *Elementary School Journal, 93*(3), 231–247.

Duffy, G. G., et al. (1987). Putting the teacher in control: Basal reading textbooks and instructional decision making. *Elementary School Journal, 87*(3), 357–366.

Duke, N. K., & Purcell-Gates, V. (2003). Genres at home and at school: Bridging the known to the new. *The Reading Teacher, 57*(1), 30–37.

Duke, N. K., Purcell-Gates, V., Hall, L. A., & Tower, C. (2006/2007). Authentic literacy activities for developing comprehension and writing. *The Reading Teacher, 60*(4), 344–355.

Durkin, D. (1966). *Children who read early.* New York: Teachers College Press.

Durkin, D. (1978). What classroom observations reveal about reading comprehension instruction. *Reading Research Quarterly, 14*(4), 481–533.

Durkin, D. (1981). Reading comprehension instruction in five basal reader series. *Reading Research Quarterly, 16*(4), 515–544.

Durkin, D. (1989). *Curriculum reform: Teaching reading in kindergarten* (Tech. Rep. No. 465).

Urbana: University of Illinois Press, Center for the Study of Reading.

Durkin, D. (1990). Dolores Durkin speaks on instruction. *The Reading Teacher, 43,* 472–476.

Dworin, J. E. (2006). The Family Stories Project: Using funds of knowledge for writing. *The Reading Teacher, 59*(6), 510–520.

Dymock, S. (2005). Teaching expository text structure awareness. *The Reading Teacher, 59*(2), 177–182.

Dzaldov, B. S., & Peterson, S. (2005). Book leveling and readers. *The Reading Teacher, 59*(3), 222–229.

Editors of the American Heritage Dictionary (1986). *Word mysteries and histories.* Boston: Houghton Mifflin.

Education Commission of the States. (2001). *Building on progress: How ready are states to implement President Bush's education plan?* Denver, CO: Author.

Eeds, M. (1989). Grand conversations: An exploration of meaning construction in study groups. *Research in the Teaching of English, 23,* 4–29.

Ehri, L. (1991). The development of the ability to read words. In R. Barr, M. Kamil, P. Mosenthal, & P. D. Pearson (Eds.), *Handbook of reading research* (Vol. 2, pp. 383–417). New York: Longman.

Ehri, L. (1997). Learning to read and learning to spell are one and the same, almost. In C. Perfetti, L. Rieben, & M. Fayol (Eds.), *Learning to spell: Research, theory, and practice across languages* (pp. 237–269). Mahwah, NJ: Lawrence Erlbaum Associates.

Ehri, L. C., & Robbins, C. (1992). Beginners need some decoding skill to read words by analogy. *Reading Research Quarterly, 27,* 13–26.

Eldredge, J. L. (1995). *Teaching decoding in holistic classrooms.* Englewood Cliffs, NJ: Merrill, An Imprint of Prentice Hall.

Elley, W. (1998). *Raising literacy levels in third world countries: A method that works.* Culver City: Language Education Associates.

Engel, T., & Streich, R. (2006). Yes, there *is* room for soup in the curriculum: Achieving accountability in a collaboratively planned writing program. *The Reading Teacher, 59*(7), 660–679.

Evans, K. S. (2001). *Literature discussion groups in the intermediate grades.* Newark, DE: International Reading Association.

Falk, B. (2000). *The heart of the matter: Using standards and assessment to learn.* Portsmouth, NH: Heinemann.

Farr, R., & Carey, R. F. (1986). *Reading: What can be measured?* (2nd ed.). Newark, DE: International Reading Association.

Farr, R., & Tone, B. (1994). *Portfolio and performance assessment: Helping students evaluate their progress as readers and writers.* Orlando: Harcourt Brace College Publishers.

Feitelson, D., Kita, B., & Goldstein, Z. (1986). Effects of listening to stories on first graders' comprehension and use of language. *Research in the Teaching of English, 20,* 339–356.

Fielding, L., Wilson, P. T. & Anderson, R. C. (1986). A new focus on free reading. The role of tradebooks in reading instruction. In T. E. Raphael (Ed.), *Contexts of school-based literacy* (pp. 149–160). New York: Random House.

Fielding, L. G., Anderson, R. C., & Pearson, P. D. (1990). How discussion questions influence children's story understanding (Tech. Report No. 490). Urbana: University of Illinois Press, Center for the Study of Reading.

Fiene, J., & McMahon, S. (2007). Assessing comprehension: A classroom-based process. *The Reading Teacher, 60*(5), 406–417.

Fisk, C., & Hurst, B. (2003). Paraphrasing for comprehension. *The Reading Teacher, 57*(2), 182–185.

Flesch, R. (1955). *Why Johnny can't read.* New York: Harper & Row.

Flippo, R. F. (2003). *Assessing readers.* Portsmouth, NH: Heinemann.

Flood, J., & Lapp, D. (1988). Conceptual mapping strategies for information texts. *The Reading Teacher, 41,* 780–783.

Flood, J., & Lapp, D. (1989). Reporting reading progress: A comparison portfolio for parents. *The Reading Teacher, 42*(7), 508–514.

Forbes, S., Poparad, M. A., & McBride, M. (2004). To err is human; to self-correct is to learn. *The Reading Teacher, 57*(6), 566–572.

Fortenberry, C. L., & Fowler, T. W. (2006–2007). Mind magnets. *The Reading Teacher, 60*(4), 373–376.

Fountas, I. C., & Pinnell, G. S. (1996). *Guided reading: Good first teaching for all children.* Portsmouth, NH: Heinemann.

Fountas, I. C., & Pinnell, G. S. (2001). *Guiding readers and writers grades 3–6.* Portsmouth, NH: Heinemann.

Fowler, G. L. (1982). Developing comprehension skills in primary grades through the use of story frames. *The Reading Teacher, 36*(2), 176–179.

Freeman, D. E., & Freeman, Y. S. (2000). *Teaching reading in multilingual classrooms.* Portsmouth, NH: Heineman.

Freeman, D. E., & Freeman, Y. S. (2001). *Between worlds: Access to second language acquisition.* Portsmouth, NH: Heinemann.

Freeman, Y. S., & Freeman, D. E. (1997). *Teaching reading and writing in Spanish in the bilingual classroom.* Portsmouth, NH: Heinemann.

Freppon, P., & Dahl, K. L. (1998). Theory and research into practice: Balanced instruction: Insights and considerations. *Reading Research Quarterly, 33*(2), 240–251.

Fries, C. (1962). *Linguistics and reading.* New York: Holt, Rinehart & Winston.

Galda, L. (1982). Assuming the spectator stance: An examination of the responses of three young readers. *Research in the Teaching of English, 16*, 1–20.

Galda, L. (1983). Research in response to literature. *Journal of Research and Development in Education, 16*, 1–7.

Gambrell, L., Pfeiffer, W., & Wilson, R. (1985). The effects of retelling upon reading comprehension and recall of text information. *Journal of Educational Research, 78*, 216–220.

Gambrell, L. B. (2004). Exploring the connection between oral language and early reading. *The Reading Teacher, 57*(5), 490–492.

Gambrell, L. B., Morrow, L. M., & Pressley, M. (2007). *Best practices in literacy instruction* (3rd ed.). New York: Guilford Press.

Gambrell, T. (1986). Growth in response to literature. *English Quarterly, 19*, 130–141.

Gammil, D. M. (2006). Learning the *write* way. *The Reading Teacher, 59*(8), 754–762.

Ganske, K., Monroe, J. K., & Strickland, D. S. (2003). Questions teachers ask about struggling readers and writers. *The Reading Teacher, 57*(2), 118–128.

Garan, E. M. (2001). Beyond the smoke and mirrors: A critique of the National Reading Panel report on phonics. *Phi Delta Kappan, 82*(7), 500–506.

Garcia, G. E. (1994). Assessing the literacy development of second language students: A focus on authentic assessment. In K. Spangenberg-Urbschat & R. Pritchard (Eds.), *Kids come in all languages: Reading instruction for ESL students* (pp. 180–205). Newark, DE: International Reading Association.

Garcia, G. E. (2000). Bilingual children's reading. In M. L. Kamil, P. B. Mosenthal, P. D. Pearson, & R. Barr (Eds.), *Handbook of reading research* (Vol. 3, pp. 813–834). Mahwah, NJ: Lawrence Erlbaum Associates.

Gaskins, I. W., Downer, M. A., Anderson, R. C., Cunningham, P. M., Gaskings, R. W., Schommer, M., & The Teachers of Benchmark School. (1988). A metacognitive approach to phonics: Using what you know to decode what you don't know. *Remedial and Special Education, 9*, 36–41.

Gentry, J. R. (1977). *My kid can't spell.* Portsmouth, NH: Heinemann.

Gentry, J. R. (2004). *The science of spelling: The explicit specifics that make great readers and writers (and spellers).* Portsmouth, NH: Heinemann.

Gentry, J. R., & Gillet, J. W. (1993). *Teaching kids to spell.* Portsmouth, NH: Heinemann.

Gill, S. R. (2006). Teaching rimes with shared reading. *The Reading Teacher, 60*(2), 191–193.

Gipe, J. P. (1978–1979). Investigating techniques for teaching word meanings. *Reading Research Quarterly, 14*, 624–644.

Goldenberg, C. (1991). Learning to read in New Zealand: The balance of skills and meaning. *Language Arts, 68*, 555–562.

Gonzalez-Bueno, M. (2003). Literacy activities for Spanish-English bilingual children. *The Reading Teacher, 57*(2), 189–192.

Good, R. H., & Kaminski, R. A. (Eds.). (2002). *Dynamic indicators of basic early literacy skills* (6th ed.). Eugene, OR: Institute for the Development of Educational Achievement.

Goodman, K., & Goodman, Y. (1991). Consumer beware! Selecting materials for whole language readers. In K. S. Goodman, L. B. Bird, & Y. M. Goodman (Eds.), *The whole language catalog* (p. 119). American School Publishers.

Goodman, K. S. (1965). A linguistic study of cues and miscues in reading. *Elementary English, 42,* 639–643.

Goodman, Y., & Burke, C. (1972). *Reading miscue inventory manual: Procedures for diagnosis and evaluation.* New York: Richard C. Owen.

Goodman, Y., Watson, D., & Burke, C. (2005). *Reading miscue inventory: From evaluation to instruction* (2nd ed.). New York: Richard C. Owen.

Grabe, M. (2006). *Integrated technology for meaningful learning* (5th ed.). Boston: Houghton Mifflin.

Grabe M., & Grabe, C. (2001). *Integrated technology for meaningful learning* (2nd ed.). Boston: Houghton Mifflin.

Graves, D. (1989). When children respond to fiction. *Language Arts, 66,* 777–783.

Graves, D., & Hansen, J. (1983). The author's chair. *Language Arts, 60,* 176–182.

Graves, D. H. (1983). *Writing: Teachers and children at work.* Exeter, NH: Heinemann Educational Books.

Graves, D. H. (1984). *A researcher learns to write.* Exeter, NH: Heinemann.

Graves, D. H. (1991). *Build a literate classroom.* Portsmouth, NH: Heinemann.

Graves, M. F. (1986). Vocabulary learning and instruction. *Review of Research in Education, 13,* 91–128.

Graves, M. F. (1987). The roles of instruction in fostering vocabulary development. In M. G. McKeown & M. E. Curtis (Eds.), *The nature of vocabulary acquisition* (pp. 165–184). New York: Lawrence Erlbaum Associates.

Graves, M. F., & Cooke, C. L. (1980). Effects of previewing difficult short stories for high school students. *Research on Reading in Secondary Schools, 6,* 28–54.

Graves, M. F., Cooke, C. L., & LaBerge, H. J. (1983). Effects of previewing difficult and short stories on low-ability junior high school students' comprehension, recall and attitude. *Reading Research Quarterly, 18,* 262–276.

Gregg, M., & Sekeres, D. C. (2006). Supporting children's reading of expository text in the geography classroom. *The Reading Teacher, 60*(2), 102–110.

Haggard, M. R. (1982). The vocabulary self-collection strategy: An active approach to word learning. *Journal of Reading, 27,* 203–207.

Haggard, M. R. (1986). The vocabulary self-collection strategy: Using student interest and world knowledge to enhance vocabulary growth. *Journal of Reading, 29,* 634–642.

Halliday, M. A. K. (1975). *Learning how to mean.* New York: Elsevier North-Holland.

Hammerberg, D. D. (2004). Comprehension instruction for socioculturally diverse classrooms: A review of what we know. *The Reading Teacher, 57*(7), 648–658.

Hansen, J. (1981). The effects of inference training and practice on young children's reading comprehension. *Reading Research Quarterly, 16,* 391–417.

Hansen, J. (1987). *When writers read.* Portsmouth, NH: Heinemann.

Harp, B. (1989). What do we know about ability grouping? *The Reading Teacher, 42,* 430–431.

Harp, B. (1991). Principles of assessment in whole language classrooms. In B. Harp (Ed.), *Assessment and evaluation in whole language programs* (pp. 35–50). Norwood, MA: Christopher-Gordon Publishers.

Harris, A. J., & Sipay, E. R. (1985). *How to increase reading ability* (8th ed.). New York: Longman.

Harris, T. L., & Hodges, R. E. (Eds.). (1995). *The literacy dictionary.* Newark, DE: International Reading Association.

Harste, J. C., Short, K. G., & Burke, C. (1988). Literature circles. In *Creating classrooms for authors* (pp. 293–304). Portsmouth, NH: Heinemann.

Harvey, S., & Goudvis, A. (2000). *Strategies that work.* York, MN: Stenhouse Publishers.

Hasbrouck, J. E., & Tindal, G. (1992, Spring). Curriculum-based oral reading fluency norms for students in grades 2 through 5. *Teaching Exceptional Children, 24,* 41–44.

Hasbrouck, J. E., & Tindal, G. (2006). Oral reading fluency norms: A valuable measurement tool for reading teachers. *The Reading Teacher, 59*(7), 636–644.

Hashey, J. M., & Connors, D. J. (2003) Learn from our journey: Reciprocal teaching action research. *The Reading Teacher, 57*(3), 224–232.

Helman, L. A. (2004). Building on the sound system of Spanish: Insights from the alphabetic spellings of English-language learners. *The Reading Teacher, 57*(5), 452–460.

Henk, W. A., Marinak, B. A., Moore, J. C., & Mallette, M. H. (2003/2004). The Writing Observation Framework: A guide for refining and validating writing instruction. *The Reading Teacher, 57*(4), 322–333.

Henry, L. A. (23006). SEARCHing for an answer: The critical role of new literacies while reading on the Internet. *The Reading Teacher, 59*(7), 614–627.

Hergenhahn, B. R., & Olson, M. H. (2004). *Introduction to the theories of learning* (7th ed.). New York: Prentice Hall.

Hickman, J. (1983). Everything considered: Response to literature in an elementary school setting. *Journal of Research and Development in Education, 16*, 8–13.

Hickman, J., & Cullinan, B. E. (1989). A point of view on literature and learning. In J. Hickman & B. E. Cullinan (Eds.), *Children's literature in the classroom: Weaving Charlotte's web* (pp. 3–12). Needham Heights, MA: Christopher-Gordon Publishers.

Hiebert, E. H. (1983). An examination of ability grouping for reading instruction. *Reading Research Quarterly, 28*, 231–255.

Hiebert, E. H., Pearson, P. D., Taylor, B. M., Richardson, V., & Paris, S. G. (1998). *Every child a reader.* Ann Arbor, MI: Center for the Improvement of Early Reading Achievement (CIERA).

Hiebert, E. H., & Taylor, B. M. (1994). *Getting reading right from the start: Effective early literacy interventions.* Boston: Allyn & Bacon.

Hill, J. D., & Flynn, K. M. (2006). *Classroom instruction that works with English language learners.* Alexandria, VA: Association for Supervision and Curriculum Development.

Hill, M. (1991). Writing summaries promotes thinking and learning across the curriculum— but why are they so difficult to write? *Journal of Reading, 34*, 536–539.

Hillocks, G. (1987a). What works in teaching composition: A meta-analysis of experimental treatment studies. *American Journal of Education, 93*, 133–170.

Hillocks, G., Jr. (1987b). Synthesis of research on teaching writing. *Educational Leadership, 45*, 71–82.

Hillocks, G., Jr., & Smith, M. W. (1991). Grammar and usage. In J. Flood, J. M. Jensen, D. Lapp, & J. R. Squire (Eds.), *Handbook of research on teaching the English language arts* (pp. 591–603). New York: Macmillan Publishing Company.

Holdaway, D. (1979). *The foundations of literacy.* Sydney: Ashton Scholastic, distributed by Heinemann, Portsmouth, NH.

Holmes, B. C., & Roser, N. L. (1987). Five ways to assess readers' prior knowledge. *The Reading Teacher, 40*, 646–649.

Huck, C. S. (1989). No wider than the heart is wide. In J. Hickman & B. E. Cullinan (Eds.), *Children's literature in the classroom: Weaving Charlotte's web* (pp. 252–262). Needham Heights, MA: Christopher-Gordon.

Hyde, A., Zemelman, S., & Daniels, H. (2005). *Best practice: Today's standards for teaching and learning in America's schools* (3rd ed.). Portsmouth, NH: Heinemann.

Hynd, C. R., & Alvermann, D. E. (1986). Prior knowledge activation in refutation and non-refutation text. In J. A. Niles & R. V. Lalik (Eds.), *The Thirty-fifth Yearbook of the National Reading Conference, Solving problems in literacy: Learners, teachers, and researchers* (pp. 55–60). Rochester, NY: National Reading Conference.

Ivey, G. (2003). "The teacher makes it more explainable" and other reasons to read aloud in the intermediate grades. *The Reading Teacher, 56*(8), 812–814.

Jenkins, J., Stein, M., & Wysocki, K. (1984). Learning vocabulary through reading. *American Education Research Journal, 21*, 767–788.

Jenkins, J. R., & Pany, D. (1981). Instructional variables in reading comprehension. In J. T. Guthrie (Ed.), *Comprehension and teaching: Research reviews.* Newark, DE: International Reading Association.

Jenkins, J. R., et al. (2003). Decodable text—Where to find it. *The Reading Teacher, 57*(2), 185–189.

Jimenez, R. T. (2004). More equitable literacy assessments for Latino students. *The Reading Teacher, 57*(6), 576–578.

Johnson, D. D., & Pearson, P. D. (1984). *Teaching reading vocabulary* (2nd ed.). New York: Holt, Rinehart & Winston.

Johnson, M. S., Kress, R. A., & Pikulski, J. J. (1987). *Informal reading inventories* (2nd ed.). Newark, DE: International Reading Association.

Johnston, P. (1981). *Prior knowledge and reading comprehension test bias.* Unpublished doctoral dissertation, Urbana: University of Illinois Press.

Johnston, P. (2003). Assessment conversations. *The Reading Teacher, 57*(1), 90–92.

Jones, J. A. (2006). Student-involved classroom libraries. *The Reading Teacher, 59*(6), 576–580.

Jones, R. C., & Thomas, T. G. (2006). Leave no discipline behind. *The Reading Teacher, 60*(1), 58–64.

Jongsma, K. (2003). Beyond beginning learners. *The Reading Teacher, 56*(6), 550–553.

Juel, C. (1991). Beginning reading. In R. Barr, M. L. Kamil, P. Mosenthal, & P. D. Pearson (Eds.), *Handbook of reading research* (Vol. 2, pp. 759–788). New York: Longman.

Juel, C., Griffith, P. L., & Gough, P. B. (1986). Acquisition of literacy: A longitudinal study of children in first and second grade. *Journal of Educational Psychology, 78,* 243–255.

Juel, C., & Minden-Cupp, C. (2000). Learning to read words: Linguistic units and instructional strategies. *Reading Research Quarterly, 35,* 458–492.

Juel, C., & Roper/Schneider, D. (1985). The influence of basal readers on first grade reading. *Reading Research Quarterly, 20,* 134–152.

Just, M. A., & Carpenter, P. A. (1987). *The psychology of reading and language comprehension.* Boston: Allyn & Bacon.

Kail, R. V., Chi, M. T. H., Ingram, A. L., & Danner, F. W. (1977). Constructive aspects of children's reading comprehension. *Child Development, 48,* 684–688.

Kaplan, R. (1966). Cultural thought patterns in intercultural education. *Language Learning, 16,* 1–20.

Keene, E. O., & Zimmermann, S. (2007). *Mosaic of thought* (2nd ed.). Portsmouth, NH: Heinemann.

Kelley, M., & Clausen-Grace, N. (2006). R[5]: The Sustained Silent Reading makeover that transformed readers. *The Reading Teacher, 60*(2), 148–156.

Kelly, P. R. (1990). Guiding young students' response to literature. *The Reading Teacher, 43,* 464–470.

Kelly, P. R., & Farnan, N. (1991). Promoting critical thinking through response logs: A reader response approach with fourth graders. In S. McCormick & J. Zutell (Eds.), *The Fortieth Yearbook of the National Reading Conference, Learner factors/teacher factors: Issues in literacy research and instruction* (pp. 277–284). Chicago: National Reading Conference.

Kern, D., Andre, S., Schilke, R., Barton, J., & McGuire, M. C. (2003). Less is more: Preparing students for state writing assessments. *The Reading Teacher, 56*(8), 816–826.

Ketch, A. (2005). Conversation: The comprehension connection. *The Reading Teacher, 59*(1), 8–13.

Khattri, N., Kane, M. B., & Reeve, A. L. (1995). How performance assessments affect teaching and learning. *Educational Leadership, 53*(3), 80–83.

Knipper, K. J., & Duggan, T. J. (2006). Writing to learn across the curriculum: Tools for comprehension in content area classes. *The Reading Teacher, 59*(5), 462–470.

Kragler, S., Walker, C. A., & Martin, L. E. (2005). Strategy instruction in primary content textbooks. *The Reading Teacher, 59*(3), 254–261.

Krashen, S. (1982). *Principles and practice in second language acquisition.* New York: Pergamon Press.

Kurkjian, C., Livingston, N., & Cobb, V. (2006). Inquiring minds want to learn: The info on nonfiction and informational series books. *The Reading Teacher, 60*(1), 89–96.

Labbo, L. D. (2005). Books and computer response activities that support literacy development. *The Reading Teacher, 59*(3), 288–292.

LaBerge, D., & Samuels, S. J. (1976). Toward a theory of automatic information processing in reading. In H. Singer & R. Ruddell (Eds.),

Theoretical models and processes of reading (pp. 548–579). Newark, DE: International Reading Association.

Lamme, L. L. (1990). Exploring the world of music through picture books. *The Reading Teacher, 44,* 294–300.

Langer, J. A. (1986). Reading, writing and understanding: An analysis of the construction of meaning. *Written Communication, 3,* 219–267.

Leal, D. J. (2005/2006). The Word Writing CAFÉ: Assessing student writing for complexity, accuracy, and fluency. *The Reading Teacher, 59*(4), 340–350.

Lenneberg, E. (1967). *Biological foundations of language.* New York: John Wiley.

Lenski, S. D., Ehlers-Zavala, F., Daniel, M. C., & Sun-Irminger, X. (2006). Assessing English-language learners in mainstream classrooms. *The Reading Teacher, 60*(1), 24–34.

Lesgold, A. M., & Curtis, M. E. (1981). Learning to read words efficiently. In A. M. Lesgold & C. A. Perfetti (Eds.), *Interactive processes in reading.* Hillsdale, NJ: Lawrence Erlbaum Associates.

Leu, Jr., D. J., Castek, J., Henry, L. A., Ciro, J., & McMullan, M. (2004). The lessons that children teach us: Integrating children's literature and the new literacies of the Internet. *The Reading Teacher, 57*(5), 497–503.

Liang, L. A., & Dole, J. A. (2006). Help with teaching reading comprehension: Comprehension frameworks. *The Reading Teacher, 59*(8), 742–753.

Liberman, I. Y., Shankweiler, D., & Liberman, A. M. (1989). The alphabetic principle and learning to read. In D. Shankweiler & I. Y. Liberman (Eds.) *Phonology and reading disability: Solving the reading puzzle* (pp. 1–33). Ann Arbor: University of Michigan Press.

Lipson, M. Y. (1982). Learning new information from text. The role of prior knowledge and reading ability. *Journal of Reading Behavior, 14,* 243–261.

Lipson, M. Y. (1983). The influence of religious affiliation on children's memory for text information. *Reading Research Quarterly, 18,* 448–457.

Lipson, M. Y. (1984). Some unexpected issues in prior knowledge and comprehension. *The Reading Teacher, 37,* 760–764.

Lipson, M. Y., & Wixson, K. K. (1986). Reading disability research: An interactionist perspective. *Review of Educational Research, 56,* 111–136.

Loban, W. D. (1963). *The language of elementary school children.* Champaign, IL: National Council of Teachers of English.

Long, T. W., & Gove, M. K. (2003/2004). How engagement strategies and literature circles promote critical response in a fourth-grade, urban classroom. *The Reading Teacher, 57*(4), 350–361.

Lorge, I., & Chall, J. S. (1963). Estimating the size of vocabularies of children and adults: An analysis of methodological issues. *Journal of Experimental Education, 32,* 147–157.

Lotherington, H., & Chow, S. (2006). Rewriting "Goldilocks" in the urban, multicultural elementary school. *The Reading Teacher, 60*(3), 242–252.

Lyon, G. R., & Chhabra, V. (2004). The science of reading research. *Educational Leadership, 61*(6), 12–17.

McCabe, P. P. (2003). Enhancing self-efficacy for high-stakes reading tests. *The Reading Teacher, 57*(1), 12–20.

McCormick, S. (1977). Should you read aloud to your children? *Language Arts, 54,* 139–143.

McGinley, W. (1988). *The role of reading and writing in the acquisition of knowledge: A study of college students' reading and writing engagements in the development of a persuasive argument.* Unpublished doctoral thesis, University of Illinois, Urbana.

McHugh, N. (1987). Teaching the domains of writing. In C. B. Olson (Ed.), *Practical ideas for teaching writing as a process* (pp. 81–87). Sacramento, CA: California State Department of Education.

McKenna, M. C., & Walpole, S. (2005). How well does assessment inform our reading instruction? *The Reading Teacher, 59*(1), 84–86.

McKenzie, M. (1985). Shared writing. In *Language matters.* London: Inner London Educational Authority.

McKeown, M. G., Beck, I. L., Omanson, R. C., & Pople, M. T. (1985). Some effects of the nature and frequency of vocabulary instruction on the knowledge and use of words. *Reading Research Quarterly, 20*(5), 522–535.

McKeown, M. G., & Curtis, M. E. (1987). *The nature of vocabulary acquisition*. Hillsdale, NJ: Lawrence Erlbaum Associates.

McLaughlin, M., & Allen, M. B. (2002). *Guided comprehension: A teaching model for grades 3–8*. Newark, DE: International Reading Association.

McMahon, S. I., Raphael, T. E., Goatley, V. J., & Pardo, L. S. (1997). *The book club connection*. Newark, DE: International Reading Association and New York: Teachers College Press.

McMackin, M. S., & Witherell, N. L. (2005). Different routes to the same destination: Drawing conclusions with tiered graphic organizers. *The Reading Teacher, 59*(3), 242–252.

McNeil, D. (1970). *The acquisition of language: The study of developmental psycholinguistics*. New York: Harper & Row Publishers.

McTavish, M. (2007). Constructing the big picture: A working class family supports their daughter's pathways to literacy. *The Reading Teacher, 60*(5), 476–485.

Malloy, J. A., & Gambrell, L. D. (2006). Approaching the unavoidable: Literacy instruction and the Internet. *The Reading Teacher, 59*(5), 482–484.

Mandler, J. M. (1984). *Stories, scripts and scenes: Aspects of schema theory*. Hillsdale, NJ: Lawrence Erlbaum Associates.

Many, J. E. (1991). The effects of stance and age level on children's literary responses. *Journal of Reading Behavior, 23*, 61–85.

Maria, K. (1988, December). *Helping fifth graders learn with science text*. Paper presented at the meeting of the National Reading Conference, Tucson, AZ.

Maria, K. (1990). *Reading comprehension instruction: Strategies and issues*. Parkton, MD: York Press.

Marino, J. L., Gould, S. M., & Haas, L. W. (1985). The effect of writing as a prereading activity on delayed recall of narrative text. *Elementary School Journal, 86*, 199–205.

Marshall, N. (1983). Using story grammar to assess reading comprehension. *The Reading Teacher, 36*, 616–620.

Martin, S. (1987, December). *The meaning-making strategies reported by provident readers and writers*.

Paper presented at the National Reading Conference, St. Petersburg, FL.

Martinez, E. B. (1987). It works! In C. B. Olson (Ed.), *Practical ideas for teaching writing as a process* (p. 23). Sacramento, CA: California State Department of Education.

Martinez, M. G., & Roser, N. L. (1991). Children's responses to literature. In J. Flood, J. M. Jensen, D. Lapp, & J. R. Squire (Eds.), *Handbook of research on teaching the English language arts* (pp. 643–654). New York: Macmillan.

Mason, J. M., & Au, K. H. (1990). *Reading instruction for today* (2nd ed.). Glenview, IL: Scott, Foresman and Company.

Massey, D. D. (2003). A comprehension checklist: What if it doesn't make sense? *The Reading Teacher, 57*(1), 81–84.

Mather, N., Sammons, J., & Schwartz, J. (2006). Adaptations of the Names Test: Easy-to-use phonics assessments. *The Reading Teacher, 60*(2), 114–122.

Meichenbaum, D. (1985). Teaching thinking: A cognitive behavioral perspective. In S. Chapman, J. Segal, & R. Glaser (Eds.), *Thinking and learning skills: Current research and open questions* (Vol. 2, pp. 407–426). Hillsdale, NJ: Lawrence Erlbaum Associates.

Meier, T. (2003). "What can't she remember that?" The importance of storybook reading in multilingual, multicultural classrooms. *The Reading Teacher, 57*(3), 242–252.

Menyuk, P. (1984). Language development and reading. In J. Flood (Ed.), *Understanding comprehension* (pp. 101–121). Newark, DE: International Reading Association.

Mesmer, H. A. E., & Griffith, P. L. (2005/2006). Everybody's selling it—But just what is explicit, systematic phonics instruction? *The Reading Teacher, 59*(4), 366–376.

Meyer, B. J. F. (1975). *The organization of prose and its effects on memory*. Amsterdam: The Hague North-Holland Press.

Meyer, B. J. F., & Freedle, R. O. (1984). Effects of discourse type on recall. *American Educational Research Journal, 21*, 121–143.

Mezynski, K. (1983). Issues concerning the acquisition of knowledge: Effects of vocabulary training on reading comprehension. *Review of Educational Research, 53,* 253–279.

Millett, N. C. (1986). *Teaching the writing process: A guide for teachers and supervisors.* Boston: Houghton Mifflin.

Moffett, J., & Wagner, B. J. (1983). *Student-centered language arts and reading, K–13* (3rd ed.). Boston: Houghton Mifflin.

Moore, D. W., Readence, J. E., & Rickelman, R. J. (1989). *Prereading activities for content area reading and learning* (2nd ed.). Newark, DE: International Reading Association.

Morrow, L. (1985). Retelling stories: A strategy for improving children's comprehension, concept of story structure, and oral language complexity. *Elementary School Journal, 85,* 647–661.

Morrow, L. M. (1989a). *Literacy development in the early years. Helping children read and write.* Englewood Cliffs, NJ: Prentice Hall.

Morrow, L. M. (1989b). Using story retelling to develop comprehension. In K. D. Muth (Ed.), *Children's comprehension of text: Research into practice* (pp. 37–58). Newark, DE: International Reading Association.

Morrow, L. M. (2003). *Organizing and managing the language arts block: A professional development guide.* New York: Guilford Press.

Moss, B. (1991). Children's nonfiction trade books: A complement to content area texts. *The Reading Teacher, 45,* 26–32.

Moss, B. (2005). Making a case and a place for effective content area literacy instruction in the elementary grades. *The Reading Teacher, 59*(1), 46–55.

Murray, D. M. (1985). *A writer teaches writing* (2nd ed.). Boston: Houghton Mifflin.

Myers, P. A. (2005–2006). The princess Storyteller; Clara Clarifier; Quincy Questioner; and the Wizard: Reciprocal teaching adapted for kindergarten students. *The Reading Teacher, 59*(4), 314–324.

Nagy, W. E., & Anderson, R. C. (1984). How many words are there in printed school English? *Reading Research Quarterly, 19,* 304–330.

Nagy, W. E. (1988). *Teaching vocabulary to improve reading comprehension.* Newark, DE/Urbana, IL: IRA/NCTE.

Nagy, W. E., & Herman, P. A. (1987). Breadth and depth of vocabulary knowledge: Implications for acquisition and instruction. In M. G. McKeown & M. E. Curtis (Eds.), *The nature of vocabulary acquisition* (pp. 19–35). Hillsdale, NJ: Lawrence Erlbaum Associates.

National Council of Teachers of English. (2001). *Language Arts* (entire issue focuses on organizing for literacy instruction), Vol. 79, No. 2. Champaign-Urbana, IL: National Council of Teachers of English.

National Council of Teachers of English (NCTE) & International Reading Association (IRA). (1996). *Standards for the English language arts.* Urbana, IL/Newark, DE: NCTE/IRA.

National PTA. (1998). *National standards for parent/family involvement programs.* Chicago: Author.

National Reading Panel. (2000a). *Teaching children to read: An evidence-based assessment of the scientific research literature on reading and its implications for reading instruction.* Washington, DC: National Institute of Child Health and Human Development.

National Reading Panel. (2000b). *Report of the National Reading Panel—Teaching children to read: An evidence-based assessment of the scientific research literature on reading and its implications for reading instruction, reports of the subgroups.* Washington, DC: National Institute of Child Health and Human Development.

Neufeld, P. (2005–2006). Comprehension instruction in content area classes. *The Reading Teacher, 59*(4), 302–312.

Nilsen, A. P., & Nilsen, D. L. J. (2003). A new spin on teaching vocabulary: A source-based approach. *The Reading Teacher, 56*(5), 436–439.

Norton, D. E. (1999). *Through the eyes of a child— An introduction to children's literature* (5th ed.). Englewood Cliffs, NJ: Prentice Hall.

Noyce, R. M., & Christie, J. F. (1989). *Integrating reading and writing instruction in grades K–8.* Boston: Allyn & Bacon.

Oczkus, L. D. (2003). *Reciprocal teaching at work.* Newark, DE: International Reading Association.

Oczkus, L. D. (2004). *Super six comprehension strategies: 35 lessons and more for reading success.* Norwood, MA: Christopher-Gordon Publishers.

Oczkus, L. D. (2007). *Guided writing: Practical lessons, powerful results.* Portsmouth, NH: Heinemann.

Ogle, D. M. (1986). K-W-L: A teaching model that develops active reading of expository text. *The Reading Teacher, 39*(6), 564–570.

Olson, C. B. (1987). *Practical ideas for teaching writing as a process.* Sacramento, CA: California State Department of Education.

Ortiz, R. W. & Ordoñez-Jasis, R. (2005). Leyendo juntos (reading together): New directions for Latino parents' early literacy involvement. *The Reading Teacher, 59*(2), 110–112.

Pace, A. J., Marshall, N., Horowitz, R., Lipson, M.Y., & Lucido, P. (1989). When prior knowledge doesn't facilitate text comprehension: An examination of some of the issues. In *The Thirty-eighth Yearbook of the National Reading Conference, Cognitive and social perspectives for literacy research and instruction* (pp. 213–224). Chicago: The National Reading Conference.

Padak, N. & Rasinski, T. (2006). Home-school partnerships in literacy education: From rhetoric to reality. *The Reading Teacher, 60*(3), 292–296.

Palincsar, A. S., & Brown, A. L. (1986). Interactive teaching to promote independent learning from text. *The Reading Teacher, 39*(8), 771–777.

Palmer, R. G., & Stewart, R. A. (2003). Nonfiction trade book use in primary grades. *The Reading Teacher, 57*(1), 38–48.

Pappas, C. C., Kiefer, B. Z., & Levstik, L. S. (1990). *An integrated language perspective in the elementary school: Theory into action.* New York: Longman.

Paratore, J. R., & Indrisano, R. (1987). Intervention assessment of reading comprehension. *The Reading Teacher, 40,* 778–783.

Paris, S. G., Cross, D. R., & Lipson, M. Y. (1984). Informed strategies for learning: A program to improve children's reading awareness and comprehension. *Journal of Educational Psychology, 76,* 1239–1252.

Paris, S. G., Lipson, M.Y., & Wixson, K. K. (1983). Becoming a strategic reader. *Contemporary Educational Psychology, 8,* 293–316.

Paris, S. G., Wasik, B. A., & Turner, J. C. (1991). The development of strategic readers. In R. Barr, M. L. Kamil, P. Mosenthal, & P. D. Pearson (Eds.), *Handbook of reading research* (Vol. 2, pp. 609–640). New York: Longman.

Parsons, L. (2001). *Response journals revisited.* Portland, ME: Stenhouse.

Pearson, P. D. (1985). Changing the face of reading comprehension instruction. *The Reading Teacher, 38,* 724–738.

Pearson, P. D., & Dole, J. A. (1987). Explicit comprehension instruction: A review of research and a new conceptualization of instruction. *Elementary School Journal, 88*(2), 151–165.

Pearson, P. D., Roehler, L. R., Dole, J. A., & Duffy, G. G. (1990). *Developing expertise in reading comprehension: What should be taught? How should it be taught?* (Tech. Rep. No. 512). Urbana: University of Illinois Press, Center for the Study of Reading.

Pearson, P. D., Roehler, L. R., Dole, J. A., & Duffy, G. G. (1992). Developing expertise in reading comprehension. In S. J. Samuels & A. E. Forstrup (Eds.), *What research has to say about reading instruction* (pp. 145–199). Newark, DE: International Reading Association.

Pearson, P. D., & Tierney, R. J. (1984). On becoming a thoughtful reader: Learning to read like a writer. In A. C. Purves & O. Niles (Eds.), *Eighty-third Yearbook of the National Society of the Study of Education, Becoming readers in a complex society* (pp. 144–173). Chicago: The University of Chicago Press.

Pehrsson, R. S., & Robinson, H. A. (1985). *The semantic organizer approach to writing and reading instruction.* Rockville, MD: Aspen Systems Corporation.

Peregoy, S. F., & Boyle, O. W. (2005). *Reading, writing and learning in ESL: A resource book for K–12 teachers* (5th ed.). Boston: Pearson/Allyn & Bacon.

Perfetti, C. (1985). *Reading ability.* New York: Oxford University Press.

Peterson, B. (2001). *Literacy pathways: Selecting books to support new readers.* Portsmouth, NH: Heinemann.

Piaget, J., & Inhelder, B. (1969). *The psychology of the child.* New York: Basic Books.

Pierce, K. (1987). Clustering in first grade. In C. B. Olson (Ed.), *Practical ideas for teaching writing as a process* (pp. 22–23). Sacramento, CA: California State Department of Education.

Pikulski, J. J. (1994). Preventing reading failure: A review of five effective programs. *The Reading Teacher, 48*(1), 30–39.

Pinnell, G. S., & Fountas, G. S. (1998). *Word matters*. Portsmouth, NH: Heinemann.

Pinnell, G. S., Fried, M. D., & Estice, R. M. (1990). Reading recovery: Learning how to make a difference. *The Reading Teacher, 43,* 282–295.

Popham, W. J. (2001). *The truth about testing*. Alexandria, VA: Association for Supervision and Curriculum.

Pressley, M. (1998). *Reading instruction that works: The case for balanced teaching*. New York: Guilford Press.

Pressley, M. (2000). What should comprehension instruction be the instruction of? In M. L. Kamil, P. B. Mosenthal, P. D. Pearson, & R. Barr (Eds.), *Handbook of reading research* (Vol. 3, pp. 545–562). Mahwah, NJ: Lawrence Erlbaum Associates.

Pressley, M., Burkell, J., Cariglia-Bull, T., Lysynchuck, L., McGoldrick, J. A., Schneider, B., Snyder, B. L., Symons, S., & Woloshyn, V. E. (1990). *Cognitive strategy instruction that really improves children's academic performance*. Cambridge, MA: Brookline Books.

Pressley, M., & Harris, K. R. (1990). What we really know about strategy instruction. *Educational Leadership, 48,* 31–34.

Pressley, M., Johnson, C. J., Symons, S., McGoldrick, J. S., & Kurita, J. A. (1989). Strategies that improve children's memory and comprehension of text. *Elementary School Journal, 90,* 3–32.

Purves, A. C. (1972). *How porcupines make love: Notes on a response-centered curriculum*. New York: Wiley.

Rasinski, T. (2006). Reading fluency instruction: Moving beyond accuracy, automaticity, and prosody. *The Reading Teacher, 59*(7), 704–706.

Rasinski, T. V. (2003). *The fluent reader*. New York: Scholastic.

Rasinski, T. V. & Hoffman, J. V. (2003). Oral reading in the school literacy curriculum. *Reading Research Quarterly, 38,* 510–522.

Read, S. (2005). First and second graders writing informational text. *The Reading Teacher, 59*(1), 36–44.

Readence, J. E., Bean, T. W., & Baldwin, R. S. (1981, 1985, 1989). *Content area reading: An integrated approach*. Dubuque, IA: Kendall/ Hunt.

Reutzel, D. R., & Cooter, R. B., Jr. (1991). Organizing for effective instruction: The reading workshop. *The Reading Teacher, 44,* 548–554.

Rhodes, L. K., & Shanklin, N. L. (1990). Miscue analysis in the classroom. *The Reading Teacher, 44,* 252–254.

Richards, J. C., & Anderson, N. A. (2003). How do you know? A strategy to help emergent readers make inferences. *The Reading Teacher, 57*(3), 290–293.

Rico, G. L. (1983). *Writing the natural way*. Los Angeles: J. P. Tracher, Inc. Distributed by Houghton Mifflin Company, Boston.

Rigg, P., & Allen, V. G. (1989). *When they don't all speak English*. Urbana, IL: National Council of Teachers of English.

Risko, V. J., & Bromley, K. (Eds.). (2001). *Collaboration for diverse learners*. Newark, DE: International Reading Association.

Roehler, L. R., & Duffy, G. G. (1991). Teacher's instructional actions. In R. Barr, M. L. Kamil, P. Mosenthal, & P. D. Pearson (Eds.), *Handbook of reading research* (Vol. 2, pp. 861–883). New York: Longman.

Rog, L. J. (2007). *Marvelous minilessons for teaching beginning writing, K–3*. Newark, DE: International Reading Association.

Rogers, T., Winters, K. L., Bryan, G., Price, J. McCormick, F., House, L., Mezzarobba, D., & Sinclaire, C. (2006). Developing the IRIS: Toward situated and valid assessment measures in collaborative professional development and school reform in literacy. *The Reading Teacher, 59*(6), 544–553.

Roget, P. (2005). St. Martin's edition of the original *Roget's thesaurus of English words and phrases*. New York: St. Martin's Press.

Rosenblatt, L. (1938/1976). *Literature as exploration*. New York: Modern Language Association.

Rosenblatt, L. (1978). *The reader, the text and the poem*. Carbondale: Southern Illinois University Press.

Rosenblatt, L. M. (1991). Literary theory. In J. Flood, J. M. Jensen, D. Lapp., & J. R. Squire (Eds.), *Handbook of research on teaching the English language arts* (pp. 57–62). New York: Macmillan Publishing Co.

Rosenshine, B. V., & Meister, C. (1994). Reciprocal teaching: A review of research. *Review of Educational Research, 64*(4), 479–530.

Routman, R. (1991). *Invitations*. Portsmouth, NH: Heinemann.

Ruddell, R. B. (1963). The effect of the similarity of oral and written patterns of language structure on reading comprehension. *Elementary English, 42,* 403–410.

Rumelhart, D. E. (1980). Schemata: The building blocks of cognition. In R. J. Spiro et al. (Eds.), *Theoretical issues in reading comprehension* (pp. 33–58). Hillsdale, NJ: Lawrence Erlbaum Associates.

Rupley, W. H., Wilson, V. L., & Nichols, W. D. (1998). Exploration of the developmental components contributing to elementary school children's reading comprehension. *Scientific Studies in Reading, 2*(2), 143–158.

Samblis, K. (2006). Think-Tac-Toe, a motivating method of increasing comprehension. *The Reading Teacher, 59*(7), 691–694.

Samuels, S. J. & Farstrup, A. E. (2006). *What research has to say about fluency instruction.* Newark, DE: International Reading Association.

Sanders, M. (1987). Literacy as "passionate attention." *Language Arts, 64,* 619–633.

Sawyer, W. (1987). Literature and literacy: A review of research. *Language Arts, 64*(1), 33–39.

Scala, M. C. (2001). *Working together: Reading and writing in inclusive classrooms.* Newark, DE: International Reading Association.

Schatz, E. K., & Baldwin, R. S. (1986). Context clues are unreliable predictors of word meanings. *Reading Research Quarterly, 21,* 439–453.

Schwartz, R. (1988). Learning to learn vocabulary in content area textbooks. *Journal of Reading, 32,* 108–118.

Schwartz, R. M., & Raphael, T. E. (1985). Concept of definition: A key to improving students' vocabulary. *The Reading Teacher, 39,* 198–203.

Seashore, R. H. (1947). How many words do children know? *The Packet, 2,* 3–17.

Sekeres, D. C. & Gregg, M. (2007). Poetry in third grade: Getting started. *The Reading Teacher, 60*(5), 466–475.

Shake, M., & Allington, R. (1985). Where do teachers' questions come from? *The Reading Teacher, 38,* 434–438.

Shanahan, T. (1988). The reading writing relationship: Seven instructional principles. *The Reading Teacher, 41,* 636–647.

Shanahan, T. (1990). Reading and writing together: What does it really mean? In T. Shanahan (Ed.), *Reading and writing together* (pp. 1–18). Norwood, MA: Christopher-Gordon Publishers.

Shanahan, T., & Lomax, R. (1988). A developmental comparison of three theoretical models of the reading-writing relationship. *Research in Teaching English, 22,* 196–212.

Short, E. J., & Ryan, E. B. (1984). Metacognitive differences between skilled and less skilled readers: Remediating deficits through story grammar and attribution training. *Journal of Educational Psychology, 76,* 225–235.

Simons, H., & Ammon, P. (1989). Child knowledge and primerese text: Mismatches and miscues. *Research in the Teaching of English, 23*(4), 380–398.

Singer, H., & Donlan, D. (1982). Active comprehension: Problem-solving schema with question generation for comprehension of complex short stories. *Reading Research Quarterly, 17,* 166–186.

Slavin, R. E. (1986). *Ability grouping and student achievement in elementary schools: A best evidence synthesis* (Report No. 1). Baltimore, MD: The Johns Hopkins University, Center for Research on Elementary and Middle Schools.

Slavin, R. E. (1990). *Cooperative learning: Theory, research and practice.* Englewood, NJ: Prentice Hall.

Sloyer, S. (1982). *Readers' theatre: Story dramatization in the classroom.* Urbana, IL: National Council of Teachers of English.

Smith, F. (1988). *Understanding reading* (4th ed.). New York: Holt, Rinehart & Winston.

Smith, L. A. (2006). Think-aloud mysteries: Using structured, sentence-by-sentence text passages to teach comprehension strategies. *The Reading Teacher, 59*(8), 764–773.

Smith, N. B. (1965). *American reading instruction.* Newark, DE: International Reading Association.

Snow, C., Burns, M. S., & Griffin, P. (Eds.) (1998). *Preventing reading difficulties in young children*. Washington, DC: National Academy Press.

Solvie, P. A. (2004). The digital whiteboard: A tool in early literacy instruction. *The Reading Teacher, 57*(5), 484–487.

Sorensen, A., & Hallinan, M. (1986). Effects of ability grouping on growth in academic achievement. *American Educational Research Journal, 23*, 519–542.

Spencer, B. H., & Guillaume, A. M. (2006). Integrating curriculum through the learning cycle: Content-based reading and vocabulary instruction. *The Reading Teacher, 60*(3), 206–219.

Spritzer, D. R. (1988). Integrating the language arts in the elementary classroom using fairy tales, fables, and traditional literature. *Oregon English, 11*, 23–26.

Stahl, S. A. (1983). Differential word knowledge and reading comprehension. *Journal of Reading Behavior, 15*, 33–50.

Stahl, S. A., & Fairbanks, M. M. (1986). The effects of vocabulary instruction: A model-based meta-analysis. *Review of Educational Research, 56*(1), 72–110.

Stahl, S. A., & Nagy, W. E. (2006). *Teaching word meanings*. Mahwah, NJ: Lawrence Erlbaum Associates, Publishers.

Stahl, S. A., & Vancil, S. J. (1986). Discussion is what makes semantic maps work in vocabulary instruction. *The Reading Teacher, 39*, 62–67.

Stanovich, K. E. (1980). Toward an interactive-compensatory model of individual differences in the development of reading fluency. *Reading Research Quarterly, 16*, 32–71.

Stanovich, K. E. (1986). Matthew effects in reading: Some consequences of individual differences in the acquisition of reading. *Reading Research Quarterly, 21*, 360–407.

Stauffer, R. G. (1969). *Teaching reading as a thinking process*. New York: Harper & Row.

Sternberg, R. J. (1987). Most vocabulary is learned from context. In M. G. McKeown & M. E. Curtis (Eds.), *The nature of vocabulary acquisition* (pp. 89–105). Hillsdale, NJ: Lawrence Erlbaum Associates.

Stevens, K. C. (1982). Can we improve reading by teaching background information? *Journal of Reading, 25*, 326–329.

Stieglitz, E. L., & Stieglitz, U. S. (1981). SAVOR the word to reinforce vocabulary in the content areas. *Journal of Reading, 25*, 46–51.

Strickland, D. (1994). Reinventing our literacy programs: Books, basics, and balance. *The Reading Teacher, 48*(4), 294–306.

Strickland, D. S. (1977). Prompting language and concept development. In B. Cullinan (Ed.), *Literature and young children*. Urbana, IL: National Council of Teachers of English.

Strickland, D. S., Ganske, K., & Monroe, J. K. (2001). *Supporting struggling readers and writers*. Portland, ME: Stenhouse Publishers.

Strickland, D. S., & Taylor, D. (1989). Family storybook reading: Implications for children, families, and curriculum. In D. S. Strickland & L. M. Morrow (Eds.), *Emerging literacy: Young children learn to read and write* (pp. 27–34). Newark, DE: International Reading Association.

Sulzby, E., & Teale, W. (1991). Emergent literacy. In R. Barr, M. L. Kamil, P. Mosenthal, & P. D. Pearson (Eds.), *Handbook of reading research* (Vol. 2, pp. 727–757). New York: Longman.

Szymusiak, K., & Sibberson, F. (Eds.) (2001), *Beyond leveled books: Supporting transitional readers in grades 2–5*. Portland, ME: Stenhouse.

Taba, H. (1967). *Teacher's handbook for elementary school social studies*. Reading, MA: Addison-Wesley.

Taylor, B., Pikulski, J. J., & Cooper, J. D. (2003). *Reading intervention for early success, levels 1 and 2*. Boston: Houghton Mifflin.

Taylor, B. M., Frye, B. J., & Maruyama, G. M. (1990). Time spent reading and reading growth. *American Educational Research Journal, 27*(2), 351–362.

Taylor, B. M., Frye, B. J., Short, R., & Shearer, B. (1992). Classroom teachers prevent reading failure among low-achieving first-grade students. *The Reading Teacher, 45*, 592–597.

Taylor, D., & Dorsey-Gaines, C. (1988). *Growing up literate*. Portsmouth, NH: Heinemann.

Taylor, D., & Strickland, D. S. (1986). *Family storybook reading*. Portsmouth, NH: Heinemann.

Teale, W. H., & Sulzby, E. (1986). *Emergent literacy: Writing and reading*. Norwood, NJ: Ablex Publishing Corporation.

Templeton, S. (1997). *Teaching the integrated language arts* (2nd ed.). Boston: Houghton Mifflin.

Thompson, A. (1990). Thinking and writing with learning logs. In N. Atwell (Ed.), *Coming to know: Writing to learn in the intermediate grades* (pp. 35–51). Portsmouth, NH: Heinemann.

Tiedt, I. M. (2000). *Teaching with picture books in the middle school*. Newark, DE: International Reading Association.

Tierney, R. J., Carter, M. A., & Desai, L. E. (1991). *Portfolio assessment in the reading-writing classroom.* Norwood, MA: Christopher-Gordon Publishers.

Tierney, R. J., & Cunningham, J. W. (1984). Research on teaching reading comprehension. In P. D. Pearson (Ed.), *Handbook of reading research* (pp. 609–655). New York: Longman.

Tierney, R. J., & Leys, M. (1984). *What is the value of connecting reading and writing?* Reading Education Report No. 55. Urbana: University of Illinois Press.

Tierney, R. J., Readence, J. E., & Dishner, E. K. (1990). *Reading strategies and practices: A compendium* (3rd ed.). Boston: Allyn & Bacon.

Tierney, R. J., & Shanahan, T. (1991). Research on the reading-writing relationship: Interactions, transactions, and outcomes. In R. Barr, M. L. Kamil, P. Mosenthal, & P. D. Pearson (Eds.), *Handbook of reading research* (Vol. 2, pp. 246–280). White Plains, NY: Longman.

Trelease, J. (2006). *The read-aloud handbook* (6th ed.). New York: Penguin Books.

Tyson, H., & Woodward, A. (1989). Why students aren't learning very much from textbooks. *Educational Leadership, 47*, 14–17.

Valencia, S. (1990a). Alternative assessment: Separating the wheat from the chaff. *The Reading Teacher, 44*, 60–61.

Valencia, S. (1990b). A portfolio approach to classroom reading assessment: The whys, whats and hows. *The Reading Teacher, 43*, 338–340.

Valencia, S., Hiebert, E. H., & Afflerbach, P. P. (Eds.). (1994). *Authentic reading assessment: Practices and possibilities.* Newark, DE: International Reading Association.

Valencia, S. W., & Buly, M. R. (2004). Behind test scores: What struggling readers really need. *The Reading Teacher, 57*(6), 520–531.

Valmont, W. J. (2003). *Technology for literacy teaching and learning.* Boston: Houghton Mifflin.

Van Leeuwen, C. A., & Gabriel, M. A. (2007). Beginning to write with word processing: Integrating writing process and technology in a primary classroom. *The Reading Teacher, 60*(5), 420–429.

Van Sluys, K., & Laman, T. T. (2006). Learning about language: Written conversations and elementary language learners. *The Reading Teacher, 60*(3), 222–233.

Vardell, S. M., Hadaway, N. L. & Young, T. A. (2006). Matching books and readers: Selecting literature for English learners. *The Reading Teacher, 59*(8), 734–741.

Veatch, J. (1966/1978). *Reading in the elementary school* (2nd ed.). New York: John Wiley.

Venezky, R. L. (1995). Literacy. In T. L. Harris & R. E. Hodges (Eds.), *The literacy dictionary* (p. 142). Newark, DE: International Reading Association.

Villano, T. L. (2005). Should social studies textbooks become history? A look at alternative methods to activate schema in the intermediate classroom. *The Reading Teacher, 59*(2), 122–130.

Villaume, S. K., & Brabham, E. G. (2003). Phonics instruction: Beyond the debate. *The Reading Teacher, 56*(5), 478–482.

Vygotsky, L. S. (1978). *Mind in society.* Cambridge, MA: Harvard University Press.

Walmsley, S. A. (1994). *Children exploring the world: Theme teaching in elementary school.* Portsmouth, NH: Heinemann.

Walmsley, S. A. (2006). Getting the big idea: A neglected goal for reading comprehension. *The Reading Teacher, 60*(3), 281–285.

Walpole, S., & McKenna, M. C. (2006). The role of informal reading inventories in assessing word recognition. *The Reading Teacher, 59*(6), 592–594.

Wasburn-Moses, L. (2006). 25 best Internet sources for teaching reading. *The Reading Teacher, 60*(1), 70–75.

Weaver, C. (1990a). *Understanding whole language.* Portsmouth, NH: Heinemann.

Weaver, C. (1990b, March 28). Weighing claims of "phonics first" advocates. *Education Week*, 32.

Weaver, C. (1994). *Understanding whole language: From principles to practice* (2nd ed.). Portsmouth, NH: Heinemann.

Weaver, C. A., & Kintsch, W. (1991). Expository text. In R. Barr, M. L. Kamil, P. Mosenthal, & P. D. Pearson (Eds.), *Handbook of reading research* (Vol. 2, pp. 230–245). New York: Longman.

Weber, R. (1991). Language diversity and reading in American society. In R. Barr, M. L. Kamil, P. Mosenthal, & P. D. Pearson (Eds.), *Handbook of reading research* (pp. 97–119). New York: Longman.

Weisberg, R. K., & Balajthy, E. (1985, December). *Effects of semantic mapping training on disabled readers' summarizing and recognition of expository text structure.* Paper presented at the National Reading Conference, San Diego, CA.

Weiss, A. S., Mangrum, C. T., & Liabre, M. M. (1986). Differential effects of differing vocabulary presentations. *Reading Research and Instruction, 25,* 265–276.

Wells, G. (1986). *The meaning makers: Children learning language and using language to learn.* Portsmouth, NH: Heinemann.

Wells, G. (1990). Creating the conditions to encourage literate thinking. *Educational Leadership, 47*(6), 13–17.

Wepner, S., Valmont, W., & Thurlow, R. (2000). *Linking literacy and technology: A guide for K–8 classrooms.* Newark, DE: International Reading Association.

Werthemer, A. (1974). Story dramatization in the reading center. *English Journal, 64,* 85–87.

White, T. G., Sowell, J., & Yanagihara, A. (1989). Teaching elementary students to use word-part clues. *The Reading Teacher, 42,* 302–308.

Wilde, S. (1990). A proposal for a new spelling curriculum. *Elementary School Journal, 90,* 275–289.

Wilde, S. (1996, November). The minilesson and assessment: From writing to spelling and back again. *Primary Voices K–6, 4*(4), 16–18.

Wilkinson, L. C., & Silliman, E. R. (2000). Classroom language and literacy learning. In M. L. Kamil, P. B. Mosenthal, P. D. Pearson, & R. Barr (Eds.), *Handbook of reading research* (Vol. 3, pp. 337–360). Mahwah, NJ: Lawrence Erlbaum Associates.

Williams, N. L., & Bauer, P. T. (2006). Pathways to affective accountability: Selecting, locating, and using children's books in elementary school classrooms. *The Reading Teacher, 60*(1), 14–22.

Winograd, P. N., & Bridge, C. A. (1986). The comprehension of important information in written prose. In J. B. Baumann (Ed.), *Teaching main idea comprehension* (pp. 18–48). Newark, DE: International Reading Association.

Wiseman, A. J., (2003). Collaboration, initiation, and rejection: The social construction of stories in a kindergarten class. *The Reading Teacher, 56*(8), 802–810.

Wixson, K. K. (1986). Vocabulary instruction and children's comprehension of basal stories. *Reading Research Quarterly, 21,* 317–329.

Wood, K. D. (1988). Techniques for assessing students' potential for learning. *The Reading Teacher, 41,* 440–447.

Wood, K. D., Lapp, D., & Flood, J. (1992). *Guiding readers through text: A review of study guides.* Newark, DE: International Reading Association.

Wright, G., Sherman, R., & Jones, T. B. (2004). Are silent reading behaviors of first graders really silent? *The Reading Teacher, 57*(5), 546–553.

Wutz, J. A., & Wedwick, L. (2005). BOOKMATCH: Scaffolding book selection for independent reading. *The Reading Teacher, 59*(1), 16–32.

Yaden, D. (1988). Understanding stories through repeated read-alouds: How many does it take? *The Reading Teacher, 41,* 556–560.

Yaden, D. B., Jr., Rowe, D. W., & MacGillivray, L. (2000). Emergent literacy: A matter (polyphony) of perspectives. In M. L. Kamil, P. B. Mosenthal, P. D. Pearson, & R. Barr (Eds.), *Handbook of reading research* (Vol. 3, pp. 425–454). Mahwah, NJ: Lawrence Erlbaum Associates.

Yopp, H. K. (1995). A test for assessing phonemic awareness in young children. *The Reading Teacher, 49,* 20–22.

Author/Source Index

Subject Index

schema theory, 77–78, 83–84
schwa, 508–509
scribble-writing, 344, 346
seating, classroom, 408
segmenting, 505
Segmenting and Blending Routines, 195–196
self-collection, vocabulary, 273–274
self-evaluation, 474–475
self-questioning, 148–149
semantic feature analysis, 252, 266–269
semantic mapping, 95, 102–104, 252, 266, 352
semantics, 186
sensory/descriptive domain, 337, 338
sentences, 188–189
sequence, in expository texts, 81, 82, 83
setting, of texts, 81
shared reading, 39, 40, 211–213
shared writing, 40, 41–42, 44, 338, 340, 361–363
sharing area, 411–412
sight vocabulary, 245
sight words, 186
social authenticity, 63
software, 252, 371
speaking area, 411
spelling, 355, 363, 365, 515
  invented or temporary, 8
  in journals, 314
  phases of, 344, 346, 347
  random letter phase of, 344, 347
  sample lesson in, 366–367
stages of literacy development, 2, 8–12
standardized tests, 458, 460, 461
standards, 3, 12
  assessment and, 458, 464
  beginning literacy instruction and, 192
  locating state, 13
  prior knowledge and, 85
  responding and, 303
  sample literacy lessons based on, 45–53, 119–133, 221–239, 279–293
  using in instruction planning, 13
  writing and, 337
standard scores, 460
state-of-the-class conferences, 436–437, 438, 441

stop and think strategy, 143
story frames, 342–344
story grammar, 150
story maps, 81, 108
strategies, 86. *See also* instructional strategies
  for decoding, 191–192
  instruction in, 156–164
  minilesson on, 164–167
  reciprocal teaching and, 163–164
  sample lessons on, 168–177
  for struggling readers, 386, 389
  for vocabulary, 258–279
strengths and needs groups, 428
structural analysis, 189–190, 192, 274–277, 384
  for teachers, 511–519
structured previews, 95, 107–111, 391
structured questions, 86
struggling readers, 375–400
  assessing progress of, 390
  comprehension by, 384–385
  content area reading for, 390–391
  core instruction for, 386–391
  decoding by, 384
  definition of, 376
  finding time for intervention with, 394–397
  identifying, 380–386
  intervention tiers for, 391–394
  oral language and, 383–384
  reading levels and, 383
  strategies and skills for, 386, 389
  who they are, 377–378
student-centered instruction, 4, 12
student strategies, 86, 87–94
  K-W-L, 87, 88, 90–92
  making connections, 92–94
  preview and predict, 87–88, 89
study guides, 38
suffixes, 249, 261, 275, 276–277, 512–513, 514
summarizing, 50, 160
  meaning construction and, 150–153
  minilesson on, 174–177
  in minilessons, 166
  as response, 301
  writing in, 342
support in advance, 429–430
support materials, 56
syllables, 515–517

syntax, 190
synthesizing, 150–153, 160

T
teachable moment, 35, 50
teacher-modeled writing framework, 440
teacher notebooks/portfolios, 424
teachers
  collaboration among, 18–19
  current research and, 17–19
  family and community involvement and, 17
  prior knowledge activation and, 85–86
  professional organizations for, 17–18
  understanding assessment and, 462
teacher sharing time, 436, 437
teacher's manuals, 56
teaching
  definition of, 14
  instructional strategies in, 14–16
  reciprocal, 149, 163–164
teaching strategies. *See* instructional strategies
technology, 15–16
  literacy blocks and, 427
  prior knowledge activation and, 118
  responding to literature with, 323
  writing process and, 355, 364, 371
texts. *See also* expository texts; narrative texts
  authentic literature, 57, 60–63
  basal series or systems, 56
  for Comprehensive Balanced Literacy Programs, 55–66
  concepts of print and, 188–189
  created, 57, 58, 59–60
  developmental appropriateness of, 61–62
  easy-to-read, 60
  evaluating, 153–156, 160
  extending, 46–48, 55
  generating and answering questions about, 148–149
  identifying important information in, 145–147
  inferencing and, 144–145
  instructional strategies and, 117
  introducing, 55